D0966389

JAMES BOSWELL

The Earlier Years

1740–1769

By Frederick A. Pottle

The Literary Career of James Boswell, Esq.,
  being the Bibliographical Materials for a Life of Boswell, 1929

Stretchers: The Story of a Hospital on the Western Front, 1929

Boswell and the Girl from Botany Bay, 1936

The Idiom of Poetry, 1941 ; revised and enlarged, 1946

Editor, singly or in collaboration, of many volumes of the journal and letters of
  James Boswell, especially of the following in the Yale Editions of the Private
  Papers of James Boswell, published by the McGraw-Hill Book Company and
  William Heinemann, Ltd.

Boswell's London Journal, 1762–1763 (1950)

Boswell in Holland, 1763–1764 (1951)

Boswell on the Grand Tour: Germany and Switzerland, 1764 (1953)

Boswell on the Grand Tour: Italy, Corsica, and France, 1765–1766
  (1955). With Frank Brady

Boswell in Search of a Wife, 1766–1769 (1956). With Frank Brady

Boswell for the Defence, 1769–1774 (1959). With William K. Wimsatt

Boswell's Journal of a Tour to the Hebrides with Samuel Johnson, LL.D.,
  1773 (1936, 1961). With Charles H. Bennett

Boswell: The Ominous Years, 1774–1776 (1963).
  With Charles Ryskamp

JAMES BOSWELL

The Earlier Years
1740–1769

FREDERICK A. POTTLE

McGRAW-HILL BOOK COMPANY

New York   Toronto   London

In memory of

GEOFFREY SCOTT

1885–1929

1 2 3 4 5 6 7 8 9   DOC DOC   8 7 6 5 4

ISBN 0-07-050578-0

Library of Congress Cataloging in Publication Data
Pottle, Frederick Albert, 1897–
  James Boswell, the earlier years, 1740–1769.
  Includes bibliographical references and index.
  1. Boswell, James, 1740–1795—Biography—Youth.
2. Authors, Scottish—18th century—Biography. I. Title.
PR3325.P62 1985   828'.609 [B]   84-10053
ISBN 0-07-050578-0

ACKNOWLEDGEMENTS

This book has been a long time in writing, and I have kept no systematic record of the aid I have received from others during its composition. If I am guilty now of invidious omissions, I beg that they may be attributed, not to ingratitude, but to the unaccountable gaps any man's memory is apt to display when pushed for comprehensive recall at short notice.

I give humble and hearty thanks:

To the John Simon Guggenheim Memorial Foundation for fellowships (1945–1946, 1952–1953) that twice enabled me to take leave from teaching for an entire year. To the Old Dominion Foundation for a grant which made possible an extraordinary leave in 1963–1964. To the American Council of Learned Societies for a grant in 1960 which paid the rental of the little car in which my wife and I rambled through Italy, happily retracing Boswell's tour of two hundred years before.

To the late Charles H. Bennett, whose unpublished collections at Yale still constitute the largest and most useful body of Boswellian annotation ever assembled.

To Robert Warnock for access to his unpublished collections on the Continental and Corsican portions of Boswell's records, as well as for general use of his unpublished Yale dissertation, *Boswell in Italy* (1933), which provided me with an annotated and indexed text of Boswell's voluminous and difficult Italian memoranda. To Joseph Foldare, on whose fine study *James Boswell and Corsica* (unpublished Yale dissertation, 1936) I have been abjectly dependent. To those other graduate students at Yale, whose contributions, made in unpublished class papers, have already been gratefully acknowledged in the volumes of the reading edition of Boswell's journal, from *Boswell in Holland* to *Boswell in Search of a Wife*. I cannot, however, pass over without specific mention John P.

Kirby's annotated and indexed text of Boswell's notes and memoranda of the London jaunt of 1769, which organized for biographical use a baffling mass of confused and overlapping material still largely unpublished.

To the long line of Yale undergraduates (bursary assistants) who doggedly typed and retyped my successive drafts: Richard S. Nutt, '47; Carl E. Jacobs, '49; Robert B. Burlin, '50; Lewis S. Ford, '55; Robert W. Mason, '56; Robert A. Carter, '58; David S. Martin, '59; Adam W. Dibbell, '61; Thomas C. Heinz, '63; Jonathan L. Price, '66; Christopher F. Givan, '66.

To my teacher and friend, the late Robert J. Menner, who read my first draft, chapter by chapter as I wrote it, and gave me encouragement that I much needed. To the late T. B. Simpson, who also read the whole of that draft in instalments, helped me with the Scottish background, and gave me expert advice on all matters touching on Scots law. To the late David Nichol Smith, who read the chapters of the first draft dealing with Boswell's childhood and youth and sent me extended and careful comments that saved me from a number of glaring errors.

To Sir James Fergusson and to N. Stanley Curnow for reading the first half of the present book in typescript and sending me detailed suggestions for revision. Though I never met Mr. Curnow, who lived in Johannesburg, South Africa, his death on 25 July last was to me a personal sorrow. He was a volunteer Boswell scholar on whose resourcefulness and learning the Boswell Office at Yale had come greatly to depend. Sir James Fergusson was also good enough to read the proofs of the second half of the book. To Neil Leonard, lawyer and general reader, my friend for close on fifty years, who read both versions carefully and helped me eliminate some of my pedantries and academicisms. To Edward Kuhn, Jr., formerly Editor-in-Chief and General Manager of the Trade Book Department of the McGraw-Hill Book Company, who also read the book in both versions and gave me useful suggestions for improvement. To A. L. Hart, Jr., formerly Senior Editor at McGraw-Hill, for a particularly perceptive and helpful reading of the typescript of the present book. To Peter Kemeny and C. S. Harvey of the editorial staff of McGraw-Hill, who have shown unfailing friendliness to a difficult text and a difficult author.

To Frederick W. Hilles, Herman W. Liebert, Benjamin F. Houston, and Harriet Chidester, who read the proofs in whole or in part. Messrs.

Hilles and Liebert had formerly been good enough to read and comment on the book in its first draft.

To Frank Brady, who has read everything—old draft, new draft, galley proofs, page proofs—and has given me a host of useful suggestions. I am happy to announce that he and I have arranged to join forces in writing the second volume of this biography.

To Delight Ansley, who has compiled the index.

To Marion S. Pottle, the only person in the world who knows all the Boswell papers.

Finally, I return thanks for help on particular matters, not elsewhere acknowledged, to Thomas G. Bergin, J. A. Christie, James C. Corson, the Dowager Lady Eliott of Stobs, Archibald S. Foord, Arthur Friedman, Joseph S. Fruton, Joyce Hemlow, E. Donald Hirsch, C. Beecher Hogan, Frederick G. Kilgour, W. S. Lewis, B. R. S. Megaw, James Ritchie, Charles Ryskamp, Lloyd G. Stevenson, Eugene M. Waith, William K. Wimsatt, and Ann Young.

F.A.P.

Yale University
1 October 1965

CONTENTS

TEXTUAL NOTE

Except in a few instances where the reason for special handling is either stated or obvious (for example, pp. 25–26, 89 below), the spelling, capitalization, and punctuation of all the quotations in the present volume are mine and not those of the sources cited. I have generally translated passages in foreign languages: with notice in the back-notes when the document is entirely in some language other than English (for example, Belle de Zuylen's letter to Boswell, 14 June 1764, all in French), sometimes silently when the document imbeds foreign phrases or sentences in an English context (for example, Boswell's Journal entry of 1 January 1765, where the narrative is in English but the conversation in French).

F.A.P.

AUTHOR'S NOTE

This book had been entirely completed in a finished draft before a belated recovery from Malahide Castle turned up the "Sketch of My Life" which Boswell, early in his twenty-fifth year, wrote for Jean Jacques Rousseau. The recovery put me in exactly the position that John Gibson Lockhart found himself in when the old cabinet at Abbotsford disclosed Sir Walter Scott's autobiographical fragment. My decision has been the same as Lockhart's: to print the Sketch, just as Boswell wrote it, for my first chapter, and to remodel my own chapters down to the end of 1764 so as to make them expansions (or, as Lockhart said, "illustrations") of Boswell's precious but too brief autobiography. The remodeling has been rendered both delightful and difficult by the complication of the materials. Boswell's Sketch, when finally recovered, was found to be accompanied by two outlines, part of a discarded first draft, and several discarded leaves from the final draft. These by no means cover the same ground as the Sketch; on the contrary, they show Boswell experimenting and discarding until his infallible sense of tune picked up the precise unifying notes—education and the casuistry of romantic passion—most likely to command the attention of the author of *Émile* and *La Nouvelle Héloïse*. Having fixed on them, he ruthlessly sacrificed everything in his outlines and first draft that could not be firmly related to his topics. The result is that, though the Sketch is much superior to the outlines and draft from a literary point of view, it omits masses of detail of the first importance to an extended biography. I have therefore used the outlines and draft (which Boswell of course preserved for just such a contingency) as raw materials in my own chapters, breaking them up, and quoting or paraphrasing as best served my purpose at the moment. The reader may here be reminded, once for all, that the Sketch and its subsidiary documents were written in French, and that what is here presented is a translation.

INTRODUCTION

James Boswell, almost in the same post, received word of the death of Dr. Johnson and a request for a four-hundred-page biography, to be ready for the press in six weeks. He had already announced that he would take his time, but he certainly did not then suppose that six and a half years would elapse before his book was published. Other biographies appeared, he was warned that the interest in Johnson was waning, he was assured that the public would not pay two guineas for any biography, he was told that nobody would read a biography in two thick volumes even if it were distributed gratis. I do not know how far it is proper for me to draw comfort from the parallels, but of one of them I cannot but be deeply conscious. This book, which covers only half of Boswell's life, has been three times as long in the writing as the *Life of Johnson*.

Indeed, I began thinking about the biography of Boswell and the problems it presents more than forty years ago, when, at the suggestion of the late Professor Chauncey B. Tinker, I chose a systematic bibliographical study of Boswell as the subject of my doctoral dissertation at Yale University. In the preface to the resulting book, published by the Clarendon Press in 1929 with the title *The Literary Career of James Boswell, Esq.*, I said that though I believed in rigorous bibliographical study for its own sake, my prime concern in compiling the book had been to lay a firmer foundation for the biography of Boswell than had previously existed.

I do not think that at the time I wrote that preface I had any very active intention of writing a life of Boswell myself. Geoffrey Scott had just brought out the first six volumes of Colonel Isham's sumptuous *Private Papers of James Boswell*, and was known to be planning a biography. His *Portrait of Zélide* had confirmed his reputation as one of the

most brilliant stylists of his day and had demonstrated his skill in biographical analysis of the summary sort, while his editorial work on Boswell's papers (especially his acute and well-informed study of the making
of the *Life of Johnson*) had shown him capable of extended and detailed
research. If he chose to do another *Portrait*, the life of Boswell would be
still to write, but if he undertook to produce a comprehensive and detailed
narrative, there was every reason to suppose that the world would get an
unsurpassable life of Boswell, a book which might well be ranked among
the few enduring literary biographies of all time.

Scott was struck down by sudden fatal illness in August 1929 before
he had written a word of the book that was so eagerly awaited. When, in
that same month, I was asked to succeed him as editor of the *Private
Papers*, I made my acceptance conditional on being allowed to use the
Isham papers for writing a biography. From 1929 on, the biography was
my Rachel, the *Private Papers* and a projected popular edition of
Boswell's journal my Leah, though it would be uncandid not to admit
that I was much fonder of my imposed spouse than Jacob is reported to
have been of his. I toiled for Laban more than the traditional fourteen
years, and was not free of my service till 1945.

Of course I had not been working constantly at Boswell during all that
time. My life from 1925 to fairly recently has been mainly devoted to teaching and the administrative chores that accompany faculty appointment in
a modern university. A disproportionate amount of my publication, to be
sure, has concerned Boswell, but over the years I have given more time
and thought to preparing myself to teach Wordsworth and Shelley than
I have to all my publication on Boswell. Boswell, by and large, has been
the delight of my summer vacations and my sabbatical leaves.

By 1945–1946 (my first sabbatical after completing my obligation to
Colonel Isham) the situation as regards Boswell's papers had become very
complicated and baffling. Many more papers had turned up since 1929:
three successive lots at Malahide Castle and one at Fettercairn House. I
had access to the Fettercairn papers only as they were calendared in Professor C. Colleer Abbott's *Catalogue*, and to the last rich recovery from
Malahide I had no access at all. But I was approaching fifty, and felt I
could wait no longer. I determined to write as finished an account as I
could of the earlier portion of Boswell's life, using the materials accessible
to me, and to correct and extend it when opportunity offered. I think I

worked on through two more summers after 1945–1946 and finished the task in 1948.

Access to the whole body of Boswell's papers was not long delayed. By heroic effort Colonel Isham reassembled the scattered archives, and in the summer of 1949 allowed them to be purchased for Yale University. But instead of the freedom to revise with which I had flattered myself, I found myself bound again, and this time by life indentures. Between 1950 and 1963 three collaborators and I brought out the eight Boswell volumes so far published in the "trade" or reading series of the Yale Editions, a drastic adaptation and enlargement of the shelved popular edition I had prepared for Colonel Isham. Revision of the biography had to wait not only on my teaching, but also on a very active continuing programme of thoughtful popularization. And I found the revision frustrating and slow. One cannot satisfactorily work masses of detailed new information into a finished historical narrative by the simple process of adding paragraphs and revising sentences here and there. I rewrote a great deal simply because the writing was more than fifteen years old when I got to it and I could not abide it, though I am by no means confident that the style that now suits me would seem better to anyone else. I often thought that it would have been easier and quicker to throw the whole thing away and start afresh. Then President Griswold of Yale reduced my teaching assignment and President Brewster reduced it further and arranged for me to have a year of extraordinary leave. I finished the text of *James Boswell, the Earlier Years* in the spring of 1964 and spent a year more in compiling the notes. I now dismiss the book with anything but frigid tranquillity.

The organizing themes or structural principles of any thoughtful biography of Boswell should be many and some of them should be fairly subtle, but I think I shall not prejudice my case with the candid reader if I define those which I have employed most prominently. First, then, and foremost, Boswell was a Scot, not an Englishman; he was a Scot of family, not a plebeian. This book begins and ends on the note of Family. Secondly, he was not an idler nor a man of leisure but a lawyer, a lawyer with a special genius for criminal practice, a lawyer for whom people in 1769 were still predicting a brilliant future. I attempt much more fully than any previous biographer has to give substance and reality to the central occupation of Boswell's life, which, as he saw things, was undoubtedly the Law. Yet, as seen by us, he was not primarily a lawyer (much less a sot or a buffoon or a neurotic), but a writer, a man whose virtues and foibles would now not interest us in the least if he had not written of them so engagingly. I have tried not to forget that my prime responsibility as a biographer of Boswell was to define and assess his literary genius.

Frederick A. Pottle

Yale University
1 October 1965

CHAPTER

I

[Sketch of the Early Life of James Boswell,
Written by Himself for Jean Jacques Rousseau,
5 December 1764]

I present you, Sir, with a sketch of my life. To men of the world who delight in reading biographies, it would be nothing, for they would find in it
few amusing adventures. But if I am not mistaken, it will be a treasure to
M. Rousseau. You who love the study of mankind so much will find in it
evidence to confirm you in your opinions. You will see in me an extraordinary example of the effects of a bad education. I have a very good
memory for the things that interest me. I have a lively imagination. I can
recall the whole development of my existence since I was able to think.
I shall give you the principal ideas. I shall not conceal my weaknesses and
follies. I shall not even conceal my crimes.

Illustrious philosopher! you shall see me completely, just as I am. You
will judge me with indulgence. You will advise me. Perhaps you will find
me worthy of your counsel.

I was born with a melancholy temperament. It is the temperament of
our family. Several of my relations have suffered from it. Yet I do not
regret that I am melancholy. It is the temperament of tender hearts, of
noble souls. But such temperaments require a very careful education.
There is danger either that they will fall into a debility which will completely destroy them, or that they will form a habit of viewing everything
in such colours as to make their lives miserable.

I was brought up very tenderly. Consequently I began at an early age
to be indisposed, and people pitied me as a very delicate child. My mother
was extremely kind, but she was too anxious when I had some small ailment. If I did not feel well, I was treated with excessive attention. I was
not made to go to school, which I detested. She gave me sweetmeats and
all sorts of pretty things to amuse me. When my health was restored, my
slavery would begin again. I knew it, and I preferred being weak and ill

1

to being strong and healthy. What a perverted notion! Nature must receive a terrible shock before it submits to such a change. In a state of Nature, a child should feel miserable in illness and joyful in health. It is for that reason that he is encouraged to struggle with his illnesses. I encouraged them; and instead of jumping and running about, I lolled in an arm-chair. I was discontented and capricious. It is surprising that I did not often say that I was ill when I was actually well. But my worthy father had impressed upon me a respect for the truth which has always remained firm in my mind. Accordingly I never lied, but I hung my head down towards the floor until I got a headache, and then I complained that I was ill.

My mother was extremely pious. She inspired me with devotion. But unfortunately she taught me Calvinism. My catechism contained the gloomiest doctrines of that system. The eternity of punishment was the first great idea I ever formed. How it made me shudder! Since fire was a material substance, I had an idea of it. I thought but rarely about the bliss of heaven because I had no idea of it. I had heard that one passed one's time there in endless praise of God, and I imagined that that meant singing psalms as in church; and singing psalms did not appeal to me. I should not have wished to go to heaven if there had been any other way of not going to hell. I imagined that the saints passed the whole of eternity in the state of mind of people recently saved from a conflagration, who congratulate themselves on being in safety while they listen to the mournful shrieks of the damned.

My mother was of that sect which believes that to be saved, each individual must experience a strong conversion. She therefore entreated me often to yield to the operations of Divine Grace; and she put in my hands a little book in which I read of the conversions of very young children. I remember that one of these children was only three years old. The servants diverted me with an infinity of stories about robbers, murderers, witches, and ghosts, so that my imagination was continually in a state of terror. I became the most timid and contemptible of beings.

However, from the age of eight to the age of twelve I enjoyed reasonably good health. I had a governor who was not without sentiment and sensibility. He began to form my mind in a manner that delighted me. He set me to reading *The Spectator;* and it was then that I acquired my first notions of taste for the fine arts and of the pleasure there is in considering the variety of human nature. I read the Roman poets, and I felt a classic enthusiasm in the romantic shades of our family's seat in the country. My governor sometimes spoke to me of religion, but in a simple and pleasing way. He told me that if I behaved well during my life, I should be happy in the other world. There I should hear beautiful music. There I should acquire the sublime knowledge that God will grant to the righteous; and there I should meet all the great men of whom I had read, and all the dear friends I had known. At last my governor put me in love with heaven, and some hope entered into my religion.

My father, who is one of the ablest and worthiest men in the world, was very busy and could not take much immediate care of my education. He did as others do and trusted me to teachers. From five to eight I attended a school, where I was very unhappy. From eight to twelve I had my first governor, and during those four years I can say that I was happy except on Sundays, when I was made to remember the terrible Being whom those about me called God. The Scots Presbyterians are excessively rigid with regard to the observance of the Sabbath. I was taken to church, where I was obliged to hear three sermons in the same day, with a great many impromptu prayers and a great many sung psalms, all rendered in a stern and doleful manner. In the evening I was made to say my catechism and to repeat psalms translated into the vilest doggerel. I was obliged by my religion "not to do my own work, speak my own words, nor think my own thoughts, on God's holy day." I tried in sincerity of heart to conform to that command; especially not to think my own thoughts. A fine exercise for a child's mind!

When I was twelve years old, my governor was appointed minister of a parish, and I was given another governor, a very honest man but harsh and without knowledge of the human mind. He had gone through the usual course of school and college. He had learned his lessons well, and all he had learned he had made part of himself. He was a dogmatist who never doubted. He felt and acted according to system. One day when I said I had a friend whom I loved more than my brothers, he called me a blockhead and said, "Do you not know how affection develops? First you love your parents, then your brothers, then you spread yourself abroad on the rest of the human race." He made me read the ancient authors, but without getting any pleasure from them. He had no other idea than to make me perform a task. When I asked him questions about the poets, for instruction or amusement—and why should I not have looked for amusement?—he lost his temper and cried out with a schoolmaster's arrogance,

"Come, come, keep at work, keep at work, don't interrupt the lesson. Time
is flying." Consequently I got the habit of reading without any profit. It
was enough to say that I had read such and such an author.

In my twelfth year I caught a very severe cold. I was given a great
many medicines, and my naturally weak stomach became so upset that
I could hardly digest anything. I confess that the fear of having to go
back to what were called my studies made me hope I could stay ill. The
greatest doctors in Scotland were called in. I was naughty enough to take
measures to prevent their medicines from having any effect on me. I could
somehow or other control the operations of my stomach, and I immediately threw up everything they made me take. I even endured blisters,
congratulating myself on not having to *work*. The Faculty decided that I
was suffering from an extraordinary nervous illness, and I confess I
laughed heartily to myself at their consultations. I was weakened in body
and mind, and my natural melancholy increased. I was sent to Moffat,
the Spa of Scotland. I was permitted a great deal of amusement. I saw
many lively people. I wished to be lively myself, and insensibly regained
my health, after having imagined that I should certainly be ill all my life.

At thirteen I was sent to the University. There I had more freedom.
The place rather pleased me, and during the three years that I was studying languages, I attained high distinction and my professors said I would
be a very great man.

My youthful desires became strong. I was horrified because of the
fear that I would sin and be damned. It came into my troubled mind
that I ought to follow the example of Origen. But that madness passed.
Unluckily a terrible hypochondria seized me at the age of sixteen. I
studied logic and metaphysics. But I became Methodist. I went back to
Moffat. There I met an old Pythagorean. I attached myself to him. I
made an obstinate resolve never to eat any flesh, and I was resolved to
suffer everything as a martyr to humanity. I looked upon the whole
human race with horror. That passed, I know not how; I think by yielding to received opinions. For even now it does not seem clear to me.

At eighteen I became a Catholic. I struggled against paternal affection, ambition, interest. I overcame them and fled to London with the
intention of hiding myself in some gloomy retreat to pass my life in
sadness. My Lord ____ made me a deist. I gave myself up to pleasure
without limit. I was in a delirium of joy. I wished to enter the Guards.
My father took me back to Scotland. I spent two years there studying

Civil Law. But my mind, once put in ferment, could never apply itself
again to solid learning. I had no inclination whatever for the Civil Law.
I learned it very superficially. My principles became more and more confused. I ended a complete sceptic. I held all things in contempt, and I
had no idea except to get through the passing day agreeably. I had
intrigues with married actresses. My fine feelings were absolutely effaced.

I was in love with the daughter of a man of the first distinction in
Scotland. She married a gentleman of great wealth. She let me see that
she loved me more than she did her husband. She made no difficulty of
granting me all. She was a subtle philosopher. She said, "I love my husband as a husband, and you as a lover, each in his own sphere. I perform
for him all the duties of a good wife. With you I give myself up to
delicious pleasures. We keep our secret. Nature has so made me that I
shall never bear children. No one suffers because of our loves. My conscience does not reproach me, and I am sure that God cannot be offended
by them." Philosophy of that sort in the mouth of a charming woman
seemed very attractive to me. But her father had heaped kindnesses on me.
Her husband was one of the most amiable of men. He insisted that I
make extended visits at his seat in the country. I was seized with the
bitterest remorse. I was unhappy. I was almost in despair, and often
wished to confess everything to Mr. _____, so as to induce him to deprive
me of my wretched life. But that would have been madness of the most
fatal sort. I opened my heart to Mrs. _____. Although she was affectionate and generous, she was set in her ideas. She reproached me for my
weakness. What could I do? I continued my criminal amour, and the
pleasures I tasted formed a counterpoise to my remorse. Sometimes even
in my very transports I imagined that heaven could not but smile on so
great a happiness between two mortals.

At twenty-two my father allowed me to go to London. I was glad to
escape from Mrs. _____'s vicinity. I made a resolve never to write to her,
and for two years we have had no news of each other excepting merely
that we were in health. At London I had an intrigue with a woman
hackneyed in the ways of gallantry. For that I could not reproach myself.
But I fell into a heartless commerce with girls who belonged to any man
who had money. For that I do reproach myself. I made the acquaintance
of a famous scholar who proved to me the truth of the Christian religion,
though his variety of Christianity was a little severe.

My father was still anxious. He wished to make me an advocate in

Scotland. Finally I consented, on condition that he would permit me to travel. I went to Utrecht. There I forced myself to study hard, but I profited little. I have never really learned how to apply myself. The blackest melancholy overwhelmed me. My gloomy ideas of religion returned, and sometimes I believed nothing at all. I thought with irresolute horror of taking my own life.

My Lord Marischal took me with him to Germany. His conversation gave me a change of ideas. His virtues brought warmth to my frozen soul. I confessed my melancholy to him. He has written to my father to allow me to travel in Italy. I expect at Neuchâtel to find my father's answer.

Sir, I have given you in haste an account of all the evil in my nature. I have told you of all the good. Tell me, is it possible for me yet to make myself a man? Tell me if I can be a worthy Scots laird. If I can—heavens, how much I fear the contrary!—if I can be virtuous in my relations with Mrs. _____. Perhaps she has changed too. O charitable philosopher, I beg you to help me. My mind is weak but my soul is strong. Kindle that soul, and the sacred fire shall never be extinguished.

CHAPTER

II

"If I can be a worthy Scots laird": it is on this note that the biography of
James Boswell should open. He was a Scot, he was the heir of an ancient
family, he was very conscious of it. By 1764 there had been eight Boswells, lairds of Auchinleck in Ayrshire, and their reigns had covered a
period of two hundred and sixty years—nearly three quarters of a century
more than the independent existence of the United States of America.
They had succeeded the Auchinlecks of that ilk in their property, the
Auchinlecks for their part having held it for at least two centuries. In
1504, the male line of the Auchinlecks having failed, the castle and
barony were presented by James IV to Thomas Boswell, a cadet of the
Boswells of Balmuto in Fife, for his good and loyal service. This was a
break in name but not a complete break in line, for Thomas's wife appears to have been a grand-daughter of the last Auchinleck of Auchinleck.

The history of the lairds of Auchinleck had not been without the
sort of violent incident that constitutes popular history—matter for Sir
Walter Scott to have woven into Waverley novels and poems like
Marmion. About the middle of the fifteenth century, James Auchinleck
was surprised and slain by his neighbour, the laird of Ochiltree, who
besieged the castle with intent to exterminate the family, but was in his
turn overpowered and hanged by the Earl of Douglas, who had hastened
to the relief of Auchinleck. In 1513, Thomas Boswell, a gentleman of
the bedchamber or squire of the body, whose recorded services ranged
from armed raids against Border thieves to morris-dancing at Christmas,
fell fighting with his king at Flodden. The second laird, David, was in
arms in the Battle of the Butts (1544); John Boswell, the third laird,
fought at Langside (1568). James, the fourth laird, got involved in a

feud with the Johnstones and had to maintain a private army of horse-
men on his estate. David, the fifth, was a warm supporter of Charles I
and paid a heavy fine rather than subscribe to the Covenant.

There is nothing extraordinary in this summary of notable incident,
drawing as it does on the record of two extremely turbulent centuries;
indeed, from Langside to the eighteenth century the public involvement
of the Boswells seems meagre. None of them attained to a title, none held
any office of state, none sat in Parliament, and their names turn up with
surprising infrequency even in the ordinary records of neighbourly business. In the biographer's time they were charged with entertaining a
pride and high estimation of themselves that seemed ridiculous in the
eyes of other people, who considered them not only as no better than any
other gentlemen's family but as a stiff and inhospitable family. It looks as
though this pride had set in early, perhaps as accompaniment to an in-
transigent political conservatism, and that the lairds had long nourished
the sense of their own superiority by deliberate aloofness.

In one respect, perhaps, their sense of distinction was not entirely
baseless. When the biographer later spoke of his pride of ancient blood,
he was clearly not confining himself to the eight Boswells to whom he was
heir male. The Boswells of Auchinleck from first to last had shown a
faculty for connecting themselves by marriage with notable houses and
notable individuals. Thomas, the founder, was an earl's grandson. David,
the second laird, married a sister (illegitimate, no doubt, but still a great
catch) of the Earl of Arran, a young nobleman of the blood royal who
was shortly afterwards proclaimed Governor of the kingdom and heir
presumptive to the throne. John Boswell, the third laird, became by his
second marriage brother-in-law both to the "upstart" Earl of Arran,
James VI's favourite, and to the wife of John Knox. James Boswell,
the fourth laird, married a grand-daughter of Janet Stewart, Lady Fleming, natural daughter of James IV and mother, by the King of France, of
"le Bâtard d'Angoulême." James Boswell, the biographer's grandfather,
brought Bruce blood into the family by marrying a daughter of the Earl
of Kincardine. The biographer's mother was a great-grand-daughter of
John Erskine, Earl of Mar, by his second countess, daughter of a Duke of
Lennox and second cousin to James VI. Whenever the biographer partic-
ularized his pride of ancient blood, he generally selected this descent and
not that through the Boswells, for it gave him his most splendid claim
to call cousins with both the Young Pretender and George III. Through

these connexions and others he was related—in some cases fairly closely
—to the representatives of a dozen of the noble houses of Scotland and
England. Study of the Boswell line itself seldom leads to the page of
public history, but if one turns to the lines into which the Boswells
married, one arrives there constantly, and not merely in such eminently
public names as Arran, Lennox, and Mar.

The fifth laird had arranged good marriages for four daughters and
had left a reduced and embarrassed estate to his nephew. We know very
little about this sixth laird and third David except that he strove valiantly
by frugality to restore the estate and kept himself very close to Auchinleck.
With his successor, the second James, the horizon suddenly opens. Charles
II and James VII have killed off Toryism and Divine Right even at
Auchinleck. The effective way now to aggrandize a family is to adjust to
the Revolution settlement, conduct one's self soberly before God and man,
and to make money. James attended the University of Glasgow, studied
law at Leyden, was admitted (or, as the Scots idiom has it, passed)
advocate, and built up one of the largest practices of the day. He freed
the barony of encumbrance, bought back portions that had been alien-
ated, and made considerable additions. A "big, strong, Gothic-looking
man," as he was once described to his grandson, he was a solid lawyer
but very slow, so slow that it used to be said that he never understood a
cause till he had lost it three times. He was given to fretfulness, melancholy, and fear of his latter end; that he could make enemies is shown
by the prayer of the old laird of Gilmillscroft, who used in his family
worship to petition the Almighty to pour down of his choicest curses on
Mr. James Boswell of Auchinleck, advocate. He had three sons: Alexander, the eldest, and twins named James and John. He made over his
estate to Alexander some time before his death, but showed notable
capriciousness in disposing of his personal or movable property. When
he died in 1749, it was found that at different times he had bequeathed
it to each of the three sons, but the will in favour of Alexander was the
latest.

Alexander was born in 1707, a year and half before Dr. Johnson.
He followed the course set by his father, studied law at Leyden, and
passed advocate. In 1748, following the abolition of hereditary jurisdic-
tions, he was appointed Sheriff of Wigtownshire, in the first group of
such appointments to be made by royal warrant. Though he held the
sheriffship only two years, he was very proud of it. Carlyle, who was born

thirteen years after Alexander Boswell's death, had heard lawyers in
Edinburgh tell how the old man in his dotage was given to prefacing his
remarks from the bench by the formula, "I, the first King's Sheriff in
Galloway." At the age of forty-seven, he attained the highest honour of
his profession, appointment as one of the fifteen judges (called "Lords")
of the Court of Session, the supreme court of Scotland for civil cases.
Six of the Fifteen constituted also the High Court of Justiciary, the
supreme criminal court, and this additional appointment he received a
year later. According to the custom of the time, he took from his estate
the style of Lord Auchinleck, a title that has perplexed many who are
not familiar with the Scottish legal system. Though it gave him the style
of "Honourable" and entitled him to be addressed as "my Lord," it
indicated only pre-eminent judicial status and was not in any sense a title
of nobility. In point of right, his wife's status was not affected by the
dignity, but custom continued for wives of Lords of Session the style of
"Lady" which had once been usual for all lairds' wives, but by 1750
was otherwise becoming obsolete. Lord Auchinleck was not a rich man,
but by the standards of the time he was in very comfortable circumstances. His estate brought in £1000 a year, and his judgeships were
worth £900 more.

By the middle of the sixteenth century the Boswells had abandoned
the old keep as a place of residence, and had constructed nearby a new
castle, in a style of architecture more elegant and domestic. This Scots
Renaissance mansion Lord Auchinleck in turn deserted, building the
present Auchinleck House, an exquisite piece of neo-classicism finished
in 1762 and now undergoing extensive restoration. He was a good
classical scholar, with an especial fondness for Anacreon and Horace.
From Horace he selected a motto to inscribe conspicuously across the front
of his new house:

> Quod petis hic est,
> Est Ulubris, animus si te non deficit aequus—

which may be paraphrased, "If you have got a good firm mind, you can
be happy at Auchinleck, remote and quiet though it be." Having acquired
the *animus aequus* himself, perhaps not without painful effort, he was
impatient with others whose efforts towards equanimity he considered
fitful or sluggish.

Lord Auchinleck was a complete Whig and a convinced, though not demonstrative, Presbyterian. He scorned modern literature, spoke broad Scots from the bench, and even in writing took no pains to avoid the Scotticisms which most of his colleagues were coming to regard as vulgar. He had an inexhaustible fund of homely anecdotes which he told without relaxing a muscle of his face, and in his pleadings and papers affected a style of unsmiling irony which was much relished by his colleagues. As a judge, he was patient, laborious, and dispassionate. He was a great friend to unhappy girls who had been seduced by young fellows that afterwards denied it, and used to say that he fathered more bastards than any man in Ayrshire. There was in all Scotland no man more respectable and few more respected than Alexander Boswell, Lord Auchinleck.

At the age of thirty he married a girl some ten years younger than himself, Euphemia Erskine, youngest daughter of Lieutenant-Colonel John Erskine, Deputy Governor of Stirling Castle. Colonel Erskine was a grandson, through the Alva line, of John Erskine, Earl of Mar (1588–1634), his grandmother, the Earl's second wife, having been Lady Marie Stuart, daughter of the Duke of Lennox. (That is, her father was first cousin to Lord Darnley, the father of King James VI.) Alexander Boswell and his wife were first cousins once removed, he being a grandson and she a great-grand-daughter of the second Earl of Kincardine and his countess, a Dutch lady of distinguished family, Veronica van Aerssen van Sommelsdyck. This reinforcement of the Sommelsdyck genes was by some thought to be imprudent, for the third Earl of Kincardine had been feeble-minded, and popular opinion traced his defectiveness to his mother. It might with equal cogency have been remarked that Veronica's eldest and youngest daughters, Lady Mary (Euphemia Erskine's mother's mother) and Lady Elizabeth (Alexander Boswell's mother) were notably able women. Lady Mary, who had married Cochrane of Ochiltree, considered herself Countess of Kincardine in her own right, and sued to be recognized as such. She was unsuccessful, but her son died a peer none the less, falling heir unexpectedly to the Cochrane earldom of Dundonald.

Euphemia Erskine was an old man's child, and her personality showed it. Colonel Erskine was approaching sixty at the time of her birth; her mother was his third wife, and he had several grandchildren by his first marriage older than any of the children of his third. Euphemia Erskine never knew her mother, Euphemia Cochrane, who died before the daughter was two years old. And the Colonel (who lived to be seventy-seven) was rendered helpless by paralysis some years before his death. Euphemia Erskine grew up in great seclusion in the Colonel's Close (now called the Palace) in the quaint old royal burgh of Culross, watched over by her formidable grandmother in Culross Abbey House up the hill, and her aunt, Lady Preston, in Valleyfield House nearby. She was, according to Boswell, "an extremely delicate girl, very hypochondriac; she had been brought up quite out of the world, and her notions were pious, visionary, and scrupulous. When she was once made to go to the theatre, she cried, and would never go again."

Though Boswell's intimacy with and need for his mother seem to have terminated with his entry into manhood, the relationship between them during his early years was extremely close. He never refers to her without tenderness: "my dear mother." The idea of her always made him feel protected and happy. To see or to think of Culross Abbey House was to have his mind serenely filled with the sentiments and affections which she roused in him in childhood; he experienced pleasant ideas when he merely met people from the part of the country where she was born. When he was a man of forty, he went to the Quakers' Meeting in Peebles Wynd, so that he might revive the agreeable mild religious impressions that he had had there in her company twenty years before. One such scene probably carries us farther back into his infantile mind than any other record we have. In 1780 the New Church in Edinburgh was renovated and the pews changed. On the last Sunday before the church was closed for the repairs, Boswell went and sat in his father's seat. "I meditated curiously on my remembering this seat almost as far back as my memory reaches—of my pious mother sitting at the head of it—of my dreary terrors of hell in it—of my having an *impression* of its being so connected with the other world as to be permanent." The figure of his mother shines in the murk of his childish terrors like a guardian angel or saint, something to hold on to, to trust, to turn to as an intercessor.

Of such parents, the worthy, ironic, strong-minded lawyer and the gentle, pious, mystical lady, James Boswell was born, in Edinburgh, presumably in the family house in Blair's Land, Parliament Close, on 29 October (New Style) 1740. It is well to remember that, though he was heir to a considerable landed estate, he was born in a town and remained at heart a town man all his life.

Edinburgh was then a city of approximately 50,000 inhabitants. On a map of the period its outline strikingly resembles the skeleton of a lizard lying with its head (the Castle Hill) to the west, and its tail (the grounds of the Abbey of Holyrood) to the east. Its prominent backbone is just a mile long; the tail section is called the Canongate. The hind legs, Leith Wynd and St. Mary's Wynd, join the backbone at the Nether Bow Port (a practicable gate, still shut at night), and extend off roughly north and south, the one leading to the city's harbour and port, the other opening into the highroad for the Border and England. The rest of the backbone is called the High Street, its western portion (the shoulders) having the additional designation of the Lawnmarket. There is no right front leg; the left, which curves in through the Corn Market, Bow Foot, and West Bow, to join the spine at the Bow Head, is called Candlemaker Row; it opens at the south end out through the Bristo Port, another of the old city gates. The Castle Rock, crowned by a magnificent fortress, rises almost 450 feet above sea-level, and everywhere except at the place where the lizard's head joins the neck, drops down in sheer rocky precipices. The backbone is the crest of a long narrow ridge which slopes gradually down from the Castle to the Abbey. The sides of the ridge (the lizard's flanks) fall away steeply north and south. Branching off at right angles to the spine and running down both flanks of the ridge, exactly like ribs, are scores of long narrow blocks of buildings separated by alleys called closes or wynds: closes (with the notable exception of the Parliament Close, a square of considerable extent) being somewhat narrower than wynds. In the tail portion, the ribs (for this lizard has ribs all the way to its tail tip) descend to thoroughfares parallel with the spine called the Backs of the Canongate; the ribs descending from the High Street terminate on the south in the Cowgate and on the north at the North Loch, a shallow artificial lake formed for the defence of the city. Most of the buildings of the Old Town are crammed into the two narrow, sharply sloping strips on each side of the ridge. The houses are enormously tall: one of them in the Parliament Close (thought by Edinburgh citizens to be the tallest inhabited building in the world) has seven storeys on the side towards the Close and twelve on the side towards the Cowgate. These towering structures, called "lands," are generally multiple tenements, each storey (called a "house") being owned by a different family. The apartments are often very elegant in their appointments, but the common stair is likely to be shabby

if not filthy. All water for domestic purposes is carried in barrels from
public conduits on the backs of porters up the stairs, and the foul water of
the household is supposed to be carried down the stairs in like manner
and poured into the sewers, which are mere open gutters alongside or
down the middle of the streets. But many a housemaid still persists, at the
stroke of ten in the evening, in throwing up a window, giving one warning shout of "Gardy loo!" and heaving the contents of the slop-barrel
into the street.

At the exact spot where the lizard's heart should be is the Parliament
Close, now coming to be known by the un-Scottish but more precisely
descriptive name of Parliament Square. The mediaeval church of St. Giles
(the principal church of the city), with its beautiful crown tower, closes
off the High Street side: it has been divided by interior partitions into
four separate kirks, of which Boswell's New Church is one. Close behind
St. Giles to the west, the Tolbooth, grim City prison, Scott's "heart of
Midlothian," almost blocks the High Street. The Parliament House, not
long since the meeting-place of the Parliament of the Kingdom and still
the place where its supreme courts sit, stands in the southwest corner of
the Close. And on the east side, a hundred yards or so from the Parliament House, are the Custom House stairs and Blair's Land, in which
Lord Auchinleck has his house, and in which Old James had owned a
house before him.

A dirty, evil-smelling, crowded, fantastic city, still very mediaeval,
commonly capped with a great cloud of smoke; a city steeped in historic
associations which a boy's lively imagination can turn into romance; a
city of surpassingly beautiful natural surroundings, from Arthur's Seat
and Salisbury Crags, which guard it like a crouching lion on the east,
round clockwise by Blackford Hill and the Braid Hills to Corstorphine
Hill and the gleaming waters of the Firth of Forth.

Boswell was not the first child of his parents, a sister Euphemia having
preceded him. When he was only three months old, he and Euphemia fell
ill with some serious malady, and Euphemia died. There is no record of
the birth of any other sister, but when he was nearly three, his mother
bore another son, John; and when he was nearly eight, a third son, David.
We know of another son who died at birth in 1754, when Boswell was
nearly fourteen, and the wide gaps between the known children's ages
hint at other similar losses.

If Boswell had been Walter Scott, we should certainly have had from him extensive personal reminiscences of the year 1745, when the Jacobite army entered Edinburgh and Prince Charles slept in Holyrood. All we in fact recover are one anecdote and one odd but obviously authentic flash of things seen and heard in the Rebellion year. A foot-note in the *Life of Johnson* (of all places) tells us that the five-year-old Boswell broke with the politics of his family and region, announced himself a Jacobite, wore a white cockade, and prayed for King James—until his grand-uncle, General Cochrane, gave him a shilling to pray for King George. And some of his verses written years later in Germany tell how "in Edina's town," before he had ever gone to school, he stared at the moustached Hessians who had come over under their prince to assist in quelling the Rebellion, and how he saw them buying breeches for themselves while Arthur's Seat resounded with their drums. He was probably not actually in the city during the Highland occupation. The only other of his too-rare backward glances that concerns the year 1745 reveals that the family spent that summer in a house in Newington, then a region of open country a mile to the south of the city. Visiting the house nearly forty years afterwards, he says that he had a very imperfect reminiscence of the particulars, but he went into a park which he clearly recollected and lay upon a little green knoll where he had lain as a child, and for a few moments felt as calm and gentle as he had then. If Alexander Boswell moved his family on the approach of the Highland army in September, he would, one thinks, have been more likely to take them to Auchinleck than back into the city, though it was not usual for Lady Auchinleck and the children to domicile at Auchinleck in Old James's lifetime. In any case, it was characteristic of Boswell, when the stirring year 1745 came up, to say nothing of the Rebellion and to try to recapture feelings associated with his mother.

Sometime during his sixth year, Boswell was placed in a private academy in the West Bow conducted by one James Mundell. Mundell's school was somewhat more advanced in its theory and methods than the famous (and still existing) High School of Edinburgh. It took children without their letters, admitted girls as well as boys, and offered a wider range of instruction ("Latin, English, Writing, and Arithmetic") than the High School, which taught only Latin. Though short-lived (it did not long survive its founder, who died in 1762), it acquired high reputation. Any one at all familiar with the history of Edinburgh in the eighteenth century will at once recognize a considerable number of names in the list of little boys who entered it at the age of five or six: heirs of noble houses, sons of professors at the University of Edinburgh, many boys who later became lawyers. At least four Lords of Session got their early schooling at Mundell's. After Mundell's death his scholars formed an association for dining together once a year. They called each other by the nicknames they had borne as children, lived over their boyish days again, and encouraged sentimentality by getting roaring drunk. Since Boswell seems rather to have enjoyed these meetings, one would have inferred that he liked the school. Actually, he attended it only two or three years and hated it all the time he was there.

At the age of eight (that is, either in 1748 or 1749) Boswell left Mundell's, and for the next four years received all his schooling at home under the direction of a domestic tutor or "governor." It was common practice in families like Alexander Boswell's to engage a divinity student to drill the children in their lessons, even when they went out to school, and it was not unheard of for a boy from one of the better families to receive all his education at home during part of his childhood. Since the removal from Mundell's occurred at just about the time of Old James Boswell's death, it may need no other explanation than Alexander Boswell's wish to have his family at Auchinleck with him during the spring vacation. But it seems likely that the decision to withdraw Boswell from Mundell's was at least partly made because of his unconquerable dislike for the school, and the alarming state of his health.

He suffered, it appears, from extreme timidity and infantile dependence on his mother. In his recollections of his earliest childhood, images of fear predominate. "Spirit crushed," says one of his outlines for the Sketch: "no noble hope. Terribly afraid of ghosts. Up to eighteen could not be alone at night. Got over it by a habit of not thinking, not by reasoning about it. Afraid of the cold and everything else. A complete poltroon in the streets of Edinburgh. . . . Black ideas even at that age. Ignorant—terrified by everything I did not understand. Stingy: truly miserable when I had to pay out money."

Parents of a small child who suffered from black ideas and fears of ghosts would probably have been well advised to keep him out of the West Bow, the most antiquated in appearance of all the streets of the city, and also the spookiest. Henry Mackenzie, a contemporary of Boswell's, says that he and his friends in the High School did not dare go there after dark unless they made a party of five or six. It was not so much ghosts in general they were afraid of as the specific apparitions of the famous warlock Major Weir and his sister Jean, who were supposed to haunt the house and close near the first bend of Bow where they were living at the time of their arrest in 1670. Sir Walter Scott says that no story of witchcraft or necromancy ever made such a lasting impression on the public mind of the city as theirs. The Major, who had at one time commanded the city guard, a tall, grim, sanctimonious man of seventy, much admired for his eloquence in extemporaneous prayer, had been strangled and burned beside the road to Leith after confessing to a life of fornication, adultery, incest, and bestiality. He would not actually assert that he had made a pact with Satan, but everybody believed that he had. His sister, the partner of one of his crimes, did declare that the Devil helped her with her spinning, and was hanged in the Grassmarket for incest and witchcraft. Among the infinity of stories about witches and ghosts with which the servants kept the child Boswell in a continuous state of terror were certainly some connected with the entry and court he had to pass every morning, for Mundell's school was in a "land" only a few yards farther down the Bow, and on the same side of the street. The folklore of Edinburgh maintained that the Major could sometimes be seen dashing out of the close in a flame of fire on a headless horse; that early in the morning one could hear the sound of a spectral coach-and-six thundering down the Bow and stopping at Weir's Close to pick up the Major and his sister, who had been spending the night in their old home; that the house (long since given over to offices and a warehouse) often resounded at night with the hum of the sister's wheel.

And the West Bow would have had other terrors for an abnormally timid child. It was the Tyburn Road of Edinburgh. Down it on foot, once or twice a year, passed a mournful procession conducting some pinioned wretch from the Tolbooth to the tall gallows in the Grassmarket: the detachment of the City Guard, the condemned man in his linen grave-clothes, the hangman in rusty black treading behind. I know of no way of finding out what happened at Mundell's school on the day of an execution, but Scott's *Heart of Midlothian* gives warrant for the conjecture that the children met as usual. Though the master would not have let them run down to the Grassmarket, where they might have got hurt in the press, he may well have allowed them to crowd to the windows of the schoolroom to see the condemned man go by. Even if he kept them at their desks, he could not have shut out awareness of what was happening. At any rate, Boswell, very early in life, acquired a deeply morbid attitude towards public executions. His own explanation of the matter in after years was that he was afraid of death, and that the spectacle of people dying helped him to quiet and fortify his own mind. The fact is that at times he was under compulsion to attend every execution he heard of and to get as close to the gallows as possible; that so far from being quieted, he suffered afterwards for several days (especially at night-time) from frightful imaginings, apparently of ghosts.

Boswell's first governor was Mr. John Dun, a young man of twenty-five when he entered the Boswell household. He came from Eskdalemuir in Dumfriesshire, and had gone through the course in divinity at the University of Edinburgh. Boswell granted him a good figure and some imagination, but was severe as to his lack of polish. "My governors," he says in a discarded portion of the Sketch, "were both men without manners, men of the meanest sort of education. They were like my father's servants. They ate at table, but they hardly dared open their mouths. I saw them treated with contempt. Yet they had authority over me, the power to inspire me with cowardly sentiments. I thought that every one who was a little better dressed than I was and could speak without fear was my superior. I trembled before a lord, and would have thought myself honoured to be a duke's coachman." In the final version of the Sketch he is a good deal more generous, but surely not generous enough. For it was Dun who set him to reading *The Spectator* and gave him his first taste for literature; it was Dun who cleared his mind of religious terrors by tactfully fixing his attention on simple and humanly pleasing ideas of heaven. Under Dun's guidance he not only read the Roman poets but was encouraged to enjoy them.

In 1748, as has already been mentioned, Alexander Boswell was appointed Sheriff of Wigtownshire. The law, which was not always observed to the letter, stipulated that a sheriff should reside for four months of the year in the county where his office lay. Alexander Boswell is said to have scrupulously fulfilled the requirement and even to have moved his family to Wigtown during the times that he was in residence. Boswell never refers to any such sojourns in Wigtownshire, and his father's preserved correspondence seems to indicate that for most of the time, at least, he led a bachelor existence as sheriff. Yet I have a feeling that Boswell had thus early seen his father laying down the law. In Scotland a sheriff is not primarily or mainly a police officer but a minor judge with power to try persons accused of a wide range of crimes and misdemeanours, and to commit others for trial by the Lords of Justiciary. The fear that Boswell always had of his father probably goes very far back into his infancy, but I suspect that it was confirmed by some early spectacle of his father as sheriff, stern on the bench, handing out whippings and imprisonments to rioters and thieves.

Though Boswell's father was effectively laird from before Boswell's birth, it does not seem likely that Boswell saw much of Auchinleck in his grandfather's lifetime. But in 1749 Old James died, and thereafter our James spent the pleasantest part of each year on his ancestral domain. The parish, by and large, is not an especially beautiful tract of country, and it has not been improved by the "bings" with which shallow coal-mines have since dotted its surface. But the grounds surrounding the house deserve Boswell's often-repeated epithet of "romantic." The Dippol burn winds through a narrow gorge one hundred and fifty feet deep, its precipitous sides covered with trees that even then were large; the bridges across it have been placed so as to make the most of the sheer drop to the stream. The old manor house, with its Gothic vaults and thick walls, was still inhabited, and nearby, at the junction of the Dippol and the Lugar, stood the dwindling ruin of the old keep perched on its sandstone rock, the streams a hundred feet below—a ruin which the eye of fancy could reconstruct with towering walls, drawbridge, and portcullis. Somewhere nearby were the ruins of an ancient chapel dedicated to St. Vincent. In the neighbourhood were other fine seats: Ballochmyle, Barskimming, Dumfries House. But in Auchinleck parish everything nourished the sense of the power and the antiquity of the Boswell family. The laird counted six hundred souls his dependents. Accompanied by his young and impressionable son, he could ride ten miles in a straight line on his own territories. But the child Boswell would not have thought, This is my father's land; or, This will all one day be mine. He would have thought, This is land of the Family. To his enthusiastic and devout mind there would have seemed little difference between the two and a half centuries of Boswell occupation and the less than six thousand years which orthodox chronology assigned to the Creation. Just as he peopled bright patches of wood and stream at Auchinleck with the nymphs and genii he was reading about in Ovid, so the eight begats of the Boswell line seemed to him to blend with those of the fifth chapter of Genesis, and in particular solemn vistas at Auchinleck he saw his grandfather, like Enoch, walking with God.

CHAPTER

III

The year 1752 (Boswell's twelfth) was critical in more ways than one. Alexander Boswell presented Mr. Dun to the parish of Auchinleck, Joseph Fergusson took Mr. Dun's place as tutor to the Boswell children, and Boswell fell seriously ill. Fergusson was somewhat older than Dun, and at the time he came into the Boswell household was an unplaced minister of thirty-three or thirty-four, still seeking a manse and consequently still unordained. Boswell's fear of him later softened into something more like amused affection, but the Sketch probably does not overstate the unhappiness he suffered when Fergusson took charge of his education. An illness, which was believed to have started as a common cold, was complicated and prolonged by his misery under Fergusson's harsh and dry method of teaching, until it ended in something really serious.

"In winter, colds," says one of the outlines. "Attacked by illness in head, stomach, etc. Cowardly, loved easy chair. Struggled against remedies. Hypochondria. Despair. All scorbutic." It is not very likely that he was the victim of actual scurvy, for children of twelve who have any choice at all in what they eat seldom suffer from that disease. And we know that the medicine of the day gave the name of scurvy to all sorts of ailments, especially identifying the "hypochondriac" and the "scorbutic" disorders. He no doubt broke out in some kind of rash or scurf, but when the doctors diagnosed his trouble as basically nervous, they were pretty certainly right.

His parents must have been dreading just such a diagnosis. Up to the time of this illness, they could have flattered themselves that he had been spoiled by an over-indulgent mother and that his delicacy was wilful, but they knew that he might have inherited a constitutional nervous weakness.

His mother was notoriously "delicate," and there had been a more-than-average incidence of melancholy, eccentricity, and actual insanity in the later generations of the Boswell family. In the drafts and outlines of the Sketch, Boswell was quite explicit about this. "My paternal grandfather," he says, "inherited a strain of hypochondria from his mother. He was indolent in youth, but his father kept him at his studies by beating him, and he became a very distinguished lawyer and made a great deal of money. Yet he was rarely happy.... He was often attacked by black melancholy; and as he had been taught to dissemble his fits of ill humour and not to overcome them, he stopped hiding them when he no longer had his father to fear.... He was always thinking of retiring from the world, but my Lady, his wife, prevented him. . . . After my Lady's death, he really did retire and lived on his estate, where he led a very quiet existence. It ought also to have been tranquil. But his black humour and the harsh ideas of religion which remained with him to his death robbed him in great part of repose." Towards the end of his life Old James was subject to morose fancies. He believed all his sons wished him dead (the three wills have already been mentioned), and talked as though he thought none of them would attend his funeral.

Old James's twins (Alexander Boswell's younger brothers) both showed signs of mental instability. James was idle, given to keeping his bed, and finally had to be put in a strait-waistcoat. John, the other twin, was an able physician, but he was decidedly eccentric. He forsook the Kirk for the more "primitive" society of the Glassites, preached the extreme doctrine of salvation by faith, demonstrated his antinomianism practically by frequenting bawdy houses, and was excommunicated by his sect, who (as Boswell says) were very strict in enforcing morality though they did not admit any efficacy in it. And Johnny, Boswell's younger brother, may already have begun to show ominous symptoms. He was to succumb to unmistakable mental derangement soon after his nineteenth birthday, and thereafter would suffer periodically for the rest of his life from violent or morose insanity.

Doctors had for some time been prescribing the water of the sulphur spring at Moffat for "scorbutic" and "scrofulous" complaints, and genteel people were already beginning to go there for relaxation as well as to drink the waters. The amusements that so entranced the child Boswell cannot have been brilliant. Moffat was a small, rude village, bearing little resemblance to a great fashionable watering-place like Bath. Visitors had

their choice of putting up at an inn (there appear to have been two, neither large) or of taking lodgings in a private house. There was as yet no
assembly room and probably no music or dancing. But there was a
bowling-green in the centre of the main street, and people must have
made parties to walk or drive out to the spring, which is a mile and a half
from the village. Moffat is set in some of the most impressive scenery of
the Border and there are fine tramps for walkers who can manage from
ten to twenty-five miles: the Devil's Beef Tub, Hart Fell, the Grey Mare's
Tail, Loch Skene. And the people in each inn or lodging probably got together for cards, for conversation, and for games, which may have seemed
homely to the adult members of the company, but would have been bliss
to a child little used to such frivolities. Mr. Fergusson went along, and
surely an ailing boy of twelve would have been accompanied by his
mother or a nanny. Besides drinking from the spring, he took warm
baths and enjoyed them, in spite of the rudeness of the apparatus provided. And he was "insensibly" cured, not by the mineral water but by
the amusements: because the gay adult company—the first he had ever
been permitted to mingle in—enchanted him, drew him out of his shyness,
and made him want to get well so that he could share in the fun. His
nervous stomach quieted down, he recovered his appetite, and his melancholy left him. Though his illness was probably not truly scorbutic, it
resembled scurvy in the spectacular promptness with which it yielded to a
corrected regimen. It was a real and terrible disease, but it could be dissipated almost at once by release from a hated routine, travel, and "a
great deal of amusement."

He was to remain all his life subject to serious recurring fits of mental
depression, but with his recovery from this illness in his thirteenth year he
threw off for ever any tendency towards physical delicacy and became
robust and active. "We never have such stomachs afterwards," he wrote
a few years later, "as we had when at college." He goes on to recount the
"rapacious haste" with which he used to scurry home after classes: "down
the Horse Wynd, up Borthwick's Close, . . . by the crowded Cross, regardless of advocates, writers, Scotch Hunters, cloth-merchants, Presbyterian ministers, country lairds, captains both by land and sea, porters,
chairmen, and cadies," and describes the agonies of impatience with which
he waited for dinner to be set on the table and for Mr. Fergusson to finish
his ample benediction. "Then did I mightily fall on, and make a meal most
prodigious."

Boswell entered the University of Edinburgh in the academic session of 1753–1754, about the time of his thirteenth birthday. He should not be regarded as particularly precocious, for fourteen was the usual age of admission then and for many years afterwards. He continued to attend classes in the University for the next six years, first completing the regular course in Arts, and then going on as a student of law.

The University of Edinburgh in the 1750s had something like five hundred students, half of them studying medicine. It had never been a religious foundation, but had been established towards the end of the sixteenth century by the City itself. There was but one undergraduate college, and the college had no dormitories or dining-hall. Students who were sons of Edinburgh families lived at home, others found lodgings with landlords in the city. Gowns were not worn, and outside of classes students were completely free to choose their own company and set their own hours. No prescription was made as to individual programs of study, but students who wished to take a degree attended certain prescribed classes and submitted to an examination. The first degree was Master of Arts. Few students actually bothered to take the degree any more, but many continued to follow the "regular" curriculum. Boswell certainly studied Latin, Greek, and Logic, and probably took the other "degree" courses: Mathematics (arithmetic, plane geometry, trigonometry, algebra), Natural Philosophy, and Moral Philosophy. He probably had a little French. After he finished the Arts course, he reported taking classes in Botany, Astronomy, and Roman Antiquities. The Roman Antiquities, which dealt with Roman institutions rather than with physical remains, was an adjunct to his class in Civil Law; the Astronomy and Botany were probably short "popular" courses taken as a relief from legal studies.

When Boswell later deplored the "narrowness" of his education (and he never ceased to do so after his first visit to London), he was not in the main expressing dissatisfaction with the curriculum of the College of Edinburgh. The narrowness he principally deplored was social: the lack, both in childhood and youth, of the firm enveloping pressure of aristocratic disciplines that might have given him the fearless, assured, unself-conscious bearing of a high-bred gentleman. He deplored his solitary education as a child under tutors of plebeian origin and unpolished manners; he deplored the fact that in the college he had attended the students were as likely to be sons of merchants as of landed gentlemen, and that the Professor of Greek said "jeel" instead of "jelly." Always nagged by a suspicion that others rated him below his true standing, he regretted deeply that he had not been sent to a school like Eton or Westminster, where his associates would have been mainly young gentlemen and his instructors men who had at least acquired a tinge of gentlemanly manners.

In point of fact, narrowness of curriculum was not the vice of the Scots universities, their weakness lying in precisely the opposite direction. Their Arts course aimed at a broad general education which could serve as the basis for later specialized study in Divinity, Medicine, or Law. Scots education was much more democratic than English; it produced fewer scholars, but the general average of learning in Scotland was considerably higher than in England.

Boswell put the matter fairly when he said in *The Journal of a Tour to the Hebrides* (18 August 1773) that he "had thought more than anybody supposed, and had a pretty good stock of general learning and knowledge." His Greek was thin. He began it at the age of fifteen, had at most only two years of formal study in it, and in later life retained not much more than enough to enable him to locate the Greek corresponding to a given passage in a translation. He professed himself unable to learn mathematics, and there is no reason to suppose that he was being overmodest. Nor does he at any time show that he had been much influenced by the study of natural science. In Latin (which he studied continuously for at least ten years) he got excellent training in every department except prosody. He never lost his knowledge of the forms, and at any period of his later life would have been able to dash off a grammatically correct Latin letter without having to consult grammar or dictionary. He appears at some period or other to have read in all the major Roman authors. His father gave him a reward (presumably in cash) for every ode of Horace he got by heart, and at one time he could repeat more than forty of them, besides passages from Horace's *Epistles* and *Satires* and from Ovid and Virgil. At least two highly respectable judges have called him a good Latinist.

Boswell probably owed a good deal more of his Latin to James Mundell, Mr. Dun, and Mr. Fergusson than he did to George Stuart, the Professor of Latin at the University. The college course which really opened his mind the most was John Stevenson's class in Logic, which he attended during the session of 1756–1757. The title "Logic" was merely a convenient short designation: Stevenson actually covered logic, metaphysics, history of philosophy, and theory of criticism. Among the works read and discussed in the course were Locke's *Essay on Human Understanding,* Aristotle's *Poetics,* Longinus *On the Sublime,* and selected French and English critics. Stevenson illustrated the critical theories by readings from ancient and modern poets, and required his students to write essays. Robertson the historian, in his own time the most admired prose writer in Scotland, always said that he was more indebted to Stevenson's lectures (especially those on Aristotle and Longinus) than to any other portion of his academic studies. Stevenson had a lasting effect on Boswell too, both for good and for evil. The metaphysics of the course proved to be merely unsettling, but the portion dealing with literature opened and enriched his mind. Stevenson not only introduced him to some of the greatest works of literature, ancient and modern, but also gave him a more coherent and comprehensive foundation for criticism than he is commonly supposed to have had.

The earliest surviving document in Boswell's hand dates from the summer of 1754, and enables us to catch a clear glimpse of him as he was when he was going on fourteen and had completed his first session at the University. It is a letter to his mother. He is at Auchinleck and she is in Edinburgh; she has recently given birth to a son, who has died. The address, in a handsome round copybook hand, "To the Right Honble My Lady Auchinleck at Edinr," shows his lifelong tendency to magnify the honours of the family. Alexander Boswell had recently (15 February 1754) been raised to the bench, but a Lord of Session rated only a simple "Honourable" and his wife not even that. Boswell's own spelling has in this case been preserved in order to indicate how little he deviates from the dictionary:

My dear Mamma,

You may be assured that your safe delivery gave me great joy. I was indeed very sorry to hear of the death of my poor little brother, but however we must be submissive to the hand of a wise Providence that superintends everything that is done here below. Perhaps the Almighty Lord and Soveraign of the Universe saw some storm impending that might have proved fatal to the aeternal salvation of his precious and immortal soul, and therefore for wise ends and purposes (though unknown to us) removed him out of this valley of tears, this world of sin and misery, into the world which is above, that New Jerusalem where there is joy and pleasures for evermore. Better it is, my dear mamma, to think that instead of, it may be, living a bad life in this world, he is now singing halelujahs

to Him that sitteth upon the throne and to the Lamb that redeemed him
and shed his precious blood for him. And besides, if he had been more
advanced in years, it would have been a much greater grief for you. . . .
Ochiltree sacrament is to be next Lord's day; the fast is tomorrow. I
design to attend all the diets. . . . I sometimes try the shooting, and have
shot two sparrows, which I know will disoblige my Lord, but as I am
sorry for my fault and am henceforth to shoot at other birds, such as mag-
pies and crows, I hope his Lordship will pardon me. . . . I am, my dear
mamma, your loving and affectionate son,

JAMES BOSWEL

Auchinleck, July 17, 1754

The most striking features of this epistle, candour and piety, are the
strains of Boswell's character attributable respectively to the training of
his father and his mother. His condolences consist entirely of evangelical
clichés, but they are genuinely felt and quite unembarrassed. He and his
mother really talked to each other in that fashion. And the ridiculous confession of crime in the shooting of sparrows is not merely a canny device
for mitigating punishment by turning himself in. Lord Auchinleck had
assumed personal responsibility for only one aspect of his child's education, but his training in that respect had been decisive. "I do not recollect," Boswell wrote at the age of forty, "having had any other valuable
principle impressed upon me by my father except a strict regard to truth,
which he impressed upon my mind by a hearty beating at an early age
when I lied, and then talking of the *dishonour* of lying. I recollect dis-
tinctly having truth and honour thus indelibly inculcated upon me by
him one evening in our house, fourth storey of Blair's Land, Parliament
Close." From early childhood Boswell was incapable of telling a lie. And
he was not merely truthful, he was accurate—a quite different matter.

It may be a mistake to attribute any other consequences to that whip-
ping. Eighteenth-century children were beaten liberally as a matter of
course, and we know that Mr. Fergusson was empowered at least to
threaten Boswell with the rod. But since we know too from one of the
outlines for the Sketch that as a small child Boswell was considered too
delicate for corporal punishment, it may be that the well-remembered
beating at an early age was the first he ever received, and that it was
more of an emotional shock than he later realized. It may have crystal-
lized the feelings of fear and inferiority that he suffered in his father's

presence, or even when he thought of him, which had been gathering from his earliest consciousness.

The spelling of the family name with one "l", as in this early signature, was a whim of Lord Auchinleck's. Generally accounted the French Bois-ville and certainly spelled Bosvile by the Founder's forbears of the fifteenth century, it had by 1600 settled down into the spellings Boswall and Boswell, the Auchinleck family preferring the latter. Lord Auchinleck chose to simplify, and his son at first naturally followed him. His reversion to the traditional spelling soon after his eighteenth birthday was one of the earliest gestures in his lifelong struggle to free himself from paternal domination.

The letter shows a purity of English style that could have been attained only by long and intelligent study. Scotsmen of the eighteenth century who wished to speak and write the language of Addison and Fielding had to learn it almost like a foreign tongue. Their own linguistic tradition was confused. Down to the beginning of the seventeenth century Scots authors made no attempt to write like Englishmen. There was no reason why they should. Scotland was a proud and independent kingdom, traditionally leagued with France and frequently at war with England. The Scots variety of English enjoyed an independent status as a literary language and boasted a large body of fine poetry and prose. After the union of the crowns, however, Scots rapidly yielded its status as an accepted literary medium, and by the eighteenth century had lost it altogether. There was, to be sure, a revival of Scots verse in authors like Ramsay, Fergusson, and Burns, but this Scots verse had then precisely the status it has now: it was considered, even in Scotland, rustic, provincial, "dialect." Scots authors of Boswell's time who wished to avoid the imputation of dialect trans-lated what they had to say into the vocabulary and idiom of the South. And they really had to translate it, for the old Scots vernacular remained vigorous as a *spoken* tongue: was in fact the kind of English used for familiar oral discourse by nearly everybody north of the Tweed. The lead-ing Scottish authors—Robertson, Hume, Blair, Beattie—all testify to the severe training that a Scotsman had to undergo if he were to write ac-ceptable English, and to the lack of confidence he always felt in his style. Boswell's writings from the time he was a mere boy show a remarkable mastery of literary English. He has Scotticisms, to be sure, but fewer, I think, than Sir Walter Scott, and Scott enjoyed the inestimable advantage of having spent a year of his childhood at Bath.

Boswell certainly was not aided in acquiring this skill by his father's precept or example. He undoubtedly learned a great deal later, at least in the way of pronunciation, from his association with actors: West Digges, James Love, Thomas Sheridan. But in 1754 he knew no actors and had seen little or nothing of the theatre. The initiators of his education in English style can only have been James Mundell and Mr. Dun. The children at Mundell's were evidently a group whose parents wished them to acquire a cultured way of speaking. Just what the "English" of the curriculum consisted of, it may now be impossible to discover, but it would be a fair guess that it included the memorization of select models of English style and the writing of English exercises. Boswell knew, and could repeat at need, a good many lines from the English poets. He may have learned some of them at Mundell's. But surely the decisive moment came when Mr. Dun put him to work on *The Spectator*. Judging from Dun's own style (we have several of his letters) he could not himself have been of much help to his pupil by way of example. But Boswell was an apt pupil, for he had a literary gift. Once embarked on the reading of English classics, he became his own teacher.

Given his early shyness and his solitary education, it is no wonder that he made no warm friendships as a child. "I found myself always a little different from my companions," he wrote in a leaf discarded from the Sketch, "and as I advanced in years, the difference increased. I found in none of them those indescribable ideas of grandeur of soul and delicacy of taste which I believed within the reach of humanity, and which I hoped I might myself one day possess. Finally, I formed an intimacy with an Englishman named Temple, of the most worthy and amiable character, and a Scot named Johnston, whose character is masculine and hearty." The fact that he feels impelled, if only momentarily, to name his friends, shows how important these friendships were to him.

He certainly met Temple and he probably met Johnston in Robert Hunter's Greek class, in the autumn of 1755. John Johnston, descendant of a clan notorious for marauding exploits in the days of the Border turbulence, was already laird of Grange, a small property in Dumfriesshire. Of all the men Boswell had extensive dealings with, he is now the most obscure; in fact, excepting a few of the Edinburgh directories, I do not remember ever having seen his name on any printed page that did not somehow or other derive from Boswell. We do not even know for certain how old he was. If two contemporary reports of the age of a younger brother are correct, then he was ten or eleven years Boswell's senior, a grown-up man of twenty-five or twenty-six belatedly embarked on a college course. It need not seem strange that Boswell at fifteen should have found an older man more attractive than most of his classmates: Boswell was then an odd, sober, priggish boy with old ideas. But it does seem odd that Boswell should never have referred to the disparity of their ages, and odder still that when we first get documentation of the relationship (1759), he should clearly be playing the dominant role.

What attracted him to Johnston in the first place was the elegance of Johnston's clothes: he was wearing a coat with a straw-coloured lining. What fostered and perpetuated the intimacy were Johnston's unshakable loyalty, his unfailing affection, and his submissiveness. Like Boswell he had ideas of becoming a lawyer (as a "writer" or solicitor rather than as an advocate); like Boswell he suffered from recurring fits of depression; like Boswell—though with much greater knowledge—he entertained a passionate regard for the history of Scotland and as much of its scenery as could be connected with great historic events; like Boswell he was a Tory and inclined to be a sentimental Jacobite.

In the course of the years Boswell actually saw a great deal more of Johnston than of any other friend, and leaned more heavily on him, but he reserved the title "my dearest and most intimate friend" for another. William Johnson Temple was an English lad, though from no farther away than Berwick upon Tweed, the son of a recent mayor of that city. He was approaching sixteen when they met, and was some months past nineteen when they parted, he to go up to Cambridge. After the summer of 1758 they saw each other rarely, but they corresponded with the warmest affection all the rest of their lives.

Temple is much less obscure than Johnston; in fact, he has his own article in *The Dictionary of National Biography*. He later became a fairly close friend of Thomas Gray; he was the grandfather of one Archbishop of Canterbury and great-grandfather of another. The later Boswell and the later Temple seem to have very little in common—Temple became a sober, retired, fussy, self-torturing clergyman-scholar—but in 1755 they must have looked pretty much alike. Temple had more charm and vigour before a conviction of failure and a family of eleven children had broken his spirit, and Boswell was then shy and puritanical. The two boys drew together because they were pious and strict in their behaviour, because they loved literature and found talk about it delightful, because they were ambitious and convinced that they would both be great men. They called each other Jimmy and Willie, took long walks together on Arthur's Seat, and poured out their hearts in unreserved converse. Temple was an Anglican. Soon after the inception of their intimacy (probably on Christmas Day, 1755), he took Boswell to a Church-of-England chapel at the foot of Carrubber's Close. Boswell never forgot the irresistible enchantment of the service. The Presbyterian worship made him think of hell; here he felt that he was in heaven.

"Melancholy temperaments," says Boswell in that discarded portion of his Sketch from which I have already quoted, "are amorous temperaments. I assure you that before the age of twelve, I experienced all that the soul can feel of that passion." His original plan had been to give Rousseau a full account of his sexual development. This he later decided against, probably because he realized that it was not so extraordinary as he liked to believe, but one of his outlines preserves a series of hints for what he planned to say. "Already [that is, before he was thirteen] in climbing trees, pleasure. Could not conceive what it was. Thought of heaven. Returned often, climbed, felt, allowed myself to fall from high branches in ecstasy—all natural. Spoke of it to the gardener. He, rigid, did not explain it. In love at the age of eight. On honour, felt the strongest emotions except those of the great cause, of which I was ignorant, or rather concerning which I did not have clear ideas." At Moffat (aged twelve) he fell deeply in love with a Miss Mackay; Mr. Fergusson ridiculed his passion. From his reading he acquired clearer ideas of the great cause. "I knew about the rites of Venus. But unfortunately I learned from a playmate the fatal practice. I was always in fear of damnation. I thought what I was doing was but a small sin, whereas fornication was horrible." He was sufficiently distressed by his defeats in his struggles with sexual appetite to ponder the example of the early Church Father Origen, who interpreted literally a text of Scripture and emasculated himself for the sake of the kingdom of heaven. "That madness passed" in a series of powerful distractions. He wanted to become a soldier, he had a return of melancholy, he became a Methodist, he had another breakdown.

CHAPTER

IV

Since Boswell, at the time he wrote the Sketch, was obviously proud of what he calls his internal changes, one might suspect that he would tend to exaggerate their complexity and inconsequentiality. Actually, the emotional shifts of his sixteenth and seventeenth years appear to have been rather more numerous and violent than the Sketch indicates. He entirely suppressed one important episode, probably because his intent was to impress Rousseau with an idea of his uniqueness, and this was the sort of thing that might have happened to any spirited youngster. "Thirteen, college, good health," says one of the outlines. "Fourteen, the same. Fifteen also. Greek class. The war began. Although timorous where firearms were concerned, set in a flame, wished to go among the Highlanders to America. It was a frenzy. My father prevented it." The news of Braddock's defeat reached Britain in August 1755; the Black Watch (an all-Highland regiment that had already seen fifteen years of service) sailed for America in April 1756, and there was a good deal of recruiting of Highland troops to form additional regiments. One of these was raised and commanded by Lieut.-Colonel Archibald Montgomerie, brother to the Earl of Eglinton and eventually Earl of Eglinton himself, an Ayrshireman well known to the family of Auchinleck. In what capacity Boswell proposed to go fight the French and Indians in the wilds of New York and Pennsylvania is not clear. The granting of commissions to boys of fifteen was not unheard of, but the subaltern officers of the Highland regiments were all Highlanders. For that matter, the men were all supposed to be Highlanders too, though some were probably not. The normal behaviour now-a-days of a boy of fifteen in such circumstances would be to run away and try to enlist under an assumed name, and that is perhaps just what Boswell did, or laid plans for doing. His diction (*among,* not

with, the Highlanders) rather supports this intepretation. But it
would have been much more romantic for a gentleman's son to enlist as
a common soldier in 1755 than it would be now, and there may have
been some capacity in which a youngster of family could accompany a
regiment in the field without actually enlisting or being commissioned.
In any case, though his scheme for going to America was perhaps fantastic,
it was more than a day-dream, for his father had to prevent him from putting it into execution.

What is important in all this is that it forces those who have previously
known a good deal about Boswell to revise their ideas about him in two
important respects. The struggle with his father must be carried farther
back into his youth, and his stubborn campaign to be a soldier must be
seen as originating in his sixteenth year, as an ardent desire for service in
the field, and not in his twentieth, as a mere device for getting to London
and staying there. This is at once more credible and more creditable than
the old view. From Boswell's fifteenth to his twenty-third year, Great
Britain was engaged in perhaps the most rousing war in all her history,
the war that brought her Canada and established her dominion over
India. Boswell was deeply stirred by the martial temper of the times, and
his response was not originally or entirely selfish.

During his first three years at the University, Boswell had been considered a highly promising student, but when he branched out from languages and literature his limitations became apparent. In the autumn of
1756, he began studying logic and metaphysics under John Stevenson,
and promptly fell prey to a horrible melancholy. The study of metaphysics
forced him to think about the problem of determinism, or, to state the
problem in the terms in which it usually presented itself to him, of God's
foreknowledge and man's free will. He found that he could not reconcile
the two logically, and with that realization lost for ever the foundations
of his peace. The suspicion that Necessity governed all his actions filled
him with an anxiety at least as shattering as that which he would have felt
if he had come to suspect that he had a cancer.

"I studied logic and metaphysics," he wrote, "but I became Methodist." The "but" indicates how we are to take the "Methodist." He does
not mean that he separated himself from the Church of Scotland; the
Methodists were not yet dissenters. He does not even mean that he became
a member of a Wesleyan religious society, for there was as yet none in
Edinburgh. He may in May 1757 have been deeply stirred by the preach-

ing of the great evangelist George Whitefield (surely not now heard for
the first time), and may even have come under Whitefield's personal influence, for Whitefield, besides preaching to thousands, set aside time for
counselling souls under distress. If any introduction were needed, he could
have had one from his uncle by marriage, Dr. Alexander Webster, minister of the Tolbooth Church, one of Whitefield's strongest supporters in
Scotland. But when he wrote, in a journal-entry summarizing his religious
changes, "Methodists next shook my passions," he must have had in mind
more than one man's teaching. Perhaps he acquired and read the standard
Methodist tracts, and then tried to observe in his private devotions the
extended periods of Scripture-reading, prayer, and self-examination which
the Methodists practised in their societies. His mother, indeed, may have
been the effective evangelist. She appears to have been interested in
Whitefield as early as 1741, and the "strong conversion" which she urged
on him as a child sounds like the distinctively Methodist doctrine of the
new birth. The details must remain conjectural, but the essence of his
"Methodism" is clear enough: he fled from the paralyzing rationalism of
metaphysics and logic into a fervid religion of the heart and salvation by
faith.

But Methodism only shook his passions without bringing certainty,
and in the summer of 1757 his melancholy had again become so alarming
that he was sent back to Moffat. His amusements this time included a
jaunt to Carlisle. Knowing his later predilection, one might have supposed
that his first contact with English soil would have been overwhelming in
its impact, but the time for that had not yet come. His hunger for spiritual
consolation could not be stilled by diversions. He wanted a prophet, and
he found one more congenial than Whitefield.

John Williamson, a self-educated sheep-farmer in the neighbourhood
of Moffat, is described by an unsympathetic contemporary as having had
more book-learning than common sense. He had read eagerly all the
books he could come at dealing with metempsychosis, mysticism, alchemy,
and mineralogy, and had become an ardent convert to the doctrine of
the transmigration of souls and consequently to the practice of vegetarianism. Though he remained a life-long bachelor, he preached polyg-
amy, maintaining that every healthy man who could afford it should have
at least three wives. Another of his tenets was that God should not be worshipped in houses built by men, but on mountains or hills surrounded by
grand or picturesque scenery. When Boswell met him, he had lost his

tenancy because of his stipulation that the sheep he sold should not be slaughtered, had been given a small annuity by the Earl of Hopetoun, and was wandering far and wide prospecting for minerals. He never found the rich mine he was looking for, but in his rambles through the wild glens in the neighbourhood of Moffat he did discover Hartfell Spa, an iron spring long believed to possess medicinal virtues. Boswell tramped the hills with him, and became his convert, perhaps the only convert he ever made.

Years ago Professor Tinker, remarking that Boswell would never be understood until people came to see in him a precursor of the Romantic Movement as well as a child of the Age of Prose, pointed to the similarity between some of his utterances and Byron's. The occasional biographical likenesses are no less startling. Byron's accounts of his passion for Mary Duff, which occurred when he was eight or nine years old, sound like expanded versions of Boswell's statement that he fell in love at the age of eight and "felt the strongest emotions except those of the great cause." And other Romantic parallels—most unlikely ones—can now be discerned. The Pythagorean episode, with its background of nervous illness, its mild old prophet, its vegetarianism, its stubborn resolve to court martyrdom, is pure Shelley. One remembers too the antagonism that existed between Shelley and his father, and one wonders whether it is not a useful analogy for considering the tension that begins at this period to build up between Boswell and Lord Auchinleck.

The chief significance of the illness of 1756–1757 was that it strengthened Boswell's conviction that he was not like other people and never would be. "The truth is, with regard to me," he wrote later, "about the age of seventeen I had a very severe illness. I became very melancholy. I imagined that I was never to get rid of it. I gave myself up as devoted to misery. I entertained a most gloomy and odd way of thinking. I was much hurt at being good for nothing in life." Undoubtedly he was much hurt; undoubtedly, too, the conviction of his own fragility brought him a certain satisfaction. This time he deliberately resisted convalescence. He would always thereafter be scanning his mind for symptoms of disorder sufficient to excuse him from distasteful duties. And of course the second nervous illness seriously affected his father's attitude. Lord Auchinleck had to balance two possibilities: either his son was behaving in a culpably flighty manner, or he was not wholly responsible. Lord Auchinleck acted on the first of these suppositions and feared secretly that the second was true.

So far as Boswell could recall, he never decisively renounced his vegetarianism or his belief in the transmigration of souls, but yielded gradually
to the opinions of those about him. He probably yielded more than he
realized to the suasions of his own body. The second illness, like the first,
had been followed by an access of physical vigour. I suspect that in this
year he attained his full stature, which would have meant a height of not
more than five feet six inches. He was a thick-set boy inclining to plumpness, physically very robust and active, with black hair and eyes and a very
dark complexion. What have commonly been considered the dominant
traits of his personality seemed suddenly now to emerge from nowhere.
The timid, priggish, prematurely grave youngster was replaced outwardly
by a vain, noisy, bouncing, odd, comical, good-humoured youth of manly
features and masculine bearing whom many men and most women found
immediately attractive. With the discovery that he had a natural power of
inspiring affection, Boswell lost his horror of the human race and the
outward signs of his bashfulness, became almost the type of hail-fellow-
well-met, the seeker after company. But the anxious child-Boswell was not
really superseded. Boswell never quite succeeded in establishing his new
figure of himself as the enduring ground of consciousness. Whenever the
environment became too threatening or his own inner drives became too
urgent, he reverted to his sense of insecurity and suffered a depression.
The famous vanity was largely self-defence through self-enhancement.
The easy manners on which every one now began to congratulate him
were in fact self-conscious and always contained an element of acting.

Boswell's last session in the Arts course at Edinburgh College (1757–
1758), a complete blank in the Sketch and all its related documents, may
be regarded as the period of pupation of his new and ostensible self. By
the end of the summer of 1758 he definitely has his wings. He is scribbling and publishing poems, he is the companion of players, he is in love
with a young lady, and he is even thinking of marriage.

The young lady whose name heads Boswell's long list of possible wives
was a Miss Martha Whyte, an eighteen-year-old orphan with a fortune
which rumour set at £30,000. Boswell reported his passion to Temple in
July 1758, anticipating incredulity. "Don't be surprised if your grave,
sedate, philosophic friend, who used to carry it so high and talk with such
a composed indifference of the beauteous sex, and whom you used to ad-
monish not to turn an old man too soon"—don't be surprised, in short,

to find him sighing after Phyllis like any other Strephon. He is modest ("I own I can have but little hopes") but he does not despair. "I have reason to believe she has a very good opinion of me. . . . O Willie! How happy should I be if she consented, some years after this, to make me blessed!" Miss Whyte, who had already rejected a future Lord Chancellor and a future Senator of the College of Justice, receives no mention whatever in Boswell's next letter to Temple, written some five months later. In the following summer she married his kinsman, the Earl of Elgin and Kincardine.

As for the scribbling, Boswell had been scribbling for some time; what made all the difference was that he was now getting some flattering attention. Professor Tinker, in a pioneering chapter of *Young Boswell,* has characterized him as "one of those unusual young persons who deliberately and by preference seek out the companionship of men twice their age." This was no doubt partly due to his inability ever to establish easy relations with his father—something we must give serious attention to later. His cleaving to John Johnston was perhaps the first expression of this need to attach himself to friends older than himself. The discipleship to John Williamson was a more picturesque instance. But his current need was for a Maecenas, and he was lucky enough to find two.

Sir David Dalrymple (who, by the way, was the future Senator of the College of Justice mentioned above as one of Miss Whyte's rejects) was fourteen years older than Boswell. Well born and possessed of a modest private fortune, he was at thirty-two a learned, accurate, and hard-working lawyer, who managed to carry on extensive antiquarian and literary pursuits. What especially charmed Boswell was his achievement in *belles-lettres.* He had been educated at Eton, had contributed papers to *The Gentleman's Magazine* and *The World,* and was a correspondent of Horace Walpole.

The other Maecenas, though to us a dimmer figure, would have seemed to Boswell even more brilliant. "Let me here express my grateful remembrance of Lord Somerville's kindness to me at a very early period," he wrote many years later. "He was the first person of high rank that took particular notice of me in the way most flattering to a young man fondly ambitious of being distinguished for his literary talents."

Lord Somerville, on the verge of sixty and in a boy's eyes venerable in age as well as rank, defined and stood model for half a dozen of Bos-

well's most passionately held ambitions. He represented Family, having
by his own efforts secured the revival of the ancient peerage of his line,
long sunk in apparently hopeless dormancy; he had gone down to London, young and unknown, and made a name for himself about Court; he
had held a commission in the Dragoons; he had rebuilt the family fortune
by two rich marriages; his intimate literary acquaintances had included
Pope and Allan Ramsay; he was the protector of the theatre in Edinburgh. He had private apartments in Holyroodhouse and went over
Boswell's manuscripts with him there, the historic setting doubling the
impact of his gracious attentions. This is a critical moment, the point at
which the significant pattern of Boswell's life begins to reveal itself, but a
biographer who tried to present it in detail would have to have recourse
to sheer fiction, for Boswell has left us concerning it only a couple of
graceful but unparticularized sentences.

If one is to understand Boswell's early involvement with the stage,
one must understand why the Edinburgh stage needed a protector.
A recent statute had proscribed unlicensed playhouses and had classed
actors who performed in such playhouses with beggars and vagrants.
General public sentiment in Scotland was still strongly opposed to stage
performances, and violence flared up whenever the attempt was made
to put the theatre in Edinburgh on a legal footing. But a sufficiently
large number of influential people were willing to scheme and support
technicalities to circumvent the law, and a tolerable company of actors
could usually be found in a decently equipped theatre near the head of
the Canongate. Theatre-goers in Edinburgh bought tickets to a concert
of music and heard a play gratis. Lord Somerville engaged the entire
theatrical company as domestic servants, and secured them from threat
of the charge of vagrancy by having them come to his house and hand
him a plate once a year.

Boswell's keen and life-long passion for the stage was certainly not
encouraged by his parents. "In my boyish days," he says, ". . . I used to
walk down the Canongate and think of players with a mixture of narrow-
minded horror and lively-minded pleasure; and used to wonder at painted
equipages and powdered ladies." The horror was a reflection of his
mother's attitude: she, as we have seen, had been to a play only once in
her life, and thought the theatre the house of the Devil. Lord Auchinleck
probably had no such scruples, but he certainly disapproved of players,

and he probably thought it inappropriate for a Senator of the College of Justice to give his countenance to an enterprise that was manifestly illegal. The example of Lord Somerville would have acted powerfully to dispel Boswell's own puritanical horror of the stage, and may have done something to allay parental disapproval. The chances are, however, that his parents knew little about his initiation. During the first four years of his university course, he seems never to have been free from family surveillance. He lived at home in Edinburgh from November to August and went to Auchinleck with the family in the summer vacation of the courts. Lord Auchinleck, no doubt, spent a good part of the spring vacation at Auchinleck on estate affairs, but Lady Auchinleck remained on in Edinburgh so as to provide Boswell with the comforts and protection of home during the whole of the university session. But in 1758 it appears to have been decided that he was old enough to fend for himself. Lady Auchinleck, with the younger boys and Mr. Fergusson, went to Auchinleck. The Edinburgh house was closed, Boswell went into lodgings, and for more than two months enjoyed complete independence. April and May constituted a very active portion of the theatrical season, and he seems to have made the most of his opportunities to attend plays.

At any rate, from his eighteenth year Boswell began to be associated with actors and actresses, with momentous results for his future. West Digges, leading man of the Edinburgh company, a handsome profligate of good family and education who had once been an officer in the Army, became his ideal of deportment. For several years one can see in Boswell's dreams of himself as he would like to be a good deal of Digges's impersonation of Macheath, a role Digges is said to have played better than any other actor in Britain. James Love, an older actor of the Edinburgh company and an excellent Falstaff, even for a time eclipsed Johnston, being referred to in a letter to Temple written near the end of 1758 as "my second-best friend."

Yet initiation into the half-guilty delights of the stage and the greenroom caused no immediate revolution in his habits. About the time of his eighteenth birthday (29 October 1758) he began the study of the law. It was, he assured Temple, a most laborious business. "From nine to ten I attend the law class; from ten to eleven, the astronomy; from eleven to one, study at home; and from one to two, attend a college upon Roman antiquities. The afternoon and evening I likeways spend in study. I never walk except on Saturdays." There is no reason to suspect that this resembles some of his later detailed programmes in being merely a schedule of what he *ought* to be doing. At the end of 1758 he was still studious and docile. But in the spring of 1759 the pattern of docility was broken for ever. A biographer can best symbolize the break by beginning a new chapter.

CHAPTER

V

When the spring of 1759 brought his second period of independence, Boswell gave himself up to the theatre with the furious and single-minded intensity that was henceforth to characterize all his enthusiasms. Before the winter season of 1758–1759 was over, the connexion between the players and the eighteen-year-old son of the worthy Lord of Session had become so notorious that he could be used as a front by a blue-stocking authoress, a cousin of his, who had written a play and was bashful or squeamish about approaching the manager directly. Lady Houston, daughter of the eighth Lord Cathcart, gave him a manuscript comedy, *The Coquettes, or the Gallant in the Closet,* with a strict injunction that she was not to be named as author, and he took it to the manager, who accepted and staged it. It was damned on the third night, "and not unjustly," Boswell cheerfully wrote later, "for it was found to be chiefly a translation of one of the bad plays of Thomas Corneille." Since he had displayed all the conventional signs of authorship, attending rehearsals and sweating out the performances in the wings—and had admittedly written the prologue—he got the laughs and sneers of the town when the piece failed. Lady Houston declined to take him off the hook. His chagrin must have been extreme, but the experience did nothing to cool his ardour for the stage. He continued to hobnob with the players, and ended by falling desperately in love with an actress. He even thought of marrying her.

Of the actress very little is known. Her name was Mrs. Cowper, and she played the leading female roles in the Edinburgh theatre from December 1758 through the summer season of 1759. She was older than Boswell, perhaps by as much as ten years, for she had been on the stage since at least 1749 and had played Sylvia in *The Recruiting Officer* at

Drury Lane in 1753. The few scraps of evidence so far turned up indicate that she came of good family but had ruined herself socially when young by marrying her music-master. She was now a widow, seems to have been a Roman Catholic, and was reputed to be virtuous.

If we were to accept implicitly the descriptions of Mrs. Cowper offered us in certain published reviews of the Edinburgh performances, summer 1759, we should have to conclude that she was indeed a paragon of beauty and charm. She is the reviewer's favourite actress; sweetness and sensibility of virtue sit on her countenance; an unaffected modest blush reddens in her face at hearing an indecent word; she has the finest person, the most agreeable face, and the politest carriage of any actress we remember to have seen on the Edinburgh stage; though she is not very quick at study, she may boast of being the perfectest actress upon any stage in the three kingdoms, etc., etc. But since Boswell, as we shall see, was almost certainly himself the reviewer, it is perhaps as well to subject these appraisals to some discount. Temple, who saw the lady perform that autumn at Newcastle, was less rhapsodical: he granted her a tolerable person and some ability as an actress, but was not much taken with her. Boswell was very circumspect about using her name (he calls her Sylvia on the one occasion that he mentions her in the surviving letters), but his attention to her was so marked that Temple had heard of it in Berwick and reported himself amazed at the transformation of his grave friend into a gallant.

Temple's grave friend was in fact demonstrating a consuming interest in human beings and human society generally. On 14 August 1759, more than two months before his nineteenth birthday, he was admitted a Freemason in the Canongate Kilwinning Lodge in Edinburgh. Dr. John Boswell, his uncle, was an enthusiastic Mason—was in fact Depute Master of the Canongate Lodge that year—but I cannot imagine that Lord Auchinleck was altogether easy about his son's entry into a brotherhood so noted for its conviviality. He must have known about it, as he must by that time have know about *The Coquettes* and Boswell's association with the players. Perhaps Dr. Boswell suggested that involvement with a hearty male group of social equals might lessen his nephew's feverish interest in actors and actresses. Something, however, suddenly convinced Lord Auchinleck that the policy of non-intervention had been carried too far. He may for the first time have heard of Mrs. Cowper; he probably discovered that his son was showing an alarming interest in Roman Catholicism. Boswell may have lingered on in Edinburgh during August, but he cer-

tainly joined the family at Auchinleck in September. Just before the opening of the University, Lord Auchinleck informed him that he was not to
return to Edinburgh as he had been planning, but was to continue his
studies at the University of Glasgow. Boswell suddenly found himself
marooned in a city where there were neither plays nor actresses.

The change implied no hardship so far as his formal education was
concerned. The buildings of the College of Edinburgh were makeshift
and mean, but Glasgow housed its university in a handsome and com-
modious seventeenth-century quadrangle, with spacious classrooms and a
court of comfortable houses for the professors. Students wore gowns (red),
some of them lived and took their meals within the College, and the place
altogether had a pleasantly collegiate flavour which the more pragmatic
College of Edinburgh lacked. And except in the department of medicine,
Glasgow at the time seems to have had the better faculty. Dr. Hercules
Lindesay, the Professor of Civil Law, attempted no publication and is now
quite forgotten, but Boswell at once recognized in him a much abler
teacher than the admittedly incompetent Robert Dick, who held the chair
in Edinburgh for almost forty years. And in Adam Smith, the recently
appointed Professor of Moral Philosophy, he encountered a seminal mind,
a mind that was to affect the course of Western thought. Two influential
books, one of them still famous, *The Theory of Moral Sentiments* (1759)
and *Inquiry into the Nature and Causes of the Wealth of Nations* (1776),
came out of the lectures in Moral Philosophy that Boswell heard in 1759–
1760. It was not, however, in ethics or political economy that Smith made
his impact on Boswell. Smith also read lectures in Rhetoric and Belles-
Lettres, dismissing contemptuously the traditional pedantries of rhetorical
classification and talking directly and practically about the marks of a
good style, which he illustrated by constant reference to English authors,
many of them living. John Stevenson's more academic prelusions may in
the long run have had as great a shaping effect on Boswell, but at the time
they seemed slack in comparison with the sallies of this original and energetic mind (Smith was in his mid-thirties). Boswell spoke of Smith more
highly than of any other teacher he had ever had, piling up adjectives
like "beautiful," "clear," "accurate," and "elegant." A remark of Smith's
that we are glad to know the minutest detail about a great man, as, for
example, that Milton wore latchets instead of buckles in his shoes, received his delighted assent. It was probably the first time his attention had
been called to the value of characteristic detail in biography. He also bore

grateful testimony to the amiability of Smith's character and his fondness for his students' company. Smith, in turn, nicely appraised his pupil's personal qualities, and afterwards told him (in a letter Boswell never tired of quoting) that he was possessed of "a happy facility of manners."

From a letter which Temple received from a common friend of his and Boswell's, Temple inferred that Boswell not only was enrolled in Smith's classes, but also was living in Smith's house. In this he seems to have been mistaken. The professors at Glasgow did often eke out their salaries by lodging and boarding students, but Smith this year was receiving a handsome fee for taking a young son of the Earl of Shelburne into his house and directing his studies, and it does not seem likely that he would have accepted other inmates. Boswell more probably lived in the house and under the supervision of James Clow, the Professor of Logic, whose chief claim to remembrance now is that the Faculty had preferred him over David Hume when the chair fell vacant in 1752.

Boswell appears at first to have taken his father's decision in good part and to have made a serious effort to do what was expected of him. He reported to John Johnston that he was leading quite an academic life: he was boarded in his lodgings, seldom went down to Auchinleck (only forty miles away), and paid few visits. The result, as might confidently have been predicted, was another fit of low spirits.

He had never been away from Edinburgh or Auchinleck for any length of time before and may have been homesick. He could hardly in any case have adjusted easily to a sudden and complete cessation of all the amusements and diversions on which he had come to depend. Glasgow in the middle of the eighteenth century was a pretty uncrowded city of elegant new buildings, clean streams, and unpolluted air, set in a landscape of great natural beauty. But it was also a narrowly commercial city, engaged in the tobacco trade with the American colonies and the sugar and rum trade with the West Indies. To those who knew Edinburgh, the manner of living there seemed coarse and vulgar. Few even of the wealthiest citizens gave dinners to any but commercial travellers or their own relations, and not half a dozen families in town had manservants. There were no postchaises nor hackney-coaches, and only three or four sedan-chairs "for carrying midwives about in the night, and old ladies to church, or to the dancing assemblies once a fortnight." Alexander ("Jupiter") Carlyle, whom I am quoting, says that during the two winters he spent at Glasgow as a student (1743–1745) there was only one concert, and that was given by a young gentleman, a student at the University, assisted by "two dancing-school fiddlers and the town waits."

There was no theatre in Glasgow at the time. One had been fitted up in 1752, and the Edinburgh company had appeared there after the end of their season in Edinburgh. But in 1753 Whitefield, preaching from an outdoor pulpit in the Cathedral churchyard, had denounced it, and it had been demolished: according to Whitefield, by the proprietor a few days later; according to the newspapers, by the infuriated mob, immediately. No other theatre was opened till 1764, and that was set on fire by the mob on the opening night.

It was possible, therefore, to keep Boswell from seeing plays presented but it was not so easy to terminate all of his connexions with the stage. In the middle of February 1760, there was published by A. Morley, in the Strand, London, a fifty-page pamphlet "by a Society of Gentlemen" entitled *A View of the Edinburgh Theatre during the Summer Season, 1759, containing an Exact List of the Several Pieces represented, and Impartial Observations on Each Performance*. It appears pretty certain that this is Boswell's first book, published when he was four months past his nineteenth birthday. The *View* collects and continues a series of reviews which had appeared in an Edinburgh newspaper (*The Edinburgh Chronicle*) during late June and early July 1759. The reader has already been enabled to sample the lyric judgements which the Society of Gentlemen handed down on Mrs. Cowper. I have always suspected that Lord Somerville encouraged the writing of the original series and perhaps even found Boswell a publisher. But some encouragement for collecting the reviews in a pamphlet may have come from a nearer source. About the time that the *View* appeared in London, the Foulis press in Glasgow brought out a small volume containing an adaptation of Thomas Southerne's play *Oroonoko* with a fulsome verse-dedication to James Boswell, Esq. The adapter, Francis Gentleman, an impecunious Irish army-officer, actor, dramatic critic, and playwright, had been a member of the Edinburgh company during the winter season of 1758–1759, serving as acting manager during part of that time, had then been dropped, and had gone to Glasgow, where he appears to have been making a meagre living by giving lessons in elocution. The two exiles, who had presumably got to know each other well during the staging of the luckless *Coquettes,* fell on each other's necks and poured their tears in common. Dedications of course were one of poor Gentleman's shifts for food (Garrick later called

him a "dirty dedicating knave"), and the verses prefixed to *Oroonoko*
called for a genteel present in guineas. If it be asked how Boswell, on the
modest allowance his father provided, could manage the lordly gesture
of setting up as patron of literature, the answer can be readily conjectured: he was letting his bills run.

Lord Auchinleck would have been deeply displeased by the *View* and
Oroonoko, for he had sent Boswell to Glasgow to get him out of the way
of just such foolishness, but he probably did not hear of either till much
more serious cause for uneasiness had arisen. In the spring of 1760 Boswell ran away to London. This was one of the few episodes of his life
about which he remained at all times secretive. The main outlines of
what happened are clear enough, but the detail can be blocked in only by
intrepid conjecture. The reader is here warned, once for all, that he should
accompany this stretch of the narrative with a constant qualification of
"perhaps" or "possibly."

Mrs. Cowper was a good woman and did not exploit Boswell's boyish
passion, as she might have done. But she was a devout Roman Catholic,
and when Boswell showed an interest in her religion, she put him in touch
with her priest in Edinburgh, the Reverend Joseph Duguid, a Jesuit, and
Father Duguid gave him some books of Roman-Catholic apologetic.
This, in 1759, laid all the parties open to penalties, and it is important to
understand just what they actually were. Under the statutes it was a
capital offence (rebellion and high treason) to apostasize or to convert
another person to Popery, but this portion of the statutes had been in
abeyance for many years. Except when urgent political considerations
came to the fore (as they did, for example, during the Jacobite rebel-
lions), Government did not molest people for simple recusancy, and did
not interfere with Roman-Catholic priests in the discreet exercise of their
function. Everybody knew where the two congregations of papists in
Edinburgh met for religious services, and who their priests were. If Mrs.
Cowper and Father Duguid had secured Boswell's conversion, no one of
the three would have run any risk of the scaffold and even the priest
would probably have escaped judicial punishment.

The political disqualifications of the statutes, however, were a different matter: they were strictly enforced. If Boswell had become a professed
Roman Catholic, he would certainly have debarred himself from any kind
of public career in the law, the Army, the Navy, the Church, or the
universities. He could not have stood for Parliament, and could not even

have voted for a candidate. He could not legally have succeeded to
Auchinleck, and could have enjoyed its revenues only through the connivance of his nearest Protestant heir.

Boswell received little or no instruction from Father Duguid, for their
meeting occurred very shortly before the beginning of the summer vacation, but he took the tracts down to Auchinleck and studied them there.
Lord Auchinleck found his son immersed in Challoner and Bossuet, and
not unnaturally took alarm. Besides being possessed of a facility of
manners, Boswell had recently been demonstrating a remarkable facility
of conversion, and the conversion of one's heir to Popery was no light
matter to a Scotsman bent on aggrandizing the family. Lord Auchinleck
attempted to refute the arguments of Rome, found Boswell stubborn, and
decided not to let him return to Edinburgh. In Glasgow there was no
resident priest, the few Catholics of that city being cared for by a
missioner who made his headquarters at Drummond Castle and got to
Glasgow only occasionally. Boswell continued to study the Catholic position from books, and at the end of February 1760 wrote to his father
informing him that he was now convinced and proposed not only to turn
Roman Catholic but also to become a monk or a priest. Lord Auchinleck
peremptorily summoned him to Edinburgh.

On 1 March 1760, after pacing the floor of his room in Glasgow for
hours while he contemplated the seriousness of his insurrection, Boswell
ran away to London, covering at least the three hundred miles from Carlisle on horseback. Arrived in London, he put up at the Lemon Tree inn
at the top of the Haymarket, "a true Scots house" kept by one Colin
Donaldson, and then took a room in the house of one Egan, a wigmaker
and Roman Catholic, "just by Oxford Chapel," where he stayed for
some days under an assumed name. During this period he lived very
frugally because he expected to be disowned and had no notion where
his next supply of cash was coming from. On arrival in London he had
gone to Thomas Meighan, a Roman-Catholic bookseller in Drury Lane,
whose shop was generally known to be a stage in the underground rail-
road for Catholic converts, and was passed on to an unidentified priest
at the Bavarian Chapel. "With a wonderful enthusiasm" he saw mass
celebrated for the first time, and was admitted into the communion of
the Church of Rome. His plan, so far as he had one, was to withdraw
to a monastery in France and become a monk, perhaps to take orders.

This is all not only rather heroic, but it is also so admirably consistent that one who knew Boswell would doubt whether it could be the whole story. It was not. He had acquired, from Lord Somerville and others, "an almost enthusiastic notion of the felicity of London," and was bent on seeing the city for its own sake; he had recently published his first book and wished to bask in the glory which he was sure would fall on him. On reaching London he had sought out a priest, but he had simultaneously sought out Samuel Derrick, a dingy fifth-rate man of letters, countryman and friend of Francis Gentleman; and Derrick, whom he later called "a little blackguard pimping dog," had shown him London "in all its variety of departments, both literary and sportive." That is, he introduced Boswell to such authors—mainly of a theatrical cast—as allowed him access, and to various ladies of the town. The neophyte who was prepared to give up all for a life of religion listened eagerly to the song of the Sirens. He experienced for the first time what he elegantly calls the melting and transporting rites of love in a room in the Blue Periwig, Southampton Street, Strand, his priestess a Miss Sally Forrester. He was at the time well advanced in his twentieth year.

Immediately on arriving in London, he had let his father know where he was. Lord Auchinleck, who either thought it unwise to give the appearance of pursuit or simply could not go the length of London at the time, took advice of his Ayrshire neighbour, the Earl of Eglinton, then residing in London, and Eglinton caused Boswell to be hunted down. Eglinton's emissary found the runaway in blackguard surroundings and company; Boswell hesitated, but finally waited on Eglinton and told him his secret in confidence. Eglinton supplied him with funds and made him emerge from obscurity. He first took handsome lodgings at a guinea a week, and then moved into Eglinton's own house in Queen Street, Mayfair. His interest in ascetic Christianity promptly waned. All this—from his elopement out of Glasgow to his delighted entry under Eglinton's roof—happened within a space of three weeks, and is as good an example as can be advanced of Boswell's famous lifelong "inconsistency": that is, of his ability to assume with complete conviction, simultaneously or in very rapid succession, attitudes generally considered to be quite incompatible.

Four years later Boswell summarized the whole business as follows: "This forenoon I took Caldwell [an Anglican priest then residing at The Hague] out to the Wood and told him the whole story of my most extraordinary life. My external changes have been pretty well, but for internal ones, I think I may enter the lists with any living being. Caldwell was struck with wonder; his amiable mind appeared very plainly. He was pleased with Lord Eglinton's method of freeing me from the gloom of superstition, although it led me to the other extreme." To put the matter in a sentence, Eglinton rescued Boswell from religious error by making him a libertine, in every sense of that word.

Alexander Montgomerie, tenth Earl of Eglinton, one of the sixteen peers representing the peerage of Scotland in the House of Lords, was well equipped to play such a part. Endowed by nature with very considerable abilities (he was one of the great agricultural innovators of his time in Ayrshire), he had once investigated the possibility of resigning his peerage so that he could enter the House of Commons and have a more distinguished political career. He was a bachelor, notoriously rakish, and on terms of easy familiarity with most of the great people of the metropolis. In particular, he was *arbiter elegantiarum* to the young Duke of York, brother to the prince who was about to ascend the throne as George III. Eglinton introduced Boswell at once "into the circles of the great, the gay, and the ingenious."

The words are Boswell's own, and are precise, as his words always are. The gay? Eglinton took him to the spring races at Newmarket and secured for him the privileges of the Jockey Club. Here he met men like the great horse-breeder Sir Richard Grosvenor, whose lady later created a first-class scandal by getting caught in an intrigue with the Duke of Cumberland; the Scots Earl of March, future Duke of Queensberry, now generally remembered as "Old Q"; Sir Charles Sedley, great-grandson of the Restoration wit of the same name, who won a Jockey Club Plate in 1776 with a ten-year-old horse, the famous Trentham—in short, the more brilliant of the sporting nobles and gentry.

The great? Eglinton introduced him to the Duke of York, and his moments with the Duke were like the most extravagant of day-dreams come true. The boy who had trembled before a lord and would have thought himself honoured to be a duke's coachman suddenly found himself rubbing shoulders with the heir presumptive to the throne of Great Britain. His Royal Highness Edward Augustus, whom Horace Walpole described memorably as "a very plain boy with strange loose eyes" was only a year and a half older than Boswell. Except for a musical talent which he shared with most of his family, he was quite undistinguished:

a loud, gay, lively young profligate whose tastes in raking were far from fastidious.

Boswell has left us some verses in which these frolics with royalty are viewed in wistful retrospect. They are bad verses, but they open a window straight into his soul:

> Oh, when my Eglinton, too good,
> Has call'd me down in cheerful mood,
> And told me in a gentle tone,
> "The Prince is here; do you make one?"
> The Royal Youth has ask'd me gay,
> "Come, Boswell, what have you to say?"
> While gladness, lighten'd in my eye,
> Has made my backwardness to fly—
> That I, without the least restraint,
> Have heard them men and manners paint!
> Talk less of books than of mankind,
> And women fickle as the wind,
> When brilliant wit and humour droll
> Flash'd instant pleasure on my soul! . . .
> How strange to think on pompous state!
> And is he really then so great?

In a tangle of erasures and false starts he laments the gulf fixed between a royal duke and a laird's son, even a laird's son who can truthfully claim descent from the grandfather of Lord Darnley:

> Oh, if he were but such as me!

Another try:

> Why is he not a youth like me
> Whom

Another:

> Why is it so? Why should this be?
> At such a distance plac'd from me?

Then, after a line so completely obliterated that it as yet remains un-recovered, four more, all in a rush:

> So very selfish was my mind
> That I have inwardly repin'd
> At the high honours on his head
> And almost wish'd him simple Ned.

The ingenious? None other than Laurence Sterne, who had just taken literary London by storm with the first two volumes of *Tristram Shandy* and was being cultivated by the great, including the Duke of York. Boswell, pondering the amazing transformation by which an obscure Yorkshire parson, a provincial like himself, had become overnight the darling of lords and bishops, drafted a long verse-letter to the author of *Tristram Shandy*. He had visited Sterne, he says, at his lodgings in the Mall, and had read to him part of a doggerel poem he had written at Newmarket. Sterne, professing to be charmed, had capered, patted him on the shoulder, and called him the son of Matthew Prior. Another realized daydream: nineteen, awkward, unknown, to have one's verses praised *viva voce* by Laurence Sterne at the height of his glory! Boswell's writings broke out at once into a violent rash of Shandyism which continued to disfigure them for several years.

He had never been so happy, so deliriously happy. Eglinton, a shrewd judge, had discerned his dominant passions and had helped him to give them all free expression for the first time. He was not really retiring and puritanical; that had all been a reflection of his narrow upbringing. He was gregarious and sensual. Fine clothes, the bustle and glitter of the metropolis, endless parties, the opportunity to combine gross physical pleasure with the refined intellectual delights of the theatre and of high conversation—these, Boswell was convinced, were what he was made for, and these were London.

Eglinton pointed out to him that he seemed better fitted to be an officer of the Guards than a monk or a lawyer, and the suggestion received his enthusiastic assent. He wrote to his father withdrawing his decision to enter the life of religion and proposed instead that Lord Auchinleck purchase him a commission. As we have seen, he had long wished to be in the Army, but his object now was not to see service in the field. He dearly wished to wear a uniform, and he found the social status of an officer attractive. But what he now wanted fundamentally was a gentlemanly profession that held the promise of keeping him in London with plenty of time to enjoy himself. He must already have renounced his allegiance to Rome, for as a professed Roman Catholic it would have been futile for him to seek a commission in the Army.

Lord Auchinleck was having trouble enough as it was in the matter of commissions. John, his second son, now in his seventeenth year, was displaying all of James's unruliness and changeableness, with none of his parts. A dull, sullen boy, he had never established an identity of his own, but picked up and stubbornly wore his older brother's attitudes, like handed-down clothes, one after another. Lord Auchinleck had decided that he was fit for nothing but the Army, and had solicited another Ayrshire friend, the Earl of Loudoun, Commander-in-Chief in America, for any kind of commission that Loudoun could manage. John had then balked, and had insisted that the commission must be in the Dragoons and in a regiment on service in Germany. Now came a request from James for a commission in a regiment of Foot Guards stationed in London or the vicinity.

Lord Auchinleck was shocked and hurt ("what have *I* done to deserve this?"), but he behaved considerately. He had allowed Boswell to remain with Eglinton and have his fling, and now, instead of vetoing by letter the proposal of a commission, he came down from Scotland himself to talk Boswell out of it. The Duke of Argyll, unofficial governor of Scotland, was the most impressive Scotsman then living. Lord Auchinleck suggested that Boswell discuss the military scheme with him, a proposal that seemed particularly appropriate because the Duke, who had served under Marlborough and had been wounded at Sheriffmuir, had studied law before he turned soldier, had sat as an extraordinary Lord of Session, and was currently Lord Justice General, that is, the nominal head of the High Court of Justiciary. Boswell was by this time more open to counsel than he would have been a few weeks earlier. His greedy draughts of venal pleasure had brought him that distemper with which Venus, when cross, takes it into her head to plague her votaries (another of his own elegant euphemisms), the distemper had developed into what he calls a nervous fever, and he was ill and abashed. He and his father went out to Whitton, and he was presented to the great man. The Duke (who had probably been rigged) took Lord Auchinleck aside and said, "My Lord, I like your son. That boy must not be shot at for three and sixpence a day." Lord Auchinleck begged Boswell to return home and take some time to consider the matter. At the end of May father and son took the road together for Scotland, pausing at Cambridge to call on Temple. The first London visit had lasted a little less than three months.

It is obvious that Boswell's conviction as regards the claims of Rome could not have gone very deep, and it is probable that the whole Roman-Catholic episode, like his Pythagoreanism, was in part inspired by a wish to be different from other people, especially his father. His formal adherence to the Church of Rome could not have lasted more than a month. Yet he was well informed as to the issues involved, and the experience left an indelible stamp on his mind. For a time he played with those latitudinarian and deistical creeds so attractive to expanding youthful minds, but to such positions the deeper layers of his being remained antipathetic. He never abandoned distinctively Christian modes of worship, and when after a few years he settled down into his final religious position, that position was a Christian orthodoxy which repudiated the exclusive claims of Rome but accepted nearly everything else in the dogma and practice of Western Catholicism. He said later that his Roman period filled him with solemn ideas, all agreeable ones. He continued occasionally throughout life to attend mass in Roman chapels, and to worship there with intense devotion. On Ash Wednesday, 1786, he went early to the Neapolitan Chapel for the imposition of ashes. He held the doctrine of purgatory to be reasonable, and in a codicil to his will requested the prayers of his friends for his departed soul. He thought on one occasion that if he were required to take the Formula (an oath for electors, designed to expose crypto-Catholics), he would disfranchise himself rather than swear that a belief in the invocation of saints and angels was unscriptural. Yet he said—sincerely—that he was no papist. After 1760 he never received communion in the Church of Rome, and there is nothing in his papers to indicate that after that date he had any inclination to subscribe to its exclusive claims.

His statement that Eglinton had freed him from the gloom of superstition was made during his brief latitudinarian period, and was perhaps meant to include release from dogma, but it is clear that what he mainly meant by superstition was the asceticism which his early religious training had enjoined and his new-found faith had extolled. He had not yet formulated that article of his personal creed which made it not merely his *right* but his *duty* to benefit by such gleams of enjoyment as life might cast on his path, but Eglinton had got him to accept it in a practical way.

One cannot help speculating whether his life would have been purer and more heroic if he had remained within the Roman fold. Certainly he could not have persisted long in a really ascetic way of life: Boswell as monk is unthinkable. He was by temperament intensely social and by physical endowment intensely sensual, a creature of ecstasy whose appetites were so ardent and whose pleasures of sense so vivid that under the best of regulation he was not likely to get through life without succumbing to the sins of intemperance and incontinence. But loyalty to a recusant religious group whose members' conduct was always under suspicious surveillance should have tended to stiffen his moral spine, or at least to make him more cautious in exposing himself to scandal. One might assume too that regular sacramental confession would have steadied him, that the firm and expert pressure of an authoritarian casuistry would have helped to reduce his excesses to something more nearly approaching decency. Boswell, an unfinished soul who never succeeded in making a completely mature adjustment between his instinctive urges and day-dreams on the one hand and the claims of the external world on the other, no doubt needed spiritual and moral authority more than most men. But this is probably to deal in ideal rather than in actual terms. There has never been any dearth of devout, licentious Catholics: witness that other convert, Rousseau's *maman,* Mme. de Warens, whose position as official proselytizer did not deter her from sleeping with her young protégés, turn and turn about. Boswell's exhibitionism, his passion for notoriety at any cost, seems central and ineradicable; and it is hard really to convince one's self that he would ever have let certain aspects of his behaviour be much influenced by consideration for others. Besides, he enjoyed confessing so much that for him the sacrament of penance might have been only another opportunity for self-indulgence.

It is safest perhaps to come to only a negative conclusion: it certainly did Boswell's moral character no good for him to be lured out of the fold so soon after he had struggled into it. It was a moral shock of the first order to be bereft so soon of his pure and solemn vision of the one true and holy church: a church that placed a rock beneath his feet and did not leave it to him to decide as to the health of his soul. Authority that does not claim infallibility may be respected and may be practically efficacious, but when the principle of infallible authority has been accepted and then rejected as an illusion, all moral authority becomes subject to sceptical scrutiny and the result may well be a progressive justification of self-indulgence. Boswell had been kept dangerously long by a sheltered upbringing from coming to grips with the world, the flesh, and the devil, and was pretty certain to go down at the first real encounter. It was deeply unfortunate that his lapse from Rome coincided with his initiation as a rake.

CHAPTER

VI

The period which Boswell had promised to take to consider his military proposals turned out to be no mere matter of days. Lord Auchinleck could not be budged from his refusal to further the Guards scheme, for he believed that it was a device for settling in London and engaging (as he said) in a life of dissipation and vice. He told Boswell that he did not like the idea of his going into the Army in any case, but that if Boswell chose to be a soldier in good earnest, he would procure him a commission in a marching regiment. Boswell declined. Lord Auchinleck then proposed that he continue the study of the law. It would be useful to him to know some law even if he never practised: landed gentlemen in Scotland often got admitted advocates without any intention of accepting briefs. A return to university study either at Edinburgh or Glasgow being now pretty much out of the question, Lord Auchinleck offered to give him a regular course of instruction himself. The course appears to have gone on for about two years. During most of that time, at least, Boswell was living at home, an unhappy and now openly rebellious young man. "I grant you," he wrote to Temple, "that my behaviour has not been entirely what it ought to be. But consider my particular situation. A young fellow whose happiness was always centred in London, who had at last got there and had begun to taste its delights, who had got his mind filled with the most gay ideas: getting into the Guards, being about Court, enjoying the happiness of the *beau monde* and the company of men of genius—in short, everything that he could wish—consider this poor fellow hauled away to the town of Edinburgh, obliged to conform to every Scotch custom or be laughed at..., his flighty imagination quite cramped, and he obliged to study *Corpus Juris Civilis* and live in his father's strict family—is there any wonder, Sir, that the unlucky dog should be somewhat fretful? Yoke a Newmarket courser to a dung-cart, and I'll lay my life on't he'll either caper and kick most confoundedly or be as stupid and restive as an old battered post-horse."

The *boulevardier* tone of the whole passage shows the thoroughness of the change that London had worked in him. He is being passionately stubborn and unreasonable and he knows it. But beneath his stubbornness is a sincere conviction, a loyalty to the deepest intuition of which he is capable. He knows that he will never be the man his father is, but he knows too that he has some gifts beyond his father's comprehension. He admits that his father's motives are kind, but he feels all the same that he is being destroyed. He *has* to resist.

It is very difficult to assess Lord Auchinleck's limitations as a father without seeming to be merely defending his son. But though our sense of protest at Boswell's egoism should certainly make us deeply sympathetic with the older man, it ought not to blind us to the fact that Lord Auchinleck was not easy to live with. He was a proud man, terribly stiff about his twin dignities of judge and head of an old family, and he resented unreasonably any action of his son's that made him the subject of gossip. He felt himself personally disgraced not merely when scandal touched a member of his family, but even when one of them got mentioned in a newspaper. Until a son of his could distinguish himself in the law—for Lord Auchinleck really had no high opinion of any profession but his own—he thought that son should stand in his shadow and remain inconspicuous. He could not sympathize with any part of Boswell's literary ambition, for he believed as a matter of course that no gentleman wrote for money, and was further convinced that modern literature was all froth and folly, and all modern writers riff-raff.

Like most fathers, he allowed no sympathetic recollection of his own youthful follies to temper his irritation at his son's wilfulness and lack of dignity. We have very few stories relating to Lord Auchinleck's youth, but there are enough of them to show that he was born neither submissive nor dignified. His father had been very severe with him. While he was in Edinburgh College, he had associated with two wild Irish lads (later expelled), and had spent too much time playing billiards with them. Old James had demanded that he give up this unprofitable company, and had beaten him heartily when he proved obstinate. As a young man on a trip to Paris (he had then advanced somewhat beyond the age that Boswell had now attained) he had displayed so flauntingly the glory of his red stockings and red-heeled shoes as to provoke mirth from a bystander. But he had put away childish things, and had forgotten that the putting away had been painful and had taken time. Though his son was now man-grown and normally jealous of his independence, he expected him to keep strict hours in the house and called him to account for his comings and goings. He disclaimed any wish to exert authority, but he was in fact never able to encourage his sons in independence nor to treat them as equals. He would not even let them *talk* freely in his presence, but awed their harmless chatter into silence.

A truly pathetic feature of the situation was that though he loved his sons and could express that love in a letter, he could not show it face to face. It was not merely giddy James who complained, over and over, that his father had no warmth of affection, that he met with biting sarcasm or icy disapproval all the unguarded demonstration that James rightly considered essential to his being. Steady David and sullen John brought the same charge. All three Boswell boys respected and admired their father enormously, and all three of them hungered for his love. But his personal manner towards them was harsh and peremptory. He made his decisions thoughtfully and with their best interests at heart, but when he announced his decisions, he did not expect them to be questioned or even discussed. He wore the red gown in his own household.

As a child, Boswell could always turn to his mother for sympathy and understanding, but the bond between them had been slackened by his growing up and especially by the events of the spring of 1760. They no longer shared the same religious beliefs and emotions; his profligacy (of which she can hardly have remained ignorant) must have shocked and hurt her deeply. But he could still count on her steady affection and tenderness; and he knew that so far as her sense of duty allowed, she would stand between him and his father.

The year following June 1760, then, was spent in study of the law, but the study was listless and often sulky. "When my father forced me down to Scotland," Boswell later wrote, "I was at first very low-spirited, although to appearance very high. I afterwards from my natural vivacity endeavoured to make myself easy; and like a man who takes to drinking to banish care, I threw myself loose as a heedless, dissipated, rattling fellow who might say or do every ridiculous thing." There was at the time a rage for raffish clubs, and when he was in London he may have heard of the most notorious of the lot, the Monks of Medmenham Abbey,

a dissolute brotherhood that numbered the emerging demagogue John
Wilkes among its members. Soon after his return to Edinburgh, he instituted a jovial society of his own known as the Soaping Club, "Every
man soap his own beard" being (at least on Boswell's testimony) contemporary slang for "Let every man indulge his own humour." The club
included some medical students, at least one Army officer, and one
buckish priest of the Church of England. (One of the medical students
was an American, Arthur Lee from Virginia, better known to history as
diplomatist than as physician.) It met every Tuesday evening at a tavern
and there engaged in adolescent orgies of drinking, singing, rattling, and
playing snip-snap-snorum, a card game about as complicated and sinister
as authors or old maid. But there were other dissipations of a less innocent
sort. Boswell had hardly recovered from the distemper he had brought
back from London when (to use his own words, reporting to Temple)
he went to a house of recreation in Edinburgh and catched a Tartar, too,
with a vengeance. This time there were serious complications, and the
cure—if it was a cure—took four months. The pain and alarm of this
bout (perhaps even the shame of undergoing treatment for such a
malady in his father's strict household) made him resolve to stay clear
of what he calls the mansions of gross sensuality, and did in fact keep
him out of them for at least a year.

But the most significant activity of the two years was not study of the
law nor raking: it was scribbling. If one is to get a proper conception of
Boswell, it is necessary to have some idea of the bulk and variety of this
early writing and of the gestures which accompanied the publication of
that portion of it that got into print. He was not (as is too often
assumed) a man who turned author at the age of fifty and wrote a
single book, *The Life of Samuel Johnson*. On the contrary, he commenced author in his teens, and was an old hand at publishing before
he ever met Johnson. Like most authors, he began with verse. His
juvenile poems (still largely unpublished) are voluminous and of considerable interest to his biographer and the editors of his papers, but they
contain no pieces worthy of salvaging as wholes for intrinsic poetic merit;
indeed, one can pick few happy phrases or fine single lines out of them.
Since Boswell obviously had a literary gift, and, first and last, wrote a
great deal in metre, the almost complete lack of distinction in his verse
must seem puzzling. He had a fine ear in music (perhaps not the same
thing as a fine ear in verse) and a good sense of rhythm, and when he

wrote without self-consciousness—that is, in familiar prose—he constantly displayed a power of original, apt, and striking metaphor. It was he, for example, who said that Christopher Smart had "shivers of genius here and there." But except for lively songs, which he sometimes turned quite neatly, and the scurrilous *Ode by Dr. Samuel Johnson to Mrs. Thrale upon their supposed approaching Nuptials,* his accomplishment in verse is simply nil. The things that were really his own, the things he really wanted to say, could not be said effectively in any of the contemporary modes of verse, or, for that matter, in verse at all. The easiness of expression which he correctly asserted to be in his power was a conversational ease that could not survive the artificialities of rhyme and metre. When he attempted verse, he had to affect a manner, and it made him artificial all the way through. He parroted, he was content with clichés. His announced preference in metaphor was for the gaudy, the overblown, the over-explicit. His poems are mere husks, coarse and empty.

One can go even farther. He was not merely limited to prose; even within prose he was limited in the ways in which he could give his talent expression fully and with integrity. He was poles removed from, let us say, Oliver Goldsmith, who could write with distinction in any of the favoured contemporary modes: poetry, the drama, the essay, the novel. Goldsmith cribbed shamelessly from other authors and made a good deal of use of autobiography. But he reshaped imaginatively what he stole and he turned autobiography into fiction. Boswell was tied to matter of fact. He could never have written a good serious poem, nor a good play, nor a good novel. He had not yet found out what it was that he *could* write. But, being possessed of literary genius, he had to write; and as poetry was the most esteemed of literary modes, he wrote poems.

It was so far a good sign that his taste in verse was up-to-date and his models contemporary. He had read with deep enjoyment most of Shakespeare and Milton and Dryden and Pope, and could quote many lines from all four, but the poets he imitated in serious verse were Thomson and Young and Shenstone and Gray and Mason. His models in humorous verse may seem more old-fashioned, but that is probably because there had been no significant innovations in the writing of light verse since Prior and Ned Ward and Gay. He began writing early. He may have been trying his hand at paraphrases from Scripture (a kind of verse affected by Sir David Dalrymple) as early as his sixteenth year, and he certainly submitted a prologue to Digges in his seventeenth, but he

seems not to have begun writing verse in quantity till his eighteenth. The
first of his extended efforts, *October, a Poem,* is a close and avowed
imitation of Thomson. The first of his pieces to be printed, so far as any
one knows, was composed in May 1758, when he was still five months
short of attaining his eighteenth birthday, and was published in *The
Scots Magazine* for August of that year. It is unsigned, runs to about
fifty lines, is a meditation on a text from Shakespeare, and is in the style
of Young's *Night Thoughts*. The title is *An Evening Walk in the Abbey-
Church of Holyroodhouse*. The opening lines may be taken as a better-
than-average example of Boswell's serious verse:

> *Now let imagination form a time*
> *When creeping murmur and the poring dark*
> *Fills the wide vessel of the universe.*
>   SHAKESPEARE
> Such is the present time, now sober Eve
> Has drawn her sable curtain o'er the earth
> And hush'd the busy world to soft repose.
> Come then, my soul, compose each faculty,
> And bid thy restless passions be at peace.
> Here's room for sacred, solemn meditation,
> Pleasing employment of the serious mind.
> Ah, what a melancholy change is here!
> This chapel, where our ancient Scottish kings
> With awful pomp and dread solemnity
> Have worship'd the Most High, must now become
> A sacrifice to desolating Time!
> This venerable roof, which oft has rung
> With the Almighty's praise, must fall a prey
> To the rude winds and Winter's stormy blasts!

The piece is in good company for the time, being flanked on one side
by an *Ode to Sleep* by Dr. John Ogilvie and on the other by a poem
entitled *The Fate of Caesar* by John Home, author of *Douglas*. In the
next number of the magazine is an ambitious *Ode to Peace* by James
Beattie, and in the number for October, one of the early compositions of
James Macpherson, still guiltless of Ossian. Fame as experienced is relative, and a youngster of seventeen who can get a poem printed in the
same page with the most highly acclaimed of the living poets of his
nation has reason to feel gratified.

His first separate publications were in prose. The earliest that has been traced was, as we have seen, *A View of the Edinburgh Theatre during the Summer Season, 1759,* which appeared in February 1760, just before he ran off to London. Although a trifle, it is no disgraceful trifle for a boy of nineteen to have written. Apart from an obvious and amusing partiality for Mrs. Cowper, it seems to give just and intelligent critiques of the various performances. The literary judgements expressed are respectable and show a considerable range of reading, not only in the drama itself, but also in books of dramatic theory. What is most interesting, the author shows that he has thought seriously about the problem of dramatic impersonation.

The verse that he wrote in London in 1760 was, as one would have expected, of a frivolous and libertine cast. One of these pieces, *The Cub at Newmarket,* has hitherto been accorded an unduly prominent place in the story of his early years because it has always been known to be his, whereas much of his other early work remained unrecognized or unstudied until fairly recently. Actually a much less interesting piece than the unpublished epistle to Sterne, the *Cub* is an extreme example of his lifelong strategy of lying down of his own accord to avoid being thrown down. While he was in the Jockey Club something happened that raised a laugh against him. As nearly as can be made out from the poem (which is not a model of narrative clarity), Boswell, who was bashful and painfully aware of the provinciality of his dress and speech, was left alone by Eglinton, unintroduced, in the vociferous throng of sporting peers and gentlemen, not one of whom he knew. He stood for a time unhappily looking on, then retreated to a corner, called for pen, paper, and ink, and began to write. Nothing could have made him more conspicuous. Sir Charles Sedley, a licensed wit, came up and subjected him to straight-faced quizzing, and some particularly corpulent and grotesque member of the Club, not now to be identified, frightened him and made him shrink. Or perhaps he merely put on an act of being frightened. At any rate, the company roared, and Boswell on the spot dashed off a doggerel tale in the manner of Prior, subjecting himself to forced and extravagant caricature. The piece assured the world that he was a good sport, though at a complete sacrifice of dignity. Boswell was proud of it, as he was always proud of anything of his that made people laugh, read it to the Duke of York and to Sterne, and tried to get it published, but without immediate success. I shall spare the reader a quotation from

The Cub at Newmarket, choosing rather to illustrate the verse of the
first London jaunt by the rakish and previously unpublished *Ode written
at Newmarket.* Miss Jeanie Wells, in Berwick Street, Soho, was another
of the handsome young ladies who (as he might have said) had par-
ticipated with him in the rites of Venus.

> When absent from my heart's delight,
> My mind seems lost in care's dark night;
> My vital spirits scarcely flow,
> Stop'd by a load of tender woe;
> And pensive melancholy tells
> How much I love the charming WELLS!
>
> When any rival's name is heard,
> My soul quick kindles at the word;
> Dire envy poisons all the place;
> Resentment flushes in my face,
> And headstrong passion loudly tells
> How much I love the charming WELLS!
>
> When in her wanton gay retreat,
> Of love the ever-mirthful seat,
> My angel, free from dang'rous wiles,
> Calls me her dear and sweetly smiles,
> Pulse-beating expectation tells
> How much I love the charming WELLS!
>
> But when, propitious to my prayer,
> Kind Venus gives the yielding fair;
> When cupids hov'ring round us play,
> And we in transport melt away,
> Oh! then my whole existence tells
> How much I love the charming WELLS!

The willingness of publishers to take the risk of Boswell's juvenile
pamphlets is testimony to a considerable journalistic knack on his part,
as his next separate publication illustrates. Shortly after he returned to
Edinburgh, Samuel Foote opened his season at the Little Theatre in the
Haymarket, London, with his own comedy, *The Minor,* a boisterous
satire on the Methodists and especially on George Whitefield. The piece
made a great stir, ran thirty-five nights, and got talked and written

about more than any work that appeared that year except *Tristram Shandy*. Boswell had not seen *The Minor* presented and in his heart disapproved of the tendency of the work, but he could not resist an opportunity to float something on the tides of controversy. *Observations, Good or Bad, Stupid or Clever, Serious or Jocular, on Squire Foote's Dramatic Entertainment intitled "The Minor," by a Genius*, a pamphlet which he later called "an idle performance, and written inconsiderately," appeared in Edinburgh in November 1760, and had enough success to induce Wilkie, a London publisher, to order a reprint. The *Observations*, though judicious, are in no way remarkable, but the pseudonym and the envelope of bantering conversation which surrounds them are of interest to a biographer. In the pseudonym "A Genius" Boswell first displays to the public the façade of impudence and self-conscious vanity with which he will henceforth screen the uncompleted structure of his breeding. The enveloping conversation illustrates the abjectness of his addiction at this time to Shandyism and reveals a fact of prime importance about Boswell himself:

Bless my soul!—are you a mimic, *Mr. Genius?*—Am I a mimic? ay, and a good one too, let me tell you.—I never was with a man in my life, who had got anything odd about him, but I could take him off in a trice.

This is Boswell's first reference to mimicry, an art which he was now practising assiduously and with enormous gusto. He was indeed a remarkable mimic; and there can be no doubt that the famous ability to reconstruct conversations from memory which he was now beginning to demonstrate was partly due to his skill in taking people off. He could stimulate the recall of words he had heard spoken by assuming the facial expression, gestures, and tone of voice of the speakers; and he could verify his reconstructions by trying them out on his muscles and viscera as well as in his brain. Foote (whom he had certainly seen in Edinburgh) probably incited him to mimicry, but he could not have learned from Foote how to express in words what the mimic gives directly by gesture. He must, I think, have been roused by Richardson, whose pervasive attention to minutely described gesture was something new in English fiction, but he no doubt learned more from Sterne, whose brilliant use of the isolated characteristic gesture, described with unparalleled verbal economy, makes Richardson seem over-emphatic and stagy. From the

biographical point of view, *Observations on "The Minor"* might well
have been entitled *Homage to Two Masters*.

Sterne was the strongest literary influence on Boswell during 1760–
1761; the strongest during the year that followed was the Hon. Andrew
Erskine, a lieutenant in the 71st Regiment of Foot, whom Boswell
sought out at Fort George in May 1761, while on the Northern Circuit
with his father.

Andrew Erskine was born in the same year as Boswell. The family
was Jacobite. His father, the fifth Earl of Kellie, took an active part in
the rebellion of 1745, but got off with three years' imprisonment because
of a general conviction that he was weak-minded. Andrew's mother—
clearly a woman of parts—was a daughter of Dr. Archibald Pitcairne,
the celebrated Jacobite physician and Latin poet. Andrew's older brother,
Thomas, sixth Earl of Kellie, was a rake and guzzler whose fiery face,
Foote said, would ripen cucumbers. He was also one of the most talented
native-born musical composers of his time in Great Britain. The family
had never been rich, and the eclipse of the fifth earl had completed its
ruin. Andrew had spent his childhood in what he himself called a blackguard state; was first sent to sea, and then entered the Army. A tall, dark,
indolent young man, painfully shy in the company of strangers, he was
capable of gay and easy impudence in letters or intimate conversation.
He was a poetaster—to borrow Boswell's characterization of Smart—
with shivers of genius, and in particular had contributed several pieces
to a miscellany, *A Collection of Original Poems by the Rev. Mr. Blacklock and Other Scotch Gentlemen*, which an enterprising Edinburgh
publisher named Donaldson had brought out in 1760. A man of good
family, a poet, a hypochondriac, an officer—he represented nearly all
the things that at the time seemed most important to Boswell.

Boswell's letter of introduction to Erskine had been furnished by his
acquaintance George Dempster, a hearty and extroverted young advocate
of twenty-nine, a public-spirited bachelor, who in the previous month
had at great expense got himself elected Member of Parliament for the
Perth burghs. Soon after the meeting at Fort George, Erskine came to
Edinburgh, and the three struck up a close friendship. In that same
summer of 1761, Thomas Sheridan, Irishman and actor, godson of Swift
and father of the much more famous Richard Brinsley Sheridan, then a
boy of ten, came to Edinburgh to give a series of lectures. Many Scots in
public life were becoming ashamed of their native Doric, and Sheridan,

a fanatical believer in the power of elocution, promised to teach a correct English pronunciation. Boswell, Erskine, and Dempster formed part of the audience of more than three hundred gentlemen who paid a guinea each to have their accents mended. Boswell and Sheridan took to each other, and in no time at all Boswell had elected Sheridan his Mentor, his Socrates, had told him all and had begged Sheridan to direct his heedless steps. Sheridan was charmed by Boswell's personality and touched by his confidence. Though he was anything but affluent, he lent Boswell five guineas to discharge a gambling debt that was giving him great distress, exacting a promise that Boswell would not play for money for the next five years. After he went back to London, Boswell sent him long confessional letters and he returned brief but affectionate replies.

Early in August there appeared with Alexander Donaldson's imprint a pamphlet containing two short poems: *An Elegy on the Death of an Amiable Young Lady* and *An Epistle from Lycidas to Menalcas.* The book is a queer affair altogether. The greater part of it—fourteen pages out of a total of twenty-four—is taken up by three "critical recommendatory letters" signed G. D., A. E., and J. B. We learn from an Advertisement that the poems had been submitted to Donaldson for inclusion in the forthcoming second volume of his miscellany, but had been found by G. D., A. E., and J. B. to be of such remarkable excellence that the author had been prevailed upon to publish them separately— accompanied by the letters. Actually, the letters are burlesques of the broadest sort, ridiculing by extravagant and ironic praise the style, diction, and even the spelling of the hapless poems. J. B.'s recommendatory letter is just as quizzing and ironic as the other two. But following J. B.'s recommendatory letter is another, a letter from the author of the poems submitting them to Donaldson. It is brief, completely serious, and is signed J. B.

Both poems were undoubtedly written with no thought of burlesque. The *Elegy* is a feeble piece on a trite subject and shocked Birkbeck Hill by recurring lapses into Scots grammar ("thou lies" instead of "thou liest"), but it was not meant to be funny. Nor was the *Epistle,* though a modern reader is bound to grin when he finds Boswell in it apostrophizing a visioned fair one by the name of Ammonia. (In 1761 Ammonia was merely a classical female name; the chemical term was not invented until twenty years later.) Boswell, in short, in the device of the commendatory letters is giving another instance of his willingness to anticipate hostile criticism by writing himself down. He is not sure whether he prefers to be known as a serious poet or as a heedless rattling fellow who might say or do every ridiculous thing, so he aims at both. If any one likes the poems, good; the letters are merely a gesture of modesty; if any one calls the poems execrable, he can point out that he has laughed at them himself. He is willing to copy any style that is popular, no matter how meretricious, and to call attention to his works by any device, no matter how undignified. (Shelley, whom I have already advanced as a parallel, did much the same thing with his *Posthumous Fragments of Margaret Nicholson.*) Boswell and Erskine were so pleased with their burlesque letters that they started a self-conscious correspondence in the same vein. Boswell kept copies of his own letters, and probably had from the first some notion of publishing them.

His next public appearance was in an extraordinary letter to Lord Eglinton which he published in *The Scots Magazine* for September 1761. Though he signed the published text merely "A Gentleman of Scotland" and reduced Eglinton to "The Earl of ***," no one who knew him or had heard of his escapade of the previous year could have had the slightest doubt as to who was the author. The coronation of George III had just occurred; Eglinton, who had been appointed one of the lords of the bedchamber at the insistent urging of the Duke of York, would have played a prominent part on that day of splendour. Boswell's object in the letter is partly to solace himself for having missed the coronation by recalling the round of pleasure of his three wonderful months in London in 1760; partly to let the world know that though he now has to study law in his father's strict family and have his flighty imagination quite cramped, he had once been caressed by the great, the gay, and the ingenious.

He acknowledges Eglinton complete master of the noble science of happiness, skilled both in theory and practice. He himself had been an apt scholar so far as his time permitted. But he is impatient for a regular course, lectures and experiments, and that cannot be till his propitious stars—Venus and probably Mars—bring him back to the delightful British metropolis.

He is generally reckoned one of the happiest men alive, for it is believed that he is about to be married to a most beautiful young lady. What a change! Not long ago people were predicting that he would be hanged; now it is all, A very pretty man! He deserves her! But what a prospect for the young lady, a pretty sort of juvenile husband will she have! How becoming will the matrimonial nightcap be to the volatile pate of Ranger![1]

He concludes with a request to be remembered to all his London acquaintance: his R____l H____ss, Sir Charles S____, Lord G____ (Sir Richard Grosvenor had been raised to the peerage), and Tristram Shandy. "He is the best companion I ever knew, and the most taking composer of sermons that I ever read. I shall write to him soon."

Boswell enjoyed playing with ideas of marriage: from the time of Martha Whyte onward he was always fancying himself head-over-heels in love with some more-or-less eligible young lady and was always writing fervent notes and making gallant addresses that stopped just short of being proposals. It is important to remember that the involved clandestine amours detailed in the chapter following this were carried on simultaneously with a number of overt and apparently feverish courtships. We know the names of three young ladies whom he enrolled at this time in his list of probationary wives: Miss Bruce, Miss Stewart, and Miss Colquhoun. Miss Bruce has not yet been singled out from the throng of maidens of that name. Margaret Stewart (of whom we shall hear more) was the eldest daughter of Sir Michael Stewart of Blackhall. Miss Colquhoun (the most likely choice for the lucky girl referred to in the letter to Eglinton) was Katherine, eldest daughter of Sir James Colquhoun of Luss, eighteen years old and quite eligible on the score of birth. Her father came from a distinguished Highland family and was generally accorded the style of baronet; her mother was an earl's sister; Lord Auchinleck was one of the trustees of Lady Colquhoun's marriage portion. I can hardly believe that Lord Auchinleck would have been really keen on a Highland marriage—his preference, one thinks, would have been an Ayrshire heiress, if possible, one whose lands marched with Auchinleck—but he may have waived some personal objections in the prospect of getting Boswell fixed. In any case, one can imagine his fury and despair at the publication of this indiscreet and extravagant letter, which, to say the least, treated the reputation of a young lady of family with reprehensible levity. Since Kitty Colquhoun will receive little further mention in this narrative, we may as well complete her matrimonial

[1] A character in a popular comedy, Benjamin Hoadly's *Suspicious Husband*, 1747. Johnson described Ranger as "a rake, a mere rake, ... a lively young fellow" (Journal, 26 March 1768).

history now. Three years later, when Boswell was on the Continent, she married Sir Roderick Mackenzie of Scatwell, who, as it happened, was a captain in the Guards.

Boswell continued in a state of active poetic fermentation. Early in December 1761, another pamphlet with Donaldson's imprint made its appearance: an *Ode to Tragedy,* by a Gentleman of Scotland, *dedicated* to James Boswell, Esq. The dedication is a more elaborate version of the gimmick used in *An Elegy on the Death of an Amiable Young Lady.* With those who merely read the advertisements of the piece in the newspapers, or who saw the book lying about but did not read it, he would at least get the reputation of being a patron of literature. The careless and uninitiated could even read the dedication and be taken in by it. Those with any degree of literary sophistication would realize at once that he was dedicating to himself. Critics of this last group who thought the *Ode* execrable might still concede that the author was quite a card.

The *Ode to Tragedy,* the most ambitious effort in verse that Boswell ever published, consists of sixteen regular ten-line stanzas, the form taken from an ode of Erskine's, who worked it up from the odes of Thomas Gray and William Mason. It provides a more ecstatic statement than any to be found in Boswell's prose of the delight he took in serious plays, and is of some slight interest to the historian of drama as a document in an acrimonious literary controversy then going on between "regular" poets like Mason and the spectacular newcomer Charles Churchill. As verse, however, it is quite dead and had better be left unquoted. For the present-day reader Boswell shows up better in the rollicking tradition of Gay, as witness the following bits from an unfinished ballad-opera which he wrote in 1760. Boswell sang well and had a real feeling for song-composition. *Give Your Son his Will,* a bit of transparent special pleading, translates Lord Auchinleck into Sir Solomon Positive, a hard-headed London citizen who is keeping his giddy but attractive son, Charles Positive, from becoming an officer in the Guards. Mr. Sagely, a man of rank and fashion (i.e., Eglinton), puts the case for spirit and adventure.

SAGELY. You must forgive me, Knight, for saying that I think you use your son very ill in imputing his inclination for the Army to such trifling motives. From the young gentleman's character, I dare believe that honour and a desire for glory are his incitements. Your Worship's concluding sneer upon the word *soldier* I don't like. To serve one's country in the capacity is undoubtedly a genteel and very respectful employment. *(Sings.)*

> A soldier surely claims regard,
> Who, leaving Pleasure's dear delights,
> 'Gainst danger, pain, and death prepar'd,
> To save his country boldly fights.
>
> No gen'rous soul was ever found
> (Though blissful Peace has milder charms)
> But ardent wish'd to be renown'd
> For glorious deeds achiev'd by arms.
>
> Albion, in trade excelling all
> The nations round, yet rules the sea;
> And by her troops imperious Gaul
> Is forc'd to bow the suppliant knee.
>
> Although her sons in each fine art
> Become more perfect ev'ry day,
> May British valour ne'er depart,
> But in our isle for ever stay. . . .

SIR SOLOMON. . . . Come, do resolve upon it. You'll find trade much more agreeable than you imagine. Consider too how advantageous and respectful it is. 'Tis that which supports the grandeur of the British nation. *(Sings.)*

> By Commerce, in glory and wealth we increase,
> By that, when the turmoils of bloody war cease,
> We happy enjoy all the blessings of Peace:
>   O the good trade of Old England, &c.
>
> A merchant esteem above all men deserves;
> 'Tis he who his country substantially serves;
> Of the politic body 'tis he gives the nerves:
>   O the good trade of Old England, &c. . . .

CHARLES. . . . My affections were always centred in the field. My ambition was to distinguish myself there. When I read in the classics the great exploits of the ancient heroes, it set my imagination on fire, and I glowed with an ardour to emulate their virtue. Perhaps I am too warm

and my expression a little florid. But I must be excused, as the subject
runs away with me. *(Sings.)*

> If Genius ean be ever known,
> Sure, Mars has mark'd me for his own.
> My constant wish has been to claim,
> By courage true, an honest fame.

(To Sir Sol.) Then, good Sir, be indulgent still:
> Give your aspiring son his will,
> And cheerful let me go, I pray,
> Over the hills and far away.

All through the autumn of 1761 the second volume of Donaldson's
Collection had been going forward; Boswell and Erskine wrote new pieces
for it and furbished old ones. When Erskine was called back to his
regiment, Boswell took over the task of correcting the proofs—a task
which Erskine said he bungled. Donaldson ran out of copy before the
volume was as thick as he thought it should be, and Boswell provided
two hundred lines more on short notice. When the book appeared in
February 1762, it contained far more pieces by Boswell and Erskine than
by any of the other contributors.

Boswell's thirty poems in the *Collection* may be roughly grouped into
five categories: graveyard poems, war poems, theatrical poems, poems addressed to Kitty Colquhoun, and (the largest group of all) what may be
called Soaping-Club verse. I shall quote two stanzas from one of the
poems in the last-named group as the best description extant of the mask
which Boswell wore to make himself easy. It was no less a mask because
it reproduced to some extent his natural features. The title is *B____, a
Song;* the air (one of those used by Gay in *The Beggar's Opera*), "To
Old Sir Simon the King." I fancy as Boswell sang it it may have been
quite entertaining.

> B____ is pleasant and gay;
>> For frolic by nature design'd,
> He heedlessly rattles away
>> When the company is to his mind.
> This maxim he says you may see,
>> We can never have corn without chaff;
> So not a bent sixpence cares he
>> Whether *with* him or *at* him you laugh.

> B_____ does women adore
>   And never once means to deceive;
> He's in love with at least half a score;
>   If they're serious, he smiles in his sleeve.
> He has all the bright fancy of youth
>   With the judgement of forty-and-five;
> In short, to declare the plain truth,
>   There is no better fellow alive.

The British Magazine dismissed Donaldson's volume in a one-sentence review: "We have seen a better collection." *The Monthly Review* was brief and contemptuous. But *The Critical Review* made amends. The collection as a whole received no very high commendation, but it was found to afford "some sparks of genius, which may one day kindle into a brighter flame." The sparks? The Hon. Andrew Erskine and James Boswell, Esq. Two of Erskine's odes were praised and one printed entire. "In the collection," continued the reviewer (who may have been Tobias Smollett himself—Boswell reported to Erskine that he had been buttering Smollett up and had got a gracious letter in reply), "we find some agreeable light pieces by J. B. Esq., such as the following song, which we take to be a good-humoured joke upon himself." There follows the entire text of *B_____, a Song*. Boswell professed himself delighted. "Had they said more, I should have thought it a burlesque." The volume contained pieces by John Home and William Julius Mickle. James Beattie had a signed poem in it, and so had James Macpherson, already famous as the "translator" of Ossian. The reviewer praised and quoted Home, but mentioned none of the others; furthermore, that same number of the *Critical* that treated Boswell so generously gave only balanced and regretful praise to the *Crazy Tales* of Sterne's friend, the ingenious Mr. Hall-Stevenson, and the *Resignation* of the aged and honoured author of *Night Thoughts*. For his continual meddling with rhyme Boswell at least had the excuse that his early poems had been praised by one of the most influential reviews of the day.

He had always intended to bring out *The Cub at Newmarket* with a dedication to the Duke of York, but had not been able to find a publisher who would take the risk of it, and did not dare himself to underwrite the cost of printing it in as handsome a style as he thought the dedication demanded. Rendered confident by the appearance of Donaldson's *Collection,* he instructed an unidentified London printer to get the copy from the Dodsleys in Pall Mall, who had had it for some time, and to print it at once. He would guarantee costs himself. "Let no expense be spared to make it genteel. Let it be done on large quarto, and a good type. Price, one shilling." The *Cub*, in a format far more elegant than it deserved, was published anonymously on 4 March 1762. Except for the fact that it sold enough copies to pay costs, it was a disappointment all round. Boswell had added a Shandyan preface and people were getting sick of Shandyan imitations. The reviewers found the humour of the piece esoteric. Worst of all, the dedication backfired. One does not dedicate to a royal duke without asking permission, but Boswell, still wandering in his day-dream of simple Ned, had done just that. The Duke was very angry, his anger brought Eglinton into a sad scrape, Eglinton was in a passion. The whole Guards scheme was threatened.

Soon after the *Collection* came out, Boswell drew up a table of contents for an entire volume of poems "to be published for me by Becket and Dehondt" (Sterne's publishers), and started making fair copy for the printer. He calculated the number of lines, and thought that "counting the blank spaces" he had enough copy to make one hundred and fifty printed pages—"a neat pocket volume." The nature of the unpublished pieces may be indicated by a selection from the titles: *Ode to Ambition, Ode to the Elves, Ode on Whistling, Ode on the Death of a Lamb;* epistles to Erskine, Lady Mackintosh, Miss Home (Lord Kames's daughter), Temple; paraphrases from Holy Scripture; prologues for *Macbeth, Love Makes a Man, The Coquettes;* songs and epigrams galore. The unpublished verse is seldom worse than the published, and is perhaps occasionally better.

For six years or so of his youth, then, Boswell regarded himself as a poet and had some encouragement in the belief. It is the usual beginning of men with literary gifts, and is not to be written off as insignificant when it proves to be a dead-end street. Writing verse nourished his conviction of literary genius, as prose writing at that age could not have done. It gave him opportunities for more frequent and more extensive publication than he could have had if he had stuck to prose; and few men who wish to be authors will ever realize their ambition unless they are encouraged by early and frequent publication. I do not know that Boswell could have avoided his destiny if he had never turned a verse, but I think it certain that his voluminous early scribblings brought him more quickly to the discovery of his true gift and made him more confident in the exercise of it.

But if that were the whole story, the proper course for a biographer would be merely to say so and to excuse himself from particularization. It is not the whole story. The most rewarding focus for a biography of Boswell is not that which makes him a neurotic or a buffoon; it is that which faces up to the central facts and presents him as an author. In the biographies of most literary men, the juvenilia can be written off cursorily as largely irrelevant: all the really characteristic writings come later. In the case of Boswell the juvenilia remain characteristic. *No Abolition of Slavery,* published when he was past fifty, is as silly as *The Cub at Newmarket. A Letter to the People of Scotland* (1785) is as extravagant and indiscreet as "An Original Letter from a Gentleman of Scotland to the Earl of * * * in London" (1761). Boswell discovered, not long after the period we are now considering, the kind of writing he was uniquely fitted for, and as time went on he developed a conscience about it. But as he acquired literary honesty and sobriety, he did not simultaneously abandon the postures he had found so delightful as a young man. To the end of his days he wrote and printed banal and doggerel verse, he puffed himself and his writings in the newspapers, he wrote letters to himself and he answered them. An account of his writing and publication during 1756–1762 is in some sort an epitome of his entire literary career.

CHAPTER

VII

On 29 October 1761 (we are now turning back some months to resume
the main biographical account) Boswell celebrated his twenty-first birthday, a date on which he had confidently expected to emerge from the detested status of young laird. He had somehow got it into his head that his
father had promised that if he was diligent in his legal studies, he might go
up to London again and pass the winter there. Sheridan, now back in
London, had proposed what he considered a tactful compromise in the
battle of wills that was making Boswell and his father so unhappy. His
plan can be recovered only by conjecture, but as it involved admission to
one of the Inns of Court in London, it presumably implied a programme
of reading and study preparatory to being called to the English bar.
As an English barrister Boswell would be able to practise in the Court of
Exchequer in Edinburgh and would be eligible for appointment to the
bench of that most respectable court. Even if he did not pursue his profession in Edinburgh, Lord Auchinleck would presumably rather have him a
lawyer practising in London than no lawyer at all. As for Boswell, the
arrangement had powerful attractions. Admission to one of the Inns of
Court cost little, would commit him to nothing, would assure him of very
pleasant living quarters; in short, would provide the ideal setting for the
kind of life he wanted to live in London. He gratefully acceded, and
Sheridan actually caused him to be entered in the Inner Temple on 19
November 1761. Boswell seems to have acted in a sincere belief that his
father had agreed to the arrangement, and was shocked and angry when
Lord Auchinleck peremptorily vetoed it. He wrote to Sheridan, indeed,
that he had more than once been on the point of running away again and
had been kept in Edinburgh only by the hope that Sheridan was going to

74

be able to arrange "an excellent Plan of Life" for him. "But if I am not in the British Metropolis next winter, may he who best plays the Prince of Denmark [i.e., Sheridan himself] despise me in this world, and the Prince of the Power of the Air roast me in the next."

To be sure, there were gratifying evidences that outside his own home his emergence into manhood was recognized. In December 1761, just after his twenty-first birthday, he was elected Junior Warden of the Canongate Kilwinning Lodge, and about the same time he was invited to become a member of the Select Society of Edinburgh. This was a distinct compliment to a youthful author, for the Select Society numbered among its members the principal established literary figures of the city (Hugh Blair, Sir David Dalrymple, David Hume, Lord Kames, Principal Robertson), and they seldom bestowed their nod on a man so much younger than themselves.

Henry Home, Lord Kames, one of Lord Auchinleck's brothers on the bench, was very kind to Boswell during this troubled period. I do not think that Boswell loved him, or that he had a really deep fondness for Boswell (it is doubtful, I should guess, whether Kames was ever deeply fond of any one but his wife), but he found Boswell amusing and promising, and had him a good deal in his home as a kindness to Lord Auchinleck. Kames was a tall, spare, hasty, arrogant man, a voluminous writer on subjects so widely diverse as agriculture and theory of poetry, sometimes coarse and profane in his speech, and in criminal trials severe to the point of brutality. But he understood Boswell better than his father did, perhaps because he was not responsible for him, perhaps because he was an author himself, perhaps because in his youth (which had been Episcopal and Jacobite) he had thought of going to Germany and enlisting in the King of Prussia's tall regiment.

Kames was a respected but not a confidential friend; in William McQuhae Boswell acquired another chum. Only three years Boswell's senior, he had come into Lord Auchinleck's household as a domestic tutor in succession to Mr. Fergusson. By that time Boswell himself had passed beyond the need of a tutor's ministrations, and was able to associate with the new governor on purely social and friendly terms. McQuhae's manliness pleased him greatly. At the University of Glasgow he had been a favourite pupil of Adam Smith; he was well educated, loved polite literature, and, though he had decided to be a clergyman in the country, was

not without a relish for the scenes of active life. The friendship was not
to endure like those with Johnston and Temple, but in 1762 it was equally
hearty.

Boswell persisted in his resolve to steer clear of the mansions of gross
sensuality, partly because his last infection (a serious one) had scared him,
partly because he had waked to the fact that he was attractive to women
and could have *bonnes fortunes* for the asking. The code of gallantry demanded that he be very circumspect in documenting affairs of this sort,
and he observed the code. The winter of 1761–1762 was as crowded,
involved, and hectic as any he ever afterwards lived through; and if a
biographer cannot make it appear so, it is because Boswell left only a
cryptic and elliptical diary (largely in cipher) instead of a detailed journal. He began studying the violin. He worked on Donaldson's *Collection*,
which was published in February; he published *An Ode to Tragedy* in
December; he published *The Cub at Newmarket* in March. Almost every
day he drank tea with or danced with or wrote to or otherwise gallanted
some highly eligible young lady: Miss Colquhoun, Miss Bruce, Miss
Stewart, Miss Thomson. (The first three of these young ladies have already been mentioned; Miss Isabella Thomson, daughter of Dr. David
Thomson, was married in the autumn of 1762 to Capt. Frederick
Bridges Schaw.) And he carried on, concurrently with all this flirting
and with each other, four separate intrigues: with two actresses, with a
lady of rank and fashion, with a "curious young little pretty" who
was probably a servant. The best way to demonstrate the complication
of his amours will be to transcribe all the entries in one week of his
notes:

WEDNESDAY [16 DECEMBER]. Tea, paradise. Think on this evening.
THURSDAY [17 DECEMBER]. Tea Kames.
FRIDAY [18 DECEMBER]. Tea Johnston.
SATURDAY [19 DECEMBER]. Dined Dundonald's, tea Lady Mackintosh.
SUNDAY [20 DECEMBER]. Dined Johnston with Schaw and Cordwell.
Tea Miss Thomson. Now easy on account of H_____.
MONDAY [21 DECEMBER]. Tea Kilravock. Next at play, *Trip to Jubilee*,
Griffith for the first night for five years. Resolved φ again in all force to
dissipate. Spoke also to A. Bravo !
TUESDAY [22 DECEMBER]. Coffee at a tavern. Supped Lord Kames.
Had sat up all night. Was with Miss T_____ forenoon.

WEDNESDAY [23 DECEMBER]. Tea Donaldson, then at play, *Incon-stant*. In the forenoon had been with ϕ; one, she two, and visited A_____.[1]

There can be little doubt that "ϕ" was adopted as symbol as being the initial letter of one of the Greek nouns meaning "love," and no doubt at all that the mistress so designated was the wife of Boswell's erstwhile second-best friend, James Love, the actor. Mrs. Love, a comic actress of some ability, probably went on the stage before Boswell was born and by 1761 must have been forty or upwards, but she was (on Boswell's testimony) very lively, smart, clever, and good-humoured. She often played Polly to Digges's Macheath. Temple implies that she and her husband made Boswell the victim of the badger game ("Recollect the sins of thy youth [Mrs. Love *deleted*], the easy compliance of the wife, the artful moderation of the husband"), but I find nothing in the documents to support such a charge. The tone of Love's dealings with Boswell (we have some of his letters) is obsequious, not at all demanding. It is true that he persuaded Boswell to make him loans amounting to £40, but Boswell at least tried to make him pay the money all back. If Love had deliberately prostituted his wife, he would certainly have managed to make more out of the transaction. Boswell's note "Resolved ϕ again" shows that the relationship was being resumed, not initiated; and his other styles for Mrs. Love, "old Canongate" and "old girl," imply condescension. Mrs. Love may have lost her heart to him, but he treated her as a convenience. On this occasion, he was returning to her in the hope that her frank and experienced love-making would moderate his troublesome passion for the woman who had admitted him to paradise on 16 December and caused the uneasiness on account of H_____ which he declared himself free of on the 20th.

That woman was, I think, the lady of rank and fashion, but before I unveil her, I should like to make a guess at the other actress, for we know

[1] Kames, Johnston, Schaw, Miss Thomson, and Donaldson have already been introduced. For Cordwell, see below, p. 464. Dundonald was Boswell's great-uncle, the Earl of Dundonald; Lady Mackintosh the Jacobite heroine who led out the Clan Chattan in 1745 when the Chief, her husband, took the side of the Government. Boswell had been flirting with her, apparently harmlessly, since the previous spring. She was at least fifteen years older than he was. Hugh Rose of Kilravock, head of the Rose family, was Sheriff of Ross. Griffith, an actor in the Edinburgh company, acted fops and fine gentlemen (John Jackson, *History of the Scottish Stage*, 1793, p. 42).

that there were at least two. The mysterious "A" of the entries for 21 and
23 December comes first into the record in May 1761, when Boswell,
then accompanying his father on the northern circuit, wrote her a letter.
By a process of deduction which I consign to the notes, I conclude that
she was Mrs. Brooke, an actress who played minor parts in the Edinburgh
theatre during 1761 and 1762. She was perhaps ten years Boswell's senior, the estranged wife of a London engraver and literary man-of-all-
work, James Brooke of Rathbone Place. "A very beautiful young woman,"
she had found her husband's ungovernable outbursts of temper intolerable,
and had left him and her three young children (one of them a godchild
of Samuel Richardson) to go on the stage. She lived with that Griffith
whom Boswell mentions in his note of 21 December as appearing in a
favourite leading role after a long absence. Later a member of the theatrical company at Norwich, she was stricken with cancer and came back to
London, where she lived on the bounty of a son-in-law, husband of
Richardson's godchild. She died in 1782.

In the Sketch which he wrote for Rousseau, Boswell makes brief and
general mention of his intrigues with actresses, detailing only the shameful,
dangerous, and thrilling affair with the daughter of a man of the first
distinction in Scotland, a man who had heaped kindnesses on him. In two
subsidiary documents the relationship with this distinguished elder becomes more intimate: he is called a "respected friend," "a worthy and distinguished friend." These details strongly suggest Lord Kames; and when
one learns further that the lady was married to an amiable gentleman of
great wealth who insisted on Boswell's visiting him at his seat in the country, the identification becomes practically certain. Jean Home, Lord and
Lady Kames's only daughter, married Patrick Heron of Kirroughtrie, a
man of considerable means with an estate near Dumfries, at the end of
October or the beginning of November 1761. We shall not be blackening
a hitherto spotless reputation if we cast her in the role of Boswell's
mistress, for Heron in 1772 divorced her, publicly presenting evidence of
her adultery with a young Army officer, and her father sent her off forthwith to France, refusing ever to see her again. Many years later her mother
with tears gave Boswell an account of the dreadful day on which she and
Lord Kames learned of their child's downfall, and tried to explain to him
how it could all have come about. Jean, she said, had been under seventeen when she married Heron; she had been much praised and made to
feel superior; he ought to have "held her in with bit and bridle," but he

was a good-natured, weak man, and she despised him. Jean met disgrace like her father's daughter; she made no denial of the charges against her and refused to weep. Boswell recorded this deeply touching confidence circumspectly but in terms, surely, that indicate sudden confrontation with a personal danger: "This was a strange subject. I kept myself steady and expatiated on that unfortunate lady's many engaging qualities. . . . I sat with [Lady Kames] till half an hour after twelve, amazed at my present vigour of mind."

Jean at sixteen was probably just as strong-willed as she was at twenty-seven, but she threw herself in Boswell's arms with shocking dispatch if I am right in seeing a reference to her in two entries (one of them quoted above) which Boswell made in his notes in the month following her marriage: "Tea, Angel, two" (3 Dec. 1761) and "Tea, paradise. Think on this evening" (16 Dec. 1761).

Boswell professed to have been greatly improved by his delicious intrigues with women of beauty, sentiment, and spirit. "Indeed, in my mind," he wrote, "there cannot be higher felicity on earth enjoyed by man than the participation of genuine reciprocal amorous affection with an amiable woman. There he has a full indulgence of all the delicate feelings and pleasures both of body and mind, while at the same time in this enchanting union he exults with a consciousness that he is the superior person. The dignity of his sex is kept up." He suffered all his life from a radical sense of insecurity and inadequacy, and sexual conquest gave him confidence and made him proud of himself. But if deeply clandestine affairs with beautiful women of family and fashion provided him with moments of the highest felicity, it was not a felicity that remained long unmixed. He had a horror of adultery, in the case of Jean Home he was ashamed of his baseness in so requiting the many kindnesses of Lord and Lady Kames, and his naturally open nature rebelled at subterfuge and lies. He was furthermore likely, in the inception of any affair with a woman not obviously his social inferior, to get excited and tense and to suffer the mortification of temporary impotency. However much he might talk about the combined and delicate pleasures of body and mind, what he really preferred in the way of sex was frank and episodic grossness which never threatened his sense of being the superior person and gave him enjoyment without the responsibilities of love. In January 1762, the affairs with "A," Mrs. Love, and Mrs. Heron all apparently active, he met something really more to his taste, a "curious young little pretty" named Peggy Doig, who—though he almost certainly did not then know it—had already had an illegitimate child. I suspect that she was a servant; certainly she was a plebeian. There were obstacles, apparently not of Peggy's providing, but by March he "made it out."

In the spring of 1762 the relations between Boswell and his father came to a crisis. Lord Auchinleck, in despair of rehabilitating his heir, talked of selling off the estate and extinguishing the Family, maintaining, in his own vigorous phrase, that it was better to snuff a candle out than leave it to stink in the socket. He was probably less moved to this decision by Boswell's amours than by his publications, his general lack of prudence and discretion, his dislike for country life and the affairs of the estate, and his unremitting demand to be allowed to go back to London. Concerning the amours, Lord Auchinleck was no doubt imperfectly informed, and in any case would not have concluded that profligacy in a young man spelled hopeless irresponsibility for the rest of his life. His threat, however, presents a puzzle which will never be solved, for it rests on a difference of legal opinion that was never taken to court. Lord Auchinleck's marriage contract, drawn while Old James was laird and signed by him, entailed the estate of Auchinleck upon the heirs male of Lord Auchinleck's marriage to Boswell's mother. When, many years later, Boswell himself was able to inspect this document, he concluded that all his father's talk of disinheriting him had been bluff, and that he had never had it in his power, even with Boswell's consent, to sell the estate or to alter the succession. Lord Auchinleck at that time said that he had another paper from his father which would have enabled him to evade the provisions of the marriage contract. Boswell could not see how either or both of them could impugn the provision in the contract, but Lord Auchinleck was a better lawyer than he was, and in any case could certainly have sold off the splendid additions which he himself had made to the property. In 1762 Boswell did not for a moment doubt that his father could do anything he threatened to do, and he made a deeply humiliating concession. He later referred to the document which Lord Auchinleck got him to copy and sign as a renunciation of his birthright, or a renunciation of his right to the family estate under his mother's contract of marriage, but when he used that language, he had not seen the marriage contract and perhaps had not looked recently at his copy of the "renunciation." This deed (7 March 1762) by implication confirmed the succession of heirs male as provided in the marriage contract, but treated Boswell personally as incompetent.

It gave his father the power, if he chose, to vest the estate in trustees after his death, Boswell to receive half the free rents and to have the right to reside in Auchinleck House, but with no say in the management of the property. He later spoke as though he had thus abased himself solely from a generous principle of preserving the Family, but the transaction involved an immediate personal solatium which must have been very attractive to him when he was struggling so hard for independence. By another document of slightly later date Lord Auchinleck formally and irrevocably granted him an allowance of £100 a year.

It must have been deeply painful to Lord Auchinleck to expose the shame of the Family to outsiders, but he was a very fair-minded man and he also probably wanted to protect himself against a possible future charge of precipitancy and harshness. He accordingly caused the deed to be witnessed by the two Edinburgh lawyers for whom he knew Boswell had the greatest respect: James Ferguson of Pitfour, Dean of the Faculty of Advocates, and Sir David Dalrymple. Dalrymple, who has already been introduced in these pages, was a man of letters; Ferguson, an Episcopalian long kept off the bench because of supposed disaffection to the Government, was universally acclaimed for probity and humanity.

At the time, Boswell seems not to have allowed the "renunciation" to depress or even to sober him. He made no mention whatever in his diary of signing the deed, recording rather on that day a very jolly dinner at Digges's house with a theatrical company, followed by supper at Lord Kames's. The diary does not tell us whether the project for complete financial independence which he formed in the days immediately following was frivolous or desperate, but it was certainly bizarre. Introduced to the recently widowed Duchess of Douglas, who met his habitual gallantries with her well-known recklessness of speech, he thought of marriage: "Resolved to propose the scheme; if it succeeds, bravo! independence; if not, a good adventure." We shall hear more of the redoubtable Duchess Peggy in due course. Just how old she was in 1762 I have been unable to discover, but since her late husband was sixty-six at the time of his death and Dr. Johnson in 1773—a year before *her* death—called her "an old lady who talks broad Scotch with a paralytic voice," I should suppose that she was not much, if any, under sixty. She was not in possession of the vast Douglas estates, but the Duke had left her a considerable sum of money, and she could quite well have provided for a second husband. The scheme, however, was short-lived. Something unsettled Boswell and he began thinking again of the Guards. This was a relapse, his London ideas since the previous autumn having centred rather in the Temple. He concluded that his plan of marrying the Duchess was "too clumsy," resolved on the Guards, and on 22 March had it out with his father. I do not know whether he obtained Lord Auchinleck's consent or announced his intention of dispensing with it and venturing forth on his small but assured allowance of a hundred pounds a year, but he emerged firm in a resolution "to set out immediately and prosecute Guards." Before he left, however, he felt bound to explain himself to Ferguson. Ferguson vindicated his reputation for persuasiveness. He predicted that Boswell, after his fling, would return to the law, and insisted that before leaving he pass his private trials as a Civilian and not run the risk of losing the gains of several years of study. Lord Auchinleck, deeply grateful for a concession which he himself had not been able to obtain, agreed (24 March 1762) that if Boswell would go to Auchinleck and study till June, he would not only grant him permission to accept a commission in the Guards, but would also, if need be, use his own interest to obtain one. Characteristically, having got what he had been fighting for, Boswell became less certain that it was what he wanted. The attractions, I suppose, of Sheridan's plan kept recurring.

Departure for Auchinleck being agreed on, he went to take leave of his various ladies. Mrs. Brooke's adieu turned out to be a *congé*: "At nine, waited on A, talked of the whole affair. She said sensibly that Rover's inconstant disposition made her unhappy, and therefore broke off.[1] Prettily conducted; friendly and letters returned." His leave-taking from Mrs. Love, not a *congé*, was shockingly broken-in upon: "At ten, ϕ. The strangest accident in bedroom; just at it when ♅ came in. 'Well, how are ye?' Such a scene! She left me, then came back, etc. I got his word of honour, but such a scene!" Who is concealed by the special symbol, I do not know, but it was clearly not Love.

A final conference with Ferguson and Dalrymple fixed him in the Guards scheme. He went off to Auchinleck, Eglinton was notified. The following letter to Erskine, as here quoted, incorporates a good deal of revision made in the following spring when he was preparing the correspondence for publication, but it is at every point dramatically ap-

---

[1] "Rover, an inconstant lover; a male flirt. *Obs.*" (*Oxford English Dictionary,* citing examples from Addison and Prior). The word had been given wide circulation earlier by Mrs. Aphra Behn's successful comedy, *The Rover* (1677).

propriate. For all its schoolboy humour, it presents with touching accuracy the full day-dream of his unchecked youthful ambition. He did not realize all these glowing fancies, but there were few of them that he ever willingly renounced.

I am indulging the most agreeable reveries imaginable. I am thinking of the brilliant scenes of happiness which I shall enjoy as an officer of the Guards. How I shall be acquainted with all the grandeur of a court and all the elegance of dress and diversions; become a favourite of ministers of state and the adoration of ladies of quality, beauty, and fortune. How many parties of pleasure shall I have in town! How many fine jaunts to the noble seats of dukes, lords, and members of Parliament in the country! I am thinking of the perfect knowledge which I shall acquire of men and manners, of the intimacies which I shall have the honour to form with the learned and ingenious in every science, and of the many amusing literary anecdotes which I shall pick up. I am thinking of making the tour of Europe and feasting on the delicious prospects of Italy and France; of feeling all the transports of a bard at Rome and writing noble poems on the banks of the Tiber. I am thinking of the distinguished honours which I shall receive at every foreign court, and of what infinite service I shall be to all my countrymen upon their travels. I am thinking of returning to England, of getting into the House of Commons, of speaking still better than Mr. Pitt, and of being made principal Secretary of State. I am thinking of having a regiment of Guards, and of making a glorious stand against an invasion by the Spaniards. I am thinking how I shall marry a lady of the highest distinction with a fortune of a hundred thousand pounds. I am thinking of my flourishing family of children: how my sons shall be men of sense and spirit and my daughters women of beauty and every amiable perfection. I am thinking of the prodigious respect which I shall receive, of the splendid books which will be dedicated to me, and the statues which will be erected to my immortal honour.

Not long before, he had written that he had never at any time been so insipid, so muddy, so standing-water like. "The country is my aversion." Now the weather is charming, he is fond of the country, he is cheerful and happy. He is expecting a letter from Eglinton which will inaugurate all these felicities, he has an assignation with Jean Heron at the circuit court at Dumfries the coming Saturday: "Saturday's our day" is the code they use with each other.

Eglinton's letter brought a shock for which he was quite unprepared. The recent publication of *The Cub at Newmarket* with its unauthorized dedication had made serious trouble between Eglinton and the Duke of York; Eglinton was vexed by Boswell's thoughtlessness and disgusted by his stipulation that the commission Eglinton was to procure for him must be in a home battalion. As Eglinton later explained, it would have been of the utmost difficulty to get a commission in the Guards at any rate, and in order to accomplish it, he would have had to make use of every argument: among the rest, that Boswell was eager for action in the field. He peremptorily demanded assurance that if he obtained a commission in a battalion on service in Germany, Boswell would accept it. Boswell's reply seemed to him evasive, and he washed his hands of the whole business.

One can hardly underestimate the depth of Boswell's dismay and anguish. He had assumed—of course too readily—that his father's opposition was the only obstacle that stood in his way; that had been removed only to reveal another barrier equally insurmountable. There was nothing for it but to go to his father, admit Eglinton's defection, and humbly entreat his father to use the interest he had promised. Lord Auchinleck, in the press and distraction of a circuit, faithfully complied and got off a letter to the Duke of Queensberry, the former patron of Gay. The Duke of Argyll, that long-time manager of Scottish affairs, was dead; Queensberry, who had been out of favour with the old king, had received distinguished marks of favour from the new one. Queensberry returned a cordial answer, promising to do what he could, but enumerating the difficulties. Lord Auchinleck, an old hand at reading political correspondence, told Boswell that Queensberry would accomplish nothing and that nobody else would either. A commission in the Guards could not be had through the Auchinleck interest alone; it would require that much interest and a good stiff sum of money besides. He had used his interest, he would not advance any money. Boswell was shaken, but refused to believe that Queensberry's cordiality meant nothing more than a desire to soften a blow.

He came up to Edinburgh in June in very bad humour, unable to fix his heart on any scheme, his views of life all dark. It seems not unreasonable to attribute some of his gloom to the fact that Peggy Doig was pregnant, whether he had already known it or only now got the news. Repentance, if he did repent, brought no reform. His note for 1 July marks a dramatic, perhaps a defiant, return of high spirits: "In rather too fine a flow, rogered ϕ forenoon and P afternoon." The indecorous word is in cipher, Boswell all his life showing a strong disinclination for speaking or writing coarse and obscene language. He turned for counsel and advice to a physician who was a fellow Mason, Dr. Cairnie, Treasurer of Canongate Kilwinning Lodge, a Jacobite who had been out in the '45 and had had to spend many years abroad in consequence. Cairnie talked over the Guards and other plans of life with him, and put him in humour with his state of unplanned parenthood. Two weeks later (23 July) he met with Cairnie and the kirk treasurer of the Canongate and made his peace with the kirk session. If he had been a plebeian in some of the country parishes of Scotland he might have had to mount the stool of repentance and would certainly have been admonished by the minister before the congregation— as Robert Burns was a quarter of a century later. But in the metropolis a milder discipline prevailed, at least for gentle folk, and he was able to get off with merely paying a fine. The kirk treasurer was unexpectedly genteel and made Boswell quite easy, but he blabbed about the matter afterwards.

Next evening, as he was supping with Lord Kames, he received a message from Eglinton saying that Eglinton was in Edinburgh and wished to see him. Kames supported him in stand-offishness, and he returned word that he would call in the morning. And he says that Kames also encouraged him in the plan of a new campaign that would by-pass Eglinton altogether. Let Lord Auchinleck supplement his allowance, give him a recommendation to the Duke of Queensberry, and permit him to go up to London for an extended stay. Face to face with the Duke, he was sure he could charm a commission out of him. When he and Eglinton met next morning, he adopted an air of ease and indifference which Eglinton at once interpreted as abjuration of his patronship.

On 30 July 1762 Boswell took and passed the private examination in Civil Law. "Was a little frightened, but it was rather an agreeable sensation, as I felt myself much in earnest. I recovered myself and really went through it easily and with applause." Lord Auchinleck afterwards told him that when he applied himself he showed as much genius for the law as any one he had ever known. Since this would have been so much the most appropriate moment to present his new plan, and I know of no evidence at all as to when he did actually present it, I shall choose to believe that he now asked Lord Auchinleck to let him go to London. In any case, whenever asked, Lord Auchinleck assented; wearily, no doubt, and with iteration of his warning that Boswell would not succeed in his quest.

There was no point in going up before the opening of Parliament brought the great people back to town. Visits to Kirroughtrie and Kames, with a fine, care-free jaunt through the southern counties of Scotland in the company of Lord and Lady Kames, would occupy most of the weeks after the middle of September, but in the mean time he had to weather out a month at Auchinleck. On 3 September, with eleven interminable days still to go, he abandoned his heavy-handed attempt at facetiousness in a letter he was writing to Erskine and uttered a thrilling cry for help. "I really can write [no wit] I am so dull. . . . Pray write to me immediately. . . . Write me an affectionate and a serious or even a dull letter. Let there be no wit in it. That I am at present incapable of, and so I hate it."

It would be wrong not to take this pain seriously and wrong to make too much of it. It was very real, and in eleven days it would have only the reality of a half-forgotten nightmare.

Boswell's journal—the central literary creation of his life—was born of his almost enthusiastic notion of the felicity of London. Since at least the end of his eighteenth year he had had spells of keeping diaries, but to judge from the surviving specimens, they had all been concise and unambitious. Throughout his life he was much given to the appointing of solemn and decisive days, days which were to mark his escape from the past and his entry into a more satisfactory state of being. 14 September 1762, the day on which he left Auchinleck for Kirroughtrie, was fixed upon by him as one of these momentous days. He would not actually set out for London for some two months, but that was so tremendous an event that he felt the need of working up to it. The record which he headed "Journal of My Jaunt, Harvest 1762"[1] was consciously begun as prologue to and training for the swelling act which he planned to record in London. It was the inception of an elaborate literary journal which he was to keep without the gap of a single day at least to the end of January 1765—nearly two thousand quarto pages of careful manuscript. It is the first of his writings in which he demonstrates his power to write so that others must read what he has written.

"Journal of My Jaunt, Harvest 1762" suffers in comparison with Boswell's later journals by not being at any point a really private record. He is writing it for the perusal of John Johnston and William McQuhae, both of whom he addresses in a self-conscious introduction. He makes too

[1] "Harvest" (pronounced "hairst" or "harst"), was once the usual Scots term for "autumn," and still survives locally.

many jocular literary allusions, and is far too much aware of the figure he is cutting. Even when the writing is up to his later standard, the matter is not. He has to distort or suppress some of his most significant episodes, and even when he writes without restraint, he suffers by comparison with his later self, for the mature Boswell is a much more interesting person than the flippant and self-satisfied cub of 1762. But after all qualification, the first of his journals remains a remarkably vivid and entertaining piece of writing, an astonishing performance for a writer only twenty-two years old. Unlike his verses, which, even when tolerable, seldom show the slightest originality, this writing is creative, a new departure in English letters. And it is to a surprising degree creative in *our* sense: its best effects fall in the area of our own interest and experimentation.

A really thoughtful analysis of the nature of Boswell's literary genius has long been overdue. It was essentially a genius for journalizing: all his really important books were quarried out of his journal. The motives that led (one can almost say compelled) him to keep a journal are many and some of them are obscure, but there is no doubt as to the central one. He had an enormous zest for living. The workings of his own mind fascinated him, and he relished every other variety of human nature. But the experience was not complete, not lived through, not wholly *realized,* until he had explored it verbally and had written it down. "I should live no more than I can record," he once wrote, "as one should not have more corn growing than one can get in."

Boswell always thought of his journal as a history of his own mind, and felt under no obligation to record external facts merely as such. One might expect therefore that he would deal rather cavalierly with circumstance, concerning himself more with the "spirit" of things than the "letter." Actually, he had an almost pedantic passion for circumstantial accuracy. Not all the circumstances go in by any means—only those that rise vividly to the area of his consciousness—but the ones that go in are scrupulously limited by historical fact.

It is this conscious and proclaimed adherence to historical fact that keeps us from recognizing in Boswell an imaginative writer of a high order. We remember Aristotle's dictum that art deals with what *ought* to have happened, and conclude that invention and imagination are synonymous terms. In point of fact, they have no necessary connexion. There are obviously two sorts of matter in Boswell's journal: matter that came to him already verbalized and matter that had nothing to do with words. Even if

we take the extreme (and, as I shall show later, erroneous) view that
Boswell was a sort of tape-recorder and deserves no praise *as artist* for the
conversations he has reported, we are still left with a vast bulk of very
vivid writing. Between perception and verbalization a great gulf is fixed;
and it requires just as much of a heave of the imagination to express non-
verbal matter of fact vividly as it does to give life to a fiction. In inventive
power Boswell is nowhere—for practical purposes he can be described as
having no inventive power at all—but in imaginative power he is the peer
of Scott and Dickens.

Aristotle's dictum is not so exclusive as it sounds. It surely does not
mean that no history can be poetry; merely that the poet (artist) who
keeps within the range of the historical is *limited*. He is dependent on his
luck or his skill in finding in real life matter with the same sort of mean-
ingful relations in it that one demands of fictions. He is something like the
really imaginative photographer. It is not likely that any day-to-day journal will be continuously great art, but considerable stretches of it may be.

And a full, honest, and penetrating history of a human mind—*any*
human mind—has an appeal beyond the appeal of art. When Dr. Johnson said that it was the biographical part of literature that he loved most,
he was not restricting himself to biographies of high literary excellence.
He meant that he loved facts about human nature as revealed in almost
any kind of intelligible account. And Boswell from the very first showed
extraordinary skill in self-analysis. His journal stands between the poles of
Pepys and Rousseau. It does not have the cool, assured, masculine tact
of Pepys, nor does it provide so lavish a recording of historical detail. It
does not have the piercing eloquence and continuous forensic warmth of
Rousseau. But Boswell is as frank and trustworthy as Pepys, and he provides self-analysis like Rousseau: self-analysis as skilful as Rousseau's in
the dissection of motives, and with a superior degree of detachment.
Rousseau's *Confessions* are an apologia, Boswell's journal is a history.

We are back at Aristotle's dictum: poetry is more philosophical and a
higher mode than history. It ought to be so, it no doubt is so, but I find
myself perversely in sympathy with Carlyle's contention that imaginative
biography is not a lower thing than fiction but is actually *better*. Do we,
in fact, receive as powerful a gratification from fictions as we do from
writing that is at once vivid *and* historical? Is Mr. Micawber more satisfying than the Dr. Johnson who emerges from Boswell's pages? Granting
that the two figures are drawn with equal skill, do we not derive an *addi-*

tional satisfaction from knowing that Boswell's Johnson is a portrait of a man who once really walked the earth? Furthermore, matter that would be tedious in a novel, because not obviously related to the plot, is of absorbing interest in a journal, largely, so far as I can see, because it really happened, because it rescues for us some little portion of the past. "The mysterious River of Existence rushes on," says Carlyle, "a new Billow thereof has arrived, and lashes wildly as ever around the old embankments; but the former Billow with *its* loud, mad eddyings, where is it?—Where!—Now this Book of Boswell's [he means *The Life of Johnson,* but what he says will apply about as well to Boswell's journal], this is precisely a revocation of the edict of Destiny; so that Time shall not utterly, not so soon by several centuries, have dominion over us. A little row of Naphthalamps, with its line of Naphtha-light, burns clear and holy through the dead Night of the Past: they who are gone are still here; though hidden they are revealed, though dead they yet speak. There it shines, that little miraculously lamplit Pathway; shedding its feebler and feebler twilight into the boundless dark Oblivion,—for all that our Johnson *touched* has become illuminated for us: on which miraculous little Pathway we can still travel, and see wonders."

I have quoted that magnificent but mannered passage not merely for what it says but also for the way in which it says it. I wanted a strongly contrasted style as a point of departure for discussing Boswell's. It may come as something of a shock to be asked to consider Boswell as a stylist. In his private journals he has, as a matter of fact, the rarest of all styles, that which seems to have no idiosyncrasies, that neither colours nor distorts. Carlyle characteristically finds the secret of Boswell's power in certain moral qualities: he had, Carlyle says, "an open loving heart." Without gainsaying this in the least, I should like also to attribute his stylistic virtues to a certain intellectual attitude, to what I might call his invincible mediocrity. What gives Boswell's writing its peculiar quality of solidity and its transparent atmosphere is that he always writes in terms of average or normal experience. Carlyle writes from anything but average habits of thought: the pages before the one I have quoted are studded with words like "transcendental" and "ideal"—words that would have made Boswell acutely uncomfortable. Boswell records a good deal of circumstantial detail, and records it accurately. But of course his journal is far more than a mere chronicle of indubitable facts: it selects and interprets. And his interpretation moves on the plane of average or normal experience, with the

result that in him we seem to see the past through no medium at all, or
at most through plate glass.

It is because Boswell's style is so scrupulously low-pitched that it affects us like the writing of a contemporary. Carlyle sounds embarrassingly
old-fashioned to ears trained to the cadences of Maugham and Heming-
way, and even the best of Boswell's contemporaries require some historical
adjustment when they are read now. Nobody doubts that the grossness of
Boswell's London Journal had something to do with its huge circulation
in our times, but it is a mistake to suppose that mere smut will make a best-
seller of any piece of writing two hundred years old. Smollett's novels are
quite as gross as *Boswell's London Journal,* but if a brand-new novel of
Smollett's, comparable in quality to *Roderick Random* or *Peregrine
Pickle,* were to turn up tomorrow, it would have little circulation outside
the relatively small group that relishes "classics." A book can compete on
equal terms with modern best-sellers only if it is written in a style expressive of modern sensibility.

The distinguishing structural features of Boswell's journal can be
summed up in the one word *dramatic*. Journals are necessarily written in
retrospect, and the normal way of writing them is to criticize the matter in
the light of later events, or at least to give the entries the emotional tone
of the moment of writing. Boswell consistently resists this undramatic
method. He did not ordinarily post his journal from day to day and was
often at a distance of months from the events he was recording. Yet he
went back and described each moment as it was lived, carefully excluding
overt reference to things that had happened later. But it would be naïve to
suppose that his knowledge of subsequent events is not affecting his writing. It helps him to select his details meaningfully, to create a significant
forward-straining tension.

Beginning with his first journal, Boswell deals lavishly in "characters":
the individuation of the people he mentions by swift and economical descriptive touches that read like stage-directions in modern printed plays.
(Printed plays of *his* day lacked such characterizations, but they had
been a feature of the printed comedy of the seventeenth century.) Mr.
Shaw, a retired solicitor whom he met at Lagwine, "is precise, starched,
and proud. Wears a dark-brown coat, a buff vest, and black breeches; has
a lank iron countenance; wears a weather-beaten scratch wig; sits erect
upon his chair and sings *Tarry Woo'* with the English accent." Dr. Coulthard, an apothecary from Carlisle, is "a true-looking Englishman with a

round-cut head and leather breeches; a jolly dog who sung us a song that the boy sings who sweeps Drury-Lane stage before the candles are lighted, to the tune of *Balance a Straw*." Miss Maxwell of Springkell is "an honest-hearted, merry, jocular girl, of size somewhat corpulent, but has a very agreeable countenance, and can walk and dance with all imaginable cleverness."

More dramatic than features, clothes, or gesture is speech; and Boswell's journal distinguishes itself from the first by the amount of characteristic conversation that it contains. It is true that in the journal of the Harvest Jaunt we get no specimens of that highest mode of his art in which the conversation of two or more speakers is cast and given stage-directions:

JOHNSON.... "I am afraid I may be one of those who shall be damned" *(looking dismally)*. DR. ADAMS. "What do you mean by damned?" JOHNSON *(passionately and loudly)*. "Sent to Hell, Sir, and punished everlastingly."

The mode of the journal of the Harvest Jaunt (for that matter, the commoner mode of Boswell's journal in general) is indirect discourse with occasional sentences or brief paragraphs quoted directly. But even here in this first journal there are long stretches that could be cast dramatically by no more radical intervention than the change of pronouns and tenses and the substitution of a speaker's name for "He said that" or "Said he." A good example is the record of a conversation lasting an hour and a half which Boswell and Erskine held with David Hume on 4 November 1762. "I have remembered," he says, "the heads and the very words of a great part of Mr. Hume's conversation with us." It will be necessary later to discuss at some length the nature of Boswell's memory and the relation which his remembered conversations bear to what actually was said. Here I shall simply assert, following his own excellent statement, that they are dramatic epitomes or miniatures. They do not preserve every word that was uttered; far from it. They probably do not preserve every topic that came up for discussion. But they invent no topics, and the important, the pivotal words, are *ipsissima verba*.

Did Boswell consciously set out to imitate anything when he began his journal of the Harvest Jaunt? Lord Hervey's *Memoirs of the Reign of George the Second*, a work which resembles his in its handling of conversation and gesture, was written before he was born, but remained in manuscript till 1848 and he could not possibly have seen it. Furthermore, the

striking similarities between Boswell and Hervey are more than out-
weighed by one great pervasive difference: Hervey's mode is consistently
satiric, as one would expect from a contemporary of Pope and Swift,
whereas Boswell is never motivated by the satiric will to correct. Even
when he dislikes people, he evokes them in his journal as complex and
plausible, admirable specimens of human nature. A study of the court-
memoir tradition (a French genre originally) might indicate that Boswell
and Hervey had common models. I do not think it very likely. When all
possible influences have been assessed, there will still remain a high degree
of originality in Boswell's journal, but he probably did have models, and
they were probably printed plays and the novels of Richardson, Smollett,
Fielding, and Sterne. Boswell, for obvious reasons, liked Fielding better
than Richardson, and would have been incredulous if some one had told
him that as author he owed a greater debt to Richardson than to any one
else, but a recent reading of *Clarissa* has convinced me that the judgement
would be true. It was Richardson—in the mode of fiction, to be sure—
who first demonstrated the values of the scrupulous short-term dramatic
stance which furnishes the prime characteristic of Boswell's journalizing.
And not only does *Clarissa* outdo all other English novels in its uncom-
promising insistence on dramatic narration, but the greatest character in
that book overtly theorizes about the method. Lovelace's phrase "writing
to the *moment*" describes exactly what Boswell was up to. When the
parallel with *Clarissa* has been suggested, one wonders indeed whether
McQuhae and Johnston of the earliest journals are not vestigial correspondents, Belfords and Anna Howes.

With the journal of the Harvest Jaunt we emerge from the twilight of
speculation into the full sunlight of Boswellian self-revelation. Good-
humoured, vain, ebullient, restless, passing in a moment from highest
spirits to deepest gloom, he moves from tenant's cottage to laird's house to
peer's mansion, subjecting each person he meets to cool but unmalicious
scrutiny.[1] He rides along muddy tracks and across lonely moors, romps
with children, talks of bullocks with the laird of Camlarg and of Pope with
Lord Marchmont. He plays his German flute and sings duets from *The*

---

[1] The tour started at Auchinleck, traversed Ayrshire, Kirkcudbrightshire, and Dumfriesshire, with a side-excursion into Wigtownshire; dipped down into Cumberland
and Northumberland, and then turned north through Berwickshire to Edinburgh.
Boswell made extended visits at Kirroughtrie, Springkell, and Kames, with briefer
stops at Lagwine, Kenmure Castle, Galloway House, and Kelhead.

Beggar's Opera, carries around apples in his hat at a Punch and Judy show, and kisses a girl in a red cloak who says she is willing to go to London with him. He takes off Lord Dumfries and David Hume to loud applause ("I had not only [Hume's] external address, but his sentiments and mode of expression"). He engages in extravagant puerile jests with Erskine and, when they are unable to get separate beds in a crowded inn, lies in the same bed with him, giggling half the night. And dispirited moments there are in plenty too; they occur whenever the glancing, irrepressible current of his lively interest is checked by monotony in his surroundings. "I am convinced that I cannot live without changes, and I believe London charms me most on account of its infinite variety, which keeps the mind lively and gay. . . . I have a flow of imagination that must not be altogether restrained, and spirits that must be fed with amusement, otherwise they will prey upon myself." As soon as he is in a house, he wants to get out of it. He runs away from Kames long before the period set for his visit is up. ("My Lord . . . seemed displeased somewhat, and asked me if I was tired already. I told him not so much so as that I wanted to be elsewhere. In short, it was an embarrassing situation, and I did not speak to him cleverly.")

To some extent this strenuously superficial tone belies the facts. Not only can he not make an honest record of the passionate and probably stormy moments which he and Jean Heron snatched for themselves at Kirroughtrie, he must misstate matters so as to pull wool over the eyes of Johnston and McQuhae. Consequently he describes Jean coolly as one who "promises to make a good wife and a very complete woman," and demurely makes mention of a walk with her "and much agreeable elegant conversation." Finally, "Mrs. Heron and I had some serious conversation before I parted with her, not to meet again in all probability for a very long time." But the faking is not thorough; even if not forewarned, the reader will feel that there is some unexplained cause of tension. Lord Kames and Heron are oblivious to what is going on, but Lady Kames, though by no means suspecting the true state of affairs, has seen something she considers improper, and vents her uneasiness in sharp and frequent scolding. The accounts of his meetings with Mrs. Love (whom he sees frequently after his return to Edinburgh, her husband being in London) must have been bowdlerized too. He had dropped her, he says, his affection having cooled, but it is quite likely that he tried to wheedle her into compliance again and found her unyielding. At any rate, their con-

versation can hardly have been so open to the world as it is here represented.

If Boswell had been free to make a full and frank record of the two
months covered by the journal of the Harvest Jaunt, his writing would
have had greater depth, but it would still have been giddy and flippant.
The literary skill and the power of self-analysis displayed in it are rare, but
the character depicted is not so uncommon. The restlessness, the keenness
of sensuous impression, the appetite for physical pleasure, the animal vi-
tality and enthusiasm, the inexhaustible ability to apply to self-chosen
tasks and the paralysis of the will in the face of tasks set by others, the unshakable conviction of genius, the day-dreams accepted as prospects, the
lack of any sense of the passing of time—these are exactly the qualities that
one would specify for any able adolescent. If Boswell at twenty-two is ab-
normal, apart from his literary genius, it is in possessing a dangerously
small reserve of moral energy and in having passed the age at which the
adolescent character is entirely appropriate. The discrepancy between his
physical and his emotional age will become more apparent. He will acquire more knowledge and greater experience, he will attain to greater
intellectual maturity, but his temperament and the deep drives of his personality will remain incorrigibly those of a brilliant, egotistic, sensual boy.

He does not yet in the least understand where his greatest gift lies.
"[Lord Kames and I] talked upon books," he says, "and the inclination
which many people, especially when young, have to be authors; which, to
be sure, is an agreeable wish, and, if one succeeds, must be very pleasing.
It is making another self which can be present in many places and is not
subject to the inconstancies of passion, which the man himself is. I told
him that I should like much to be distinguished in that way: that I was
sure that I had genius, and was not deficient in easiness of expression, but
was at a loss for something to say, and, when I set myself seriously to think
of writing, that I wanted a subject." Kames advised him to try lively
periodical papers. Actually, bond unknown to him had been given, and he
had already found his subject. It was his journal, that unrecognized, name-
less work of art which an irresistible impulse was forcing him to create.

His other "production," Peggy Doig's child, was due to arrive at the
end of November. He did not propose to wait for the event, but he saw to
it that proper provisions were made for her lying-in and for putting the
baby out at nurse, and he left £10 for Peggy's use with Dr. Cairnie. It
had been agreed that the final arrangements for his departure should be

made as soon as his father came to town for the Winter Session. Lord Auchinleck arrived on 8 November, and Boswell waited on him. It must have been a deeply discouraging time for the worthy judge. His eldest son was showing himself flighty and irresponsible, and he had just received word that his second son, John, now a lieutenant in the Army, was disordered in his intellect and confined in a hospital at Plymouth. He declined to discuss details, but referred Boswell to Lady Auchinleck's uncle, Commissioner Cochrane, who told him that Lord Auchinleck would pay his debts and would increase his allowance to £200 a year. On Sunday 14 November he went to the English Chapel (he had pointedly absented himself from Presbyterian worship the week before, it being Sacrament Sunday), dined with Lord Somerville, sat with West Digges, and supped with Lord Kames. Next morning he had a long serious conversation with his father and mother. "They were very kind to me. I felt parental affection was very strong towards me, and I felt a very warm filial regard for them." He had not seen his mother at all between 14 September and 10 November, and he was never to see her again. "At ten I got into my chaise, and away I went. As I passed the Cross, the cadies and chairmen bowed and seemed to say, 'God prosper long our noble Boswell.'" But there were solemn leave-takings still to be performed. At the foot of the Canongate, just before turning left towards Portobello and the highway for England, he stopped the chaise, walked into Holyroodhouse, went round the piazzas, and bowed three times: to the Palace, to the stone-work crown over the gate, to the Chapel. In the court before the Palace he bowed three times to Arthur's Seat, "that lofty romantic mountain on which I have so often strayed in my days of youth, indulged meditation, and felt the raptures of a soul filled with ideas of the magnificence of God and his creation." The young man who is joyfully running away from Scotland is very much a Scot.

CHAPTER

VIII

The chaise attains the summit of Highgate and the great panorama of London opens out below. Boswell, all life and joy, repeats the soliloquy from Addison's *Cato* on the immortality of the soul, and composes extempore a song about an amorous encounter with a pretty girl. "I gave three huzzas, and we went briskly in."

The combination of modes is symbolic of the whole London journal of 1762–1763. "Mr. Addison's character in sentiment, mixed with a little of the gaiety of Sir Richard Steele and the manners of Mr. Digges, were the ideas which I aimed to realize." The Spectator strolls and Macheath prances: they alternate, they blend.

But Macheath's caperings must not be allowed to run into money. Boswell is determined to be independent, and that means that he must not exceed or anticipate his allowance by a penny. His very first act is to draw up a budget for the coming year, debating and fixing the proportions of his various expenditures. "A genteel lodging in a good part of the town is absolutely necessary." (Lodging £50.) "I would have a suit of clean linens every day." (Washing £7.) "I would have my hair dressed every day, or pretty often." (Hairdressing £6.) "I have just £43 left for coach-hire, diversion, and the tavern, which I shall find a very slight allowance." (Amusements receive no separate item in the budget—he must manage out of whatever is left over.)

Deprived of his father's oversight and incessant scrupulous admonition, he devises a substitute. Just before he goes to bed each night, or the first thing in the morning before he puts on his clothes, he writes out a memorandum telling himself what to eat, what to wear, what to read, what supplies to get in, where to walk, where to dine, what schemes of gallantry to pursue. The directions extend even to what he shall say, what

gestures he shall use, how he shall *feel*. "(4 December) Be comfortable
yet genteel.... (31 December) Then Louisa; be warm and press home,
and talk gently and Digges-like. Acquire an easy dignity and black liveliness of behaviour like him.... (6 March) Breakfast on fine muffins and
[enjoy] good taste of flour.... Pray remember, and mark it on separate
paper, how happy you now are in the full enjoyment of liberty. Summer
will come when all Scots will be gone. Then you'll grow more English and
fine.... (21 March) Then call Lady M. and propose fairly, and say
you'll do all in your power to make happy.... (6 April) Then home, read
Hume, and dress in frock-suit and five-shilling diced stockings and clean
shirt.... (30 April) Bring up fortnight's journal and letters, so as to be
clear on May Day. Now be sure to do this.... (30 May) Then Piazza
and Miss Temple, and behave nice and romantic and bold.... If you go
[to] Edinburgh, you're ruined." Above all, over and over, "Be *retenu*."[1]

"A genteel lodging in a good part of the town": that meant Westminster. Boswell took rooms with Mr. Terry, chamber-keeper to the Commissioners for Trade and Plantations, up two pairs of stairs in Downing
Street, just across the way from the house where so many of Britain's
prime ministers have resided. The rent was forty guineas a year, well
within the sum allowed by his budget, but he fretted about it, and the
landlord, rather than lose him ("as I was extremely agreeable to the
family") reduced it to £22, and later knocked off something more when
Boswell gave up one of his rooms to another tenant. Boswell relished intensely his independence, his comfortable bed, his neat dining-room, the
easy access to St. James's Park.

The wide-eyed *étourdissement* of 1760 has given way to a planned
and savoured Epicureanism. "There is something to me very agreeable
in having my time laid out in some method." Each day up about eight, a
brisk walk round the Park, breakfast alone in his own dining-room; then
perhaps a call on the Duke of Queensberry about his commission, or a
stroll to the City; dinner with his newly met relatives the Goulds in South
Audley Street, or with the Sheridans in Henrietta Street, Covent Garden,
or (not without misgivings) with the hamely Erskine clan, gathered for
the winter with Andrew's sister, Lady Betty Macfarlane, in Leicester
Square. If he has no invitation or feels not up to company, he dines with
the Terrys at a fixed rate of a shilling, or at a chop-house. On Saturdays
he goes regularly to the Spectator's coffee-house, Child's, in St. Paul's

[1] Reserved, discreet.

Church-yard, to listen to the talk of citizens and physicians. It is for him what a sketching-expedition is for a painter. He has no notebook before him, but he selects in his head, and enters his sketches later in his journal:

I CITIZEN. Pray, Doctor, what became of that patient of yours? Was not her skull fractured?
PHYSICIAN. Yes. To pieces. However, I got her cured.
I CITIZEN. Good Lord.

Occasionally a play; once a cock-fight; evening parties frequently at Lady Northumberland's; home by eleven and to bed. No suppers, no late hours, next to no drinking. And hours and hours spent happily at home, writing, mainly on the journal, which he is sending in weekly instalments to Johnston.

And the rule at times becomes really ascetic. At the end of December his funds run out because he has had to spend a good part of his quarter's allowance in getting up to London and has made a genteel loan to a lady —of which more later. For a week and more, when he has no invitations, he dines in his room on bread and cheese, glowing with the satisfaction of living within his means.

He has a secret which shores him up and fills him with pride. Shortly after he had settled in London, word had come from Johnston that Peggy Doig had been delivered of a son. "I feel myself dignified somehow.... God bless him." The boy is christened—Charles, after the Royal Martyr— by an Anglican clergyman, and turned over to a foster-mother. "By all means," writes Boswell, "let the nurse give my child the surname of Boswell immediately. I am not ashamed of him."

Continence is no part of his prudent and rational plan, merely economy and safety. He had gone to Mrs. Love as soon as she came up and had tried all his blandishments—in vain. About the middle of December he opened a campaign against another actress whom he had known slightly in Edinburgh, a Mrs. Lewis, to whom in his journal he assigns the name Louisa. She played minor roles at Covent Garden, was handsome and intelligent, and just twenty-four years old. The journal provides day-by-day bulletins on his siege and her eventual capitulation. 14 December, he called on her; 17 December, he respectfully declared his passion; 20 December, she accepted the loan of two guineas to meet a dun and allowed him to embrace her warmly; 22 December, he went with the prospect of consummating his bliss but was tense and incapable and she wanted more time to recollect herself; 26 December, she announced that they should wait a week, and if he were then of the same opinion, she would make him blessed; 1 January, he claimed the fulfilment of her promise and began to take gross liberties, she appointed the following afternoon, when her landlady would be at church; 2 January, he was again languid and unready and wasted so much of the hour that when at last he felt himself a man the landlady was on the stairs; 4 January, she agreed to spend the night with him at an inn the following Saturday; 7 January, she announced a postponement for physical reasons; 12 January (at last!) they met in the Piazzas of Covent Garden and drove in a hackney-coach to the Black Lion, Water Lane, Fleet Street, where he had engaged a room for Mr. and Mrs. Digges. They supped agreeably while the bells of St. Bride's rang their merry chimes nearby, he withdrew while the maid helped her undress, he took a candle and walked out to the yard. "The night was very dark and very cold. I experienced for some minutes the rigours of the season, and called into my mind many terrible ideas of hardships, that I might make a transition from such dreary thoughts to the most gay and delicious feelings. . . . I came softly into the room, and in a sweet delirium slipped into bed. . . . Good Heavens, what a loose did we give to amorous dalliance! . . . Five times was I fairly lost in supreme rapture." Next day: "So we parted. Thus was this conquest completed to my highest satisfaction. . . . I really conducted this affair with a manliness and prudence that pleased me very much. The whole expense was just eighteen shillings."

Louisa is infatuated, and he continues their intrigue, but as usual he is disgusted by possession and alarmed by the prospect of being tied down. The next night but one after the Black Lion he plans a more brilliant conquest. At Northumberland House a lady of quality whom he calls Lady Mirabel—a middle-aged widow with whom he is slightly acquainted—strikes the ball back smartly when he serves to her:

BOSWELL. . . . Pray, don't you think the meetings here of people of fashion very dull? There seems to be no communication between men and women. They seldom speak to each other.

LADY MIRABEL. True, but when they do speak, they speak to the purpose. . . .

BOSWELL. You must know, Madam, I run up and down this town just like a wild colt.

LADY MIRABEL. Why, Sir, then, don't you stray into my stable, amongst others?

But he had balanced his account of expenses in that affair of Louisa a little prematurely. One week lacking a day after the paradisial night at the Black Lion, he felt twinges of an ominous sort. Next day, no doubt of it: "Too, too plain was Signor Gonorrhoea." He taxed Louisa to her face with gross treachery; she, pale as ashes, admitted that she had once been in a bad way, but swore that for fifteen months she had been quite well and for six had had no connexion with any man but himself. She was probably telling him the complete truth as she knew it: she had no symptoms, but may unwittingly have been a carrier. May, because there seems a distinct possibility that Boswell himself had been harbouring a dormant infection since the unusually severe attack of the summer of 1760, and that the strenuous gallantry of which he was so proud had rendered it active again. But Boswell (who had the backing of Surgeon Douglas) was implacable and brutal. He dispatched her a letter demanding the return of his two guineas. "I neither *paid* it for prostitution nor *gave* it in charity. . . . I want no letters. Send the money sealed up. I have nothing more to say to you." A sealed packet was delivered by Louisa's maid, precisely as stipulated; inside, two guineas, not a single word written. End of the connexion with the fair Louisa which had been so flattering to his ego and from which he had expected "at least a winter's safe copulation." Five weeks of enforced seclusion, the ministrations of Douglas, five guineas to pay. He began sealing his letters to Johnston with black wax.

As a matter of fact, enforced seclusion was not all mournful. Boswell has admitted that he liked system: he also was deeply relieved to be freed temporarily from the obligation to bustle and rattle and intrigue. There is no portion of the London journal that on the whole shows deeper contentment than this.

I move like very clock-work. At eight in the morning Molly lights the fire, sweeps and dresses my dining-room. Then she calls me up and lets me know what o'clock it is. I lie some time in bed indulging indolence, which in that way, when the mind is easy and cheerful, is most pleasing. I then slip on my clothes loosely, easily, and quickly, and come into my dining-room. I pull my bell. The maid lays a milk-white napkin upon the table and sets the things for breakfast. I then take some light amusing book and breakfast and read for an hour or more, gently pleasing both my palate and my mental taste. Breakfast over, I feel myself gay and lively. I go to the window and am entertained with the people passing by, all intent on different schemes. . . . My day is in general diversified with reading of different kinds, playing on the violin, writing, chatting with my friends. Even the taking of medicines serves to make time go on with less heaviness.

He can feel the effect of calmness and system in his writing:

Upon my word, my journal goes charmingly on at present. . . . How easily and cleverly do I write just now! I am really pleased with myself; words come skipping to me like lambs upon Moffat Hill; and I turn my periods smoothly and imperceptibly, like a skilful wheelwright turning tops in a turning-loom. There's fancy! There's simile! In short, I am at present a genius.

A genius undoubtedly. Few stretches of his journal show so many good consecutive pages as that which covers the period from his arrival in London in the middle of November 1762 to his emergence from confinement at the end of the following February. The reason is not far to seek: he had time enough so that he could make journal-writing his main activity, or at least could concern himself as much with recording the events of his life as with experiencing them. It is our misfortune that Boswell could so seldom act out his conviction that he should have no more corn growing than he could get into the barn. Generally speaking, the journal was relegated to such moments as he could snatch from business, spare from pleasure, or redeem from despondency. But during the London jaunt of 1762–1763 he had no business beyond the occasional solicitation of the Duke of Queensberry and Lady Northumberland, and up to the end of February he was not dissipated—did not waste his energies aimlessly—and was not much troubled with low spirits. It was a season of sober regularity, and the journal benefited.

Of course he wrote other things besides the journal; things that looked to immediate publication. Mrs. Sheridan, his Mentor's wife, a homely, sensible, clever Irishwoman who had won general acclaim two years before with a novel, *Memoirs of Miss Sidney Bidulph,* had just completed a new comedy, *The Discovery,* and transported him by asking him to write a prologue for its forthcoming performance. She seemed at first satisfied with the lines he hammered out. But after he had regaled his mind with

images of Garrick declaiming his verses from the stage of Drury Lane and
had peacocked before the Erskines and the Dempsters, Sheridan rejected
his offering roughly, going so far as to call it very bad, and resorting to
acrimony and ridicule when asked to specify. Boswell managed to behave
with seeming good humour to Sheridan's face, but he was deeply hurt and
never forgave him. After the middle of January 1763, he seldom mentions
his erstwhile Socrates without some expression of dislike. Garrick, meanwhile, was being very kind to him, and he transferred to Garrick the
affection and respect which he had hitherto felt for Sheridan. It was a
great pity, for Sheridan, though wrongheaded and positive, was a kind-
hearted man, and he and his wife were unaffectedly hospitable.

Erskine, as we have seen, was in town, waiting for his regiment to be
"broke," and Dempster was there as a Member of Parliament. On 19
January (an extremely cold day, besides being that on which Boswell
learned for certain that he was ill) the three tramped by prearrangement
from one end of London to the other, dined at Dolly's Chop-house, and
then went to the opening of David Mallet's tragedy *Elvira* with intention
of procuring its damnation if they could. Mallet was deservedly unpopular on various grounds, but his chief offences in the eyes of our young
gentlemen were that he had changed his distinctively Scots name of
Malloch, that he had trained himself to speak English without an accent,
and that he styled himself Esquire. (He was the son of a crofter—a member of the proscribed clan of Macgregor, at that—and in his youth had
been janitor of the High School in Edinburgh.) Having planted themselves in the middle of the pit, armed with oaken cudgels, cat-calls, and
borrowed names, they strove to sway the audience, but were borne down
by the concerted applause of the author and thirty friends seated nearby.
(Among the *claque,* still unknown to Boswell, was that young Edward
Gibbon, whose life in one aspect had so strangely resembled Boswell's
own.) Having hissed valiantly but in vain, they withdrew for supper at
Lady Betty Macfarlane's and there found themselves so fertile in sallies of
wit against *Elvira* and its author that they decided to preserve them for
the world. Erskine made a draft, they revised it in joint sessions, and it
was brought out as a sixpenny pamphlet on 27 January by Flexney, publisher of the spectacular satirist, Charles Churchill, then at the summit of
his fame. The title was *Critical Strictures on the New Tragedy of "Elvira,"
written by Mr. David Malloch.* The general tone and style of the piece,
as one would expect, are Erskine's, the following being a fair sample:

In the fifth act we were melted with the sight of two young children, which the King embraced, which the Prince embraced, which Elvira embraced. . . . We would suggest to Mr. Malloch the useful hint of introducing in some of his future productions the whole Foundling Hospital, which, with a well-painted scene of the edifice itself, would certainly call forth the warmest tears of pity and the bitterest emotions of distress; especially when we consider that many of the parents of these unfortunate babes would probably be spectators of this interesting scene.

Boswell (who went into retirement between the writing of *Critical Strictures* and its publication) confessed himself much pleased with the performance and instructed himself to relish the review in the *Critical.* It consisted of a single sentence: "We shall bestow no farther notice on these strictures than to say they appear to be the crude efforts of envy, petulance, and self-conceit." This provided an epithet for each author, and Boswell says that the three of them had a humorous dispute as to how they should be assigned.

Strict confinement for five weeks gave him time and to spare for literary pursuits. He had planned to do some systematic reading while he was in London, but would probably never have got to it if it had not been for his illness. (Dr. John Pringle, his father's staunch friend and his own sensible if somewhat acid counsellor, summarized the situation for him in a wry jest: "He that runs may read.") He now set himself to the six volumes of Hume's *History of England* (recently completed), making notes on each volume to send to his father. He began a comedy and he wrote some essays. One of the essays has survived, the other pieces appear to have been lost. But he did bring to publication a work of more ambitious scope than anything he had yet attempted.

Nothing he had written now seemed to him better worth the attention of the public than the strenuously facetious letters which he had been writing to Erskine since the summer of 1761. He proposed to Erskine that they should give the correspondence some polishing and print it—with their names. Erskine was horrified. Flexney (who had not found *Critical Strictures* very profitable) was lukewarm or less. But Boswell bore all before him, and by the time he was free to range again the copy had gone to the printer and he was expecting proofs. *Letters between the Honourable Andrew Erskine and James Boswell, Esq.*, a pretty little book of 156 pages, was published on 12 April 1763, price three shillings. It was the first of Boswell's publications (six pamphlets to date, besides the poems in

Donaldson's miscellany) to bear his name; it was also the first considerable expression of his wish, later recorded in his journal, that nothing that concerned himself should be secret. Many of the letters are dated from the specific seats of Kellie, New Tarbet, and Auchinleck; they all bear the full signatures of James Boswell and Andrew Erskine; and though both authors have too much of a tendency to turn letters into ranting essays, both manage to divulge a good deal of their own private concerns. One letter of Boswell's contains an affectionate characterization of himself. Worse than that, the impudent allusions to other people which had been a principal feature of the original letters had not been removed in revision, nor had the names been effectively disguised. Persons known to the English public, such as Lord Kames, Adam Smith, John Home, Thomas Sheridan, Samuel Derrick, and David Hume, appear with their full names. Others are reduced to initials, but to readers in Edinburgh there would have been little mystery in Lady B____, D____r, Mr. M____, etc.

Indeed, the most outrageous of all the allusions are those to "Mr. M____," Erskine's elderly brother-in-law, the laird of Macfarlane, in whose London house Erskine was staying while the letters were being revised. The "Mr." itself was intended to annoy: Macfarlane as head of the clan—*the* Macfarlane—was properly addressed and referred to without mistering, and he was known to be stiff in matters of punctilio. Readers of the *Letters* were informed that his seat of New Tarbet could not conveniently lodge above a dozen people, and that one could get to the entrance only by skipping through a dirty puddle. All the old wheezes about Highlanders were repeated. "Lady B____," Erskine writes, "entreats that you would come here and spend the Christmas holidays. . . . We are all, thank God, in general pretty clear of the itch just now, and most of us not near so lousy as we used to be, so I think you may venture." "Miss C____" was mentioned more than once, and Boswell rejoiced that "people" had failed in their scheme to get him married. Donaldson could read that his children stood in need of correction, Sheridan that he *sometimes* spoke sense, John Home that he had written *one* good play, Lord Kames that his style was obscure. In short, the book was a fair portent of the indiscretions of the *Journal of a Tour to the Hebrides* and *The Life of Johnson*.

The dismay with which the work was greeted by the authors' acquaintances in London is reflected in a "History of Erskine and Boswell's

Letters" which Boswell wrote in the days following the publication. Eglinton the rake and Hugh Blair the professor and divine were equally shocked, and had their contrasted modes of speech recorded with equal nicety.

It is clear that Boswell did not learn to record conversation by practicing on Johnson, for he had not yet met Johnson.

EGLINTON. "Upon my soul, Jamie, I would not take the direction of you upon any account, for as much as I like you, except you would agree to give over that damned publishing. . . . By G____, I heard it asserted today in a public assembly that you had done it for money. Your father would give you none, and Erskine's regiment was going to be broke. I wonder really at Erskine, for he seems to be a douce,[1] sagacious fellow." BOSWELL. "Poor fellow! My Lord, I've led him into the scrape. I've persuaded him." EGLINTON. "He cannot be very sensible if you have persuaded him. You must get it suppressed, or put in an advertisement in the papers denying it. By the Lord, it's a thing Dean Swift could not do— to publish a collection of letters upon nothing. Nor Madam Sévigné either." BOSWELL. "My Lord, hers are very fine." EGLINTON. "Yes, a few at the beginning; but when you read on, you think her a d____ned tiresome bitch." . . .

BLAIR. . . . "I'm really vexed at the publication." BOSWELL. "O Doctor, I'm sure they are innocent." BLAIR. "They are not only innocent, Sir, but very lively. But the world will not take them as you give them. You know the letters of remarkable men, such as Pope to Swift, Cicero to Brutus, are much sought after. We there see men who have made a great noise in the world, as it were in their night-gowns. But what are you to the world? It is true, you may say, 'Here are we, the Hon. Andrew Erskine and James Boswell, Esq., who will publish our letters, which shall have as much wit, perhaps, as any, and then let your great people publish theirs.' But it does not carry that look. It appears to those who do not know you as if you were two vain, forward young men that would be pert and disagreeable and whom one would wish to keep out of the way of. Now God knows you have nothing of that. It is a mere *lusus*."[2]

Lord Auchinleck, unhappy man, opened his newspaper at Jedburgh, on the circuit, and found before him a review of the *Letters*, quoting one of Boswell's as a specimen. He was deeply mortified. "Though it might pass between two intimate young lads in the same way that people over a bottle will be vastly entertained with one another's rant, it was extremely

[1] Sober.   [2] Freak.

odd to send such a piece to the press to be perused by all and sundry." At Dumfries, the next town on the circuit, he heard of Boswell's taking off Lord Dumfries and others the previous autumn, and concluded that Boswell was deliberately trying to shame him. "The offices I hold entitle me to some respect, and I get it beyond my merit from all that know me except from you, who by the laws of God, nature, gratitude, and interest are bound to do what you can to make me happy, in place of striving, as it were, to find out the things will be most galling to me and making these your pursuit."

The book received prominent mention in the reviews. The *Critical Review* was supercilious and condescending, but the *Monthly* (Ralph Griffiths, the editor-in-chief, wrote the review himself) struck exactly the note Boswell and Erskine would have desiderated: "This honourable and ingenious duumvirate appear to be officers in the Army; young men, fresh from North Britain, full of blood, full of spirits, and full of *fun*. *Vive la bagatelle* is their maxim." *The Public Advertiser* ran a kind notice. But the most interesting of all the reviews (perhaps the one that Lord Auchinleck saw?) appeared in *The London Chronicle*. After a really discerning analysis, it ends with a prediction which has been brilliantly fulfilled so far as one of the authors is concerned: "Upon the whole, we would recommend this collection as a book of true genius, from the authors of which we may expect many future agreeable productions." Boswell wrote that review himself.

By the time the *Letters* appeared, Boswell had waked, reluctantly but completely, from his day-dream. The hope which political inexperience had allowed him to draw from the Duke's letter survived several meetings with the Duke himself. Queensberry, polite, kind-hearted, indecisive, repeated the roll of difficulties but said he would keep on trying: he would apply to the Commander-in-Chief (who was Colonel of the First Foot Guards), he would speak to the Secretary at War. He went to the country and sent a firm letter saying that the affair could not be managed; back in London he allowed Boswell to push him into saying that he would try again. By that time Boswell had little hopes of him. He concluded, and was to believe to the end of his days, that the Duke was in secret league with his father to keep him from getting what he wanted. Surely he was unjust. If Lord Auchinleck had consistently opposed the Guards scheme in every way, he might very well have asked Queensberry not to further it, but he would surely not have done so after promising to use his interest.

There were plenty of other people who could have told Queensberry that Auchinleck did not really want the ensigncy he had solicited. But Boswell was enraged and violent. His first impulse on getting Queensberry's firm letter was to punish his father by enlisting as a private in the Horse or Foot Guards, or by going off to India in the ranks. His next was to keep his head, be patient, and continue his campaign under the patronage of Lady Northumberland. But though she fed him with encouragement, as the Duke had not, she seemed never to take any actual measures, and when he got out of confinement and resumed his calls, he ran into unmistakable evidence that she was avoiding him.

It was the discarded patron Eglinton who finally did exert himself in Boswell's behalf. Since the previous spring, Boswell had been convinced that Eglinton had neglected him and consequently he had determined to meet him only in a social way. But Eglinton was kind to him during his confinement, a long, frank conversation ensued, and they were reconciled. Eglinton offered to intercede with Lord Bute, the Prime Minister, and did so. He gave Bute a copy of Boswell's unpublished *Ode to Ambition*, presented a brief letter from Boswell which he himself had drafted, and told Boswell's story in the most favourable style he could muster. Bute gave the answer which Eglinton must have expected: it was impossible to get anybody a commission in the Guards through influence alone; such commissions could be had only through money *and* influence. But if Boswell wanted a commission in an ordinary marching regiment, that could be managed. Boswell would not hear of the proposal unless it meant that his regiment would soon be disbanded and its officers discharged from duty on half pay.

EGLINTON. "If you get your commission in a young regiment, you will be broke of course. If in an old, you will get numbers who will be willing to exchange a half-pay commission for yours and give you some money into the bargain." BOSWELL. "Well, my Lord, remember you must settle the affair for me, for London leave will I not."

Within less than a week Bute sent Eglinton a note saying that he had mentioned to the King Mr. Boswell's case, and that His Majesty would not fail to order that Boswell should have "a pair colours." Boswell wrote vengefully to John Johnston that his father had little thought of his "stealing this half-pay march," but though he did not act promptly and decisively, he finally declined Bute's offer. I do not think it at all certain that he would really have accepted a commission in the Guards, either. The dream had been terribly real to him, but he was bound to wake from it sooner or later. During his confinement, when he had had plenty of time to think things over, he had drawn up a statement of the advantages of his father's plan which had convinced him for a day and had left him shaken afterwards. What he probably wanted deep down in his mind was to prove his independence by getting assurance of the commission and then to put his father under obligation by declining it. At any rate, the half-pay scheme for staying in London was an intolerably shabby substitute for the glowing dream. His hopes had one last flare-up. Lord Northumberland was being sent to Ireland as Lord Lieutenant. Perhaps Boswell could accompany him as aide-de-camp, get promotion in Ireland, and thence step into the Guards? Lady Northumberland was polite but evasive: Eglinton characterized the note she sent as just "three blue beans in a blue bladder." After that (22 April 1763) Boswell's stubborn will to stay on in London yielded more and more to a wish to be on good terms with his father.

For Lord Auchinleck had stopped answering his letters. His dissatisfaction with Boswell's avowed lack of interest in Scotland and determination (as Lord Auchinleck would have put it) to hang on idly in London had been converted into cold rage by Boswell's assertion of a right to independence. The controversy started with Boswell's private papers: letters and perhaps some journal notes. Boswell had intended to leave them with John Johnston, but when Johnston had failed to appear in Edinburgh to see him off, he had sealed them in four parcels and left them with his mother for Johnston to pick up. Johnston, following Boswell's instructions, had called at Lord Auchinleck's house and obtained delivery of the papers from David Boswell. He found that some one had broken the seals, but did not tell Boswell this immediately. When Lord Auchinleck learned that the papers had escaped from family custody, he was very angry, apparently gave David a dressing down, and took Boswell severely to task. He could not very well admit that he knew the parcels to be full of dangerous stuff, but he had somehow by legitimate means learned that Boswell was keeping a journal, and he progressed from general strictures on the rashness of trusting one's boon companions with one's secrets to specific complaints of Boswell's keeping a detailed record of his follies and showing it to McQuhae and Johnston as though he were proud of it. Boswell for his part progressed from remonstrances which Johnston thought

submissive to others which Lord Auchinleck considered defiant and contemptuous. There was actually more bitterness in the controversy than got
stated in the letters, for Boswell did not tax his father with the broken
seals, though Johnston finally told him about them, and Lord Auchinleck
did not say "I told you so" when the minister of Ochiltree, in whose house
McQuhae was staying, repeated to him various highly indiscreet passages
from the journal of the harvest jaunt. Lord Auchinleck wrote no more and
began to talk openly and violently of selling the estate. Dr. Boswell and
McQuhae warned Boswell, Lady Auchinleck sent one of her rare letters,
urging conciliation and assuring Boswell that his father was deeply in
earnest. Boswell dragged on defiant, obstinate, deeply unhappy. "My
father's displeasure hangs over me; the airy forms of gaiety and pleasure
that glittered before my fancy are vanished or hid in clouds of discontent,
and wherever I turn my thoughts I can find no certain joy." About the
middle of May he wrote his father "a most warm letter"—"warm"
probably meaning earnest rather than disputatious—saying that if his
father could have no peace of mind unless Boswell returned to Scotland,
Boswell would make the sacrifice; that nevertheless he begged to be allowed to choose his own way of life for some years, in order that he might
settle more effectually. He asked Dr. Pringle and Sir David Dalrymple to
intercede for him. "It is not from the fear of being disinherited (which
he threatens) that I am anxious. I am thoughtless enough not to mind
that. But my affection for him makes me very unhappy at the thoughts
of offending him." On 30 May 1763 Lord Auchinleck broke his three-
months' silence, apparently without prompting from any one but Lady
Auchinleck. He admitted that he had been pondering extreme measures:

Indeed, finding that I could be of no use to you, I had determined
to abandon you, to free myself as much as possible from sharing your
ignominy, and to take the strongest and most public steps for declaring
to the world that I was come to this resolution. . . . Be assured of this; for
even I, who am your father and who, while you trod the paths of virtue
and discretion was bound up in you and carried on all my projects with
a view to you, in whom I flattered myself to find a representative worthy
of this respectable family—I say even I by your strange conduct had
come to the resolution of selling all off, from the principle that it is
better to snuff a candle out than leave it to stink in a socket.

The law, he said, was still his choice for Boswell: if Boswell followed
that way of life, he might be respected and useful, might get into Parlia-

ment, might confer places instead of begging them. But if he was bent on getting into the Army and had the offer of an ensigncy in a marching regiment, "though I am far from liking the thing, if better cannot be, take it, and hold by that as your business for life. But be more on your guard for the future against mimicry, journals, and publications."

Boswell received this Spartan pronouncement meekly and even gratefully; called it "a very kind letter," and put himself in his father's hands. His only stipulation was that he be allowed a foreign tour before he settled down. It was agreed that he should study Civil Law for a winter at a Dutch university, and should then be allowed to visit Paris and some of the German courts. The year in Holland was normal procedure. Scots law, which is quite different from the English, makes much of Roman law, and the Dutch civilians were the great masters of the subject. Lord Auchinleck and Old James Boswell had attended the University of Leyden; Utrecht was selected for Boswell on the advice of Sir David Dalrymple, who had studied there and thought it might suit Boswell better as having a gayer social life.

While Boswell's private drama of indecision and gloom was being played out (23 April to 16 May 1763), the most stirring public events of the year were being enacted in London. John Wilkes, the squinting, witty, profligate M.P. and demagogue who was shrewdly advancing his own political game by playing on the unpopularity of the Scots and the governments of Bute and Grenville, had been conducting since June of the previous year a daringly abusive periodical called *The North Briton*. In the number for 23 April he had characterized certain references to the Peace in the recent speech from the throne (19 April) as "the most abandoned instance of ministerial effrontery ever attempted to be imposed upon mankind" and had insinuated that the King, in consenting to read the speech, had countenanced a deliberate lie. The Government, with the hearty approval of the King, ignored the convention that the responsibility for a speech from the throne rests with the ministers, and ordered the prosecution of the writer of the paper. Since it was ostensibly anonymous, proceedings in the ordinary course were impossible. The two secretaries of state accordingly issued a general warrant (that is, a warrant naming no particular person) for the apprehension of the authors, and on this warrant Wilkes was taken into custody (30 April). The legality of a general warrant would in any case have been questionable, and the use of such a warrant for the arrest of a Member of Parliament made the matter doubly grave. A writ of *habeas corpus* was applied for, but as there was some delay in issuing it, the secretaries committed Wilkes to the Tower and held him there incommunicado. His house was ransacked and his personal papers seized, and at the King's express orders his commission in the militia was cancelled. On the morning of 3 May he was taken from the Tower and brought before the bar of the Court of Common Pleas. The hearings not being completed on that day, he was offered his liberty on bail, and on his refusing to provide it, was sent back to the Tower.

That morning of 3 May Boswell walked up to the Tower to see Wilkes brought out, but arrived too late. Having determined to see prisoners of some sort, he made a detour to Newgate on his way back to Westminster. In the court of the prison were a number of "strange blackguard beings with sad countenances," acquaintances and friends of two oddly assorted criminals who were to be executed the next morning. As he stood there in the court the condemned pair passed near him on the way to chapel. Hannah Diego, "a big unconcerned being" convicted of theft, was a common enough type, but in Paul Lewis, a young highwayman, Boswell with shock and horror saw an image of his heart's ideal, overpowered, shackled, about to be deprived of breath:

Paul, who had been in the sea-service and was called Captain, was a genteel, spirited young fellow. He was just a Macheath. He was dressed in a white coat and blue silk vest and silver, with his hair neatly queued and a silver-laced hat, smartly cocked. An acquaintance asked him how he was. He said, "Very well"; quite resigned. Poor fellow! I really took a great concern for him, and wished to relieve him. He walked firmly and with a good air, with his chains rattling upon him, to the chapel.

All that afternoon Newgate lay on Boswell like a black cloud, Lewis always coming across him. At night he got his barber to try to read him to sleep with Hume's *History;* the barber made clumsy work of it and he lay in sad concern. Next day, though he knew he would suffer for it, his compulsion drove him in "a sort of horrid eagerness" to Tyburn to witness Paul's behaviour in the last extremity. "I got upon a scaffold very near the fatal tree, so that [I] could clearly see all the dismal scene. There was a most prodigious crowd of spectators. I was most terribly shocked and thrown into a very deep melancholy." For three nights he was subject to such gloomy terrors that he dared not sleep by himself and had to beg a bed of Dempster or half of one from Erskine.

This is the first execution reported in his journal, and if it was not the first he had ever witnessed, was certainly a kind of indulgence he had very seldom allowed himself. On most occasions his fear of the horrors he knew he would suffer if he went, automatically overruled his horrid eagerness to go. It was certainly the first execution he had seen at Tyburn, though hardly the first he could have seen there. On 15 June five convicts (one of them a boy of fifteen) suffered, but he was not present.

On 6 May Wilkes was again taken before the Court, and was discharged on the ground of his privilege as a Member of Parliament. A huge mob which had gathered outside the Court to applaud followed him to his house in Great George Street. Boswell saw him bowing from a window.

MONDAY [16 MAY]. Send breeches [to] mend by barber's boy. You are now on good plan. Breakfast neat today: toast, rolls, and butter, easily and not too laughable. Then L[ove]'s and get money, or first finish journal. Keep plan in mind and be in earnest. Keep in this fine frame, and be directed by Temple. At night see Pringle. Go to Piazza and take some negus e'er you go; or go cool and take letter and bid him settle all, but not too fast.[1]

This memorandum is remarkable for what it does *not* contain. When Boswell wrote it, he could not know that this was to be the most memorable day of his life. He was at last to meet Samuel Johnson.

On the whole, he had not been particularly active in extending the circle of his literary acquaintance during this visit to London, his main concern being to make or strengthen connexions with the great people who might help him to a commission. But he did very much want to meet Johnson, and he had done what he could to bring a meeting about. He had for years been reading Johnson with delight, and had formed in his mind a venerated image of him living in London in "a state of solemn elevated abstraction." This showed independence, for his critical Mentors, Kames, Adam Smith, and Hugh Blair, all disparaged Johnson's writing as heavy and pedantic. Gentleman had told him what Johnson looked like,

[1] Boswell is to breakfast in his rooms with Temple and his brother, and their parties tended to get noisy. The letter he was taking to show Pringle was that in which he sued for terms of surrender from his father. Pringle was to be empowered to negotiate, but was so to arrange matters that Boswell could stay on some time more in London. The Piazza was a coffee-house in Covent Garden.

Derrick in 1760 had promised to introduce him, but to Boswell's keen disappointment had never seemed to be able to manage it. One of the things that attached him to Sheridan in 1761 was their common admiration for Johnson and Sheridan's friendship with him. Sheridan boasted of talking with Johnson till two or three in the morning and assured Boswell that when he came to London he should have many opportunities of meeting him at his home. But when Boswell did get to London, he found that Sheridan and Johnson were no longer speaking. Johnson, on hearing that Sheridan had been granted a pension by the Crown, had exclaimed, "What! have they given *him* a pension? Then it is time for me to give up mine"—an indefensible outburst of spleen, for Johnson owed his own pension in some degree to Sheridan's intercession. Ossian Macpherson had maliciously reported Johnson's remark, without telling Sheridan (what would perhaps not have mended matters) that Johnson, after a pause, had added, "However, I am glad that Mr. Sheridan has a pension, for he is a very good man." Johnson later made overtures for reconciliation, but Sheridan stiffly refused ever to meet him again. Boswell then tried Tom Davies, who said that nothing was simpler: if Boswell would dine with Davies on Christmas Day, he would meet Johnson and some other interesting men of letters. But on Christmas Day Johnson failed to put in an appearance, and Boswell had to solace himself with Robert Dodsley and Oliver Goldsmith. It was through Davies that he finally did meet Johnson nearly five months later, but the meeting happened by chance.

Johnson was at this time in his fifty-fourth year, a huge, slovenly, near-sighted scholar, his face scarred by scrofula, his body distorted by compulsive tics, his speech interspersed with absent-minded clucks and mutterings. He had married at twenty-six a florid widow twenty years older than himself, and for eleven years now had been a widower, mourning in solitude his beloved Tetty. A man of vast learning, most of it gained outside the schools, he had failed as a school-teacher and had finally fought his way to eminence and the independence of a modest pension by the unlikely profession of bookseller's hack. He had published two fine gloomy poems and a tragedy which he now admitted he had thought better of than it deserved. He had compiled the best English dictionary, a work which underlies much subsequent lexicography. In his best-known literary works—two series of essays, *The Rambler* and *The Idler,* and a short Oriental novel, *Rasselas*—he had forsaken the agreeable chit-chat and graceful didacticism of Addison and Steele for forthright lay sermons, mournful, eloquent, ironically humorous, cast in that ponderous but precise style which no one else has ever attempted without making it ridiculous, and which even in Johnson too often raises the image of the unwieldy elephant wreathing his lithe proboscis. *Rasselas* expounded his favourite text, sincerely held, that human life is everywhere a state in which much is to be endured and little to be enjoyed. Though he was given to occasional huge hilarity, his temperament was gloomy to the point of despair. He had had to struggle all his life with low-grade chronic disease which made his days uncomfortable and his nights a horror; and he laboured under a constant and apparently justified fear of insanity. Though naturally sceptical, he had won his way to firm Christian faith but not to serenity of mind. He lived under a constant unutterable horror of death, and was tortured by remorse of conscience which the known frailties of his life seem insufficient to explain. A profound moralist and a heroically good man, he was slothful, dilatory, splenetic, and greedy. The days when he had gone hungry and had walked the streets at night because he lacked the price of a meal and a bed were now far behind him, but he retained an effective sense of pity for the needy and the unfortunate, and a lively and unfastidious interest in all the varieties of human nature. But he was a very formidable man. He had had to fight to make his way, and he remained a gladiator. Talk had become his real profession, and when he talked for victory, he subscribed to no rules whatever. He could turn at the drop of a hat from utterances of serene wisdom to the most outrageous sophistry or the most brutal use of *argumentum ad hominem.*

On Monday 16 May 1763, as Boswell, after drinking tea, was sitting in the parlour behind Davies's bookshop, Johnson came unexpectedly into the shop and advanced on the parlour. Davies, watching the shop through the glass door, struck a stage posture and announced his coming in such a tone as he would have used if he had been playing Horatio in *Hamlet* and was announcing the Ghost. Boswell, caught unprepared and deeply agitated, had only time to observe that the object of his veneration was much more dreadful than he had expected ("a very big man . . . troubled with sore eyes, the palsy, and the king's evil . . . very slovenly in his dress . . . most uncouth voice") before Johnson was upon him and Davies was pronouncing his name: "Mr. Boswell." He decided on a gambit that involved Johnson's notorious prejudice against the Scots:

"Don't tell him where I come from." "From Scotland," cried Davies mischievously. "Mr. Johnson," said Boswell, "I do indeed come from Scotland, but I cannot help it." It was a very bad opening. Like all robust and fearless men, Johnson was irritated by the appearance of timidity or disloyalty in others. It was true that he had a prejudice against the Scots, but he never visited it on individual Scotsmen unless they adopted a defensive attitude. He looked at Boswell coldly and said, "That, Sir, I find, is what a very great many of your countrymen cannot help." Boswell, of course, had meant that he could not help his nationality; Johnson implied that he had fled from starvation or imprisonment. Having swept from the board far more pieces than the poor little pawn which Boswell had offered, Johnson turned to Davies and complained that Garrick had refused him an order for the play. Boswell, eager to get into the conversation and retrieve himself, burst out with, "O Sir, I cannot think Mr. Garrick would grudge such a trifle to you." "Sir," replied Johnson with a stern look, "I have known David Garrick longer than you have done, and I know no right you have to talk to me on the subject."

Boswell had probably never been treated so in his entire life by a stranger. In Scotland people always knew his family, or at least were aware of his father's standing, and were therefore constrained to treat him politely until he gave them reason to do otherwise. Among the Scots in London he enjoyed the same privilege. No part of the popular apprehension of Boswell's character is more mistaken than that which makes him out a social climber. He came from an excellent family, and he was always careful in the matter of introductions. If he dispensed with formal letters, he still tried to arrange matters so that his rank in society would be explicitly stated. Davies had been of no help to him at all. Davies's recommendation was in any case of dubious weight: he had been an actor, and Johnson followed the conventions of his time in thinking that no man who was or had been on the stage could be quite a gentleman. For all Johnson knew, this young Scot was some fledgling hack who had run away from his debts in Scotland, and he was certainly not going to allow a raw Grub-street recruit to bandy words with him about David Garrick.

Boswell was stunned and hurt and not a little angry. ("His dogmatical roughness of manners is disagreeable," he wrote in his journal.) But he realized that he had been *gauche,* and he had great capacity for making allowances. Johnson's acquaintance meant so much to him that he was

not going to give up the struggle without throwing in his reserves: so he
took the affront with apparent good humour and sat quietly studying the
field. Johnson soon made a complaisant appeal to him, as he always did
when he had been rough to people and they did not fight back; Boswell
gratefully moved in. Within a few minutes he was leading the conversation. Davies told him when Johnson left that he was sure Johnson liked
him. The great friendship had begun.

Its strength was tested immediately. Eight days later Boswell went to
call for the first time on Bonnell Thornton, a young literary man whom
he had admired from afar and had discovered to be the author of *The
Public Advertiser*'s generous review of *Letters between the Hon. Andrew
Erskine and James Boswell, Esq.* While he was there, Wilkes, Charles
Churchill, and Robert Lloyd dropped in, and he found himself unexpectedly in the presence of all the "London wits" save one—George
Colman, whom he had met a few days earlier at Garrick's. Thornton,
Colman, Lloyd, Churchill, and Wilkes made a group which a literary neophyte with a strong appetite for contemporary fame might well have regarded as the most exciting to be found in Britain, and Boswell must have
been highly gratified to find himself in their company. Thornton, Colman,
and Lloyd (all Old Westminsters) belonged to a Nonsense Club which
may have been the pattern for his own Soaping Club; he and Erskine had
certainly patterned their literary partnership on that of Thornton and
Colman (*The Connoisseur, The St. James's Chronicle*) and on that of
Colman and Lloyd (*Odes to Obscurity and Oblivion*). Wilkes's tie with
the rest of the group was Churchill, another Old Westminster. Churchill,
a burly clergyman turned rake, besides being Wilkes's assistant in *The
North Briton,* was also the most discussed poet of the day, having brought
out a series of poems that entitle him still to be regarded as the most
powerful verse-satirist between Pope and Burns. Both Wilkes and
Churchill, from political motives, had subjected Scotland and individual
Scots to the most savage kind of abuse. Boswell, who certainly resented
most of the anti-Scots prejudice he was encountering in London, appears
not to have been nettled by the anti-Scottishness of *The North Briton*:
he relished its poignant acrimony (his phrase), and for weeks had been
devouring each number as it appeared. The notorious Wilkes, when one
met him face to face, was the most pleasant of companions. He liked Boswell from the start, encouraged him to make more of the acquaintance,
and offered to correspond with him. But Boswell made a memorandum to

"go on with Geniuses moderately." His efforts to cultivate Thornton, Colman, Lloyd, and Churchill were not vigorous. He got on easy enough terms with Wilkes to ask him for some franks "to astonish a few staunch North Britons," but their real intimacy was to come later. It would be an exaggeration to say that his meeting with Johnson had converted him instantly to discipleship, for in the month following that meeting he called on Johnson only twice. But it is pretty clear that the "Geniuses" seemed less enchanting to him than they would have if he had met them before he met Johnson.

At any rate, he excused himself from the wits and went directly to call on Johnson in his chambers in the Temple; was courteously received and asked to stay longer. On his third call, Johnson cried out with warmth, "Give me your hand. I have taken a liking to you." It was not in the least surprising. Johnson liked to associate with young people: as he himself said, he hated to think he was growing old, and young friends last longer. "I love the young dogs of this age: they have more wit and humour and knowledge of life than we had." Boswell was an attractive young dog: he was frank and manly and good-humoured; he was well bred and he came of a good family. Johnson, though a sturdy plebeian, did not hesitate to say that, other things being equal, superior birth was a positive value. His favourite young dogs when Boswell appeared on the scene were Topham Beauclerk, a duke's grandson, and Bennet Langton, whose ancestor was thought to have had a grant of free warren from Henry II.

And Boswell had appealed to him in another way very hard for any good man to resist. He had opened his heart and told Johnson the whole story of his most extraordinary life: his religious changes, his struggles with his father, his sexual dissipations. He had put himself in Johnson's hands and had begged for counsel.

The memoranda for the winter and spring appear to be a full statement of Boswell's moral goals, and down to the first of April they contain little morality that is not either complacently rakish or grossly prudential. One wonders what his principles had really been like before Eglinton went to work on him in 1760, what sort of effective moral training his parents, tutors, and pastors had really given him. That as a boy he had considered irregular sexual connexions deeply sinful is clear from the Sketch and its outlines, but sin for him seems then to have had little reality apart from the material hell which was threatened as its punishment. ("I was horrified because of the fear that I would sin and be

damned.") When he adopted less gloomy notions concerning life beyond
the grave, he was preparing for a time when the sense of sin too could be
repudiated as a mere bugbear. His mother's mystical piety, it may be
feared, dealt more with techniques of worship than with the making of
moral choices. To follow Joubert's nice distinction, she probably taught
him piety but not religion. As for his father's influence, there is no doubt
about that at all. Boswell complained, with justice, that his father never
impressed upon him any valuable *principle* of morality except a strict
regard for truth. For the rest he insisted only on the *appearance* of virtue:
let men see you grave, industrious, prudent, grown up. Boswell's conscience had been talking very much like Lord Auchinleck.

What I mean can best be shown by putting these memoranda of Boswell's against that odd collection of sublimity and triviality which we
know as Johnson's *Prayers and Meditations*. Johnson brings himself
shuddering and groaning to the bar of an ascetic Christian morality: his
ideas find their natural expression in the terminology of good and evil, sin,
contrition, repentance, grace, salvation. Not one of those terms occurs in
Boswell's. He never urges himself simply and solely to eschew evil and do
good. It is rather, don't be silly, don't be flashy, don't make yourself cheap,
do make yourself agreeable to yourself and other people. If admonitions to
avoid vice occur, it is for prudential reasons: the consequences of vice
may be painful. The most astonishing of all the memoranda are those
which combine directions for church-going with schemes of gallantry.
Amorous reverie in church (which Boswell also reports) is by no means
uncommon, but one does not often find a man coolly and deliberately
writing out *beforehand* Sunday plans like the following:

SUNDAY [28 NOVEMBER]. Dress. Have barber, and hair dressed. Then
D[ouglas]'s and advise. Then the General's and go to the Duke's; or if he
is not come, to St. James's church. Home before three; dine. If not church
forenoon, at four. Then L[ove]'s, as he's at Club, and try old Canongate. . . .

SUNDAY [2 JANUARY] Go at eight to King's Chapel. Home at nine
and dress, and order dinner at two. [George] Home[1] at ten, and be easy
and grave. Then after he goes, go to church; or if not, write journal till
dinner. At three go up to Louisa. Have porter at dinner. Be warm and
fine and consummate bliss. . . .

[1] Lord Kames's son and heir.

SUNDAY [20 MARCH]. Breakfast always home Sunday. Before ten, St.
Clement's and give penny for seat. Be fine: have white silks, but walk
little. Then Eglinton's and consult, and determine nothing out of London
but what is broke, and insist on seeing Lord Bute, so then you can tell him
your story. Then go Lady Mirabel's and try siege fairly. . . .

As a matter of fact, there is no evidence that after the débâcle of the
Louisa affair he really put his heart into the pursuit of Lady Mirabel or
any of the other women of beauty, sentiment, and spirit whom he set
down in his memoranda as possibilities for delicious intrigue. Some three
weeks after he got out of confinement, he followed up a direction he had
made earlier, went to the Green Canister (Mrs. Philips) in Half Moon
Street, laid in a supply of the articles which contemporary slang de-
nominated "armour," and thereafter allowed himself frequent recourse
to street girls—in taverns, in the Park, down a lane, once on Westminster
Bridge. There is, to be sure, some self-reproach. Temple, whom he had
been looking for ever since he arrived in London, turned up the day before Easter (3 April), and the friends were together for a longer period
than they had been since 1758 or would ever be again. The memoranda
now begin to show considerable uneasiness: "Promise to Temple no
debauchery"; "Call Temple, confess errors, and not only resolve but
promise, so as to be under his power"; "Take Temple privately by himself and own your depravity, and how vexed you are, and promise never
more to indulge low venery. This last *thief* and *monster* [she had picked
his pocket of his handkerchief] may cure you completely." But the parallel
record in the journal shows that he was more bothered by the brutishness
of his behaviour than by its wickedness: "I was shocked to think that I had
been intimately united with a low, abandoned, perjured, pilfering creature. I determined to do so no more; but if the Cyprian fury should seize
me, to participate my amorous flame with a genteel girl."

On the very day on which he recorded those last sentences in his journal (18 June) he wrote in his memoranda, "At one call Johnson [he
spells it Johnston]. Be fine and appoint him to sup with you next week.
Think of telling him your imbecility, your disposition to ridicule, and take
his advice." When he met Johnson a week later, he made a much more
ample confession than he had intended. Three weeks later he was writing,
"Since my being honoured with the friendship of Mr. Johnson, I have
more seriously considered the duties of morality and religion and the dignity of human nature. I have considered that promiscuous concubinage is

certainly wrong. It is contributing one's share towards bringing confusion and misery into society; and it is a transgression of the laws of the Almighty Creator, who has ordained marriage for the mutual comfort of the sexes and the procreation and right educating of children."

Better principles did not immediately produce better behaviour. The passage I have just quoted continues, "Notwithstanding of these reflections, I have stooped to mean profligacy even yesterday." Like most of us, Boswell thought abstinence possible only if buttressed by a magic date and prepared for by a surfeit, or at least by a process of tapering off. He would turn the new leaf on the day he left England. But once he had written down his conclusion that promiscuous concubinage was wrong, the tone both of memoranda and journal changed. After that, no cool, detailed plans for sexual indulgence, no delighted records of heroic raking, such as the occasions when he solaced his existence with two pretty little girls in the Shakespeare's Head, or roared from St. James's Park to St. Paul's Church-yard on the King's birthnight. Only the brief, shamefaced admission of yielding to appetite and the resolve to put up a stronger resistance next time. It is the pattern his journal is going to show through most of the rest of his life.

Weakness of will undoubtedly, but not *general* lack of will power. It may well be that there is no such thing as a man of generally weak will. The man of character applies his will-power to the things that are socially approved; the derelict wills as powerfully but in an eccentric fashion. One does not have to look far to see where Boswell's powers of choice and decision were going during the summer of 1763. A few days before he was to leave London, Johnson proposed that they make an all-day's river-excursion to Greenwich in order to have time to discuss plans for the programme of study Boswell was to follow at Utrecht.

We stayed so long at Greenwich [Boswell wrote] that our sail up the river in our return to London was by no means so pleasant as in the morning, for the night air was so cold that it made me shiver. I was the more sensible of it from having sat up all the night before recollecting and writing in my journal what I thought worthy of preservation; an exertion which, during the first part of my acquaintance with Johnson, I frequently made. I remember having sat up four nights in one week without being much incommoded in the day time.

If one said of a poet or a novelist that he was regularly defeated in his efforts to attain to chastity, but that he frequently sat up four nights in a week to write, the remark would seem commonplace. If it does not seem so in the case of Boswell, it is because we are still underestimating the urgency of his literary gift.

Any one reading the London journal of 1762–1763 with recourse to none of the other documents in the archives, would probably conclude that Boswell's eight months in London had been happily spent. It is quite certain that, except for the first few weeks, while he could live in the dream of his Guards scheme, they had been far from happy. At least after the end of February, he had been frustrated, insecure, bored, and latterly ashamed of himself. He told Sir David Dalrymple that he had been in a "miserable unsettled way," and in later life he was unable to read the journal of the period without being sickened by it. What sickened him was not his youthful debauchery but the unsettled state of mind, his "sickly weakness" when he cast off authority. It was with deep relief that he surrendered to Johnson's intellectual and moral domination ("You will smile to think of the association of so enormous a genius with one so slender") and his father's control. He made careful arrangements with John Johnston for the support of his child out of monies owed him by Love, Temple, and Sir David Dalrymple, and wrote the last of his London memoranda:

Set out for Harwich like Father, grave and comfortable. Be alert all along, yet composed. Speak little, make no intimates. Be in earnest to improve. It is not you alone concerned but your worthy father. Be reserved in grief, you'll be so in joy. Go abroad with a manly resolution to improve, and correspond with Johnson. Be grateful to him. See to[1] attain a fixed and consistent character, to have dignity. Never despair.

Johnson, on the return from Greenwich, had offered to accompany him to Harwich and see him out of England—an uncomfortable two-day journey with a solitary return in order to cheer and strengthen a confused young man whom he had known only a few weeks. At the inn at Colchester, where they spent the night, a moth flew into the candle-flame, and he seized upon the incident as a symbol: "That creature was its own tormentor, and I believe its name was Boswell." At Harwich he took Boswell to the church and made him say his prayers. The account of their parting in the *Life of Johnson* is one of Boswell's greatest passages; it

[1] Be solicitous to.

would be impossible to change or to add a word without upsetting its delicate balance of pathos and humor:

I said, "I hope, Sir, you will not forget me in my absence." JOHNSON. "Nay, Sir, it is more likely you should forget me than that I should forget you." As the vessel put out to sea, I kept my eyes upon him for a considerable time while he remained rolling his majestic frame in his usual manner; and at last I perceived him walk back into the town, and he disappeared.

CHAPTER

IX

Boswell had whirled into London in a post-chaise, cheering; he crawled into Utrecht in a canal boat, without huzzas. The campaign for making a new man out of James Boswell had got off to a very bad start.

It was not his fault for not having got ready a role for himself. He had written up the lines for his Holland act thoughtfully and with care. He had an aim, and he had a model. The aim: primarily, to become regular, sedate, and pious; secondarily, to learn French, study law, and improve his Latin and Greek. The model, a composite of Lord Auchinleck, Sir David Dalrymple, and Samuel Johnson. The role was all right. The trouble was that he seemed decidedly miscast in it.

He had left London gloomy and apprehensive, and the crossing had made him seasick. It was a shock to find himself in a country where hardly any one could speak his language. At Rotterdam a boyish Scots merchant of good family, Archibald Stewart, cheered him up, but Leyden, where he paused a few days trying to amuse himself with sight-seeing, depressed him worse than Glasgow had ever done. He moved on to Utrecht—nine hours on that sluggish *trek schuit* with no companions— and fell into the worst despondency he had ever known. He had made the mistake of coming a month before the University opened, and of arriving on a Saturday. They put him up in a high bedroom with old furniture and fed him there in solitude. Nearby, the bells of the Cathedral tower played dreary psalm tunes every hour, recalling the ennui and terror of his childhood. Next day—Sunday—was worse. He had nothing to do and could find nobody in Utrecht to talk to except the clerk of the English-speaking Calvinist church—not a sympathetic type. He thought he would go mad, thought he had gone mad, and ran frantically up and down unfamiliar streets weeping and crying out without restraint. Next day he fled ignominiously back to Rotterdam (if one can be said to flee on a boat moving three miles an hour), begged Stewart to do something for him, and sent out frantic appeals for help to Johnson, to Dempster, and to Temple.

Johnson made no reply. He had just demonstrated his sympathy and regard by accompanying Boswell to Harwich, and he always rebelled at the demand of a prompt reply to a letter. He was also disgusted by the abandon of Boswell's misery, and probably thought the expression of it exaggerated. But Stewart and Dempster and Temple made no doubt that Boswell was in a very serious state, indeed, and came to his relief promptly and with no scolding. Stewart—who was hardly more than a chance acquaintance—took him into his own house and surrounded him with soothing attentions. Dempster was in Paris. Boswell begged him to come to Brussels, and without waiting to write, Dempster posted two hundred miles to the meeting. No Boswell. Boswell had meantime prescribed for himself a brief tour of Holland with a young American, John Morgan, a recent M.D. of Edinburgh. Dempster made no complaint of four wasted days or four hundred miles of useless posting. He waited a day in Brussels, and then sent a long kind letter. Of course, he said, the whole Dutch scheme had been a mistake. But couldn't Boswell stand it for a couple of months before going to a French academy? "In the mean time, I should think you might amuse yourself in acquiring the French, keeping a journal and writing your friends, and debauching a Dutch girl." Temple, in a letter sent by return post, assured Boswell that the source of all his woes was idleness, and that if he would only put himself on a regular plan of study, he would recover his spirits. And even though he did not write, Johnson furnished the decisive word. Boswell turned to *The Rambler,* and found there several papers that seemed written expressly for his needs. He was especially roused by one sentence in which Johnson stated his doubt "whether a soul well principled will not be separated sooner than subdued." Boswell went resolutely back to Utrecht, engaged the first personal servant he had ever had (an old, gentle, fumbling Swiss named François Mazerac), and rented an apartment in, or connected with, the Keizershof, an inn on the Cathedral Square, just opposite the great tower with its dreary bells. He intended to give his part another try.

"I am now at a foreign university, or rather in a foreign city where I have an opportunity of acquiring knowledge," he wrote to Temple, but his arrangements actually showed little eagerness to exploit the advantages of being in a foreign country and specifically in Utrecht. He had to take steps at once to acquire French, for until he had French he was excluded from all polite intercourse. His best plan would have been to avoid English-speaking companions (the fact that he was the only British student in the University that year was so far all to the good) and take lodgings with a French-speaking family. Instead, partly out of soreness of mind, partly out of scepticism as to the value of the education offered him by Utrecht manners, he took a house of his own and then insulated himself further by making familiars of two Scotsmen. The Reverend Robert Brown, British agent and pastor of the English-speaking (Presbyterian) church in Utrecht, was a man whom Boswell might have wanted to meet in any case, for he had corresponded with Sterne and had attracted enough of Voltaire's attention to get named in one of his poems, with an unfriendly foot-note. He had married a Swiss girl, daughter of an expatriate Scots baronet, and also had a younger sister of his wife's living in his house; the ladies spoke French and had no English. The Browns eked out their income by taking lodgers and boarders, among them one Rose, a Scot, closely related to the Laird of Kilravock. He may have come over as a student in the University, but was now taking no courses; he later took orders in the Church of England. Boswell arranged to dine daily with the Browns, ostensibly for French conversation. Brown became his mentor, Rose his intimate friend. Or rather, since none of Boswell's relationships in Holland was entirely without reserve, it might be truer to say that he made Brown and Rose substitutes-on-the-spot for Johnson and Temple.

So, too, the repugnance to formal Dutch colleges which he had brought with him from England caused him to lay out his programme of studies with less reference to the University of Utrecht than one might have expected. Latin literature and Scots law he decided to read by himself, Greek under the direction of Rose. As French master he engaged one Caron, the clerk of the English church, who had done him so little good on that awful first Sunday in Utrecht, but who at least spoke English. To the University he turned for a single "college," that in Civil Law conducted by Christian Heinrich Trotz, a genial Prussian who not only lectured in Latin but used that language in letters and conversation. Boswell's one concession to student life was to join a club of Hungarians who met on Saturday evenings and gossiped in Latin. He later engaged a fencing-master, an old Italian who gave his age as ninety-four, and said he had fought in the Battle of the Boyne.

The fact that he could have carried on the greater part of this plan of study just as well in England as in Holland does not mean that he did not take it seriously. The memoranda bristle with ferocious time-tables: be waked at 6:30, read Latin from 7 to 8, write French from 8 to 9, breakfast from 9 to 10, Latin again from 10 to 11; 11 to 12 get shaved and dressed, 12 to 1 Trotz's lecture, 1 to 3 walk and dine, 3 to 4 French master, 4 to 5 Greek, 5 to 6 coffee, 6 to 7 study Civil Law, 7 to 8 Scots Law, 8 to 10 read French. *Then* journal and letters and other books. He soon discovered the unwisdom of keeping himself at such a stretch ("You must allow three hours every evening for amusement"), but if amusements were to be tolerated, they had to be modest and of good repute. No more roaring or drabbing. He might attend card-assemblies in the homes of people of fashion, go to concerts, and make jaunts to The Hague in vacation time. Otherwise only walking and an occasional game of shuttlecock with Mlle. Kinloch, Mrs. Brown's sister. Billiards were out. He was very fond of the game, but in Holland it was considered disreputable. Smoking, on the other hand, was permitted to gentlemen. He experimented with tobacco and came to relish it.

His schedule provided four hours for French and three for law, but even Lord Auchinleck would have concurred in the proportion. Every morning he wrote his French theme—one or two quarto pages on any subject that came into his head. He read approved French works such as Voltaire's *Universal History,* marking and memorizing the unfamiliar words. At Brown's he was supposed to speak only French. He helped organize a weekly literary society, where only French was permitted and the members took turns in reading formal discourses.

The fact is that the schedules rather understate the amount of system he managed to subject himself to. Every morning, seven days a week, as he had done in London, he wrote a memorandum giving directions for the day ahead, only now he began each memorandum by reviewing his actions of the day before and deciding what could have been done better. He tried to make each day's entry fill just one octavo page. Six days in the week he wrote his French theme, exactly one or two large quarto pages. Every night, Sundays included, he wrote ten lines (no more, no less) of heroic verse, apparently with no other object than to acquire facility in English composition. He kept a register of letters sent and received, a full daily expense account, and a special account of sums won and lost at cards.

For such a radical change of habits he felt his brief daily admonitions inadequate, and kept reminding himself to compile something more elaborate and exhaustive. Finally, on 15 October 1763 he drafted his outsize memorandum, which he titled characteristically "Inviolable Plan"; he directed himself to read it over every morning at breakfast and to carry it with him in his trunk when he travelled.

You have got an excellent heart and bright parts. You are born to a respectable station in life. You are bound to do the duties of a *Laird* of Auchinleck. For some years past you have been idle, dissipated, absurd, and unhappy. Let those years be thought of no more. You are now determined to form yourself into a man. Formerly all your resolutions were overturned by a fit of the spleen. You believed that you had a real distemper. On your first coming to Utrecht, you yielded to that idea. You endured severe torment. You was pitiful and wretched. You was in danger of utter ruin. This severe shock has proved of the highest advantage. Your friend Temple showed you that idleness was your sole disease. The Rambler showed you that vacuity, gloom, and fretfulness were the causes of your woe, and that you was only afflicted as others are. He furnished you with principles of philosophy and piety to support the soul at all times. You returned to Utrecht determined. You studied with diligence. You grew quite well. This is a certain fact. You must never forget it. Nor attempt to plead a real incurable distemper, for you cured it when it was at its very worst merely by following a proper plan with diligence and activity. This is a great era in your life, for from this time you fairly set out upon solid principles to be a man. Your worthy father has the greatest affection for you and has suffered much from your follies. You are now to make reparation by a rational and prudent conduct. Your dear mother is anxious to see you do well. All your friends and relations expect that you will be an honour to them and will be useful to them as a lawyer, and make them happy as an agreeable private gentleman. You have been long without a fixed plan and have felt the misery of being unsettled. You are now come abroad at a distance from company with whom you lived as a frivolous and as a ludicrous fellow. You are to attain habits of study, so that you may have constant entertainment by yourself, nor be at the mercy of every company; and to attain propriety of conduct, that you may be respected. You are not to set yourself to work to become stiff and unnatural. You must avoid affectation. You must act as you ought to do in the general tenor of life, and that will establish your character. Lesser things will form of course. Remember that idleness renders you quite unhappy. That then your imagination broods over dreary ideas of its own forming, and you become contemptible and wretched. Let this be no more. Let your mind be filled with nobler principles. Remember religion and morality. Remember the dignity of human nature. Remember everything may be endured. Have a sense of piety ever on your mind, and be ever mindful that this is subject to no change, but will last you as long as life and support you at death. Elevate your soul by prayer and contemplation without mystical enthusiasm. Preserve a just, clear, and agreeable idea of the divine Christian religion.

That is less than half of it, but it will suffice.

Even his schemes for publication took their colour from the new and sober pattern of his life, became in fact quite Dutch. The young man with a passion for light, agreeable pieces now planned a Scots dictionary and a translation into Latin of John Erskine's *Principles of the Law of Scotland.* Neither was carried much beyond the planning stage, but that they should even have been planned indicates a profound change in values. Actually, he gave over publishing completely, and pretty much restricted his writing to letters, his journal, and voluminous exercises.

He preserved the exercises; fortunately, for they have values other than that of proving his industry. The least interesting thing about the French themes is their French. Boswell soon came to speak and write French fluently and confidently, but he never mastered its idioms nor the nice points of its grammar. His French, even at its best, is Boswellian English literally translated; and it is in translation that the themes ought to be read. Since he wrote on the first subject that came into his head and that first subject was likely to be Boswell, they abound in glancing recollections of events in his past not elsewhere recorded, and in analyses of his tastes and opinions which he would have thought too trifling for his journal. We learn from them that he took warm baths at Moffat when he was first sent there as a child, and that one of his greatest pleasures in life is to soak his feet in warm water; that Eglinton had told him he had a better ear than all but three members of the famous Catch Club in London; that his breeches had once been mended while he had them on by the most famous beauty in the north of Scotland ("I must confess, however, that it was only in one of the knees"); that as a boy he had loved to distraction a cousin of his, a beauty of capricious temper who had beaten him; that he is fat; that he thinks he was badly educated ("They taught me the ancient languages, but they did not teach me things"); that he never beats his servant; that he likes to sleep with his head very high and always asks for two pillows; that he loves the Scots vernacular literature; that it is terribly hard for him to get up in the morning; and that he is no longer proud of his one-time intimacy with the Duke of York. "The Duke of York was not a man of worth nor of extraordinary genius. He was given over to debauchery and sometimes associated with the vilest of the human race. I knew him only very little and he never did me the least service."

As one reads these dashing and inconsequential *causeries,* one has a feeling of talent wasted for lack of a proper model. The accepted public *genres* of Boswell's day offered him none that quite suited him. The formal essay, of course, was in high favour, and he did later try his hand in an essay-series of some length, but *The Hypochondriack* has its eye too closely on *The Rambler* to be a fully happy expression of Boswell's genius. These French themes, for all that they are mere space-fillers, have an ebullience, a gaiety, a conversational charm that makes one feel that he might have written far better essays than *The Hypochondriack* if some-body had shown him a compelling alternative to the eighteenth-century sententious mode. Sententiousness, from which his journal, once it becomes private, is free, is a real vice of his public style, and it is a vice that came from imitating an inappropriate model: Johnson. Johnson could always make a commonplace memorable, but Boswell's sententious pronounce-ments lack acuteness of expression as well as novelty. Waywardness suits him better. But the models that would have done him the most good were forty years off in the essays of Lamb and Hazlitt.

Leonard Bacon once said that as verse Boswell's ten-line poems are comically bad; he would have permitted me, I think, to say that some of them are charmingly bad. They were written at top speed (the whole point was to get them done as soon as possible) on any topic that chanced to present itself, and, like the French themes, occasionally turn a spotlight into areas of his past which would otherwise be quite dark for us. For example, we learn from them how he saw the Hessians who had been brought in to help put down the Rebellion buying breeches for themselves and making Arthur's Seat resound with their drums; how Mr. Fergusson used to punish him for not being prepared in his lesson by hanging the fire-tongs around his neck.

His letters for the period may not have averaged more than one a week, but they were written with care and are extremely long, four large folio pages being the common measure. The journal of the period must have been a document of considerable charm, though because of the lack of variety in the subject-matter, it is not likely to have attained the literary distinction of the London journal. We have to resort to speculation, for it was lost in Boswell's own life-time. But we know its length: it ran to 536 large quarto pages.

Indeed, it is important here to emphasize quantity, the sheer *amount* of writing that Boswell managed to do at Utrecht. Though he could already write well, he was training himself to write better, and his exercises contributed to the formation of one of the easiest and most rapid styles of the century. One can turn over page after page in his letters or his journal without finding a single false start or a correction.

Geoffrey Scott's witty remark that Boswell kept his good resolutions by writing them down and redressed his backslidings by copying them out is not too severe if applied to Boswell's life as a whole, but it is not a fair summary of his behaviour while he was in Holland. During those ten months he was by heroic effort modest, studious, frugal, reserved, and chaste. The memoranda soon pass from anxious nagging to surprised and affectionate approval. "You was a little irregular yesterday, but it was but for one day to see the Utrecht concert. You don't like it, and you're not to go any more." "Yesterday was an excellent day. Remember it with satisfaction. You did all your business well and with spirit." "You did charmingly yesterday. You attended well to everything." "You have struggled, you have conquered." "You are now happily free from sickly ideas of vice." "Yesterday you did very well. You read an immensity of Greek. You was *retenu* yet cheerful at table. It was a dismal day and you eat too much wild duck, so was a little gloomy. However, you said not a word of it, nor have you said a word of it near these three months." "Yesterday you did delightfully. You did not commit one fault in any respect the whole day." "Yesterday you did just as well as you could wish. Upon my word, you are a fine fellow."

Utrecht agreed. The odd and amusing young Scotsman at Bart's (the Keizershof) was soon on the invitation lists of all the ladies of fashion. No Briton since Sir David Dalrymple had been so universally sought after.

The peak of his satisfaction came in December when he laid aside his books and claimed the reward he had been dangling before himself ever since September—three weeks of brilliant dissipation (his own words) at The Hague. The exuberance of his zest spilled over into sketches of the same sort as the Saturday dialogues at Child's Coffee-house:

Scene, M. Spaen's house

COLONEL SPAEN. Well, Sir, will you sit beside my wife?

BOSWELL. If I may venture to *part* the ladies.[1]

MME. SPAEN. I am afraid, Sir, that my hoop is in your way.

BOSWELL. Not at all, Madame, but I fear that I am in the way of your hoop.

He received distinguished attention and warm regard from his noble kinsman Heer van Sommelsdyck; he was presented to the young Prince of Orange; on Christmas Day, in the Chapel of the British Ambassador, he received the sacrament for the first time in the Church of England. The religious observance is properly listed as the climax of his joys, but it would be wrong to give the impression that it was a hasty or merely sentimental gesture. He had been thoughtfully considering committing himself for some time—perhaps from early in his acquaintance with Johnson—and had gone to the Ambassador's chaplain beforehand to state his case and make sure that he had done everything that was expected of him.

He saw the sights, he went to the theatre, he attended dinners and balls unnumbered.

To a man of system, dissipation even so brilliant as that of The Hague could not fail to present some uneasy moments. He came back to Utrecht with real pleasure ("Arrived happy and comfortable"), but things were never the same again. He was heading into one of his periods of depression. He found it hard to buckle down to his studies. He was distracted by a brief but violent passion for a young widow, Mme. Geelvinck, and when the passion was providentially interrupted by her departure for The Hague, he recorded himself hippish,[2] gaunt, weak, relaxed, insipid, and gloomy. He caught a bad cold and felt so wretched that he began to question the reality of his late satisfactions. "After dinner you said 'twas hard that in this world of woe your greatest quantum of happiness had been enjoyed in vice. . . . Brown said, 'What! have you been happier in vice than in virtue?' 'Yes.' "

A few days later he received word from John Johnston that his little boy, Charles, was dead. Though he had never seen the child, he was deeply affected. Thereafter the memoranda are an almost continuous

---

[1] The company is sitting down to table, Boswell between Mme. Spaen and the Countess of Nassau-Ouwerkerke.

[2] Low-spirited, depressed. (From *hypo*chondria.)

wail of misery. "You was so bad as really to think of despairing." "Yesterday you awaked as dismal as mortal could be." "You was direfully melancholy and had the last and most dreadful thoughts. You came home and prayed." "You was very bad after dinner and shuddered with dire ideas." "You awaked in great disorder, thinking that you was dying, and exclaiming, 'There's no more of it ! 'Tis all over !' " "Confused and changed and desperate." "Dreadful." "Gloomy." "Bad." "Very bad. You got up as dreary as a dromedary." "You awaked shocked, having dreamt you was condemned to be hanged." "In a kind of delirium." "Desperate. This day, *Easter,* rouse. Be Johnson. You've done no harm. Be *retenu,* &c. *What* am I?"

As usual, when these fits were on him, he got no comfort from religion, and had to stand fascinated while the old horror Necessity crept up to devour him. None of his friends particularly wanted to argue predestination, but he forced them to: Rose, Brown, even one of the Hungarians. His extreme gesture to escape from the coils furnishes stuff for the most dramatic of the memoranda: "You went out to fields, and in view of the tower, drew your sword glittering in the sun, and on your knee swore that if there is a fatality, then that was also ordained; but if you had free will, as you believed, you swore and called the Great G____ to witness that although you're melancholy, you'll stand it . . . and not own it." He is swearing on the hilt of his sword, like his knightly ancestors.

The many people who have thought that Boswell's "hypochondria" was an affectation would not have thought so if they had read his Utrecht memoranda. These sincere (and utterly private) pages record no luxury of grief, they show us rather a soul in torment, struggling, resisting, attempting every means of escape. He groans and wails, but he tries hard to keep his groans and wails to himself. "Show that you are Boswell, a true soldier. Take your post." The pattern of this winter is the shape of a real and recurring malady. It cast its shadow over much of his life, and it must be envisaged if one is to understand him.

The Boswellian hypochondria was a state of mental irresolution and languor, a sick suspicion that he had no power over the operations of his own mind. But this impression of inability to act was accompanied by extremely vivid ideas of activity: he was tortured by strong ineffectual desires and loaded with regrets and self-accusation. He envied the condition of every man he met, and imagined that every one thought meanly of him. Labour of any sort was painful to him, but his fear of the contempt of others would never let him quite give up the struggle with his accustomed tasks, and he toiled on with the feelings of a slave, "not animated by inclination, but goaded by fear."

When he was in mental health, he was a creature of extraordinary zest. Not only were his pleasures keen and fresh, but he was *conscious* of his pleasures, he stood apart savouring them. In his states of depression everything that had formerly given him joy seemed to him quite indifferent: he repeated over and over Hamlet's lines, "How weary, stale, flat, and unprofitable seem to me all the uses of this world." But his insensibility to joy bred no numbness to sensations of pain. When he was gloomy, his mind was abnormally tender and irritable—a peculiarly painful affliction for a man who had trained himself always to appear good-humoured.

One may well wonder why Boswell, with his insatiable appetite for sensual pleasures, was so tortured by the doctrine of Necessity. Why did he not embrace fatalism, float down the tide of sense, and disclaim responsibility? He did not because so much of his life was spent in pain. When he was depressed, he could get no comfort out of the assurances of religion or the recollection that he always *had* recovered, but he still had to cling to the bleak conviction that he was ill, that struggling somehow or other *must* help matters. Necessity could just as well condemn him to a life of unrelieved misery as restore him to health; and when he was under a cloud, that was what he was sure Necessity *would* do. He *had* to struggle, he *had* to try to break loose. If he admitted that he was powerless, then he was literally and perhaps for ever damned.

The attacks were generally sudden in their onset. He might go to bed in good spirits and wake up, after confused and horrible dreams, in a state of depression that would last for weeks. And the emergence into good spirits was generally as abrupt. The figure of the sun entering and emerging from a thick cloud is a sound one.

Two Dutch doctors whom he consulted—both of them men of some distinction—told him he had bad nerves and recommended exercise and attention to diet, but it does not really appear that improper care of his body had much to do with his attacks. He was sedentary and careless about exercise, but he had great muscular vigour and at almost any period of his life could wear other people down by his energy and resilience. Until he was past forty, his frame would endure almost any amount of punishment. It was, indeed, his own belief that he could improve the state of his mind by punishing his body. Twice during the worst part of his fit of low spirits

at Utrecht he changed the current of his ideas by sitting up very late, or by
not going to bed at all.

But perhaps the relief was not really so much caused by loss of sleep as
by relaxation of routine. What made him at times so desperately unhappy
was not, so far as I can judge, the manic-depressive psychosis. Both his
melancholy and his high spirits were excessive, but his alternations of
gloom and high spirits do not follow a true cyclic pattern, and can be too
readily explained by what was happening to him at the moment. Nor, to
change twentieth-century jargon for eighteenth, was the source of his
trouble acrimonious juices and lax solids—the diagnosis of one of the
Dutch physicians. His fits of low spirits did not come from the weather,
from idleness, from drinking, from sexual excess, from remorse of conscience. They came from frustration: frustration of his overweening ambition by any course of life which did not promise to make him a Great
Man *soon;* frustration of his urges to pleasure by the prudent and monotonous routine of respectability. His power of sublimation was very
limited. And in the unending struggle between instinct and conscience,
his responsible conscious self (the self he addresses in the memoranda as
"you") got sadly lacerated. To use an attractive Freudian metaphor which
does seem to illuminate Boswell's case, he had to drain off a dangerous
amount of the energy of his conscious self to balance the opposed charge
of the repressed urge to pleasure. His attacks came on suddenly because
the balance of his moral energy gave out suddenly: there is no such thing
as being a little bankrupt. The relief came as suddenly, not because of any
pouring in of reserve energy, but because his conscience had finally told
the poor beaten responsible self *to let go.* Make him a Great Man, send
him upon a jaunt in which he can experience change, excitement, constant
agitation, and you restore him as by a magic infusion. And he will never
get so tired and inelastic that the formula will not work.

Be good, be prudent, be sober, be systematic, be constantly industrious,
and you will be happy, said his father and everybody else. In Utrecht he
gave the formula a good hard try and it didn't work. And it didn't fail
because he hadn't dealt sufficiently firmly with himself on his return from
The Hague. The old childhood weakness had revealed itself again. His
limit of systematic application was about ten weeks, and he had reached
the limit.

What does a man do when he toils and prays and hangs on by his
teeth, and life only gets blacker and blacker until he wakes in the morning

out of dreams that he is about to be hanged or that he is actually suffering the pains of death? Johnson would have said: Life is a state in which much is to be endured and little to be enjoyed. Johnson would have said: I know not whether a soul well principled will not be separated sooner than subdued. And he would doggedly have fronted the pain and the darkness.

Boswell was no such hero. To do him justice, he could not have acquired the equipment for moral heroism. From the first of his journal to the last, appearing here, appearing there, probably never with a completely good conscience, is the plea that he is different, that he inherited a vile constitution, that his mind really cannot stand the ordinary ways of life, that he must have change and excitement; finally, that it is not merely his *right* but his *duty* to have such gleams of enjoyment as life allows him. The peculiar pathos of the Utrecht memoranda rises from the fact that they show Boswell for more than eight months refusing to tolerate such reflections.

Boswell in reform forswore gallantry no less than drabbing. When, early in his stay in Utrecht, the Countess of Nassau-Beverweerd, an elegant blue-stocking of thirty married to a man more than twice her age, took him under her protection and introduced him to the assemblies and private parties of the *noblesse,* he admitted that the prospect of having to resist temptation was cheering, but he wrote memoranda counselling piety and chastity. As it turned out, the Countess disappointed him by never trying his virtue. She was *galante,* but she already had a lover, and was quite content to have Boswell on his own high-minded terms so long as he showed no interest in any other woman. She could be jealous, though, and when Boswell began paying more than casual attentions to Mme. Geelvinck, she punished him by pretending not to understand his French. Vile spite, low cunning, thought Boswell, who thereafter called her "a very so-so *vrouw*," and rejoiced at knocking a pair of ducats out of her pocket at cards. "This turned up her Dutch nose."

Reform, of course, was rather favourable to schemes of marriage, and while he was in Holland he played with no fewer than three such schemes. The first was a whim, but it was very characteristic. Soon after he landed in Holland he wrote to both Temple and John Johnston, begging their advice. Archibald Stewart, the young Rotterdam merchant who had been so kind to him, was brother to the Margaret Stewart whom he had gallanted in the winter of 1761–1762. Though she had shared his attentions with Kitty Colquhoun and Miss Bruce, he now maintained that while he was in Scotland she was the only woman he could ever think of as a wife. He had put her and all Scots maidens out of his mind when he decided on an English marriage, but now, having had her good qualities recalled by talking with her brother, he wonders whether he ought to let such a prize slip. She is sensible, she is amiable, she has been in London, she can read and talk, she plays the harpsichord, she has £5000 for her fortune. "I could write postscripts in her brother's letters, and take many ways to find out how she would like the scheme. . . . Will it fix me to a rational plan, and shall I begin to beat about the bush?" By the time he got Temple's reply, he had already realized the absurdity of the scheme of a courtship in postscripts. "I have a strange turn towards marriage," he wrote. "I have distressed you with consultations upon that head from the beginning of our friendship." All the same, when he read in a newspaper in the following spring of Miss Stewart's marriage to his cousin, Sir William Maxwell of Springkell, he admitted that he was galled.

His passion for Catharina Elisabeth Geelvinck, *"la veuve,"* was a good deal more serious. She was a young Dutchwoman of noble birth, only two years older than he was, married at eighteen and a widow at nineteen, tender, beautiful, very rich, with a six-year-old son whom she adored, and a crowd of suitors whom she allowed to dangle. Boswell dreamed of her, recorded his "love and fiery imagination," paid court to and flattered her child (he even got himself invited to a party for children so that he could talk to Mme. Geelvinck without competition from the pack of suitors), and courted her in impassioned French. But he never quite made a forthright proposal of marriage.

BOSWELL. How old were you when you first truly fell in love?

MME. GEELVINCK. Really ! That is certainly being frank.

BOSWELL. Oh, how happy I am ! And since you have been a widow, have you ever been in love?

MME. GEELVINCK. No. Really !

BOSWELL. But, Madame, I am very much in love. I adore you. Will you make a distinction between yourself as Mme. Geelvinck and yourself as my friend, and give me your advice?

MME. GEELVINCK. Yes. But I am truly sorry. My advice is to cure your passion.

BOSWELL. But, Madame, how?

MME. GEELVINCK. You have been in love before?

BOSWELL. Yes, I have been in love before, but those passions had no foundation. I could always call reason in to cure them. But I believe I have never really been in love before now.

MME. GEELVINCK. Oh, fancy that !

It was his conclusion that she was delicious but impregnable. When she left for a visit to The Hague, he got up early after a sad night of sickness from a disordered stomach, took a dram, and went out to the city gate, where he made interest with the soldier on guard to let him stand in the sentry-box and see her pass. "She looked angelic, and that glimpse was ravishing. You then treated sentinel with geneva.[1] You stood on ramparts and saw her disappear. You was quite torn with love." Troilus and Cressid. But this Cressid returned; and when she did, he told her (no doubt to her relief) that he "adored her but would not marry her for the world. *Le sentiment est changé.*" She was later twice married, she never bore the name of Boswell.

The most important of his *égarements du coeur* while he was in Holland—the most amusing of all his courtships—was that which sent him, fascinated and repelled, after that extraordinary young woman, Belle de Zuylen. Isabella Agneta Elisabeth van Tuyll van Serooskerken, to give her her full name, or Zélide, to give her the literary style she herself affected at the time and which Boswell invariably uses, was born in the same year as Boswell to one of the oldest families in Holland, a family with a stately town-house in Utrecht, and a moated castle at Zuylen on the Vecht, a few miles outside. She was proficient in mathematics, had mastered Newton, had a good knowledge of Latin, Greek, and English, and wrote French well enough to impress the French. And she was not plain and unfeminine. Her figure was too tall and her hands too large to meet the eighteenth-century specifications of beauty, but she had good features and a beautiful neck which she admitted she was a little too fond of displaying. Her mind ran circles around Boswell's, but it was emphatically a woman's mind, intuitive, subtle, ironic, mocking. Though in temperament she was *aristocrate* to the bone and despised unshapeliness and vulgarity, she had freed her mind completely from the timidity and reserve befitting her maiden state, and had acquired a general reputation of unconventionality. "*That*—a young lady?" protested the dowagers whom she had offended by her published satire on their pride of rank, and they did not know the half of it. From the age of twenty she had been carrying on a clandestine

[1] Gin.

exchange of letters with a Swiss officer in the Dutch service named Constant d'Hermenches, a married man much her senior with a great reputation as a lady-killer. The correspondence by great good luck has survived, and shows nothing of passion on either side. She wished to refer her analyses of herself and other people to the judgement of a mind as frank and sceptical as her own, and with greater worldly experience; he felt himself sufficiently rewarded by letters as well written (so he said) as Voltaire's.

Frankness and truth—truth defined within the strictest lines of eighteenth-century rationalism—marked everything she said or wrote. Her devastating irony played first on her own irrationalities and then on those of other people. On the prerogatives of rank, as we have seen, she cast a satiric eye; she could not accept a revealed religion and said so; she was willing to debate the necessity and even the value of female chastity.

Yet she wanted very much to get married, for only by marriage could she escape from the conventions which held her a prisoner. In fact, the main concern of her life was to find a husband. But she was having a signal lack of success, for if she liked a suitor, she either scared him off by her tendency to lead, or she felt it her duty to discourage him as being too good—her own words—for sacrifice on the altar of matrimony. What she thought she wanted was a marriage of convenience, and for some time she and d'Hermenches had been scheming ways of persuading d'Hermenches's friend the Marquis de Bellegarde, a Savoyard, to make a firm proposal. She had even written a letter for the Marquis to copy and present to her father. But Bellegarde was disposed to set a rather high price on his title, and her father was deeply opposed to a Catholic marriage. Boswell appeared on the scene. If he had been really sure that he wanted to marry her and had behaved with reasonable circumspection, he might very well have made her Mrs. Boswell.

He came well recommended; his family, though less ancient and distinguished than hers, had a sufficient number of quarterings. Her father and mother were fond of him. Belle (whose younger sister was already married and a mother) clearly ought to be married soon, and among the suitors she could be brought to show an interest in, Boswell looked better than merely possible. She had taken to him at first sight because he was comical and warm-hearted, because, as she later told him, she found him odd and lovable. For all she or any one else in Utrecht could see, he was a sober, pious, industrious young man, very methodical and well behaved, and desperately eager to make the most of himself. He was vain, admittedly, but so was she, and she found his vanity refreshing. She did not even mind that he was a prig and something of a pedant; that he rebuked her endlessly for her animation and imprudence. For he was frank, he was honest, he could be made to come down from his high horse with a grin to engage in irresponsible gaiety. He was an escape from the boredom of her placid existence, and she was grateful to him for the good he did her.

Almost at the beginning of their acquaintance Boswell inscribed her as a probationer in his list of possible wives. She had family, she had money, he admired her, he liked her, sometimes he felt tender towards her. But she was so unpredictable and often so unsatisfactory! If she could be persuaded to be a little more *retenue*, if she could be brought to entertain a more respectful attitude towards male dignity, she might do. Meanwhile he courted Mme. Geelvinck, who roused his amorous interest by coyness and flattered his masculine pride by deference. "You was shocked or rather offended with [Zélide's] unlimited vivacity. You was on your guard"; "Zélide was *nervish*. You saw she would make a sad wife and propagate wretches"—memoranda like these are characteristic of his feelings towards her up to the very end of his stay in Utrecht.

Trotz's college was to end in June. In April Boswell got a letter from his father confirming the promised reward. Though Lord Auchinleck was depreciatory ("In general I must tell you that travelling is a very useless thing. . . . I could wish to see you 'gainst winter at home"), he was explicit; Boswell might have his choice of a trip through Flanders to Paris or a tour of some of the German courts. The old Earl Marischal of Scotland, who was at the time in Scotland, had recommended the courts of Brunswick, Prussia, and Baden-Durlach. Boswell wrote at once to Temple, confiding to him plans which he certainly had not yet shared with his father: "I shall set out from Utrecht about the middle of June. I shall make the tour of the Netherlands, from thence proceed to Germany, where I shall visit the Courts of Brunswick and Lüneburg,[1] and about the end of August arrive at Berlin. I shall pass a month there. In the end of September I shall go to the Court of Baden-Durlach, from thence through Switzerland to Geneva. I shall visit Rousseau and Voltaire, and about the middle of November shall cross the Alps and get fairly into Italy. I shall there pass a delicious winter, and in April shall pass the Pyrenees and get

[1] Hanover.

into Spain, remain there a couple of months, and at last come to Paris.
Upon this plan, I cannot expect to be in Britain before the autumn of
1765. . . . Perhaps I allow myself too little time for it. However, I may
perhaps prevail with my father to allow me more time. When a son is at
a distance, he can have great influence upon an affectionate parent."

Lord Auchinleck's letter did not clear Boswell's mental sky by any
means, but it caused a sudden break in the clouds; and thereafter the prevailing gloom might at any time be shot through by glorious flashes of joy.
Boswell began again to record delight, ecstasy, fiery vivacious blood. And,
as could have been predicted, he began also to record more serious moral
struggles. His previous admonitions to continence had been negatives:
"Let not Satan tempt you as Cupid," he had written oddly but sincerely
in the midst of his passion for Mme. Geelvinck, following with instructions
not to go to Amsterdam to a bawdy-house. On the day after he received
his father's letter, he wrote, "Think if God really forbids girls"; and when
the lurking thought of Amsterdam turns up again, it is in the positive style
of the London memoranda: "Go to Amsterdam and try Dutch girl Friday, and see what moderate Venus will do." On Thursday he consulted a
distinguished physician in Utrecht, Johannes David Hahn—it is odd that
he did not go to him sooner—and received the answer he was hoping for:
"Women are necessary when one has been accustomed, or retention will
influence the brain." Next day he did go to Amsterdam and trailed fret-
fully through blackguard *speelhuizen* and mean brothels in dirty lanes, but
could not overcome his fastidiousness, his fear of infection, and what he
petulantly called his low scruples. He came back to Utrecht with his record of continence intact but precarious.

On 4 June 1764, being then at The Hague, where he had gone to meet
two Scots acquaintances and attend a magnificent ball given by the British Ambassador on the King's birthday, Boswell received letters informing
him that the old Earl Marischal was coming through Utrecht, and that
he was to travel in his company to Berlin. "Never was man happier than
I. . . . I was very, very gay." George Keith, tenth Earl Marischal of Scotland, at this time something over seventy, was a valiant old Jacobite who
had been one of the leaders of the Rebellion of 1715 and the lesser upris-
ing of 1719. Attainted, wounded, and barely escaping with his life, he
had continued to work for the restoration of the Chevalier until just before the '45, when he gave the Stuarts up as hopeless and entered the service of Prussia. As one of Frederick the Great's most trusted counsellors,

he had been Prussian Ambassador to the Courts of France and Spain, and Governor of the Principality of Neuchâtel. In 1759, because of valuable service done for the British government, he had been pardoned and allowed to inherit estates in Scotland; his title had not been restored, but nobody called him anything but Lord Marischal. He had been in Scotland arranging his affairs with the intention of ending his days there, when he received a letter from Frederick begging him to return: "If I had ships, I should consider making a descent on Scotland to steal off my *cher mylord* and bring him hither. . . . I am yours with heart and soul." He had sold his properties, and was on his way back to his royal master. Always shrewd, brave, and kind, his sojourn in Spain had made him stately, his association with Frederick ironic. The news that he was to become the intimate of such a man was enough to dispel Boswell's clouds for good.

Now that the time of his parting was really at hand, he found that leaving Belle de Zuylen was going to be harder than he had imagined. He hired a handsome chaise and drove out along the sleepy Vecht to Zuylen for a Sunday afternoon call. "I was in solid spirits in the old *château,* but rather too odd was I; for I talked of my pride, and wishing to be a king. Zélide and I were left alone. She owned to me that she was hypochondriac, and that she had no religion other than that of the adoration of one God. In short, she discovered an unhinged mind. Yet I loved her." So the journal; but in the notes he had written, "You would be miserable with her. Yet she is to write, and loves you." They met in Utrecht on the two following days ("She was *échauffée* but sweet. . . . Yet she rattled so much that she really vexed me"), and she gave him an unpublished play of hers to read. His interest was not lessened by the assurance of one of their common acquaintances that she was in love with him, nor by a warning from Dr. Hahn that she would always be *une malheureuse demoiselle,* the slave of her fancy.

Lord Marischal arrived on 13 June, with him his adopted daughter, Mme. de Froment, "a Turkish lady," Boswell explains, "who was taken prisoner by Marshal Keith at the siege of Ochakov." He could have been even more romantic and kept within the bounds of history, or at least within the bounds of history as related—without references—by Lord Marischal's most voluminous biographer, Mrs. Cuthell. James Francis Edward Keith, Lord Marischal's younger brother, a Prussian Field Marshal and Frederick the Great's most trusted general, had fallen at Hochkirch in 1758. Before entering Frederick's employ, he had held com-

mands in the Spanish and the Russian services, and as general of infantry
in the war between Russia and the Turks had been second in command
at the siege of Ochakov (1737). Ochakov fell, but he himself was seriously wounded in the knee. As he rode through the town, where the Rus-
sians were slaughtering the Turks indiscriminately, a Turkish child clung
to his stirrup and allowed herself to be dragged to safety. She was the
daughter of a chief janissary, and her name was Emet-Ulla. Lord Marischal had assumed responsibility for her, had become fond of her, and had
brought her up as his own daughter. Recently she had requested Protestant baptism, and had married an officer in the Sardinian service. Her
age is uncertain, but thirty-nine would be a fair guess. She did not talk
about her romantic past; in fact, she was indolent and did not talk about
much of anything.

Lord Marischal intended to tarry in Utrecht only a day or two. Consequently on 14 June 1764 Boswell drove out to take his congé. "Zélide
and I had a long conversation. She said she did not care for respect. She
liked to have everybody free with her, and that they should tell her her
faults. I told her that this was very wrong, for she would hardly find a husband of merit [the memoranda at this point say, "*I* for instance"] who had
not some pride, and would not be hurt at finding people so free with his
wife. I owned to her that I was very sorry to leave her. She gave me many
a tender look."

Actually, besides lecturing her unmercifully as to the kind of husband
she ought to marry, he had taxed her with being in love with him, and had
invited her to write to him and admit it. He need not have been so complacent, but he was not mistaken in thinking that she was genuinely
touched. After he had gone she stood by herself some moments in a deep
reverie, and that night started writing him one of those long inimitable
letters of hers in which so many virtues combine: delicacy of perception,
clarity and firmness of thought, absence of coyness and affectation, flash-
ing irony. He had asked her to tell him how she felt about him? Well, she
has had him enough in her mind the last three or four days so that she has
thought less often of Bellegarde; she has had him in her mind because he
appeared to be suffering a lover's agitation, otherwise he would not have
given her a moment's distraction. "I am affected by your departure, I
have thought of you all the evening. I find you odd and lovable. I have a
higher regard for you than for any one, and I am proud of being your
friend. Are you not satisfied?"

She repeats without reserve her rationalist notions about marriage. "I do not regard the advice of selecting a cold husband as the wisest of your propositions. If I am much in love with my husband and he with me, it is at least possible that I shall not fall in love with another; if we were but little in love, I would certainly love some one else. My spirit is formed to have strong feelings, and will assuredly not escape its destiny.... What would d'Hermenches and his like say if such a letter as this were to fall into their hands!... But I am writing to Cato. Cato's friend is very unlike him, but loves him much." She invited his correspondence, but with the stipulation of strict secrecy: "Write to me, not often, but write long letters and address them to Spruyt, the bookseller.... Give me always your exact address for towns where you intend a long visit. Be very careful and remember that all my peace of mind depends on it. Do not ever be so absent-minded as to send your letters to my father's house."

The letter was of the sort one posts after the recipient is at a safe distance. But Boswell characteristically provided an anti-climax. On 17 June, the evening of his last day in Utrecht, he drove out again to Zuylen with Lord Marischal. "Zélide said to me, 'What, are you back? *Nous avons dit des adieux touchants.*' She gave me a letter which she had written to me on my departure and bid me not read it till I was just going. She ... seemed much agitated, said she had never been in love, but said that *one* might meet with an amiable man, etc., etc., etc., for whom *one* might feel a strong affection which would probably be lasting, *but* this amiable man might not have the same affection for *one*. In short, she spoke too plain to leave me in doubt that she *really* loved me. But then away she went with her wild fancy, saying that she thought only of the present moment. 'I had rather feel than think. I should like to have a husband who would let me go away sometimes to amuse myself.' In short, she seemed a frantic libertine.... She gave me her hand at parting, and the tender tear stood crystal in her eye. Poor Zélide!"

Poor Boswell rather, vain and fatuous Boswell thus to condescend to Belle de Zuylen. One who knows her later history must compare him very unfavourably with that other odd and lovable young man, not yet born, who twenty-five years hence will sit at her feet. "Madame de Charrière's outlook on life was so original and lively," wrote Benjamin Constant, "her contempt for conventional prejudices so profound, her intellect so forceful, her superiority to average human nature so vigorous and assured, that for me, a boy of twenty, as eccentric and scornful as herself, her company was

a joy such as I had never yet known. I gave myself up to it rapturously."
Yet the comparison shows Boswell prejudiced rather than obtuse. He saw
in Belle de Zuylen just about what young Constant did, but that contempt
for the modes of the world which entranced Constant antagonized him
and made him question her superiority. In one of his French themes he
tells how a common acquaintance of theirs at The Hague had maintained
that she sacrificed probity to subtlety and brilliance. "I would give a great
deal," he wrote, "to cure myself of the weakness of being too much influenced by other people's opinions. Reynst changed to some extent my idea
of Zélide. Yet I fought like her champion. I said, 'That young lady makes
me feel very humble when I find her so much above me in wit, in learning,
in good sense.' 'Pardon me,' said Reynst, 'she lacks good sense and consequently she goes wrong. A man who has not half her wit and learning
may still be above her.' I made no reply. I thought it very true and also a
very good thing, for if it were not for that failing, Zélide would have absolute power. Her dominion over men would be unbounded, and she would
overthrow the dignity of the male sex."

Boswell's attitude towards women, at this time and later, was grossly
conventional. Johnson, for all his rough exterior, loved blue-stocking society: he could discern literary talent in women and was always encouraging it. But Boswell, though he was attracted to every variety of greatness
in men, no matter how unconventional, actually disliked superior intelligence in women. It intimidated him, it made him fear for "the dignity
of his sex." For him all women were females—potential mistresses or potential wives. If a woman was not on his matrimonial list, the one quality
he looked for in her was the power to allure and enchant. If she *was* on
his list, he wanted that quality too (accompanied, of course, by a decent
appearance of modesty), but it was even more important that she be a
mother, a nurse, a comfortable friend, ever ready to soothe his temper and
be complaisant. He did not expect or desire her to furnish intellectual conversation, which he could get elsewhere.

He was up all night packing and writing letters, and some time after
midnight wrote her a short note. No doubt he thought it magnanimous,
but except for one phrase it is complacent and priggish: "You say that
I 'appear to you to have the agitation of a lover.' I am extremely sorry
for this. My sincerity, or perhaps my extreme simplicity, prevents me
from leaving Utrecht without frankly enlightening you on this subject.
. . . I admire your mind. I love your goodness. But I am not in love with

you. I swear to you that I am not. I speak strongly because you have given me reason to think that your peace of mind may be involved. In such circumstances one must not stand on ceremony."

She replied that same evening: "So much the better, my friend, all the better if I made a mistake. I am not in the least mortified by having remained in error for three days. . . . What I wrote on Thursday evening was perfectly true when I wrote it; on Friday it appeared to me less true. I had slept well; I was no longer clear whether I had believed myself to be a little inclined to be in love with you: all that appeared more or less a dream. On Sunday it appeared to me more or less an untruth. I felt some scruple in giving you my letter; I would have liked to have torn off the first page. But that would have been to destroy it all. I thought, 'The date is my justification. What I wrote in the evening on Thursday is what I thought in the evening on Thursday. With Mr. Boswell there is no need of prudence. Give him the letter. It is an act of frankness, it is the diary of the heart of a live and feeling woman.' . . . My friendship is yours for ever: count on it however much you may think me fickle. I count on the stability of your feelings as on that of the rocks which God placed on the surface of the earth when he created the world." There is more—much more—of it. To abridge a letter of Belle de Zuylen is like trying to abridge a brook. But Boswell was gone. The letter passed him somewhere on the road and he got it at Brunswick.

18 June 1764, seven o'clock in the morning. François is not leaving Utrecht, and Boswell has engaged a new servant, Jacob Hänni, a Bernois. He has told François that as he has given him a character as a servant, he wants François to give him one as master, marking equally the good and the bad. François hands it to him, sealed, according to instructions. Boswell could not read it till he was out of sight, but we can read it now. It says that Monsieur is a good and kind master, is generous to the poor, does not speak evil of others, and is very punctual in the duties of religion; but that he is extremely careless about leaving his watch and his money lying about with the door unlocked, invites guests and is not at home punctually to receive them, studies too hard, and goes to bed too late. "As for me, I believe I shall never forget Monsieur." A coach and four drives into the Cathedral Square; Boswell takes his place with venerable Scot and silent Turk, Jacob climbs up outside. School is out, and the whining school-boy has flung away his satchel.

CHAPTER

Boswell's "tour" in Germany extended over five months, from 19 June to 20 November 1764, but about half the time he was stationary in Berlin. From Utrecht he travelled eastward in Lord Marischal's company by way of Hanover and Brunswick to Potsdam, and, except for a jaunt back to Brunswick in August, he remained at Berlin and Potsdam from early July until the end of September. Then he struck out south-west towards Geneva, planning to visit as many courts as a short allowance of time and money would permit.

Germany in the eighteenth century offered the traveller little between the extremes of gilt rococo and the common *Stube,* where unwashed plebeians snored in the straw. The roads were atrocious, the public conveyances nothing but great high-wheeled uncovered carts, with boards laid across for seats, and, except in cities of some size, there were no inns where one could get a bed, let alone a room to one's self. But the courts were really very splendid places, with staffs of officials and a display of buildings, painting, and music out of all proportion to their size. Boswell's German was woefully thin (he spelled it like Dutch, which shows that he never made any formal study of it), but the linguistic barrier seldom bothered him. The court language was French, the native German speech, like the native German culture, being considered too homely for exalted display.

A twentieth-century reader finds it difficult to take seriously a country with sixty or more sovereign princes, some of them, like the Prince of Anhalt-Zerbst, boasting armies of less than two hundred men. In theory, of course, these principalities formed one state, the Holy Roman Empire, with an Emperor at Vienna and a Diet of princes at Regensburg. Nine great princes, the hereditary Electors, chose the Emperor. (Before Boswell left London he had on three occasions seen one of the nine, the Elector of Hanover, who happened to be King of Great Britain. On his tour he was presented to two more, the Elector of Saxony and the Elector Palatine. He saw a fourth, Frederick the Great of Prussia, Elector of Brandenburg.) But for a long time now the Empire had been the loosest sort of federation of virtually independent principalities and free cities, the Emperor outside his own fief exercising few powers except the granting of titles. The territories of the Electors were of considerable extent and descended undivided, but the other princes held their principalities as personal possessions, and divided them as they pleased. Boswell visited two Anhalts, two Badens, two Brunswicks, and two Saxonys; there were actually at the time five duchies of Saxony besides the Electorate. But a very considerable prestige attached even to the smallest courts. I have allowed myself above to join with Boswell in sneering at the Prince of Anhalt-Zerbst. But that prince's sister had been considered good enough to marry the heir to the Russian throne, and in 1764 was Empress of Russia in her own right—the redoubtable Catherine.

The trip from Utrecht to Potsdam may be taken as an epitome of the whole German tour. Boswell was travelling in as comfortable a style as the country permitted (a private coach and four), and under the protection of an honoured friend of the King of Prussia, who owned a good deal of the territory through which they were passing. On 24 June he slept on straw spread on the floor of a barn, surrounded by cows and horses; three days later he dined in the Palace of Brunswick with the ducal court, opposite him at table Duke Ferdinand, who had commanded the allied forces at the battle of Minden. ("He absolutely electrified me. Every time that I looked at him, I felt a noble shock.")

Boswell had probably assumed (or at least had hoped) that Lord Marischal would keep him under his wing and serve as his active protector and patron at the Court of Prussia. He did not yet understand the limitations of friendship with Frederick the Great. Arrived in Potsdam, the old man presented him to Frederick's nephew and heir, the Prince of Prussia, arranged for him to see the Palace, Sans Souci, and the Picture-Gallery—and then politely gave him to understand that he was on his own. Boswell went on to Berlin and rented rooms in a private house in the old part of the city. No more devotion to books; the aim now was perfection in the manly disciplines. He entered an "academy" (that is, a riding-school) and got a French fencing-master to continue the ministra-

tions of the veteran of the Boyne. He was very happy. Berlin he thought
the finest city he had ever seen, and his apartment came up to all his con-
ceptions of elegance. Carl David Kircheisen, his landlord, was President
of the City Council; he and his wife were people of culture, friendly and
hearty. They treated Boswell as a member of the family, and introduced
him to their friends. They had two children living at home, a boy of
fifteen and a girl of seventeen, both of whom Boswell found good company. He romped with Friedrich and flirted with Caroline, who knew
exactly how to handle him. Andrew Mitchell, the British Minister, a
Scotsman and old friend of Lord Auchinleck, proved amiable and easy,
very different from stiff Sir Joey Yorke at The Hague. Even the bankers
to whom he had been referred, Herr Schickler and Herr Splitgerber,
made parties of pleasure for him. He rode in the Kircheisens' chaise, he
strolled Unter den Linden, he whirled in a private carousel, spearing at
rings with a pole. ("I was blockhead enough to bet against a lady an écu
—three shillings—each ring. I lost eighteen écus.") This part of the journal is all *Gemütlichkeit,* a succession of German idyls. "We had at ten
o'clock a collation in the garden; three or four tables with cold meat and
pastry and sweetmeats and fruits and wine of different sorts. Behmer [his
host] was a big, gallant *allemand;* his wife, hearty even to excess. She
was a most singular figure. She had no cap, and her hair dangled about
her head. While she ran from table to table with bottles in her hand and
health most florid in her face, she seemed quite a female Bacchanalian."

The admonitions in his daily memoranda to be Addison or Steele or
West Digges or Sir David Dalrymple or Samuel Johnson taper off and
practically disappear. A new and portentous model, the Spanish grandee,
does step into his pages from his conversations with Lord Marischal, and
will long remain there, but this Spaniard is part of his true self that he
wishes to develop, not an alien role. The long-delayed declaration of independence finally comes on 20 July 1764, three months before his
twenty-fourth birthday. The occasion was another *fête champêtre.* "I
danced a great deal and was in true gay, vigorous spirits. . . . I was
rather too singular. Why not? I am in reality an original character. Let
me moderate and cultivate my originality. God would not have formed
such a diversity of men if he had intended that they should all come up
to a certain standard. . . . Let me then be Boswell and render him as
fine a fellow as possible." And again (9 August 1764) : "I saw my error
in suffering so much from the contemplation of others. I can never be

them; therefore let me not vainly attempt it in imagination. . . . I must be Mr. Boswell of Auchinleck and no other. Let me make him as perfect as possible." He will continue to try on masks but he will no longer act as though he feared that he has no features of his own.

Shortly after he reached Berlin, he sent Belle de Zuylen through the hands of Bookseller Spruyt, as stipulated, a huge letter, seventeen pages long, all in English. He begins by telling her how perfectly methodical he is (he is slow in replying because he *planned* it that way), and then settles down to an unsparing criticism of her character. She lacks prudence, she thinks too much of pleasure, she disdains religion. "Pray make a firm resolution never to think of metaphysics. Speculations of that kind are absurd in a man, but in a woman are more absurd than I choose to express." He throws back at her her libertine remarks about love and marriage. "Ah, poor Zélide!" It is no good her saying she was not in love with him; he knows the signs. "But I am too generous not to undeceive you. . . . I would not be married to you to be a king."

That sounds sufficiently final, but of course he has to take it all back, striking a pose that is absolute Dogberry: "I have assumed the person of Mentor. . . . Perhaps I judge too hardly of you. . . . Defend yourself. Tell me that I am the severe Cato." Could she humble herself? Could she acquire the subaltern talents? (She had said, "You are very right to say that I should be worth nothing as your wife. . . . I have no subaltern talents.") Could she be cheerful? Live in the country six months in the year? Bridle her tongue? Give spirits to her husband when he is melancholy? "If you can, you may be happy with the sort of man that I once described to you. Adieu."

He sealed the letter and then broke it open to bully her some more. "Answer me this one question. If I had pretended a passion for you . . . answer me: would you not have gone with me to the world's end? . . . You do not know yourself if you say you would not have done this."

He sent the letter off and confidently awaited her reply. None was forthcoming.

His months in Germany were as free of practical efforts towards seduction and gallantry as those in Holland had been. "Since I left England," he wrote to Temple on 23 July, "I have been as chaste as an anchorite. Now my mean scruples are gone, but rational morality directs me to do no harm to others or to myself. I have not yet had an opportunity of indulging my amorous genius. But I have hopes." He was, in fact, combining paradisial fantasies of fresh, healthy Teutonic *houris* to be his in the next town with uneasy motions towards coarse and dangerous nymphs whom he could have any time he chose. And the memoranda, to which one always turns for a full report on the tensions in his conscience, show that the ascetic impulses which he liked to consider mean scruples had by no means been wholly exorcised. "Swore new virtuous conduct" (19 June, setting out from Utrecht); "Adore God, be good" (25 June, after hearing mass at Minden); "Pursue Plan. Forget dreary ideas and sensual Turkish ones. Be Johnson. But take fresh German, etc." (5 July, entering Berlin, the sensual Turkish ideas caused by the proximity of Emet-Ulla). Finally, quite in the London style, "This day, church. Be grave and think, and at nine for health—" (15 July). That evening, after being presented at Monbijou to the Queen of Prussia, he came home, changed from court dress, and went out to the street. But he had been unable to furnish himself with one of those articles which Mrs. Phillips in London had so obligingly dispensed, and when he found that the "black girl" whom he picked up did not have one either, he left her and came home. The memoranda continue in the vein of prudence: "Marry not, but think to have fine Saxon girls, etc." (21 July); "*Chase libertine fancies.* Happiness upon whole as Milton's 'wedded love' " (25 July—two days after the letter to Temple mentioned at the beginning of this paragraph); "You must be constant to one good woman" (4 August); "Remembered Mother, her tender care, and resolved to be good-humoured, and by superior strength of mind to make her gay. This is real. Write her so, and God will assist you. . . . Have a care or health and purse ruin. You're well, and can be with no girls except sure ones" (9 August). On 3 September he asked his German friends to take him to a Berlin bawdy-house. "We found a poor little house, an old bawd, and one whore. I was satisfied with what I saw."

A few days later the *houri* put in her appearance—though it must be admitted that she came in disappointingly unparadisial guise. He had sat up all night writing, partly to get caught up on his journal and letters, partly to punish himself for "extravagant rodomontading" with Caroline Kircheisen and her mother. "Grievous was it to the flesh till seven in the morning, when my blood took a fine flow. I was quite drunk with brisk spirits, and about eight, in came a woman with a basket of chocolate to sell. [One wonders how she got into the Herr President's house at that hour. Perhaps Boswell's apartment had its own entrance from the street?]

I toyed with her and found she was with child. Oho! a safe piece. Into my closet. 'Habs er ein Man?' 'Ja, in den Guards bei Potsdam.'[1] To bed directly. In a minute—over. I rose cool and astonished, half angry, half laughing. I sent her off. Bless me, have I now committed adultery? . . . Should I now torment myself with speculations on sin, and on losing in one morning the merits of a year's chastity? . . . I am sorry that this accident has happened, I know not how. Let it go. I'll think no more of it. Divine Being! Pardon the errors of a weak mortal. Give me more steadiness. Let me grow more perfect." The lapse caused him much more distress of conscience than these quietist resolves indicate. A later entry of the journal shows that he composed a discourse against fornication "quite like an old Scots minister" and read it aloud to scare himself. He was putting himself on the stool of repentance and giving himself such a reproof as a parishioner might have received from Mr. Moody at Riccarton or Mr. Auld at Mauchline. But strict habit was not so easily reestablished. Almost immediately he had to record another encounter with a street girl, which probably did not go all lengths but was certainly intimate. It would be a long time before he would be able to claim the merit of a year's abstinence.

Boswell's great object in Berlin was of course to be presented to Frederick the Great. One might have thought he would have encountered no difficulties. England (with Hanover) had been Frederick's only ally in the late war, Andrew Mitchell was Frederick's friend, and nobody was on closer terms of intimacy with him than Lord Marischal. But in 1764 Frederick did not love Englishmen—Bute, he thought, had let him down in his hour of greatest peril—and in any case he was very cavalier in the matter of presentations. He disliked the routine ceremonial of courts and gave himself very little concern about such matters, spending his days in public business, the parade, and the relaxations he really enjoyed: playing the flute, listening to concerts, and talking with male friends. Presentations were made at the Palace in Berlin on the rare occasions when he appeared there and let it be known that he was accessible, and in the summer of 1764 he was almost continuously at Potsdam. Neither Lord Marischal nor Andrew Mitchell would have thought of asking him to break his rule for anybody, let alone a young unknown like Boswell.

At first matters seemed hopeful. The Prince of Prussia had made pro-

---

[1] "Have you a husband?" "Yes, in the Guards at Potsdam."

posals of marriage to the daughter of the Duke of Brunswick, and soon after Boswell settled in Berlin, the Court of Brunswick arrived for the formal betrothal. At Mitchell's advice Boswell hurried over to Potsdam to see the entertainments, and there, on the Parade, he got his first view of the King: "It was a glorious sight. He was dressed in a suit of plain blue, with a star, and a plain hat with a white feather. He had in his hand a cane. The sun shone bright. He stood before his palace with an air of iron confidence that could not be opposed." But Mitchell had been misinformed about the entertainments, which were all being held in Berlin. On the evening of 15 July Mitchell carried him to Monbijou and presented him to Frederick's much-neglected Queen and the rest of the Court. "She has been handsome, and is very amiable, although she stammers most sadly. I was presented to I don't know how many princes and princesses." But Frederick was not among them. A week later he did show up for splendid entertainments at Charlottenburg, but no strangers were invited to dine or sup with the Courts, and no presentations were made. Boswell was near the King in the garden at a concert, and for a moment thought (so he says) of throwing himself at his feet and telling him how much he wished to hear him speak. Fortunately he was able to control the impulse; Frederick might have cut him with his cane, certainly would have had him ejected from the garden. His disappointment was somewhat assuaged by the very flattering notice of the Duke of Brunswick, who recognized him in the crowd, called him out and shook his hand, and expressed pleasure on hearing that he was coming back to Brunswick for the *foire*.

On 27 July Mitchell again took him to the Queen's court at Monbijou: still no Frederick. Boswell now began to think that he had better bestir himself, and wrote one of his long cajoling letters to Henri Alexandre de Catt, the King's reader, formerly tutor to Belle de Zuylen's brothers. "I am not satisfied with having seen the King. If it is possible, I should like to hear him speak. . . . It is certain that I am not a great man, but I have an enthusiastic love of great men, and I derive a kind of glory from it."

He hoped, of course, that De Catt would be so much taken by the letter that he would show it to the King, and with that in view he composed a paragraph intended to flatter Frederick's vanity as an author, and to draw him into an argument. Does De Catt know that Boswell is reading Frederick's poems every morning? "Has he not fired my soul?"

But how could he uphold the gloomy doctrine of annihilation, as he did in his epistle to Marshal Keith? "Ah, no, great King! You shall never be destroyed. Not only shall your name live for ever, but your soul shall be immortal too; and I shall certainly speak to you in the other world, though I may not in this."

The King is leaving for Silesia, Boswell is leaving for Brunswick ("a court . . . where I have received extraordinary attentions"), isn't there a chance that he can be presented in the small time remaining? De Catt sent a polite reply confirming the edict of no presentations at Potsdam but (apparently) promising to mention Boswell to the King.

Boswell's second visit to the Court of Brunswick lasted two full weeks and should have been a draught of unalloyed bliss. He was repeatedly invited to dine with the Court; he attended operas and operettas (he was sitting in the Duke's *loge* with the ladies of the Court when he made his resolve to be Mr. Boswell of Auchinleck and no other), he attended French comedies and German comedies, he attended grand Sunday services in the Duke's Chapel. "I heard a psalm performed with magnificent music, eunuchs and other singers from the opera, an organ, a French horn, flutes, fiddles, trumpets. It was quite heaven. . . . We had a prodigious company to dine at Court, and a most magnificent dinner. . . . Grand music played in an apartment adjoining, and round the table was a vast crowd of spectators. I confess that I was supremely elevated. I had the utmost pleasure of contrast by considering at this hour is assembled Auchinleck kirk, and many a whine and many a sad look is found therein." He talked religion with Abt Jerusalem, the Hereditary Prince's tutor. He danced a minuet with the Hereditary Princess, sister of George III, he danced with Princess Elizabeth, the future Queen of Prussia. But towards the end of his stay he confessed to ennui and disappointment. Twice the Marshal had failed to ask him to stay for supper. The Duke had been gracious but not demonstrative. "I expected still more civilities than I received, because forsooth the Duke spoke to me at Charlottenburg. I magnify all events in my own favour, and with the wind of vanity blow them up to size immense." It is the old persistent day-dream of James and Ned: of a prince who will grant him not merely civilities but unreserved personal affection.

He remained nearly a month more in Berlin, but he was growing tired of the place and his boredom translated itself into moods of bad temper which he described variously as unruly, fiery, angry, and splenetic.

One of them landed him in serious trouble. A professor named Castillon whom he had known at Utrecht had got him invited to a dinner given by a French captain of artillery named Durand: it had been a dreary affair, but he felt bound to join with Castillon in repaying it. The house at Stralau where they met was not to his liking, he was bored and sulky, and he showed his spleen by railing against the French. Durand, his guest, promptly called him a scoundrel. The affair was made up by what a twentieth-century reader would regard as candid and sensible dealing (he made a public apology, and Durand followed suit), but it left a rankling doubt in Boswell's mind which he later tried to get Rousseau to resolve, a doubt that is reflected in all the many discussions of the morality of duelling in *The Life of Johnson*. It was the first of seven occasions in his life when he was either challenged or thought he ought to challenge some one else, seven opportunities for combat that ended in explanations rather than pistols at twenty paces. He could never quite persuade himself that his candid dealing had satisfied the gentlemanly code. How much of his will to be reasonable was due to his constitutional timidity?

But his main conscious concern during that last month in Berlin was the inflexibility of will displayed by the Laird of Auchinleck and the King of Prussia. The fact that he could not deal with his father face to face did not seem to him a handicap but the contrary, for in personal conference his father could always cow and silence him. But he knew, as his letter to De Catt indicates, that he had a very pretty power of epistolary persuasion, and he enjoyed exercising it. "Manage Father with affection," he had written in the memoranda, but the letter he had finally sent his parent requesting a tour of Italy had failed to budge him in the least. Lord Auchinleck had replied, as before, that a tour of some of the German courts or a visit to Paris was the utmost that he would sanction. This meant that Boswell had to start farther back and manage Andrew Mitchell and Lord Marischal to manage Lord Auchinleck. Mitchell had meantime left Berlin and was at Spa on his way back to England. Boswell's letter to him is one of the best in his cajoling series. The letter to De Catt had struck the tone of naïve hero-worship, that to Lord Auchinleck had made artful use of affection, this one is deferential but manly. "Your departure is a good deal unlucky for me, not only as it deprives me of conversation which gave me uncommon pleasure and insensibly accustomed me to rational thinking and honourable sentiment, but because I now particularly stand in need of your prudent and kind counsel with respect to my travels. . . . I own that the words of the Apostle Paul, 'I must see Rome,' are strongly *borne in* upon my mind. . . . I would beg, Sir, that you may write to my father your opinion as to this matter."

The management of Lord Marischal was a more delicate piece of work. Boswell needed his intercession with both laird and King, but felt that it would be pushing to make two requests at the same time; for that matter, to make any request bluntly. And he did not feel like assuming a mask. The letter he sent was for the greater part a quite sincere and heartfelt protest against the formality and coldness of his old friend's manner. Boswell says that he feels an honest warm regard for him, reveres his principles, honours his character. Why does Lord Marischal repress his ardour? Why does he not allow him to show his respect and affection? The request is slipped in casually and almost parenthetically in the last paragraph: "As my father is anxious to have me at home as soon as possible, I would wish to make the most of my time. I beg to know if it will be possible for me to hear the King talk. Cannot your Lordship procure me that satisfaction?"

The letter pleased the old man and put him and Boswell permanently on relaxed and intimate terms. But when they met, Lord Marischal appears not to have referred in any way to the request for an interview with Frederick, and Boswell appears to have had manners enough not to bring the topic up himself. They talked about Boswell's future, and Lord Marischal counselled him to fall in with his father's plans for the law. The opportunity for the second request had risen in the most natural fashion. "Then, my Lord, will you write to him, that in the mean time he may allow me to travel a year?" "I will." And he did, promptly, not only recommending the tour in Italy, but also suggesting an addition to Boswell's allowance of two hundred pounds extraordinary. Mitchell wrote too. Boswell could not know his father's answer for certain till he got to Geneva, but he left Berlin in a confident mood.

The monarch remained unbowed, but to the very end Boswell refused to admit defeat. Two days before his departure, having halted at Potsdam to take final leave of Lord Marischal, he appeared at the parade of the Prince of Prussia wearing a Scots blue bonnet. He says he had a whim to appear as a Scots gentleman, but his main intention must surely have been to make himself so conspicuous that the King would have to notice him. The Prince of Prussia noticed and made inquiries, but the King never once looked in Boswell's direction. Next morning he called on

General Friedrich von Wylich, whom he had known for some time, and got Wylich's promise to present him on the Parade if an opportunity offered. "But an opportunity did not present itself. This King is feared like a wild beast. I am quite out of conceit with monarchy." This was not so much the major social defeat of Boswell's life as the only one. So far as I can recall, Frederick the Great of Prussia was the only person Boswell ever set himself seriously to meet without meeting.

He left Berlin and Potsdam with tender feelings. All in all, it had been the happiest summer he had ever spent.

Before I quit this house, let me mark some ideas which I shall like to recall. The President's regular employment. The easy uniformity of the family. Three machines.[1] Five good horses. The courtyard with the walnut tree. The stork. The little temple of ease. Curtzin, the neat little maid. . . .

I took leave of [Lord Marischal] with a most respectful and affectionate embrace, saying, "My Lord, you may always reckon upon me as upon a most faithful servant." My heart was big when I took my last adieu of the venerable Scots nobleman. I yet hope to see him again. I almost cried. At this moment the tears are in my eyes. I dined at Froment's and took leave of my poor Turk with regret. Well, she and I have passed curious hours together. . . . I mounted the post-wagon. I found it cold and really hard enough. Courage.

Boswell had already been received at the Courts of Brunswick and Prussia; on his tour after leaving Berlin he was presented at seven more: Anhalt-Dessau, Saxony, Saxe-Gotha-Altenburg, Hesse-Kassel, the Palatinate, Baden-Durlach, and Baden-Baden. He passed through Coswig, the residence of the Prince of Anhalt-Zerbst, and Mainz, where the Elector of Mainz held his Court, but in both cases went on without presenting his credentials when he heard that the sovereign was not at home. He made a jaunt to Wittenberg to see the graves of Luther and Melanchthon, visited the universities of Halle and Leipzig, and took in the free city of Frankfurt-am-Main. There is perhaps no other document extant that transmits so vividly as his journal the feel of German *Kleinstaaterei* at the middle of the eighteenth century, but the biographer can offer as summary only a selection of episodes and aspects that particularly illustrate Boswell's character.

[1] Carriages.

At Coswig, his first court after leaving Berlin, he drew a blank. The Prince of Anhalt-Zerbst, who commanded a regiment in the Austrian service, was at Vienna. Boswell, as he says, being a good deal diverted by "the appearance of his little dirty town, his castle, and his sentinels with sentry-boxes painted in lozenges of different colours"—also, one suspects, splenetic because of his disappointment—went about asking all the sentries how many troops the Prince had. (The answer, as he already knew, was 150 foot and 30 horse.) A soldier, hearing his outlandish German, decided that he was a foreign spy, and had him arrested. The burgomaster could not speak French and Boswell could not really speak German, but fortunately one of the soldiers—a Leipzig student gone wrong —could speak Latin, and procured his discharge.

The Prince of Anhalt-Dessau was not at home either, but the honours of the Court were cordially and splendidly performed in his absence. Boswell rode to a stag-hunt, was given the stag's foot as a mark of distinction, and came back with an oak-garland on his hat. Dessau, he thought, though a good deal grander than Auchinleck, was still the best sort of model for a Scots laird. His wife later was to rebuke him for explicitly comparing himself to a German prince.

He had planned when he got to Wittenberg to write Samuel Johnson a letter with his paper resting on the tomb of Melanchthon. The tomb proved to be a mere slab in the pavement, but he showed his lifelong readiness to sacrifice dignity to authenticity of circumstance. Having called for pen and ink, he lay flat on his stomach and wrote his letter in that posture.

The University of Leipzig so pleased him that he regretted he had not studied there; at any rate, he said, he would go home, marry, and send a son. (He was very tenacious of these apparent whims. Thirty-one years later his heir Alexander appeared at Leipzig, according to promise.) At Leipzig, too, he met his greatest German authors: Johann Christoph Gottsched and Christian Fürchtegott Gellert. They seem rather obscure now, but were about as good as he could have managed unless he had gone far off his route to Breslau, where Lessing was. In 1764 Herder was only twenty, Goethe fifteen, Schiller five; Klopstock was at Copenhagen.

The Court of Saxony was in mourning when he arrived, and he had not provided himself with a black coat. Told by the Envoy (Philip Stanhope, the son to whom Lord Chesterfield addressed the famous letters) that he could not go to Court, he put a cockade in his hat, tied a piece of crape round his sleeve, and got himself presented as an English officer. ("The Elector's Master of Horse . . . looked at my coat and said, 'Sir, that is not a uniform.' I replied, 'No, Sir, not properly speaking. But in our country, if you have a red coat, you are an officer; it is enough.' ")

At Gotha he dazzled the Court in a suit of flowered velvet of five colours which he had kept pristine for the occasion: the Princess made him come to her table and said, "M. Boswell! Mais, vous êtes beau!" Gotha, like Dessau, was a comfortable, easy, cordial court.

Mannheim was a quite different affair. The Elector Palatine, Karl Theodor, Chancellor of the Electoral College, was very high and mighty: he provided magnificent entertainments but seldom invited strangers to dine. Boswell did not get asked once. He wrote sarcastic verses about the Elector, and drafted a long ironical letter to his Grand Chambellan comparing the politeness of Mannheim with the rudeness of Brunswick. ("The family of Brunswick is only a minor family, almost unknown in Europe. It is true that it has produced heroes of the greatest distinction and that it has made the most illustrious of alliances. But that is nothing to the Elector Palatine. Show me another prince in Europe who has a face as black as his. . . . It is that that constitutes his Highness' unique glory.") But as the memoranda at that point contain injunctions of caution, he may not actually have sent this peevish epistle.

He relished the extremes of elegance and squalor which the tour provided: they suited a taste which was both Scots and personal. He loved splendour, the elaborate and stately ceremonial of courts. He loved to be clean, to deck himself in velvet of five colours and to preen himself conspicuously. He was charmed by a country where he could assume the style of Baron without claiming more than German heraldry would have granted to a gentleman of his standing. It did his feudal soul good to drive along in a state coach and see the common people bowing to the earth. But there was also an earthy streak in his composition that made it positive pleasure to him to ride muffled up through the night in a jolting cart, to sleep in his clothes ten nights running, to sleep in haylofts and on the floors of inns. Baron Boswell of Auchinleck resembles Whitehead's simile for an electron: he appears just outside a city gate, but can be located nowhere in between. On the road he is replaced by a coarse, resilient, penny-pinching young fellow who enjoys roughing it.

This lack of consistent bearing was a source of irritation to his new servant, a very different sort of chap from gentle François. Jacob Hänni was honest and intelligent, but independent and outspoken. He thought Boswell ought to keep his place, especially with Jacob himself. He did not approve of the alternations from baron to blackguard, and he resented Boswell's attention to the collection and stowing away of the luggage. Before Geneva was reached, there had been two or three sharp collisions.

Boswell's plan for his tour of courts, as we have seen, called for much more than mere contact with the great. Somewhere along the way he would find the reality of which the Duke of York had been the false image. "Since I have been in Germany it has been my ardent wish to find a prince of merit who might take a real regard for me, and with whose ennobling friendship I might be honoured all my life." It would not have been like his fates to deny him any fulfilment of his dream, but it was very like them to keep him waiting and then to grant ambiguously. At Karlsruhe, the next to the last of the courts he was to visit, it seemed to him that he had met the prince he had been looking for. Karl Friedrich, Margrave of Baden-Durlach, was one of the most intelligent princes of his day. Voltaire visited him frequently, but unlike Frederick the Great, that other patron of Voltaire, he supported the new German literature. He was interested in agricultural theory and attempted (unsuccessfully) to put the teaching of the Physiocrats into practice. He spoke English and was even willing to try writing it. His court had little of the pomp and splendour of Brunswick, Dresden, or Mannheim, and was frequented by no such throng of courtiers. He had scholarly tastes, collected books and medals, and enjoyed arguing on fate and free will. He took to Boswell at once, talked very freely and familiarly with him, and instructed his librarian to grant him special privileges. He even offered to correspond with him after he had left.

Boswell ought, one thinks, to have felt that this was very gratifying progress for an association that had lasted only two or three days, but he was not willing to leave well alone. Karl Friedrich had instituted an order; Boswell determined to be a knight of the Order of Fidelity, and to wear a star and a ribbon. When the Margrave offered to correspond with him, he thought he would surely be granted the order, but no mention of it was made. Just a week at Karlsruhe, and he was presented to take leave.

The Prince said, "I cannot ask you to stay longer, as I am afraid you would tire." I said, by no means, but I was a little hurried at present, and would return again and pass a longer time. I then took courage and said, "Sir, I have a favour to ask of you, a very great favour, I don't know whether I should mention it." I was quite the courtier, for I appeared modest and embarrassed, when in reality I was perfectly unconcerned. He said, "What, Sir?" I replied, "Your Highness told me that a good gentleman might have your Highness's order. Sir, might I presume to ask you that, if I bring you proof of my being a very good gentleman, I may obtain the order?" He paused. I looked at him steadily. He answered, "I shall think of it." I said, "Sir, you have already been so good to me that I flatter myself that I have the merit for obtaining such a favour. As to my rank, I can assure you that I am a very old gentleman" (some days ago I had given his Highness a history of my family) "and it may sound strange, but, Sir, I can count kindred with my Sovereign from my being related to the family of Lennox and the royal family of Stuart. . . . If you grant me this favour, you will make me happy for life, in adding honour to my family; and I shall be proud to wear in my own country the Order of Fidelity of such a prince." He seemed pleased. I said, "I hope, Sir, you do not take amiss my having mentioned this. I was anxious to obtain it, and I thought it was pity to want what I valued so highly, for want of boldness to ask it." He said, "Let me have your genealogy attested, and when you return, we shall see." Oh, I shall have it.

Boswell the sprightly companion of princes of course found time occasionally to be Boswell the bemused and reluctant lover. Though Belle de Zuylen had warned him that she could not write frequently ("Clandestine letters keep me up too late; I look to your guidance to cure me of this libertine habit"), he had left Berlin deeply piqued by her silence, which he attributed to a fit of the sulks. At Dessau, again through Bookseller Spruyt, he dispatched an addendum to his enormous indictment. Nearly three months had gone by, he reminded her, since he invited her to call him Cato, and she had not written a word. Of course she was offended by his frankness, but what did that say for *her* vaunted candour? In any case, he knew he was right. "Do not tell me you have never experienced feelings for me more lively and tender than those of friendship. Say it as much as you please, I shall not believe you." At Gotha he felt a void in his heart which she seemed to fill; at Kassel the Flemish pictures made him wonder again whether he did not want to marry her. At any rate, he wanted to *hear* from her. "Write," he had concluded his Dessau letter, "if it were only to say, 'I shall never write to you again.' " Surely, he thought, she will rise to that, and I shall find a letter from her when I get to Switzerland.

As usual, he entertained concurrent paradisial fancies; and the fancies, as in Holland, turned unbearably sordid when he tried to realize them. "Think to have fine Saxon girls," he had written in a memorandum at Berlin before the episode of the soldier's wife. He had already seen enough of Berlin street-walkers to cause him to advance his visioned *houris* to the future and to lands further south. "Saxon" presumably meant "Dresden," but when he had got as far on the road as Leipzig, the vision had moved on again to the horizon, and he enjoined himself to "swear solemn with drawn sword" to—well, to have no unarmoured dealings with women—"nisi Swiss lass." But at Dresden the fantasy revived: he instructed himself to "have sweet lass" and attempted to carry out the injunction. It was all very disappointing. The lasses were pickpockets and he was afraid of them; he dared venture only what he later called "lesser lascivious sports." There were three of these episodes in two days. After the first he wrote, "Wrong, low, punish, but in Suisse have sweet girl"; after the last, "Swore never to be with girl till you see Rousseau." The name of a new Mentor has appeared in Boswell's records. The Rambler has yielded to the author of *Émile* and *La Nouvelle Héloïse*.

CHAPTER

XI

On 3 December 1764, a young gentleman riding a small and reluctant horse came up the Val de Travers from the direction of Neuchâtel. He was travelling alone and had no luggage except a *Reisesack,* containing some shirts. Arrived at the village of Môtiers, he put up at the inn in the Maison de Village, withdrew, and wrote busily for some time. Then he changed his shirt, dined, and gave the maid a letter, telling her to deliver it at a house in the village and to leave immediately, saying she would come back for an answer. While he was waiting for his reply, he walked out by the side of the little river Areuse, gazing at the frowning rocks, the clustering pines, and the glittering snow, preparing himself for the interview which he hoped would follow. As he strolled pensive, he was an incongruous spot of sophisticated colour against the snowy slopes and the dark rushing water: coat and waistcoat of scarlet trimmed with gold lace, greatcoat of green camlet with collar and cuffs of fox's fur, hat with a solid gold lace, or at least a lace that *looked* as though it were solid. James Boswell, after making dutiful notes on the antiquities of Bâle, Soleure, and Berne, is laying siege to Jean Jacques Rousseau. In half an hour ("one of the most remarkable that I ever passed") he returns to the inn and finds that the maid has a card for him. "I am ill," it says, "in pain, really in no state to receive visits. Yet I cannot deny myself to Mr. Boswell, provided that he will remember the state of my health and make his visit short." Relieved and at the same time alarmed by the word "short," he hurries to the meeting. Thérèse Le Vasseur, whom we are surprised to find described as "a little, lively, neat French girl" (she was forty-three years old), admits him and conducts him up a darkish stair. She opens a door and Boswell thinks, now I shall see him. But he is only in a room that serves as vestibule and kitchen, and it is empty. Then the door to another room opens, and there stands the wild philosopher himself, a genteel dark-complexioned man in a cassock-like gown, wearing a nightcap. "Many, many thanks," says James Boswell, and walks in.

"I am a Scots gentleman of ancient family," his letter had said. "Now you know my rank. I am twenty-four years old. Now you know my age. Sixteen months ago I left Great Britain a completely insular being, knowing hardly a word of French. I have been in Holland and in Germany, but not yet in France. You will therefore excuse my handling of the language. I am travelling with a genuine desire to improve myself. I have come here in the hope of seeing you. . . .

"I present myself, Sir, as a man of singular merit, as a man with a feeling heart, a sensitive and melancholy spirit. Ah! if all that I have suffered does not give me singular merit in the eyes of M. Rousseau, why was I made as I am? Why did he write as he has written? . . . Your books, Sir, have melted my heart, have elevated my soul, have fired my imagination. . . .

"I learn with deep regret, Sir, that you are often indisposed. Perhaps you are so at present. But I beg you not to let that prevent you from receiving me. You will find in me a simplicity that will put you to no trouble, a cordiality that may help you forget your pains.

"I have much to tell you. Though I am still a young man, I have experienced such a variety of existence as will strike you with wonder. I am in a serious and delicate situation concerning which I ardently desire the counsel of the author of the *Nouvelle Héloïse*. If you are the charitable being I believe you to be, you cannot hesitate to grant it. Open your door, then, Sir, to a man who dares tell you that he deserves to enter it. Place your confidence in a stranger who is different. You will not regret it."

The whole thing was sheer bravura. Boswell had a note from Lord Marischal asking him to present his compliments to Rousseau and to report on Rousseau's health, not an outright letter of introduction, but one which would certainly have opened Rousseau's door. He had also at Neuchâtel provided himself with a letter to the Lord of the Manor of Val de Travers, M. Martinet, who, he had been assured, could introduce him without difficulty. But to a romantic genius such methods seemed intolerably conventional. Great soul should speak directly to great soul and be recognized. And to a sportsman whose game was difficult men, such methods seemed ignobly easy. To have sent round Lord Marischal's note would have been just like going after the great trout with a bunch of worms. He was likely never again to meet such a challenge to his skill. Better make a brilliant and difficult cast even if he risked going away with an empty creel.

He had prepared a letter to Rousseau at Neuchâtel and came with it in his pocket. But he had stopped at the half-way inn at Brot for a glass of wine, and had chatted with the inn-keeper's daughter there, and she had scared him. Rousseau, she said, was besieged by an incredible number of people who came out of sheer curiosity to get a sight of him. He did not like to be stared at like a freak in a sideshow ("a man with two heads"), and besides, he was ill, really ill. Boswell began to wonder if his letter was particular enough. At Môtiers he rewrote it twice more before he sent it off. The final version made explicit reference to his rank in society (in the first he had called himself merely "a good Scot"), and took the risk of referring to Rousseau's illness. It was, he thought, really a masterpiece. "I shall ever preserve it as a proof that my soul can be sublime." And in fact he had wound a very effective lure. Rousseau had by this time received scores of letters praising his books and insisting on the unique claim of the writer of each to encroach on his time, but nobody before had told him that he was a man of singular merit, a man who *deserved* to meet him.

It is Boswell's virtue to have taught us the importance of circumstance, of setting. Generally he provided it himself, but in this case we can profitably add a good deal to what he set down, for he really did not know very much about Rousseau's history. In particular, he did not know how much drama there was in the timing of his visit.

Jean Jacques Rousseau was born in Geneva in 1712, and was consequently fifty-two years old when Boswell penetrated his retreat at Môtiers. After having spent the first thirty-eight years of his life in obscurity as footman, teacher, secretary, musical composer, copier of music, hack writer, and vagabond, he emerged into fame with a *Discourse on the Arts and Sciences,* in which he maintained with infectious eloquence the paradox that man in the savage state is better and happier than man in the state of advanced civilization. In three large works, *La Nouvelle Héloïse,*[1] *Émile,* and *Du Contrat social,* all published within a period

---

[1] "The New Héloïse," with reference to the famous twelfth-century lovers Abélard and Héloïse. Julie, the heroine of Rousseau's story, was seduced by her teacher, Saint-Preux, as Héloïse had been by Abélard.

of eighteen months in 1761–1762, he had presented revolutionary views on all the topics most important to humankind: government, education, religion, sexual morals, family life. The central story of *La Nouvelle Héloïse* is enacted in the impressive region of the Lake of Geneva, and in that book, to a greater extent than ever before in literature, natural scenery had been made expressive of intense and expansive emotion. Rousseau became at once the most powerful force in European letters, and consequently came into violent collision with both Church and State. For some years before the publication of *Émile* (a section of which, entitled "The Creed of the Savoyard Vicar," contains the fullest statement of his views on religion), he had been living in Paris, and he published the book there with the assurance of protection from powerful friends. It was promptly condemned, and an order issued for his arrest. With the connivance of the authorities, he fled to Yverdon, a dependency of the state of Berne. The religious doctrines of *Émile* were quite as repugnant to orthodox Calvinists as to Catholics. Geneva, his native city, condemned him, and brought pressure on Berne to order his expulsion. In July 1762 he took refuge in Môtiers, a small mountain village near Yverdon, but in the territory of Neuchâtel, which was at that time a principality of the King of Prussia. The governor was none other than our old friend Lord Marischal, who extended to the harassed author his own tactful friendship and the guarantee of Frederick's protection. Rousseau's gratitude was intense. Other people, he said, had been willing to serve him in their own fashion; Lord Marischal had served him as Rousseau wished to be served. He called him father, protector, friend, the only man on earth to whom he owed an obligation.

Boswell's account of his first meeting with Samuel Johnson, as he recorded it in 1763, is thinner than the account of the same scene in the *Life of Johnson*, but it differs from it only as a sketch differs from an easel picture. In 1763 Boswell's knowledge of the facts of Johnson's life was imperfect but it was representative; nothing he learned later forced him to revise fundamentally his impression of Johnson's character. But if he had ever published his interviews with Rousseau, as he talked of doing down to the end of his life, he would have placed them in a frame of reference very different from that of his original record. If we are to see Rousseau as Boswell saw him at the end of 1764, we must erase from our minds nearly everything we know about his private life. The *Confessions* were not yet written; many of the more scabrous de-

tails of Rousseau's past were unknown even to some of his closest associates. Some twenty years before he had taken as concubine an illiterate
French girl, Thérèse Le Vasseur, a servant at an inn. According to Rousseau's own account, which there seems no good reason to doubt, Thérèse,
between 1746 and 1755, bore him five children. All, immediately on
their birth, were placed in the Foundling Hospital in Paris. Rousseau's
justification at the time was that he was so wretchedly poor and Thérèse's
relations were such a bad lot that he thought the children would have
a better chance in the Foundling Hospital than in his own care. He *was*
very poor and he appears to have been justified in his judgement of
Thérèse's relations, but he probably also at that period of his life had
about the same kind of qualms in sending infants to the Foundling Hospital that a reasonably kind-hearted person today would feel in sending
kittens to the Humane Society. Later, he passed through an intense
moral struggle and emerged as the "savage philosopher," genuinely ascetic in practice as well as in theory. In 1761 he had caused a search to
be made for the abandoned children, but none of them could be found.
At that time he had told Madame de Luxembourg, who actually conducted the search, that he had ceased intercourse with Thérèse some time
since, though she remained on as his housekeeper and nurse, and was
treated with respect and affection.

At Môtiers Rousseau was briefly situated in what for him were nearly
ideal conditions. He suffered from a compulsion to quarrel sooner or
later with every one who put him under obligation, and at Môtiers he
was better able than at Paris to fend for himself. He could spend more
uninterrupted time at his desk there, an important consideration for a
man whose pen furnished all his income. As a recluse he could manage
somewhat better his chronic physical complaint, a constriction or con-
gestion of the urethra which caused frequent painful urination and kept
him at all times uneasy. At Môtiers, he could, for example, wear with
less embarrassing notice the Armenian caftan which he had found more
comfortable and convenient than breeches. And beyond all this, he loved
the country for its own sake, both as affording an outlet for his nature-
mysticism and as providing an opportunity for his hobby of botanizing.

In brief, when Boswell in his letter called Rousseau's house "the retreat of exquisite genius and elevated piety," he was not saying something
he did not believe, and he was probably not using the word "piety" in
an unduly sophisticated sense. He met Rousseau at the very height of

Rousseau's brief unclouded fame: saw him as a fearless and virtuous philosopher, persecuted by civil tyranny and ecclesiastical bigotry, a figure deserving the homage of the young, the generous, and the ardent.

It adds poignancy to our reading of the interviews if we realize how near the eclipse was. Rousseau could probably have gone on enjoying his retreat at Môtiers indefinitely if he had been willing to refrain from polemics, but Rousseau could as easily have refrained from breathing as from controversy. He published a reply to the Archbishop of Paris, in which he continued to air his religious views; he defiantly and publicly renounced his Genevan citizenship, and he encouraged a numerous party of supporters at Geneva to initiate a democratic revolt against the Government. A member of the Genevan Council named Tronchin had defended the condemnation of *Émile* in *Letters written from the Country,* and Rousseau had replied in *Letters Written from the Mountain,* an eloquent and inflammatory attack on the ruling oligarchy of the city. Though Boswell did not know it, he had himself played a small part in the unrolling action. A young French engraver named Boily whom he allowed to share his carriage from Strasbourg to Bâle was carrying advance copies of this work from the publisher to Rousseau. *Lettres écrites de la montagne* appeared in Geneva on 18 December 1764, three days after Boswell took final leave of Rousseau. Nine days after that (27 December 1764) Voltaire struck Rousseau down with a scurrilous anonymous pamphlet, *How the Citizens Feel,* ostensibly the work of a Genevan pastor. It published the story of the abandoned children, attributed Rousseau's complaint to venereal disease, and accused him of abusing Thérèse and of causing her mother's death by his heartless behaviour. Rousseau read this pamphlet on 31 December, and from that time was a broken man. The remaining fourteen years of his life were mainly spent in flights from persecutors, who seem, after 1765, to have been wholly imaginary. If Boswell had come only a trifle later, his interviews would probably have been far less interesting and valuable. There is not much chance that they would have contained, for example, anything like the gentle and charming domestic idyll in which they culminate.

Boswell had left England with the intention of visiting Voltaire and Rousseau, but there is no clear evidence that he had actually read any of Rousseau before the spring of 1764, at Utrecht. Then, a reading of "The Creed of the Savoyard Vicar" had helped him out of his depression by relaxing the severity of his religious convictions at the very time that

Gaubius and Hahn were giving him more comfortable notions of sexual morality. When he left Berlin towards the end of September, he counselled himself not merely to visit Rousseau but also to consult him concerning his melancholy; and to protect himself in the mean time from further sordid fiascos such as those of Dresden, he had invoked the sanctions of the as-yet-unmet Mentor. At Gotha he began to prepare for the interview by really digging into Rousseau's writings; and as he came down to Neuchâtel (a period of roughly six weeks), he read straight through the *Nouvelle Héloïse* and *Émile*. He had intended only to equip himself with enough knowledge to ask good questions—"prepare for Rousseau," say the memoranda over and over—but he experienced a violent conversion. He arrived at Môtiers not merely a patient, but also a disciple and a penitent.

Boswell managed to obtain no fewer than six interviews on five different days. Getting Rousseau to talk easily and at length was a most difficult and delicate negotiation. In his attitude towards talk, as in most things, Rousseau was the exact opposite of Johnson. Johnson hated writing, but was grateful for any excuse to prolong conversation. His talk was conscious art, and he was a giant at it. Rousseau was a giant when he had a pen in his hand, but he was shy, and he felt that talking was a waste of a valuable commodity. He was very temperamental: naturally warm-hearted, expansive, and charming, he might at any moment become bored with a visitor and turn him out.

ROUSSEAU. "I have seen the Scottish Highlanders in France. I love the Scots; not because my Lord Marischal is one of them but because he praises them. *You* are irksome to me. It's my nature. I cannot help it." BOSWELL. "Do not stand on ceremony with me." ROUSSEAU. "Go away."

His natural restlessness was increased by his physical complaint. He had given up doctors, but treated himself periodically with a probe or dilator. On one of their meetings, when Boswell was admitted for a moment only, he found him "sitting in great pain," the instrument either just used or actually *in situ*. A man suffering that kind of pain, a man who (as he told Boswell) needs a chamber-pot every other minute, presents great difficulties to an interviewer who wants to get a moral *summa*. Hence the six interviews. In every one of them Boswell had to fight for time: he was told that he must make his call short, he was told

to lay his watch on the table, he was dismissed brusquely, he was told
that if he came back he might not be admitted. But he managed by
good-humoured impudence to amuse Rousseau and to extend his time.

ROUSSEAU. "Now go away." BOSWELL. "Not yet. I will leave at three
o'clock. I have still five-and-twenty minutes." ROUSSEAU. "But I can't
give you five-and-twenty minutes." BOSWELL. "I shall be giving you even
more than that." ROUSSEAU. "What! of my own time? All the kings on
earth cannot give me my own time." BOSWELL. "But if I had stayed
till tomorrow, I should have had five-and-twenty minutes, and next day
another five-and-twenty. I am not taking those minutes. I am making
you a present of them." ROUSSEAU. "Oh! since you don't steal my money,
you are giving it to me." He then repeated part of a French satire ending with, "And whatever they leave you, they count as a gift." BOSWELL.
"Pray speak for me, Mademoiselle. [*To Rousseau.*] I have an excellent
friend here." ROUSSEAU. "Nay, but this is a league." BOSWELL. "No
league at all." Mademoiselle said, "Gentlemen, I will tell you the moment
the clock strikes."

It was, in fact, a league. Boswell had been thoughtfully attentive to
Thérèse, and he had a winning way with women of her class. As he
left after the second interview, she had told him that he could come
morning and evening, and he had complacently recorded in his memoranda, "She your friend." Thérèse was lonesome and bored; she liked
gay people, and Boswell promised diversion. Though she was illiterate
and rather stupid, she had a considerable idea of her own importance,
and she managed Rousseau more than he was willing to admit.

THÉRÈSE. "M. Rousseau has a high regard for you. The first time
you came, I said to him, 'That gentleman has an honest face. I am sure
you will like him.' " BOSWELL. "Mademoiselle is a good judge." THÉRÈSE.
"Yes, I have seen strangers enough in these twenty-two years that I
have been with M. Rousseau, and I assure you that I have sent many
of them packing simply because I did not fancy their way of talking."

He asked her how he could repay her, and with no coyness she suggested a garnet necklace. It was duly sent, the cost eight crowns.

Boswell never found time to write out a really finished version of
his interviews with Rousseau, and he recorded the conversation in his

imperfect French, but even with these limitations the interviews contain some of the finest specimens of his art.

ROUSSEAU. "When I speak of kings, I do not include the King of Prussia. He is a king *tout à fait unique*. That force of his! Sir, that's the great thing, to have force. Revenge even. You can always find matter to make something out of. But when force is lacking, when everything is small and split up, there's no hope." . . .
ROUSSEAU. "Sir, I have no liking for the world. I live here in a world of fantasies [*chimères*], and I cannot bear the world as it is." BOSWELL. "But when you come across other fantasts, are they not to your liking?" ROUSSEAU. "Why, Sir, they don't have the same fantasies that I do." . . .
BOSWELL. "Is it possible to live amongst other men and retain one's singularity?" ROUSSEAU. "Yes, I have done it." BOSWELL. "But to remain on good terms with them?" ROUSSEAU. "Oh, if you want to be a wolf, you must howl.—I attach very little importance to· books." BOSWELL. "Even to your own books?" ROUSSEAU. "Oh, they are just rigmarole." BOSWELL. "Now you are howling." ROUSSEAU. "When I put my trust in books, I was tossed about as you are—though it is rather by talking that you have been tossed. I had nothing stable here" *(striking his head)* "before I began to meditate." BOSWELL. "But you would not have meditated to such good purpose if you had not read." ROUSSEAU. "No. I should have meditated to better purpose if I had begun sooner." . . .
I said, "You say nothing in regard to a child's duties towards his parents. You tell us nothing of your Émile's father." ROUSSEAU. "Oh, he hadn't any. He didn't exist." . . .
I gave him very fully the character of Mr. Johnson. He said with force, "I should like that man. I should respect him. I would not disturb his principles if I could. I should like to see him, but from a distance, for fear he might maul me." I told him how averse Mr. Johnson was to write, and how he had his levee. "Ah," said he, "I understand. He is a man who enjoys holding forth." I told him Mr. Johnson's *bon mot* upon the innovators: that Truth is a cow that will yield them no more milk, and so they are gone to milk the bull. He said, "He would detest me. He would say, 'Here is a corrupter, a man who comes here to milk the bull.' "

Boswell showed some rashness in repeating Johnson's witticism and Rousseau great acuteness in appropriating it, for it was precisely with reference to Rousseau and Hume that Johnson had made the remark.

Boswell's patience and tact paid off so well that on the last day he got himself invited to dinner. In his account of this dinner in Rousseau's kitchen, he gives us a more detailed and charming domestic sketch than can be found anywhere else in the whole mass of records left by Rousseau's visitors. Thérèse was an excellent cook—Boswell listed all the dishes. Rousseau was unusually vivacious. Dinner had been set early to allow time for talk. When Boswell forgot himself and became too ceremonious—"May I help you to this?" "May I help myself to some more of that?"—Rousseau replied, "No, Sir, I can help myself," or "Is your arm long enough?" This led to a long discussion on manners, authority, and respect, culminating in this delightful *genre* piece:

ROUSSEAU. "Do you like cats?" BOSWELL. "No."[1] ROUSSEAU. "I was sure of it. It is my test of character. There you have the despotic instinct of men. They do not like cats because the cat is free and will never consent to become a slave. He will do nothing to your order, as the other animals do." BOSWELL. "Nor a hen, neither." ROUSSEAU. "A hen would obey your orders if you could make her understand them. But a cat will understand you perfectly and not obey." BOSWELL. "But a cat is ungrateful and treacherous." ROUSSEAU. "No. That's all untrue. A cat is an animal that can be very much attached to you: he will do anything you please out of friendship. I have a cat here. He has been brought up with my dog and they play together. The cat will give the dog a tap with his tail, and the dog will offer him his paw." He described the playing of his dog and cat with exquisite eloquence, as a fine painter draws a small piece. He put some victuals on a trencher and made his dog dance round it. He sung to him a lively air with a sweet voice and great taste. "You see the ballet. It is not a gala performance but a pretty one all the same." I think the dog's name was Sultan. He stroked and fed him, and with an arch air said, "He is not much *respected*, but he gets well looked after."

But it cannot be too many times repeated that no tête-à-tête between Boswell and a great man is a mere miscellaneous collection of striking remarks. There is association in all such conversations, and the association is Boswell's. In this case he had come with the intention of making Rous-

[1] Boswell in fact had a positive antipathy to cats strong enough to make him uneasy all the time he was in the same room with one. Readers of the *Life of Johnson* will remember how this adds spice to the delicious account of Dr. Johnson and his cat Hodge (Collection between March and April 1783: Hill-Powell ed. iv. 197).

seau his confessor, and the conversations throughout show him trying, in
the face of alarmingly resourceful resistance, to manoeuvre Rousseau into
the box. Rousseau was on pins and needles to get back to his desk. Unlike
Johnson, he disliked the role of personal mentor, and Boswell's letter had
warned him what to expect.

In the first interview Boswell probably hoped merely to make a favourable impression and to establish a re-entry. Perhaps taking his cue from
Milord Edouard Bomston in the *Nouvelle Héloïse* (Rousseau's own
sketch of what he conceived the ideal English character to be), he
eschewed formal politeness and adopted an air of bluff and ingenuous
frankness. Within a few minutes after his admission to the sanctuary, he
was seizing Rousseau by the hand and thumping him on the shoulder.
That worked very well. As soon as he was sure that he had really pleased
him, he mentioned Lord Marischal and Lord Marischal's note. If Rousseau had been suspicious, Boswell would have been in an awkward position, for he had forgotten to bring the note with him. But Rousseau waved
all doubts aside and spoke of the old hero with tender affection. After
that, he could hardly refuse Boswell one more visit, for he had let him in
on his own credentials and now owed him something on Lord Marischal's.
Also, Boswell reminded him of the promise he had made to Lord Marischal to write the life of the Scots patriot Andrew Fletcher of Saltoun, and
he had asked Boswell if he would give him materials—another excuse to
Boswell for coming back. Boswell was chased away, but he had inserted
his wedge firmly.

Rousseau monopolized the second conversation (4 December) with
a long and brilliant character of the Abbé de Saint-Pierre, and Boswell
deservedly lost his chance when he was forced to admit that he had not
read Rousseau's *Plan for Perpetual Peace Drawn from the Papers of the
Abbé de Saint-Pierre*. Rousseau smilingly sent him off with a presentation
copy. But he paused at the door for some gallant attention to Thérèse and
got her assurance, already mentioned, that he could come back any time
he chose. He wrote in his memoranda the next morning, "This day be
serious with Rousseau. Learn."

At the third interview (5 December), accordingly, he began confessing almost as soon as he had crossed the threshold.

I told him how I had turned Roman Catholic and had intended to
hide myself in a convent in France. He said, "What folly! I too was

Catholic in my youth. I changed, and then I changed back again. I returned to Geneva and was readmitted to the Protestant Church. I went again among Catholics, and said to them, 'I am no longer one of you,' and I got on with them excellently." I stopped him in the middle of the room and I said to him, "But tell me sincerely, are you a Christian?" I looked at him with a searching eye. His countenance was no less animated. Each stood steady and watched the other's looks. He struck his breast, and replied, "Yes. I pride myself on being one." . . . BOSWELL. "But tell me, do you suffer from melancholy?" ROUSSEAU. "I was born placid. I have no natural disposition to melancholy. My misfortunes have infected me with it." BOSWELL. "I, for my part, suffer from it severely. And how can I be happy, I who have done so much evil?" ROUSSEAU. "Begin your life anew. God is good, for he is just. Do good. You will cancel all the debt of evil. Say to yourself in the morning, 'Come now, I am going to *pay off* so much evil.' Six well-spent years will pay off all the evil you have committed." BOSWELL. "But what do you think of cloisters, penances, and remedies of that sort?" ROUSSEAU. "Mummeries, all of them, invented by men. Do not be guided by men's judgements or you will find yourself tossed to and fro perpetually. Do not base your life on the judgements of others; first, because they are as likely to be mistaken as you are, and further because you cannot know that they are telling you their true thoughts: they may be impelled by motives of interest or convention to talk to you in a way not corresponding to what they really think." BOSWELL. "Will *you*, Sir, assume direction of me?" ROUSSEAU. [*Recovering himself and instantly on the defensive.*] "I cannot. I can be responsible only for myself." BOSWELL. "But I shall come back." ROUSSEAU. "I don't promise to see you. I am in pain. I need a chamber-pot every other minute." BOSWELL. "Yes, you will see me." ROUSSEAU. "Be off; and a good journey to you."

Out; and the confession hardly begun. Was he to be denied the opportunity to tell about Sally Forrester and Jeanie Wells? About Mrs. Love and Mrs. Brooke, about Mrs. Heron and Peggy Doig, about his illegitimate son? About Louisa and the street-girls and the soldier's wife at Berlin? He had gained some wonderful remarks, but how could he resume the conversation? Rousseau, it was only too clear, was just not going to listen to an extended confession. But could he resist *reading* it? He had been unable not to read Boswell's letter to him. The correct method undoubtedly. Boswell would write a confessional sketch of his life, leave the document with Rousseau, go away for a week, and then come back for reproof and counsel. He returned to the inn and wrote furiously all afternoon, the final result being the sketch with which this book opens, which he sent to Rousseau with a covering letter:

If you can, I beseech you to help me. I am leaving you a sketch of my life. It is hastily written. In it you have merely the facts; had I entered on feelings, I should have been too diffuse. You do not like to be disturbed by any one's company, but perhaps you may admit my papers. After all that I have done, I still have my health, I still have for the most part a very healthy mind, I have a soul that incites me to be a man. Oh, vouchsafe to save a true Scot! Lord Marischal is old. That illustrious Scottish oak must soon fall. You love that ancient country. Save a sapling from it. . . .
You will have the goodness to return my sketch.
During my fit of melancholy at Utrecht, I made the acquaintance of a young lady, very rich and of the first rank. I behaved in such a way as to be honoured with the reputation of being a philosopher. Oh, how deceitful appearances are! If you wish to amuse yourself by reading some pieces written by that young lady, you will find them in a little packet apart. I should very much like to have your opinion of her character.

December night had fallen outside, it was raining, and he had a considerable stretch of mountain road to traverse without a guide. But he paused to write a vaunting letter to John Johnston:

I feel an enthusiasm beyond expression. Good heaven! Am I so elevated? Where is gloom? Where is discontent? Where are all the little vexations of the world? O Johnston! wert thou but here! I am in a beautiful wild valley surrounded by immense mountains. I am just setting out for Neuchâtel. . . . I am to be alone on horseback in a dark winter night, while the earth is covered with snow. My present sentiments give me a force and a vigour like the lion in the desert.

At six o'clock he mounted his little horse, and with the wind roaring through the desolate rocks and the rain flooding his path, rode down the Val de Travers. At the half-way house at Brot, three hours later, he turned in for the night. He and the host's daughter—she who had scared him with the tales of how difficult Rousseau was—sang together a long popular ballad versifying the story of the *Nouvelle Héloïse*. "Though the song is written in a ludicrous style, the recollection of the events made me cry."
At Neuchâtel he received a great packet of letters which had been forwarded from Geneva: one from Lord Auchinleck granting him per-

mission to go to Italy for four months, none from Belle de Zuylen. He went to call on Belle's former governess, Mlle. Prevost, who had supervised Belle's education for ten years and had taken her to Geneva. Mlle. Prevost had a portrait of her charge which revived all his tender feelings. "I loved her." But when she showed him a letter in which Belle referred complacently to the "shocking" tales she had written and called Constant d'Hermenches her "generous friend," his love changed to jealousy and disapproval. "A vapourish, unprincipled girl. Glad not to have her."

He stopped overnight at Colombier, where Lord Marischal had had his residence while he was governor, and where part of his queer family (a Turk and a Kalmuck) were still quartered. If some one had told him that the manor-house across the road from the *Château* would not many years hence receive Belle de Zuylen as its mistress, he would have been incredulous but perhaps not much distressed. For the fine fresh lass of his amorous fantasies had actually turned up. The inn at Colombier was kept by the father of Emet-Ulla's maid, Lisette, and Lisette's sister, Caton, had served his dinner. When he asked her what seems to have been his stock question to pretty maids at inns, how would she like to go to Scotland with him? she had instantly taken him up. She was married, with two pretty children, but she had never loved her husband, and he had deserted her. She was so eager to leave Colombier, she said, that she would accompany Boswell anywhere, with no stipulations. He was gratified but taken aback, for his fantasies had not envisaged anything quite so permanent, especially with an Italian tour in prospect. He declined to close at once, but said he would write back if on consideration he found the arrangement suitable. That he did give it some thought is shown by a memorandum of topics to discuss with Rousseau which he drew up a day or two later: "Suppose not slave to appetites, more than in marriage, but will have Swiss girl, amiable, &c. Quite adventure. [Would name my natural sons] Marischal Boswell, Rousseau Boswell. Anxious to see if children sound ere marry. Hurt nobody." But, as we shall see, when he actually got to discuss the topic of sexual relations with Rousseau, his scheme had become much more comprehensive. Poor Caton is never mentioned again in the journal or the surviving letters.

After spending three days in Yverdon and the vicinity visiting Mr. Brown's father-in-law, Sir James Kinloch, and his connexions, he headed back (14 December) for Môtiers. This time his route lay over summits deep in snow, and he needed a guide. When he called, Rousseau was undergoing, or had just undergone, the treatment of the probe, and would see him only for a moment. But he had read the sketch.

ROUSSEAU. "I have read your memoir. . . . Come back in the afternoon. But put your watch on the table." BOSWELL. "For how long?" ROUSSEAU. "A quarter of an hour, and no longer." BOSWELL. "Twenty minutes." ROUSSEAU. "Be off with you!—Ha! Ha!" Notwithstanding the pain he was in, he was touched with my singular sally and laughed most really. He had a gay look immediately.

Returning at four, Boswell allowed no time to be lost. He had run over in his mind the topics he wished to have Rousseau discuss, and had jotted down a list: suicide, hypochondria, concubinage, Scots familiarity, his future career. When Rousseau inveighed against books (the passage is quoted above), Boswell said that but for the "Savoyard Vicar" he would never have had such agreeable ideas of the Christian religion. But he was bothered by questions of practical conduct, concerning which that nobly simple document was perhaps a trifle vague.

BOSWELL. "Morals appear to me uncertain. For instance, I should like to have thirty women. Could I not satisfy that desire?" ROUSSEAU. "No!" BOSWELL. "Why not?" ROUSSEAU. "Ha! Ha! If Mademoiselle were not here, I would give you a most ample reason why not." BOSWELL. "But consider: if I am rich, I can take a number of girls; I get them with child [*Thérèse at this point gets up and leaves.* ROUSSEAU. "See now, you are driving Mademoiselle out of the room."], propagation is thus increased. I give them dowries, and I marry them off to good peasants who are very happy to have them. Thus they become wives at the same age as would have been the case if they had remained virgins, and I, on my side, have had the benefit of enjoying a great variety of women." ROUSSEAU. "Oh, you will be landed in jealousies, betrayals, and treachery." BOSWELL. "But cannot I follow the Oriental usage?" ROUSSEAU. "In the Orient the women are kept shut up, and that means keeping slaves. And, mark you, their women do nothing but harm, whereas ours do much good, for they do a great deal of work." BOSWELL. "I should like to follow the example of the old Patriarchs, worthy men whose memory I hold in respect."

It is out at last, and it is a real question, not an ingenious trap for a memorable pronouncement, like "If, Sir, you were shut up in a castle and a new-born child with you, what would you do?" He has presented his persistent day-dream of male potency under its three recurring guises: Feudal, Oriental, Biblical. He was sexually very vigorous, and his habit of self-admiration caused him to regard his potency as almost inspired. He wanted some respected moralist to convince him that a man with such a gift might exercise it innocently. Though he was drawn more than he realized to the unidyllic commerce of the streets (precisely because, among other things, it *was* brutish, sordid, dangerous, and forbidden), his dream of felicity was a vigorous but innocent pastoral idyll: himself a grave and potent young Patriarch surrounded by thirty handsome concubines and an unspecified number of sturdy children. If Rousseau had not created this idyll in his mind, he had at least done much to give it warmth and the feeling of virtue.

The great maxim was to follow nature. Well, what *was* Nature in the matter of sexual relations? Was man naturally monogamous or was he a polygynous animal who had been perverted by civilization? The Abbé de Saint-Pierre, whose arrangements Rousseau had described without con- demnation, had followed a program not unlike that proposed by Boswell. Boswell was hardly to blame for inferring that a return to nature meant literally a return to one of those more primitive forms of social organization which Rousseau had depicted with such nostalgic fervour, for the majority of Rousseau's readers have come away from his books with just that im- pression. Rousseau's poetry has always been more powerful than his dialectic. But actually he had never meant to teach a literal return either to Tahiti or to the Age of the Patriarchs, and he promptly gave Boswell his true doctrine. Modern man cannot escape from his heritage, but he can return to Nature *within* his civilization, that is, can so change his will (or have it changed) that he can recover the moral balance that constituted the happiness of more primitive times. Especially, he must restore the true equality of men. And that, Rousseau had come to believe, was more likely to be accomplished by the authority of a just state than by religion or man's instinct to pity. In spite of his own highly individualistic be- haviour and his progressive disillusion with existing governments, he really wished to convince people that their salvation lay in enlightened citizen- ship. "But are you not a citizen? You must not pick and choose, one law here and another law there; you must take the laws of your own society. Do your duty as a citizen and if you hold fast, you will win respect. I should not talk about it, but I would do it." He went on, with reference to Jean Heron:

ROUSSEAU. "And as for your lady, when you go back to Scotland, you will say, 'Madam, such conduct is against my conscience, and there shall be no more of it.' She will applaud you; if not, she is to be despised." BOSWELL. "But suppose her passion is still lively, and she threatens to tell her husband what has happened unless I agree to continue our intrigue?" ROUSSEAU. "In the first place, she will not tell him. In the second, you have no right to do evil for the sake of good." BOSWELL. "True. None the less, I can imagine some very embarrassing situations. And pray tell me, how can I expiate the evil I have done?" ROUSSEAU. "O Sir, there is no expiation of evil except good."

Boswell maintained his doctrine of atonement through suffering, but almost immediately swung the conversation back to his main topic. One must take the laws of society: very well, of what society? "When I get to France and Italy, may I not indulge in the gallantries usual to those countries, where husbands do not resent your making love to their wives? Nay, should I not be happier as the citizen of such a nation?" Rousseau was forced to invoke sanctions which can hardly be derived from notions of political justice:

ROUSSEAU. "They are corpses. Do you want to be a corpse?" (He was right.) BOSWELL. "But tell me, has a virtuous man any true advantage, is he really better off than a man given up to sensuality?" ROUSSEAU. "We cannot doubt that we are spiritual beings; and when the soul escapes from this prison, from this flesh, the virtuous man will find things to his liking. He will enjoy the contemplation of happy souls, nobly employed. He will say, 'I have already lived a life like that.' Whereas those who experience nothing but the vile passions which have their origin in the body, will be dissatisfied by the spectacle of pleasures which they have no means of enjoying."

It is hard to believe that the allotted fifteen minutes had not already been stretched to something nearer an hour, but Boswell went on to one more of his topics, his choice of a profession. This soon shifted to the more basic question, how could he get on easier terms with his father? Rousseau said that their present joint activities, such as supervising the planting at Auchinleck, were too serious. They should have a common amusement that would put them on an equal footing, for example, shooting. "A shot is missed and a joke is made of it without any infringement of respect. You enjoy a freedom which you take for granted." Shrewd and excellent advice, but Lord Auchinleck had no amusements beyond planting and the Greek and Roman classics. The conversation having now become decent, Thérèse came back, Boswell was invited to dinner next day, and he and Thérèse went off together to distribute charity to a poor woman with a great many children. And he drew up another list of topics to discuss.

The last day (15 December), the day of the dinner, was the most delightful of the whole series. Rousseau was gay, discouraged inquiries about his health, and did not begin to fidget for two hours and a half. They talked on parents and children, *The Spectator* (Rousseau praised it but expressed dislike of its allegories), Samuel Johnson, Corsica, cats, religion, and Voltaire. But the subject which Boswell's record develops at greatest length is that of respect: the life-long jangle in Boswell's nature between feudal pride and the desire to meet all men at their own level, even to play the clown. Rousseau's pungent simplicity, though it had delighted him, had also shocked him, and he definitely did not agree with his egalitarian notions.

ROUSSEAU. "I confess that I like to be respected, but only in matters of importance." BOSWELL. "You are so simple. I expected to find you quite different from this: the Great Rousseau. . . . I expected to find you enthroned and talking with a grave authority." ROUSSEAU. "Uttering oracles? Ha! Ha! Ha!" BOSWELL. "Yes, and that I should be much in awe of you. And really your simplicity might lay you open to attack: it might be said, 'M. Rousseau does not make himself sufficiently respected.' In Scotland, I assure you, a very different tone must be taken to escape from the shocking familiarity which is prevalent in that country. Upon my word, I cannot put up with it. Should I not be justified in forestalling it by fighting a duel with the first man who should treat me so, and thus live at peace for the rest of my life?" ROUSSEAU. "No. That is not allowable. It is not right to stake one's life on such follies. Life is given us for objects of importance. Pay no heed to what such men say. They will get tired of talking to a man who does not answer them." BOSWELL. "If you were in Scotland, they would begin at the very start by calling you Rousseau; or they would say, 'Jean Jacques, how are ye?' with the utmost familiarity." ROUSSEAU. "That is perhaps a good thing." BOSWELL. "But they would say, 'Poh, Jean-Jacques, pourquoi toutes ces fantaisies? Vous êtes un joli homme d'avoir tant de prétentions. Allons, allons, venez vivre dans la société comme les autres.' And they would say it to you with a sourness which I am quite unable to imitate for you." ROUSSEAU. "Oh, that's bad." (There he felt the thistle, when it was applied to himself on the tender part. It was just as if I had said, "Hoot, Johnie Rousseau man, what for hae ye sae mony figmagairies?[1] Ye're a bonny man indeed to mauk siccan a wark; set ye up. Canna ye just live like ither fowk?" . . .) BOSWELL. "I have leanings towards despotism, let me tell you. On our estate I am like an ancient baron, and I insist on respect from the tenants." ROUSSEAU. "But when you see an old man with white hair, do you, as a young man, have no feelings at all? Have you no respect for age?" BOSWELL. "Yes. I have even on many occasions been most affable. I have talked quite freely with the tenants." ROUSSEAU. "Yes, you forgot yourself and became a man." BOSWELL. "But I was sorry for it afterwards. I used to think, I have lowered myself." ROUSSEAU. "Ha! Ha! Ha!"

The lists of topics to be discussed show that Boswell had intended to tell Rousseau about his poems and the seven hundred pages of journal he had written, but either he found no way to introduce them, or Rousseau made no significant comment. In the final five-and-twenty minutes which he extorted from Rousseau,[2] he did, however, refer in highly interesting fashion to another of his accomplishments:

BOSWELL. "In the old days I was a great mimic. I could imitate every one I saw. But I have left it off." ROUSSEAU. "It is a dangerous talent, for it compels one to seize upon all that is small in a character." BOSWELL. "True. But I assure you there was a nobleness about my art, I carried mimicry to such a point of perfection. I was a kind of virtuoso. When I espied any singular character, I would say, 'He must be added to my collection.' " He laughed with all his nerves: "You are an odd character."

By now three o'clock had struck and Thérèse came to say that Boswell's guide was waiting for him. Rousseau embraced him and kissed him.

ROUSSEAU. "Good-bye. You are a fine fellow." BOSWELL. "You have shown me great goodness. But I deserved it." ROUSSEAU. "Yes. You are malicious, but 'tis a pleasant malice, a malice I don't dislike. Write and tell me how you are." BOSWELL. "And you will write to me?" . . . ROUS-SEAU. "Yes." BOSWELL. "Good-bye. If you are still living in seven years, I shall return to Switzerland from Scotland to see you." ROUSSEAU. "Do so. We shall be old acquaintances." BOSWELL. "One word more. Can I feel sure that I am held to you by a thread, even if of the finest? By a hair?" *(Seizing a hair of my head.)* ROUSSEAU. "Yes. Remember always that

[1] Whims, crotchets.
[2] See above, p. 169.

there are points at which are souls are bound." BOSWELL. "It is enough. I, with my melancholy, I who often look on myself as a despicable being, as a good-for-nothing creature who should make his exit from life—I shall be upheld for ever by the thought that I am bound to M. Rousseau. Good-bye. Bravo! I shall *live* to the end of my days." ROUSSEAU. "That is undoubtedly a thing one must do. Good-bye."

The seemingly spontaneous exit-lines had in fact been planned, perhaps rehearsed. In his list of topics to discuss, Boswell had written, "I tell you that the idea of being bound even by the finest thread to the most enlightened of philosophers, the noblest of souls, will always uphold me, all my life." And the sentiment about living to the end of one's days was lifted from a passage in *Émile,* in which Rousseau urges his reader to dismiss his doctors and live according to Nature: "Suffer; die or get well; but in any case *live* to your last hour." Rousseau had pretended not to recognize his own work, but he had played up very prettily to the figure of the bound souls.

At the inn the landlady noticed the seriousness of Boswell's expression and thought he was crying. As he rode back past Rousseau's house, Thérèse, who was standing at the door to catch one more glimpse of the scarlet and gold, waved and cried, *"Bon voyage.* Write to us." And James Boswell rode and scrambled back to Yverdon, wondering how the day he had just passed would appear to his mind some years hence.

It would appear very different before even one year had run its course. His own figure of being joined by a thread was more accurate than Rousseau's of being lashed at a number of points. The thread was religion. Rousseau's doctrines in 1764 received his full assent and probably always formed a submerged element in the orthodox creed to which he later subscribed. He was surprised on his return to England to hear Johnson call Rousseau a bad man who ought to be transported to the colonies; and years later he let Rousseau off gently in a book which is not remarkable for charity towards free-thinkers, Protestant non-conformists, and liberal Anglicans. "I cannot help admiring [the *Profession de foi du vicaire savoyard*]," he wrote in the *Life of Johnson,* "as the performance of a man full of sincere reverential submission to Divine mystery, though beset with perplexing doubts: a state of mind to be viewed with pity rather than with anger." To scepticism either of the ironic or the hard and destructive sort he soon grew bitterly hostile, but Rousseau's tender and devout scepticism never became uncongenial to his mind. Rousseau worshipped where he could not prove; he made religion principally worship. And Rousseau's further tendency to make morality a passion probably received a permanent assent in Boswell's heart even though he soon came to repudiate it formally. Like Rousseau, he was an unbridled egoist. A gospel justifying originality and spontaneity, a gospel proclaiming the goodness of instinct and impulse—at least in his own case—would always have his sympathy.

There were other Rousseauistic influences, but they were much more temporary. In his developed character Boswell was the kind of man who, as he once said, could properly enjoy a prospect of the country only if he saw it across Piccadilly. Yet in this period of conjunction his soul lighted up with fire from the neighbouring luminary. As he stood in urban scarlet and gold by the side of the pastoral Areuse, he transferred his feelings to the landscape and received them back quite in the mode of Saint-Preux: the rocks frowned and the pines clustered as they had never before done in his experience. And he carried away a fading glow. The idyllic pictures of the life of the *prisca gens mortalium* in Corsica which he was soon to draw are suffused with the unmistakable tender light of Jean Jacques. The Hebridean journal written six years later has nothing whatever of that gleam.

So, too, in *An Account of Corsica* he used an amount of Rousseauistic political vocabulary that must have made him uncomfortable after 1789, as it did Johnson at the time the book was published. He was essentially a Tory, aristocrat, and monarchist, with almost mediaeval notions of subordination—anything but an egalitarian. What delighted him in the Corsican social scene was really its unreformed feudalism, not its approximation to the state of nature.

And Rousseau's sensual mysticism, his exaltation of the sexual passion into a kind of religious aspiration, was not merely too refined for Boswell's practice, it was also out of accord with his real principles. He once said that sexual intercourse made him humane, polite, and generous; he even associated love and music with adoration; but one feels that if he had been as acute and honest in theorizing as he was in observing, his reasons would have been common-sense and physiological, not mystical. His characteristic attitude towards sex was direct and uncomplicated in the extreme, and sorted ill with Rousseau's refinements. *La Nouvelle Héloïse* inflamed his imagination with visions of passionate romantic love and at the same time filled him with disgust for venal and casual fruition; the anti-Rousseauists will say it is no accident that just at this time the memoranda contain the only clear indications in Boswell's surviving papers of a recourse to what, in one of the drafts for his Sketch, he called "the fatal practice."

But our realization of Boswell's fundamental lack of capacity for Rousseauism should not make us doubt the sincerity of his discipleship in 1764. He came to Môtiers as to an oracle, and more. The Master, he hoped, would not merely tell him what virtue was, but would also fill him with virtue; would transform his will and save him from vacillation and the bleak hunger of self-denial. Rousseau, that much maligned man, gave him austere and lofty counsel, but it had no effect on him at all. It is only fair to add that, so far as sins of appetite were concerned, nobody in the long run had any effect on him, not even Johnson. He would always attach himself to great and good men; he would always sincerely seek their counsel; he would always, except for two brief shining eras of his life, yield to sensual temptation with no more than routine contrition. When the Holland campaign petered out in the swamps of misery, the shape of Boswell's future was evident. He would always be a weak good man.

CHAPTER

XII

Boswell liked Lausanne ("a fine, airy, agreeable place"), but he detested Geneva for its Calvinism, its republican manners, and its bitter denigration of Rousseau. One great compensation was to find letters from Rousseau and the Margrave of Baden-Durlach waiting for him there. Karl Friedrich's was very gracious: it was in his own hand and in English, and asked Boswell to write freely and without ceremony. Rousseau's was hardly more than a covering letter for another which Boswell was to deliver to Alexandre Deleyre, a friend of Rousseau's at Parma, but the letter to Deleyre was open, and in it Boswell read a very flattering characterization of himself. Since Rousseau later told Deleyre that he had not meant for Boswell to see what he had written, we may conclude that the characterization was sincere. Elated with these spoils, Boswell turned at once to schemes of further conquest.

"Voltaire! Rousseau! immortal names!"—so Temple had written as far back as 1759, proposing that Boswell and he should go together to Geneva to study. Lord Auchinleck had considered the proposal most inappropriate, but Boswell had clung with his usual tenacity to the idea of meeting Europe's two greatest authors. In the previous April, at Utrecht, he had confidently written, "I shall visit Rousseau and Voltaire," and he continued to repeat the assertion in his letters and journal. Less than two weeks after he had parted from Rousseau—on the day before Christmas, 1764, to be exact—a coach deposited him at Voltaire's door. He had laid siege to the philosopher of Môtiers in the glory of scarlet and gold; he approached the poet of Ferney in the milder effulgence of sea-green and silver. And he came with a conventional and proper letter of introduction (it was from Constant d'Hermenches) in his hand.

For Voltaire was a very different kind of celebrity from either the

uncouth moralist of the Temple or the prickly hermit of Môtiers. To begin
with, he was far more famous and powerful than either of them. In
English-speaking countries at the present day the only works of Voltaire
that come readily to the mind of the ordinary reader are the short prose
tales like *Candide,* but in 1764 one thought of him first of all as epic and
dramatic poet (he wrote over fifty plays, among them some of the most
admired tragedies in the French classical tradition); then also as historian,
philosopher, critic, and controversialist. His works, as collected a few years
after Boswell's visit, ran to more than forty volumes. His entire life had
been spent in sniping from not-too-precarious hide-outs at the political
and religious orthodoxy of his country. He was a deist, but a deist of the
hard-minded variety, and never passed up an opportunity to mock at all
particular scriptures and all particular religions. Ferney was only four
miles from Geneva, but it was on French soil. There Voltaire could enjoy
both the social liberty of France and the political liberty of Geneva; and
he had prepared for the possibility that these states might turn on him
simultaneously by purchasing other houses in the Canton of Vaud and the
Kingdom of Sardinia, both close at hand. His writings and his shrewd
business dealings had brought him great wealth, and he lived in a *château*
like a seigneur, amidst a constant crowd of guests. Boswell had no reason
to fear that he would not be admitted. Yet he had some bad moments.

Not one but two or three footmen met him at the door and showed him
into a very elegant room. One of them took the letter and returned with
the statement (obviously given with pleasure) that M. de Voltaire was
abed and that he was very much annoyed if he was disturbed while lying
down. Anxiety on Boswell's part. Several ladies and gentlemen came into
the room and engaged him in conversation. At last the door of Voltaire's
apartment opened and Boswell, surveying the septuagenarian Monarch of
Letters with eager attention, found him just as he had imagined him from
his many portraits: skeleton-thin, in slate-blue dressing gown cut like a
great-coat, toothless, with a long nose, and with eyes of unearthly brilliance
peering out of his three-knotted wig, under a nightcap. He received Boswell with dignity and an air of the world, sat erect in a chair, simpering
as he spoke, and Boswell was in conversation with the most renowned man
of letters in the world. "He was not in spirits, nor I neither. All I presented
was the 'foolish face of wondering praise.'"

His difficulty in talking with Rousseau consisted merely in getting
admitted: once there he had topics enough to present. But this was no

Mentor. Boswell came to Voltaire with no confession to make, expected no magic pronouncement that would enable him to live to the end of his days. This was merely a great man, from whom, in a short space of time, he had to elicit just as many memorable remarks as he could. Voltaire, in spite of not being in spirits, was very obliging and produced a pretty series of those dry ironic jokes which were his forte: painting will never succeed in Scotland because a man cannot paint well when his feet are cold; Boswell and Johnson may go to the Hebrides if they do not insist on his accompanying them; he no longer speaks English because in order to speak English one must place one's tongue between one's teeth and he has lost his teeth; *un chargé d'affaires n'est guère chargé*.[1]

Dinner was announced. Voltaire did not dine with the company, and as the gates of Geneva were closed at five, Boswell had to hurry away after eating without seeing more of his host. It was altogether rather disappointing. He had met Voltaire, he had talked with him half an hour, and he had not got him to speak on a single important subject.

Next day—Christmas—in Geneva was a duplication with differences of the afternoon at Môtiers when he wrote the "Sketch of My Life." To put Voltaire properly to the question he would have to get invited to stay overnight under the great man's roof. A letter was obviously called for, but it would have to be very different in tone and approach from the document that had sapped Rousseau's defences. Imagine trying to captivate the agile and mocking intelligence of Voltaire with that kind of ingenuous self-revelation! It would have to be brief, it would have to be witty, it had better be impudent and a little off-colour. And since Voltaire prided himself on his English (Boswell had got him to speak English in spite of his jest about the missing teeth), it had better be in English. And it would have to be directed ostensibly to the lady of Voltaire's house, his niece Mme. Denis. She had been kind and attentive to Boswell at dinner, and fortunately she spoke—or at least read—English too.

I must beg your interest, Madam, in obtaining for me a very great favour from M. de Voltaire. I intend to have the honour of returning to Ferney Wednesday or Thursday. The gates of this sober city shut at a most early, I had very near said a most absurd, hour, so that one is obliged to post away after dinner before the illustrious landlord has had time to shine upon his guests. Besides, I believe M. de Voltaire is in opposition to

[1] An untranslatable pun on two meanings of the word *chargé:* "put in charge" and "overloaded." Literally, "an ambassador's substitute is hardly overworked."

our sun, for he rises in the evening. Yesterday he shot forth some rays. Some bright sparks fell from him. I am happy to have seen so much. But I greatly wish to behold him in full blaze.

Is it then possible, Madam, that I may be allowed to lodge one night under the roof of M. de Voltaire? I am a hardy and a vigorous Scot. You may mount me to the highest and coldest garret. I shall not even refuse to sleep upon two chairs in the bedchamber of your maid. I saw her pass through the room where we sat before dinner.

I beg you may let me know if the favour which I ask is granted, that I may bring a nightcap with me.

He sent the letter off by an express and dashed out to church, but the service was over and he heard only a voluntary on the organ. Back came the express with an answer: it was in English and in Voltaire's hand, though it professed to be from Mme. Denis: "You will do us much honour and pleasure. We have few beds, but you will not sleep on two chairs. My uncle, though very sick, hath guessed at your merit. I know it more, because I have seen you longer." He spent the rest of the day in high spirits at letters and journal, even passing up his dinner. One of the letters, in spite of his recent assertion that he was glad to be done with her, was to Belle de Zuylen. This time, instead of using the agreed clandestine route, he sent his reproaches, sealed, in a letter straight to her father.

I wrote you a long letter from Berlin. I gave you such advice as I imagined would help make you happy. You made me no reply. I feared I had spoken of your conduct in terms that were too wounding. I wrote to you from Dessau to tender you my excuses. Once more you did not write.

Mademoiselle, I am proud, and I shall be proud always. You ought to be flattered by my attachment. I know not if I ought to have been equally flattered by yours. A man who has a mind and a heart like mine is rare. A woman with many talents is not so rare. Perhaps I blame you unreasonably. Perhaps you are able to give me an explanation of your conduct towards me. O Zélide! I believed you to be without the weaknesses of your sex. I had almost come to count upon your heart. I had almost—

He returned to Ferney on the 27th, this time in his flowered velvet, and found himself very genteelly lodged. "My room was handsome. The bed, purple cloth lined with white quilted satin; the chimney piece, marble, and ornamented above with the picture of a French toilet." Every guest was master of his own room, and a trusty servant laid a fire and set out candles as they were called for. "Everything put me fully in mind of a decent Scots house, and I thought surely the master of the family must go to church and do as public institutions require; and then I made my transition to the real master, the celebrated Voltaire, the infidel, the author of so many deistical pieces and of the *Pucelle d'Orléans*."

Voltaire came out for a few minutes before dinner but did not dine; when the company returned from dinner, he had gone back to his room. The company amused themselves: "Some sat snug by the fire, some chatted, some sung, some played the guitar, some played at shuttlecock." This was just like any other house in the country, and Boswell was bored and restless. Between seven and eight Voltaire appeared again and called for his domestic Jesuit, Père Adam, to play chess with him. The account had better be continued in the words of Boswell's vaunting report to Temple, an enormous letter written next morning on all eight sides of four folio leaves of Voltaire's paper—a gazette that cost Temple four shillings in postage:

I placed myself by him. I touched the keys in unison with his imagination. I wish you had heard the music. He was all brilliance. He gave me continued flashes of wit. I got him to speak English, which he does in a degree that made me now and then start up and cry, "Upon my soul, this is astonishing." [The journal shows that Voltaire scolded Boswell sharply for talking too fast, implying that it was a fault of all Englishmen. Boswell replied that Englishmen made the same charge against the French. VOLTAIRE. "Well, at any rate, *I* don't. I speak slowly, that's what I do (*c'est ce que fais moi*)."] When he talked our language, he was animated with the soul of a Briton. He had bold flights. He had humour. He had an extravagance; he had a forcible oddity of style that the most comical of our *dramatis personae* could not have exceeded. He swore bloodily, as was the fashion when he was in England. He hummed a ballad, he repeated nonsense. Then he talked of our Constitution with a noble enthusiasm. I was proud to hear this from the mouth of an illustrious Frenchman. At last we came upon religion. Then did he rage. The company went to supper. M. de Voltaire and I remained in the drawing-room with a great Bible before us; and if ever two mortal men disputed with vehemence, we did. Yes, upon that occasion he was one individual and I another. For a certain portion of time there was a fair opposition between Voltaire and Boswell. The daring bursts of his ridicule confounded my understanding. He stood like an orator of ancient Rome. Tully was never more agitated than he was. He went too far. His aged frame trembled beneath him. He cried,

"Oh, I am very sick; my head turns round," and he let himself gently fall upon an easy chair. He recovered. I resumed our conversation, but changed the tone. I talked to him serious and earnest. I demanded of him an honest confession of his real sentiments. He gave it me with candour, and with a mild eloquence which touched my heart. I did not believe him capable of thinking in the manner that he declared to me was "from the bottom of his heart." He expressed his veneration—his love—of the Supreme Being, and his entire resignation to the will of Him who is all-wise. He expressed his desire to resemble the Author of Goodness by being good himself. His sentiments go no farther. He does not inflame his mind with grand hopes of the immortality of the soul. He says it may be, but he knows nothing of it. And his mind is in perfect tranquillity. I was moved; I was sorry. I doubted his sincerity. I called to him with emotion, "Are you sincere? Are you really sincere?" He answered, "Before God, I am." Then with the fire of him whose tragedies have so often shone on the theatre of Paris, he said, "I suffer much. But I suffer with patience and resignation; not as a Christian, but as a man." Temple, was not this an interesting scene? Would a journey from Scotland to Ferney have been too much to obtain such a remarkable interview?

We have no further record of the vehement dispute conducted by the aged Voltaire and the youthful Boswell for an hour and a half in the draw-ing-room at Ferney with the great Bible open between them. It is an hilarious picture, one that Sir Max Beerbohm ought to have turned his hand to: "James Boswell attempts to convert the Sage of Ferney to the Christian Religion." The moment to choose would be that in which the wily old champion, having seen with astonishment and incredulity the missiles of ridicule which had sunk many a weightier craft glancing harm-lessly off the sides of this small iron-clad, simulates a fainting-fit and sinks down in his chair, a pathetic frail old figure in a nightcap, perhaps—who knows?—in his last gasp. He was an accomplished actor and he no doubt put on a good show, but he did not know his man. No exclamations of shocked and contrite commiseration, no chafing of hands, no scurrying for a glass of water. Nothing. He cracks one eye and there sits Boswell in his flowered velvet, imperturbable, waiting. "He recovered. I resumed our conversation." And the conversation went on now as Boswell wished it to, "serious and earnest." He got a sincere profession of faith from the man who preferred on such occasions to keep to the role of scintil-lating mockery. A most formidable man, too; a man who could and would have cracked Boswell like a louse if he had felt his tactics to be merely the brutal insensibility which has so often been attributed to him. Voltaire was amazed, he was puzzled, but he was not angry. He was amused, both at Boswell and himself. He realized, as other great men had, that this odd, eager young man with his infectious grin and his solemn ideas had stuff in him. He saluted genius which he could not define and capitulated gracefully. "For a certain portion of time there was a fair opposition between Voltaire and Boswell."

The company drifted back from dinner and Voltaire retired. Mme. Denis insisted that Boswell should not miss his supper and had a small table set up for him in the drawing-room, and he ate in solitary magnificence, surrounded by the guests, who looked at him "with complacency and without envy."

Boswell slept at Ferney two nights and stayed on until after dinner of the third day. He walked in Voltaire's garden, he inspected Voltaire's theatre, he looked at Voltaire's library, he attended mass in Voltaire's church. He talked with Voltaire several times. Voltaire gave himself out to be very ill on the last day of Boswell's visit, and had not appeared as the time approached for Boswell's departure. Boswell begged to take leave of him, and he came into the drawing-room. Boswell characterized the final half-hour conversation as "singular and solemn."

BOSWELL. "When I came to see you, I thought to see a very great, but a very bad, man." VOLTAIRE. "You are very sincere." BOSWELL. "Yes, but the same sincerity makes me own that I find the contrary. Only, your *Dictionnaire philosophique* troubles me. For instance, the article *Ame,* the Soul—" VOLTAIRE. "That is a good article." BOSWELL. "No. Excuse me. Is it not a pleasing imagination? Is it not more noble?" VOLTAIRE. "Yes. You have a noble desire to be King of Europe. I wish it for you, and I ask your protection. But it is not probable." BOSWELL. "No, but all cannot be the one, and all may be the other. Like Addison's Cato, we can all say, 'It must be so,' till death reveals the truth about immortality." VOLTAIRE. "But before we say that this soul will exist, let us know what it is. I know not the cause. I cannot judge. I cannot be a juryman. Cicero says, *potius optandum quam probandum.*[1] We are ignorant beings. We are puppets of Providence. I am a poor Punch." BOSWELL. "Would you have no public worship?" VOLTAIRE. "Yes, with all my heart. Let us meet four times a year in a grand temple, with music, and thank God for all

---

[1] "Matter of faith rather than of demonstration." Either Voltaire or Boswell seems to have erred in attributing the phrase to Cicero.

his gifts. There is one sun. There is one God. Let us have one religion. Then all mankind will be brethren." BOSWELL. "May I write in English, and you'll answer?" VOLTAIRE. "Yes. Farewell."

After recording his farewells, Boswell expatiated in a complacent paragraph of self-analysis, the longest that has yet appeared in the journal:

Well, I must here pause, and as an impartial philosopher decide concerning myself. What a singular being do I find myself! Let this my journal show what variety my mind is capable of. But am I not well received everywhere? Am I not particularly taken notice of by men of the most distinguished genius? And why? I have neither profound knowledge, strong judgement, nor constant gaiety. But I have a noble soul, which still shines forth, a certain degree of knowledge, a multiplicity of ideas of all kinds, an original humour and turn of expression, and, I really believe, a remarkable knowledge of human nature.... With this, I have a pliant ease of manners which must please. I can tune myself so to the tone of any bearable man I am with that he is as much at freedom as with another self, and, till I am gone, cannot imagine me a stranger.

It is a very shrewd remark. Most of us have the power to derive pleasure and instruction from fictional characters whose principles we disapprove of, but few of us are able or willing to tune ourselves to the tone of living men whose wills we find set against our own. Boswell approached living men almost with the security and lack of emotional involvement with which other men read books. A man can engage in animated debate with the other self in his own mind, but he is not likely to quarrel with it. And the doctrine of the other self explains also the vividness and solidity of Boswell's characterizations. He really did tune himself so that for a time he stood inside the other man's mind, giving its content the generous and understanding judgement a man accords to himself. If he prepared for an interview with an author by reading that author's books, it was because he wanted to get as nearly in tune as possible beforehand. His technique involved much more than flattery and the asking of teasing questions.

It is commonly assumed that he displayed this sympathy only for those in whose reflected light he might hope to shine: the Johnsons, the Rousseaus, the Voltaires, the Paolis. This is to mistake the facts. Any one who has read his journal remembers as among its more memorable passages those in which he has recorded his conversations with obscure chance-met acquaintances who cross the scene only once: old red-faced fat gentlewomen, elegant ladies' maids, common soldiers, coroners, hatters, coachmen, inn-keepers, convicts, drabs—all with the same precision of characteristic phrase that marks the conversations with Johnson. He would even have understood Keats's claim to have taken part in the existence of the sparrow outside his window and to have picked about the gravel. Did he not once, in no stoical vein but in sheer exuberance of sympathy, wish to be the whinstone on the face of a mountain, if it were possible for him to be conscious of it, and to brave the elements by glorious insensibility?

Because of this sympathy, we should be very careful how we style his interlocutors "victims." It is true that he sometimes roused Johnson to revolt ("I will not be baited with *what,* and *why;* what is this? what is that? why is a cow's tail long? why is a fox's tail bushy?") but it must be remembered that Johnson was an irascible and unpredictable man who often knocked other people than Boswell down for using with him tactics to which he ordinarily responded with benign complacency. By and large, Johnson *enjoyed* his conversations with Boswell: they were to him exhilarating and refreshing. Most of the time he *liked* to be asked why a fox's tail is bushy. With Boswell tuned to him, he had an opportunity to display the recesses of his mind to another self, and in the recesses of his mind there were many odd things. The same could be said of Voltaire.

Another pair of keen young eyes, as it happened, was observing Voltaire at precisely this same time, and through those eyes we are able to see Boswell's scenes with a different composition; able by contrasting Boswell with this other young man to see Boswell's limitations and to define his virtues. In his journal for 27 December 1764 Boswell mentions the presence at Ferney of the Chevalier de Boufflers, "a fine, lively young fellow and mighty ingenious." It is a mark either of Boswell's ignorance or of a drastic revision of his youthful dreams that he was able to dismiss so casually a man who has been called the spoiled darling of Europe. Stanislas Jean de Boufflers was the son of the Marquise de Boufflers, favourite of Stanislas I, formerly King of Poland and now Duke of Lorraine by the bounty of his son-in-law, Louis XV. Born only two years before Boswell, Boufflers had already realized most of the ambitions which dominated Boswell's heart during his Guards period. He rode like a centaur, he was a gallant and seasoned officer, he painted portraits with real distinction, he was reputed to have enjoyed more *bonnes fortunes* than any man of his time. Destined for the church and an abbé from childhood, he had concurred with alacrity in a request that he withdraw from the seminary of Saint-Sulpice because of the authorship of certain licentious poems and a prose tale of decidedly unchurchly tone: *Aline, ou la Reine de Golconde,* which is said to have inspired Madame de Pompadour to construct the little rustic farm and gardens of the Petit Trianon. He embraced the profession of arms but retained his benefices by entering the military order of the Knights of Malta. While Boswell was teasing his father for a commission and languishing in London, Boufflers was fighting the German campaign. Everywhere he went he tossed off little Voltairian anacreontics, of which one may be quoted to show his incomparable superiority to Boswell in the matter of versifying:

> Faisons l'amour, faisons la guerre,
> Ces deux métiers sont pleins d'attraits.
> La guerre au monde est un peu chère;
> L'amour en rembourse les frais.
> Que l'ennemi, que la bergère
> Soient tour à tour serrés de près.
> Eh! mes amis, peut-on mieux faire,
> Quand on a dépeuplé la terre,
> Que de la repeupler après?[1]

This autumn he had taken it into his head to go to see Voltaire, an old friend of Stanislas and his mother, and to have adventures on the way. Before arriving at Ferney he would make a tour of Switzerland *incognito,* travelling as Monsieur Charles, an itinerant artist, painting portraits of ladies and making love to them. From Switzerland he was sending his mother a series of traveller's letters, charming, witty, ironical,

---

[1] Let us make love, let us make war:
Both gallant trades have charms for men.
War costs the world a trifle dear,
Love brings the balance up again.
Embrace the foe, embrace the fair,
From close encounter ne'er refrain.
Ah, friends, what better deed is there,
After unpeopling the sphere,
Than to repeople it again?

perceptive; letters that show at every turn a keen and mature intelligence and that perfect urbanity and sense of proportion which Boswell yearned for so painfully and would never achieve. One cannot read these letters without feeling how much older, how much cleverer, how much more civilized this young man is than Boswell; how egregious is Boswell's vanity and how oblivious he is to the values that other people discern as a matter of course. He thinks of himself as engaging more of Voltaire's attention than he actually does. Voltaire was gracious to Boswell, but of course he was a hundred times more taken by Boufflers. He was matching rhymes with the Chevalier as gay and improper as Boufflers's own, and in several letters of the period expresses his admiration and affection for this brilliant scapegrace—even his envy of him: "The Chevalier de Boufflers is one of the most original creatures in the world. He paints charmingly in pastel. Sometimes he rides off all alone at five in the morning to go paint women at Lausanne; he exploits his models. From there he rushes off to do the same at Geneva, and from Geneva he comes back to me to rest from the fatigues of his labours among the Huguenots." Boswell when he was at Ferney copied out and sent Voltaire some of *his* verses. It makes one wince to think of those pretentious empty things lying on Voltaire's desk beside the irreverent but graceful and original lines that Boufflers was sending him.

Yet in spite of the fact that Boufflers is superior in so many attractive social qualities, Boswell is much the greater literary genius. "Sir," Rousseau had said, "there's the great thing: to have force. You can always find matter to make something out of. But when force is lacking, when everything is small and split up, there's no hope." There is one answer to the great Macaulayan paradox if anybody wants it: whatever attractive qualities Boswell may have lacked, whatever unattractive qualities he may have had, he possessed force. Crude, perhaps; canalized, certainly; but an irresistible elemental force that could not be deflected or absorbed. Boufflers did too many things gracefully ever to do one thing supremely well. Like Belle de Zuylen, he was always quenching his enthusiasm with irony; he was too well-bred to take himself seriously. Boswell was protected by his egotism—by what Geoffrey Scott called his saturation with himself—from that kind of reserve which keeps a man from exploiting his own special gift in the presence of more obvious kinds of greatness. He had no illusions as to the fantastic intellectual disparity (another phrase of Scott's) between himself and Voltaire, but he insisted that he had powers by which he could for a time hold his own with him, and he was right. Boufflers's reports on Voltaire are charming but they say nothing that a score of other observers have not said. Boswell's, for all that they are confined and in some ways imperceptive, are of the first importance.

He had discussed Voltaire with Rousseau, but there is nothing to show that he brought up Rousseau's name at Ferney. He could not have known that the infamous *Sentiment des citoyens,* which appeared on the day he went back to Voltaire's house with an invitation to spend the night (27 December) was by his host. Rousseau had begun as a warm-hearted admirer of his brilliant elder, but had come gradually to abhor his mocking scepticism. His animosity was sharpened when in 1755 Voltaire settled at Les Délices, just outside the gates of Geneva, became the city's idol, built a private theatre, and stirred up his friend d'Alembert to attack the Genevan prohibition of dramatic performances. Rousseau, instigated partly by jealousy but in the main by sincere conviction, replied to d'Alembert in a famous *Letter* in which he accused Voltaire of corrupting the Spartan virtue of his native city. In 1760 he sent one of his characteristically brilliant and savage letters to Voltaire himself: "In short, I hate you, since you will have it so." That ended the matter so far as he was concerned. It was his habit to quarrel very freely, but he was incapable of subterfuges or of practical actions to harm an enemy. In attacking Voltaire he had foolishly pitted himself against one of the most tenacious, devious, and ruthless adversaries in Europe. Voltaire began, under a pseudonym, by subjecting the *Héloïse* to coarse ridicule, and was probably instrumental in bringing about the Genevan condemnation of *Émile.* His personal physician, Dr. Théodore Tronchin, cousin of the author of *Letters written from the Country,* was one of four or five living persons who knew the sad secret of Rousseau's abandoned infants. He seems directly or indirectly to have handed the information to Voltaire, who was not slow to make use of it.

There is nothing to show whether or not Boswell read the *Sentiment des citoyens,* but he ultimately got all the scandal. The Bailiff of Yverdon (Victor de Gingins) told him that Rousseau thought it no crime to have a mistress; that he was always talking about citizenship and the law and always treating himself as an exception. In Geneva, after his first call on Voltaire, Boswell had to spend the evening in a company where Rousseau was abused. His record shows how unwilling he still was to believe anything against his idol. "There were a good many men here who railed against Rousseau on account of his *Lettres écrites de la montagne*. Their fury was a high farce to my philosophic mind. One of them was arrant idiot enough to say of the illustrious author, 'He's a brute with brains, a horse with brains, an ox with brains.' 'A snake rather,' said a foolish female with a lisping tone. Powers of absurdity! did your influence ever extend farther? I said, 'On my word, it is time for me to leave this company. What, can *women* speak so against the author of the *Nouvelle Héloïse?* "

On the eve of his departure from Geneva (31 December) he answered the letter he had received from Rousseau a week earlier. If any doubts as to Rousseau's character had found lodging in his mind, he certainly does not show it. He says that he considers Geneva an Athens during the persecution of Socrates, and quotes Rousseau's verdict that there are points at which their souls are bound together ("What glory for me!"). His confidence in Rousseau as Mentor is unshaken, most of the letter being taken up with the posing of questions which he had not been able to get to in their conversations. Should he apply seriously to music—up to a certain point? If so, what instrument? ("I play on the flute a little, but I think it beneath me. Two years ago I began to learn to play the violin, but I found it so difficult that I gave it up.") Shall he not be able to soothe his old age with the notes of his lyre? And there is an unreported episode of his past which troubles him (here a long account of the brush with Capt. Durand at Berlin). What is Rousseau's opinion of duels?

But an attack on Rousseau that he heard the next day (New Year's, 1765) was not so easily brushed off. There was a story current that Voltaire was afraid of death, that on at least one occasion when he thought himself dying he had whined and recanted. He had assured Boswell that this was a lie, and had referred him for the facts to Dr. Tronchin. Boswell thought the matter so important that he arranged to see Tronchin on the morning of his departure, though he had to make his call at eight o'clock, wearing his boots. Tronchin ("a stately, handsome man, with a good air and great ease") said, yes, it was quite true. Voltaire was by no means consistent and had no fixed principles, but the story that he had whimpered in the face of death was utterly false. Much of the time when he was well he was a good deist, and the more ill he was, the better deist he became. "Illness makes him think more of God as merciful." Concerning

Rousseau, Tronchin spoke in the exact tone of the *Sentiment des citoyens:* "He said Rousseau was 'an arrogant, ambitious, wicked rascal, who has written with a dagger dipped in the blood of his fellow citizens. A man ruined by venereal diseases, a man who affects austerity of morals and at the same time keeps a mistress. I used to be his friend, but when I found that rather than be under obligation to any one, he exposed his own children, I was not willing to see any more of him.' This shocked me, but I recollected that Tronchin was connected with the Geneva magistracy, whom Rousseau has so keenly attacked. Tronchin saw that I was hurt at hearing such a character of my admired Rousseau, and said, 'I have plucked a feather from your happiness.' I replied, 'It will grow again.'"

Yet he did not write to Rousseau again for more than four months, and when he did write, he had a favour to ask—a letter of recommendation to the Corsicans. He did not send off his next letter—a huge confession of his debaucheries and gallantries in Italy, written at the end of the tour—and his draft for this letter shows him already capable of raillery at Rousseau's weaknesses. When, early in 1766, he met Rousseau again, his enthusiasm had quite evaporated: he saw him as a great literary genius but as a weak and faulty man. His disillusionment had been accelerated, as we shall see, by consciousness of having done Rousseau an injury, but it is probable that it was set in irreversible motion that morning in Geneva by Tronchin's revelations.

At eleven he was off in a chaise mounted so high before that he was "thrown back like a bishop in his studying chair." Before him, over the Alps, lay Italy, the last stage (as he supposed) in his education.

CHAPTER

XIII

Boswell's response to Arthur's Seat may justly be called Romantic, but the feelings he had in the Mount Cenis pass—or at least the feelings of his transit that he chose afterwards to record—were mere Addisonian *clichés*. He thought of Hannibal, he quoted Juvenal and Virgil. "The prospect was horribly grand. The snow was sometimes six foot deep, but the road had been well hardened by passengers. I saw the chamois at a distance, of whose skin is made the shambo or shammy leather." In fact, he devoted more space to description of the "Alps machine" (a cord-chair slung between poles, carried at a trot by four bearers) and his reception at the Pilgrims' Hostel on the heights than he did to the scenery. He crossed, after attending mass, on the Feast of the Epiphany, which in 1765 fell on a Sunday—double satisfaction to one brought up to scorn church feasts and not to travel on the Sabbath. On the evening of 7 January 1765 he alighted at the Bonne Femme in Turin, his beckoning vision of an Italian tour near at hand and almost real. He was, as usual, prepared to do what was expected of him.

Geoffrey Scott's *espiègle* summary—pedantic in Holland, princely in Germany, philosophic in Switzerland, amorous in Italy—brings out more effectively than a less witty statement would the serious motive of self-education that informed all Boswell's impersonations, but it over-simplifies the Italian role. He was in a state of high sexual effervescence throughout his stay in Italy, but for the most part, as Scott himself says, his inclinations led him down paths where joys were undelayed and vanity secure from rebuff. There was nothing new about this, and it was not an act. The role of courtly gallant was one that he assumed only sporadically, principally as he was entering the country and leaving it. The chief responsibilities that he felt in Italy, as his records abundantly demon-

.strate, were to see with his own eyes the sites connected with the Roman poets who had furnished the greater part of his education, to refresh his Christian faith by participating in the ceremonies of the Mother Church of the West in the city of the apostles, and to form a correct taste by the systematic study of antique and modern art. Courts— and Italy was as much a patchwork of courts as Germany—were no longer a matter of vivid concern to him nor was he primarily concerned to seek out Italy's living great men. He went, an enchanted pilgrim from Thule, to pluck lemons and oranges from the tree, to stare at the Falls of Velino, to clamber up Vesuvius. He went to visit Virgil's birthplace and tomb, to tread the soil of Horace's Sabine farm, to toss flowers into the Bandusian fount. He went for the Easter mass in St. Peter's. He went to admire the Laocoön and the Apollo Belvedere, to trail through churches and palaces without number, to pore on pictures by the Carracci, by Correggio, by Guercino, by Guido, by Michelangelo, by Perugino, by Raphael, by Tintoretto, by Titian. And to make reams of notes like these:

> Yesterday well. . . . Saw some churches in Ecles St. Agn — fine martyrdom — In dominic church Inscrip on picture St. T. Aquin — Coeur [i.e. choeur, "choir"] fine inlaid wood — old and new test & Apoc Saw several pieces — then Palazio _____ very numerous and valuable Then Ranusi some fine Tapestry given by Louis 14 to Cardinal of this house Pope's Legate — prodigious rooms Lustres like stars — Then Palaz. St. Pier — Rhenis fort manier. Pierre et Paul superb. . . .[1]

This sort of dutiful notation ("a bad Baedeker" as one critic has styled it) cannot be presented in quantity in a biography, but it should be assumed for practically every day of the Italian tour.

Boswell went to Italy to be conformed to the Grand Style, but in 1765 Grand Style covered more things than painting. Every well-born Englishman who went south of the Alps in that era seems to have as-

---

[1] Memorandum dated 5 Feb. 1765, at Bologna. Boswell is recording visits to the church of S. Agnese, where he saw a martyrdom of the saint by Domenichino, and to the church of S. Domenico, where he noted an inscription on Guercino's portrait of St. Thomas Aquinas and inspected the inlaid choir-stalls. He records visits to the Palazzo Ranuzzi and the Palazzo Sampieri; the palazzo of which he could not recall the name was probably the Palazzo Zambeccari. "Rhenis fort manier" identifies his guidebook as Charles Cochin's *Voyage d'Italie* (ii.171, 172 in the edition of 1769).

sumed that a really complete tour included at least one Italian countess. Rousseau's austere counsel was not likely to blast Boswell's luxuriant and deeply rooted fantasy of high Italian romantic intrigue. Such affairs were probably wrong (in his present frame of devout scepticism even that did not seem certain), but they were certainly educational, and at such a juncture much must be granted to education. His schemes of courtly love revived with warmer air, indeed engrossed his attention by the time he got to Turin.

Colonel Chaillet at Neuchâtel, a friend of Lord Marischal's, had given him a letter of recommendation to the Countess of San Gillio, whose husband, a natural son of the late King of Sardinia, was a prominent figure in the court at Turin. While Boswell was crossing Savoy, he fell in with a high-born young officer in the Sardinian service who told him that Mme. di San Gillio "had lovers." Boswell promptly made a memorandum counselling himself not to "yield to a creature whom many have had," but added one of his characteristic saving clauses: "if not very charming." The lady turned out to be past fifty, but not unappetizing. Casanova says that she superintended all the theatrical intrigues in town; another observer reported that she had a fondness for young Englishmen, and had recently inspired a violent passion in Lord Charles Spencer and Sir Brooke Boothby. (Lord Charles was of Boswell's age.) She at once attached Boswell to her as a *cicisbeo,* and he dismissed his scruples. Her age, he thought, might even be an advantage, for he did not plan to stay long in Turin and would have to cut corners. "I began throwing out hints at the opera. I sat vis-à-vis to her and pressed her legs with mine, which she took very graciously. . . . This night (the third of our acquaintance) I made plain addresses to Mme. St. Gilles, who refused me like one who wished to have me."

Perhaps she did, for women generally found Boswell attractive, and an older woman might well have felt that if she took him as a lover, some of his ridiculous but precious youth might rub off on her. Still, a veteran of intrigue in one of the more brilliant courts of Europe was not likely to lose her head completely, and unless she did, she was not likely to forgo the attentions that were her due. Boswell told her straight out that he was young, strong, and vigorous and that she would do well to accept his services, giving her to understand that he proposed to spare purse and sentiment, and to follow a strictly love-and-run policy. The least she could have expected on these terms would have been fidelity, but he did not

accord her even that. On the very night that he made his plain addresses
to her he met a younger and more beautiful countess, Mme. di Borgaretto, and fell "madly in love" with her. Two days later (again in a box
at the opera) he made his declaration, and was amazed to find it "received with the most pleasing politeness." After assuring him in a loud
voice that it could not be, for she already had a lover—the Neapolitan
Minister, Count Pignatelli, in whose box they were sitting—she whispered to him to come next day at three. He was so full of his promised
bliss that he sat up all night. But he had not been discreet enough in their
very public conversation, and in the morning he got a note saying that
people were talking and that he must stay away. He dispatched a frantic
letter of the ritual sort, following it with at least three more. "Baneful and
delicious madness! O Love!" Mme. di San Gillio had of course observed
his attentions to the Borgaretto, and now gave him his *congé* in the style
most calculated to hurt: "I think you have been a book-worm. You ought
to go back to your books. You should not attempt the profession of gallantry, for if you do, you will be terribly taken in. Mind your health and
your purse, for you don't know the world." He was forced to acknowledge a hit, for all the comforting recollection that he had once had four
successful intrigues running concurrently. "This abominable woman
spoke very true upon the whole. I have too much warmth ever to have the
cunning necessary for a general commerce with the corrupted human
race."

He had met Mme. di San Gillio on the 8th of the month, Mme.
di Borgaretto on the 10th. On the 17th he was introduced to Mme. di
Scarnafigi, a singular lady, very debauched. "But I took a fancy to her."
He was still pursuing the Borgaretto, and on the 18th, with two more
swains, was allowed to assist at her toilet. "She dressed before us, changing even her shirt. We indeed saw no harm, but this scene entirely cured
my passion for her." On the 19th (his usual limit of the third day following an introduction) he made explicit advances to Mme. di Scarnafigi,
who at first seemed propitious, but on the following evening refused him
the slightest liberties and advised him to go away. "O Rousseau, how am
I fallen since I was with thee! I wrote a long letter to Mme. S——,
entreating her pity and all that." The ironic tag from *The Rehearsal*
shows that he was quite aware of the ridiculous aspect of his operatics,
and his self-possession further appears in his thrifty re-use of a fine phrase
from one of his letters to Mme. di Borgaretto: "Ah! when we abandon

ourselves to pleasures under the veil of darkness, what transports, what
ecstasy will be ours! . . . O Love, baneful and delicious madness, I feel
you and am your slave."

The ladies who qualified as respectable under the code of Turin had
not been affronted by his direct advances; the very debauched lady
could not afford to be so liberal. Mme. di Scarnafigi sent a word-of-
mouth message by Boswell's valet that if she had known the letter was
of such a nature, she would not have opened it. When he sent back next
day to recover it, she told the valet to tell him she had thrown it into the
fire. "Here was the extreme of mortification for me. I was quite sunk."
There was nothing more to detain him in Turin, and he set out at once.
As he passed through the city gate, he saw a crowd running to see a thief
hanged, got out of his chaise, and went close up to the gallows, "thinking
that the feelings of horror might destroy those of chagrin. . . . I then went
into a church and kneeled with great devotion before an altar splendidly
lighted up. Here then I felt three successive scenes: raging love, gloomy
horror, grand devotion. The horror indeed I only *should* have felt."

The raging love was no doubt a genuine passion, for Boswell could
inflame his mind very easily, but he could hardly have maintained that it
sprang from starved appetite. A Captain Billon, who had introduced him
to Mme. di Borgaretto and had encouraged him to think that he might
have her, had descended to pimping of a more earthy sort and twice during Boswell's stay in Turin had supplied him with willing girls. The dike
so painfully erected in Holland was breached and levelled. After Turin,
Boswell's records resume the old pattern of prudent resolves, greedy purchased indulgence, shame-faced comment, fresh resolves. The *Don Giovanni* costume was packed up, but it was not forgotten.

The two weeks in Turin were of course not entirely devoted to the
fiasco of the three countesses. Boswell was presented to the King of Sardinia (Charles Emmanuel I, a great-grandson of Charles I of England,
Scotland, and Ireland), he attended the opera and grand public balls,
he discussed the Trinity and debated the doctrine of eternal punishment
with John Turberville Needham, Roman Catholic priest and scientist.
And he crossed trails with John Wilkes, now an outlaw.

Ever since his triumphant discharge by Lord Chief Justice Pratt in
May of 1763, Wilkes had been the storm-centre of British politics. The
first efforts of the Government to crush him had been extraordinarily
clumsy, and had only resulted in making him more formidable than ever.

But the Government was determined not to yield, and in the autumn of 1763 moved to expel him from the House of Commons and so to strip him of the privilege that was shielding him from prosecution as the author of No. 45 of *The North Briton*. Wilkes had recklessly strengthened the Government's hand by printing at his private press a few copies of a pamphlet of violently obscene and blasphemous poems with notes purporting to have been written by Bishop Warburton. He was now charged simultaneously in the two houses of Parliament with seditious libel and with obscene and blasphemous libel, was found guilty, and was expelled early in 1764. The Opposition, though generally dissociating itself from him personally, resisted this action strenuously on the ground of principle. Once expelled, he was indicted in correct form in the Court of King's Bench, but failed to put in an appearance. He had left England at the end of 1763 to visit his daughter in Paris, and refused to return. His plea was ill-health, a plea not without foundation, for he had suffered a painful and dangerous wound in a duel with a Government M.P. whom he had attacked in *The North Briton*. When this excuse was roughly rejected, he decided that he was sure to receive a long gaol-sentence if he went back, and that he had better remain where he was. He was convicted on both charges and outlawed when he failed to appear for sentencing.

When chance brought him and Boswell into the same city in 1765, he had reason to be morose. His sojourn in Paris had not been unpleasant: he had been fêted by the *philosophes* and countenanced by the Court, and his lonely hours had been solaced by a beautiful Italian courtesan, Gertrude Corradini, for whom he probably felt more affection than he ordinarily allowed himself in arrangements of this sort. But early in November 1764 he had suffered a shocking blow: his friend and literary partner Charles Churchill, who had come over to Boulogne to visit him, had taken typhus and had died in his arms. Corradini, alleging herself to be too delicate for a winter in Paris, had preceded him into Italy, with a promise to wait for him at Turin. But at Turin he had been disappointed: Corradini, complaining of rheumatism, had gone on to Bologna.

It was in these circumstances that he received, by the hands of a messenger, a note from the odd and eager young Scotsman he had known two years before in London. The note was jocular but elaborately cautious. It said in effect that Boswell very much desired Wilkes's company, but would not call upon him because it would not be decent; would

Wilkes come to Boswell? If so, he would be very welcome. Wilkes did call, but not at the appointed hour, and Boswell missed him; he only saw him in the distance, high up in a box at the opera. He went home and wrote another note repeating his invitation, but Wilkes had gone to bed before it was delivered, and left Turin next day. Boswell stayed on for twelve days more, having just opened his campaign on Mme. di San Gillio.

But the letters had had their effect. Even if Wilkes's personal sorrow and vexation had not made him lonely and unhappy, he would have been grateful just then for notice from somebody from home. For all his abuse of the Government, he was English to the core, and he was by nature genial and social. If he had been in England—even though in gaol there—he would have been able to exercise his wit and charm on a circle of devoted friends. But here the English all avoided him, either because they abhorred his principles or because they feared the consequences of associating with a man under sentence of outlawry.

He was also of course captivated by the ingenuous impudence of Boswell's approach, an approach which was actually as considered and artful as that to Rousseau had been. Boswell never for a moment acquiesced, or seemed to acquiesce, in Wilkes's scurrilities. He assured him that as a monarchist and Scot of Scots he abhorred his politics, but he also told him that he loved him for his wit, his gaiety, and his elegance.

Boswell's leisurely progress from Turin to Rome occupied three weeks and a half: he paused at Milan, Piacenza, Parma, Reggio, Modena, Bologna, Rimini, Fano, Ancona, Loreto, Spoleto, Terni, and Castelnuovo. From Giuseppe Bartoli, Antiquary to the King at Turin, he had received a letter of introduction to an archaeologist at Milan named Giuseppe Allegranza. Allegranza was a Dominican friar, and he gave Boswell a letter to a member of his order at Bologna. From there on, in Italy, Boswell was passed from the protection of one Dominican house to another. When he paused for some time in a place, he secured lodgings in an inn, but if he were merely stopping overnight, he accepted the Dominicans' hospitality. The association was rewarding on both sides. The fathers (many of whom were Irish) were pleased by his friendliness and good humour, and he respected their learning and was grateful for their kindness. They quizzed him mildly about the "devout scepticism" he had taken over from Rousseau's Vicar, but tactfully avoided polemics.

At Parma he made a most congenial acquaintance. Rousseau had given him a letter of recommendation to a friend and disciple there, Alexandre Deleyre, a Frenchman, one of the remarkable band of scholars whom the Duke had assembled for the education of his young son, Ferdinand, a grandson of both Louis XV of France and Philip V of Spain. Through Deleyre he met the Prince's preceptor-in-chief, Étienne Bonnot de Condillac, and his brother, the Abbé de Mably, and chatted with Condillac on the sensationalist psychology, of which Condillac was the chief European exponent. Condillac was, in fact, as famous a man as was to be found anywhere in Italy, but he interested Boswell much less than the now-obscure author to whom Rousseau had recommended him. Deleyre professed himself an atheist, but he radiated friendliness and sympathy, gave Boswell kind and sensible advice about his melancholy, and wrote a report on him to Rousseau that shows more than perfunctory concern. "I conceived for him," Deleyre says, "an immediate and lasting affection."

"I was struck with everything," Boswell later wrote to Rousseau of his trip from Turin to Rome, but the thing that rose to his memory as he wrote the letter was not pictures or buildings. "I visited many monasteries, including those of the strictest orders. I shall never forget an hour that I spent in conversation with the Prior and other reverend fathers of a Carthusian convent near Bologna. I encouraged in myself a sceptical but reverent superstition, which by a mysterious—an inexplicable—mixture of feelings calmed my uneasy mind." Boswell had asked the monks how they managed if they got melancholy. He also on that same day called on the famous female scholar, Laura Maria Caterina Bassi, who lectured in the University of Bologna on philosophy, mathematics, and physics. She struck him as "old" (she was only fifty-four) and "curious," and he noted that it gave him the spleen to see professors again. He was tremendously impressed with the Holy House of Loreto, which was shown to him by an English Jesuit, and wrote a letter to John Johnston from the church itself. "I am in a most pleasing solemn frame, and, upon my soul, I cannot refuse some devotion to this miraculous habitation."

As he was getting his luggage through the customs at Rome (which he reached on 15 February) he met Wilkes on the same errand. They embraced, but could see little of each other, for Wilkes was about to set out for Naples. This fell in very well with Boswell's own plans, which were to stop in Rome for what remained of the Carnival, use up most of Lent in a tour to Naples, and get back to Rome in time for the ceremonies of Holy Week.

Rome was a let-down. He had no such feelings on coming through the Campagna as he had had in 1762 in descending Highgate, and the rapture he felt in St. Peter's was not quite spontaneous. The chief shows of the Carnival were the parade of masks and the races in the Corso—riderless horses dashing straight up the street, spectators tumbling out of their way—and these turned out to be disappointing, too, for he could see hardly anything from the place he had hired. A little Frenchman, seeing his discomfiture and taking him for a countryman, introduced himself as Guillaume Martin, student of painting in the French Academy at Rome, and invited him to come see the next race from his own room in the Academy's building. "You can see the middle of the street quite well from there." Boswell accepted the invitation and from Martin's attic window saw the races on both Shrove Monday and Shrove Tuesday. On the latter day, Boswell having apparently made inquiries, his new acquaintance offered to lead him to girls. The three sisters Cazenove were not at home, but Boswell and his guide found a "charming girl," sister to a nun, near the palazzo of Cardinal Colonna. The mother, who served as bawd, talked of the "vocation" of both her children. Lenten abstinence did not discharge the debt of Mardi Gras indulgence: on the morning of Ash Wednesday Boswell made resolves to be less stingy ("Nothing debases mind like narrowness"), to be a Spaniard, and to have a girl every day. On the three days following he more than met his obligation under the last article, jotting down outlays for "girls"—each time in the plural. But either he could not overcome narrowness or he yielded to the taste for progressively grosser indulgence which we have already noted as characteristic of him, for his *"fille charmante"* at fourteen paoli (7s.) on 19 February and his *"des filles"* at a sequin (10s.) on 20 February gave way abruptly to *"des filles"* at three and four paoli (18d., 2s.) respectively, on the 21st and 22nd. And on 24 February, though the expenditure was ten paoli, the entry is an emphatic MONSTRE. For the first time in two years he had attained a surfeit of sex. "Recover," he wrote in the memoranda. "Be self." It was an injunction that he had frequent cause to repeat. Next day he set out for Naples.

The road was rough and slow, the weather hot, and for two days he was hipped and peevish, disputing with Jacob and ashamed of his weaknesses. But when, probably at Mola di Gaeta, he came upon his first garden of oranges and lemons, the frame of mind he had hoped would be his in Italy suddenly blossomed. "Walked among them as among apples and pears at Auchinleck. Mounted tree and pulled. What luxury!" "Well. . . . Quite joyous. . . . Fine night's rest lulled by romantic Italian sea. . . . Gusto. . . . For once in your life, you are perfectly satisfied with self" —the notes and memoranda begin to sing for the first time since he had crossed the Alps.

He presented himself to William Hamilton, the English plenipotentiary (Emma would not appear on the scene for twenty years), he visited Herculaneum and Pompeii, he made a pilgrimage to Virgil's tomb ("cut a wreath of laurel and . . . a wreath of ivy"), he ascended Vesuvius ("smoke; saw hardly anything"), he broke out with "a prodigious scurvy" (probably prickly heat), he ran after girls, he bought objects of virtu though he had sworn that he would resist *that* weakness. But his main object was Wilkes; and to Wilkes's conversation he devoted more pages of notes than to that of any one else he met on the Continent after Rousseau and Voltaire. Unfortunately, he never wrote up the notes, and an editor cannot expand and develop them as he would have done, especially cannot add the stage-directions which give the final touch of conviction to Boswellian reporting. Even so, a good deal can be confidently recovered, and the resulting dialogues constitute the best recording extant of the candid and indecent conversation of John Wilkes.

WEDNESDAY 6 MARCH [*Wilkes is calling on Boswell in his lodgings at Bertollo's, "Strada Andalusia al Mare"; Boswell had earlier in the day been at Pozzuoli, Lake Avernus, and Baia.*] WILKES. . . . "At school and college I never read; I was always among women. At Leyden my father gave me as much money as I pleased. I had three or four whores, and was drunk every night. I had a sore head the morning after and then I read. I'm capable of sitting thirty hours over a table to study.—My original plan for *The North Briton* was to make it a grave revolutionary paper, seasoned each time with a character from the Court list.—I hated my wife, but was the civilest husband to her. Since I love this girl [Corradini], I'm not hurt by her follies—her stupid mother and her foolish cousin. In these connexions, there's no good mother in any case. I keep my eyes open and my pockets shut."

THURSDAY 14 MARCH [*Boswell, after ascending Vesuvius, is dining with Wilkes at Stefano's, "a large good house on the banks of the sea . . . the island of Capri . . . just opposite."*] WILKES. "I have never a moment in my life been low-spirited." BOSWELL. "What shall I do to get life over?" WILKES. "While there's all ancient and modern learning and all the arts and sciences, there's enough for life even if it lasted three thousand years." BOSWELL. "But the problems of Fate and Free Will?" WILKES. "Let 'em alone." . . . BOSWELL. "Why do you keep company with me?" WILKES. "You're an original genius. But they'll spoil you. Paris will lop the luxuriances from you.—I talked much to Baxter of the immateriality of the soul and read his two quarto volumes, and have never thought of the matter since.[1] But I always take the sacrament.— Dissipation and profligacy . . . renew the mind. I wrote my best *North Briton* in bed with Betsy Green."

FRIDAY 15 MARCH [*Wilkes and Boswell, mounted on asses and pushed by porters—the eighteenth-century version of a funicular—are laboriously scaling the height of Vomero to inspect a villa Wilkes is thinking of renting.*] WILKES. "I am always happy. I thank God for good health, good spirits, and the love of books. . . . A man who has not money to gratify his passions does right to govern them. He who can indulge them does better. Thank Heaven for having given me the love of women. To many she gives not the noble passion of lust."

Except for the plaintive query about Fate and Free Will, there is little evidence in these conversations that Boswell is leading. Wilkes, gay, irrepressible, and inconsequential, is talking most of the time and Boswell is listening. Certainly he is not encouraging Wilkes in bawdy: Wilkes himself granted that and was puzzled by it. "You too like the thing almost as well as I do," he wrote later, "but you dislike the talk and laugh about it, of which I am perhaps too fond." Nor did Boswell for a moment consider Wilkes a mentor to whom he should open out all his problems of conscience. He thought him a great original; he admired his manliness, his cheerfulness, his classical learning, his wit, his generosity; but he thought him also a deeply unprincipled and immoral man—and told him so to his face. His affection for Wilkes is another striking case—perhaps the most striking that could be adduced—of his power of combining sympathy with adverse moral judgement.

Wilkes's affection is harder to explain, but one thing is certain: he was the first person who ever assessed Boswell's peculiar gift correctly

[1] Andrew Baxter, author of *An Inquiry into the Nature of the Human Soul*, was a Scots philosopher, much older than Wilkes, whom Wilkes met and captivated at Spa in 1744.

and encouraged him to exploit it. Everybody else wanted to make Boswell over; Wilkes saw that he was *sui generis,* and that to lop his luxuriances would be to spoil him. He recognized Boswell's powers of sympathetic adjustment for what they were. "You're the most liberal man I ever met with," he said; "a citizen of the world. . . . I shall never forget your civilities to me. You are engraved on my heart." Long before any one else, he recognized that Boswell's letters and journal were significant art, not the mere exercises that Boswell himself considered them. "I want *your* letters at Naples. You must go on. Publish what you have by you."

On the day that Boswell wrote down Wilkes's remark about the noble passion of lust, he received a magnificent packet of letters: from his father, from Temple, from M. de Sommelsdyck, from M. de Zuylen, from Voltaire, and—at last—from Belle de Zuylen. If there had been one from the Margrave of Baden-Durlach, the score would have been perfect. M. de Zuylen had faithfully discharged his trust and had handed on unopened the plaintive epistle that Boswell had penned in Geneva on Christmas Day. Belle replied that she had been much pleased with everything in the first part of his huge letter from Berlin, not so well pleased with his scolding and hectoring. "I found passages copied from my letters, passages . . . written to you (as I thought I might safely do) in thoughtless confidence. These were sent back to me with severe refutation, each one made the excuse for some humiliating admonition as inconsiderate as it was needless. . . . But that is not all. You went on repeating, ringing all the possible changes on the words, that I was in love with you, or that I had been in love with you, that my feelings were those of love. You wanted me to admit this, you were determined to hear me say it and say it again. I find this a very strange whim in a man who does not love me and thinks it incumbent on him (from motives of delicacy) to tell me so in the most vigorous and express terms." She had at once begun a reply, but was interrupted and upset by a strange proposal of marriage. She named no names. She was blaming herself, none the less, for not writing, when she got the letter Boswell had sent from Dessau. "Once more I found myself ordered by you to confess that I had felt a passionate desire for you. I was shocked and saddened to find"—here it comes, Dogberry, as you asked for it— "in a friend whom I thought of as young and sensible, the puerile vanity of a coxcomb coupled with the arrogant rigidity of an old Cato. . . . My dear Boswell, I will not answer for it that my talk, my tone, my glance may never have kindled with you. If it happened,

forget it. I have written you letters with the spirit and freedom of a headlong imagination, which, with a trustworthy friend, shakes off the yoke
of constraint that is laid on our sex. Burn them. But never lose the memory of so many talks when each in his own fashion was reasonable and
both were sincere; when the pair of us were equally light-hearted: I, well
content in the flattery of your attachment, and you as happy to count me
your friend *as if there were something rare about a woman with many
talents.*[1] Keep that memory, I say, and be sure that my tenderness, my
esteem, I would even say my respect, are yours always.—But in talking
like this I have lost track of some sentence I left incomplete. Oh, yes; I
was telling you that I wanted to answer your letters. I would have done it
—I would have sent you a few lines at least—in spite of my new worries
and complications, if you had given me your address at Geneva. But you
never did."

So he had to forgive her, and that revived the old tenderness; and the
old tenderness raised the old question whether he wanted to marry her or
not. She certainly had genius ("more genius," he wrote to Temple, "than
any woman I ever saw, and more acquired perfections"), but what about
her character? *Did* she really love him? He had left Belle's "portrait" of
herself and the two letters he then had with Rousseau, along with his own
sketch, probably in the hope that Rousseau would tell him, and he now
took Wilkes's opinion, reading out to him parts of the letter he had just
received and perhaps bits of the earlier ones. Wilkes's verdict was confident: she was certainly in love with him; his recommendation terse and
characteristic: "You've been topped. Go home by Holland and roger
her. You might be in her." Boswell, who of course kept possible wives
and possible mistresses in utterly separate compartments in his mind, decided that it would be madness to marry her. "She has weak nerves. I
know the misery of that distemper, and will therefore choose a wife of a
sound constitution, that my children may at least inherit health."

The letter from Voltaire was a masterpiece of irony, a wonderful
trophy. Boswell had written to the great man from Turin reminding him
of their spirited debate on the immortality of the soul. Voltaire replied in
English: "You seem solicitous about that pretty thing called soul. I do
protest you, I know nothing of it, nor whether it is, nor what it is, nor
what it shall be. Young scholars and priests know all that perfectly. For
my part, I am but a very ignorant fellow." But whatever soul might be,

[1] She is quoting from his letter of 25 December 1764. See above, p. 187.

his soul had a great regard for Boswell's. "When you will make a turn into our deserts, you shall find me (if alive) ready to show you my respect and obsequiousness." To reply properly either to the ironist at Utrecht or to the ironist at Ferney called for greater deliberation and more leisure than he could muster while he was in Naples, and he put both letters away to think about and to answer later.

On 20 March Boswell headed back for Rome, taking the route by Caserta and Old Capua; at Formia he inspected the so-called villa of Cicero which he had by-passed on the way down. He arrived back in Rome on 24 March, and remained there nearly twelve weeks. On the very day of his return he got in touch with Colin Morison, a resident Scots antiquary whose services he had probably already engaged, and next day began a systematic private course in what were called the "antiquities" of the place, actually a survey of everything considered worth seeing in the way of ancient remains and modern art. Morison appears to have been his daily companion for a month or more. Together they peered down on old Rome from the roof of the Palazzo Senatorio on the Capitol, viewed the Forum, clambered over the Colosseum and the imperial ruins of the Palatine, inspected ancient statues and Renaissance palaces with their ingenious water-works and gardens like spread periwigs, and pored over acres of canvas from Raphael to Pompeo Batoni. Boswell also engaged a teacher in Italian, one Abate Dossi, and according to his own account was soon jabbering ("jargonnant") the new language at such a rate as to make him forget his French. But the absence of daily themes and other written exercises of the Utrecht sort makes it pretty clear that for some months his ambition did not extend much beyond a rough and ready Italian for conversational use. His expense account continued for some months to be kept in French.

The actual functions of Papal Rome enclosed, interrupted, and completed the imagined pomps of the Caesars. Boswell and Morison started their tour on the Feast of the Annunciation. Before ascending the Capitol that day, they had already witnessed a spectacle reminiscent of a triumph: the cavalcade of Pope Clement XIII riding on a richly caparisoned white mule to Santa Maria sopra Minerva, preceded by his cardinals and followed by a long train of richly dressed lay dignitaries. Flowers showered down from balconies draped in scarlet, and every one in the street kneeled. The main feature of the service in the church was a procession of poor girls to whom the Pope gave dowries from a fund called the San-

tissima Annunziata: some of the girls were to be married, some to become nuns. Boswell noticed that nearly all the pretty ones planned to take
the veil. On Palm Sunday (31 March) he was in the Pope's chapel at
Monte Cavallo (the Quirinal) to see the ceremony of the distribution of
the palms and the great procession out of the chapel and in again. He
attended the Maundy Thursday mass in the Sistine Chapel at the Vatican on 4 April, saw the Host carried in procession to the altar of repose
in the Pauline Chapel, the public Papal malediction and benediction
from the gallery over the porch of St. Peter's, and then the ceremony in
which the Pope washed the feet of thirteen poor priests and served them
at table. (He did it, Boswell said, with mingled grandeur and modesty:
"looked jolly landlord, and smiled when he gave to drink.") After going
back in the evening to see the illuminated cross at St. Peter's and hear
tenebrae chanted in the Sistine Chapel, he had had a day of it: "Quite
tired; sunk to bed." Finally, of course, he attended the Easter mass at
St. Peter's (7 April). "Immense crowd, fine day. Superb high mass. . . .
Most grave and pious, quite sure there must be some truth beyond skies.
. . . Elevation noble. Procession. Pope kneeled and prayed. Whole crowd
on knees. Universal silence, perfect devotion. Was quite in frame;
thought it *one* way of adoring the Father of the Universe, and was certain no hell for ever. Then up, stood just by Pope's chair when he gave
blessing. Grand, the whole place crowded with people." He wrote to
Rousseau afterwards that he was never more nobly happy than on that
day.

The arrangements necessary for him to attend the Maundy Thursday
service had been made by a Scots cleric, the Abbé Peter Grant, and it was
probably also Grant who arranged for him to be in the Pope's chapel on
Palm Sunday. The Abbé was Agent in Rome for the Scots Mission, an
important office but one that left him a good deal of free time; and
though he was a staunch Jacobite, he served as a sort of ecclesiastical
cicerone to visiting Britons of every political stamp. Boswell on first meeting him thought him an excellent, obliging, hearty character." He was of
about Lord Auchinleck's age.

Grant arranged for him to be presented in private audience to the
Pope at Monte Cavallo on 13 May, along with three other Britons: a
knight from Lancashire, a gentleman from Derbyshire, and a third as yet
unidentified. "In antechamber, off sword, etc. Then in and kneelings and
kiss of slipper, rich with gold." Grant apparently made the presentations

himself; Boswell, in the antechamber, appointed himself master of ceremonies. He put the knight at the head of the line, but caused himself to
be presented as "Baron Boswell." He also attempted to make some conversation in Italian, which was the language the Pope chose to speak. He
says that he put his foot in his mouth, but the extremely cryptic nature of
the notes makes it as yet impossible to say just how. The Pope made a
pleasant remark about his beginning to speak the language, and Boswell
kneeled his way out, with delightful thoughts of the distance he had
travelled from his Presbyterian childhood.

Finally, on 26 May Grant went out with him to Frascati to see Cardinal York, the Pretender's younger son, pontificate at a splendid Whitsunday mass. A special memorandum shows Boswell preparing himself
with appropriate instructions: "Up betimes. Shave and dress, green and
silver. Well with Abbé; talk on religion, large. Prepare mind for grand
function. . . . Look up to God. Adore in church without affectation, fer-
vently. Get near Cardinal, and think of Grange and old Scots kings, and
Chapel of Holyrood." The record of the "function" itself is much briefer,
but reveals intense satisfaction: "Mass, Jesuits. Then grand Cardinal
York. British arms. Old Scots royal blood, majestic and elegant. All the
assembly, face as face of angel. Fine voice, quite noble, smiled as he
passed."

The motives for the Frascati jaunt were of course as much Jacobite as
religious. Indeed, except for the group of artists soon to be mentioned,
Boswell in Rome associated mainly with Jacobites. He had laid out for
himself a programme of serious study in the Utrecht fashion ("Day, antiquities, night, write") and did not wish to be diverted from it by a time-
consuming round of tavern dinners and drinking-parties. He was deeply
disappointed with the *conversazioni* and parties of the Roman nobles to
which his introductions gained him admittance: they were formal, glittering, and (as it seemed to him) cold and empty. "They have scarcely
any real society." Cardinal Orsini, to whom he had been highly recommended, received him politely, but never once asked him to dine. He was
all his life strangely silent about an honour which the *letterati* of Rome
conferred upon him. Among his papers is an imposing diploma which
declares that the *nobile ed erudito* Signor Giacomo Boswell, Barone
d'Auchinlech in Iscozia, having been proposed by our fellow shepherds,
Carillo Maratonio and Filandro Lampidiano, has been elected an Arcadian shepherd with the name of Icaro Tarsense (Icarus of Tarsus) at

a general meeting of the Collegio d'Arcadia held in the Parrhasian Grove on the neomenia of Sciroforione, fourth year of the 635th Olympiad. The proposer, Carillo Maratonio, remains unidentified; the seconder, Filandro Lampidiano, was the Abbé Grant. The Collegio d'Arcadia, a national literary academy founded in 1690 to combat the extravagances of effete Marinism, had accomplished an important work in the first half of the eighteenth century and still bore an honoured name. Metastasio and Goldoni were among its members, and its diploma would later be accepted by Alfieri and Canova. It was customary to elect visiting celebrities: Angelica Kauffmann was an Arcadian, and so, at a later date, would Goethe be. One would have thought that Boswell would have been enchanted to attend meetings in the Parrhasian Grove (an elegant outdoor amphitheatre on the Gianicolo erected through the bounty of John V of Portugal); that he might even have offered to exercise the right, which the diploma granted him, of reciting his verses there. He may have thought that Arcadian membership was too freely bestowed on visiting Britons and Americans to constitute much of an honour—the Duke of Dorset had the accolade, but so also had Dr. John Morgan, the *fat bonhomme* with whom he had toured Holland—or he may have been bullied into a low opinion of the Arcadia by the terrible-tempered Giuseppe Baretti, whom he met at Venice just at the time the diploma came into his hands. Baretti was certainly at that time pouring vitriol on the society. Whatever the cause, Boswell, who continued to yearn for the Margrave's star, never, so far as is known, subscribed himself Icaro Tarsense or let the world know that he, too, had been in Arcadia.

What he actually found most satisfactory in the way of Roman society was the card-parties given at the home of an Italian lady with a Scots surname. Agata Gigli, Mrs. Colin Erskine, was the widow of a painter-son of Sir Alexander Erskine of Cambo; Sir Alexander had been out in the '15, and Mrs. Erskine's home seems to have been the social centre of James's disconsolate court. Mrs. Erskine had a son and daughter, the daughter Clementina named for James's Queen, the son Charles, a young man of Boswell's age, already an abbé and destined to become a cardinal. As a cousin, Boswell would have looked the Erskines up in any case, but he came back because he liked the house and the company. Every Sunday evening from early April till his departure from Rome in the middle of June, he went to Mrs. Erskine's, paid out a sequin or more but without repining, and rubbed shoulders with the few remaining members of James's entourage, with Irish and Scots abbés and friars, and with young English Jacobite squires on their travels.

Writing cautiously to his elderly Scots friend Sir Alexander Dick, he reported that he had had the pleasure of forming the acquaintance of a cousin of Sir Alexander's, "who resides at Rome as secretary to a Scots gentleman of very ancient family." Andrew Lumisden had been private secretary to Charles Edward in the '45. After adventures that would have made good material for a novel by Scott or Stevenson, he had escaped to the Continent and made his way to Rome, where he secured his appointment with the titular James III and VIII. Boswell was never offered a presentation to the Scots gentleman of very ancient family, then bed-ridden and much failed mentally, and would certainly have declined one if it had been offered. But he made the acquaintance of Lumisden soon after his return from Naples, formed a firm friendship with him, and sat with him many hours in the Scots gentleman's palace (the Muti, at the north end of the Piazza dei Santi Apostoli). He had gone there originally, fearful of treason, to see if he could borrow a copy of Robertson's *Scotland* (we shall soon see why he wanted it), found Lumisden a fine specimen of the worthy, clear-headed Scot, classical and genteel, without a trace of political rancour or fanaticism, and came back again and again for sensible friendly advice or quiet talks about Derby and Culloden. Lumisden immediately took to him and described him to a correspondent as a young gentleman of great talent and merit; to his brother-in-law and fellow Jacobite, the engraver Robert Strange, he wrote that he had a particular esteem for Boswell, and that he was beloved by all his acquaintances. This was probably true of the acquaintances Boswell shared with Lumisden himself, but was certainly not true of the run of visiting Britons. Most of them, true to the description Lady Mary Wortley Montagu had given of them twenty-five years before, kept an inviolable fidelity to the language their nurses had taught them, shone in obscure coffee-houses, and met only one another. They distrusted Boswell because of his marked preference for outlaws of various descriptions, and they disliked him because he avoided tavern sociability, spoke Italian, and went out seriously each day to look at ruins and pictures. Boswell returned Lumisden's affection and held him in respect; in Lumisden's company he felt somewhat as he did when he was with Johnson.

Lumisden was an active and accurate antiquary (he was writing a book on the antiquities of Rome), and, finding Boswell responsive, arranged for him the most exciting of all his Roman jaunts, one of the spiritual peaks of his year in Italy. For an eighteenth-century gentleman who knew by heart more than forty of the odes of Horace as well as many passages from the epistles, no spot of Italian soil could be a more urgent object of pilgrimage than the famous Sabine farm, that little nook of land where the poet felt happier than anywhere else. On 17 May Boswell made the usual tour to Tivoli and was shown not only the villa of Horace but also the Bandusian fount. This was generous measure, for Horace does not say that his famous spring was on or near his farm; in fact, does not specify any location for it at all. To find the spring near the villa, however, coincided with Boswell's expectation, as it probably would with that of any present-day reader who should master Horace without archaeological notes. He "relished fully Horace and repeated him on the spot," especially declaiming "O fons Bandusiae." He sacrificed no kid and poured no wine, but he did toss in elderberry blooms ("non sine floribus"), and he pocketed three stones to take home to Auchinleck.

Just a week later he was back with Lumisden for an excursion beyond Tivoli to Vicovaro and up the Licenza valley. This may have been the plan all along, but I doubt it. I think that Boswell had reported his Horatian rites to Lumisden, and that Lumisden had told him that though he might possibly have seen the Bandusian spring, he had missed the villa by more than ten miles. The notion that Horace had a villa at Tivoli, fostered by the guides because they wanted a definite and accessible ruin to show, really had little to recommend it. The true Sabine farm lay up in the hills beyond Tivoli; and an Italian scholar had recently published a book maintaining that vestiges of Horace's very villa could be seen a little south of the modern village of Licenza. I think that Lumisden had read this book but had not yet visited the site; and that he now proposed that he and Boswell should be among the first of their countrymen to make the authentic Sabine pilgrimage. They left Rome very early in the morning, drove to Tivoli and then to Vicovaro (Horace's Varia), where they left their chaise. "Took horses and guide and left Mandela on *gauche* and went up to Rocca Giovane, little village. Another guide. Sad mountainous roads like Auchinleck turnpike. Came to *fons idoneus,* Lucretilis behind. Saw ruins; fell on knees and uttered some enthusiastic words." He would behave similarly thirty years hence when shown the Shakespeare manuscripts impudently faked by seventeen-year-old William

Henry Ireland; this time the relics were probably authentic. A critic whose concern is literature will be less inclined to deplore the absurdity of his enthusiasm than to give thanks for what Carlyle called his loving heart, the generosity of his response. The fact that he had *planned* it so ("Horace jaunt. . . . At villa be in enthusiasm") does not make it any less sincere.

The other member of the Pretender's staff whom Boswell saw most of was his chief physician, Dr. James Murray, "little Murray," as he twice affectionately calls him. On his return from Naples he had consulted Murray professionally about the disfiguring "scurvy" on his neck and chin, and Murray had prescribed lenitives. Boswell liked the old man and after that had him frequently for dinner. At the end of April he had to consult him about a more serious ailment than prickly heat. In his report to Rousseau, he talked as though his raking in Rome had been pagan and joyous: "I sallied forth of an evening like an imperious lion, and I had a little French painter,[1] a young academician, always vain, always alert, always gay, who served as my jackal. I remembered the rakish behaviour of Horace and other amorous Roman poets, and I thought that one might well allow one's self a little indulgence in a city where there were prostitutes licensed by the Cardinal Vicar." The expense account had earlier struck the Horatian note by entering all outlays for carnal relaxation under the heading *badinage*, but the memoranda are more sober, and I think not merely because they reflect the qualms of the morning after.

FRIDAY 12 APRIL. Yesterday walked to Genzano.[2] Saw Capuchins' prospect, but dusky. Alban Mount noble. Lake curious. Genzano fine, Cesarini avenues. Lake Nemi rich. Albano. Ariccia, church of Bernini. Then monuments. Morison quite sulky; low to dispute with him. You have seen how vain, how impossible to make others as you, so from hence never dispute. Be firm. Night, new girl.[3] Swear no women for week. Labour hard.

[1] Guillaume Martin. See above, p. 206.
[2] From Frascati, where he had made a two-days' jaunt with Morison and Gavin Hamilton, the painter, soon to be introduced. The distance is 7½ or eight miles. They were probably followed by their chaise, which took them to Albano and Ariccia, and then back to Rome.
[3] Perhaps another of the three Cazenove sisters (above, p. 206). On 21 May he "went to Cazenove's and had third girl" (Mem. 22 May 1765).

SUNDAY 14 APRIL. Yesterday morning, churches and villas. Morison played trick at Medici with Niobe. . . . Evening, Martin and with girl. Vexed. Resolve sober for week. Today mass, etc.

The leaf bearing the notes for 26, 27, 28, and 29 April has disappeared in some flurry of family censorship, but the expense account indicates an orgy on the 27th: *badinages* totalling the extraordinary sum of four sequins. Martin is hovering in the background on either side of the hiatus. Murray was summoned on the 29th to see Boswell, whom he found in bed. "Alas, real disease." A couple of days more revealed the added indignity of crab-lice. In London two years before he had been confined to his room for a full five weeks, but this time he was out in three days and roaring again in twelve: "SUNDAY 12 MAY. Yesterday . . . after dinner went to Corso like one *enragé* and amused for last time. You're never to go back. . . . *Now* swear no *libertinages* except Florentine lady." Murray's bill was ten sequins or £5, the same as Surgeon Douglas's. Italian sunshine probably accounted for the quicker recovery.

But Boswell in Rome, it cannot be too often repeated, was primarily a student of art and archaeology. Though licentious, he was not at all dissipated in the sense in which he himself would have used the word. If he raked, it was as relaxation from a serious course of sight-seeing and note-taking. He chummed with Jacobites, not because they were Jacobites but because they were Scots and because some of the members of the group were so useful to him in his studies. The inhabitants of Rome whom he actively sought out were artists and archaeologists, but as at Utrecht, during his other study-period, he allowed himself little time for pursuit of the merely great. We should be glad to have fuller notes of his two extended tête-à-têtes with Johann Joachim Winckelmann, who showed him through the Villa Albani, where Winckelmann, who was Cardinal Albani's librarian, had written his *Geschichte der Kunst des Alterthums*. Boswell records no remark of the great historian of ancient art, and his emphatic pronouncement that Winckelmann had fine and classical taste is less memorable than his note that the garden looked like a spread periwig. Nor do we find more than the conventional in his note on Angelica Kauffmann, the beautiful girl who at the age of twenty-three had acquired a reputation as painter somewhat in excess of her actual merits. When he was introduced to her, promptly on his arrival in Rome, he paid the usual tribute to her beauty by declaring himself "quite in love," but never went back to allow his passion to mature. He visited the studio of Pompeo Batoni, the painter then in greatest practice in Rome (he is said to have painted twenty-two sovereigns), but noted only that he saw him draw the drapery for the portrait of General Gordon, now at Fyvie Castle. The "drapery" is a kilt and plaid of Huntly tartan, and we should be glad to know whether Batoni painted it himself or merely designed and drew it for an assistant to paint.

The first Briton Boswell met in Rome was John Wilkes; the first he sought out was Nathaniel Dance, brother of his old friend Love. Dance, who later added the name Holland and attained the honour of a baronetcy, was a portrait painter of some distinction, a foundation member of the Royal Academy. He introduced Boswell immediately to St. Peter's and to Angelica Kauffmann (for whom he entertained a hopeless passion), and was very attentive to him for some days. No close friendship developed, partly, I think, because Dance was offended by Boswell's marked attentions to Wilkes.

Boswell's closest association among the artists at Rome was, as one might have predicted, with a fellow Scot of good family, Gavin Hamilton, of the Hamiltons of Murdieston. Hamilton, who is now best known for his excavations of Hadrian's Villa, was in 1765 in considerable repute as a history painter with a fondness for classical subjects. Boswell looked him up at his studio four days after his arrival in Rome, and was much impressed by a picture he saw there which Hamilton was painting on a commission from the Duke of Bedford, "Achilles dragging the Body of Hector at his Chariot Wheels." He left for Naples soon after this, but called on Hamilton on the very evening of his return. He had decided at Naples to emulate the Duke of Bedford, and on this evening proposed that Hamilton should paint *him* a large picture, not from *The Iliad,* but from Scottish history. He felt the need of reviewing Robertson's *History of Scotland* for a subject, but had no copy of the book; Morison suggested that he borrow one from Andrew Lumisden. It was this errand which on 26 March took him, fearful of treason, to the Muti Palace and initiated his warm friendship with Lumisden. The subject selected was "Mary Queen of Scots resigning her Crown"; Lumisden promised to lend a miniature of Queen Mary for Hamilton to use in drawing the face of the principal figure. Hamilton, not unnaturally uneasy about accepting such a commission from a young fellow of Boswell's prospects, had to question him bluntly to make sure that he understood what he was letting himself in for. Boswell's replies were lordly in the extreme.

HAMILTON. "But are you really to have this picture?" BOSWELL. "Indeed am I. Am I to have it?" *(taking him by the hand).* "Yes, if you please. Make it full size and neglect nothing. As I'm to have a picture, don't mind price. I shall not stand for £100 more or less." HAMILTON. "Don't talk of price. I don't intend to make you pay much money for this picture. I shall make a great deal by the print. I like your spirit in bespeaking a picture. In our country it is only men of the greatest fortunes, as Lord Hopetoun, who do so." BOSWELL. "No, Sir, I could not be satisfied if you did it a farthing cheaper for me than for another. Were I in a certain rank of life, I would ask you to make me a present of it. But I am rich enough." HAMILTON. "I shall do it for £150." BOSWELL. "No. £200." HAMILTON. "You may pay me just as you can, by degrees." BOSWELL. "In Scotland they'll talk against me: 'What! is he bespeaking history pictures?' "

He went to his lodgings feeling a veritable genius and was recalled sharply to reality by a letter from his father which he characterized as "somewhat disagreeable."

The letter is lost, but a later one which has survived indicates its tenor well enough. "This much I can say," wrote his alarmed parent, "that you have spent a vast deal of money; for since you left Geneva in January last you have got no less than £460 sterling, which is much beyond what my income can afford, and much beyond what the sons of gentlemen near double my estate have spent on such a tour." The year in Italy all told cannot have cost much less than £500, by no means including the fee for "Mary Queen of Scots resigning her Crown," which was not delivered for eleven years and was a disappointment when it did arrive. The expense account shows that Boswell lived frugally enough (he indeed acquired among his fellow Britons the reputation of being penurious), but in the four months from his arrival in Rome in the middle of February to his departure in the middle of June, he spent at least £100 for objects of modern and allegedly ancient art. His commonest heading for such expenditures is *antiquités,* but he sometimes specifies: *vases étrusques, Pénates, boîte de lave de Vésuve, statue d'Hercule.* He must have shipped home a ton of marble. He bought several liturgical and devotional manuscripts and an expensive book of engraved views of Paestum. He commissioned a seal (subject, a Vestal; cost, about £7) from the lapidary Pick-ler. And he sat twice for his portrait.

Britons of substance visiting Rome got themselves painted by Pompeo Batoni. Boswell's acquaintance, Col. (later Gen.) the Hon. John J. William Gordon, son of the Earl of Aberdeen, was having himself done full-length by Batoni, as we have seen; eight years earlier Sir Adam Fergusson of Kilkerran, Boswell's Ayrshire neighbour, had sat to Batoni for a half-length. Perhaps because of his ducal commitment to Gavin Hamilton, perhaps because Batoni was engaged for the period of his stay in Rome, he decided to economize in this article, and went to George Willison, a young Scots student in Rome, and got from him an excellent portrait in Batoni's manner at a fraction of Batoni's fee. It is odd that he did not meet Willison sooner, for Willison was first cousin to George Dempster and is said to have pursued his studies in Rome on Dempster's bounty. Be that as it may, Willison dined with Boswell on 2 May with Hamilton and Dr. Murray, and on 4 May Boswell began sittings. ("This day at nine, Willison's, and sit—a plain, bold, serious attitude.") The costume, save for the breeches, was that which he had worn when he first visited Rousseau: a scarlet suit with gold lace and a sage-green cloak trimmed with brown fox. He had originally planned to have only a head, but Willison pleaded earnestly for a half-length, which would enable him to introduce some Batonisque emblems indicative of both adventure and meditation. Boswell, wearing his cloak and holding his hat, sits on a boulder under an overhanging rock on a wild sea-coast; on a branch of a small tree growing out of a cleft in the rock perches a small owl. (Batoni's portrait of Colonel Gordon had the Colosseum in the background and a figure of Minerva on the right.) Boswell liked the idea, but consulted Lumisden and Hamilton before he acceded to it. It was at one point agreed to include some "lines" by Boswell (probably a legible manuscript of ten-line verses), but this scheme, which Boswell thought "noble," was fortunately abandoned. Willison worked rapidly on the picture and seems to have had it finished, or nearly so, by the time Boswell left Rome on 14 June.

As the portrait progressed, Boswell decided to have a miniature painted for John Johnston. This task he entrusted to another young Scots painter in Rome, James Alves, whom he clearly had had no previous dealings with. The miniature was based on Willison's portrait, but Boswell gave Alves three sittings. He paid Willison about £15 and Alves about £6.

The miniature, which was sent back to Britain through Lumisden and his brother-in-law Robert Strange and was no doubt delivered to Johnston, has dropped out of sight; the portrait, though separated from the Auchinleck collection, remained in the possession of Boswell's descendants until it was bequeathed to the National Portrait Gallery of Scotland in 1913. Apart from the jejune engraving showing him in the costume of an armed Corsican chief which was made four years later for inclusion in a magazine, it is the only portrait of him as a young man that we possess, and it is a most satisfying one. This biographer could wish for no better visual embodiment of the idea of Boswell he has tried to present through words: odd, eager, egotistical, boyish, sensual—and attractive. For the purposes of this book it is a pity that the well-known portrait by Reynolds cannot be completely forgotten. It is a fine portrait, but it shows Boswell at forty-five.

Correspondence was now more of an obligation than it had been at Utrecht. The Register records two letters sent from Naples and forty-five sent from Rome during the period from 15 February to 13 June, and the list is certainly not complete. His much-pondered reply to Voltaire, when he came to write it, turned out rather ponderous in wit and solemn in sentiment. He said that receiving a letter from Voltaire was like getting one from Abraham ("whose reality you doubt of"), and he continued the argument about the Soul. Something more in the vein of sleeping on two chairs in the maid's bedchamber would have served his turn better.

He probably had no strong hopes of engaging the Monarch of Letters in a regular correspondence, and was not unduly disappointed when no further word from Ferney was forthcoming. But he was puzzled and disappointed by the silence of the Margrave of Baden-Durlach. It will be remembered that at Geneva he had received a singularly gracious epistle from Karl Friedrich in English, saying that Karl Friedrich would value his correspondence and asking him always to write without ceremony. He had written a rather pompous and fussy letter of compliment from Turin, ending by informing His Most Serene Highness that he planned to be back in Karlsruhe in May with an attested genealogical tree and that he was indulging the agreeable idea of being honoured with the star of the Order of Fidelity. On 11 May in Rome he wrote again, this time a simple, friendly letter of news of himself, expressing uneasiness that he had had no further word from Karl Friedrich, but reasserting his intention of returning to Karlsruhe, which he thought would be so soon as July. Though the letter from Turin may well have been lost in the post, this one from

Rome certainly reached its destination. But no answer came from the Margrave.

Of the long letter to Belle de Zuylen which he sent from Rome on 3 April, only a discarded postscript survives, and we have to guess the tenor of the letter itself from Belle's reply, written on 25 May.[1] He exempted her from saying or believing that she was in love with him, confessed his raking in general terms, asked to have his letters returned, and refused to feel contrite for being systematic and having old-fashioned ideas. The discarded postscript, if it had been sent, would have completely reversed the whole in typical Boswellian fashion. He is prepared, it says, to make a recital which will surprise her; though he will speak without choosing his words, she will not blame him this time. She has not sufficiently entered into the character of her proud and amiable Scot; she has advanced a considerable way on the path, but if she had gone some steps further ... if she had trusted him *fully* and spoken everything out. . . . He decided that caution was the wiser course and suppressed it, but it is clear that he was not really prepared to regard her as no more than a friend and confidante. Try as he would, he could not dismiss from his mind the recurring agreeable reverie which presented her as his daily helpmeet and mistress of Auchinleck.

[1] Received by Boswell at Florence, 11 August 1765 (Register of Letters).

CHAPTER

XIV

If the author of an historical novel had presented his fictitious hero in quick succession as the crony of John Wilkes and the bosom friend of the son of Wilkes's chief opponent, the plot would have been reprobated by the critics as "contrived"—something as unconvincing as Sir Walter Scott's bringing Edward Waverley in on both sides of the Rebellion of 1745. But history actually did devise that plot for Boswell and he accepted the offered role. Three months after saying good-bye to Wilkes in Naples he left Rome as the travelling companion of Lord Mountstuart, eldest son of the Earl of Bute.

He had been introduced to Mountstuart on the day before he left Rome for Naples, and at Naples he could have improved the acquaintance, for Mountstuart soon followed; put up, in fact, in the same hotel as Wilkes. To cultivate Wilkes and Mountstuart simultaneously would have been too *outré* even for a Boswell: he saw all he could of Wilkes and left Mountstuart alone. But when Mountstuart returned to Rome at the end of April, he made a note to see him often "as a good lad," found that Mountstuart liked him, and thereafter was in Mountstuart's company two days out of three. The course in "antiquities" should by now have been over, but he extended his stay for two weeks—to see a few more palaces and churches, to get his portrait painted, to be presented to the Pope, to make the jaunts to the environs of Rome which his strict schedule had hitherto prevented—and he then continued to linger on because the friendship with Mountstuart was so flattering and looked so promising. Simple Ned had been a day-dream; the Margrave was beginning to fade into unreality; but even the hard-headed judge his father would have to agree that if Lord Mountstuart offered friendship, it was plain practical good sense to accept it. Lord Bute was no longer in the Government but he was still considered to be the King's friend, and regardless of how Government might change, his son's political prospects looked brilliant. Mountstuart begged Boswell to go with him on a jaunt to see Tivoli, talked freely with him about his own education ("There is not one Englishman to whom I could have talked in this way"), finally invited Boswell to be his companion for the remainder of his Italian tour. Boswell had doubts, but when Mountstuart asked him a second time, he agreed if Mountstuart would manage his father. Mountstuart wrote at once to William Mure, Baron of Exchequer, a respected friend of Lord Auchinleck's, requesting him to arrange matters. "Boswell is an excellent lad, full of spirit and noble sentiments; and (as the world goes) it ought to be reckoned a fortunate thing for him going with me, and indeed fortunate for myself." At three o'clock in the morning of 14 June 1765 Mountstuart's party left Rome headed for Venice. It will be useful to pause a moment and look somewhat closely at the four members of that party.

John Stuart, by courtesy styled Viscount Mountstuart, lacked nearly a month of being twenty-one. He was handsome, charming, and imperious; possibly able (he was a grandson of Lady Mary Wortley Montagu), certainly lazy. He counted on a brilliant career, but was too self-assured and indolent to worry about it or anything else. His state was princely: he expected people to make allowances for him.

Because of his youth, Mountstuart was under tutelage: he had a "governor" to manage his tour and keep a tactful eye on him and a tutor to read him lectures in history and prepare him for a career in diplomacy. The governor, Lt.-Colonel James Edmonstone, a veteran of many years' active service, was a Scot of good family, a favourite correspondent of David Hume and a very distant cousin to Boswell, who almost certainly knew him before they met in Rome. He was in his forties. Boswell assigns him the adjectives honest, hearty, worthy, and homely (adjectives, by the way, which he would have thought appropriate for his friend Johnston), but complains of his occasional resort to rough Scots familiarity. Edmonstone seldom interfered in the bickerings of his younger companions, but when he did his word was decisive.

Paul Henri Mallet, the tutor, a Swiss not quite thirty-five years old, was already a *littérateur* and historian of considerable reputation. Having gone to Copenhagen as a very young man to teach French *belles-lettres*, he had written a history of Denmark, and in preparation for it had learned the Scandinavian languages—an unusual accomplishment, then as now, for a French-speaking scholar. The *Histoire de Danemark* resulted in commissions for official histories from the houses of Brunswick and Hesse and led to his appointment as tutor of the Prince Royal of Denmark and to an offer (declined) from Catherine the Great to superintend the education of the Grand Duke Paul. He was uncomplaisant and outspoken, morose through natural hypochondria, homesickness, and the daily frustration of trying to keep a spoiled and indolent young nobleman to a serious programme of study.

Boswell, as we have seen, was well aware of the difficulties in the situation. Edmonstone's roughness had already caused him to write a memorandum telling himself sternly not to tolerate any more of such behaviour. He and Mallet had bristled almost at first meeting and were well on the way towards hating each other. To begin with, Mallet was an informed and determined enemy of Rousseau. "A sad Genevois without subordination" (to quote Boswell's bitter early characterization of him), he sneered at Boswell's pride of birth, and as a systematic scholar derided his jaunty pretensions to knowledge. And in his relations with Mountstuart, Boswell had already had plenty of opportunity to discover how difficult in practice he was going to find that patronage for which his feudal soul truly yearned. The Boswells of Auchinleck nourished an inflated sense of family pride: they thought of themselves as somehow better than other families. Throughout his life Boswell strove vainly to combine sincere belief in political subordination with an intuitive conviction that a Boswell of Auchinleck was as good as anybody. He wanted a political patron to whom he could surrender one part of himself as unreservedly as he had surrendered another part to Johnson, but his stiff family pride would never suffer itself to be bent for long. The result, in all his dealings with political Great Men, was an alternation of undignified prostrations and equally undignified hostilities, of fawning and defiance.

This association, too, was to be more than mere patronage: it meant living for weeks in the enforced intimacy of carriage and bedroom. Boswell knew that he was not up to his usual level of complaisance. In his ferocious concentration on his Italian studies he had, as he later admitted, isolated himself, formed exaggerated ideas of his own importance, and grown touchy and irritable. And in any case, he had reason to fear that his domestic manners were not those of a finished gentleman. He had never learned to spend money as a gentleman should, but oscillated between extravagance and meanness: between commissioning historical paintings and avoiding his share of a reckoning. And he had a really coarse streak in his composition that caused him occasionally to prefer low people and low pleasures. By travelling alone he could avoid a kind of observation he wished to be free of. Jacob (who was ill with a fever and had been left in Rome) had for months been trying to get him to behave like a proper milord, and had especially urged him to find a proper travelling companion. He had got one now, and he was not at all sure whether he could hold up his end of the arrangement.

Trouble developed immediately. The weather was atrociously hot (hence the departures before dawn) and Mountstuart was determined not to get out of the chaise to look at anything or to permit his companions to do so. On the second day out, at Foligno, he lost his temper because Boswell and the Colonel went for a walk through the town and delayed supper. Next day, between Foligno and Macerata, Boswell got into a rage because Mountstuart insisted on calling him "Jamie," a style of address he loathed. Thereafter his companions addressed him as "Baron," and he called Mountstuart "Your Excellency." At Pesaro there was a row about the line of route. Boswell and the Colonel wished to visit the little republic of San Marino, Mountstuart and Mallet did not. After having agreed to go on with one of the carriages to Rimini and wait there while Boswell and the Colonel made the side-excursion, Mountstuart changed his mind, sulked after the horses were put to, and said he was going straight on to Bologna. Mallet, as usual, sided with his pupil. On this one occasion, the Colonel interposed, called Mallet insolent, and rebuked Mountstuart, who instantly yielded. Boswell and Mountstuart exchanged sarcastic letters and rode silent side by side in the same chaise. At Ferrara there was a violent dispute as to whether the party should stay long enough to explore the town; Mallet, who had been furious with the Colonel for his harsh words, now joined with him in blaming all the dissension on Boswell. At Padua Boswell talked back, maintaining that he had as many ideas as Mallet and really got cut down: "You know no one branch of learning. You never read. I don't mean to make you angry, but among young men of education I have never found a single one who had as few ideas as you do."

Because of what Horace Walpole called "the heats and nauseous air" of Venice, the Venetian people of fashion were in midsummer mainly to be found in Padua, and a good deal of opera and grand entertaining was crammed into the four days that Mountstuart's party paused there. On his last day in Padua, Boswell, partly to meet a very famous man, partly to get personal professional advice, made a call on Giambattista Morgagni, the great anatomist of the University of Padua, then in his eighty-fourth year. Morgagni, a "fine, decent old man," first talking Italian and then Latin—a measure of Boswell's fluency in Italian at the period—advised him to discontinue the syringe, live soberly, take little exercise, and let his urethral catarrh clear up of itself. "A physician takes his cue from Nature, who does things step by step, never by leaps and bounds." For "scurvy" Morgagni recommended rhubarb and goat's milk; for hypochondria (from which he himself had suffered) horseback exercise. He thought he had studied too hard: "I have passed my life," he said, "amidst books and cadavers."

At Venice, though there was a dearth of people of fashion, there were buildings and paintings to see, and to these Boswell applied himself with his usual persistence. The mere list is as dead as all mere lists are, but he confers life on two bits of it by noting that he roared out Pierre's speech from *Venice Preserved* ("Cursed be your senate!") in the Great Council Hall of the Doge's Palace, and that he "strolled" all one morning in a gondola. Charmed at first by the novelty and beauty of a city set in the sea, he soon wearied of continual travel by water, "shut up in those lugubrious gondolas."

Mountstuart's party had been met at Padua by an old friend of Lord Bute's, General William Graeme, the Scots commander-in-chief of the land forces of the Republic, and Graeme had invited them while in Venice to make his palazzo their home. Boswell grabbed a good room and commented bitterly on Mallet's impudence in assuming that he had equal rights of choice. Mallet showed great forbearance in not leaking the information (he apparently never did) that whereas Boswell *called* himself a Baron, he himself really *was* one, having been ennobled by the King of Denmark. All the same, he had got to the stage of continual cutting rudeness. He told Boswell that the ideas of which he was so proud were false and that he was without system; that he had no genuine attachment to any one and no real friends. Boswell ("shocked with wonder that a wretch could think so" of him), replied with more feeling than wit that he had a very low opinion of Mallet: "I have never lived in peace with a man of whom I had such a low opinion."

General Graeme, by the testimony of both Boswell and Lady Mary Wortley Montagu, was an admirable representative of his nation, but the official representatives of Great Britain in Venice were a pretty ripe lot.

Joseph Smith, the retired consul, now ninety or over, appears in Casanova's *Memoirs* as confidant if not accessory in a plot by the Resident to
seduce a beautiful nun away from Casanova. Smith's first wife, an opera-
singer, had been rich but mentally unstable, and some people suspected
him of marrying her with the intention of putting her under restraint and
using her fortune to amass the fine collection of books and pictures which
he sold to George III in 1762 for £20,000. The Resident, John Murray,
was an amatory gladiator for whom Casanova expressed admiration; he
said that Murray looked like a Bacchus by Rubens, and Lady Mary maintained that he had started life as a smuggler. Murray arranged for his sister to become Smith's second wife when Smith was past eighty, in order
(as was held) that he might obtain an interest in Smith's collection. John
Udney, Smith's successor as consul, had been Corradini's protector before
Wilkes took her up. He brought Boswell up to date on a current scan-
dalous rumour. At the end of May, irritated because Wilkes, who was sup-
porting Corradini's mother and uncle, would not also settle £2000 on
her, Corradini had decamped for Bologna with all of her own effects and
some of Wilkes's. Udney—one can only guess as to how he got them—
showed Boswell the letter which Corradini had left for Wilkes and the
congé that Wilkes had sent after her. Boswell, who did not yet believe the
rumour of Corradini's thefts, was deeply shocked: "Thought him *now*
worthless in private life; agreeable, to be sure, or he could not be so
vicious, but in moral balance really good for nothing."

Even if there had been no slacking of assiduity on his part, Boswell
while in Italy would perhaps have failed through thin pickings and accident to meet a really first-rate Italian man of letters. Goldoni and Metastasio—the only Italian writers of *belles-lettres* of the day who enjoyed
European reputation—were respectively at Paris and Vienna. Boswell did
not meet Parini, though for all I know to the contrary he could have done
so on one or both of the occasions when he was at Milan. He may not
have heard of him (*Il Mattino* had appeared so recently as 1763), or he
may not have been able to find time in the two crowded days he spent in
Milan. Or Parini may have been temporarily out of town. We have
evidence of Boswell's persistence in these matters in the case of the Abate
Melchiorre Cesarotti, the translator of Ossian. Boswell tried to see him in
Padua, somehow missed him, and wrote suggesting that they meet at Dolo
on the Naviglio di Brenta, half way between Padua and Venice—a
twenty-six-mile round trip for both parties. Waked, according to instruc-

tions, by a hoarse gondolier at four in the morning after having been in bed only an hour and a half, he tried to sleep on the way out in the gondola but felt as miserable as in a Dutch *trekschuit*. Cesarotti, a "round, lively Italian," read his own verses "with immense enthusiasm and propriety." He was accompanied by his Italianized English friend Charles Sackville, who had first roused his interest in English studies and had paid for the publication of the Ossian—a man one would like to know more about. On the way back, as Boswell had stipulated when he hired them, the hoarse gondoliers sang Venetian ballads.

He also sought out Giuseppe Marc' Antonio Baretti, notorious for the recent suppression of his slashing review *La frusta letteraria,* though Boswell was undoubtedly more interested in him as friend, translator, and correspondent of Johnson, with whom he had established an intimacy during an extended residence in London. Baretti ("curious Italian") was assiduous in showing Boswell the sights of Venice, and allowed him to read three long letters which Johnson had sent him ("rich"). He was in a miserable state of mind, as well he might be after his repeated crushing encounters with censorship, and was about to leave Venice for Ancona (in the Papal States), where he hoped to be able to continue his review. He believed, as he told Boswell, that the Devil created man: "as man dies like a dog, let him lie like a dog." In a letter sent when Boswell left the city, he urged him to go straight home. "Why should you lose your time far from your glorious island, and why should you still wander about a country whose manners, politics, and religion are so trifling, so nonsensical, and so corrupted?" Boswell was later to conceive for him a dislike bordering on hatred, but in Venice his delight in meeting an admirer of Johnson made him quite overlook the ferocity of Baretti's manners. He introduced him to Mountstuart, who afterwards sarcastically referred to him as "your Venetian hero," and was amused when Baretti characterized Mallet as a watchmaker and Edmonstone as a farmer. He confided in Baretti his doubts as to whether he should have become Mountstuart's companion, and was relieved when Baretti said that Johnson, had he been in Boswell's place, would have done as Boswell had done.

The climactic interchange between Mallet and Boswell was, fittingly enough, over Johnson, and Baretti precipitated it. On the morning of his first call he had filled Boswell's head with enthusiastic ideas of Johnson, which Mallet, at breakfast later that day, had poured cold water on. He said that his *valet de chambre* could match Johnson's eloquence, and maintained the superiority of Hume's style. Boswell got furiously angry. "When you see him, you will get down on your knees. David Hume is a child in comparison with him. His Dictionary is great philosophy: in it you have all the axiomatical knowledge of the language, all the obscurities and perplexities reduced to clear ideas." A hot debate ensued. "M. Mallet, if you provoke me, I shall have to squash you."

It seems strange that we have no record of any meeting at Venice between Boswell and Count Gasparo Gozzi, the essayist, or with his brother Carlo, the writer of comedies, for Baretti at that time had a very high opinion of Carlo's work and lived on terms of personal intimacy with Gasparo. Also, one would have expected Boswell to have been eager to meet a man called "the Italian Addison." We cannot completely rule out the possibility of a meeting, for Boswell's journal-notes for 10 and 11 July are missing, having fallen prey to some fit of family scrupulousness. But probably the Gozzi were just out of town.

The centre of Boswell's social operations while he was in Venice was the "superb" palazzo on the Grand Canal, near Santa Chiara, of Resident Murray, whose wife, an "old English lady," was styled Lady Wentworth because of her previous marriage to an English baronet. Mountstuart (or Graeme) also did a lot of entertaining in the General's palazzo. On 2 July, at one of these dinners at home, Boswell met a Mme. Michieli, a friend of Lady Mary Wortley Montagu's, gay, lively, and *appétissante*, though somewhat advanced in years. He marked her, called on her that very afternoon, and began an assault exactly in the style of his Turin *amours*. But this one, though it ended without victory, just as those had, left him with a very different impression of the lady's character. Mme. Michieli liked him and did not dissemble her liking; she endured from him gross familiarities and most unflattering bluntness. She told him first, preserving her gaiety, that she would no more choose to take a lover for a fortnight than a good cook: she might suffer too much when she lost him. But when Boswell went all lengths with her, she confessed that she had never been *galante* at all. "Once I was in danger, but I escaped. I admit that I am prejudiced, but it would make me wretched." He had the grace to be touched with her goodness and to desist from his importunities.

He was not likely, however, to leave the city of pleasure without some fleshly solace. "My fancy," he afterwards wrote, "was roused by the glittering tales I had heard of the Venetian courtesans. I went to see them, *et militavi non sine gloria,*[1] but the wounds of my Roman campaigns were barely healed when I received fresh ones at Venice. What is worse, my Lord Mountstuart was of the party. He saw that I was excited and asked what I was up to. I told him that I was going to take a look at the girls, to taste the pleasures of Venice and get to know the world, but I begged him not to go. As you can well imagine, we went together. A pretty dancer was our common flame, and my Lord catched a Tartar as well as I. A fine piece of witless behaviour!"

Voilà une belle étourderie indeed. Though Mountstuart was quite as much a rake as Boswell, he had probably been a good deal more fastidious, and in any case he was four years younger. The main argument advanced by Boswell and Mountstuart for Boswell's joining the party had been that Boswell was going to be a steadying influence: was to keep Mountstuart to his studies and discourage him from flighty behaviour of all sorts. It had long been clear that as encourager to studies, Boswell was worse than useless: Mountstuart and he had taken hardly any lessons since the party left Rome. In fact, instead of humbly and eagerly listening to Mallet's words of wisdom, Boswell had endlessly and pertinaciously attacked Mallet's opinions, a situation which an even less irritable pedagogue would have found intolerable. And now, so far from keeping Mountstuart to paths of virtue, he had himself led him astray, with damage—perhaps serious—to his health. Edmonstone took Boswell sharply to task, and thereafter had little respect or affection for him. His report when he got back to Scotland was that Boswell was a mischief-making lad, vain and penurious.

General Graeme, who was sometimes vexed and sometimes diverted by the quarrels of his guests, offered his country-house at Monigo for a quiet cure, and the party removed there on 13 July. (On the way, Boswell made a side-trip from Mestre to Mogliano to call on old Consul Smith, whom he had missed in Venice.) But only two days later, while Resident Murray was dining with them, letters arrived: Lord Bute was summoning Mountstuart home. Boswell was never given a clear statement of Bute's reasons, but it is not hard to advance plausible ones. The fall of Grenville's ministry had been imminent for more than a month (it had actually occurred on 10 July), and it was only common prudence for a young man thinking of a great political future to be on hand when ministers were shuffled and posts given out.

[1] "And I fought, not without glory" (Horace, *Odes,* III.xxvi.2).

Boswell, all contrition when he knew that his association with Mountstuart was so nearly over, vowed reform, and so probably did his companions, but to no avail. The very next day Boswell got into a sad humour, "laughed at Odoacer and all history," cut the Colonel down with jokes, and went to bed early. The day after that Mountstuart took his turn: "Sir, you behave ill to me, one day proud, one day flattering. You are not to be depended on. . . . From this day, I shall have no more to do with you."

On 22 July Mountstuart's party headed back for Turin by way of Vicenza, Verona, and Brescia. Boswell resolved to go along as far as Milan, though it meant retracing part of his former route. The first three days were relaxed and friendly. Mountstuart said, "I shall miss you much on the road, Baron." But on the fourth (the day of their arrival at Milan) disputes broke out again, and Mountstuart added that, though he should always esteem Boswell, he was most disagreeable to live with. Boswell late that night or early the next morning made a last desperate resolve to set matters right. "Have long conference with my Lord and own being in wrong, not for obstinacy but loose conduct. Say sorry, and you'll be on guard." When he waked Mountstuart he felt quite happy and complaisant, but after loitering through the morning and visiting the cathedral again (he had been there in January) he suffered a change of ideas and returned home touchy and bristling. Suffering from an intolerable sense of ill usage, he pitched into Mountstuart: "You have behaved ill to me. I'm sorry I did not put a stop to it at first. I'm glad we now quarrel. I wished it." At the same time he was sorry and afraid he was being too sorry. The last dinner was eaten in open hostility: the Colonel ("honest, homely man!") was rough and announced that he meant to be rough. He recapitulated all Boswell's bad behaviour and Boswell grudgingly admitted it. The moment for leave-taking arrived. "BOSWELL. 'If you don't like me you'll never like anybody.' MOUNTSTUART. 'Baron, are you sorry?' BOSWELL. 'More than you thought.'" The Colonel called him a geck (foolish) man, and said that if he wanted to maintain a real friendship with Mountstuart, he should not have been so familiar. Mallet professed to retain no hard feelings, and they were gone. Boswell sat for an hour dull and weak. He had really had more affection for Mountstuart than Mountstuart had had for him. He felt very much discouraged and dissatisfied with himself.

Mountstuart's unexpected recall caught Boswell in a situation from

which no artful letter was likely to extricate him. Lord Auchinleck had
originally granted him four months in Italy, and had then, on Boswell's
earnest plea, granted an extension of a month to enable him to complete
the full course in antiquities at Rome. Boswell had been so penetrated by
his father's goodness that he had planned to follow his instructions to the
letter, and accordingly early in May began counselling himself to wind up
his affairs and leave Rome. Before the month was up, Mountstuart had
proposed that they travel together. Mountstuart himself (through Baron
Mure) asked that Boswell's time be extended, and Boswell left Rome with
a clear conscience, feeling sure that his father would never refuse to assent
to an arrangement which promised to provide him with so eligible a
patron.

But when Mountstuart was recalled, Boswell knew perfectly well that
his father would expect him to come home, too. Though Lord Auchinleck
was prepared to make a prudent investment in political interest, he took
a very dim view of the values of foreign travel, considered simply as such:
"There is no end nor use of strolling through the world to see sights before unseen, whether of man, beasts, birds, or things." But now that Boswell had been granted permission to see a good deal more of Italy and
had inflamed his mind with the prospect, he simply would not accept a
disappointment. He wanted to go back to Parma, he wanted to see
Florence, he had business in Siena, and he had half decided to go to
Corsica. Accordingly, knowing that a request for an extension would certainly be refused, he pretended to think that his father would allow him to
stay for as much time as he would have had if Mountstuart's tour had
not been interrupted, and took care that he should not be informed otherwise. "Your conduct astonishes and amazes me," wrote his father many
months later. "I have wrote letters on the back of letters to you telling
you to come home. Whether any of them have reached you, I cannot say.
It is possible not; for one thing is most extraordinary in your conduct: you
give me no notice where you will be when any letter I can write may
reach you but leave me to guess." The period of dutiful submission and
parental approval is over; Boswell is again the headstrong and self-justify-
ing son who ran away to London, and Lord Auchinleck is again the anxious and sarcastic parent.

His goal now was Parma, but he did not hurry thither, nor did he
take the direct route. In Milan he had met a seal-cutter named Grassi who
told him that a brother of his, Padre Serafino Grassi, had been for fifteen

years a monk in the Certosa (Charterhouse) of Pavia, and Boswell determined at once to give himself the satisfaction of the study of a mind so much warmed by piety. He also wished to see the site of the battle of Pavia (1525) and to call upon the distinguished Jesuit mathematician, astronomer, and physicist, Ruggiero Giuseppe Boscovich, at the University there. Then, too, being so near, he could not think of passing up Cremona, which Virgil mentions in a line which he could recall but could not explain (*Mantua vae miserae nimium vicina Cremonae*), nor Mantua, the very birth-place of the poet. Pavia was a disappointment, for it was a day of retreat at the Certosa and the Prior would not let Padre Grassi come out, Boscovich was not at home, and nobody knew where the field of the battle of Pavia was. Cremona seems to have been in no way memorable: the only report we have of Boswell's visit is that he did *not* go "to look at Cremona fiddles." But Mantua furnished a peak of feeling to go with the Easter mass and the Sabine farm. Having taken boat five miles down the Mincio to the village of Pietole, the supposed birth-place of Virgil, he wrote on the spot a long classical letter to Wilkes, matching the scene before his delighted eyes with the consecrated phrases of the First and Ninth Eclogues: *patulae fagi, fronde super viridi.*

Gay Wilkes, congratulate with me; an hour of felicity is invaluable to a man whom melancholy clouds so much. Here as I sit I am perfectly well. Time rolls back his volume. I am really existing in the age of Virgil, when man had organs framed for manly enjoyment and a mind unbroken by dreary speculation: when he lived happy and died in hope. Will you tell me, is humanity really the same now that it was then? And is it only our own faults that we are not as happy as the old Romans?

Boswell had felt the need of a confessor for some time, and ever since Venice the needle of his spirit had been pointing towards Parma: "Consult all with Deleyre." He arrived at Parma for the second time on 1 August and remained there nearly a week. Deleyre was as amiable and sympathetic as ever, and Boswell unloaded on him all the burden of his perplexities and his misdoings. He told him about Belle de Zuylen, his troubles with his father, his campaign for the Margrave's star, the unhappy story of the duel he had so narrowly avoided in Germany. He showed him his journal, confessed his licentious behaviour and asked for a dispensation to continue it so far as to have gallantries in Italy. Deleyre, whom Boswell could not budge from his placid atheism, told him he was made for misery. "I ought to have your principles with my conduct, and you ought to have my conduct with your principles." They parted tender and sad.

Boswell's way to Florence lay back through Modena and Bologna and then over the Apennines by the highroad through the Passo della Raticosa and the Passo della Futa. Like all English travellers he paused to see the subterranean fires at Pietramala. He arrived on 10 August and stayed for a fortnight.

Boswell, with his usual flair, arrived in Florence at a most exciting time. Since 1737 the Grand Duchy of Tuscany had been a fief of Francis I, Holy Roman Emperor and husband of Maria Theresa, but Francis had always been an absentee sovereign, ruling by a regent or governor. It had been announced as early as 1763 that Francis's second son, Leopold, who was to marry the Spanish Infanta, would be made his father's lieutenant in Tuscany, and would succeed as Grand Duke on his father's death. The city was in a ferment of preparation for the arrival of the young archduke and his princess, when—during Boswell's actual stay in the city—the Emperor died, the news raising for a few hours in Florence a flurry of intense concern as to whether Leopold would now be made Grand Duke. (He was.)

Tuscany was one of the four states of Italy to which Great Britain sent an envoy or resident minister, and the resident at Florence, Sir Horace Mann, was by far the most seasoned diplomat in the Italian service, having held the post at Florence since the year of Boswell's birth. For these reasons and perhaps others, there was at Florence a higher concentration of British notables than Boswell had encountered at any other Italian city. His Sommelsdyck cousin Earl Cowper was, indeed, beginning to look like a permanent resident, having arrived as a traveller in his father's lifetime, fallen hopelessly in love with a married Marchesa, and never gone home again. Lord Beauchamp, the handsome young son of the Marquess of Hertford, was there; so was Earl Tylney, a rich Englishman with an Irish peerage; so was Colonel Isaac Barré, the warrior and opposition orator from whom Wilkes-Barre, Pennsylvania, gets half its name; so was Baron Wallmoden, the son of George II's Hanoverian mistress, the Countess of Yarmouth, and reputed son of George II himself; so was the Hon. Peregrine Bertie, younger son of the Earl of Abingdon, Captain in H. M. Navy; so was the Hon. Keith Stewart, younger son of the Earl of Galloway, another Navy captain, whom Boswell had already run into at Cremona. Mann was very polite and hospitable, and Boswell was much at his house, characterizing him as "neat-talking," and recording hints for an anecdote of his about a witch who said the Lord's Prayer not only backwards and forwards, but sideways. Boswell was charmed with Beauchamp ("wished to have such a son"), dined round the circle of notables, was presented to and dined by Marshal Botta Adorno, the Governor, and was perhaps sketched or painted by Thomas Patch. He attended a meeting of the famous Accademia della Crusca in a room in which the furniture all allegorized the Academy's name ("Crusca" = "bran") : the president sat on a millstone; the members' seats were baskets, the table was a kneading trough, the lectern a bolter. The evening's discourse (by an abbé) was on the subject of fire; the President squinted a little but was genteel; Boswell escaped in half an hour. He went to see the lions and tigers in the Grand Duke's menagerie, and was "amused and agitated just enough" by the news of the Emperor's death. He met Giovanni Lami, antiquary and historian, who was publishing a literary review, and was very much impressed with a Padre Gentili ("the first shrewd Dominican you've met") to whom he had an introduction from Allegranza. After having repeatedly called on Lord Cowper and being repeatedly told that Cowper was not at home, he caught him in company one evening at Mann's and backed him into a corner for serious family talk—first explaining their relationship, of which Cowper was not aware. He assured Boswell that his siren ("a siren," Boswell remarked, *"en fort bon point"*) had lost her allure, and that he was staying on in Italy simply because he had made many close friendships there and had no friends in England. He thought his duty would oblige him to return to England before the year was out. (As a matter of fact, he married in Florence a young English gentlewoman and sent his children to England to be educated, but never went home himself. Grand Duke Leopold got his brother the Emperor to make him a count of the Holy Roman Empire, it is said because of an attachment to his countess.)

Deleyre had given Boswell a letter of introduction to the Marquis Venturi, a Parmese friend of his at Florence, and Venturi (a "green, neat man ... *quite virtuous*" who subscribed to the Savoyard creed) had been most assiduous in showing Boswell the glories of Florence: the library and chapel of San Lorenzo, the Uffizi, the menagerie and Boboli gardens, the Palazzo Medici, the Cascine, Santa Maria Novella, the Accademia della Crusca. Vigorous and systematic sight-seeing may be assumed.

Yet for all his activity, Boswell's two weeks in Florence do not seem to have been happy. On arrival he had found Jacob, whom he had not seen for nearly two months, and Jacob was "just as before: rude." He found a letter from his father waiting him, and reported his "ideas changed"—a Boswellian *cliché* which means that he had become suddenly and deeply depressed. Next day he received a second batch of letters: another from Lord Auchinleck, one from Belle de Zuylen, one from Rousseau. "No effect. Ideas quite changed." He thought that the Florentines (especially Florentine women) were proud and that their eye was to an unpleasant degree on the main chance. He was melancholy, weak and young, cold and gloomy, tired, dreary; he argued about free will, he reminded himself that all was fancy and that he should never yield to the opinions of others as to how to spend his short life. The fretfulness in society which had plagued him ever since he crossed the Alps was still much in force. He made various frantic resolves to maintain strict behaviour, but finally ("quite furious") rushed out to the bridge and picked up two girls. Modern censorship has obscured some of the detail of this unintentional and horrid parody of the *Vita Nuova*,[1] but the result is clear. He had a recurrence of symptoms, and had to send for an old Irish doctor who looked after the ills of the British in Florence. Dr. Tyrrell, who made him laugh by calling the women "poor craiturs," told him he was infectious and could not honourably engage in gallantries. Boswell made a note to dismiss the old man ("Say you don't wish he should be seen here, and you only want little advice") but he did counsel himself to "ask condoms for Siena."

All in all, his best memories of Florence centred in another Scotsman, Lord Hertford's chaplain, Dr. James Traill, who later in this same year on Hertford's becoming Lord Lieutenant of Ireland was made Bishop of Down and Connor. A bland, cheerful, accommodating man, he got Boswell to talk about his Scots Dictionary, and was able to make even bugbears like Divine Prescience seem tolerable. At Traill's Boswell heard Nicholas Dothel, a Lorrainer, play the flute, was captivated by his playing, and engaged Dothel to teach him the instrument. When he left Florence, Traill told him not to marry a female wit (Boswell must have discussed Belle de Zuylen) and gave him a flute that the world was to hear of.

Boswell left Florence for Siena on 24 August and probably went there

---

[1] Actually, as I now find, a horrid anticipation of Henry Holiday's well-known painting (1883) of the meeting of Dante and Beatrice. Dante (*Vita Nuova*, § III) does not specify a bridge.

fast and directly; he stayed in Siena an unplanned five weeks. The beckoning vision of Italian gallantry which he had followed so long as a mere mirage floated down to earth and merged with the actual scene. The frustrations melted, the mean self-doubtings fell away, the dream came true. He was very happy, and very, very proud of himself.

Boswell's determination to visit Siena was not due in any large measure to a still unsatisfied appetite for buildings and pictures. He came almost desperately in a final attempt to bag a countess. Mountstuart had heated his fancy with an account of a brilliant intrigue he had had there with a high-born lady named Porzia Sansedoni, whose husband was Chamberlain, or chief ceremonial representative in Siena, of the Grand Duke of Tuscany. ("The Gothic *Palazzo Sansedoni,* on the N. side of the piazza, with its battlements and tower, dates from the 13–14th centuries." —Baedeker.) Boswell begged Mountstuart for a letter of introduction and came to try his luck on the same range.

The Sienese, he found, had no court and no calculated ostentation; they were free from the pride and self-seeking coldness of the Florentines. He was the only foreigner in the city, and could have been very lonely, but they accepted his recommendation and received him cordially and naturally. He had a pleasant apartment adorned with mirrors and pictures. ("The portrait of a lady hangs over the door of my bedchamber, and this lady looks as though she were my lady-in-waiting. She stands in a majestic attitude, gesturing with her hand as though to say, 'This is where the Signor Cavaliere sleeps.' ") His appetite was hearty, he was pleased with Sienese food, he drank the local wine with gusto. The sun shone bright, his illness evaporated. The Abate Crocchi, who said mass daily but was gentle with lovers, dined with him and taught him Italian. He read Ariosto two hours every day. His music-master came every afternoon to teach him singing and the flute. He spoke only Italian, he wrote reams of chatty Italian exercises.

Porzia did not want him, but was willing to keep him dangling; she professed to have lost her heart so completely to Mountstuart that she could not bear the thought of a rival or successor. Boswell's line was eloquent, ingenious, and fantastic. They both loved Mountstuart, and how could they better express this common love than by giving themselves to each other? "Oh, if that could happen, how much closer would be the bonds which knit me to my amiable friend, penetrated, as we should both be, with the same sentiments for yourself; beloved, as we should both be, by *la cara Porzia!* How beautiful would be the mixture of tender feeling between the three of us!'" He persuaded himself that he was madly in love, and he actually did suffer some uneasiness.

But he was master enough of himself to hedge, just as he had done in Turin. Among several Sienese ladies whom he had met at about the same time as Porzia, one had been especially friendly. Her name was Girolama (familiarly Moma or Momina) Piccolomini, and her husband Orazio Piccolomini, a scion of the most renowned of all Sienese families, was Capitano di Popolo, an office roughly equivalent to mayor. Boswell, with no passion whatever in his heart, made ardent and despairing declarations to her too. "I lied to her certainly no fewer than a hundred times a day. ... My *valet de place,* a lout who could neither read nor write, was sent off with his face turned towards the east to carry a letter to Signora A in his right-hand pocket and a letter for Signora B in his left."

At the end of the fortnight Porzia's defences remained unsapped, but Momina surprised and embarrassed him by unconditional surrender: "Ebbene, mi fido a voi." The stalwart and experienced lover who had so bragged of his prowess went in trepidation to consummate his bliss—and had to confess inability. Momina laughed at his rueful apologies, but she generously accepted his protestations of passion and was kind and tender.

Boswell soon mastered his bashfulness and became a delightful lover, and his gratitude for Momina's kindness developed into genuine tenderness and respect. He abandoned his design on Porzia, got his letters back from her, and for some eighteen days gave himself up entirely to his "dear little mistress." Being Boswell, he of course promptly confessed his perfidy. "She reproached me tenderly. ... But from that time on she had complete confidence in me."

It will be remembered that at Florence he had received a letter from Belle de Zuylen. Her budget of ironic chat had ended by at last naming the mysterious suitor about whom she had been dropping hints for more than a year, and what she said about him sounded pretty final. "I shall perhaps marry early next winter the Marquis de Bellegarde, colonel in our Service, with fine estates in Savoy and a house at Chambéry; a Roman Catholic whose children must be Catholics, a man of forty, a man with brains, kind and good-natured. ... Do not accuse me and do not condemn me. ... If one day you want further explanations and justifications, you shall have them. Good-bye, my dear Boswell." Boswell had been a good deal put out and hurt by this apparent *congé,* but when he received the letter, he was too "changed" and gloomy to cope with it. He answered it now from Girolama's arms, let us hope magnanimously. We shall probably never know, for he did not keep a copy.

We have portraits of neither Porzia nor Girolama—the Palazzo Sansedoni and the Palazzo Piccolomini have passed into other hands and the family pictures have been dispersed or lost—but some facts can be adduced. Porzia was thirty-five and the mother of three children; she had "noble manners," was cool, aloof, and probably beautiful. Girolama was either thirty-three or thirty-eight (her husband was fifty) and had had four children. She was small, merry, intensely feminine, and probably had the vivid kind of face that people call "interesting" rather than "beautiful." We do not have to guess about her gestures and the turn of her speech, for Boswell has fixed these for us in a little "Sienese Sketch," which shows her surrounded by a completely male circle, and with her *cavalieri serventi* at her elbow:[1]

MOMA. Good day, gentlemen. Good day, Tiburzio. You didn't go to the country? Sor Silvio, another fan. That will do nicely. Bino, please wind this watch....

TIBURZIO. You are always working at something, Signora Girolama. You never seem to get tired.

MOMA. As a matter of fact, I enjoy knitting a few pairs of stockings, so I work as I talk. It isn't hard, it doesn't tire me, it doesn't hurt my eyes.

GIACOMO. I wish I had a wife like you.

TIBURZIO. Bravo, Signor Giacomo. You are right. A most excellent lady....

SILVIO. The Mayor told me you are dining today at the Town Hall. If you feel sleepy afterwards, there's a good bed there.

MOMA. For shame, Silvio! You think of nothing but beds and sleeping.—I want to go home at once.

GIACOMO. I shall go tomorrow to pay my respects to the Mayor.

MOMA. For shame! Come and see me instead.

In the letters she sent to Boswell after he left Siena, she mingled outbursts of grief and loneliness with commissions for silk stockings at Leghorn and the makings of a gown at Paris ("thirty-two ells of cloth ... with a

[1] Tiburzio's last name was Spannocchi, Bino was Bernardino Ghini-Bandinelli. Silvio (Porzia Sansedoni's brother) also bore a double name, Gori-Pannilini. Giacomo (= James) is of course Boswell.

watered ground, the colour . . . should be throat-of-pigeon"). She shows
the aristocrat in her carefree attitude towards spelling and her ability to
paraphrase Dante appropriately: "Non vi è maggior dolore che recordarsi
delle felicità in tempo di miserie."

She had had lovers before, but she told Boswell with obvious sincerity
that he was the first for whom she had ever felt a true passion. "They took
me out of the convent and married me at sixteen, when I did not have
the slightest idea of what marriage was about. I was a complete innocent.
When I was put to bed with my husband, I found *stuff*[1] beside me and
thought it was an animal. . . . My husband is considerably older than I
am, a man whom I cannot respect, let alone love, for if truth must be told,
he is anything but a man of parts, indeed is most uncouth." Though she
regretted her inability to attain the heights of conjugal virtue concerning
which Boswell (of course) lectured her, she had no scruple about their
relationship, for it was completely within the code in which she had been
brought up. She went to mass and made Boswell go with her.

She was gay, she was tender, she was fierce, she was scornful ("Go
and visit the barbarians; it's just the right place for you"), she was pro-
tective, she was at all times utterly in love. Yet she was perfectly clear-eyed
about him. "The good in you," she once remarked, "amazes me as much
as the bad." When he spiced his transports by moral readings from the
Nouvelle Héloïse, she punctured him with sharp common sense. "You and
that Rousseau of yours are just alike. Birds of a feather. You talk all the
time about virtue and then go and do wrong."

She wanted their affair to go on for ever; he of course began to form
plans for retreat as soon as he had possessed her. His feeling for her was
proprietary enough to make him deeply jealous of her former lovers—
one of whom was always at their *conversazioni*—but if all time had been
at his disposal, he was not one to emulate his cousin Cowper. He had
written in one of his letters to Porzia, "I wish it were over. . . . It is not the
ecstasy of a moment but the delicious memory of a whole lifetime that I so
ardently desire." This is extravagant but not all specious. He was very uneasy in the prospect of any enduring sexual relationship, even if illicit.

A week beforehand, "firm though sad," he had informed Momina of
the day of his departure. She took it very hard, dismissing his talk about
eternal friendship as twaddle. She reluctantly consented to his going as far
as Leghorn, but then he absolutely must come back.

[1] "*Roba,*" a word of great range of meaning.

SUNDAY [29 SEPTEMBER]. Yesterday morning rose by eight; was firm and philosophical and calm. Put all in order. At ten Momina. She was quite tendered down, for she had not slept. You told her you was resolved. She said, "You go on adding happiness to happiness, but you leave me here always to go from bad to worse, for in a few years my youth will be gone, and I am among people who mean nothing to me." . . . You took her to bed and with mild courage did it fine. Both happy. She begged return from Livorno. But you was reserved. She shed tears without affectation, and promised fidelity. Her *allegria* returned by fits. [Poor Momina, laughing with the tears on her lashes!] You was like Spanish cavalier and promised eternal friendship. You had been in cathedral first. Leave quite in confusion. At twelve, found chaise at port. Half well, half ill all day. Night, bad inn.

He is off: to Lucca, to Pisa (where he viewed the leaning tower "and with great modesty proposed doubt if the wind had not bowed it"), to Leghorn. His goal is Corsica; he has come to Leghorn to arrange his cruise. Keith Stewart has told him that he may get captured by Barbary corsairs and spend the rest of his days in the galleys; hence a British passport seems expedient. His luck for the unique does not desert him. Commodore Harrison, in command of the British squadron in the Mediterranean, is lying in the bay of Leghorn, his ship no other than the *Centurion* in which Anson had circumnavigated the globe. He gives Boswell a very ample and particular passport with an impressive red seal, telling him at the same time that he will hardly need it, for the "Turks" have stopped making trouble.

Early on the morning of 11 October 1765, a small bark plying to Cap Corso left the harbour of Leghorn under a light wind. Aboard was James Boswell, his education completed, about to emerge from obscurity into delightful notoriety. Henceforth for many a long year the names of Boswell and Corsica will be united.

CHAPTER

XV

In the account of his tour which he afterwards published, Boswell says that he had "wished for something more than just the common course of what is called the tour of Europe," and allowed his readers to infer that he had planned to go to Corsica from the time that he left England. Actually, the vague "something more" did not become the definite "Corsica" until he met Rousseau. There was excellent reason why the conversation with Rousseau should have furnished him with the suggestion that he later made such good use of. Rousseau at the end of 1764 was full of the subject of Corsica, and on subjects that interested him Rousseau could be very persuasive.

Not, of course, that Corsica was any private discovery of Jean Jacques. In the eyes of Europe for some twenty-five years the political future of Corsica had been a matter of the most lively interest and concern. The Corsicans—no doubt because of the mountainous character of most of their terrain—were extraordinary for having preserved a national identity and a fierce spirit of independence through all the successive dominations to which they had been subject. Etruscans, Carthaginians, Romans, Goths, Vandals, the Byzantine Empire, Franks, and Saracens had held the island without really subduing it. The Pisans, who were given the sovereignty by the Pope at the end of the eleventh century, seemed, in retrospect at least, to have been better masters than any of the others. Then in the fourteenth century Corsica came under the sway of the Republic of Genoa, and for four hundred years was governed with singular harshness and cynicism. The Kingdom of Corsica (it had been so styled ever since Moorish times, nobody quite knew why) was to the Genoese sheer property to be exploited; in fact during part of the time the governing body had been the Bank of San Giorgio, a commercial corporation of Genoa, and not the Doge and Senate. Revolts and conspiracies, headed by a series of adventurers and patriots, notably the brilliant Sampiero da Bastelica (d. 1567), had been bloody and chronic. Half, at least, of the fighting had been domestic, for Corsicans, notorious for the vendetta, were just as restive under native overlords as under the Genoese bureaucracy. By the eighteenth century it had become evident that the Corsicans, if left to themselves, were going to drive the Genoese out, and each of the Mediterranean powers began moves to secure the sovereignty of the island for itself, or at least to prevent it from falling into the hands of a rival. For a time it seemed politic to all parties to preserve the *status quo* by lending aid to the waning Genoese Republic. In 1729, when a serious revolt broke out, the Emperor Charles VI sent in German troops; in 1738 France sent in French. On both occasions the Corsicans promptly revolted as soon as the "pacifying" troops had been withdrawn. In 1736, that is, between the German and the French occupations, occurred the bizarre episode of Corsica's only king. Theodor von Neuhof, a German baron and adventurer, arrived from Tunis in a vessel flying the British flag. He was got up in a scarlet fur-trimmed caftan, full trousers, and peaked shoes, and he carried richly decorated pistols stuck in a silken girdle, but he topped off this Moorish garb with a long curled European wig and broad-brimmed cocked hat, and his sword was a long Toledo blade. He called himself Grandee of Spain, Lord of England, Peer of France, Baron of the Empire, and Prince of the Papal See; he brought arms and other stores and offered further aid to the islanders if they would make him king. They had no objection to doing so, for they had recently offered the sovereignty without result to the King of Sardinia, the Pope, and the King of Spain, and would have offered it to any power on earth that would have helped them expel the Genoese. King Theodore was personally valiant, but none of the great powers underwrote his cause with the money and stores he had hoped for. He left the island within a few months, hovered vainly about Corsica for several years, drifted finally to London, fell into a debtors' prison, and died in the most abject poverty, having registered the Kingdom of Corsica for the benefit of his creditors.

As early as 1735 the French government had secretly adopted a definite plan and a firm policy with regard to Corsica: to annex it ultimately, but only by cession or purchase from Genoa, and then only at the request of an ostensibly respectable party within the island itself. Great Britain had followed its usual course of taking the cue from circumstance. In the year of King Theodore (1736), wishing to confirm the country's then peaceful relations with France, Queen Caroline as Regent had issued a proclamation prohibiting any of His Majesty's subjects from furnishing provisions or assistance to "the malcontents of Corsica." Four years later the War of the Austrian Succession aligned Great Britain with Austria and Sardinia against France, Spain, and Genoa, and for a few years inclined British policy in the Mediterranean to schemes of Corsican intervention. In 1743 a British squadron carried Theodore back to L'Île Rousse, but the King declined to land. In 1745 Great Britain joined Austria and Sardinia in a campaign to establish Charles Emmanuel as sovereign of the island, Great Britain presumably to pick up some naval bases. A British squadron shelled and took Bastia and St.-Florent, according to agreement, but then withdrew from the campaign. This defection was due partly to a conviction that the Austrians and the Sardinians were not fulfilling their engagements as to money and troops, and partly to disgust at the domestic broils of the Corsicans. Count Domenico Rivarola, a Corsican in the employ of Sardinia, whom the expedition had brought in as Generalissimo, proved not to have the confidence of Gaffori and Matra, the actual leaders of the insurgent band in the island, and after capturing Bastia, the Corsicans had taken to shooting each other. Mainly, however, Great Britain shifted its policy because the death of the King of Spain in July 1746 seemed to offer the opportunity for a separate peace with his successor, and the British government wanted Corsica to bargain with. The Anglo-Austro-Sardinian campaign against Corsica was later revived, but nothing had come of it when the war ended. The peace of Aix-la-Chapelle (18 October 1748) restored the *status quo*. Corsica was confirmed to Genoa and the island was ruled by a French expeditionary force, with the usual insurrection when the expedition was withdrawn. France left garrisons to help the Genoese hold the fortified coastal towns, and granted Genoa a subsidy for raising gradual replacements.

After the War of the Austrian Succession, the British government seems to have acquiesced in France's patient manoeuvring and to have written Corsica off its books. There was a tendency, since Britain had intervened with unsuccessful issue, to rate Corsica as worthless both commercially and militarily, and to consider its people savages. Corsica formed no part of Great Britain's plans in the Seven Years' War, and when that war ended in 1763, the British government was even induced, as part of the treaty of peace, to issue a proclamation similar to Queen Caroline's, branding the Corsicans as malcontents and rebels, and forbidding British nationals to give them aid and comfort under pain of the imputation of treason.

Since 1729 the insurgent Corsicans had been headed by a succession of elected chiefs or generals, among whom the name of Paoli had long been prominent. In 1735 Giacinto Paoli had been chosen one of three "generals of the people." Together the generals had introduced a democratic constitution, had supported the experiment of King Theodore, and had resumed the direction of the insurgent state when it became clear that Theodore's monarchy was a fiasco. Giacinto Paoli fought against the French invasion of 1738 for some months, but then, either having lost his nerve or having decided that further resistance would merely lacerate the country to no good end, surrendered to the French and was allowed to go into exile. With him he took his younger son, Pasquale, a boy of fourteen. His elder son, Clemente, mystical, austere, intrepid, fanatical—a sort of Catholic Roundhead—remained behind in active resistance. When, in 1753, Genoa secured the assassination of Gian Pietro Gaffori, sole general of the island after 1748 and one of the most formidable of the whole succession, Clemente was chosen one of a quadrumvirate to head the government, and was then offered the supreme power in his own person. He declined, feeling that his abilities were purely military, but he probably suggested his brother. At any rate, Pasquale Paoli was offered the generalship of the nation, and arrived in Corsica early in 1755. He was then just thirty years old.

Giacinto Paoli, on leaving Corsica, had entered the military service of the Kingdom of Naples, where he was given the rank of lieutenant-colonel. Pasquale received an extended education as cadet in the Royal Academy of Naples. He read repeatedly and with passionate attention the great classical historians Thucydides, Livy, Tacitus, and Polybius; he pored over the *Lives* of Plutarch; he seems to have committed to memory most of the great epic of Virgil. Antonio Genovesi, the well-known Neapolitan philosopher and political economist, trained him in liberal political theory. At the age of twenty-four he too entered the military service of Naples, but he had seen only garrison duty and indeed had not risen above the rank of second lieutenant when he was recalled to head the government of his native land.

The title of "General" which he bore is likely to give a distorted impression of his real achievement. It is doubtful whether Paoli, though a

competent strategist, was one of the greatest even of Corsican fighters:
history seems to place Sampiero, Gaffori, and even his own brother Clemente above him in this respect. Pasquale Paoli was primarily a legisla-
tor and political economist; he was everything that the title "Father of his
Country" implies. The best historical analogue would probably be King
Alfred. He saw clearly that something more than guerrilla warfare, however intrepid, was necessary to make Corsica a free country. The curse of
Corsican politics had always been internecine strife and treachery: Sampiero and Gaffori had both been assassinated by Corsicans. Paoli, like his
predecessors, drove the Genoese back to the fortified towns, but he then
proceeded to reduce Corsican anarchy to civilized order. Combining firmness with magnanimity, he suppressed revolts or won over dissidents by the
overwhelming force of his personality; he abolished the oppressive power
of the feudal lords and stamped out the vendetta. He created a new port
as an outlet for the nation's commerce, and built ships; he encouraged
agriculture and introduced new crops. He brought in a printing-press and
founded a university. In military matters his will was supreme; as regards
the other departments of the state he was in theory merely the chief execu-
tive under a constitution which anticipated strikingly by many years the
central features of the constitutions both of the United States and of Revolutionary France. In fact, because of the enthusiastic devotion of his people, he was a dictator; but he was a dictator who was earnestly striving to
lead his country towards self-government. In the brief ten years of his
generalship, he had probably brought Corsica farther on the road to
practical independence than all his predecessors of the preceding century
and a half.

A generation profoundly stirred by theories of the progressive corruption of governments and the glories of the state of nature, found that it no
longer had to look to the remote past or the world of ideas for its example
of the good state, or at least of a state which held promise of becoming
good. Just as Macpherson's Ossian had arrived in the nick of time to
realize contemporary theories about primitive poetry, so in the early six-
ties of the eighteenth century Corsica was being recommended to men's
consciousness as the embodiment of all that was hopeful in enlightened,
up-to-date political theory. But precise information was still sadly lacking.
In 1764 and 1765 the ordinary European had only the vaguest notion
of what had been happening in Corsica in the last decade, and had practically no means of finding out. Incredible as it seems to an age accustomed

to great organized news-services with their scrambling correspondents, no Briton capable of making a coherent and literate report had as yet been beyond the coast towns of Corsica. English merchants had traded with Corsica time out of mind; English men-of-war had touched there and on one occasion (as we have seen) had even bombarded two of its ports. But Boswell laid claim to be the first British gentleman to reach the interior of Corsica, and his claim has never been disputed.

Rousseau had had much to do with bringing Corsica to the attention of the age. In the *Contrat social* (1762) he had remarked that, in the midst of almost hopeless governmental corruption, there was one country still capable of legislation, and that he had a presentiment that the little island of Corsica would one day astonish Europe. Matteo Buttafoco, a Corsican in the service of the French, had written to him in the autumn of 1764 urging him to come to Corsica and draw up a constitution for the nation. The invitation to visit Corsica was somewhat cautiously seconded by Paoli, though he seems not to have known of it until after it had been made. He had no intention of giving Rousseau *carte blanche* to remodel the government, which was being satisfactorily shaped under his own direction, but he was very much alive to the prestige which Rousseau could give his cause as historian and propagandist. Rousseau, however, through no fault of his own, believed that he had been officially solicited to be Corsica's Lycurgus: that he had received the most flattering kind of commission which could possibly come to a political theorist and reformer. It was nothing less than the opportunity to write a new *Republic* with a guarantee of seeing his ideal tried out.

Boswell and Rousseau must have said more about Corsica than the journal records; at some point in the conversation Boswell in more than jest must have announced his determination to include the island in his tour and must have secured from Rousseau the promise of a letter of introduction to Paoli. On 11 May, when (as he thought) he was winding up his affairs in Rome and preparing to turn homeward, he had written to Rousseau telling him that he had almost finished his tour of Italy, that he had promised to see Deleyre again, and that before embarking for France from Genoa he was determined to go to Corsica, "as I told you at Môtiers." He therefore begged Rousseau to send the letter of introduction. If he did not get it, he was going to show as a passport the note he had received from Rousseau at Geneva: "It will be odd if I get hanged as a spy." Mountstuart's invitation caused a radical revision of his plans. In letters

which he wrote in July from Venice to Deleyre and Johnston, he said he
was going from Leghorn to Genoa, and from Genoa to France—no mention of Corsica. But when at Parma he and Deleyre talked about Rousseau, the scheme returned upon his mind with irresistible force, and he
wrote in his memoranda, "You must see Corsica." At Florence he found
the letter from Rousseau that he had begged for waiting for him, and that
clinched the matter. Corsica he must see, though he ought long since to
have started for home, and Corsica he did see even after granting himself
five additional undutiful weeks in Siena.

His first plan had been to embark from Genoa. But at Florence, Keith
Stewart had not only scared him about the danger of being captured by
Barbary pirates, but had further warned him against the Genoese, presumably suggesting that they might detain him at Genoa if they knew that
he proposed to visit the insurgents. Then, too, if he sailed from Genoa, he
would probably be landed at Bastia, and, the Genoese apart, he did not
know whether he would be permitted to pass from Bastia into the interior.
In 1756, by the first treaty of Compiègne, France had renewed its subsidy
to Genoa, but had increased the number of French troops in Corsica. In
August 1764 (only a few months before the time we are now considering)
she had granted new subsidies and had assumed the entire defence of
Bastia, Ajaccio, Calvi, Algajola, and St.-Florent. Nobody could tell Boswell much about the relations between the French commander and
Paoli's nation. It seemed better to land on a part of the coast held by the
insurgents, and for this the regular route was from Leghorn to Cap Corse.
Boswell arranged passage on a small merchant bark owned by a Corsican
of Pino who exported wine to Leghorn; it flew the Tuscan flag and had
a Livornese master. Two nights before his departure he had the good
fortune to meet Count Antonio Rivarola, the Sardinian consul at Leghorn, a Corsican and son of a former general of the kingdom, the generalissimo whom the British had supported in 1745. Rivarola gave him
some extremely useful letters of introduction; he also (though Boswell
never suspected it) arranged to have all his movements in Corsica
watched and reported for the King of Sardinia.

There was so little wind that the passage took two days. Boswell was
sick a little at first and found the berth allotted him in the cabin intolerable
because of "mosquitoes and other vermin," but the crew made a bed for
him on the deck, a Corsican played on a cither and he joined in with his
flute; at sunset the whole company sang the Ave Maria "with great de-

votion and some melody." The idyllic tone, struck at the beginning of the tour, was to persist.

There was, as a matter of fact, complete freedom of communication between the towns held by the French and the insurgents, because the French were looking forward to annexation in the not distant future and wished to placate the Corsicans as much as possible. If Boswell had known this, had further known where Paoli was at the moment, and had been able to arrange passage to Ajaccio, he could have put himself in the presence of the Corsican chief with a ride of less than thirty-five miles. But it is doubtful whether he would have shortened and simplified his route even if his information had been better. He wanted to see a great man and witness the birth of a nation, but he also very definitely wanted to make a tour of Corsica and see a country which nobody else had seen. He would in any case, I think, have penetrated to the nationalist capital, Corte, which is roughly in the centre of the island. As it turned out, he traversed three fourths of the length of Corsica from north to south. Landing at Centuri, on the western side of the tip of Cap Corse, he came down the west coast by Morsiglia, Pino, Nonza, and Patrimonio, his trail probably following much the line of the present road. Then he struck almost directly south to Corte by Oletta and Murato. Arriving at Corte, he found that Paoli was presiding over a circuit court at Sollacarò "beyond the mountains," that is, west of the great mountain chain that divides Corsica from north-west to south-east, and about as far south of Corte as Corte is south of Centuri. Again following a nearly straight line, he headed for Sollacarò by way of Bocognano, Bastelica, and Ornano. The total length of Corsica from north to south in a straight line is about 115 miles. Boswell's route to Sollacarò must have amounted to more than 100. He covered it in eight days, with a stop-over of one day in Corte. Outside the garrison towns there were no inns. He sometimes passed the night at the houses of gentlemen to whom he had letters of recommendation, but more frequently stopped at monasteries.

What strikes a modern reader as extraordinary is that he should have made so little special preparation for an extended trip into the interior of a country like Corsica. The island is a continuation, not of the Apennines, but of the Alps. In its confined space are packed about forty peaks of more than 6,500 feet, some rising close to 9,000 feet. In fact, except for one narrow strip of alluvial land on the east coast which Boswell did not visit, the whole island is violently mountainous. In 1765 there were no made roads. People travelled on foot or on the backs of diminutive horses, mules, and asses by rough trails cutting through the dense undergrowth of the lower slopes (the *maquis*), and zig-zagging up over the lofty cols. One can now go all the way from Centuri to Sollacarò by good motor-road, but the route is more circuitous than Boswell's. Even now if one set out to retrace Boswell's route exactly, one would have to take to trails for which a modern traveller would think hobnailed shoes and knapsack obligatory. Boswell, so far as we know, got no special clothes or boots; he set sail for Corsica with his servant and all his usual luggage. He threaded the *maquis* and toiled up mountains in the effulgence of scarlet and gold; in his portmanteau was a full formal suit of black. Though he himself, apparently not unwillingly, covered much of the road on foot, he saw to it that the several pieces of his luggage were carried wherever he went, sometimes by pack-animals, more often on the heads of sturdy women. He came back from Corsica with both great-toes painfully sore. This affliction, which he would suffer from for years, may safely be attributed to ingrown nails caused by much walking down mountain trails in riding-boots.

Boswell, though robust and active, was a city boy with a city boy's attitudes, but in this instance his behaviour was merely typical of the eighteenth century. We have so developed the comfort and speed of transportation that there are no longer any points of similarity between, let us say, a trip by Pullman or jet across the Continent and a fishing expedition deep into the Rockies. In the eighteenth century, however, all travel was at times so arduous that the difference between touring Germany and touring Corsica seemed only one of degree. Boswell's contemporaries applauded the originality of his quest and would have admired his intrepidity in risking capture by pirates or arrest as a spy if there had been any risk, but his willingness to traverse two hundred miles or more of very difficult and savage terrain, largely on foot, does not seem to have struck them as remarkable.

Corsica stirred the Romantic sensibility to almost unparalleled virtuosity of word-painting. A reader who came to Boswell's published account of his Corsican jaunt after reading several of these Romantic tours would probably conclude that Boswell's feeling about extravagant landscapes was quite typical of the Age of Reason. Such a reader would be wrong. To a young man who once wrote that he would like to be whinstone on the face of a mountain so as to brave the elements by glorious insensibility, mountains could never have been mere horrid or disgusting protuberances. Boswell's sensibility in this respect was not nearly so advanced as Thomas Gray's, but it was much more advanced than Samuel Johnson's. Read first for purposes of orientation an early twentieth-century impression, and then consider several vignettes from Boswell's *Tour:*

Mountains crowd in upon the road, and the lofty Incudine, with its rich vesture of green and grey, of purple and crimson, with a fairy gossamer mantilla of cloud thrown over its brows of white, seems to march from the north as though to bar the way. Nature has been wildly extravagant in tossing torrent and tree, rock and stream, mountain and valley in vast spendthrift profusion. It is as though she had gilded and gladdened into a garden a corner of cosmic chaos. Twisting through age-old forests of chestnut-trees, ... through clumps of lofty, meagre pines and giant fern plots, now cutting its way through a huge Jove-thrown boulder, then narrowing to cling desperately to a steep, *maquis*-covered mountain-side, flower-brightened, the road takes its way. Far above are the bare hilltops, where winter has but lately loosened her grasp, and from which she has hurled spring torrents down to the peaceful vale below, torrents which have cut deep paths for themselves in the road. Down, deep down, stream and waterfall play, and through a maze of shrubs and trees come their musical murmurs; the stroke of the woodman and his song echo through the glades; the birds are busy with their music; scattered like stars are wild flowers and berries; and everywhere, thrown between forest leaves and through boulder-clefts, flashes living gold from the sun's eastern mints.[1]

Here is Boswell:

[*From Morsiglia to Pino.*] I got a man with an ass to carry my baggage. But such a road I never saw. It was absolutely scrambling along the face of a rock overhanging the sea, upon a path sometimes not above a foot broad. I thought the ass rather retarded me, so I prevailed with the man to take my portmanteau and other things on his back....

From Murato to Corte, I travelled through a wild, mountainous, rocky country, diversified with some large valleys. I got little beasts for me

[1] George Renwick, *Romantic Corsica*, 1909, pp. 103–104, describing the road from Zonza to Solenzara. Muirhead's *Southern France with Corsica* forty-five years later notes that this road is "not practicable for cars."

and my servant, sometimes horses, but oftener mules or asses. We had no bridles but cords fixed round their necks, with which we managed them as well as we could. . . .

[*Beyond Corte: the spectacular region from Venaco to Vizzavona.*] Next morning I set out in very good order, having excellent mules and active, clever Corsican guides. The worthy fathers of the convent, who treated me in the kindest manner while I was their guest, would also give me some provisions for my journey; so they put up a gourd of their best wine and some delicious pomegranates. My Corsican guides appeared so hearty that I often got down and walked along with them, doing just what I saw them do. When we grew hungry, we threw stones among the thick branches of the chestnut trees which overshadowed us, and in that manner we brought down a shower of chestnuts, with which we filled our pockets and went on, eating them with great relish; and when this made us thirsty, we lay down by the side of the first brook, put our mouths to the stream, and drank sufficiently. It was just being for a little while one of the "*prisca gens mortalium,* the primitive race of men," who ran about in the woods eating acorns and drinking water. . . .

My journey over the mountains was very entertaining. I passed some immense ridges and vast woods. I was in great health and spirits, and fully able to enter into the ideas of the brave rude men whom I found in all quarters.

Boswell more than once deplored his deficiency in expressing visible objects, but the fact that he deplored it proves that his perception was in advance of his idiom. That road in Cap Corse does not force from him the almost painful outcry of Walpole ("But the road, West, the road!"); it is such a road as he never saw, it was absolutely scrambling. The Gorge of the Vecchio and the Col de Vizzavona (3,870 feet) do not move him to verbal raptures. They are merely "very entertaining"—a word that nobody born after 1800 could ever have used in such a connexion. Also, the way the attention in all the extracts is fixed on creature comforts and the varieties of human nature is perhaps rather eighteenth-century. But this young man in great health and spirits, exhilarated and released by muscular exertion in a primitive landscape, moved by peak, stream, and forest to feelings of delight which he is content to leave organic and un-analyzed—he is much more like us than Johnson or Walpole or the Romantics.

In sight of Sollacarò and the end of his pilgrimage, Boswell experienced very severe anxiety. All along his route he had been hearing from the islanders accounts which raised Paoli almost above humanity. This was no retired and uncourtly scholar to be won over by tact and unobtrusive flattery, no literary man to be hooked with the bait of adroit composition, no bored princeling for whom bait was unnecessary. Boswell, it will be remembered, had failed to secure an interview with Frederick the Great, and he may well have wondered what he would have said to Frederick if he had been introduced to him; more pertinently what that terrible old figure in the plain blue uniform would have said to *him*. This, perhaps, was a man like Frederick; almost certainly more like Frederick than like Johnson, Rousseau, Voltaire, or the Margrave of Baden. How could he account for his singular visit? Would he be permitted to speak to Paoli at all? If he was permitted, would he not be dismissed after a moment of frigid courtesy? Were the letters he had brought (Rousseau's and another from Count Rivarola) sufficient? Would it not be better to turn around and go home?

Of course he went forward, passed through the guards, and after very little delay was ushered into a room where Paoli was standing alone. He saw a tall, strongly-built man of forty, rather splendidly dressed in green and gold; a man with thinning reddish-blond hair and blue eyes, the most piercing eyes he had ever had turned on him; a man of noble and courtly bearing, polite but extremely reserved. Paoli read the letters from Rivarola and Rousseau without unbending, and he and Boswell walked backwards and forwards through the room for ten minutes, hardly saying a word, while Paoli scanned him "with a steadfast, keen, and penetrating eye, as if he searched my very soul." It was, on Boswell's testimony, the most severe trial he had ever been put to. At length Boswell ventured a compliment obviously prepared and rehearsed in advance ("Sir, I am upon my travels, and have lately visited Rome. I am come from seeing the ruins of one brave and free people; I now see the rise of another"), Paoli received it graciously, but with the sensible remark that Corsica aspired only for independence and had no hope and no chance of empire. Some of the Corsican nobles came into the room, dinner was announced, and Boswell was seated next to the General. The trial was over; Boswell had been approved. "Paoli became more affable with me. I made myself known to him. I forgot the great distance between us, and had every day some hours of private conversation with him."

By great good luck we have Paoli's own account of this meeting: it was recorded, with some attempt to reproduce his pronunciation and idiom, by Fanny Burney, an anecdotist with an incurable habit of over-dramatizing but who probably in this case sticks fairly close to fact.

He came to my country, and he fetched me some letter of recommending him; but I was of the belief he might be an impostor, and I supposed in my minte he was an espy; for I look away from him, and in a moment I look to him again, and I behold his tablets. Oh! he was to the work of writing down all I say! Indeed I was angry. But soon I discover he was no impostor and no espy; and I only find I was myself the monster he had come to discern. Oh! is a very good man; I love him indeed; so cheerful! so gay! so pleasant! but at the first, oh! I was indeed angry.

It is from this passage and a remark in one of Mrs. Piozzi's *Anecdotes* that posterity has derived its favorite legend of Boswell: that he pursued famous people with a notebook and wrote down their remarks on the spot. That legend Professor Tinker and Geoffrey Scott have exploded, as far as it is possible to explode any legend. The vast bulk of Boswell's notes were made, not in notebooks but on loose sheets of paper; they were made not on the spot but late at night in the privacy of his own room; they were almost invariably written in ink, not pencil. But there is evidence that on rare occasions Boswell did jot down something—probably no more than a word or two—in company; and this may have been one of the occasions. It is most unlikely that he resorted to so tactless a trick during that terrible ten minutes of the General's preliminary inspection, or later when the General had begun to unbend but the two of them were alone in the room; it is just possible that he did make a note later when the room filled, or during the course of the dinner. But it is much more probable that in Corsica, having nothing else to do, he wrote up his notes directly on retiring from the General's presence, and that Paoli came upon him one day when he was making a record of a conversation concluded only a few minutes before.

It is useless to berate history for relegating some of her greatest sons to comparative obscurity because it was their misfortune to head unsuccessful revolutions in countries that never established their independence. No one now will ever succeed in convincing the world that Paoli was as great a character as George Washington, and that, given the opportunity that Washington had, his fame would now shine as bright. But it appears really to be so. We are not confined to Boswell's memoirs in forming our judgement; a great many of Paoli's letters have been printed, and they confirm

Boswell's portrait at every point. Though Paoli had a low opinion of wit
that was glittering but superficial ("Je ne puis souffrir longtemps les
diseurs de bons mots," [1] he told Boswell), he had a real gift of eloquence.
His letters, and even his conversation as reported by Boswell, ring like
Roman oratory: "I reached the point where almost no one stood by me
but my brother, and I did not yield: shall I yield now when there is a
gleam of hope? *Ah, let them think me more honest or more ambitious!*"

Boswell had never heard anything like that from the lips of living man,
nor was he ever again to establish intimacy with any human creature so
magnanimous. He had at last met a hero; a hero the like of whom, as
William Pitt later remarked, was now to be found only in the pages of
Plutarch. Fiery, energetic, clear-eyed aspirant for the highest ranks of
fame ("I have an unspeakable pride," he told Boswell), Paoli remained
in the era of the encyclopedists a man of unshakable Catholic belief and
serene Christian faith. He seems never to have doubted for a moment that
it was God's will that Corsica should be free, nor that he was the elected
agent of God's purpose. ("I am no bigot, but I am persuaded, nay,
thoroughly convinced by a thousand particular proofs, that our war has
the protection of Heaven; from that is born my certainty of a happy
issue.") He speaks as easily and naturally of the operations of the Holy
Spirit as of those of the Corsican Assembly. Chastity in the eighteenth century was not expected of heads of states, however pious (Paoli could have
exchanged his title of general for that of king at any time he had had a
mind to), but he remained, through an exceptionally long life, a celibate
immune to sexual scandal. Yet he was not, like his brother Clemente,
a fighting monk; he was very much a man of the world, full-blooded,
ardent, literate, and courtly. Making all allowance for the projected devotion and awe which had raised him in the eyes of his followers almost
above human stature, it is clear that his presence was intrinsically impressive, that there was in it that element of the incalculable—even the formidable—which, more than goodness or unusual intellectual power, makes
the crowd single out one of its number as great. To traitors he spoke with a
fierceness and a darkness of brow that Boswell (who witnessed such a
scene) describes as awful. He was universally credited with seeing the
future in dreams, and told Boswell that he believed himself in fact to
have the gift of prophetic vision.

In the days that Boswell spent at Sollacarò he came closer to realizing

---

[1] "I cannot endure long the sayers of good things" (Boswell's translation).

his fantasies of greatness than at any other period of his life. As soon as Paoli was disabused of the notion that Boswell was a spy, he set about encouraging the suspicions of the genuine spies that he was an accredited envoy from the British government. He lodged him in the house of the local feudal chief, Colonna d'Istria, which was ruinous but magnificent, and surrounded him with all the pomp that he could muster. Boswell's morning chocolate was served up on a silver salver adorned with the arms of Corsica; he dined and supped at the General's table. The Corsican nobles came to pay their respects, and whenever he went abroad, he was attended by a party of guards. Boswell rides out, "mounted on Paoli's own horse, with rich furniture of crimson velvet, with broad gold lace, and . . . my guards marching along with me": it is a climax in his life. He is styled "the English ambassador" by the peasants and soldiers and gravely plays the role. "I did everything in my power to make them fond of the British, and bid them hope for an alliance with us."

Of course, being Boswell, he tries on other masks. He gets a Corsican dress made and wears it; Paoli presents him with his own pistols to complete the costume. He performs on the flute for his honest natural visitors "one or two Italians airs, and then some of our beautiful old Scots tunes. . . . The Corsicans were charmed with the specimens I gave them, though I may now say that they were very indifferently performed." He sings them Garrick's nautical ballad, "Heart of oak," and translates it into Italian. " 'Cuore di quercia,' cried they, 'bravo Inglese.' It was quite a joyous riot. I fancied myself to be a recruiting sea-officer. I fancied all my chorus of Corsicans aboard the British fleet."

Whatever the differences in young Boswell's method of approach to a great man, the ensuing conversations always drift in one direction. His daily interviews with Paoli show, even through a published record that was meant to conceal it, the old familiar pattern: enthusiastic and humble attention to the remarks of a remarkable man; the swift establishment of so perfect a *rapport* that within a matter of hours the overworked General of the Corsicans is listening with deep sympathy to the unreserved outpourings of Boswell's troubled soul. Are licentious pleasures permissible? Should I get married? What can I do about my melancholy constitution and my fear concerning free-will? He tells Paoli about Samuel Johnson and repeats some of his sayings; Paoli is delighted and translates them into Italian for the rest of the company. When he says good-bye Paoli asks him to write: "Remember that I am your friend." "I dare not transcribe from my private notes the feelings which I had at this interview. I should perhaps appear too enthusiastic. I took leave of Paoli with regret and agitation, not without some hopes of seeing him again. From having known intimately so exalted a character, my sentiments of human nature were raised; while, by a sort of contagion, I felt an honest ardour to distinguish myself and be useful, as far as my situation and abilities would allow; and I was, for the rest of my life, set free from a slavish timidity in the presence of great men, for where shall I find a man greater than Paoli?"

Paoli was a politician; had he found Boswell a bore and a nuisance, he would still have flattered him if he had thought there was any possibility that Boswell might help his cause in Britain. But subsequent events prove that he was quite sincere in proclaiming himself Boswell's friend. Within the space of a day or two he had felt himself strongly attracted to this eager and agreeable young man; and the interest of that first meeting developed into a deep affection which endured for the rest of Boswell's life. One element in his later attitude was undoubtedly simple gratitude for Boswell's energetic defence of the Corsican cause in his book and in the newspapers, but gratitude alone would never account for a feeling so tender. It was a paternal feeling, and rather oddly so, for Paoli was only fifteen years older than Boswell and only forty when the two first met. In the years that followed, the influence of the General of the Corsicans was perhaps more powerful for good in Boswell's life than that of any other person except his wife. Paoli advised him, admonished him, chided him, but he never once showed anger towards him.

The old house of Colonna d'Istria was much decayed and let in wind and rain. Boswell, starting off from Sollacarò in persistent bad weather, soon found that the heavy cold he knew he had was only prelude to something much worse—malaria. Burning with fever, racked with chills, continually drenched with rain, he felt the trip back to be long, hard, and not very entertaining. Ill and light-headed, he sometimes lost the power to enter into the ideas of his brave rude companions: he railed at the stupidity of one of the Corsican guards whom Paoli had insisted on sending with him, "a strange iron-coloured fearless creature" who had told him casually how he once manoeuvred so as to shoot two Genoese through the head with one bullet. His old friends the Franciscan fathers at Corte were most solicitous, and he spent some days there nursing himself. He wanted to write to Johnson of his adventures, but the monastery did not provide that physical contact with the spirit of Corsican independence which his superstitious soul demanded. Between bouts of the ague, he walked into Corte so that he could write the letter from Paoli's house. From Corte his route led to Bastia, for Paoli had not only assured him that it was safe to go there, but had even given him a letter of recommendation to the Comte de Marbeuf, the French commander. He went by way of Rostino in the hope of seeing Clemente de Paoli, but missed him; at Vescovato he met and was entertained by that same Colonel Buttafoco who had solicited Rousseau's aid in drafting a constitution for Corsica. Buttafoco went with him to Bastia and introduced him to Marbeuf. The brilliance of Marbeuf's levee in the old Citadel delighted him: "It was like passing at once from ... the mountains of Corsica to the banks of the Seine."

Marbeuf, discovering his illness when his ague forced him to ask for a chair, made him take a room in his own house, put him under the care of the army physician and surgeon, and took as thoughtful a charge of him as though he had been a near relation. In twelve days he was certified able to travel again. He had spent more time in bed at Bastia than he had at Sollacarò in the company of the General of the Corsicans.

He set sail at last for Genoa, but there were to be further delay and more agitation. A tempest forced the bark on which he had taken passage to seek harbour at the little Genoese island of Capraia, an almost soilless rock about eighteen miles east of Cap Corse, and kept him storm-bound there for more than a week. He lodged with the Franciscans and tried to keep off ennui by writing a minute account of the island. The device failed. He wrangled with Jacob, who had scolded him again for stinginess, and worked himself up to a fury of coarse invective (in Italian) against the master of the felucca he counted on to take him to the mainland because he suspected the man of unnecessary lingering. When the felucca did sail, he was sick and scared. On 30 November 1765, just fifty days after his embarkation from Leghorn, he coasted, still seasick, into the harbour of Genoa. "Land, overjoyed." A packet of letters was awaiting him: three, "all love," from Girolama; three, not all love, from his father. "Your conduct astonishes and amazes me. ... I have wrote letters on the back of letters to you, telling you to come home." As far back as August, Lord Auchinleck had suffered a complete stoppage of urine and had been at death's door; while Boswell was dallying at Siena, he had been lying in pain and uncertainty at Auchinleck and Glasgow. "This my state, I should think, will make you incline to accelerate your return, because I hope you have impressions of filial duty, besides knowing of what consequence it is to you in after life that I, before I die, come to be satisfied, from what I see of your conduct, that you are become a man such as I and your other friends could wish you to be." He must, of course, obey his father's command now that it had caught up with him; to do him justice, he wanted now to obey it. There could be no long sojourn in Genoa, and there was much to see there. But he found time to write and send off to one of his Dominican friends, Padre Pio Clemente Vasco of Bologna, a paragraph for the Italian gazettes, saying that Mr. Boswell, a Scots gentleman upon his travels over Europe, had been in Corsica, and that the politicians of Italy were aroused. The Corsican campaign was on.

CHAPTER

XVI

As far back as Brunswick, Boswell had announced his intention of being Mr. Boswell of Auchinleck and no other. His difficulty in achieving identity was due not merely to excessive mobility and lack of self-confidence but also in large part to the lack of a public uniqueness to match and justify the surge of unique value his own feelings assured him of. Now he had it. "I am no longer that delicate, anxious being who complained to you in the Val de Travers," he wrote to Rousseau. "I am a man. I think for myself." Other men made Continental tours, other men scribbled and published, other men even could boast of familiar acquaintance with Samuel Johnson and Jean Jacques Rousseau. But nobody else had been over the mountains to Paoli; nobody else could talk with authority of the little isle which was one day to astonish Europe. Boswell once records a wish that he had the noble force of Johnson, but he has emerged for ever from the fantasy of being Sir Richard Steele or West Digges. As Scipio is Africanus, as Johnson is Dictionary Johnson, so Boswell is now and will remain Corsica Boswell. He has grown up as much as he ever will.

On the morning after his arrival in Genoa, he called on the British consul, James Hollford, and opened his campaign ("Talked of Corsican affairs plainly"); then he waited on the French *chargé d'affaires* and was invited to dinner. There, a Genoese secretary of state increased his self-esteem by revealing that he had been under the surveillance of Genoese spies all the time he had been in Corsica: "Sir, you have made me tremble, although I never saw you before." "Do you know," he wrote delightedly to John Johnston, "I have had my own fears at Genoa. . . . I am pretty certain that the noble merchants of this despicable republic would have been well pleased to have had a stiletto slipped into my back, or to have got me into prison and very quietly given me a little poison. But the British flag makes them tremble, and good Captain Robinson of the *Vulture* rides at anchor in their port." If the dagger, the chain, and the poisoned bowl are rodomontade, they are rodomontade that John Dick, the seasoned consul at Leghorn, encouraged him in, and there can be no doubt that he had caused a great flurry in the foreign offices. Count Rivarola's reports at Turin record a rumour that the Doge had him in for questioning. This seems hardly likely, for Boswell says nothing of it in the published *Tour,* and there is no reason why he should have suppressed so flattering an attention. His notes mention no presentation, but there evidently was one, for he recorded uneasiness on being told that he had kept the Doge waiting.

The notes on churches, palaces, and pictures are kept up with un-flagging industry and with new self-confidence. Genoa being favoured by more northerly nations as a winter resort, his ten days there also record meetings with an extraordinary number of visiting notables. He had a letter of introduction to the French astronomer Joseph Jérôme Lalande, who was preparing a guide to Italy (published in 1769 in eight little volumes) which is wonderfully useful for extending and explaining Bos-well's own cryptic record. Count Hessenstein, illegitimate son of Frederick I of Sweden, he thought a "sweet, lively young man"; he does not char-acterize Henry Ellis, explorer of Hudson Bay and successively Governor of Georgia and Nova Scotia. Two Englishmen who probably interested him more were John Symonds, later Gray's successor in the chair of Modern History at Cambridge, and the ambiguous young cleric-nobleman from whom all the Bristol hotels ultimately derive their name: Frederick Augustus Hervey, son of Pope's "Sporus," later simultaneously Bishop of Derry and Earl of Bristol. To Symonds and Hervey Boswell talked Cor-sica so effectively that they both made excursions there themselves.

Boswell came up the Riviera to Marseilles, struck north to Avignon and from Avignon made a side-excursion to Nîmes and Montpellier, re-turned through Nîmes to catch the Marseilles-Lyons mail-wagon at Pont St.-Esprit north of Avignon, and then went on to Paris in the diligence. His original plan had been to go as far as Antibes by felucca, but after the vessel had been held up twice by unfavourable winds, he took to the land at Noli, letting Jacob and the luggage continue by water. The trip was memorable for certain dispatches he sent off from Marseilles, for his stop in Avignon, and for troubles with his toe-nails, his dog, and his servant.

At Genoa a surgeon had operated on one of his toes and had afforded him some relief, but he was travelling mainly on horseback to save money, and by the time he got to Aix both nails were in the flesh and his jack-boots were torture. The surgeons he sent for at Montpellier and Lyons scared him: the first, "as awkward and bouncing a dog as if he had been bred a blacksmith," he dismissed when he saw how the fellow looked at his toes; the second, "a fat and an alarming dog," gravely recommended pulling out one of the offending nails altogether but was allowed only to apply a plaster. One of the toes got infected and the whole foot swelled alarmingly; by the time Boswell reached Lyons he could not walk across the room and had to forgo sight-seeing altogether. At Paris a more competent surgeon took him in charge, warning him that a complete cure would take time. The treatment was efficacious, for we hear no more of sore toes for many years.

The dog, who bore the name Jachone, was (like the painful toe-nails) a Corsican souvenir. To protect himself from assassination, Paoli kept five or six large fierce dogs, "something between a mastiff and a strong shep-herd's dog," constantly about him. When Boswell took his leave at Solla-carò, Paoli presented him with one of these animals. Boswell's treatment of Jachone has done more than all his debaucheries to blast his character in the eyes of the British nation. He kept the dog on very short rations and forbade Jacob or any one else to feed him; when the poor brute held back on his leash or ran away to haunt butchers' stalls and snatch pieces of meat (as he repeatedly did), he beat him systematically and unmerci-fully. These beatings have been taken to reveal a sadistic streak in Boswell's make-up. That he actually suffered from any such perversion seems most unlikely. The Jachone episode is isolated and uncharacteristic. There is nothing to indicate that Boswell had a way with animals (he confessed to a positive antipathy for cats), but in the years following he was the owner of many horses and many dogs, and he left no record of having beaten any of them. His casual directions concerning the care of the horses at Auchinleck after he became laird show some ignorance but no lack of consideration. He often inflicted mental pain on others through self-absorption and inability to deny himself pleasure, but deliberate acts of physical cruelty seem simply not to have been in his nature. He never struck his wife or the servants, as Pepys often did; he records only one beating administered by him to one of his children (he beat Sandy once for lying, as his father had beaten him); on the rare occasions when liquor made him savage, he restricted his violence to smashing the furniture and throwing things about. Jachone was full-grown and intractable, and it seems fair to conclude that Boswell had been told in Corsica that he could induce him to follow on foot back to England only by disciplining him severely, keeping him hungry, and convincing him that he was going to be fed only from Boswell's own hand. When Boswell (at Toulon) decided that the beating was accomplishing nothing, he stopped it. "I saw that it was to no purpose to beat the brute, as he did not understand what I meant, being very stupid. I therefore resolved to carry him along with me just like a trunk or a packet that could move of itself." At the rougher inns he slept with Jachone on his bed or in his arms; at Lyons, where this would not have been tolerated, he caused a soft bed of hay to be made for the animal in a corner of the room. Poor Jachone failed to keep up with the stage-coach, and was lost somewhere near Auxerre. Boswell later struck the worst of the beatings out of the manuscript, surely not from motives of prudence (consider what he left in), but because he himself found the passages painful to read. He was ashamed, perhaps not of having beaten a dog, but of having done it in anger and with relish. He may also by that time have learned how much food a large dog really needs.

Jacob, that uncomplaisant Swiss, was not above lecturing Boswell for his own good, and Boswell gave him almost daily opportunity. He had never submitted to the convention that masters have places as well as servants, alternated between stiff authority and expansive familiarity, snooped in areas that were Jacob's responsibility, and was for ever putting Jacob to the question. There had been wrangling ("changling" is Boswell's word) almost from the first, and on the trip up from Genoa Boswell's narrowness in the article of food for Jacob (who wanted capon and Madeira) and his severities to Jachone brought Jacob to the point of revolt and downright rudeness. He fed the dog against positive orders and said if his brother had behaved as Boswell was behaving he would have thrashed him. Boswell wanted to turn him off on the spot, but was unable to because he owed him a considerable sum for wages and was short of money. Jacob's most extended lecture occurred as the pair jogged sluggishly along between Fréjus and Le Luc. He told Boswell that he had been badly brought up and did not have the manners befitting his station. "Every man ought to keep to his own class according to his quality. You would like to behave just like a peasant. And you force a servant to speak as he should not, because you torment him with questions. You want to know everything to the very bottom." Boswell paid him off in Lyons, Jacob by that time having himself decided that he did not wish to go on to Paris. The parting was rather awkward, for Boswell was not magnanimous enough to forgo *his* chance to lecture. "I told him that I regarded him as a very worthy man, but that I was, however, glad that he left me, for after having rebelled and been so free, it was impossible he could be a good servant for one of my disposition. He seemed angry a little at this. He made awkward speeches as how he wished to have served me better, and was sorry for having ever offended me, and was much obliged to me for my goodness to him, etc. Thus was I at last separated from my Swiss governor. I wished him sincerely all happiness."

An entry in Boswell's Register of Letters on 23 December, when he was at Marseilles, marks the beginning of one of the most elaborate and extended campaigns of puffing and propaganda ever to engage the attention of a man of letters. We have already seen that at Genoa he had taken steps to get notice of his Corsican adventure inserted in the Italian gazettes. The entry at Marseilles is "Mr. Wilkie," and it is repeated just a month later when Boswell was in Paris. John Wilkie was the publisher of *The London Chronicle,* an English newspaper of wide circulation, and what Boswell sent him must have been a series of dated news-paragraphs which Wilkie was to "release" separately in successive issues of the paper. They began to appear on 7 January 1766, more than a month before Boswell landed in England, and were (to use the terminology which Boswell himself later employed in indexing them in his own file of the *Chronicle*) a mixture of "fact" and "invention." The serious and persisting object of this campaign was to work up so much sympathy for the Corsican cause in England that the Government would be forced to reverse its policy of non-intervention; the immediate object was to make England aware of the existence of James Boswell, Esq., and to puff the book on Corsica which he was already planning to write. Our concern at the moment is only with that phase of the campaign which ended when Boswell arrived in London in February 1766.

Since the Proclamation of 1763, in which Great Britain had agreed to consider the Corsicans malcontents and rebels, very little concerning Corsica had appeared in the British press. Boswell started the campaign with a letter purporting to have been sent in by a correspondent in England, briefly summarizing the political situation in Corsica and pointing out the importance of the island in a military way. Then, with due attention to dramatic suspense, he developed a narrative of intrigue in a series of letters purportedly sent from various Italian cities in various Italian states, all actually written by James Boswell, Esq., in Marseilles and Paris. The "inventions" became more romantic and interesting, until, just as Boswell reached London, they were dispelled as baseless rumours, leaving only the "facts," of which there had been a considerable number. To summarize some of the more interesting paragraphs:

Rome, 5 December (appearing in London on 9 January, Boswell on the road from Lyons to Paris). There have been rumours that Great Britain was planning to send an embassy to Corsica; well, a British subject has actually been there. He is Mr. Boswell, a Scots gentleman upon his travels over Europe. He met Paoli, and was treated with every mark of distinction. He says he went to Corsica merely out of curiosity, but the politicians of Italy think they can see more important reasons for his visit. The Genoese are not a little alarmed. People in this part of the world are curious to know what will really be the consequence of Mr. Boswell's tour to Corsica.

Florence, 16 December (appearing in London on 23 January, Boswell in Paris). We think we now know the true motives of the late mysterious expedition into Corsica. Mr. B., with some of his friends, had worked out a scheme for getting the Young Chevalier made King of Corsica, and went over to sound out Paoli concerning it. The Chevalier knew nothing of this notable plot.

Genoa, 2 January (appearing in London on 6 February, Boswell at Calais). Colonel Matra and Captain Grimaldi, of our service, who took refuge with the Sieur Boswell in Capraia, say that they could learn nothing from him as to his motives, but report that he had a great many papers, about which he seemed anxious.

Leghorn, 3 January (appearing in London on 11 February, Boswell on the road from Dover to London). Nothing could prove the weakness of the Genoese more than their fears about Mr. Boswell's tour. Why suppose that it indicates any political interest in Corsica on the part of the British government? Isn't the curiosity of an observant traveller enough reason for such a tour?

Turin, 6 January (appearing in London on 13 February, Boswell two days in London). There is no truth whatever in the rumours that Mr. Boswell is really a desperate adventurer named Macdonald. He is a gentleman of fortune upon his travels, a friend of the celebrated Rousseau. We don't think he had any instructions from his Court to treat with Paoli, but we hope he will nevertheless be able to undeceive his countrymen with regard to the Corsican nation.

London, 15 February. Yesterday (actually on 11 February) James Boswell, Esq., arrived in town from his travels.

This summary having got us some seven weeks ahead of the narrative, we now return to 24 December and Avignon.

Boswell hurried and pushed through various annoying obstacles to reach Avignon in time for the first mass of Christmas and just made it, arriving in town about eleven in the evening and going straight to the Cathedral as soon as he had deposited his luggage at his inn. Next morning he went to mass again, and then presented a letter of introduction from Andrew Lumisden to a notable Scots Jacobite in Avignon. James Murray, second son of Lord Stormont, advocate and M.P., had taken part in the Rebellion of 1715 when he was a young man of twenty-five, and had now been in exile for fifty years. His sister Marjory, widow of John Hay, one of the Pretender's generals, herself formerly one of the principal ladies of the Pretender's court, lived with him. He bore the Jacobite style of Earl of Dunbar and she that of Countess of Inverness. The fact that their younger brother, William, had kept clear of overt Jacobitism, had gone to Oxford, and had risen to be Lord Mansfield, Lord Chief Justice of the King's Bench, added spice to the meeting. Both Lord Dunbar and Lady Inverness were pathetically pleased by Boswell's call, asked him to family dinner, and entertained him freely and unaffectedly with Jacobite anecdotes and gossip, of which nobody had a larger or more authentic store. It had been Boswell's intention to leave next day, but Lord Dunbar would hear none of it. " 'You're not absolutely pressed?' BOSWELL. 'No.' DUNBAR. 'Will you give us another day?' BOSWELL. 'Indeed will I, my Lord, with all my heart.' " Dunbar wrote on the 28th to Lumisden, thanking him for having procured him so valuable an acquaintance.

The natural and almost constant power of being agreeable to others is an aspect of Boswell's character that a biographer ought to render imaginatively ("dramatize") and keep constantly to the fore. Indeed, in justice to the facts, he ought probably to make it the prevailing impression of his book. Many years ago, when Boswell's journal was still to me a fresh and overwhelming experience, I said that a biography of

Boswell ought to give its readers no more—and no less—than an impression of what life felt like to Boswell. But surely that is only half of the obligation that rests on a biographer of Boswell. The outer or public Boswell was as real and as important as the inner or private, and should be as graphically presented. The difficulty is that Boswell has himself dramatized the private aspect ("the state of my own mind") with incomparable vividness, but of necessity provides only inferences and second-hand testimony concerning the public. Lovableness, agreeableness are not part of what life feels like to a man himself, they are part of what he feels like to other people. And there exist very few genuinely imaginative recordings of the public Boswell; almost none except for one or two paragraphs by Fanny Burney, who did not feel his charm and cast him as a merely comic character. As a result, the biographer who wishes to do justice to Boswell's agreeableness must write against Boswell himself, and will always be defeated. Do what one will, Boswell's own enormous private record is always going to make his life seem scrappy, furtive, gross, and unlovely. There would be nothing to deplore in that if one could with equal force present Boswell's charm, his affableness, his good humour, his genuine good will. The combination would be a kind of biography like Boswell's own *Life of Johnson,* infinitely superior to the kind that debunks or the kind that draws a decent veil. But in fact a twentieth-century biographer can do little more than *tell* his readers about Boswell's amiability. He can *enact* for them his wrangling with his servant, his dog-beatings, and his whoring.

Of the whoring the first instance occurs four months after Boswell left Florence, and would not be worth specifying if it did not mark a moral crisis, something like the episode of the soldier's wife at Berlin when he lost the merit of a year's chastity. Duncan Drummond, a young artillery officer whom he had met in Genoa, had counselled him when he was at Marseilles to look up a Mademoiselle Susette, "a very good girl whom he kept a long time, and had with him eight months at Minorca." Boswell felt an obligation of fidelity to Girolama, Paoli had earnestly counselled chastity and an early marriage, and Boswell had made his twenty-fifth birthday (29 October 1765, just after he had left Paoli) the occasion of a serious resolve not to run any risks with his health. But at Marseilles he wavered, got a *valet de place* to take him to Susette's lodgings, and passed the night with her. "She was so little that I had an idea as if she was a child, and had not much inclination for her. I recalled my charming Signora at Siena, and was disgusted at all women but her, and angry at myself for being in the arms of another." Next day (a Sunday): "I found I was now above being taken in by whores. I viewed with pity the irregularities of humanity. I went to hear mass, but was too late." Actually, the consequence of the "irregularity" was precisely that of the affair in Berlin: the resumption of the old licentious routine.

For some months now he had known that Rousseau had left his retreat at Môtiers, but he did not know where he was or what his plans were. Mme. Boy de la Tour, Rousseau's landlady in Môtiers, lived in Lyons, and from her he was able to get some precise information. Following the disclosures of Voltaire's *Sentiment des citoyens*, a pastor at Môtiers had preached against Rousseau, and stones had been thrown at his house. Rousseau, in a state of alarm that grew steadily more morbid, fled from Frederick's protection to the little island of Saint-Pierre in the neighbouring canton of Berne; after six weeks, being asked by the authorities to leave, he moved on to Strasbourg, ill and with no plan beyond that of getting out of Switzerland altogether. There he received a cordial letter from David Hume, at the moment Secretary to the British Embassy in Paris, inviting him to seek asylum in England. He had gone on to join Hume in Paris, and Mme. Boy de la Tour thought he was still there. Boswell dashed off an enthusiastic letter in which he proposed a perfect satisfaction to himself in introducing Rousseau to Johnson and in escorting him to Auchinleck. "How impatient I am to see you and to tell you a thousand enchanting anecdotes of Corsica!" On arriving in Paris a week later, he took a cab the moment he had picked up his luggage and went in search of Rousseau. But he was too late: on the very day that Boswell wrote his letter from Lyons, Rousseau and Hume had left for England. Boswell was told, however, that Thérèse was expected. Rousseau had left her behind in Switzerland till he should be able to make definite arrangements, and she was now on her way to Paris.

Rousseau, Belle de Zuylen, and Wilkes, three major threads in the pattern of Boswell's European web, all play prominently on the surface in Paris. Boswell later told Belle that it was in the island of Corsica that he made up his mind that he loved her; evidently his discussions with Paoli about marriage had been specific. Paoli's earnest counsel to

marry soon had made Belle again a vivid object of speculation and feeling, since for months all the ideas of marriage Boswell had entertained
had been associated with her. While he lay ill at Bastia with plenty of
time for self-questioning, he no doubt blamed himself for having beat
a retreat without ever having really made an attack. He expected to
learn when he got to Genoa whether or not Belle was still free, but
found there no letter from her and none from her father. On the day
after he landed, he wrote in his notes, "Thought to offer marriage to
Zélide. Mad." He probably wrote to M. de Zuylen, expressing fear that
he had offended him and begging for explicit information as to the
progress of Bellegarde's suit. While he was writing this letter, apparently,
he had an impulse to make a formal proposal but decided that such a
course would be rash; better wait in the hope that at Paris he would
have a letter enlightening him as to the last seven months of van Tuyll
family history. At Paris not only did he find a gracious letter from M.
de Zuylen, but he also met for the first time Belle's brother Willem,
M. de Zuylen's heir, a young man of twenty-two. M. de Zuylen said
that he and his wife were holding up their consent till they had positive
assurance that a mixed marriage would be valid in Savoy, and indicated
that they did not in any case like the prospect of a Catholic son-in-law.
Willem told Boswell that he thought he might make Belle a very good
husband, and that the proposed union with Bellegarde was a mere
mariage de convenance for which nobody—not even Belle herself—was
very eager. On 15 January 1766 Boswell sat in all day and wrote to
M. de Zuylen a letter which he himself calls magnificent: it fills twenty-
six quarto pages and contains over three thousand words. He tells him
that in Holland he had been very fond of Zélide but had never been
in love with her; that is, he had never felt for her "that madness of
passion which is unaccountable to reason." But Zélide, he was sure, had
felt such passion for him. With the most scrupulous probity he had informed her that he was simply her devoted friend, and that he would
be charmed to see her married to some other worthy man. He had not
told her the whole truth, which was that he had "always had a leaning
towards a marriage" with her himself; and since he was undecided and
was assured that several satisfactory alliances were open to her, he had
resolved to stand aside. "And I swear to you that in so acting I had the
pride of an heroic soul." When he heard of Bellegarde, he was at first
put out, but reconciled himself to the prospect. His conversations with

Willem have changed things a good deal. Perhaps Zélide still likes him better than anybody else.

"My dear and respectable Sir, here is my proposal." Find out whether Zélide would still give him her preference. *If* she would (he didn't want her if she didn't still love him), and *if* no engagement, however slight, had been concluded with M. de Bellegarde, and *if* M. de Zuylen approves of him above all others as a son-in-law, he would like to propose marriage. But there would have to be assurances even more binding than the forms of the church.

I should require a clear and express agreement. I should require an oath, taken in your presence, Sir, and before two of her brothers, that she would always remain faithful, that she would never design to see, or have any exchange of letters with, any one of whom her husband and her brothers disapproved; and that without their approbation she would neither publish nor cause to be acted any of her literary compositions; and, finally, she must promise never to speak against the established religion or customs of the country she might find herself in. If she would promise all that for my sake, I would marry her tomorrow and thank heaven for it—supposing my father were to give his consent. . . . I picture with the most heartfelt satisfaction an alliance between the family of de Tuyll and that of Auchinleck. And you, my dear and respectable Sir, perhaps will see it in the same light. You will embrace me as your son, and my children will call you grandfather, and Madame de Zuylen would possess an authority over me, and would be well pleased with her dear daughter, and my friends would become my brothers-in-law, and all of you would come and visit us in Scotland, and every two or three years we would come to Utrecht. . . . I know not by what association of ideas the rich pastures where your cows graze appear to me like the fields of the pious patriarchs. The amiable Belle would be my Rebekah.

A good peroration, but of course he is not finished: he proceeds to vacillate and to hedge.

To speak clearly, [Zélide's] heart is more precious to me than her mind, and it is rather what I hope she will become than what she actually is that I desire to marry. . . . Sir, I am proud, very proud, and it is perhaps to my pride that I owe my best virtues. What a pride is this which makes me refuse to petition for a young lady's hand until I have the certainty that she prefers me to all the world! . . . Sir, since being in Corsica, since making such proof of my talents and address, I am more proud than ever. I have a right to look to a distinguished career; I am worthy to make one of the best matches in England. . . . But it must not be forgotten that I am a hypochondriac, as she is, and that it might be a grave error to unite two victims of that malady. . . . I have many faults. . . . My knowledge is very restricted. I have an excess of self-esteem, I cannot apply myself to study. . . . I have no sufficient zest for life I have the greatest imaginable difficulty in overcoming avarice. . . . I do not covet riches; I have only the low weakness of wishing to make little savings. I should require a prudent wife, a good housekeeper. . . . Judge, my worthy friend, if Zélide is capable of ever becoming such an one? Judge, I beg you, if she would not be happier with M. de B_____. . . . I have at least this one consolation, that if my marriage with her were to prove unhappy, it could not be worse than I *fear*. . . . Listen. You know Mademoiselle, you know me, and all the circumstances of the case. As a man of honour, I ask you to decide for us.

He hopes, if M. de Zuylen gives him encouragement, to plead his suit in person. But come what may, let not the magnificent letter be lost to its author.

I beg for the earliest possible reply. If *jacta est alea* [1] and I may no longer indulge the thought of our marriage, I beg you to return me this letter. If you are of opinion that the alliance might be brought about, keep the letter, and when I pay my visit, you will give it me or allow me to take a copy of it, for I shall always be curious to recall how I expressed myself in an affair of this consequence.

"I have no doubts about obtaining my father's consent," he wrote, but actually he could not have been so confident. Lord Auchinleck, on receiving Boswell's assurance from Genoa that he meant to obey orders and was on his way home, had written with considerable complaisance saying that his health was better and that Boswell might stay a month in Paris if he chose. Boswell now wrote asking permission to go home by way of Holland and make formal proposals. The writing of the letter made him impatient to realize his scheme; he wanted to set out at once and told his father he might not wait for a reply. He did wait, but before he had heard in the business from either M. de Zuylen or Lord Auchinleck, he received news that put a jaunt to Holland out of the question.

1 "If the die is cast."

Wilkes, still an outlaw, was in Paris, living in style on the bounty of the Rockingham Whigs and the French government. Boswell and he resumed their old bantering relationship: Boswell told Wilkes about his tour to Corsica, Wilkes told Boswell about his visit to Voltaire. And Wilkes proved a kind and useful friend in a time of great and unexpected need. Boswell spent most of Friday 24 January getting his trunk through the Customs. A young fellow there gave him the names of some of the best bordellos, and he promptly got a cab-driver to take him to Mme. Hecquet's. With "Mlle. Constance, tall, quite French lady," he feigned innocence and she promised to show him the sights. The events of the next day are recorded simply as "Evening, Montigny's; sad work." (The Hôtel Montigny was another well-known brothel.) Next day, Sunday 26 January, after attending both mass at the convent church of the Théatins and a Church-of-England service at the chapel of the British Ambassador ("Sermon made you gloomy or rather tired"), he went to Wilkes's lodgings, picked up a copy of *The St. James's Chronicle,* and read in it a notice of his mother's death. He was stunned, for Lord Auchinleck's last letter, though reporting an indisposition, had expressed no alarm, and Boswell within the week had received from his mother —who wrote to him very infrequently—a letter which only hindsight could interpret as ominous. His immediate reaction was to refuse to take into his mind the dreadful thing he had read. Since newspapers did sometimes report people dead prematurely or with no warrant at all, he told himself that he could not *know* that the news was true till he had had a letter from home; and till he should *know,* he would try to push it out of his mind by engrossing excitements. Telling no one of his anxiety, he went to dinner at the Dutch ambassador's and engaged in animated discourse on Corsica; then at six o'clock "as in fever" he rushed back to Mme. Hecquet's. "Constance elegant." That evening, face to face again with his anxiety, he wrote a long letter to Temple assuring him of his affection and begging for sympathy. Next morning his mail did produce the dreaded letter from his father: Lady Auchinleck had died on 11 January, the day before Boswell reached Paris. She had had from the first of her illness a fixed persuasion that she was going to die of it, and had no doubt intended the letter she sent Boswell as a last farewell, though she can hardly have said as much directly. Boswell was stupefied. He stayed in all morning, wept in bursts, addressed prayers to her as to a saint, and sang Italian airs softly to soothe himself.

He was twenty-five years old, but this was the first serious bereavement
he had ever experienced. His recourse to orgy to dispel anxiety has had
plenty of parallels, but his recording of the orgy, not without his usual
tone of wonder at his own variety, approaches the unique. Wilkes, who
would quite have approved this part of his recipe for dissipating grief,
was solicitous and sympathetic, and Boswell was always deeply grateful
to him for it. In parting they returned to their old vein of raillery, but
Wilkes remained unusually complaisant. When Boswell said, "You'll
think as I do one day," Wilkes replied that Boswell would probably come
round to his views in politics, he to Boswell's in religion. It was not good
prophecy, and was probably not seriously meant.

Boswell forthwith abandoned or postponed his scheme of returning
to Utrecht to accept the capitulation of Belle de Zuylen and prepared
to go directly home to comfort his father. Samuel Johnson had gone
down to Harwich with him to see him out of England; his travelling
companion when he came back into it was in ludicrous contrast to the
Great Cham. Thérèse Le Vasseur had arrived, and Boswell went to pay
his respects. She was distraught at the prospect of making her way alone
to London, and fairly clutched at Boswell: "Mon Dieu, Monsieur, if
we could go together!" He told her he had come to propose it. On 30
January 1766, after having been up all night writing letters (no fewer
than sixteen) and keeping the post-horses waiting three hours while
he packed, he picked up Thérèse at the Hôtel de Luxembourg and set
off for Calais.

Boswell's sight-seeing in Paris was surprisingly restricted and conventional: he felt an obligation to explore it diligently on its wicked side
only. He went to the Palais du Luxembourg and was told that it was not
the day to see the gallery; he went to the Palais Royal and found it
so dark that he could see nothing. And that, literally, was all. He attended mass in two churches, but if he entered (or even saw) Notre
Dame, he makes no mention of it. The notes also record not a single
attempt to meet a distinguished Frenchman or to move in French society. His principal associates besides Wilkes were Lumisden's brother-in-
law, Robert Strange the engraver, and the knot of Scots Jacobites in
and about the Scots College, then much saddened by news (just received)
of the death of the titular James III. Nothing he saw in Paris roused
him so much as the Stuart relics (now largely lost) which Principal
Gordon of the Scots College showed him. The most important addition

he made in Paris to his list of notables was an Englishman—Horace Walpole. Boswell, who had declined a letter of introduction from Sir David Dalrymple to Walpole in 1760 on the ground that he was not of sufficient importance to interest the chatelain of Strawberry Hill, now felt that his Corsican adventure justified him in leaving a "card" soliciting an acquaintance. He did not warm particularly to Walpole ("lean, genteel man"), but his notes show interest and respect. Walpole, whose "card" in reply is a masterpiece of the polite "come and see if you can find me at home" invitation, disliked him on sight, and later told Gray that Boswell had "forced himself upon me at Paris in spite of my teeth and my doors." It was inevitable that Walpole's fastidiousness and elegance should be offended by Boswell's pushing affability and his utter lack of reserve.

Boswell's ignoble failure to exploit the cultural and social glories of Paris may have been due in part to his lameness, to the intense cold, about which he had been complaining ever since he left the Riviera, and to Mountstuart's failure (later to be discussed) to provide him with letters of recommendation, but was no doubt mainly attributable to the let-down which most foreigners experience when they come to Paris from an extended and conscientious tour of Italy. It is gratifying to one who has panted after Boswell in Italy to find that even he was content to loll about Paris and associate himself with people who spoke his own tongue.

From the other side of the water David Hume wrote to the Comtesse de Boufflers, "I learn that Mademoiselle sets out post, in company with a friend of mine; a young gentleman very good-humoured, very agreeable, and very mad. He visited Rousseau in his mountains, who gave him a recommendation to Paoli, the King of Corsica, where this gentleman, whose name is Boswell, went last summer in search of adventures. He has such a rage for literature that I dread some event fatal to our friend's honour. You remember the story of Terentia, who was first married to Cicero, then to Sallust, and at last, in her old age, married a young nobleman who imagined that she must possess some secret which would convey to him eloquence and genius."

This was probably in intent no more than fooling of the elegantly bawdy sort that Hume sometimes affected, but it turned out to be prophecy. Boswell started with no thought of gallanting in his head. He was absorbed by grief, his mind continually waking with a start from reveries in which he imagined his mother alive. Thérèse now did not seem so agreeable as she had in the Val de Travers: she whined too much and behaved like a servant. Still, she was a unique source of information about a great man, and when Boswell was not sunk in his gloomy personal reverie, he questioned her about Rousseau: "Talked much of Rousseau always."

So ends the entry for 31 January, recording the events of the previous day. Boswell and Thérèse disappear into an eleven-day black-out imposed by family censorship. One extremely thin ray of light pierces the darkness: Boswell sent five letters from Calais on 5 or 6 and 7 February. When he and Thérèse emerge into the light again, they are at Dover, it is 11 February, and the entry (which is dated 12 February) begins, "Yesterday morning had gone to bed very early, and had done it once: thirteen in all." The late Colonel Isham, who assembled the Boswell archives and initiated their publication, claimed to have read the missing pages of the notes at Malahide in 1927 just prior to their destruction, which he said he witnessed; and I have twice printed circumstantial reconstructions of the deleted passage which he professed to supply from memory. Briefly stated, his report ran that the intimacy of travel precipitated an intrigue almost at once; that Thérèse stunned and humiliated Boswell by telling him that he was hasty, self-absorbed, and clumsy, much inferior to Rousseau as a lover; that she offered to instruct him in the art of love, and started a full course of lectures and demonstrations; that he became bored and tried to get her to talk about Rousseau, so that he could collect some *dicta philosophi* for his journal; that she would not be deflected, and he had to take the full course. The narrative is amusing and apparently appropriate, but I cannot any longer be certain that it is not a brilliant historical fiction by a highly imaginative man who knew Boswell's journal forward and backward. Both versions of the story say that Boswell had to invoke Dutch courage before climbing into bed, and the later and more developed version says that his first encounter found him incapable. This would be very Boswellian if the intrigue had been in the grand style or even a genteel one, but it does not seem as though Boswell would have suffered incapacity with a female of Thérèse's status. And I also find it suspicious that the story makes no mention of certain circumstances which could not have been invented by analogy with other portions of the journal and ought surely to have figured prominently in Boswell's notes. He left Paris on the morning of

30 January, having notified Temple, in one of the sixteen letters which he had stayed up all night to write, that he hoped to be in London on Monday or Tuesday, that is, on 3 or 4 February. He was in fact mistaken or misinformed as to the day on which the packet sailed. The usual day of arrival in London of the mail from France that winter was not Monday (or Tuesday) as he was assuming, but Friday (or Saturday). The mail for the week of 26 January reached London on Friday the 31st, which meant that the packet sailed before Boswell could have got to Calais. As there was only one packet a week, he would have had at best to wait four or five days. But the next sailing was delayed two or three days more, apparently because of a bad storm, and the mail did not get through to London again till Tuesday 11 February, the twelfth day after Boswell left Paris. I cannot believe that Boswell's notes did not mention his mishap and enforced wait emphatically and repeatedly; and it is very hard for me to believe that Colonel Isham, if he had read about Boswell's missing the boat, would either have forgotten such an amusing detail or have suppressed it in the retelling. One wonders whether the affair between Boswell and Thérèse did not actually develop out of their common *ennui* at being shut up by bad weather day after day in an inn in a small provincial city.

On its physical side the affair contains nothing surprising so far as Boswell was concerned. Thérèse was forty-five years old, had probably been the mother of five children, and was vulgar, illiterate, shrewish, and deceitful. It is reported on respectable authority that she was so stupid that she could barely learn to tell the time of day by a clock. But the common impression that she was ugly and aged in her appearance should yield to Boswell's own report: his impression of her at Môtiers had been that "she was a little, lively, neat French girl." He had previously in his affairs shown something of a preference for women older than himself. Thérèse was not much, if any, older than Mrs. Love.

What does cause some surprise is that he should have so repaid Rousseau's very real kindnesses to him. He had been falling out of love with his Mentor for a long time, his respect may have received the final blow from Walpole's characterization of Rousseau as a mountebank with great parts, and he was certainly disgusted ("Quackery this") with recent complaining letters of Rousseau that Thérèse had shown him. Thérèse was technically a free woman. Rousseau had never offered her marriage, had never pretended fidelity, and seems by this time to have renounced her bed. But all this does not change the fact that he would have regarded the affair as a betrayal and would have been deeply hurt by it; nor that Boswell had recently written him a disciple's letter, long and cordial ("I am always yours as I was at Môtiers"); nor that Boswell had accepted a relation of trust with regard to Thérèse, a sort of guardianship. On the only occasion when he had an opportunity to make a practical return for Rousseau's kindness, he behaved grossly, furtively, and meanly. Wilkes would have justified his conduct, and that is as much as one can say for it.

During his enforced stay at Calais, Boswell wrote a grieved but manly Finis to his hopes of a star from the Margrave of Baden-Durlach. It will be remembered that he had received at Geneva an informal and extremely friendly letter in English from Karl Friedrich, saying that the Margrave valued his correspondence very much and wished him to write openly and freely. Boswell replied from Turin in January; getting no answer, he wrote again, with growing uneasiness, from Rome in May and from Siena in August. He says now that the Margrave's silence has caused him to decide against a second visit to Karlsruhe, and he takes Karl Friedrich gently to task for "that fickleness to which the great are so unhappily subject." It seems likely that His Most Serene Highness was, so far as Boswell was concerned, not fickle but managed. The letters that Boswell sent from Turin and Calais may have been lost in the post, but the other two certainly got to Karlsruhe, for they still repose in the Grand-Ducal Family Archives there. With them is the file-copy of a letter in English dated 24 May 1768 from Karl Friedrich to "Sir Boswell of Auchinleck" saying that from the time Boswell left Karlsruhe, Karl Friedrich heard nothing of him till the notices of his return to England appeared in the newspapers. "I am glad of your being now more at leisure to renew our correspondence, interrupted by your travels. For to judge from the affectuous mind you once showed to me, I dare hope that it is no oblivion which stopped the courses of this literary commerce. . . . After having enjoyed your agreeable and instructive conversation I am now deprived of, I should be too much at a loss if you did not make me amends for by writing. In this sweet expectation, I am, with all my heart, Sir, your affectionate. . . ." There is nothing whatever in the Boswell papers to show that Boswell ever received this singularly gracious epistle; and it is very hard to believe that if he had received from a reigning German prince a letter ending "you affectionate," the expressions of his gratification would all have disappeared. The likeliest explanation is that Karl Friedrich's secretaries disapproved of this familiar English correspondence and "forgot" to show the Margrave Boswell's letters before they filed them, and likewise "forgot" to post the Margrave's to Boswell, though they made and filed a copy. It is sad to think that Boswell may have lost his star and his princely correspondent through mere bureaucratic meddling, because it all seems so unnecessary. But to such insignificant casualty all biography is subject, and it would be better to reserve one's regret for weightier miscarriages.

We, too, had better pause at Calais to resolve the suspense as regards Belle de Zuylen. Lord Auchinleck and M. de Zuylen replied to Boswell's letters on the same day, 30 January, the day he left Paris. Lord Auchinleck had been deeply offended by the tone of Boswell's of the 15th (which of course arrived after Lady Auchinleck's death, though it was written in ignorance of it) and enraged by the newspaper items concerning Boswell's Corsican expedition, especially that which connected him with the Young Pretender. It was his notion, as he told Boswell's brother David, that when the publishers of the London papers ran out of copy, they said to one another, "Now, let us have a joke at Boswell." Actually, he must have had a strong and justified suspicion that Boswell was writing the paragraphs himself. He called Boswell's request for his permission to enter into treaty for Belle's hand a "very strange proposal," and said he hoped the news of his mother's death had "immediately put an end to that fermentation" and made him think seriously what he owed "to duty, to gratitude, and to interest."

If that be so, all is well. But if, contrary to expectation, you shall be unmoved, and go on in pursuit of a scheme which you in your unstayed state are absolutely unfit for at present, and a scheme, which, abstracting from that, is improper and would be ruinous—a foreigner, a *bel esprit* and one who even in your own opinion has not solidity enough for this country—what can you expect from me? All that I need say further is that as I gave you a full allowance to answer your expenses in every place you were in and you have got all that advanced and considerably more; and as I ordered you one hundred pounds at Paris, which was to defray your expense the few days you stayed there and bring you over to London; if you shall employ that money for other purposes, it is what I cannot prevent, but I acquaint you that I am to answer no more of your bills, either for one purpose or another. I hope there will be no occasion for this last *caveat,* as I hope you will show yourself a dutiful and affectionate son, as I have been, and wish to continue, your affectionate father.

The newspaper paragraphs and the proposal to wed Belle de Zuylen, in short, had put Lord Auchinleck very close to, if not actually in, his old disinheriting mood.

M. de Zuylen's letter was in as complete contrast as could be imagined. He thanked Boswell ("a man of birth and intellectual distinction who remains attached to his good principles of religion and virtue, who dares declare his position with firmness and conducts himself accordingly") for having spoken so helpfully to Willem, who was suffering from his first venereal infection. "You made a strong impression on him." He thanks Boswell for his confidence in telling him so much about himself; he is honoured by the proposal that he, as impartial judge, should decide whether Belle and Boswell were suited to each other. But he has not faced that difficult decision, nor has he even told Belle of Boswell's letter, for Boswell's instructions were that his suit should not be prosecuted unless Belle were completely free and liked him better than any one else. Bellegarde's case is *not* settled. There still remain grave problems to be solved, but Belle does "have a disposition to say yes if the marriage is feasible." So he will keep Boswell's letter, "because it richly deserves it, and also so that you can re-read it here." It was months before Boswell saw either the blunt veto from his father or the courtly report of no progress from M. de Zuylen, but the interruption of his scheme assured its quietus. By the time he got to London he was glad he had been saved from his rash impulse to overlook Belle's defects. When it became clear that he was not coming to Utrecht, M. de Zuylen sent him back his letter through Robert Brown.

It is gratifying to learn that on the morning of parting Boswell "was really affectionate" to Thérèse, and "was good to her" during the fatiguing ride in the fly to London. He delivered her to Hume that night, and the next morning carried her out to Chiswick, where Rousseau was staying. Their reunion he found rather disgusting. "*Quanta oscula,*[1] etc.! He seemed so oldish and weak you had no longer your enthusiasm for him." Boswell had promised Thérèse on his honour that he would not

[1] "Such kissing!"

tell anyone of their affair "till after her death or that of the philosopher," and he kept his word, deceiving even Temple. Whether Thérèse herself kept her lips sealed is less certain, as we shall see. In any case, the personal relationship between Rousseau and Boswell, whom Boswell now saw for the last time, is at an end. It had begun for Boswell in an orgy of sentiment; it had ended in disillusion, disgust, and a bland feeling of superiority.

Not at all so the relationship with Johnson. From Chiswick Boswell went straight to Fleet Street and burst in on Johnson like a long-absent son. "Johnson received you with open arms. You kneeled and asked blessing. Miss Williams glad of your return. When she went out, he hugged you to him like a sack, and grumbled, 'I hope we shall pass many years of regard.' " It is true that the seasoned and superior traveller had to get his eyes adjusted even to Colossus: "You for some minutes saw him not so immense as before, but it came back."

Out of the fleeting, restless, unbounded waves of the Boswellian record heaves the great sullen rock. Until it appears, we have not realized how weary we were for its emergence, for the sight and sound of the waves breaking on something hard, massive, fixed, prejudiced.

You told him he looked ten years younger, and that Davies had said he now got up at eight. JOHNSON. "Why, Sir, if I were a friend of John James Rousseau, then everything that concerned me would be of importance. As it is, Sir, it concerns nobody but myself." You quoted Wilkes for something. JOHNSON. "It seems you have kept very good company abroad—Wilkes and Rousseau!" BOSWELL. "My dear Sir, you don't call Rousseau bad company? Do you really think him a bad man?" JOHNSON. "Sir, if you are to talk jestingly of this, I don't talk with you. If you would be serious, I think him one of the worst of men; a rascal who ought to be hunted out of society as he has been. Three or four nations have expelled him; and it is a shame that he is protected in this country." . . . You said, "Sir, I don't deny but his novel may do harm, but I cannot think his intention was bad." JOHNSON. "Sir, that will not do. We cannot prove any man's intention to be bad. You may shoot a man through the head, and say you intended to miss him, but the judge will order you to be hanged. The want of intention, when evil is committed, will not be sustained in a court of justice. If you are no better lawyer than that, Bos, we must send you back to Utrecht. Sir, Rousseau is a very bad man. I would sooner sign a sentence for his transportation than for that of any felon who has gone from the Old Bailey these many years. Yes, I should like to have him work in the plantations." BOSWELL. "Sir, do you think him as bad a man as Voltaire?" JOHNSON. "Why, it is difficult to settle the proportion of iniquity between 'em."

Boswell's stay in London was short, but it was lucky in its timing. Temple was in town for a few days; he had given up his design of being a lawyer and had returned to Cambridge to qualify himself for ordination. He had been reading improper books ("Hume and Helvétius and other modern philosophers") and did not believe the Thirty-nine Articles which he was going to subscribe. Boswell, though a little hurt by this, found his sympathies with his friend confirmed and deepened by absence; it amazed him to find that Temple had kept pace with him without the advantage of travel. Dempster was on hand; so was Lord Eglinton; so was Lord Mountstuart. Of his old cronies, only Erskine was not in London, and he had recently sent a long letter. Boswell made up for his absence by getting out the published volume of their letters, which he had not seen for two and a half years. He found it childish: "Could not bear your own, except one or two: in general, mere forced extravagance and no real humour." He thought better of Erskine's, but had clearly outgrown that relationship and thought he had outgrown that era in his style. Dempster had acquired "a real ministerial look," and Boswell was pleased to find the conversation less free on both sides. He was pleased by Lord Eglinton's fine house, but felt quite detached from his old concern for "interest and worldly vanities . . . a Johnson in comparison of former days." Mountstuart was angry with him and for better cause than their juvenile bickerings about San Marino. Boswell had written to him from Genoa asking him for letters of recommendation in Paris. Dr. John Pringle, to whom Lord Auchinleck had confided his worries, had begged Mountstuart to try to get Boswell to come home with no further delay. Mountstuart had written accordingly, not actually refusing the letters, but not sending them, and pressing urgently for Boswell's return. Boswell, in a fury at what he considered officious meddling, had sent him one of the very few rude letters of his that we know of. He announced his complete independence, recklessly dispelling the cherished dream of Stuart patronage: "I shall never again ask the smallest favour of you." Pringle (and Andrew Mitchell, whom Boswell unexpectedly found at Pringle's) told him he was completely in the wrong and must apologize; Boswell was "outrageous." He told Mountstuart himself that he could not see that he had been wrong, but that he was sorry that Mountstuart had been offended. And that was as far as he would go. When Mountstuart kept up the prince, Boswell brought him down by asking him how he got his Venetian infection cured. His spirited request of Mountstuart not to be angry any more finally produced a grudging avowal from Mountstuart that he didn't care sixpence about the whole matter. Poor-spirited, Boswell thought. The striking feature of the interview was that Boswell seems really to have felt no trace of deference. Of course he would later.

In 1763, in London, Boswell had been introduced to an eighteen-year-old ensign in the Guards, William Bosville, who told him that he was the eldest son of an ancient family in Yorkshire, and that Bosville and Boswell were the same name, both being variants of the Norman Boisville. Boswell now met the family of the man whom he came (on shaky genealogical grounds) to regard as his chief. Godfrey Bosville of Gunthwaite in the West Riding, a shrewd, solid, hearty squire of engaging manners and considerable parts, extended to him a permanent invitation to family dinner and gave him a no less permanent affection. The eldest daughter, Elizabeth Diana, was a great beauty ("black hair, charming complexion, quite modest"), and Boswell set her down at once as a matrimonial possibility, within five days going so far as to request a portrait, which Mrs. Bosville gently refused.

Eglinton got Boswell for the first time presented at Court. George III (whose one conversational gambit seems to have been to ask people when they had come to town and when they planned to leave) said, "Lately come over?" and that was all. Boswell was quite easy, not a bit struck, but liked it. In visualizing the scene, one must see the King as a young man, not much older than Boswell.

The climax of all was Boswell's interview with William Pitt, the Great Commoner. When Boswell, in Corsica, had asked Paoli what he could do to repay him for his kindness, Paoli had said, "Only undeceive your Court. Tell them what you have seen here. They will be curious to ask you. A man come from Corsica will be like a man come from the Antipodes." The main thing was somehow to secure the repeal of that hated proclamation of 1763 in which Great Britain had stigmatized the Corsicans as rebels and had forbidden intercourse with them. It was even rumoured that Great Britain was about to enter into a commercial alliance with Genoa, a step which would make the cause of Corsican independence even more difficult. Pitt was not in the Cabinet, but if he could be persuaded to speak for Corsica, he could perhaps do more than anybody else. He was by far the most famous living Englishman; he had humbled France in the world-wide struggle recently concluded; he was the great champion of the American colonies. He might very soon be prime minister again. It was reasonable to infer that he would be against the proclamation, for though it had been issued by Grenville's government, it was in line with the foreign policy established by Bute, whose peace with France Pitt had considered pusillanimous.

Boswell had been in London less than a week when he wrote to Pitt asking an audience. The letter, "a clean neat short" one, cost him a good deal of labour, for Temple warned him that he wrote in too swelling a style and made him throw out "many bouncing sallies." Pitt, who was suffering cruelly from the gout, replied from Hayes, expressing doubts of the propriety of receiving communications from Paoli, but not refusing an interview. He had recently appeared in the House of Commons and had made several remarkable speeches urging that the Stamp Act be "absolutely, totally, and immediately" repealed. The bill for repeal was finally brought to a vote on 21 February; Pitt, though far from well, had gone up for the division. The debate lasted till half-past one in the morning of the twenty-second, when the motion for repeal was carried. Cheering mobs followed Pitt's carriage to the Duke of Grafton's house in Bond Street, where he was staying. At nine o'clock Boswell was at the door; told that Pitt was not up, he said he would come back. At eleven o'clock he returned and was ushered into the great man's presence. A tall man dressed in black, with a white nightcap; his foot, wrapped in flannel, resting on a stool. Ashamed to say he had never read Rousseau; would do so now. Laughed at Voltaire's saying that there was only a king and a half in Europe—the King of Prussia and the King of Sardinia; ventured to improve on the witticism by rating Frederick a king and a half and the others just kings. Asked if it would have been possible to have forced the Stamp Act on the Americans, replied in the negative. "Abstracting from the equity of the cause, it would not have been possible. They are all united. . . . If severe measures were ever to be used, it must be done when they are divided; but let us use them with indulgence and they'll always find it their interest to be with us." He had heard of Boswell, had in fact seen an account in the foreign press of his being in Corsica.

PITT. "Now, Sir, I will explain to you how I cannot properly receive communications from General de Paoli, for I am a Privy Councillor, and have taken an oath to hear nothing from any foreign power that may concern Great Britain without declaring it to the King and Council. Now, Sir, it is in your breast to judge whether what you have to say is of a nature fit to be told or not. I shall be very happy to hear your accounts of the island as a traveller. Some time hence things may turn about, and I may be at liberty to receive communications from Corsica, and then I shall be very happy to hear all you have to say. I am now just a private member of Parliament. I had once, Mr. Boswell, something to do in the affairs of this nation. But when they had come to me in distress and perplexity—'Think for us, act for us, venture for us!' and I had thought, acted, and ventured—for 'em then to come and tell me, 'Now you must think as we choose!' When I had rolled the stone to the top of the hill, then!" . . . BOSWELL. "Sir, General de Paoli said—" PITT. "Sir, you'll remember my situation." BOSWELL. "Pray, Sir, may I ask if you never received a letter from General de Paoli?" PITT. "Never, Sir." BOSWELL. "Why then, Sir, after the Proclamation he wrote to you, and, as he has the highest admiration of your character, he was most sensibly hurt to be neglected by Mr. Pitt." PITT. "Sir, I never received his letter. I suppose *those next the King* have taken care it should not be delivered. I could not have answered it, could not have been in correspondence with General de Paoli, but I should have taken care to let him know my regard for him. Sir, I should be sorry that in any corner of the world, however distant or however small, it should be suspected that I could ever be indifferent to the cause of liberty."

It is absurd to think that Boswell could record only Johnson. That is not in the least the Johnsonian cadence: it is the unmistakable eloquence of Pitt, and Boswell had to get himself impregnated with the Pittian ether in one exposure of an hour or less. And the interview is not preserved in a carefully worked-over manuscript. It is a long rough note, written at headlong speed. There are many abbreviated words but only one correction or substitution: in the last sentence but one Boswell originally wrote "attachment to him" instead of "regard for him."

Of the remaining week that Boswell stayed in London, he appears to have left no memorial whatever. Early in March he set off for Edinburgh in the fly, leaving it at Newcastle to see his brother John, who was being boarded with a dissenting clergyman there in order to keep his now obvious mental derangement as much as possible from the eyes of the world.

At Berwick he paused again to reconnoitre Miss Anne Stow, the young lady about whom Temple was suffering matrimonial vacillation in an almost Boswellian manner. She was Temple's cousin, and the family thought her too good for him. When Boswell sent a card asking permission to call, Anne's elder sister burned it before the messenger's face. Not at all put down ("You know my way, Temple"), he knocked at the door, walked in, and put the young lady through her paces. He reported from Haddington to Temple, who understandably did not thank him for his meddling.

On the threshold of re-entry into his native city, he paused to sum up the gains of an absence of more than three years. "I am the friend of Johnson and of Paoli, the gallant of Signora _____, am looked after by Mr. Pitt, and will probably marry Miss Bosville." The Scots accent is incredibly hard to bear: "I think the people are affecting to talk in as disagreeable a manner as they can." But he is anxious to see his father, and is prepared for small sufferings as well as great. "I am now just going upon service, resolved for everything, and solemnly sworn to the strictest duty."

CHAPTER

XVII

Since Boswell, always retaining a childlike faith in miraculous transformations, never based his expectations of the future on past experience, he probably more than once cherished the day-dream of a home-coming in which his father would play to the full the role assigned him in the parable. It is safe to infer that nothing of the sort happened. Lord Auchinleck did not run to meet him while he was yet a great way off, did not even hug him to him like a sack. But though he almost certainly allowed himself no unseemly display of emotion, it does look as though he did sincerely try to indicate affection and a willingness to wipe the slate. It was a promising circumstance that the Winter Session was in its last week when Boswell arrived, and that the two men could go down to Auchinleck together almost at once. The sense of their common loss, so much sharper in the fine empty new house than in Blair's Land, heightened their tenderness. Boswell set himself to console his father and to conform studiously to his inclinations. Lord Auchinleck talked whole evenings of the Family—the topic on which he could come nearest to shedding formality—and as a shy gesture of confidence continued through his own lairdship a manuscript history of the Family which Old James had begun. This little autobiography, though dry and homiletic, must have seemed to Boswell a tremendous relaxation of his father's usual reserve.

He also offered—surely another great concession—personally to coach Boswell for the examination in Scots law which Boswell had to pass before he could be admitted advocate. Unfortunately, the course was made a college by the inclusion of another student, Claud Boswell of Balmuto. Claud was the son of Lord Auchinleck's uncle, but the generations had got out of step, and he was younger than Boswell, a very steady and regular young man, sobered and somewhat cowed by having grown up the only boy in a household of women—his mother and three much older maiden sisters. One cannot help wondering whether Lord Auchinleck had not at the last lost his nerve and invited Claud out of a fear that six weeks of daily and undiluted intimacy with his own son would be more than he could bear.

As could have been predicted, Boswell suffered low spirits on arriving at Auchinleck, but escaped from gloom almost at once by falling delightfully in love with the chambermaid. Euphemia Bruce was the daughter of the gardener, James Bruce, a worthy man whose father also had been a trusted servant of the house, and she had been named for Lady Auchinleck. As children she and Boswell had paddled in the burn and pulled the gowans together (we have his word for it), and for years he had been taking her for granted. Now he suddenly saw that she was an angelic creature with the most amiable face and the prettiest foot and ankle; she was more graceful, he realized, with a besom,[1] than ever shepherdess was with a crook; she had even read a great deal. He helped her dust the library and left surreptitious notes for her under the table-cloth, but never considered seduction a possibility. "In plain words," he wrote to Temple, "I am mad enough to indulge imaginations of marrying her. Only think of the proud Boswell, with all that you know of him, the fervent adorer of a country girl of three and twenty. I rave about her. I was never so much in love as I am now. My fancy is quite inflamed. It riots in extravagance."

His professions are comic—he knows it—but not utterly absurd. He knows that his tediously avowed passions for women of social status equal or superior to his own have been largely factitious, whereas the attraction he feels for pretty chambermaids is strong, direct, honest, and (as it seems to him) wholesome.

I am not fit for marriage in all the forms. A lady would not be compliant enough, and would oblige me to harass myself with an endless repetition of external ceremony and a most woeful maintaining of *proper conduct*. Whereas my dear girl would be grateful for my attachment, would be devoted to me in every respect, would live with me just as a mistress, without the disgrace and remorse.

He never got over wanting a wife with whom he could live just as with a mistress, but he knows well enough that this scheme of marrying the gardener's daughter is a will o' the wisp—"it would kill my father." The delirium would do for a summer, but only a strong imagination could have

[1] Broom.

made him think it would last for life. "I will rouse my philosophic spirit
and fly from this fascination. I am going to Moffat for a month. Absence
will break the enchantment."

Absence alone would perhaps have sufficed, but he actually broke the
matrimonial spell by subjecting himself to one that was equally potent and
a great deal less high-minded. His ostensible reason for the month's retreat to Moffat was the persistence or recurrence on his skin of "scurvy
spots" (prickly heat? eczema?) which he diagnosed as a legacy from the
warmer climates of Europe. For these he bathed and drank the waters
and took a good deal of exercise with his chum Johnston, probably feeling
very superior to the callow youngster of nine years before who had trailed
about with the old Pythagorean and listened to lectures on vegetarianism
and the transmigration of souls. He apparently intended to continue his
studies, and perhaps did read some law, but the whole Moffat episode was
essentially a junket or holiday, and he could hardly have planned it without some hopes, however fleeting, of a *bonne chance*. At any rate, he col-
lided with one promptly on his arrival. Within a week he was writing to
Temple that his scheme of marrying a chambermaid was like a dream that
is past; he was still considering Miss Bosville, but had struck Belle de
Zuylen off his list, his father having convinced him that she would never
do at Auchinleck. (He did not mention Girolama, for Girolama was not
a matrimonial possibility, but he had recently been regaled with two passionate epistles from her.) His reason for being so free of Euphemia was a
luscious young grass-widow whose expectations of Moffat matched his
own. "I am quite devoted to her. . . . When we meet, you shall hear of
Elysium. Love reconciles me to the Scots accent. . . . I am all health, affection, and gratitude. . . . I shall be attached to the generous woman for
ever."

Some day we may know more about the lady's background and family
history, for though Boswell generally refers to her by blanks and pseudonyms—"Miss ____," "La Cara," latterly "Circe" and "Laïs"—he on one
occasion so far forgot decorum as to write out her real name: Mrs. Dodds.
She was probably the wife or daughter of a small laird, for she was known
not only to Boswell's city friends but also to his Ayrshire acquaintances,
and she had income enough to live at Moffat or in Edinburgh, but her
rompishness and ill breeding indicate no great experience of polite society.
She was separated from her husband and her three children, and her husband, who was said to have used her badly, was living with another

woman, but she appears not to have been divorced. She was young, lively, black-haired, reckless, paradisial in bed, and generous; she had had lovers before, but she did not by any means sell herself. If she yielded instantly to Boswell's advances, it was because she liked him on sight and was as ardent and direct as he was. When he returned to Edinburgh in June, she took lodgings there so as to continue their connexion. But she retained her independence, refusing to accept any presents of money from him. Boswell (who continued to live in his father's house) believed that his father was unaware of his amorous arrangements, as probably for a time he was, but the confidence and frankness of the earlier weeks were now flawed by surreptitiousness and a secret.

Before he left Scotland in 1762, Boswell had passed the examination in Civil Law, the most serious part of his trials for admission to the Faculty of Advocates. He had still to pass trials in Scots Law, to compose and present a brief printed Latin thesis expounding one of the titles of the Pandects, and to stand a public examination on the thesis. He passed the examination in Scots Law on 11 July, went to bed with a smart recurrence of malaria, and passed the examination on his thesis on the 26th. Since he always found himself most alive when most on the stretch, July 1766 must have remained in his memory a wonderfully bright, whirling, feverish spot of time. The thesis was on Tit. X, Lib. XXXIII of the Pandects, *De supellectile legata* ("Legacies of Household Furniture") and was not a work of deep research. Only one thing about it is now interesting, and that is its long and fulsome dedication to Lord Mountstuart, "viro nobilissimo, ornatissimo, . . . atavis edito regibus, excelsae familiae de BUTE spei alterae,"[1] etc., etc. He rushed off a copy to Johnson who cuffed him for professions he considered insincere ("Why did you dedicate it to a man whom I know you do not much love?") and made strictures on his Latin. Boswell sent back a long and sturdy defence, which was sophistical on some points but clearly proved Johnson captious on others. Twenty-five years later he printed the dedication and both letters in the *Life of Johnson*, his avowed reason for dragging in the dedication being that Johnson's strictures made no sense without the text to which they referred. His real reasons, no doubt, were to remind Mountstuart (now Bute) of a debt long unpaid, and to show the world that he was capable of a pretty piece of Latinity. If the public examination on the thesis was conducted as it

[1] "A man most noble, most illustrious, sprung from royal progenitors, second hope of the lofty Family of Bute."

now is (it is not likely in any case to have been more exacting), it consisted merely of reading in Latin previously prepared answers to three challenges which Boswell himself had drafted and given to three of his friends beforehand.

26 July, the day on which Boswell "passed advocate," was a Saturday, so that his putting on the gown was delayed to Tuesday the 29th, the next day on which the Court of Session sat. Kindly old William Wilson, Writer to the Signet, gave him a cause and a guinea. Though he had come in at the very end of the session, he got ten causes and picked up eight guineas before the Court rose eleven days later. He was by now disposed to think very well of the law, though two promotions that had occurred just before he went to Moffat were bitters in his cup of satisfaction and ominous for the future. The Lord Advocate, Thomas Miller of Barskimming, an Ayrshire neighbour whom the Boswells of Auchinleck considered their inferior in blood and antiquity, was promoted Lord Justice-Clerk, that is, was jumped to the second-best appointment on the bench, over the heads of Lord Auchinleck and four other Justiciary lords, some of whom had seen many years of service. And Henry Dundas, the Lord President's young half-brother, aged twenty-four, whom Boswell and Temple had looked down on in Edinburgh College as a coarse, unlettered dog but who had been digging into the law while Boswell was cavorting on the Continent, was made Solicitor-General before Boswell—his senior by eighteen months—had even passed advocate. Boswell at this time, with unshaken confidence in his own powers and a sense of unlimited time, was merely plaintive in his resentment, but the jealousy was never resolved and was destined to bring him quite soon into unpleasant collision with Miller, and eventually with Dundas.

For the next seventeen years Boswell followed the practice of the law in Edinburgh with complete regularity and a fair degree of assiduity. It is almost as difficult to fix in a reader's mind a lively impression of him as an ambitious and busy lawyer as it is to transmit a realized sense of his personal attractiveness. The popular or Macaulayan image, which makes him an imbecile, can be peremptorily dismissed as uninformed, but it is not so easy to dismiss the informed view which makes him an idler. Since Boswell's own two Johnsonian books undoubtedly show him for considerable periods of time in many different years giving little or no attention to his legal practice, his idleness has become as fixed an attribute as his notebook. But the notebook is now known to be apocryphal, and it behoves us to limit the idleness. The best way to begin a discussion of Boswell's career as a lawyer is to ask the reader to look at the dates in the *Life of Johnson.* After July 1766, all the conversations in which Boswell himself is represented as taking part will be seen to fall either between 12 March and 11 June or between 12 August and 11 November—that is, in the vacations of the Court of Session. From 1766 to 1783 Boswell did not once absent himself from Edinburgh during term time. For six months of every year he was busily engaged in a daily routine of studying, dictating, consulting, and arguing in court. It is true that if he had devoted more of the vacations to study, he might have gone farther in his profession than he did, but that is not to impugn his regularity and the seriousness of his application while the Court was sitting.

Though the Scots system of law, of court procedures and terminology, differ considerably from those of the rest of the English-speaking world, non-Scottish readers of this book need make only a few adjustments in their notions of what it means to be a lawyer in order to have an adequate imaginative comprehension of Boswell's professional manner of life. American readers need to be told that his legal business, by and large, did not concern itself with the drawing of wills and deeds, with giving legal advice directly to clients, or even with the managing of law cases (*causes* is the usual Scots term). Those functions, in Scotland as in England, were performed by a different kind of lawyer, the kind called "solicitor" in England and present-day Scotland, but in Scotland in Boswell's time always "writer." Writers prepared and managed causes, but were not qualified to present them in court. For that they employed and briefed lawyers of Boswell's kind, "advocates" in Scotland, "barristers" in England. Writers served an apprenticeship and usually had less formal education than advocates, who had generally completed the Arts course in a university and had often studied in Holland. (Holland, because, as has already been said, Scots law was based on the Roman Civil Law, and the Dutch were traditionally the great commentators on Roman Law.) The profession of writer, especially of the superior class of writer called Writer to the Signet, was likely to be more lucrative, but the profession of advocate was considered more "liberal." It was also more ambitious. The high law offices of the Crown (Lord Advocate, Solicitor-General) were reserved for advocates; only advocates could serve as sheriffs of counties; in practice only advocates were raised to the bench as Lords of Session. Some portion of Boswell's daily business was devoted to writing answers to memorials—statements of fact drawn up by writers requesting his legal opinion—but for much the greater part his practice consisted of oral or written arguments in litigations actually before the Court of Session, or of the defence of clients actually being prosecuted before the High Court of Justiciary. He was a courtroom, not an office, lawyer.

Yet, though a courtroom lawyer, he wrote (or dictated) more and spoke less than most American courtroom lawyers do. Causes in the Court of Session (the supreme court of Scotland for civil causes) were all tried without juries, generally in the first instance in the "Outer House" before a single judge, who summarily pronounced a judgement ("interlocutor") which he might later amend or reverse as further representations were made to him. From this single judge ("the Lord Ordinary") appeal could be taken to "the Inner House," the whole bench of fifteen judges sitting with the Lord President at their head. The first arguments in causes before the Ordinaries were usually oral, but in all the later stages the Lord Ordinary was likely to demand written papers which he could study at home. The arguments addressed to the Inner House were generally not only written but also printed. Boswell estimated that half an advocate's business in the Court of Session was done in writing.

The High Court of Justiciary had a bench of six, with the Lord Justice-Clerk at their head, but tried all causes by juries. Each cause offered counsel two opportunities for forensic eloquence *viva voce:* "the pleading to the relevancy," in which counsel for the Crown and counsel for the defence "stated on either part the arguments in point of law and evidence in point of fact against and in favour of the criminal," and "the charge to the jury." The bench took a more active part in formulating the evidence than in English or American courts, the presiding judge digesting for the record both evidence in chief and evidence in cross-examination into a summary narrative which he and the witness signed.

Lastly, Scots advocates did not maintain offices or chambers. Boswell studied and prepared papers at home, often getting up at six in the morning to dictate to his clerk, and he saw clients there or perhaps more often at a tavern. Consultations were held at taverns, in the Advocates' Library, at the home of the agent, or the home of one of the counsel. An advocate did not wait at home for business, but appeared, vested in black gown and white horse-hair wig, in the Parliament Hall five days each week as the clock struck nine. If Boswell had no cause to attend to, he joined the other unemployed advocates pacing back and forth in the Hall. It was customary to engage more than one advocate, even in litigations of small consequence.

Ever since the appearance of Macaulay's high-coloured and exaggerated characterizations, most people, though they may know that Boswell was a member of the Faculty of Advocates, refuse to believe that anybody ever gave him any business. Since the detailing of Boswell's hopes, struggles, and final despair as a lawyer will occupy the greater part of the remainder of this chronicle, it would be out of place to engage here in an extended inquiry into the degree of his success. This does, however, seem to be the place for a flat statement that he enjoyed good general practice for nearly twenty years, and for the recording of an informed guess that his percentage of victories was at least as high as that of several of his friends—MacLaurin, Nairne, Gordon—who were raised to the bench. Of his oral arguments (by contemporary testimony his more brilliant performances) no full transcripts survive, but a good many of his printed papers are preserved in the libraries of Edinburgh. I do not know that they have ever been systematically studied by any one capable of pronouncing on their legal competence, but I can at least report that they are sober and workmanlike. Though his fees did not place him among the reigning advocates of his day, they were clearly better than average. The obvious literary analogue is in his favour: the fees he received in his first full year at the bar considerably exceed the fees that Walter Scott drew in his fifth. And it is definitely not true, as has been more than hinted, that his causes were different from those handled by his colleagues, were all somehow ridiculous or fantastic. His criminal practice, which will be adequately illustrated by trials I shall have occasion to discuss in the course of this narrative, was in every way representative of Scots criminal practice generally. He was never senior counsel in a civil cause involving vast amounts of property, but the causes he pleaded by himself embodied exactly the same legal issues on a smaller scale as those underlying the great causes. A biographer is forced to assert the solidity and routine dullness of most of Boswell's civil causes, for few readers could be induced to pay heed to a true demonstration. It is, however, perhaps possible to illustrate this side of his practice by the summary of one early cause turned up in a random search of the records.

KERR V. THOMSONS. Hugh Thomson, minister at Kilmaurs, Ayrshire, died in 1731. He owned certain heritable property [real estate] in and around Kilmaurs. Three of his children survived him: Martha, wife of

Robert Kerr, writer in Kilmarnock; Margaret, wife of David Smyton
(or Smeaton), minister in the [dissenting] anti-burgher church in Kilmaurs; and Lilias, wife of Gavin Bryce, merchant in Glasgow. By Scots
law the property was equally divisible between these three as heirs-por-
tioner. But the widow held a liferent interest in one half of it, and when
she was over eighty, she became a convert to Smyton's brand of independent Presbyterianism, and by her influence the property was let to
Smyton as a tenant. On her death, Hugh Kerr, writer in Paisley, son of
Martha and Robert Kerr, as representative of his deceased mother,
brought (23 June 1766) a summons of division against his aunts. This
called for a division of the property, and for its being forthwith let by
public roup [auction] till the division should be made. Hugh Kerr also
claimed a right of praecipuum [right of the eldest heir-portioner to the
principal dwelling place] as representing the eldest daughter. There was
no dispute about the question of division; the questions at issue were the
roup and the praecipuum. Hugh Kerr claimed that the property was let
to Smyton at an unduly low rent and should be let by roup immediately.
The defenders[1] (whom Boswell represented) claimed that it should not be
let without the unanimous consent of all three proprietors; that in any case
Smyton was entitled to a year's warning; that the right of praecipuum
was applicable only to large estates or to property which had been in a
family for a long time; finally, that Hugh Kerr's right was defeated by
certain deeds executed by Hugh Thomson. The Lord Ordinary found for
the defenders in a series of interlocutors. Hugh Kerr carried the cause to
the Session, but eventually sold his right to a third party and withdrew his
petition. A final interlocutor, 5 March 1768, ruled no expenses to either
party. The bitterness with which the cause was fought over comparatively
small issues suggests a strong dash of *odium theologicum*. The process
contains about thirty documents. Boswell and the opposing advocate, William Wallace, Professor of Scots Law in the university and later Sheriff
of Ayrshire, made verbal pleadings on 3 December 1766 and Boswell appeared in court on several other occasions; the process contains written
Representations, a Memorial, a Petition, and Answers (altogether, forty-
six pages) signed by Boswell, of dates from c. 3 February 1767 to 29
February 1768. Boswell's fees amounted to twelve guineas.

   Like other lawyers, Boswell usually took causes without particular concern for the subject matter. Since he invited Erskine and Johnston to come
hear him plead the following "curious cause," it is probable that he took

---

[1] Defender = defendant; pursuer = plaintiff.

it mainly for fun—as an opportunity to repeat Billingsgate in court and comment on it with grave and shocked seriousness.

ROBERTSON V. STORRIE. James Storrie, late tide-waiter [customs collector] in Saltcoats, now in Irvine, was charged with slander before the Commissary Court of Glasgow by Jean Robertson, wife of Robert Boyd, sailor in Saltcoats. [Boyd was at the time in America.] He was alleged to have called her an adulterous whore, adulterous bitch, who had given him the clap, etc. The Commissary Court decreet, 28 August 1766, ordered him to pay £30 Scots [£2.10.0 sterling] to Jean Robertson and £10 Scots to the Procurator-Fiscal [Public Prosecutor]; he was also ordered to apologize in open court. For failing to do this he incurred a further £30 penalty to Jean Robertson. The record shows that there had been bad blood between the two for some time. Storrie alleged that Jean Robertson was a friend of smugglers, and gave this as the reason for her enmity. They had been bound in mutual lawburrows [legal securities not to do each other injury] and finally had given bond to be of good behaviour towards each other. Storrie obtained letters of suspension [appealed to the Court of Session], 28 October 1766. Boswell represented Jean Robertson, William Wallace represented Storrie. The cause came up on 27 January 1767 and was adjourned at Storrie's request. Boswell appearing on 3 and 7 February and the other party being absent, the Lord Ordinary found the decreet orderly and modified Storrie's expenses as £3 sterling. On 17 February 1767 Wallace lodged a Representation asking the Lord Ordinary to review these interlocutors. Boswell lodged Answers (14 pages). On 12 June 1767 the Lord Ordinary, having considered the Representation and Answers, adhered to the former interlocutor. Boswell's fee was a guinea.

Just as the Summer Session rose, Boswell received his last letter from the great writer whom he had not long since addressed as "illustrious philosopher" and to whom he had issued a rhapsodic invitation to visit Auchinleck. As we have seen, what remained of his sense of discipleship had evaporated completely on the February morning when he had surrendered Thérèse to Rousseau's embraces at Chiswick. Though he remained in London more than two weeks after that, he seems not to have gone back to see Rousseau again. Rousseau, by letter, taxed him with neglect, and he repelled the charge, but the tone of his letter was one of persiflage. In March, Rousseau and Thérèse had gone to live in Staffordshire, in a cottage furnished by an admirer. Thérèse, who had no English at all, hated England and worked on Rousseau's all-too-active sense of persecution. Further cause for paranoid apprehension was furnished by the English newspapers, which Rousseau, though he was not fluent in English, seems to have combed for references to himself. Horace Walpole, as far back as Rousseau's transit of Paris, had composed in French a malicious squib which purported to be a letter from Frederick the Great to Rousseau, inviting him to Potsdam and promising him persecution on a royal scale. This got published in *The St. James's Chronicle* for 3 April 1766 and was followed by others in the same vein, notably by a biting fable, *Le Débiteur de pilules* ("The Pill Pedlar"), actually written by Gibbon's Swiss friend Georges Deyverdun but by Rousseau attributed to his old enemy d'Alembert. It is to be feared that Boswell wrote some of the other newspaper banter of the time, not directly attacking Rousseau but treating his singularities with levity. Though Hume had got Rousseau a pension from the Crown and was innocent of any disloyalty worse than private expressions of dismay at Rousseau's prickliness, Rousseau persuaded himself that Hume had leagued with Walpole and d'Alembert to destroy him. He may also have imagined that Boswell was in the plot, for he knew that Boswell and Hume were acquainted (Boswell's letters, in fact, were coming to him through Hume), and Thérèse may have tattled, though probably not to the extent of admitting her own frailty. On 10 July Rousseau wrote Hume a long and violent letter accusing him of treachery, and on 4 August he wrote Boswell a short and mysterious note which Boswell called peevish and professed to consider mad. Boswell instantly sent off replies to Rousseau and Thérèse (both missing), but appears to have received no further communication from either. Certainly Rousseau never explained his grievance. Hume (unwisely, as most people thought) published his correspondence with Rousseau in order to vindicate himself. Boswell wrote a few more anonymous newspaper squibs ridiculing Hume and Rousseau impartially. Rousseau remained in his cottage till the following summer (1767), growing constantly more disturbed and suspicious. Finally, under a delusion that he was being held prisoner, he made a frantic dash for the coast, was assisted by the authorities to leave the country, and went to France, where he was allowed to remain in peace. He went on writing the *Confessions,* married Thérèse in a left-handed fashion, and died of a stroke in 1778.

It is impossible to approve or to justify Boswell's contributions to the Hume-Rousseau quarrel. Granted that it was only honest and manly to withdraw from a discipleship he no longer felt, his gratitude for Rousseau's real kindnesses to him should have kept him from public gibes, however apposite. We are dealing here with an odd, disquieting, and permanent trait of Boswell's personality, what he himself would have called his irrepressible gaiety of fancy. By 1767 he had already begun to consider it no real disloyalty to his acquaintances to exercise his imagination in ludicrous inventions concerning them. What is more remarkable, he maintained that they should not mind his publishing such inventions in the newspapers provided he did it anonymously. Newspaper publication of this sort he held to be as blameless as irresponsible thoughts that come and go; it gave him intense and inexplicable satisfaction.

Boswell had little more than arrived at Auchinleck for the vacation than he was forced to take to his bed again with chills and fever. Though he had more than one relapse during the autumn, he was able to attend parts at least of the Western and Southern Circuits of the Justiciary Court. Young lawyers working up a practice were glad to accept court appointment on the circuits as counsel for poor clients. At Glasgow, on 13 September 1766, he was given his first criminal client, and threw himself with ardour into a cause which was destined to affect his whole career. John Reid, a poor man of bad reputation ("habit and repute a common thief") was accused of stealing no fewer than one hundred and twenty sheep from a farm in Peeblesshire, driving them off to Glasgow, and there offering them for sale to the butchers. The charge was of course capital. It could not be denied that the sheep were stolen, but Reid persisted in maintaining that he had them in a flock from another man who commissioned him to drive them to Glasgow and sell them. Boswell and his fellow advocate Bannatyne MacLeod believed he might be telling the truth, and on the grounds that Reid had not been assigned an agent in time to collect his evidences, and that the jury in Glasgow was hostile, they managed to get the trial postponed and the venue shifted to Edinburgh. It is clear from the papers that Boswell preserved that he furnished all the energy of the defence and did most of the speaking.

At Ayr on 11 October a client of his named James Haddow was convicted on two counts of house-breaking and two days later was sentenced to be hanged. Haddow was unquestionably guilty, but he had borne a good character until recently, when he had fallen in with bad company. He was very young and very simple, and Boswell was moved by his father's distress. Besides, the old man stated indignantly that the Lord Advocate had promised him that his son should escape with a sentence of transportation. Boswell, who was satisfied that the lad had had a fair trial, was no longer professionally concerned, and was required by legal etiquette to stand aside and let matters take their course. But he could never keep himself from emotional involvement in capital causes affecting poor people, and he began, on the very threshold of his career, the dangerous practice of extra-legal manoeuvring. He did not speak to the Lord Advocate or the Lord Justice-Clerk, and did not even make representations to the Duke of Queensberry, who, as Lord Justice-General, was titular head of the Justiciary Court. But he wrote, and gave to Haddow's father, a moving letter addressed to the Duchess of Douglas, imploring her to intercede: "For God's sake, my Lady Duchess, be earnest." It is not known whether she did or not, but James Haddow was granted a reprieve and escaped the gallows. And Boswell began the accumulation of one of the most moving sections of his archives, a bale of legal papers relating to clients of his who were tried for their lives. The issue was not often even so comparatively happy as with James Haddow. Most of these clients were hanged in spite of all his efforts.

It is clear that tensions were building up again between Boswell and his father. As far back as the autumn of 1764 Boswell had written to Sir David Dalrymple (now raised to the bench as Lord Hailes) asking him to present to Lord Auchinleck the four conditions on which he would consent to come back to Scotland and be a lawyer. First, his father must stop treating him as a young laird, that is, as a boy undergoing discipline and instruction to fit him for his station in life. Secondly, he must not require him any longer to live under the parental roof but must allow him a domicile of his own. Thirdly, he must permit him to worship in a Church-of-England chapel. And fourthly, he must indulge him in a jaunt to London once every year. As earnest of a real wish for reconciliation, Boswell had dropped his more *outré* demands of Anglicanism and London, but he had expected that after he had lived with his father for a decent length of time to console him, his father would himself propose separate quarters. He was dismayed and hurt when Lord Auchinleck made clear that he had no intention of ever releasing him till one or the other of them got married. But he gave up this point too, having convinced himself that it was his duty to live with his father and be careful of him in his lonely and unprotected state. And at last he accepted the fact that his father's character was not going to change on the fundamental issue of authority: "He must have his son in a great degree of subjection to him."

By autumn Lord Auchinleck was giving him such a dose of young-lairdism that both his uncle and his brother were moved to tender their sympathy. "As to your choice of the ague before the spleen," wrote Dr. Boswell, "I agree with you and think your father has it . . . oftener far than good humour." "I do assure you, my dear brother," wrote David, "I feel for you very much in regard to the galling manner in which you are treated. . . . I know that the causes of your unhappiness are in general—nay, perhaps all—trifling, but I know they are innumerable; and a continued pain, though minute, is ten times more difficult to be borne by a man of resolution than one calamitous misfortune." On the way back to Edinburgh with his father for the Winter Session, Boswell paused at Dalzell, the seat of the family of Hamiltons which had produced his great-grandmother, and was moved in a long memorandum written in Italian to specify the nature of his continued pain.

Solemn anniversaries have great influence on an imaginative mind like mine. One hundred years ago that pious lady Anna Hamilton came from this house to the Family of Auchinleck. Seriously touched by this reflection, I resolve to reach an agreement with my father, to make a friendly covenant that he is never to ridicule you or say harsh things to you before others, but is to tell you all in private. It is just that now you have arrived at the independence of a rational being, he should make some sacrifice too; and for this get his promise and his hand and trust in them securely. But let it be agreed that when he forgets, you are to remind him. On your side, promise that you will always be attentive to all his inclinations, assure him that you are sufficiently master of yourself to be able to forgo any gratification whatsoever when your duty calls you to stand by him, and that you are able to live without any other aim than the ancient Family and Corsica. Having made this accord, you will be united, you will be loyal to each other, and you will keep this wonderful change secret from the world. They will see the effects of it, and your father and you will say, "We are happy together," but the world will not know the reason. In consequence, he will tell you all his affairs in confidence. You will be calm and proud under his protection, the ancient Family will be honoured, and whether he die or you die, you will have consolation and hope in God of a better life.

The syntax is incoherent (even more so than appears in the translation) and the tenses are not quite certain, but later statements of Boswell do seem to indicate that he had got up courage to speak in a manly fashion to his father about his father's habitual sarcasms and censoriousness, and that Lord Auchinleck, in an equally manly fashion, had promised to treat him with greater courtesy and to take him more fully into his confidence. For a few months both men sincerely professed themselves to be happy in their relations with each other. The league of friendship was soon infringed on both sides, but it is gratifying to know that in the long desert years ahead both could recall one oasis.

CHAPTER

XVIII

"What strength of mind you have had this winter, to go through so much business and at the same time have so violent a passion!" So Boswell on 18 March 1767, savouring the Winter Session before taking flight for Auchinleck. It had been a dreadful winter, ice nine inches thick, muir and dale levelled with snow, and the birds starving. But in frost and snow Boswell had glowed incandescent. Mrs. Dodds, presumably on hand since November, could not receive male callers privately in the house where she was boarded, but Boswell rented a rendezvous in the house of a sober widow, and she came there most obligingly whenever he sent for her. He called it Philippi, the retreat for his hours of Paphian bliss, his stately and witty phrase rebuking the vulgarity of a later age that would style such conveniences love-nests. He revived his old model of the passionate Spaniard ("Be Spaniard: girl every day"), but his ultimate analogue was the Herculean Antony. Philippi proved not domestic, not exclusive, enough, and he rented a house of his own against Whitsunday, paying over for it the fees of an entire session.

The business he admired himself for having transacted was by no means all in the line of his profession. Ever since he got back to Scotland he had been reading and extracting for the book on Corsica he intended to write, and had been sending off letters to Paoli, Rivarola, and John Dick, who were collecting printed and manuscript materials for him. He continued to write for the newspapers, his production in the first part of 1767 averaging better than six paragraphs a month. His prime object, an extremely ambitious one, was to secure a reversal of the policy of the British government and to make Great Britain the avowed protector of a free Corsica. But of course he did not intend to be self-effacing. He saw more clearly than any of the people from whom he was asking advice that Corsica was ripe for literary exploitation and that he was uniquely equipped to do the exploiting. He set out to sell Corsica to the British public and at the same time to fix his own name to Corsica like a trade-mark.

He had left the Duke of Grafton's door on 23 February 1766 with a happy conviction that any government headed by Pitt would repeal the hated Proclamation of 1763. In the following summer Pitt (no longer, alas, the Great Commoner) was asked to form a ministry but no action regarding Corsica emerged. Boswell waited for a few weeks and then wrote a brief letter: would my Lord Chatham not now befriend a noble and unfortunate little nation? No answer. After a decent interval he wrote again and more pressingly. This time Pitt replied with reasonable promptness and crushing clarity: "I see not the least ground at present for this country to interfere with any justice in the affairs of Corsica." Boswell wrote one more letter, mainly about his proposed book, but by the time it reached Pitt, Pitt had sunk into a state of prostration from which he did not emerge during the rest of his ministry. Having failed to secure action by direct pressure on the head of government, Boswell now began to work up pressure from below by means of the newspapers. It was a serious campaign, shrewdly conducted, but it had the predictable Boswellian trimmings. In so brief a résumé as must here suffice, it seems best to move from its more fanciful to its more serious aspects, and to collect matter that was scattered serially over more than half a year.

Among the Corsican troops who stormed the island of Capraia (so ran a paragraph in *The London Chronicle*) were several English soldiers whose valour contributed greatly to the success of the expedition. A few days later the *Chronicle* printed a letter from one of these English lads, Sam Jones by name. Sam is of the tribe of Joseph Leman and Honour Blackmore: "We haiv littel pai to signifi but enuff of good vittals and drink, sweet mutton as any on the downs, and the best of wyns as plenty as smal bir in old Ingland." Two days after that, came a letter from "A. E.," thanking the *Chronicle* for printing Sam Jones's letter: "I rejoice to see that the British and the Corsicans do so well together.... I shall carefully lay by the soldier's letter; such original unaffected sallies give us the justest ideas." All three items entirely by Boswell.

There was also the dashing and mysterious Corsican courier, Signor

Romanzo, who moved across Europe a precursor of d'Artagnan. He was first heard of from Hamburg on New Year's Day: he had called on the Earl Marischal and Sir Andrew Mitchell, His Britannic Majesty's ambassador to the court of Prussia. By the first of March he was at The Hague, where he stayed a week. He had a long audience with Sir Joseph Yorke, British ambassador, to whom he was introduced by the Reverend Mr. Richardson, his Excellency's chaplain. He next turned up at Utrecht, and then he came to London, where he was seen on the Royal Exchange. His stay in England was fruitful, for when he returned to The Hague his *maître d'hôtel* gave out that he had secured £100,000 extraordinary credit from the English merchants. He was extremely loyal to his British friends. At Marseilles, when a French duke said something in his presence disrespectful to the British nation and their monarch, Signor Romanzo replied that the British were a nation of men and their king the best prince in Europe. The Duke called him out and was severely wounded. When Signor Romanzo reported back to Paoli in Corsica, Paoli insisted that the conversation should be in English. In this long series (seven paragraphs, January–June 1767), though most of the persons mentioned were real people, Signor Romanzo was a pure invention of James Boswell. He was a great success, and his story was picked up and reprinted by many other newspapers (including some on the Continent), and the magazines.

Signor Romanzo's mission was only one of many entertaining political inventions concerning Corsica that one could read in *The London Chronicle*. The Grand Duke of Tuscany was about to establish the independence of Corsica; a quadruple alliance in favour of Corsica was being discussed in Europe; the Genoese admitted that the Corsicans were winning; the King of Prussia had written a very elegant poem entitled *L'Éloge des corses;* the Dey of Algiers had sent his agent, Mahomet Ruza Beg, with particular dispatches to Paoli; Prince Heraclius of Georgia had sent Paoli six beautiful camels, etc., etc.

"I do believe," wrote Boswell in *An Account of Corsica,* "an English newspaper is the most various and extraordinary composition that mankind ever produced. An English newspaper, while it informs the judicious of what is really doing in Europe, can keep pace with the wildest fancy in feigned adventures, and amuse the most desultory taste with essays on all subjects and in every style."

The word "fancy" brings us back to the problem I have broached in discussing Boswell's newspaper squibs on Hume and Rousseau, which belong to this same period. How are we to reconcile the responsible James Boswell, Esq., with his sober, almost obsessive regard for minute circumstantial accuracy, his literary tact and his literary taste, and the anonymous irresponsible writer for the newspapers who delights in the coarsely indelicate, the broadly ludicrous, the unsubtly fantastic? Clearly in the newspapers he is consciously writing down and clearly he is often writing with no thought of promoting anything. In this spring of 1767, sandwiched between a notice that an artist was going to Corsica to paint a portrait of Paoli (true: his name was Henry Benbridge, he was an American, and Boswell was paying the bill) and a factual extract of a letter from Mr. Boswell concerning the island of Capraia, which the Corsicans had recently taken from the Genoese, *The London Chronicle* presented two quite gratuitous and disinterested inventions. An "extract of a letter from Newcastle" tells how two sailors, streaking down from London in a purchased post-chaise to visit their girls, refused to stop to have their wheels greased ("Damn it, she has had tar enough for all the voyage"), and burst into flames as they entered Newcastle; the second recounts the tragic tale of a young officer who slaughtered his bride on the morning after their marriage in a fit of lunacy. Below the first, in his own file of the *Chronicle,* Boswell recorded what was surely for him the pay-off: "My Lord Dumfries believed this story of the tars and told it often and often." Did Boswell enjoy seeing himself in print so much that he got satisfaction out of sheer publication, whether recognized as his or not? Was his object to set traps for the unwary, his satisfaction coming when people repeated the paragraphs in his presence as facts, he laughing inwardly? Did he relish the sense of manipulating others so much that he was willing to descend to the level of gratuitous misinformation? Did he like the reputation of writing widely for the newspapers, a masked and Protean figure whose hand might be anywhere? Was it all just a part of his wish to write so that people would have to read him, not merely people of literary sophistication but also people whose reading never got beyond the news? Were the inventions a compensation for the sacrifice of fancy demanded by judicious habits of mind and responsible sticking to the facts? One can only speculate, but in the really important matter we are left in no doubt. Instead of dulling Boswell's perception of fact, the fictions sharpened it. Three volumes of his file of *The London Chronicle* are provided with manuscript indexes of his own contributions, in which he has carefully distinguished the "facts" from the "inventions."

It would be easy to conclude that only naïve and stupid people were taken in by Boswell's historical inventions, but the conclusion would be wrong. The saga of Signor Romanzo was gravely epitomized in the *Neue Genealogisch-Historische Nachrichten* of Leipzig, which practically certified its authenticity for future researchers. In an amusing passage in his journal Boswell tells how he once found Thomas Percy, the distinguished editor of *Reliques of Ancient English Poetry,* trying by the most approved research techniques to locate for General Paoli an unpublished defence of the Corsicans by Dr. John ("Estimate") Brown, a defence which Boswell himself had invented and had long since forgotten about.

The Corsican inventions (even Prince Heraclius's camels) of course all had some serious purpose. They were shrewdly devised to catch the attention of the public and, as our jargon would have it, to improve the public image of Corsica, which in England was generally assumed to be a savage land inhabited by dangerous malcontents. Once interest had been focussed, once Corsica had been made to seem civilized and important, facts in some quantity could safely be presented. And Boswell gave facts in plenty, or at least provided plenty of Corsican news that *he* had not slanted. As early as 4 October 1766, *The London Chronicle,* in a paragraph clearly composed by Boswell himself, announced that though in future the *Chronicle* would continue to print reports about Corsica "for the authenticity of which we cannot absolutely answer," it would also from time to time present its readers with extracts from *The Corsican Gazette,* published by the Corsican Government. Readers were assured that they could trust implicitly anything appearing under that heading. On two later occasions the *Chronicle* informed its readers that the articles appearing as *Corsican Gazette* or *Corsican Intelligence* were furnished by Mr. Boswell, to whom regular information was transmitted by order of General Paoli. The guaranteed articles, which were extensive in scope, were widely copied by other newspapers and were generally believed to be the only completely trustworthy news of Corsica.

And of course the newspaper paragraphs were all advance publicity for the proposed book. Again, as early as 11 October 1766, *The London Chronicle* announced "that Mr. Boswell is soon to publish an account of the island of Corsica, with memoirs of General Paoli." Follow-ups appeared at regular intervals. An ingenious indirect device kept the plug Corsica-Mr. Boswell recurring through the *Chronicle* for a period of seven months. At the beginning of 1767 a letter signed "J. B." requested verse translations of two epigrams on Corsica by the Roman philosopher Seneca. Readers were delighted to oblige. As each version appeared, "J. B." commented on it and referred to the book on Corsica which he had in hand. To make sure that no one should fail to identify "J. B.," he sent in a translation himself over the pseudonym "Humilis, Plymouth," with a letter saying that he did not really expect Mr. Boswell to insert his careless verses in his *Account of Corsica*. Finally, in August, Boswell, signing his full name and dating from Edinburgh, asked "Patricius," the author of the version he had selected, to identify himself so that his name might be included in *An Account of Corsica*. "Patricius" turned out to be a lad of nineteen, one Thomas Day, who was later to win fame as an educational theorist with a Rousseauistic book entitled *Sandford and Merton*.

After the beginning of the Session on 12 November 1766, Corsica and the newspapers had to be fitted into the interstices of a very tight routine. Boswell was coming into great employment; undoubtedly, as he wrote to Temple, he had been kept very throng.[1] "My clerk comes to me every morning at six, and I have dictated to him forty folio pages in one day." By the end of the Session he had made eighty-four guineas. He had pleaded a cause against Henry Dundas and the great Robert Macqueen and had been praised from the bench by Lord Gardenstone; even Dundas had admitted that his reply was masterly. Lord Hailes told him that in one cause he had drawn a paper with as unfair a state of the facts as Lockhart could have done, a backhanded compliment, for Alexander Lockhart, Dean of Faculty, was rated at the time the most successful lawyer at the Scottish bar. Boswell's causes before the Court of Session—solid, humdrum litigations concerning property —must be assumed as the matter of his crowded daily activity, but call for no more detail in his biography than they receive in his journal notes. There is much more stuff of biography in his occasional practice before the Court of Justiciary.

John Reid's trial finally came up on 15 December, he by that time having lain in gaol for nearly six months in Stirling, Glasgow, and Edinburgh. Boswell gave him an allowance for food to match that of the

[1] Busy.

City while he was at Glasgow, and no doubt continued his bounty after
Reid was transferred to the Tolbooth in Edinburgh. He also gave him
some kind of devotional book with an inscription saying that if he could
not save him from punishment in this world, he hoped at least to assist
him in obtaining mercy in the world to come. He persuaded another
advocate, Andrew Crosbie, to come in with him and MacLeod, Crosbie
having a reputation for this sort of case. The Lord Advocate clapped on
a second charge of sheep-stealing committed as far back as 1763. Reid
lost his nerve and proposed to settle for transportation, but was persuaded to stick it out. At the trial, which lasted from nine in the morning
till one that night, the Crown presented many witnesses and the Lord
Advocate, the Solicitor-General, and three other advocates spoke for the
prosecution. Reid bore a bad character, he was found with the number
of sheep that had been stolen on a road leading from the farm where
the theft occurred, and he did not pretend that the sheep were his own.
Boswell and his associates presented no witnesses but attacked the case
of the prosecution on purely legal grounds. The official manuscript record (process) does not report the speeches of counsel, but it is clear from
the general applause that Boswell received that it was he who charged
the jury, and his own subsequent comments leave little doubt as to the
line he took. Reid, he maintained, was being convicted on his character
and purely circumstantial evidence. The jury was impressed and returned the Scots verdict of "Not proven," much to the indignation of
the judges, who in a body denounced it as preposterous. It was a great
personal triumph for Boswell, whose strategy and eloquence were widely
applauded, but it did not bode well for his professional future. No one
in Edinburgh could make a career of criminal practice: there were not
criminal causes enough, and few of the accused in criminal causes could
pay a lawyer anything. An ambitious man got out of that sort of work
just as soon as he could, and while he was in it was careful not to appear over-zealous. Lawyers who worried about, or showed zeal for, poor
clients under vehement suspicion of sheep-stealing were thought not to
be quite sound. Crosbie, one of the most brilliant lawyers of his generation, had already pretty much put himself out of the running for a judge-
ship by his pertinacity in securing for poor prisoners all the advantages
that the law allowed them. Only very rarely and then sometimes with
deep misgivings did Boswell take the side of the prosecution in a criminal
cause, though most advocates, if asked, were as ready to assist the Crown

as to defend the prisoner. It was a tribute to his heart but not to his head that at the very outset he made Crosbie his model rather than the Lord Justice-Clerk, Robert Macqueen, or Ilay Campbell.

A week later, again in the Justiciary Court, he helped Crosbie put brakes on the automatic turning of the wheels of justice. Joseph Taylor, an Englishman, was capitally indicted for stealing three mares. The alleged crime had occurred near Carlisle, but he had been apprehended on the Scottish side of the border, where he had made a confession which the Crown proposed to use against him. On the reading of the indictment, Boswell pleaded that the crime, if committed, was outside the jurisdiction of the Court. This held up the disposition of the cause for almost three months while the Court received oral and written pleadings. Crosbie turned in an Information of seventy-eight folio pages, going at great length into questions of international law and the statutes of England and Scotland. When the Court found the indictment relevant, as it ultimately did, Taylor petitioned for banishment to the plantations and was sentenced accordingly. It is impossible to say how much he really gained by the technicalities.

Considering the desperate nature of these causes, Boswell was bound before very long to lose a client. On 9 February 1767 he defended Robert Hay, a young soldier not more than twenty-two years old, who was charged with having assaulted a sailor in the Cowgate and with having robbed him of £2 and a silver watch. The evidence of Hay's guilt was that he had tried to sell the watch on the day after the robbery. The facts seem to have been that John Butterfield, drummer in the 44th Regiment of Foot, had persuaded Hay, while drunk, to go along with him on a foray; that Hay had stood watch while Butterfield committed the assault and the robbery and had accepted the watch as his share of the spoil. In view of his youth and simplicity and the practical certainty that he had not been the principal assailant, he could probably have obtained a transportation pardon if he had been willing to incriminate Butterfield, but this the principle of honour among thieves forbade him to do. He did not tell Boswell the truth, but rather tried to shift the blame to a soldier named Robertson, presumably because Robertson already had one or more capital charges laid against him and there was good reason to think that he could not be produced. Boswell did what he could with this unconvincing plea, adding the standard clichés that Hay was the favourite son of an old and distressed mother whose gray hairs must be brought with sorrow to the grave should her unfortunate son be condemned, and that he had never in his life been drunk before the night of the robbery. The jury brought in a unanimous verdict of guilty (in Scotland a majority is enough for a conviction), but so far responded to Boswell's eloquence as to recommend mercy. The judges imposed a sentence of death by hanging, and it rested with them whether the recommendation of mercy should be forwarded or not. Boswell talked seriously to Hay on the day following his condemnation, advising him to clear the innocent but not to impeach a companion if the relationship had been one of trust. Hay told him nothing, but nine days later revealed the whole story, Butterfield by that time having got to Ireland. Boswell then forwarded a petition for clemency to the King, saying he did so because there was reason to fear that the judges would not transmit the jury's recommendation of mercy because they were angry at Hay for his tergiversations. The petition was of course hopeless. Boswell visited Hay at least once more and found him attended by his mother (she really was aged) and his wife, refusing food and drink and sunk in a paralysis of terror. His fate was made to seem even harder by the fact that another client of Boswell's, tried on a charge of cow-stealing a week later than Hay and sentenced to die with him, did get his sentence changed to banishment for life. Boswell did not witness Hay's execution, because he had gone to Auchinleck by the time it occurred, but he commissioned David to attend and make a report, and he had fears of ghosts after reading David's letter. He made no systematic collection of his papers in civil causes, but he did of those connected with his capital criminal trials, and the group of papers on poor Robert Hay set the generally macabre tone of the whole. It was harder for him if his criminal clients were poor. "Why it is, I know not," he wrote after seeing Hay in prison, "but we compassionate less a genteel man." One may guess that one reason, at least, was his ingrained sense of feudal responsibility.

He did not collect the papers in his civil causes and rarely discussed those causes in his journal because they seldom gave him that sense of heightened consciousness that he considered worth putting into words. But in one civil cause at this time he did allow his passions violent play, and it was one that he was not professionally engaged in: the great Douglas Cause. It is impossible here to give more than the barest sketch of that tremendous action which has been called the greatest trial in

Scottish history affecting civil status, but some notice of the human issues it presented is necessary if one is to understand Boswell's involvement.

In the year 1761 a thirteen-year-old boy named Archibald Steuart had been served heir to the huge estates of the Duke of Douglas, and had taken the Douglas name. Next year another small boy, the Duke of Hamilton, brought suit to have this service set aside, and his cause was joined with two others to the same effect brought by his brother Lord Douglas Hamilton and by Sir Hew Dalrymple, one of the Duke's heirs-at-law. All three claimed that Archibald Steuart was in fact not the nephew of the Duke of Douglas, as he was represented to be, but the son of a poor French artisan, abducted or purchased as an infant by the Duke's sister and her husband in order to impose on the Duke and to inherit his property. The moving spirit on the Hamilton side was the beautiful (widowed) young Irish Duchess of Hamilton, *née* Elizabeth Gunning; Archibald Douglas had the warm support of the Duke of Queensberry and the eccentric old Duchess of Douglas.

The story of young Douglas's birth, even as told by his partisans, was sufficiently extraordinary. Lady Jane Douglas, the Duke's only sister, after remaining single to the age of forty-eight, had entered into a clandestine but valid marriage with Col. John Steuart, a penniless Jacobite adventurer of good family, eleven years her senior. The marriage was not divulged because the Duke hated Steuart, and the couple lived on the Continent on Lady Jane's small allowance. On 10 July 1748, according to their story, in Paris, in the lodgings of a woman who let rooms to casual patients, attended by her husband, one confidential female servant or companion of long standing, and a French army surgeon, Lady Jane gave birth to twin sons, Archibald and Sholto. Sholto died at the age of four, Lady Jane herself died in 1753 when Archibald was five years old. Colonel Steuart, having meantime succeeded to the baronetcy of Grandtully, saw Archibald inducted into the Douglas estates, but he also had died before 1767.

The Hamilton lawyers had been able to subject this story to very damaging scrutiny. The defender could not produce Mme. La Brune, at whose house in the Faubourg St. Germain his birth was alleged to have taken place, nor could he locate her establishment. The Pierre Delamarre whose existence his lawyers proved differed from Sir John's surgeon La Marr in almost everything but name. In the month when the twins were said to have been born, in Paris, a male infant two weeks old had been abducted (one suspects really purchased) by foreigners from Nicholas Mignon, a poor glass-worker and his wife. Sholto had not actually appeared in the Steuarts' company till November 1749, it having been given out that he had been left at nurse because he was too delicate to travel. Somewhere about that time, in Paris, a child twenty months old was carried off from the family of an acrobat named Sanry, again by foreigners. Archibald Steuart had been served heir on the evidence of Lady Jane's companion, Helen Hewit, who swore that she had been present at his birth, and by four letters in French purporting to have been written by the surgeon to Sir John, stating that he had delivered Lady Jane of twins. It seemed clear that these letters were the concoction of some English-speaking person, presumably of Sir John himself.

Boswell, with his fanatical devotion to the principle of male succession and with the "two doses of Hamilton blood" which he afterwards bragged of when presented to the Duke of Hamilton, might well have been expected to take the Hamilton side. Actually, he was a violent Douglasian. The "principle of Family" is a complex of so many passions that the outcome of its application to cases is unpredictable. The House of Douglas, in spite of its late sorry representative (the Duke had been a man of weak intellect, violent, unsocial, and unforgiving) was the proudest house in all Scotland. The very mention of the name caused Boswell's knees to slacken and he oftener than not wrote it in the over-size characters he otherwise reserved for the Deity: Douglas. Boswell did not want the great House of Douglas to be submerged in the House of Hamilton. To him the boyish figure of Archibald Douglas was a symbol of Family itself, fighting for its life in a degenerate world.

More than that, though Boswell may never have admitted it to himself, Archibald Douglas was a symbol of his own deepest grievance. To a Douglasian, the Cause came down to a vicious attempt to prove the true heir a changeling. Metaphorically, that was what his own differences with his father had amounted to: a reiterated and destroying charge that he was not a true son of Auchinleck.

The weight of circumstantial evidence was strongly on the Hamilton side. Assuming fraud, one could compose a completely reasonable narrative of events. Assuming that Archibald Douglas really was the son of Lady Jane Douglas, one had to settle for a narrative riddled with improbabilities, irrationalities, mysteries, and coincidences. The intellectuals —David Hume and Adam Smith may serve as examples—were almost to a man Hamiltonians. But Boswell, as we have seen, was rather repelled than attracted by the drawing of confident reasonable conclusions from circumstantial evidence. And he always reacted violently to any attempt to infringe a status that had been sanctioned by law. To him, as to many other thoughtful Douglasians, the cause was primarily one of law and only secondarily one of fact. The law does not demand certainty as regards filiation, for certainty as to a man's parentage can almost never be had. In general, all that a man needs to enable him to claim his birthright is the acknowledgement of two married persons that he is their child and his being commonly reputed to be such. Archibald Douglas's filiation had not been legally challenged in the lifetime of his reputed mother, the person whose testimony on his behalf would have been most useful. He had proved his filiation by due process of law and had been inducted legally into his estate. There was therefore strong legal presumption in his favour, and nothing short of over-whelming demonstration of fraud could be accepted as adequate to over-balance it. Better tolerate some doubt in this individual case than shake the sacred principle of birthright. And the evidence of the pursuers, whatever puzzles it might pose as to Sir John's and Lady Jane's actions, was far from being overwhelming proof of fraud. That there were co-incidences, mysteries, lies, and (possibly) even forgery in the story might be admitted. Should one expect candour and reasonableness of behaviour from an improvident, imaginative, scatter-brained old soldier of fortune and a woman near her hour whose first pregnancy had occurred when she was fifty years old? Did the perplexing obscurity of Sir John's and Lady Jane's movements in Paris need any explanation except that they made great plans but arrived there with almost no money? The very gaps and discrepancies in the story, when one knew the characters of Sir John and Lady Jane, testified to its essential truth. In just such an implausible manner might they have been expected to behave.

Finally, Boswell sided with the mob in being a Douglasian because the opportunities for generous sentiment were all on that side. The Douglas story was studded with pathetic scenes: Lady Jane, disowned by her brother, begging a pittance from the Crown ("presumptive heiress of a great estate and family . . . I want bread"); Sir John, immured, to avoid arrest for debt, six days of every week within the rules of King's

Bench Prison, Lady Jane sending him tidbits for his dinner and gallant notes about the "little men"; Lady Jane, a babe in either hand, turned rudely away from the gate of Bothwell Castle; Archibald, aged five, on the Duke's orders dragged sobbing from the mourning coach at his mother's funeral. The story of young Douglas's life was so much like a fairy tale of the oppressed princeling that it almost automatically cast the Hamiltons in the role of the wicked oppressor. And indeed, if young Douglas *was* a princeling, he and his mother had very definitely been oppressed. Until rough-tongued, warm-hearted Duchess Peggie—a braid-Scots fairy godmother—had married the unattractive old Duke in order to circumvent the Hamiltons, the Duke had been governed by a domestic keeper, a tool of the Hamiltons, one White of Stockbriggs. It was said that when Lady Jane appeared with her babes at the gate, Stockbriggs had locked the Duke up so that he might not succumb to generous feeling. And the whole Hamilton action against Douglas looked, or could be made to look, like an expensive piece of spite. Neither the Duke nor his brother could have touched a penny of the Douglas estate simply by turning Archibald Douglas out of it. To have inherited, they would have had to get certain cancelled settlements of the Duke of Douglas reinstated, and it was highly doubtful whether they would ever be able to do so.

Unpopular already on these grounds, the Hamilton cause was rendered odious to the mob by the way in which the evidence of the French witnesses had been collected. Whether Boswell himself was really disturbed by this aspect of the case I do not know, but he endlessly represented it as iniquitous for popular effect. The French witnesses who gave evidence heard a completely *ex parte* (Hamiltonian) narrative read to them as though it were established fact, and gave depositions in consequence, no lawyer for Douglas being present. Worse, the *ex parte* narrative was issued by the Archbishop of Paris, was read in all the churches, and all persons who knew of any matters mentioned in it were enjoined to come forward and give testimony. The witnesses were for the most part wretchedly poor and probably eager to be bought; even when perjury was not invited, the action, it was said, was intended to lead and intimidate witnesses and to fix their testimony in the sense prejudicial to Douglas. It was in every way French (the war with France was only just over), Popish, and detestable.

Boswell had shown no interest in the Cause when he met young

Douglas, a Westminster boy, in London in 1762, nor again when Andrew Stuart and William Nairne, the Duke of Hamilton's agent and one of his advocates, came through Holland collecting evidence in 1764. He probably did not become a Douglasian until after he had passed advocate and had begun to hear the Cause pleaded and discussed by his fellow lawyers. Since it had then been grinding on for better than three years and a half and was approaching a judgement, he could hardly ever have expected to be engaged as counsel. In his own words, he volunteered and "took care to keep the newspapers and other publications incessantly warm with various writings, both in prose and verse, all tending to touch the heart and rouse the parental and sympathetic feelings." I recall no reference to the Cause in his papers earlier than 14 February 1767, but by that time he is already a volunteer.

The counsel for both sides having completed their pleadings in the summer of 1766, the Court of Session had called for printed memorials, and these had just been submitted, two huge quarto volumes, each as big as an unabridged dictionary. The Hamilton memorial had been compiled by an Ayrshire laird, Sir Adam Fergusson of Kilkerran, a conscientious advocate whose knowledge of mathematics was rather more extensive than his sense of humour. In one section of his eight-hundred-page argument he had computed the odds against Archibald's and Sholto's being other than the "abducted" children of Mignon and Sanry, and had come out with the figure 11,533,394,545,595,999 to 1. Boswell, pouncing on this bit of unessential pedantry, made it the text for a derisive ballad, "The Hamilton Cause." He showed it to Lord Hailes, who admitted that it was witty but told him to burn it: "You'll make yourself enemies." Boswell was momentarily intimidated, but could not convince himself that anybody would resent his gaiety of fancy. He showed it to Sir Adam himself and to Hume, who assured him that it had no venom. Thus encouraged, he sang it (no doubt in gown and wig) to an admiring circle in the Parliament House, felt himself filled with the *vivida vis* of Wilkes, and resolved to follow his own plan, which of course was to publish. *The Hamilton Cause* is one of his better songs:

> Alas! my poor brethren, poor sons of the laws,
> You're all knock'd o' the head by the Hamilton cause;
> No more can you live by your noisy vocation,
> The plan now is silent and slow calculation.
> *Derry down down,* etc.

You may e'en make a bonfire of Bankton and Stair,
And betake you to Sherwin, to Cocker, and Mair;[1]
The Roman Twelve Tables exploded shall be,
The table of *Multiplication* for me.
   Derry down down, etc.

Succeeding lines are a string of arithmetical *doubles entendres:* Sir Adam wants *reduction* but fears *division*[2]; the light-headed ladies who think him not gay must surely now admit that he *figures away.* (Sir Adam, whom Burns was later to call "chaste Kilkerran," seems never to have taken any interest in women.) This is, to say the least, patronizing; and the Duchess of Hamilton would not have found the last stanza without venom:

Like Samson of old, I confess we now find
That *our beauty* has charms which have made us all blind;
So in rage and despair, with a terrible joy,
The house we'll pull down, and the law we'll destroy.
   Derry down down, etc.

It may not be amiss to remind the reader that though I have traced some aspects of Boswell's newspaper publication into the summer of 1767, the present chapter has been mainly concerned with his activities during the short period from November 1766 to March 1767. Nor to remind the reader also that the activities which the limitations of intelligible narrative force me to develop one after the other were all in fact running concurrently. Legal practice, Corsica, Douglas Cause, Mrs. Dodds were one kaleidoscopic action moving at a pitch of excitement that bordered on frenzy. "What a variety you have made of Edinburgh!" Boswell says to himself, and the reader must echo his note of admiration. During the year 1767 there seems to have been no limit either to the amount of work he could perform or of pleasure he could encompass. And this feverish existence, which to most men would seem appallingly wasteful, was to Boswell, during the period of his vigour, a state to be desired and cherished. Life to be worth living must move

---

[1] "You may burn your law books and search for arguments in texts of mathematics."
[2] He wants Archibald Douglas's service as heir declared void, but he is afraid that even if the Duke of Hamilton wins his cause in the Court of Session, he will lose it in the House of Lords.

on the plane of ecstasy. "The sound and perfect human being," he said to Dr. Hugh Blair, "can sit under a spreading tree like the Spaniard, playing on his guitar, his mistress by him, and glowing with gratitude to his God. Music, love, adoration! There is a soul."

The variety, it will be noted, included no schemes of marriage. Belle de Zuylen was certainly not in his thoughts when he pictured himself with guitar and mistress underneath the bough. At the moment he wrote those words, she was in fact in London; had been there four months and would be there two more. She had come over as the guest of General Eliott and his lady (Eliott, the defender of Gibraltar during the War of American Independence, is now better known by his later title of Lord Heathfield), and was having a great social whirl. Dr. Pringle had been called in to prescribe for her and had been captivated; David Hume was to dine with her in lodgings; Lord March had paid her equivocal attentions. Boswell could have gone to London to see her when the court rose in March but never discussed it as a possibility. Either Pringle or Eliott (they were both Scots of family) could surely have arranged for her to visit Scotland under proper protection if a visit had been desired. But Boswell did not propose a visit; in fact, though he was in correspondence with her brothers, he did not write once to her and she did not write to him. That they were both willing to invite the imputation of coolness is clearer than the reasons why they should have done so. Boswell appears to have been piqued by her silence; Pringle reported to Lord Auchinleck that she talked of his son without either resentment or attachment. What her real feelings were we have no way of knowing, but Boswell, since his return to Britain, had never wavered in declaring himself glad that the van Tuyll treaty was off, and now went so far as to say he was well rid of her. He was also becoming restive in Elysium.

Mrs. Dodds, though she truly loved him and was willing to make sacrifices in matters she thought important, could not be brought to treat him with that respectful deference which he considered his due, and delighted in teasing him. She reduced him to a torment of brooding jealousy by pretending to be receiving letters from another lover, and charmed him into gaiety by wearing a black dress and letting the candles burn during their love-making. But she would have done better to keep him to assignations at Philippi and not to let him rent a house for her. The very day after he had fixed on one, he confessed that he felt too much like a married man, and from that point on the raptures of the record alternate with recriminations and expressions of indifference. Early in March he was admitting to Temple a resolution to be free:

I am . . . uneasy about her. Furnishing a house and maintaining her with a maid will cost me a great deal of money. And it is too like marriage, or too much a settled plan of licentiousness. . . . How am I tormented because my charmer has formerly loved others! I am disgusted to think of it. My lively imagination often represents her former lovers in actual enjoyment of her. My desire fails, I am unfit for love. Besides, she is ill-bred, quite a rompish girl. She debases my dignity. She has no refinement. . . . I wish I could get off, and yet how awkward would it be!

He went to her with parting in his thoughts and told her he was very unhappy, but would not tell her why. She was much affected and gave up the house; he secured it again. She charged him with using her ill and said she was determined to leave him and go and live in the north of England. He was torn between a prudent resolve to let her go and passion which he could see she shared:

I took her in my arms. I told her what made me miserable. . . . She said I should not mind her faults before I knew her, since her conduct was now most circumspect. We renewed our fondness. She owned she loved me more than she had ever done her husband. All was again well. . . . I embraced her with transport.

The transports were superficial, the wish to escape from a relationship that was too like marriage, too much a settled plan of licentiousness, extended much deeper and was really not dismissed. "I cannot in honour draw back," he had said, but there were ways to elude the imputation of dishonour. That very evening he gave a bachelor supper to pay off a bet he had made before he left Scotland in 1762: "a guinea that I should not catch the venereal disorder for three years." There was a great deal of drinking, he got so intoxicated as to lose all scruple, went to a low house in an alley where he knew a common girl lodged, and like a brute ("as I was") lay with her all night. He confined himself, as he believed, to safe excesses, but by noon of the next day found evidence of infection. He had an assignation for that evening with Mrs. Dodds and was forced to tell her his shocking story.

I took courage. I told her how drunk I had been. I told the consequences. I lay down and kissed her feet. I said I was unworthy of any other favour.... She bid me rise.... She said she forgave me. She kissed me.

Boswell's reputation for drinking is so firmly established that even careful readers of the present book might fail to realize that this is the first occasion in the story so far (Boswell being now in his twenty-seventh year) on which it has been necessary to say anything at all about his consumption of alcohol. As a matter of fact, Boswell was, by any standards, abstemious in wine up to the time he became an advocate. The Faculty were a hard-drinking lot, and he carelessly adopted hard drinking along with his other professional habits. It was for him the most disastrous of practices, for, as he himself realized, he had a bad head for liquor, and could easily develop a dangerous craving for and dependence on it. But one should never think of him as a drunkard in the period covered by the present volume. He was a social (never a solitary) drinker who occasionally got spectacularly drunk.

That his symptoms were those of acute gonorrhoea was confirmed by a surgeon and physician whom he consulted; that he could have developed acute gonorrhoea within twelve hours or less from the time of exposure is contrary to all medical testimony. He seems not to have taken medical advice for several days, and may perhaps have mistaken for gonorrhoea some other inflammation which was duly succeeded or reinforced by gonorrhoea, but it seems much more likely, as I have suggested above, that the cure of his second bout of the disease had not been complete, and that on the present occasion he had raised a chronic latent infection to the acute stage by charging his blood with alcohol and indulging repeatedly in a rough and irritating mode of relief.

Since the recovery of the Boswell papers, a vast deal of solemn nonsense has been written about Boswell's sexual constitution, commentators showing a monotonous fondness for the pathological term "satyriasis." The Kinsey Report should put an end to all that. Boswell would undoubtedly have qualified as a "high-rating person" in Dr. Kinsey's amusingly neutral terminology, but he would by no means have rated as "sexually extreme." His sexual potency was above average, but in its physiological aspect it was no more pathological than a runner's speed or a boxer's strength. Boswell conceived of sex almost entirely in terms of pleasure, and, as I have already remarked, what he really preferred in the way of sex was frank and episodic grossness without responsibility. Prostitutes attracted him: in his stumblings about low alleys he was unconsciously trying to find his way back again to the pristine bliss of his encounter with Miss Sally Forrester. Though he talked endlessly about marriage, he was actually running away from marriage. Even *settled* licentiousness scared him. He wanted to be free to range, to be a rake, and if scruples bothered him, he stilled them by drinking. For nothing is clearer in the repeated episodes in which Boswell whores while drunk than that he let himself get drunk in order to have a defence for whoring.

Though in their physical basis his amours were even excessively healthy, there is something in his mental attitude towards them that strikes one as not quite right. He likes confessing too well, he derives pleasure from abjectness. The prostrations before Mrs. Dodds and the foot-kissings are an extreme example of attitudes that enter unpleasantly at times even into the *Life of Johnson*. Some part of this self-exposure is no doubt due to a habit of honesty, an ingrained repugnance to deceit, but much of it is inverted boasting and is to be identified as exhibitionism. And there is that other surprising strain in his journal and letters which one hesitates to define for fear that one may be imagining things: his actual enjoyment of venereal invalidism. Part of it boasting again (the wounds of the veteran who has fought *non sine gloria*), part perhaps the conscience-soothing acceptance of punishment?

The rising of the Session on 11 March spelled a separation: Boswell to go to Auchinleck with his father, Mrs. Dodds to return to Moffat. Boswell saw her almost every day after his disaster, oscillated between disapproval and delirium, parted with great fondness in hopes of meeting, and simultaneously prepared, with delicious agony of mind, to make the parting final. He took advice of everybody—John Johnston, Lady Betty Macfarlane, Andrew Erskine, Lord Monboddo, Lord Hailes, Dr. Blair, brother David—admitting his feverish infatuation but (as he thought) concealing the "paradisial completion" of the affair. All, as he hoped they would, urged him to break free. John Johnston told him he had no morals, Lord Monboddo quoted Horace on Ulysses and Circe, thus giving him a new name for poor Mrs. Dodds. On the morning of the departure for Auchinleck (19 March, Mrs. Dodds having left two days earlier) he believed himself close to distraction: "Waked in tender anguish. What, shall I give her up? Your melting moments rushed on your mind. Her generosity—ah! For some seconds a real fit of delirium, tossing in your distempered mind instant self-destruction. Bless me! Is this possible? It was literally true. Got up, roused, grew better." On the way down, at Sornbeg (the trip took three days because of heavy snow) he finished and sent off a huge involved epistle to Mrs. Dodds, laying down terms which he expected her to refuse indignantly. Two days later (a Sunday, at Auchinleck) he lay long abed and reflected comfortably on being free of Laïs. That evening he asked himself with astonishment whether the friend of Paoli had really spent an entire winter the slave of a woman without one elegant quality.

On another Sunday, just three weeks earlier, Miss Catherine Blair, heiress of Adamton, had sat in the Boswell family seat in the New Church in Edinburgh. On that occasion Boswell had merely remarked that she was a handsome stately woman with a good countenance—an odd description in view of the fact that she was only eighteen years old. A few days later—at the height of his frenzy for Mrs. Dodds—he noted that he liked Miss Blair "more and more without any fever." By the end of the month, having, as he supposed, broken the spell of Circe, he was thinking that he might possibly marry Miss Blair. She was an Ayrshire heiress, her estate (which was worth between two and three hundred a year) was near Auchinleck, she was his own fourth cousin, Lord Auchinleck had been her guardian, was fond of her, would approve highly of her as a daughter-in-law. "No bad scheme this," Boswell wrote to Temple. "I think a very good one. But I will not be in a hurry. There is plenty of time." And indeed, there will be time.

XIX

"I wished I could write now as when I wrote my *Account of Corsica*," lamented Boswell in December 1784, when he received almost simultaneously the news of Johnson's death and a request from his publisher that he have a biography of four hundred pages ready within six weeks. He might well have looked wistfully back to 1767 as the period when his vigour and confidence stood at their peak. On 23 March (the first weekday following his arrival at Auchinleck), sitting in the grand new library, his body not unpleasantly indisposed and his mind sound after the fever of love, he began where most authors end, and wrote the Introduction to his *Account of Corsica*. It was his intention to write steadily on day by day and every day except Sunday, and to complete the *Account* by the time the Session sat down again on 12 June. He not only succeeded, but also managed to carry through the entire task with zest and high spirits. His manuscript turned out to be copy for about 260 octavo pages.

In fact, he finished most of the writing during the month of April, and even in those four weeks there were many interruptions. His clerk Brown arrived, and he dictated law papers. Clients called, and he gave them his time. He read the memorials in the Douglas Cause, which his father had brought down to study, and conceived a brilliantly impudent scheme for indulging his gaiety of fancy and striking a blow for Douglas at the same time. Any published *ex parte* handling of the cause before the judges had rendered their decision would have been punishable as contempt of court, but how about allegorizing an *ex parte* statement and daring the Court to prove it more than a fiction? *Dorando,* a pamphlet of fifty pages in rather large print, was dictated to Brown, largely if not entirely on two days. It is a popular and shamelessly partial narrative of the Douglas Cause, presented under the transparent disguise of a Spanish tale. (The prime suggestion, no doubt, came from Walpole's *Castle of Otranto, a Story,* which had appeared a little over two years before. Spanish colouring was adopted because Boswell had been thinking about Lord Marischal.) The dim-witted and homicidal old Duke of Douglas becomes Don Carlos of Dorando, a melancholy but amiable recluse; his redoubtable Duchess is transformed into the tender Donna Eleanora. Lady Jane is Lady Maria, the princely name of Hamilton is degraded to Arvidoso, a blend presumably intended to convey notions of extensive acres and greed for more. The story is not unskilfully adapted to the capacities of the vulgar. The shabby-genteel narrative of the wanderings of Lady Jane and her old-soldier husband is embellished with the colours of a sentimental novel, the characters are operaticized, and we are given much pathetic conversation and resounding oratory. The story sweeps on beyond the actual events to a triumph for young Dorando. The President of the Senate of Seville [Robert Dundas, Lord President of the Court of Session] proclaims his firm conviction of the justice of Dorando's cause, and the Senate finds for him without one dissenting vote. "The Arvidoso train gnashed their teeth in rage and despair," and appealed to the Grandees of Madrid [the House of Lords]. There, "the greatest minister that Spain ever saw" [Pitt, now Earl of Chatham] subjected them to menacing rebuke:

What have we before us? A daring attempt to render our children uncertain. If adulterers have been thought worthy of death, what punishment do those deserve who would introduce what is still more dangerous to society? A few wives may be unfaithful, but every wife may be attacked like the Princess of Dorando. . . . I tremble, I shudder at the consequences. . . . No, signors! While my blood is warm, I hope Spain shall never adopt such unjustifiable measures. . . . I think we should award the defendant very large costs of suit.

Boswell was not content to let the story end there. In a boar-hunt, Dorando saves the life of young Arvidoso, Arvidoso generously admits that he always thought the cause injurious, and through his lips Boswell wings his final dart at the beautiful Gunning: "I have only to ask one favour of you, my dear prince, which is that you may not give my mother as much trouble as our family has given yours."

Boswell felt himself in great vigour of genius while he dictated this extravaganza; Brown was so overcome with admiration as frequently to break out into plaudits: "That's grand!"

Next day, at Cumnock, Boswell further reinforced the sense of his own importance by becoming a laird in his own right. The large muirland farm of Dalblair, bordering on the Auchinleck estate, was up at auction, and he resolved, with Lord Auchinleck's backing, to bid for it. The property fell to him for £2410, plus an annuity which he thought he could compound for £80. Lord Auchinleck took him by the hand as Dalblair and next morning provided a special dainty for his breakfast as a parish laird. On the morning before the sale, writing to Sir Alexander Dick, he indulged in the kind of classical pun they both delighted in. He needed, he said, a sinking-fund for the guineas he was earning by the law; now Dalblair was certainly a *fundus* (Latin, "farm"), and a *fundus* was certainly a fund. And as a great part of Dalblair consisted of peatbog and standing water, it might very properly be called a *sinking* fund. To Lord President Dundas (who had recently sent a complaisant reply to a letter in which he had confessed his illness) he was even more jubilant: "I have just now bought a little estate of about £100 a year, to be a sinking-fund for my consultation-guineas. What shall we say of this world when an idle, dissipated, runaway fellow whom your Lordship knows will appear in the charter chest of his family to have been a sedate, diligent young man buying land before he had been a year an advocate?" How much this impressed the Lord President is not recorded, but it would impress us more if we did not know that Boswell had actually sunk his fees of the last Session in house-rent for Mrs. Dodds, and was planning to borrow the entire purchase price of Dalblair. And the prim respectful letter to the Lord President, written on the very day that *Dorando* went off to the printer, provides especially stark illustration of the double standard that Boswell allowed his liveliness of fancy to justify.

On 27 April, *Corsica* going on pleasantly, he received after dinner a reply from Mrs. Dodds to the hedging labyrinthine dismission he had sent her from Sornbeg more than five weeks earlier. Her silence in the mean time had probably indicated grieved or indignant acquiescence, but an unexpected development has forced her to decline her *congé*: she is with child. Boswell is delighted; it appears that not only had neither of them taken any precautions against pregnancy, but that he *wanted* a child and had been unhappy when none had put in an appearance. The irony of circumstance had arranged that their parting embrace should be fertile.

Boswell resolved to behave with honour and generosity and pleased his fancy with a thousand airy plans. "I also got a proof of *Dorando*. What a variety of *productions!*" Both he and Mrs. Dodds being very dark in complexion, he began referring to his expected child as "the black boy" or "Edward the Black Prince."

May passed in a whirl of visiting and being visited, and in the mingled round of social gaiety and professional keenness occasioned by circuit courts at Dumfries and Ayr. Lord Auchinleck presided. Boswell approached Dumfries with misgivings presumably caused by the fact that he and Jean Heron had held some of their dangerous trysts there, and that he would have to meet her and perhaps be reproached for his infidelity. He mentions breakfasting at her mother-in-law's, but names neither her nor her husband, though cryptic references to his own firmness and the phrase "Saturday's our day" may adumbrate the confrontation he dreaded.

As he rode from Auchinleck to the court at Ayr he made another song:

The Douglas Cause

We grant you, gentlemen, your suit
    Must be pronounc'd the Cause of Causes;
We've studied with sufficient care
    Your Parts, your Sections, and your Pauses.

We own your tale is finely told,
    We own your conduct has been glorious;
But you'll excuse us if we own
    We think you'll hardly be victorious.

No birth must henceforth be believ'd
    Unless proclaim'd by sound of trumpet,
And ev'ry dame of high degree
    Become as brazen as a strumpet. . . .

Who e'er denied that fifty is
    Less giv'n to sport than five-and-twenty?
And who could not from Paris bring
    Blank books and tavern-bills in plenty?

We've read how children have been own'd
    By rings, by bracelets, and by lockets;

> But now to dispossess an heir
>   Proofs may be found in Falstaff's pockets. . . .[1]

"The Hamilton Cause" had appeared in *The Scots Magazine* for March; "The Douglas Cause" he circulated as a broadside. A better song than either, enclosed in a letter to John Johnston on 28 May, seems not to have reached print till our own time:

> Gif ye a dainty mailing want
> And idleseat prefer to working,
> Ablins ye'll get it by a plea
> That far aff owr the seas is lurking.
>
> Gang ye your ways to Paris town,
> Blow in the lug o' lown and sorner,
> And Ise be caition yese bring hame
> An *enlèvement* frae ilka corner.
>
> French proofs! Howt, man, gae haud your tongue!
> For to sic proofs nae judge e'er lippens;
> Gowpins o' gowd your cause has cost,
> And after aw it's no worth tippence.
>
> Tho' your Memorial's braw and lang,
> And tho' your Sequel, like a curple,
> Would keep it sicker steeve and tight,
> 'Twill faw before the men in purple.
>
> Your *procureurs* may by their art
> Cast glamour in the een o' dunces,
> But conscience, callants! The Fifteen
> Are owr auld-farrand for the munsies.
>
> Since ye a worthy lady's name
> Wi' muckle foul abuse hae pelted,

---

[1] By an entry of charges for food and wine from the register of a hotel in Paris where Lady Jane and her husband admitted staying before moving to Mme. La Brune's, the Hamilton party were trying to prove that the Steuarts had in fact been there on the day on which the birth was alleged to have taken place. Boswell confronted this entry with the reckoning for capon and sack which Prince Hal abstracted from Falstaff's pocket (*1 Henry IV*, II.iv, end).

By jinks! I'd turn up aw your tails
And hae you aw fu' soundly belted.[1]

It may be, as Virginia Woolf was disposed to conclude, that the charm
conferred by Scots is often no more than adventitious, but surely for Boswell's verse Scots makes a substantial difference. His other Douglas-Cause
ballads are clever, but do not attain to anything like such vigour and wit
as this. Working, lurking; sorner, corner; lippens, tippence; curple,
purple: Byron would have admired these rhymes, and Burns would not
have disdained a line like "Blow in the lug o' lown and sorner." It is a
pity that Boswell did not affect Scots more. He would never have been a
Fergusson or a Burns, but if he had written his verses in Scots, they would
at least always have been continuously entertaining.

At Ayr, by defending two groups of "meal rioters," he got an initiation
into the human problems attendant on what we now call the Industrial
Revolution. The government policy of price supports made it more profitable to export oat and barley flour than to sell it locally. The "rioters,"
members of the working class in towns, when nobody would sell them the
flour that was the staple of their existence, formed organized mobs to
appropriate and sell stocks that were being collected to send out of the
country. He won six acquittals. To this unhappy business an opportunity
to conduct the appeal of the "Kilmarnock necromancing Irishwoman"
no doubt furnished some relief. Nelly Barcly *alias* Buchanan *alias* Taylor,
with her family, had been ordered to leave Kilmarnock on pain of being
put in the pillory and drummed out of town as often as she reappeared,
because she took money for revealing secrets and telling people where lost
or stolen articles could be found. Boswell won her a new trial. His

[1] If you want a nice farm and prefer idleness to working, perhaps you'll get it by a
law-suit that is lurking far off over the seas.

Go your way to Paris town, whisper in the ear of ragamuffin and sponger, and
I'll guarantee that you'll prove an abduction from every corner.

French proofs! Hush, man, go hold your tongue, for no judge ever trusts such
proofs! Your cause has cost handfuls of gold and after all it's not worth tuppence.

Though your Memorial's fine and long, and though your Sequel, like a crupper,
would hold it sure, firm, and tight, 'twill fall before the Lords of Session [who wear
purple gowns with cape and facings of crimson].

Your French lawyers by their art may cast a spell in the eyes of dunces, but faith,
lads, the Fifteen are too sagacious for the monsieurs.

Since you have pelted a worthy lady's name with a great deal of foul abuse, by
jinks! I'd turn up all your tails and have you all most soundly belted.

activities in behalf of two other prisoners, Hay and McClure, procured from the Lord Advocate letters of liberation for them and a lecture
for himself. After more than hinting that Boswell was privy to the spiriting
away of a material witness, Montgomery goes on: "It is your duty to
defend your clients, and I observe your zeal in doing so upon every occasion with great pleasure and satisfaction, but it is both your duty and
mine to wish a detection of the persons guilty of so foul a crime." Hay had
been identified by William Harris, merchant in Ayr, as one of the four
men who (he said) had ambushed him and two companions—Alexander
Gordon, Surveyor of the Customs at Ayr, and John McMurtrie, extraordinary tide-waiter there—on the evening of 6 March opposite Fullarton House, had fired several shots at them, killing Harris's mare, and when
his companions rode off to save themselves, had threatened his life, believing him to be Gordon. It was McMurtrie the tide-waiter who had been
"spirited away," and Montgomery apparently thought the evidence
inadequate for a conviction without McMurtrie's testimony. He however
reaffirmed his intention to bring Hay and McClure to trial if he obtained
fresh evidence, but he appears not to have got it, for though Boswell
noted a further Justiciary Court consultation in the following July, the
record of the Court lists no prosecution. His combined fees on the two
occasions totalled four guineas. The extraordinary feature of this allegedly
fortuitous collision of Hay and Harris so far as we are concerned is that
Boswell ultimately served as counsel for both men and that both were
hanged: Harris in 1770 for extensive counterfeiting of bank-notes, and
Hay in 1780 for poisoning an entire family with arsenic.

Early in the week of 7 June, Boswell and his father returned to Edinburgh for the Summer Session. While he was attending the court at Ayr,
he had ridden out to Adamton and surveyed the estate (Miss Blair not
being at home), and a week later he and Claud Boswell had gone back and
fetched Miss Blair and her mother for a four-days' visit at Auchinleck. On
the day the Session sat down, having just received a letter from Temple
announcing that he was in Berwick and proposed to pay him a visit, Boswell in an ecstasy of delight summed up all the matters on which he needed
his friend's advice:

The lady in my neighbourhood is the finest woman I have ever
seen. . . . In our romantic groves I adored her like a divinity. . . . My father
is very desirous I should marry her. All my relations, all my neighbours
approve of it. She looked quite at home in the house of Auchinleck. Her

picture would be an ornament to the gallery. Her children would be all Boswells and Temples, and as fine women as these are excellent men. And now, my friend, my best adviser comes to hear me talk of her and to fix my wavering mind. I must tell you my Italian angel is constant. I had a letter from her but a few days ago which made my cry. . . . My late Circe, Mrs. _____, is with child. What a fellow am I!

It was arranged that Temple should come on 29 June, a week in which Boswell would be relatively clear of business. It was an unusually crowded time, with Lord Auchinleck scheduled to sit in the Outer House as Lord Ordinary. ("You must know that the absurdity of mankind makes nineteen out of twenty employ the son of the judge before whom their cause is heard.") The Douglas Cause was approaching a decision, and Boswell, besides attending the hearings, was stepping up his volunteer activities. *Dorando* was published on 15 June and within two weeks reached a third edition. It was probably at this time that "The Douglas Cause" was put in circulation as a broadside. And the newspapers were being supplied with an exuberant series of Douglas-Cause inventions. On 19 May *The London Chronicle* had informed the public that the judges would sit in one of the large rooms of the Palace of Holyroodhouse for the determination of the Cause; scaffoldings would be erected to accommodate the public, and an admission fee of half a guinea would be charged, the money to go to the Royal Infirmary. This piece of misinformation, which has duly found its way into most of the serious studies of the Cause, was probably intended to tease the Hamilton party, the Duke of Hamilton being Hereditary Keeper of the Palace. Another invention in the same issue of the *Chronicle* may have been designed to tease the Lord President, but probably originated in sheer impishness. It announced that five eminent shorthand writers were about to set out from London for Edinburgh to make a report of the speeches of the Lords of Session in the Douglas Cause. (Such reports were illegal.) On 16 June *The Edinburgh Advertiser* took over with interesting further notice of these shorthand men, sent in by an obliging correspondent in Berwick who had seen and talked with them. Their names, it appeared, were Cust, Garnet, Tracy, Selwyn, and Burridge. The *Advertiser* for the 19th gave extended descriptions. Mr. Noel Burridge may serve as a specimen:

Mr. Burridge . . . wears a brown coat and a cut wig, and looks as grave as a parish clerk, yet over his bottle he has the most droll and ludicrous sallies, and when he turns that cut wig of his, you would laugh for a whole evening. His life has been one continued scene of strange adventures. He is a Cornishman by birth, and lived a good while among the miners. He has been a proselyte to all sects of religion. He was long an attendant at the Popish chapels in London. He next went over to Pennsylvania and joined the Quakers, and on his return to England he commenced Methodist. . . . In the year 1745 he was employed as a spy by the Government, and by letting himself down a chimney at Derby and keeping himself concealed, he with the help of a dark lanthorn wrote down many secrets of the rebel chiefs. In one place where none but ladies were admitted, he went in properly dressed, and with a fountain-pen in shape of a fan he took down with white ink on the bottom of a French song the whole conversation without so much as being perceived by those about him.

Readers of the *Advertiser* were assured that it would be impossible to detect the shorthand men and exclude them from the Court. They would appear as men of the highest quality; they might even all disguise themselves as women. A stop-press postscript, ostensibly added by the editor, reports their actual arrival in the Canongate. On 23 June the Lords examined Isabel Walker, one of Lady Jane's maids, the only person still living who was accused of having been party to the alleged crime of *partus suppositio*. "Her examination," wrote Boswell to Temple, "will be solemn and important." Three days later the *Advertiser* printed a letter from Noel Burridge himself, communicated by the obliging correspondent in Berwick. He and his companions, he said, had been in the Court, "but instead of the Cause, we had only the examination of a witness, at whom they were going to ask a parcel of French and Dutch questions in cookery, which would have played the devil with us." The determination was postponed, and he and his friends proposed to set out ("disguised like English riders"[1]) on a jaunt to the Highlands. Then, on 7 July (the day on which the judges began delivering their opinions) a letter from Inveraray written by Algernon Cust ("poor Burridge has sprained his thumb") told how they had met one Donald Macquire who had the second-sight. At that point the series stopped, for the Lord President had cited all the publishers of newspapers in the City of Edinburgh for contempt of court. Their offences included not only the printing of the paragraphs on the shorthand men but also their comments on *Dorando*.

Boswell had by no means trusted to chance and its own merits to bring

[1] Commercial travellers.

that masterpiece to the attention of the public, but had contributed to the newspapers, day by day, a series of anonymous puffs, in the guise of reviews, containing extensive extracts from the work itself. Readers were told that the story could not but greatly interest every feeling heart, that it contained many interesting and beautiful passages, that it left the mind to overflow with benevolent sentiments, that its reception did honour to the country. The best puff of all, though not relevant to the issue of contempt of court, appeared in *The London Chronicle*. The anonymous reviewer (Boswell himself) "cannot help observing that if the hand of M. Rousseau, guided by my Lord Marischal of Scotland, is not here, *Dorando* is at least the production of no ordinary genius."

The Lord President appears to have made no attempt to suppress the book itself, probably because of the notorious difficulty of proving allegory in any narrative that is intelligible by itself and contains nothing that makes sense only in terms of a second meaning. The newspapers, in comments practically all written by Boswell, had however explicitly treated *Dorando* as an allegory of the Douglas Cause. Dundas accordingly passed over Drummond, the Edinburgh bookseller who had exposed all three editions of *Dorando* for sale and had put his name to the third as publisher, and haled into court the publishers of all four Edinburgh newspapers. Practically every word of every article that Dundas objected to had flowed from the pen of James Boswell, Esq. Dundas was probably ill advised in his action, but contemporary articles *not* written by Boswell show that thoughtful members of the public considered *Dorando* a dangerous book. "I see," says "A" in *The Scots Magazine,* "that some of the reviewers have represented *Dorando* as a *contemptible* performance. I cannot help differing from them. I think it artfully wrote and very eloquent, for as the end of eloquence is to persuade, it does not consist in any one particular manner of speaking or writing, but in adapting the manner to the taste and capacity of those for whom it is intended. . . . And it is amazing how great an effect this pamphlet, and other such arts used by the favourers of the defendant, have had. . . . The writing and publishing that pamphlet was a manifest attempt to bias the judges by the hopes of great popularity in case of their giving their decree for the defendant, and the fears of a general odium in case of their deciding for the plaintiffs." The temper of the mob had grown ugly. Threatening letters had been sent, windows had been broken, and walls daubed with intimidating libels.

On 7 July, with public interest at a climax, the judges of the Court of Session began delivering their opinions. The Lord Justice-Clerk and Lord Hailes had been counsel for the Hamilton party (the pursuers) before their elevation to the bench, and Lords Gardenstone and Monboddo had been counsel for Douglas (the defender). No one of the four disqualified himself, and all four found for the party from which they had earlier accepted fees. The balance of opinion see-sawed back and forth through the following week: the Lord President for the pursuers; Lords Strichen, Kames, Auchinleck, and Coalston for the defender; Lords Barjarg, Alemoor, Eliock, and Stonefield for the pursuers; Lords Pitfour and Gardenstone for the defender; Lords Kennet, Hailes, and the Lord Justice-Clerk for the pursuers; Lord Monboddo for the defender. On 14 July the Lord President (who voted only in case of a tie) called for the votes: seven for the pursuers, seven for the defender. He then gave his casting-vote for the pursuers. Archibald Douglas had lost his case in the Court of Session. There was intense popular indignation, the Lord President receiving letters threatening his life. The Dorando train gnashed their teeth and appealed to the House of Lords.

The publishers of the four Edinburgh newspapers being then summoned to answer to the charge of contempt of court, James Boswell performed the most impudent act of a life not unremarkable for impudent actions. As counsel for *The Edinburgh Advertiser,* he handed in a printed memorial excusing the *Advertiser* for having published the letters relating to the shorthand men. The Court, which can hardly have been in doubt as to the identity of the real culprit, had to submit to further genteel ribbing:

As to the extract of a letter from Berwick, the matter stands thus. It was a thing commonly reported in town that a set of shorthand writers were come from London in order to take notes in the Douglas Cause. An article of intelligence of that kind had some time before appeared in *The London Chronicle,* and in former papers published in this place their arrival had been mentioned and an humorous description of their genealogy and characters had been given. The memorialist will indeed acknowledge that he never did inquire into the truth of this report. He considered it as a harmless piece of intelligence very proper for a newspaper; and as the description of these stenographers seemed to have pleased many of his readers, he did not imagine that his inserting the letter . . . could have given the smallest offence. . . . He is now indeed sorry to find, upon looking it over with more attention, . . . that something appears to have been said in it relative to the examination of a witness with a degree of levity that is not suitable to the dignity and solemnity observed in courts of justice.

The publishers were dismissed with a rebuke, and Boswell, in a tone of demure sarcasm, reported the proceedings in the *Advertiser.* But he was not yet through. A month later, in an article signed "Tribunus" covering the whole front page of *The London Chronicle,* he begged some learned judicious correspondent to tell him whether the Lord President had not exceeded his powers. The article makes use of the tactics he would have adopted if any attempt had been made to prosecute the publisher of *Dorando.* How, he asks, could it be proved that *Dorando* was the Douglas Cause? The Lord President had said that the speech of the Chief Justice of the Court of Seville was a speech put into his own mouth. Now, as it happened, *Dorando* from beginning to end was a most mild and genteel performance, and the speeches in it were such as no man need be ashamed of. But suppose the author of *Dorando* had made the Chief Justice a blockhead and had made him speak arrant nonsense. Suppose he had called him a rogue and a rascal. Could this have been punished as an offence against the Court of Session? "I believe not. For by the same rule, every author of a tale or allegory into which fools and rogues are intro- duced might be liable to punishment, provided any man in power should cry, '*That was levelled at me.*' "[1] And when no answer was forthcoming, Boswell wrote one himself over the signature "Jacob Giles," a supposed English barrister, equally full of malicious pleasantries.

I have again misrepresented the swirling, incongruous, existential variety of Boswell's consciousness by isolating one narrative pattern and carrying it forward without reference to other events with which it was in fact entangled. "Jacob Giles's" letter appeared on 15 October 1767, and we have now to turn back again to the end of June, the Douglas Cause

---

[1]   When you censure the age,
             Be cautious and sage,
        Lest the courtiers offended should be;

         If you mention vice or bribe,
            'Tis so pat to all the tribe,
        Each cries, "That was levell'd at me!"
             (*The Beggar's Opera,* Air 30)

undecided and Boswell bubbling over with joy ("Well, I never was happier") at the prospect of Temple's visit. He got off three letters in two weeks to his friend, now only one post day off, the last reaching him on the eve of his departure.

I would not cloud the present frame of my mind with any gloomy reflection that concerns either you or myself. It is better to communicate them when we meet, when our mutual sympathy and friendly warmth may temper and relieve them. In the mean time I must tell you that on Tuesday last [23 June], drinking Miss Blair's health (for that is the name of my angelic princess), I got myself quite intoxicated, went to a bawdy-house, and passed a whole night in the arms of a whore. She indeed was a fine, strong, spirited girl, a whore worthy of Boswell if Boswell must have a whore, and I apprehend no bad consequences. But I am abashed and determined to keep the strictest watch over my passions.

Of Temple's week in Edinburgh we have no record whatever, but we have a pretty good notion of the way he spent the week following, while the Lords of Session were delivering their opinions in the Douglas Cause. Boswell had insisted that he *must* see Miss Blair, and since she was at Adamton and Boswell could not leave Edinburgh, that meant that Temple must go down to Ayrshire ("You are a stranger, and may do a romantic thing") like a royal envoy, with a sheet of instructions in his pocket:

WEDNESDAY. [*Temple at Auchinleck.*] Breakfast at eight; set out at nine. Thomas will bring you to Adamton a little after eleven. Send up your name; if possible, put up your horses there (they can have cut grass); if not, Thomas will take them to Mountain, a place a mile off, and come back and wait at dinner. Give Miss Blair my letter. Salute her and her mother; ask to walk. See the Place fully; think what improvements should be made. Talk of my mare, the purse, the chocolate.[1] Tell you are my very old and intimate friend. Praise me for my good qualities (you know them), but talk also how odd, how inconstant, how impetuous, how much accustomed to women of intrigue. Ask gravely, "Pray, don't you imagine there is something of madness in that family?" Talk of my various travels —German princes—Voltaire and Rousseau. Talk of my father, my strong desire to have my own house. Observe her well. See how amiable. Judge if

[1] Miss Blair had given Boswell some chocolate (To Sir Alexander Dick, 21 Aug. 1767), but the mare and the purse are unexplained. Perhaps she had netted him a purse and he had given or lent her a mare.

she would be happy with your friend. Think of me as the great man at Adamton—quite classical, too! Study the mother. Remember well what passes. Stay tea. At six, order horses and go to Newmilns, two miles from Loudoun, but if they press you to stay all night, do it. Be a man of as much ease as possible. Consider what a romantic expedition you are on. Take notes. Perhaps you now fix me for life.

Mrs. Dodds arrived in town about the same time as Temple—to occupy, let us hope, that house that Boswell had rented—and Boswell, though he had so recently referred to her as "my late Circe," promptly returned to her arms. He had assumed too soon that his escapade of 23 June was to have no bad consequences. On 29 July he reported to Temple that he was an unhappy man.

I have got a disease from which I suffer severely. It has been long of appearing and is a heavy one. I shall stay a month here after the Session rises, and be cured. I am patient under it, as a just retribution for my licentiousness. But I greatly fear that Mrs. _____ is infected, for I have been with her several times since my debauch, and once within less than a week of the full appearance of mischief. In her present situation the consequences will be dreadful, for besides the pain that she must endure, an innocent being cannot fail to be injured. Will you forgive me, Temple, for exclaiming that all this evil is too much for the offence of my getting drunk because I would drink Miss Blair's health every round in a large bumper? But general laws often seem hard in particular cases. I am not, however, certain that Mrs. _____ will be ill. I would fain hope that she may have escaped. I have told her the risk she runs. Her good temper is astonishing. She does not upbraid me in the least degree.

Mrs. Dodds, after being thought out of danger ("O Temple, what an escape!") did share his misfortune, but it is not upon record that she upbraided him. Poor Circe has been tamed by gravidity; she romps no more. She comes cheerfully and drinks tea with him once or twice a week in his confinement (in Lord Auchinleck's house, apparently, but Lord Auchinleck had by that time gone to Ayrshire), and the connexion keeps him reasonable in his attachment to the Princess. That phrase (Boswell's own) indicates nicely the degree and quality of his commitment. He was thinking more seriously of marriage than he had ever done before, and he was rationally convinced that Miss Blair was a more generally appropriate match than Euphemia Bruce, or Belle de Zuylen, or even Elizabeth Diana

Bosville: "Here *ev'ry* flow'r is united."[1] But he was certainly not deeply in love and he was no more than "entertained" by Temple's report that a "formal Nabob" (William Fullarton of Rosemount, an Ayrshire surgeon who had returned from India with a competence) was hovering about Adamton. In short, he wrote flighty, ambiguous letters which he relayed to Temple, and played hard to get. And as might have been expected, having proclaimed his choice fixed on the Princess, he took steps to remove that coolness between himself and Belle de Zuylen which he had not long since declared to be so much to his satisfaction. Robert Brown came over for a brief visit to his native land, and when he went back to Utrecht, Boswell gave him a letter for Belle soliciting a renewal of correspondence. I do not know how he justified or explained his two-years' silence, but her response shows that he must have been reasonably complaisant. He may have told her, as he certainly told Brown, that he had thoughts of revisiting Utrecht in the following summer.

His stay in town lengthened. A cold combined with his distemper to bring on a fever, he spent several days in bed in a really alarming state, and when the fever abated, the distemper continued obstinate. He did not get away from Edinburgh till 13 October—two whole months of involuntary tarrying in a house from which his father and most of the servants had departed.

He had plenty of interesting work to keep him entertained, for the *Account of Corsica* was in the press, and he was compiling for the printer the *Journal of a Tour to Corsica* which was to accompany it. Early in August, the firm of Edward and Charles Dilly in London had purchased the copyright of the book for one hundred guineas, with an agreement that the first edition should be printed in Scotland under Boswell's supervision. How the association came about is not known. The Dillys were not the publishers one would have predicted for Boswell: they were Whigs and Dissenters, sold a good many books in America, and had no great reputation in the field of literature. Probably their Whig sympathies and con-

[1] My heart was so free,
   It rov'd like the bee
      Till Polly my passion requited;
   I sipp'd each flow'r,
   I chang'd ev'ry hour,
      But here ev'ry flow'r is united.
      (Macheath's song, *The Beggar's Opera*, Air 15)

nexions attracted them to a book which, first and last, had a great deal—
Johnson thought too much—to say about liberty. But however the associa-
tion came about, it proved profitable and most agreeable on both sides.
Edward Dilly, a cordial and loquacious but extremely shrewd man of
business, found in Boswell an author after his own heart. On 15 August
1767, just after he and Boswell had concluded their contract, *The London
Chronicle* printed Boswell's signed letter concerning the translations of
Seneca's epigrams on Corsica which he wanted for his forthcoming book.[1]
Two weeks later the *Chronicle* gave space to an importunate letter signed
"B. M.," purporting to come from Oxford:

Of all history, that of nations struggling in trying and difficult times
in the great cause of freedom is surely the most interesting; and therefore
I confess I am very impatient for the publication of *An Account of Corsica*
by Mr. Boswell. It is now a year and a half since all the gazettes in Europe
announced the tour made by that gentleman to Corsica and his interviews
with the illustrious General Paoli, and it is some time since your paper has
told us that a book was preparing for the press in which we might expect
to see a full and authentic relation of the affairs of the brave islanders. If
it is not improper, I would beg, Sir, that you may insert this, as it may
perhaps furnish an additional motive to hasten the publication.

Dilly correctly identified the source of this communication, and wrote
to applaud:

I saw a letter in *The London Chronicle* of last Thursday relative to
the publication: it is dated from Oxford and signed "B. M." . . . From
what I can judge of the letter, I apprehend that this Oxonian is now upon
a visit at Edinburgh and lodges in or near the Parliament Close. Possibly
Mr. Boswell may know him; and if he should be happy in his acquaintance, please to inform him that I am well pleased with the letter, and shall
esteem it as a favour if he will now and then send a letter to the printer of
the different London papers, and likewise of the Scots papers, upon the
same subject.

Robert and Andrew Foulis of Glasgow, who had printed the first and
second editions of *Dorando,* were selected also to print the *Account* and
acknowledged receipt of a good part of the copy on 21 August. Proofs
were arriving by 2 September. By that time the *Journal of a Tour to*

[1] See above, p. 308.

Corsica was probably completely written out and in the hands of various advisers. Lord Hailes read the whole book and made suggestions for revision, and Boswell also had the advice of Lord Monboddo, of Sir Alexander Dick, and of Temple. A clerical friend of Temple's, Christopher Wyvill, who later acquired some fame as a reforming politician, was persuaded to read the *Journal* and comment through the post. The Dedication of the book is dated from Auchinleck on Boswell's twenty-seventh birthday (29 October 1767), but it is clear that Foulis did not get all the copy until well into November, and did not complete the printing before the end of December.

Meanwhile, in the interstices of proofs and voluminous correspondence concerning the volume, Boswell had compiled and published two more small books on the Douglas Cause.

Douglas's counsel had from the first realized that their best witness was Lady Jane herself. Her sufferings elicited sympathy, time had sorted out the evidence and preserved little that did not show her as admirable and appealing, and she could not be cross-examined. The most moving portion of the Douglas Proof was a series of letters which she had written to her husband during the time that his poverty kept him confined within the rules of King's Bench. The Hamilton counsel never questioned their genuineness, and the casual way in which they were recovered after her death—in an old cloak-bag which Colonel Steuart had left in pawn with a landlord—seemed to preclude the possibility of their having been written for effect. Why, asked the defence, if Lady Jane and her husband were confederates in a desperate crime, did they drop no hint of it in these utterly private letters? Intrepidity and a certain kind of hard magnanimity might consort with such guilt, but would domestic tenderness and simple unaffected piety? Lady Jane sends Sir John her last half-crown to buy him "a little rappee"; she consoles him with the news that "the little men are, I bless God, very happy"; she counsels him to put his trust in Heaven, "for God never disappoints those that entirely depend on him." Thomas Carlyle, coming on these letters in 1860, said that the reports of the speeches of the Lords of Session left him quite in doubt as to the right and wrong of the case, but Lady Jane's letters "nearly altogether convinced" him "that *spuriousness* was inconceivable on the part of two such persons, especially on her part." So enormously effective in lay judgement is the right kind of character testimony ("Does he *look* as though he did it?"), but as buried in the Douglas Proof the letters were inaccessible to the general public. To Boswell it was obvious that they ought to be reprinted separately and cheaply.

He had started advance publicity for such a volume in *The London Chronicle* some two weeks before the decision of the Court of Session (the decision was sure to be appealed, whichever side won), and appears to have had the copy well in hand by the end of August. *Letters of the Right Honourable Lady Jane Douglas,* an octavo of 160 pages with a very crowded title page, appeared at the end of November. The letters were skilfully and not very scrupulously abridged to heighten the pathos of Lady Jane's story, "dying declarations" of Lady Jane, Sir John, and Helen Hewit were appended, and the whole concluded with "A Cool and Candid Inquiry how far such Declarations should weigh with the Rational Part of Mankind." Readers who knew the facts would—depending on their allegiance—have been either affronted or amused by title-page mottoes taken from the speeches of Lord Alemoor and Lord Hailes, and by an Introductory Preface "partly taken from a case drawn up by Alexander Lockhart, Esq., Dean of the Faculty of Advocates." Alemoor and Hailes had been among the eight judges who had voted *against* Douglas, and Lockhart was chief of counsel for the Duke of Hamilton.

Another book—by Boswell's estimation his *magnum opus* in the Douglas Cause, the only one he claimed publicly though he published it anonymously—appeared a few days before the *Letters of Lady Jane Douglas.* "With a labour of which few are capable," he afterwards wrote, "he compressed the substance of the immense volumes of proofs and arguments into an [80-page] octavo pamphlet, which he published with the title of *The Essence of the Douglas Cause;* and as it was thus made intelligible without a tedious study, we may ascribe to this pamphlet a great share of the popularity on Mr. Douglas's side, which was of infinite consequence when a division of the House of Lords upon an appeal was apprehended; not to mention that its effect was said to be considerable in a certain important quarter." I assume that by the "certain important quarter" Lord Mansfield was meant, but the reader is free to make his own identification. *The Essence of the Douglas Cause,* a calm, dignified, systematic, and lucid presentation of the case for Archibald Douglas, follows in the main the lines of Lord Auchinleck's opinion in the Court of Session. In the more than thirteen months which elapsed before the House of Lords decided the appeal, Boswell made some further scattering efforts in the newspapers to touch the heart and rouse the parental and sympathetic feelings, but in the main his campaign for Douglas ended with the *Essence* and the *Letters*.

On 13 October, after being kept two entire months in Edinburgh by his course of medicines, Boswell was declared perfectly recovered and set off with his brother David for a shortened holiday at Auchinleck. Their way lay by Bothwell Castle, the principal Douglas residence. Boswell stipulated a warm, orthodox room, and the Duchess sent back word that the warmest bed in the house was her own, and that he would be welcomed there. David, aged nineteen, was getting his last view of Auchinleck for a long time. Having completed his apprenticeship with a banking-house in Edinburgh, he was on his way to Glasgow and London and thence to Spain, where he proposed to settle as a merchant. Boswell devised for his going forth a solemn ritual of investiture on the crumbling walls of the Old Castle. Having collected as chaplains Mr. Dun and Mr. Fergusson (the latter from a distance of sixty miles or more), and having secured the attendance as retainers of James Bruce and his four sons, their ages ranging from 15 to 6, he put David through a ritual in which David solemnly promised always to be faithful to the ancient Family of Auchinleck and was invested with a ring "according to the usage of the Family." The document, with its four witnessing signatures, signed by David and sealed with the seal of investiture, was of course both drafted and engrossed by "James Boswell, Esquire, my eldest brother and heir of the Family." David gave the perfect finishing touch thirteen years later when, on returning from Spain, he added a cautious ratification explaining that the usage of oath and ring was not of immemorial antiquity, but had begun with himself.

However embarrassed literal-minded David may have been by this ceremony, he was nevertheless constrained by Boswell's enthusiasm to play his role, and so were the no-longer-youthful ministers of Auchinleck and Tundergarth. But the Representative of the Family—the person to whom the oath was theoretically taken—was conspicuously absent and was probably not even advised of the occasion. One easily imagines the withering sarcasm with which Lord Auchinleck would in any case have met a proposal that he preside at such puerilities, but Boswell had special reason for thinking that his father would not be sympathetic. Lord Auchinleck was deeply dissatisfied with him. It is not surprising that two bouts of venereal infection within six months should have strained Lord Auchinleck's patience, but it is surprising that he should have exclaimed against Boswell's profligacy (as we know he did) to a woman, Mrs. Montgomerie-Cuninghame. She was his niece, to be sure, but he had not hitherto made her free of his intimate reasons for displeasure with his heir. His deep disquiet rose from a conviction that Boswell was publishing again. Even granting that he did not know or suspect the full extent of Boswell's dealings with the newspapers, he could not help seeing there things calculated to enrage him. There had been one particularly improper paragraph: Boswell, writing in *The London Chronicle* over his own name to report the siege of Capraia, had attributed his delay in bringing out his book on Corsica to "the unavoidable occupations of a laborious employment." For a young man less than nine months at the bar thus to announce himself burdened with business was vaunting and unprofessional. And one can imagine how galling Lord Auchinleck would have found the pleasantries of his brethren on the bench when they had before them Boswell's defence of *The Edinburgh Advertiser* in the matter of the shorthand men.

On such grounds Lord Auchinleck might have been offended and have had our sympathy, but unfortunately he seems to have been even more moved by the old unreasonable jealousy of his son's independence. He was infuriated when Boswell asserted his wish to be *primus Mantuae* (first, not in Rome, but in a lesser place), and confessed his inability to take the kind of interest in Auchinleck that Lord Auchinleck demanded so long as it remained another man's property. The comfortable rapport of the previous spring was breached, and would never again be restored.

CHAPTER

XX

It had been in the cards since August that so soon as Boswell was discharged by his surgeon, he should go to Adamton and throw himself at the Princess's feet. But, as we have seen, the infection proved stubborn, the date of his departure was repeatedly postponed, and he continued to conduct his suit by letters. To these fervent but elaborately non-committal missives he expected replies by return post, and when they were not forthcoming, he found the lady's conduct mysterious and her motives impenetrable. The lady condescended to excuse herself once, proving her silence a mere accident (his letter had lain eight days in the post-office); but after that she wrote no more. By the time Boswell got to Auchinleck she was three long letters in his debt. He assumed that she had accepted the Nabob, fretted for ten days, and then, not to seem sullen, wrote wishing her joy. She replied in the easiest fashion imaginable that he had no occasion. He then wrote "a strange, sultanic letter, very cool and very formal" and delayed for almost three weeks going to pay his respects; in fact, put off his visit to the latest possible date before returning to Edinburgh. The letters which he wrote to Temple during this year contain a series of dramatic sketches not inferior to the best in his journal. Here he is, writing from the bedroom at Adamton where Temple also had slept:

I have been here one night. She has insisted on my staying another. I am dressed in green and gold. I have my chaise in which I sit alone like Mr. Gray, and Thomas rides by me in a claret-coloured suit with a silver-laced hat. But the Princess and I have not yet made up our quarrel. She talks lightly of it. I am resolved to have a serious conversation with her tomorrow morning. If she can still remain indifferent as to what has given me much pain, she is not the woman I thought her, and from tomorrow morning shall I be severed from her as a lover.

343

Miss Blair, threatened with this deprivation, remained perfectly self-possessed and cool while Boswell stammered in unwonted confusion: "she did not appear in the least inclined to own herself in the wrong." Nor could she be brought to any sense of guilt by a strong letter sent back from Auchinleck. Let her go, wrote Boswell to Temple: "I from this moment resolve to think no more of her." But of course when he scratched one entry from his card, he had to review the other contenders: "Do you know, I had a letter from Zélide the other day, written in English, and showing that an old flame is easily rekindled. . . . Ah, my friend, shall I have Miss Bosville?"

The very next day, re-reading the Princess's letter on the road back to Edinburgh, he saw it in a quite different light. What she had written, he now thought, was right in every respect. She had not answered him because she had expected him to arrive in person on the heels of each successive letter, and had only shown proper spirit in refusing to own herself in the wrong when she was conscious of no fault. "I love her, Temple, with my whole heart. I am entirely in her power." And he passes to resolves which we could have predicted and to reflections that take us by surprise, though they ought not to:

Temple, I wish to be at last an uniform, pretty man. I am astonishingly so already; but I wish to be a man who deserves Miss B_____. . . . I am always for fixing some period for my perfection as far as possible. Let it be when my *Account of Corsica* is published. I shall then have a character which I must support. I will swear like an ancient disciple of Pythagoras to observe silence. I will be grave and reserved, though cheerful and communicative of what is *verum atque decens*.[1] One great fault of mine is talking at random. I will guard against it.

"I am astonishingly so already": it is a measure of the central difficulty of Boswellian biography that even those who are in possession of the evidence have to remind themselves that a statement like this is not preposterous. We realize, of course, that the perfection he desiderates is merely one of manners (Boswell's gentlemanly ideal always tolerated—indeed stipulated—a strong dash of rakishness), but putting moral issues to one side, the fact remains that we derive from his accounts of himself a prevailing impression of social eccentricity, not one of the general solidity and manliness ("an uniform, pretty man") which he is here claiming for himself.

[1] "Right and seemly" (Horace, *Epistles*, I.i.11).

Yet he was quite right and our impression is wrong. Everybody who knew him in 1767 thought him a socially clever young man of good parts and remarkably engaging manners, no wilder than many others in the professional group with which he associated, though certainly more given to talking about his wildness than others were. He was not deceived in thinking that he had gone far towards acquiring the bearing and mental frame of a shrewd and judicious counsellor-at-law, and he was perhaps not mistaken in thinking that he could make himself still more regular and prudent. That it seems otherwise to us is due to the literary shaping of his own autobiographical records. His journal preserves the moments of heightened emotional charge, not the routine; his letters to Temple formalize the welter of his life in recognized literary modes. In those letters his vision of Boswell vis-à-vis Catherine Blair was prevailingly comic. We are the gainers by some very lively writing, and shall do no essential harm to that episode if we leave it within the frame in which he set it, but we should show ourselves naïve if we took such a selective sketch as a total portrait.

Though we do not know just when Boswell became for the second time a father, it is clear that the Adamton visit fell in the concluding days of Mrs. Dodds's pregnancy. In the letter (8 November 1767) in which Boswell announced his emancipation from Miss Blair, he cited the gardener's daughter and "Mrs. D_____" as proofs that his heart would mend. "By the by," he continued, "the latter shared in my late misfortune, but she is quite well again, and in a fortnight hence I expect a young friend, who if a male is to be George Keith after my good Lord Marischal, who has accepted of being his name-father." One cannot help speculating whether Miss Blair's coolness may not have reflected more knowledge of Boswell's intimate concerns than she was supposed to have. I doubt if she knew anything about Mrs. Dodds, for Boswell had really been close-mouthed on that score, but he—and, for that matter, his father—had revealed the nature of his indisposition to so many people that it is not at all unlikely that Miss Blair had got word of it. Boswell never discussed what effect this might have on his chances. Either he assumed that information of that sort never reached maiden's ears, or, more probably, that any sensible girl would accept that kind of illness as a male commonplace.

He had an opportunity for reviving his jest about the variety of his *productions*. The theatre in Edinburgh, as we have seen, operated illegally

under the cover of various fictions. After a great deal of tumult and opposition, a royal patent for a theatre in Edinburgh had been obtained, and
a well-known Covent Garden actor, David Ross, had secured appointment
as patentee and manager. Though Ross was the son of a Writer to the
Signet and uncle to a laird, he was personally unknown in Edinburgh,
and a powerful group combined to oppose him. Boswell did not know him
personally, but took his side, and Ross, partly in gratitude, partly as a
compliment, asked him to write the prologue for the opening of the
theatre, now styled the Theatre Royal, on 9 December 1767. Boswell
consequently had the satisfaction of hearing the first legal dramatic performance in Scotland introduced with rhymes of his own. Lord Mansfield
later called his prologue "a very good copy of verses"; Johnson, I think,
might have said, "Sir, it was no doubt adequate to the occasion." Though
there are no lines in it that come anywhere near the best in its model,
Johnson's own "Prologue at the Opening of the Theatre in Drury Lane,
1747," it is all firm, clear, emphatic verse. One might paraphrase Johnson
on Mason and say that there are now and then in it some good imitations
of Johnson's stock manner:

> The Thistle springs promiscuous with the Rose . . .
> To play elusive with unlicens'd mask . . .

It duly appeared in most of the newspapers and magazines of the day, and
probably received wider circulation in Boswell's life-time than any other
of his efforts in verse.

Miss Blair sent a verbal message that she was still his friend, but
preserved epistolary silence for more than five weeks, while Boswell strove
to break his chain. When she came to Edinburgh (unfortunately not in
time to hear Ross recite the Prologue), she assured Boswell, as she had
before, that if there was any quarrel, it was all of his own making. He
accompanied her to *Othello,* sitting close behind her and pressing his hand
against her waist at the most affecting scenes; she wept for Desdemona,
but declined to melt for Boswell. A female cousin took it upon herself to
tell him that Miss Blair and her mother did not know what to make of
him: he seemed bent on gaining the lady's affections without a firm proposal of marriage. This was of course quite true; and if he had fixed Miss
Blair in a confession of love, he would probably have lectured her on her
short-comings as he had lectured Belle de Zuylen. Boswell's description of

what followed is his masterpiece in the Congrevian mode, and acquires even more of a Restoration flavour if one reads it equipped with two pieces of information which he chose to present as appendix: firstly, that he had been as wild as ever and had catched another memorandum of vice ("but a very slight one"), and secondly, that Mrs. Dodds had brought him—not George Keith, a future nabob, but—a fine, healthy little girl whom he had named Sally.

On Monday forenoon [21 December 1767] I waited on Miss B_____; I found her alone, and she did not seem distant. I told her that I was most sincerely in love with her, and that I only dreaded those faults which I had acknowledged to her. I asked her seriously if she now believed me in earnest. She said she did. I then asked her to be candid and fair, as I had been with her, and to tell me if she had any particular liking for me. What think you, Temple, was her answer? *No.* "I really," said she, "have no particular liking for you. I like many people as well as you." (Temple, you must have it in the genuine dialogue.) BOSWELL. "Do you indeed? Well, I cannot help it. I am obliged to you for telling me so in time. I am sorry for it." PRINCESS. "I like Jeanie Maxwell" (Duchess of Gordon) "better than you." BOSWELL. "Very well. But do you like no man better than me?" PRINCESS. "No." BOSWELL. "Is it possible that you may like me better than other men?" PRINCESS. "I don't know what is possible." (By this time I had risen and placed myself by her, and was in real agitation.) BOSWELL. "I'll tell you what, my dear Miss Blair. I love you so much that I am very unhappy. If you cannot love me, I must if possible endeavour to forget you. What would you have me do?" PRINCESS. "I really don't know what you should do." BOSWELL. "It is certainly possible that you *may* love me, and if you shall ever do so, I shall be the happiest man in the world. Will you make a fair bargain with me? If you should happen to love me, will you own it?" PRINCESS. "Yes." BOSWELL. "And if you should happen to love another, will you tell me immediately and help me to make myself easy?" PRINCESS. "Yes, I will." BOSWELL. "Well, you are very good" (often squeezing and kissing her fine hand while she looked at me with those beautiful black eyes). PRINCESS. "I may tell you as a cousin what I would not tell to another man." BOSWELL. "You may indeed. You are very fond of Auchinleck; that is one good circumstance." PRINCESS. "I confess I am. I wish I liked you as well as I do Auchinleck." BOSWELL. "I have told you how fond I am of you. But unless you like me sincerely, I have too much spirit to ask you to live with me. . . . If I could have you at this moment for my wife, I would not."

PRINCESS. "I should not like to put myself in your offer, though." . . .
Temple where am I now ? . . . What does the girl mean ?

"What strength of mind you have had this winter, to go through
so much business and at the same time have so violent a passion!"—
one wishes that Boswell had made his summary at the end of the *annus
mirabilis* instead of after a mere two months and a half of it. Mrs. Dodds,
Sally, the Princess, common girls, three different bouts of gonorrhoea;
John Reid, Robert Hay, meal rioters, nearly a hundred civil causes;
*Dorando, The Essence of the Douglas Cause, Letters of Lady Jane
Douglas,* ballads, shorthand men; a 400-page book on Corsica written
and seen through the press, paragraphs galore of "fact" and "invention"
in the newspapers—no later single year in Boswell's life will show so much
variety and perhaps none will show so much achievement.

1768 brought intense cold, a great number of political causes precipitated by the forthcoming general election, and a recurrence of Lord
Auchinleck's old complaint which put him for some hours in fear of
death and caused him to advise Boswell as for the last time. Marry Miss
Blair; retire to Auchinleck if he did not succeed at the bar; look out
for John and David; be a worthy man; keep up the character of the
Family. Boswell was terribly concerned and firmly resolved to do as
his father wished, "though" (the reservation is very characteristic) "in
somewhat a different taste in life." Towards Mrs. Dodds, whom he had
told Temple he should take the greatest care of but have no more in
keeping, he now professed to act from principle alone, in fact, to be
tired of her. But it was not like him to reduce complications in one area
without increasing them in another. On 10 January, having that very
day heard a rumour that Miss Blair was to marry Sir Alexander Gilmour
(M.P., £1600 a year of estate with a Court appointment worth £1000
more), he set himself to rekindle the flame in Belle de Zuylen. He laid
before her all his perplexities concerning Catherine Blair: fine girl—
heiress—admirable wife for him—doesn't like him but professes to like
nobody else—he has heard a rumour but hopes it is not true—and
modulated from that into a tender and respectful admission that in spite
of all his protests to the contrary, he had once been in love with Belle
herself. He had realized the state of his heart in Corsica, but the question
as to how they would do together had been presenting itself to him in
and out of season ever since his days in Holland. What does *she* think?

Would they have made a success of marriage? A few days later, with the backing of Lord Eglinton who gave him very sensible advice about both Catherine Blair and Miss Bosville ("a cow fed in fine Lowland parks was unco bonny, but turned lean and scabbed when she was turned out to the wild hills"), he wrote to the Heiress demanding in high terms to know if she was engaged "and if she was disengaged and did not write me so, I should *upon honour* consider it to be the same thing as if she was engaged." Miss Blair, as usual when he tried to intimidate her, paid no heed to him whatever.

One must imagine all this happening in the hurry of business with its fatigues, anxieties, and harassments and with the usual unapproved procedures for relaxing tension. Consider a four-day sample. 16 January, walking home from convoying Lord Eglinton to his lodging after a late dinner, he allowed a street girl to pick him up though he was still ill. 17 January, Lord Auchinleck scolded him for being out so late ("I bore with him quite calmly"); he consulted with Macqueen and three other lawyers about the defence next day of John Raybould, who was being tried on the capital charge of counterfeiting bank-notes; he went to bed at nine so that he could rise early next morning. 18 January, he got up at three, wrote a reply in a political cause and prepared a charge to the jury for Raybould; sat through the forenoon in the Justiciary Court listening to a dull reading of the decreet of Raybould's previous trial in the Court of Session; went home for dinner and a little wine, wrote another reply. Henry Dundas charged for the Crown, Boswell was uneasy and frightened. "I however began, and was soon warm and in spirits, and recollected all my arguments. I really spoke well for above half an hour. I saw my imperfections, and hoped in time to make a real good speaker." The jury unanimously found Raybould guilty. That evening another consultation in another cause. 19 January, annual meeting of the Faculty of Advocates ("felt myself *Mr. James Boswell,* comfortable and secure"), and dinner at Clerihue's. Many toasts to ladies, including one proposed by the Dean, "A young lady just in her teens—Miss Corsica!"

I drank too much. I went to a close in the Luckenbooths to seek a girl whom I had once seen in the street. I found a natural daughter of the late Lord Kinnaird, a fine lass. I stayed an hour and a half with her and drank malaga and was most amorous, being so well that no infection remained. I felt now that the indifference of the Heiress had cured me, and I was indifferent as to her. I was so happy with Jeany Kinnaird that I very philosophically reasoned that there was to me so much virtue mixed with licentious love that perhaps I might be privileged. For it made me humane, polite, generous. But then lawful love with a woman I really like would make me still better.

He has found his way back for some enchanted minutes to Sally Forrester and knows his happiness; he is really not sure that what he says about lawful love is true. One does not grudge him Jeany Kinnaird, but one does sigh when one sees him a few days later slipping into bed again with Mrs. Dodds. There is no more talk of Mark Antony, quite given up to violent love; he says he "renewed gallantry," and was clearly using her as a convenience. The relapse happened characteristically on a Sunday (31 January 1768), after a forenoon in church and an elegant dinner of fashionable people gathered to meet the author of *The Essence of the Douglas Cause*.

Miss Blair returned to Edinburgh some time that week. On the following Sunday, after going twice to divine service (Church of Scotland forenoon, Episcopalian chapel afternoon) Boswell met Fullarton, the Nabob, who proposed that they should go together and call on the Heiress. They did, and found her not surprisingly reserved and distant. Boswell took to Fullarton, carried him to supper at Mrs. Montgomerie-Cuninghame's, and then withdrew with him to drink claret at Clerihue's. They joked a great deal about "their" heiress and at two in the morning agreed to go successively and make formal proposals. On the way home Boswell roused Mrs. Dodds and subjected her to amorous attentions; between nine and ten he called on Miss Blair. He asked if she was engaged to Sir Alexander Gilmour, she said he should not believe everything he heard, and why did he ask? Because, he replied, if she were not engaged, he would take a good deal of trouble to make himself agreeable. She said she need not take the trouble. Had he, then, he asked, no chance? She said no. He repeated his question, she repeated her answer. He made her give him breakfast, and she lectured him for talking about her with so little reserve. The Nabob made his call at twelve and was treated with great coldness. Boswell, writing a long report to Temple the same day ("All is over between Miss Blair and me") showed himself detached enough to compose "A Crambo Song[1] on Losing My Mistress":

[1] Song with recurring rhyme-word.

Although I be an honest laird,
In person rather strong and brawny,
For me the Heiress never car'd,
For she would have the knight, Sir Sawney.

And when with ardent vows I swore,
Loud as Sir Jonathan Trelawny,[1]
The Heiress showed me to the door,
And said she'd have the knight, Sir Sawney.

She told me with a scornful look
I was as ugly as a tawny;[2]
For she a better fish could hook,
The rich and gallant knight, Sir Sawney.

N.B. I can find no more rhymes to "Sawney."

Five days later (13 February 1768) Mrs. Dodds, whom Boswell had ever since her confinement been calling "Sally's mother," appears in a style that leads one to expect that she will again take a more central role in the narrative. Boswell dined at the Lord Justice-Clerk's in a party composed mainly of judges, drank freely, and after five "went to Sally's mother and renewed. She told me she was again, she believed, as before. I was a little embarrassed, but just submitted my mind to it." That evening he had a consultation, got more wine, and went back. "She really looked pretty." Actually, with that entry the curtain drops on Mrs. Dodds and stays down for more than a year. On 31 March 1769, Boswell, writing from Auchinleck to John Johnston in Edinburgh, says he had done nothing for his black friend for these many weeks, which he admits to be very wrong. He sends a draft for £10, the money to be delivered to her through Alexander Hamilton, surgeon, who is to tell her that Boswell's reason for not seeing her for some time is that he has resolved to take no part "in a certain dispute." The dispute remains unexplained. Then on 23 June 1769 Boswell consulted with Johnston and Dr. Cairnie as to "managing with economy that unlucky affair of Mrs. ____." And that is all.

The sudden eclipse of Sally and her mother in the records cannot mean that they dropped overnight out of Boswell's life; it means rather

[1] A militant bishop who opposed James II. In a contemporary doggerel poem cited by *The Dictionary of National Biography* he is styled "a spiritual dragoon."
[2] A brown-skinned person, a "tawny-moor," originally applied to the natives of northern Africa.

that he has made one of his rare but effective decisions to be secretive. What happened to Boswell's lively mistress and her child is the prime mystery of his biography. We are, of course, not without means of inference, for Boswell, before the descent of his self-imposed black-out, had several times put himself on record as to what he felt his responsibilities to be. If we remind ourselves that these inferences can never be more than plausible, there will be no harm, and perhaps there may be some value, in making them explicit.

It seems fairly clear that if Sally had not put in an appearance, Boswell would have felt no obligations to Mrs. Dodds beyond keeping her free of expense on his account and not deserting her abruptly or unfeelingly. Even if he had not been able to reconcile her completely to their parting, he would probably not have felt obligated to make a settlement on her or to tender her a *douceur*. He had not seduced her, in any proper sense of the term. Her life had been irregular before she met him, and she had accepted him as a lover with full awareness of what was involved. She would have resented any suggestion that her favours had been purchased, and had even shown reluctance to accept presents.

The pregnancy considerably increased Boswell's responsibilities. To Temple, whose attitude towards Mrs. Dodds ("that vulgar creature") was consistently unsympathetic, Boswell repeatedly stated his obligation to be kind to her while she was bearing his child and to take the greatest care of her at the time of her delivery. He does not make clear whether he thought that her being his child's mother gave her a continuing claim on him, but my impression is that he did not. If he had supported her during her pregnancy, paid all the expenses of her delivery, and had taken the baby completely off her hands, I think he would have considered her situation at parting essentially no different from what it would have been if there had been no child in the case. That appears to have been his attitude towards Peggy Doig, though his statement that Peggy had "been well taken care of" is admittedly ambiguous.

For Sally he would have accepted continuing responsibility: we have assurance of this from the previous case of Charles, from his delight in hearing that Mrs. Dodds was pregnant, from his enlisting of Lord Marischal as godfather, and from his obvious pride in the child ("the finest little girl I ever saw"). He had recorded some of his plans for Charles: at nurse for some years, then a private school in England, then nothing to be wanting to accomplish him for whatever his genius might lead him to.

This was no doubt rather youthful and grandiose, but it looks as though his plans for his second child, if a boy, were far from sordid. "Bonny wark, Colonel," Lord Marischal had written, "getting the lassies wi' bairns, and worse to yoursel. . . . Get well; take care of Keith Boswell, who in time I hope shall become a nabob." Boswell put on record his conviction that illegitimate daughters should not receive the advantages of daughters of the house, but I do not know that he ever made any positive statements as to how they should be nurtured. My guess is that if he had had his choice, he would have caused an illegitimate daughter of his own to be brought up in the country under his own supervision and fitted to become the wife of a tenant or minor laird. This would have required some regular annual outlay of money; and if Sally had lived down to the time when Boswell began to make regular surveys of his income and expenditures (we have many such surveys after 1774), we should expect to find Sally listed, or some mysterious annual obligation that might be Sally. Nothing of the sort occurs. It seems quite certain that Boswell was not contributing any significant sum to her support after 1774.

Two explanations suggest themselves. The first, and in many ways the most plausible, is that Sally died in extreme infancy, as we know Charles did. Infant mortality was high where children enjoyed every advantage (Sir Walter Scott was one of twelve children, of whom only six survived infancy; Gibbon was the only one of seven children born to his parents who lived more than a few months), and in the case of babies farmed out at nurse the death rate ran much higher. But we cannot ignore the possibility that Boswell funded his obligation by purchasing an annuity. We have no financial statements for his reckless bachelor years, but we know that Lord Auchinleck paid off a debt of more than £1200 for him in 1776, and to this debt a settlement on Mrs. Dodds may have contributed.

In view of the complications that a second pregnancy would introduce into a situation that is already at the verge of useful speculation, I prefer to believe that Mrs. Dodds was mistaken in suspecting (13 February 1768) that she was "as before." The sum of £10 sent to her in March 1769, with Boswell's acknowledgement that he had been "very wrong" in not sending it sooner, suggests to me that she still had the care of Sally. And Boswell's talk about "managing with economy that unlucky affair of Mrs. ____" in June 1769 sounds to me as though it were proposed at that time to purchase an annuity for Mrs. Dodds or to pay off her claim in a lump sum. Possibly Boswell declined to assume continuing responsibility for Sally unless Mrs. Dodds gave her up, and Mrs. Dodds refused to part with her. In such a case, where Boswell could not have complete control of his child's nurture and education, it seems not unlikely that he would have attempted a settlement of some sort with a disclaimer of further responsibility. I still think, however, that Sally died young. With all his faults and sins, Boswell was an affectionate and responsible father; indeed, it is in the role of father that he was most consistently admirable. I cannot believe that if Sally grew up (she would have been twenty-seven at the time of Boswell's death) he would not have kept track of her; and if he had had glimpses of her in those later years, I cannot believe that there would not be some evidence of it in his journal. The evidence would no doubt be cryptic, but I think I should recognize it.

We do not have to look far for the cause of his decision to suppress further mention of his irregular family. He had said that he would swear to observe silence when the *Account of Corsica* was published, and he carried out his vow in the disconcertingly literal fashion that he was occasionally capable of. His last recorded visit to Mrs. Dodds occurred on 13 February. On the 15th, he heard from Dilly that the *Account* was ready for publication, and ordered copies issued for sale in Scotland. On the 18th, "My book was published this day, and felt my own importance." He opened the Ayrshire ball at Fortune's that evening with the Countess of Crawford.

I was quite as I wished to be, only I am positive I had not so high an opinion of myself as other people had. I look back with wonder on the mysterious and respectful notions I used to have of authors. I felt that I was still subject to attacks of feverish love, but I also knew that my mind is now firm enough soon to recover its tone.

The access of firmness extended to emotional assaults which he has not listed. His account of his first Tyburn execution—the hanging of the handsome young highwayman Paul Lewis in 1763—furnishes a paradigm of his attitudes with regard to executions before this time. His curiosity to see the melancholy spectacle was so strong, he says, that he could not resist it; he had a sort of horrid eagerness to be there. He got on a scaffold very near the fatal tree so that he could clearly see all the dismal scene; he was terribly shocked and thrown into a very deep melancholy. Gloomy terrors came upon him so much as night approached that he fled from his solitary lodging and begged half a bed from Erskine. Even on the second and third nights, he was still so much in horror that he had to appeal to Dempster's and Erskine's kindness. Now, though the compulsion to attend remains, the horror at the sight of inflicted death is much more manageable. And he now begins the macabre practice of exhorting the condemned man and quizzing him as to how he expects to feel in the moment of dissolution.

His client Raybould—the second he had lost to the gallows—had been lying in gaol for the statutory month and was to be hanged on 24 February. Boswell had suffered much less emotional involvement with him than he had with Robert Hay, partly because Raybould was guilty as charged and did not bother to deny it, partly because he was a genteel man and hence not naturally to Boswell such an object of pity as he would have been if he had been rustic and simple. But a few nights before the fatal day he had a vivid dream of Raybould under sentence of death, his gloom persisted, and he resolved to try to cure his gloomy imagination by stuffing his mind with the reality. Beyond a terribly clanking door, in the dim light of a farthing candle, he found his client sitting quite composed, one leg fastened by a travelling chain to an iron bar that traversed the cell from wall to wall a little above the floor. He read to him from the 1st epistle of St. John and discoursed ("very appositely," he says) on the subject of fear. This was quite gratuitous so far as Raybould was concerned, but it was of course his own fear he was trying to dispel, and with very little regard for Raybould's feelings. He went on to describe to him how prostrated and desperate Robert Hay had been ("all for *fear*, just terror for dying"), and pressed him as to whether he wasn't after all really *a little* afraid of the pain of dying? Raybould remaining at ease and even smiling, Boswell suddenly thought how amazing it would be if a man in his situation should really laugh.

> With the nicest care of a diligent student of human nature, I as decently as possible first smiled as he did, and gradually cherished the risible exertion till he and I together fairly laughed. How strange!

At the execution, which he saw from the window of a merchant in the Grassmarket who had invited him, he professed to feel very little, but his final comment is revealing. That evening, coming home from *The Beggar's Opera* and late drinking of wine, "I was a little dreary, but it went off and I slept well." It was the first time in his life that he was able to sleep after seeing a man hanged.

Next day the post brought from Belle de Zuylen the long-awaited answer to the letter in which he had attempted to kindle her anew. It was in her very best rallying vein:

Permit me to remark that you certainly take your time in everything you do. You waited to fall in love with me till you were in the Isle of Corsica, and you waited to tell me so till you were in love with another woman and had proposed marriage to her. That, I repeat, is certainly to take one's time. . . . A strictly logical person who should read our letters would perhaps not find you too rational, but I do not wish to put my friend under constraint. Everything his singularity may prompt him to tell me shall be well received. The imagination is so mad that when one permits one's self to say all that it suggests, one necessarily says mad things, and what harm in that? I see none. I read your belated endearments with pleasure, with a smile.

Boswell replied with surprising tact and humility, granting her the right to rally him. He recapitulated the long indecisive story of the ups and downs of his affection for her and the episode of the Heiress. That is all over. "I am therefore a free man, and you cannot again tell me, 'You certainly take your time.' " Seriously, does she think they would live happier as correspondents or as partners for life? If the latter, "let us consider it in all lights and contrive how we could possibly make the old people on each side of the water agree to it." On 23 February he wrote a graceful letter to Horace Walpole, accompanying a presentation copy of *An Account of Corsica*. Walpole, though his opinion of the book was moderate, sent a "noble" reply (unfortunately unrecovered), and Boswell also had flattering letters from Garrick, from Mrs. Macaulay, and from Lord Lyttelton, both the latter pair being at the moment in great fame as historians.

On 16 March, the Session dutifully finished, he started off for London to savour the success of his book and to propagandize for Corsica. The change of scene provides an opportunity for some extended comment on his first important publication.

Corsica satisfied the expectations which Boswell's advance publicity had raised for it. The first edition was sold out in six weeks, and a second, hastily printed in London, was advertised for the first of April. This met the demand for a year. The third edition was out on the first day of May 1769, with the announcement that "Mr. Boswell's *Account of Corsica* has been so well received by the public that two numerous editions of 3500 copies have been sold within the space of a few months; and the book is so highly esteemed abroad that it has been translated into the French and Dutch languages and printed at Amsterdam and Lausanne." If Boswell had been writing a year later, he could have been even more complacent. Besides the Dillys' three editions, there was an unauthorized Irish reprint that ran through at least three more; and the full list of published translations included another French version (an abridgement), two German versions (one abridged), and an Italian version. The complete French version had at least two editions, the German, three. Three other partial or complete translations into French are known to have been made: one (apparently complete) made for the use of the French prime minister, the Duc de Choiseul; one (probably of the *Tour* only) made for Mme. du Deffand by her secretary Wiart; one of unknown extent by Belle de Zuylen. A translation into Russian was begun, but abandoned on the death of the translator. The book had a considerable sale in America.

As one would expect from this, *An Account of Corsica* figured very prominently in the reviews. *The Gentleman's Magazine* accorded it more space than any other book for the year; the *Critical* and *Monthly* agreed in giving a little more space to the third volume of Blackstone's *Commentaries,* but handled Boswell expansively. (The *Monthly's* review was in two instalments and ran to nineteen pages.) Guthrie and Griffiths, the editors-in-chief of the two reviews, wrote the articles for their magazines personally. In its sale *Corsica* was the eighteenth-century equivalent of a book-club selection. And the further analogy of the present-day digests was not wanting. Newspapers and reviews printed long extracts, one monthly magazine in fact giving its readers in five instalments a slightly condensed version of half the book. A great many people who never looked into *Corsica* itself must have known something about its contents.

The reviews were not merely long, they were surprisingly laudatory. Both Guthrie and Griffiths (who may be taken as typical) were amused by the fervour of Boswell's passion for liberty and by that quality of his writing which is commonly called naïveté. Both commented on his Scotticisms (Griffiths printed a list). Guthrie thought he had been too profuse in compliments to his friends, Griffiths rallied him on his reactionary notions about spelling (of which more later). Both indicated not merely approval of the book but also respect for its author. "We hope," concluded Griffiths, ". . . that our author will take in good part these *fescue* remarks,[1]

[1] Remarks of the sort that a teacher would point out in an exercise. ("Fescue" = pointer.)

which proceed from no ill-will to him as a man or as a writer. In the first respect we, indeed, esteem him for the amiableness of his private character, of which we have heard frequent mention from those who are personally acquainted with him; and we really admire him for even the extravagance of his love of liberty and his extreme regard for the brave Corsicans. As a writer, too, with all his inaccuracies and peculiarities, we are not a little pleased with him. He has a lively, entertaining manner; he has a competent share of classical learning; and he has acquired a degree of good taste, which, when ripened by time and corrected by experience, may enable him to make a considerable figure in polite literature."

Corsica does indeed show some pedantries which its author makes more absurd by the obvious pride he takes in them. In an attempt to be dignified, he has occasionally become pompous and stilted and has fallen into Scotticisms (generally Scots legalisms) from which his journal and letters of the period are free. The *Account of Corsica,* though on the whole simple and easy, is the least easy in style of Boswell's books. In his preface he smugly disclaims any intention of making "an ostentatious display of learning," but he has clearly tried to locate and pull in—even if by the hair—every allusion to Corsica in every Greek and Roman classic and in practically every other author who wrote in the Latin tongue. Though the passages are all either paraphrased or translated, the originals are given *in extenso,* sometimes at the foot of the page but too often in the text. The result, as Georges Deyverdun and Edward Gibbon, the most acid of Boswell's reviewers, remarked, was "that kind of erudition which costs little and is worth less." The long extracts in Greek types, which Boswell himself could probably read only with difficulty, give a false impression of a book which can actually be read without knowledge of any language but English.

Boswell's erudition was no doubt of the *ad hoc* variety attainable by any one who has access to a good library, but one who saw his classical preoccupation as a personal oddity would betray ignorance of the literary modes of the century. Joseph Addison had assumed out of hand that the correct way to write a travel book on Italy was to start by making a systematic collection of everything the Roman poets had said about the places one proposed to visit. In following the lead of the admired *Remarks on Several Parts of Italy* (which he himself had used as a guide) Boswell was showing himself conservative in his choice of models. His conservatism appears even more strikingly in another feature of the book to which he complacently directed attention in his preface: the orthography. It had become the style, he said, to omit the *k* after *c* in such words as *publick* and the *u* in words like *honour*. Johnson in his Dictionary had been careful to preserve the final *k* "as a mark of Saxon original," and for the most part had preserved the *u*, though in some words he had omitted it. Boswell says that he himself has not only preserved the *k*, but has also taken it upon himself to insert the *u* in all words, ultimately of Latin origin, that came into English through the French. "An attention to this may appear trivial. But I own I am one of those who are curious in the formation of language in its various modes, and therefore wish that the affinity of English with other tongues may not be forgotten. If this work should at any future period be reprinted, I hope that care will be taken of my orthography."

"Boswell," once wrote Professor Lounsbury, "resembled most of the ardent partisans of the ending *our* in the fact that his curiosity in the formation of language had never been rewarded by any intelligent knowledge of it." He was no student of English etymology himself and could not have found anywhere in print the historical collections which he would have had to have if he were to realize his ambitious programme with any rigour. His remark about "Saxon original" shows complete misapprehension. Yet his injunction to spare his spelling has been piously observed by his editors, so that in the best editions of the *Life of Johnson* we still read not only of *publick* and *musick* and *physick* but also of *authours, professours,* and *spectatours*. I have ignored it in this book, I confess with considerable pleasure. One could not find a better test than this for differentiating Boswell's judgement from Johnson's. Boswell's spelling is nothing but Johnson's rules consistently enforced. Johnson, however, a man of vast common sense, after stating his rules, deferred in many cases to general usage. He knew, as some one has well remarked, that complete consistency in matters of this sort is not merely impossible, it is offensive. His disciple was very apt to be rigorously and pompously consistent in things that were not worth bothering about. From 1768 on, he made a valiant attempt to restore *u*'s and *k*'s, though frequent lapses both in his books and his manuscripts show that this new system required a conscious effort on his part and a constant warfare with the compositor.

From any time after 1765 it could have been confidently predicted that Boswell would be somewhat ostentatious in the profession of religious and moral orthodoxy. The section of *An Account of Corsica* in which he discussed the sexual morality of the islanders gave him an opportunity for really splendid rigour: "Their morals are strict and chaste to an uncommon degree, owing in part to good principles unhurt by luxury, and partly to the exercise of private revenge against such as violate the honour of their women. This last may to some appear rude and barbarous, but I hold it to be wise and noble. Better occasional murders than frequent adulteries. Better cut off a rotten branch now and then than that the whole of the society should be corrupted."

Under any circumstances such sentiments would set one back on one's heels, but they are particularly jolting as coming from a man who has had another man's wife in keeping for the better part of two years past. Boswell's insistence that a man's principles are not to be inferred from his conduct is notorious, and it seems also to be a fact that he wrote this astonishing passage in the flush of virtue attendant on temporary separation from his Circe. I suspect, however, that neither of these explanations applies here, and that the right explanation is one that goes a considerable way towards removing the discrepancy between Boswell's professions and his behaviour. I think he is simply using the term "adultery" in a sense much narrower than that of the dictionary. Twice, in reply to Temple's strictures, he had denied, and apparently quite seriously, that his relation with Mrs. Dodds was adultery in any proper sense. Adultery, he maintained, was not all sexual behaviour between a legally married person and some one not his or her spouse. Adultery was infidelity, deceit, the confusion of offspring. "There is a baseness in all deceit which my soul is virtuous enough ever to abhor, and therefore I look with horror on adultery." He had not seduced Mrs. Dodds from her vow of fidelity to her husband, and she had not deceived her husband in accepting him as a lover. The husband (so Boswell said) had used her shockingly, had deserted her, and was living with another woman. Consequently, though her relation with Boswell was vicious, she was free of the imputation of adultery. It cannot be maintained that Boswell always strictly lived up to his avowed principle of never attempting to debauch an innocent girl or a faithful wife, but he tried to hard enough to earn him in anybody's book the right to profess the principle. The sanguinary Puritanism of "Better occasional murders than frequent adulteries" is quite in line with his generally reactionary notions on the score of family. But it can well be supposed that it gave the reviewers cause for amused comment. And John Wilkes digressed in a published political letter to rally "James Boswell,

Esq., of Auchinleck in Ayrshire, that primitive Christian," and to "wonder at such an assertion from a gentleman, a man of humanity, and an *Englishman,* for so I call him, as he chose to be our countryman abroad, though not at home."

These pedantries and quaintnesses granted, *An Account of Corsica* is still a very pleasant book. Sir George Otto Trevelyan as late as 1880 maintained that it was by far the best account of the island that had ever been published. He thereby betrayed the fact that he had not read very widely in the French and Italian histories of Corsica, but his remark still remains an impressive testimony to Boswell's charm. The fact is that, for everything that concerns Corsican geography, natural history, and political history down to 1741 (i.e., the greater part of the first two chapters) the *Account* is a skilful but hasty and superficial compilation, based principally (as Boswell frankly admitted) on two recent French books the authors of which had served in Corsica with the French army in 1738–41. For the remainder (roughly half) of the *Account,* the part dealing with Paoli's rise to power and struggles against the Genoese, "The present state of Corsica with respect to government, religion, arms, commerce, learning," etc., Boswell had manuscript materials furnished by Paoli, Rivarola, and others closely in touch with the revolutionary government. This matter is still of primary historical value. Even when it is suspect as to accuracy, it shows "what the Corsicans wished to believe—or at any rate what the Corsicans wished the world to believe." No serious student of the history of Corsica will ever be able to ignore this portion of Boswell's *Account,* but there is no reason to suppose that the *Account* will ever again be much read by any but serious students.

At least two critics immediately proclaimed the superiority of the *Tour.* Guthrie, in the *Critical,* remarked that it was more valuable because it was more original: "because it could not be the result of reading or information." This verdict Johnson confirmed in the best known of all the criticisms of *Corsica:*

Your History is like other histories, but your Journal is in a very high degree curious and delightful. There is between the History and the Journal that difference which there will always be found between notions borrowed from without and notions generated within. Your History was copied from books; your Journal rose out of your own experience and observation. You express images which operated strongly upon yourself, and you have impressed them with great force upon your readers. I know not

whether I could name any narrative by which curiosity is better excited
or better gratified.

Boswell, with characteristic clear-headedness where his own writings were
concerned, had known this all along. "The last part of my work, entitled
the *Journal of a Tour to Corsica,* is, in my opinion, the most valuable," he
had written to Temple while the book was still in the press.

The eighteenth-century printings of the *Account* will probably furnish
as many copies of that work as will ever be needed, but the *Tour* should
always be kept in print. It is not Boswell at his best, because he has not
yet learned to trust his journal and has reworked his notes into a continuous narrative without dates. There has been ruthless elimination of the
detail which makes a genuine Boswellian journal so absorbing. The *Journal of a Tour to Corsica* is in every way a more slender, less mature piece
of work than the *Journal of a Tour to the Hebrides,* which (in its original
form) was written only six years later. What endears it to Boswellians is
perhaps first its youthfulness, its unflagging high spirits, then this very
quality of thinness, of charming simplicity. Illustrations will serve better
than comment:

After supper therefore the Prior walked with me to Corte, to the house
of the Great Chancellor, who ordered the passport to be made out immediately, and while his secretary was writing it, entertained me by reading
to me some of the minutes of the General Consulta. When the passport was
finished and ready to have the seal put to it, I was much pleased with a
beautiful simple incident. The Chancellor desired a little boy who was
playing in the room by us to run to his mother and bring the great seal of
the kingdom. I thought myself in the house of a Cincinnatus.

(The equally charming passage about the *prisca gens mortalium,* quoted
above on p. 254, follows this immediately.)

The main purpose of the *Tour* was to evoke powerfully certain emotions concerning Paoli and his Corsicans. That it did evoke them is indicated by an entry in the journal of John Wesley, who goes some way towards defining them: "At intervals read Mr. Boswell's *Account of Corsica.*
But what a scene is opened therein! How little did we know of that brave
people! How much less were we acquainted with the character of their
general, Pascal Paoli: as great a lover of his country as Epaminondas, and
as great a general as Hannibal!" Boswell had not left it to his readers to

draw such parallels. He had studded his text with names like Themisto-
cles, Lycurgus, Numa, Solon, and Scipio, and had ended his volume with
the fine remark of Pitt that Paoli was one of those men who are no longer
to be found but in the lives of Plutarch. One would like to know whether
it was that remark of Pitt that set the tone for Boswell's "memoirs of
Paoli," or whether Boswell, by skilful manoeuvring, got Pitt to say what he
wanted said and which he knew would come with greater weight from
Pitt than from himself. At any rate, his portrait of Paoli is much more
Plutarchian than his portrait of Johnson. In a way this was inevitable.
Paoli was a statesman and a general; he had taken the hero of Virgil and
the great men of Plutarch as his models and talked about them constantly.
He really had a heroic manner and a Roman style. But there are clear,
though not abundant, indications in Boswell's papers that, if he had
chosen, he could have presented Paoli in something much more like the
Flemish style which he had already adopted for Johnson in his journal
and was later to carry over into the *Life of Johnson*. Paoli had a pungent
wit which did not disdain occasional homeliness or vulgarity. On one occasion when he thought Johnson too obsequious to a peer who was praising
him, he said that Johnson held down his head to have the full pail of flattery poured on. Boswell's surviving outline for the "memoirs of Paoli"
shows him deciding that though it was "quite proper" for Paoli to adopt
a more distant bearing before a crowd and soldiers under arms, it was
"not for public view." So, too, he omitted some anecdote of Paoli's that
dealt with "cows and fishes," and suppressed the General's remark that
when he tried to write down his thronging thoughts he "only got in a
sweat."

If one wants to be sure of making people like one's hero, one had better use the Plutarchian method. The Flemish portrait leaves no one indifferent, but cannot be counted on always to rouse feelings of approbation.
Many, perhaps most, of the readers of the *Life of Johnson* conceive for
Johnson a fondness that may develop into profound respect, even into
veneration. But some intelligent and sensitive readers hate Boswell's Johnson at first sight and on further acquaintance are only confirmed in their
dislike. To them he seems a dirty, opinionated, wilful—even brutal—old
man. The Plutarchian *Journal of a Tour to Corsica* produced no such double reaction. It would be possible to collect pages and pages of contemporary comment to prove this, but Wesley's record will suffice. The reading
public felt for Paoli (whom they knew *solely* through Boswell's book) a

pitch of veneration for which their own term might have been "enthusiastic."

The *Tour,* like the later Johnsonian studies, also evoked strong emotion towards Boswell himself. We are familiar with the emotional reaction produced by the Boswell presented in the *Life of Johnson.* It is generally friendly but always amused, and even when it stops short of the Macaulayan attitude, usually has in it an element of condescension and contempt. Present-day readers who peruse the ephemeral publications of the year 1768 and a few years after will be amazed by the extravagance of personal regard which sensible people on all sides testified to concerning the author of *An Account of Corsica.* At least half a dozen people addressed serious poetical tributes to him. Edward Burnaby Greene, who had earlier gained some notoriety by poems in which he was proud to confess that his pen o'erflowed with gall when Scotland was his theme, produced an ode in which he called on Truth to

> proclaim a baffled Genoa's groan,
> And grace a classic isle with Boswells of her own.

Capel Lofft, dubbing Paoli Corsica's Alfred, said that

> Clio taught
> His acts, his image, to her BOSWELL's thought.

In the academic retreats of Warrington, Anna Letitia Aikin—better known as that Mrs. Barbauld who told Coleridge that *The Ancient Mariner* did not have moral enough—was moved to compose a blank-verse poem in which the young historian of Corsica is presented as a gallant and noble figure:

> Such were the working thoughts which swell'd the breast
> Of generous BOSWELL, when with nobler aim
> And views beyond the narrow beaten track
> By trivial fancy trod, he turned his course . . .
> To animated forms of patriot zeal
> Warm in the living majesty of virtue.

The climax is provided by the Reverend Robert Colvill, who, in a simile drawn from the most famous English tragedy of the century, equates Paoli with Cato and Boswell with Juba, the Numidian Lion:

> So when proud Caesar [Louis XV] stretch'd his iron rod,
> Expelling Freedom from her fam'd abode,
> The Mauritanian [J. Boswell], smit with virtue's charms,
> Ador'd the Goddess in her Cato's [Paoli's] arms;
> Arrang'd his myriads, kindling at the call
> To humble Caesar or with Cato fall.

No one is upon oath in poetical compositions, but it was not merely versi-
fiers who said things like that. Worldly, cynical old Mme. du Deffand
wrote to Horace Walpole that she was madly in love with Boswell. "He
has an excellent heart, his soul is all virtue. I shall be on my guard not to
show the enthusiasm I have for his book." James Burgh, a hard-headed,
loud-voiced Whig schoolmaster who wrote essays in defence of the American colonies, printed a panegyric in *The London Chronicle:* "I do not
know of any publication better calculated to rouse in the breasts of degenerate E——men the expiring flame of patriotism than Mr. Boswell's
Account of Corsica. I do not know the author, but I venerate and I love
the man who shows such love and such veneration for the illustrious Paoli;
and I would with pleasure travel an hundred miles to thank Mr. Boswell
in person for his worthy labour, which I would wish to be very attentively
perused by every man in Britain." General Oglethorpe, founder of the
colony of Georgia and senior general of the British Army, hunted Boswell
up in London on his first visit to the metropolis after the publication of
Corsica and asked the honour of shaking his hand. "My name, Sir," said
the grand old man, "is Oglethorpe, and I wish to be acquainted with
you."

When I spoke above of Boswell's charming simplicity, I used the
phrase with some uneasiness because of a suspicion that the reader would
think that I considered the simplicity unconscious. It was not. A man who
in his private memoranda counsels himself to "behave nice and romantic
and bold" is not likely to have been actually ingenuous on any occasion or
in any description he ever wrote of himself. The simplicity was genuine,
just as Byron's Titanism was genuine, but like Byron's Titanism it was a
deliberate simplification of character for literary ends. And like any other
simplification of the sort it ran risks: in particular, to use the jargon now
in vogue, it was vulnerable to ironic contemplation. The great majority of
the readers of *Corsica* reacted just as Boswell wanted them to. Like Miss
Aikin, they thought his enthusiastic and humble veneration of Paoli not
silly but "generous." They were not disposed to think him a fool because

he everywhere made Paoli magnanimous and himself eager, unformed, and obsequious. But there were then, and have been at all times since, sensibilities in which such simplification and subordination of self raises only contempt for the man who practises it. Deyverdun and Gibbon, though clearly themselves of this party, at least allow a choice: "All classes of readers will have derived pleasure from a kind of ingenuousness which either prejudices us in the author's favour or makes us laugh at him." Horace Walpole and Thomas Gray allow no choice; and with Horace Walpole and Thomas Gray particularly in mind as exemplars of this sensibility, I may perhaps characterize it as Etonian. Its motto, if not exactly *nil admirari,* is at least *nil admirari ultra quam satis est.* Men of the Etonian sensibility never wear their hearts on their sleeves, never "speak out." And they are made acutely uncomfortable by authors who do. Thomas Gray's comment on *Corsica* states with the felicity one would have expected from that reserved and exquisite artist the perennial verdict of a long line of critics on Boswell as author. The position is usually called Macaulayan from its most flamboyant spokesman, but all of Macaulay is implied in this letter of Gray's to Walpole:

Mr. Boswell's book . . . has pleased and moved me strangely, all (I mean) that relates to Paoli. He is a man born two thousand years after his time! The pamphlet proves, what I have always maintained, that any fool may write a most valuable book by chance if he will only tell us what he heard and saw with veracity. Of Mr. Boswell's truth I have not the least suspicion, because I am sure he could invent nothing of this kind. The true title of this part of his work is "A Dialogue Between a Green Goose and a Hero."[1]

It is not my intention anywhere in this book to argue with those who feel contempt for the private character of Boswell, or, as we commonly say, for Boswell the man. The choice between liking and disliking another human being is legitimately arbitrary. Though the list of Boswell's friends is a long and impressive one, plenty of people who knew him in the flesh held him in contempt, and plenty of people who have known him only by his writing have felt the same way. Nor shall I disagree with any man who calls Boswell a fool, if he means by the term that Boswell often made bad practical choices, behaved foolishly, showed weakness of will. Boswell un-

---

[1] A green goose is a goose under four months old, a large gosling.

doubtedly was that kind of fool. But that is not what Gray means. He means, "Any man, *no matter how limited in intelligence, no matter how deficient in literary ability,* may write a most valuable book by chance if he will [notice that Gray does not say "can"] tell us what he heard and saw with veracity." That, of course, is a false theory of literature. Good books are never written by chance. The author of a great book is by definition a great author. Wisdom, virtue, magnanimity do not get themselves automatically recorded by a green goose who is unaware of the quality of what he has recorded. He may in his practical choices be a very foolish man, but if he gives you a book that breathes magnanimity, it can only have happened first, because he had a mind and a heart capable of understanding magnanimity, and secondly, because he had the rare power of expressing magnanimity in words, had literary genius of a high order. Gray, who had a keen and subtle mind, ought to have been able to analyse better. He should have been able to see that the "memoirs of Paoli" were no stenographic transcription and that Boswell in a very real sense *was* "inventing" both sides of the "dialogue" that moved him so strangely. He was not inventing the topics of Paoli's conversation, and, as Gray suspected, could not have invented them, but he was reconstructing the scene imaginatively, was making a work of dramatic art out of a sprawling series of words, which, if Gray could have overheard it, would have moved him much less than Boswell's rendering.

By the publication of *An Account of Corsica* Boswell became at twenty-seven a literary figure of international reputation. His book could be read in five languages and was the concern of statesmen. For a certain period of time far more people knew about him than knew about Goldsmith or Johnson. When in 1789 he concluded that Sir John Hawkins meant to show ill-will when he referred to him merely as "Mr. James Boswell, a native of Scotland" (instead of "Mr. James Boswell, the well-known author of *An Account of Corsica*"), he was certainly justified. In the Preface to the first edition of his book he had expressed an ardent desire for literary fame. In the Preface to the third edition, written a year later, he was able to report that his wildest hopes had been realized. "I have obtained my desire; and whatever clouds may overcast my days, I can now walk here [at Auchinleck] among the rocks and woods of my ancestors with an agreeable consciousness that I have done something worthy." "It is amazing," he wrote about the same time in his journal, "how much and how universally I have made myself admired. This is an absolute fact. I am certain of it; and with an honest pride I will rejoice in it." For many years he was to be known as Corsica Boswell, and though he was to publish two greater books, he was never again to be so admired, never again to take such unalloyed satisfaction in his fame. The world, he was to find, has greater respect for the press-agent of a nation than for the author of the greatest of biographies. "I said to General Paoli," he wrote in 1783, "it was wonderful how much Corsica had done for me, how far I had got in the world by having been there. I had got upon a rock in Corsica and jumped into the middle of life."

CHAPTER

XXI

Boswell set out on his fourth visit to London happily conscious of a firmer mind and a superior character. No furtive runaway planning to hide his head in a monastery, no cap-in-hand suppliant for favours of the great, no self-recommended envoy from a dubious nation, he comes a settled lawyer who has made two hundred pounds in a year, a man cloaked with the mysterious authority of successful authorship. His coming has been heralded (by himself) in the London newspapers, and his arrival will be duly announced. He travels leisurely and in style, his chaise-companion one of the contractors for paving the streets of London, his volunteer Master Household a macer of the Court of Session who gallops ahead and bullies waiters, postilions, and ostlers for him. And for the first time in more than two years, he finds time to write a continuously literary journal, a journal of space for his wandering, of distinctness for his luxury. It is the first of the long happy series of spring-vacation London journals from which he was later to quarry the conversations that give most of the sparkle to the *Life of Johnson*.

In a coffee-house in York he falls incognito into conversation about Corsica with a Sir George Armytage; Sir George's information seems gratifyingly familiar.

So I asked him if the Corsicans had any seaports. "Oh, yes, Sir," said he, "very good ones. Why, Boswell's *Account of Corsica* tells you all that." "Sir?" said I, "what is that?" "Why, Sir," said he, "a book just now published." . . . "But, Sir," said I, "can we believe what he says?" "Yes, Sir," said Sir George, "the book is authentic and very accurate."

He explores the state of his mind in two of those exhaustively detailed circumstantial metaphors of which he always had too high an opinion. His mind, he thinks, is a room, hung now with flimsy chintz and gaudy paper, but his walls are good, they will bear any sort of hangings. They have, in fact, often been substantially hung, but up to now he has changed his furniture as whim suggested. His mind is a lodging-house, and his lodgers have been highly miscellaneous: lawyers, Presbyterian ministers, Methodists, Roman clergy, Deists.

I am forced to own that my rooms have been occupied by women of the town and by some ladies of abandoned manners. But I am resolved that by degrees there shall be only decent people and innocent, gay lodgers.

By degrees yes, sometime yes, but he certainly does not intend to start tapering off now. He has left behind a pretty, lively little girl named Mary whom he has recently promoted into Mrs. Dodds's place, and hopes (not very confidently) to find faithful on his return; he approaches London nursing a keen appetite for raking. His trunk barely unpacked, he sallies forth "like a roaring lion" after girls, and he continues to roar through a series of remarkably crowded days.

He stages a cordial and stately ceremony of investiture for John Dick, the obliging consul at Leghorn, intermediary of all his correspondence with Paoli and indefatigable collector of materials for his book. Dick believed himself to be heir male to Sir Alexander's ancestor, Sir William Dick of Braid, Lord Provost of Edinburgh, and as such heir male, heir *de jure* to a dormant baronetcy conferred on Sir William c. 1640. The court of Tuscany having become more punctilious with the advent of a resident Grand Duke, he had come to feel that the title would be professionally useful to him, and had made the trip to England in the hope of getting it revived. It is clear from his correspondence with Boswell that his case was far from satisfactory: he could present documentary proof neither that he was Sir William's heir male nor that Sir William had ever been a baronet in the first place. But, as he pointed out, only he himself was involved, for he had no children; and he proposed simply to assume the title if enough of a show of formal procedure could be provided to satisfy the King. Boswell and Sir Alexander, cooperating enthusiastically and none too scrupulously, had worked out a pedigree for him, and had caused him to be served heir to Sir William; and Boswell now came bearing the Latin retour of the jury and a collection of other gratifying ceremonial appurtenances, including a miniature of Sir William. His investiture of the Consul and his lady with their titles at their house on the evening of his arrival, recalling his recent investiture of brother David with a ring on the ruins of the Old Castle, was no doubt bustling and pompous, but it would be wrong not to recognize it also as an effusion of generosity and pure good will. Lady Dick, accepting it as such, presented him with a princely sword.

He went a second time to Tyburn. The execution, at which two ill-assorted criminals suffered, was in every way the most satisfactory that he ever witnessed. Benjamin Payne, footpad, a scrawny boy of nineteen or twenty in mean clothes and a red nightcap, presented the usual spectacle of penitence and almost lethal terror, but James Gibson, attorney and forger, a neatly dressed man of fifty, exceeded all Boswell could imagine of calmness and manly resolution. He had been allowed to come with his friends in a mourning coach to the place of execution, and he stood with a perfect composure in the cart with the rope around his neck, sucking an orange while the Newgate ordinary read prayers. He made death seem a very easy matter. Boswell was so impressed that he worked up the account in his journal into an essay which he published in *The Public Advertiser* over the pseudonym "Mortalis." In the journal he had for the first time admitted his obsession: "It is a curious turn, but I never can resist seeing executions." In the essay he puts this in the form, "I feel an irresistible impulse to be present at every execution," and subjects his motives to extended analysis. He cannot with complete conviction repel the Lucretian charge that his reason for liking to see others in acute physical distress is that it enables him to savour his own security, though he would like to think, with the Abbé Du Bos, that his pleasure in such scenes really involves no element of comparison but merely testifies to the universal wish to be moved. He feels quite certain that he is not more hard-hearted than other people.

When I first attended executions, I was shocked to the greatest degree. I was in a manner convulsed with pity and terror, and for several days, but especially nights, after, I was in a very dismal situation. Still, however, I persisted in attending them, and by degree my sensibility abated, so that I can now see one with great composure, and my mind is not afterwards haunted with frightful thoughts, though for a while a certain degree of gloom remains upon it.

The main motive, he is sure, that drives him to executions is a profound and abiding concern with death, his own death. He wants as often as pos-

sible to witness "the various effects of the near approach of death," so that
by studying them he can learn to quiet and fortify his own mind.

It does not sound very convincing. Is it really true that one can cure
one's self of deep fears dating from one's infancy by exposing one's self at
all opportunities to scenes of terror? If examples count, why should Mr.
Gibson's manly composure be more effective than Benjamin Payne's pitiful funk? Even more puzzling is Boswell's statement in the journal that
during an execution he was always imagining himself the condemned man
and thinking how much better he could manage things: "I never saw a
man hanged but I thought I could behave better than he did, except Mr.
Gibson." Surely one would have expected him to say the exact opposite:
that he never saw a man hanged but he feared his own behaviour would
be more grovelling. How could he feel a sense of superiority at the very
time that he was convulsed with pity and terror at another man's agony?
I do not know, but I feel pretty certain that what was giving Boswell his
new composure in the face of spectacles of death had not come by degrees
but suddenly on 18 February 1768, and that it was a confirmed sense of
identity resulting from the world's assurance that he had done something
important. In any case, there can be no doubt that the composure is there.
His account of his first Tyburn execution in 1763 was little more than a
shuddering constricted ejaculation of his own horror; this account, with
its firm, bright, characterizing detail, is as hearty as any other portion of
the journal during an unusually hearty period.

He met his publishers. Life could have held few more wholly satisfactory moments for Boswell than that in which he strode into the Dillys' shop
in the Poultry and announced himself as the author of that extremely successful book, *An Account of Corsica*. The Dillys strike one instantly as
having been invented by Charles Dickens; one even has a feeling that one
has already seen them all depicted somewhere in Cruikshank's plates.
There are four of them, three bachelors and a maiden lady, though Boswell does not on this occasion meet the head of the family, Squire John,
whose Dingley Dell is at nearby Southill. All of them are well under
forty: John 37, Edward 35, Charles 29, Martha 26. Edward talks incessantly and vivaciously, letting off squibs of keen, quick, shrill sound close
to one's ears; Charles is tall, smartish, civil, quite of the City form; Martha
is a neat little young lady, smart rather than pretty, with a handsome
(probably huge) headdress. They have finished dinner, but in no more
time than it takes to ask a question, Boswell is being served a plate of sub-

stantial mutton and potatoes. For the rest of his life he will be treated in
that hospitable house with the respect due to high character and the
cordiality usually reserved for blood relations.

Boswell's new friends accompanied him to Guildhall to see the poll for
members of Parliament: on the hustings Lord Mayor Harley, Beckford,
Trecothick, Glyn—and Wilkes. Weary of exile and short allowance,
Wilkes had returned to London early in February. The Government had
ignored him. He addressed an insultingly informal appeal for pardon to
the King, and was still ignored. The general election coming on, he presented himself as candidate for the City of London. The enthusiasm of
the mob was unbounded, but unfortunately few of the mob had votes.
(Being told that one of his supporters had proved a turncoat, Wilkes replied, "Impossible. Not one of them has a coat to turn.") This is the year
of Wilkes's first Middlesex election and the "massacre" of St. George's
Fields, and Boswell was in London during the entire period. A series of
Boswellian reports on Wilkes's conversation during this crucial spring
would be beyond price. But Boswell seems to have taken for granted that,
whatever infringements of propriety he might permit himself with Wilkes
abroad, he was in England to have no personal dealings with Wilkes so
long as he remained under judicial sentence. He remarked on the confusion and uproar of the mob shouting "Wilkes and Liberty," on the true
London countenances of the candidates, on his own curious feelings at
seeing Wilkes in London and recollecting their meetings in Italy and Paris,
but he made no attempt to speak to him, and did not even wave his hand.
He had always sincerely reprobated Wilkes's politics. He was now an advocate, with something more than a layman's responsibility for avoiding social intimacy with persons in the shadow of the law. He wanted, in good
time, to be a candidate for Parliament himself, and he knew that any Scot
who let himself be seen in Wilkes's company while Wilkes was an outlaw
or the inmate of a gaol would be seriously hurting his chances. These are
all good, prudent reasons, but it is impossible not to be impatient with
them. Boswell might better have passed up some of his less rewarding
imprudences for this really splendid one. The best that can be said for
him—I shall recur to this—is that he knew that association with Wilkes
would diminish his usefulness as a propagandist for Corsica.

Two days later, coming through Bloomsbury Square, he had the extraordinary fortune to be mistaken for Wilkes by a Middlesex voter. He
did not resemble Wilkes in the least in face or figure, but his rather con-

spicuous dress of green and gold seems to have been similar to one that
Wilkes had worn on the hustings. He seized the opportunity for one of his
old Soaping Club exercises of mimicry and shaving, and walked his voter
half a mile or more, discoursing of liberty and general warrants "and I
don't know what all." Among other things he told the voter (between
themselves) that the King really thought very well of him. Half way down
Long Acre he dropped the role and announced that, so far from being
Wilkes, he was a Scotsman. Johnson later was angry with him for not borrowing money from the man.

Boswell would in any case have made one of his first calls on Dr. (now
Sir John) Pringle, but in a letter he had just received he had particular
matter to discuss. Belle de Zuylen had sent a very sensible proposal that if
he had any serious thoughts of her, he ought to come over to see her.
They should meet without any engagement and judge whether they were
likely to make a success of living together. Sir John, who had now himself
experienced Belle's charm, was better disposed towards the marriage than
he had formerly been, and Boswell wrote to his father begging permission
to go to Utrecht.

On the way down to London, though he had considered marriage and
was determined to have a good match, he had still balanced between Belle
and Miss Bosville, an off-and-on candidate ever since he had met her in
London two years before. Dining with the Bosvilles on 25 March, the day
after his conference with Sir John, he learned that Miss Bosville was no
longer his to command: she was engaged to Sir Alexander Macdonald of
Sleat. So far as we know, she never knew the honour that Boswell proposed for her. He seems to have accepted the news with great equanimity,
being at the time much taken up with the scheme of revisiting Utrecht.
For the moment his matrimonial list had reduced itself miraculously to the
sole name of Belle de Zuylen.

He had supper and a long expectation-raising conversation with William Guthrie, editor-in-chief of *The Critical Review,* whose review of *An
Account of Corsica* was due to appear in a few days. Guthrie, an old gentleman in a white coat with a crimson satin waistcoat and a bag-wig,
called him a genius: "A thousand people might have thought of making
themselves famous before one would have thought of Corsica."

Johnson, he had found on his arrival, was not in London but was
visiting his friend Robert Chambers, Vinerian Professor of Laws at
Oxford. He was considerably in the dark as to the state of Johnson's

feelings towards him. Johnson had shown extraordinary marks of affection and had grumbled a wish for many years of regard, but he had not answered any of Boswell's letters for a long time—not, in fact, since August 1766, when he had made strictures on his Latinity and had roughly advised him to drop his scheme of writing on Corsica. ("You have no materials which others have not, or may not have. You have, somehow or other, warmed your imagination. . . . Mind your own affairs, and leave the Corsicans to theirs.") Boswell had assumed that he would certainly write on receiving a presentation copy of *An Account of Corsica,* in which he was very highly spoken of, but he had taken no notice of it. On getting to London, Boswell heard that Johnson was certainly displeased at him for printing part of one of his letters without permission; whether he was otherwise offended, or, worse, had merely grown indifferent, could be determined only by a meeting face to face. He resolved to go to Oxford and explore the situation. Johnson greeted him as warmly as ever, took him in his arms and kissed him "on both sides of the head," and was tremendously pleased to learn that Boswell had made a trip to Oxford just to see him, and that he had made two hundred pounds a year as a lawyer. "What, Bozzy? Two hundred pounds? A great deal." He had, in fact, three days before written Boswell a letter, but had sent it to Scotland. It was very brief, asked why he should write to a man who published letters of his friends without leave, and wished he would empty his head of Corsica, "which I think has filled it rather too long," but it made clear that the long silence had been completely unmotivated, and it ended with the usual assurance of affection. Boswell got from him over this week-end several of his most memorable dicta. Can a lawyer plead a cause he knows to be bad without hurting his principles of honesty? "Sir, you do not know it to be good or bad till the judge determines it." Is it not hard that one deviation from chastity should so absolutely ruin a woman? "Why, no, Sir. The great principle which every woman is taught is to keep her legs together." What happens to the birds that disappear during the winter? "Swallows certainly sleep all the winter. A number of them conglobulate together, by flying round and round, and then all in a heap throw themselves under water and lie in the bed of a river." Were not Belle de Zuylen's superior talents an objection in a wife? "Sir, you need not be afraid; marry her. Before a year goes about, you'll find that reason much weaker and that wit not near so bright."

Wilkes had failed of election for the City of London, but he was also standing for the County of Middlesex, which at that time included a large part of the metropolis. When Boswell took the fly for Oxford on Saturday 26 March, he passed through Brentford, the shire town and seat of the poll. The first ten miles of the road from London were in the possession of Wilkes's mob, pouring down to Brentford, roaring "Wilkes and Liberty" and chalking their slogan of "No. 45" on every coach or chaise that passed. When he started back on Tuesday morning, he heard with astonishment at Bensington that Wilkes had been elected on the previous day by a considerable majority. By being out of London he had missed a very pretty riot. The mob, streaming back through Westminster to the City, had broken the windows of Lord Bute's house in Mayfair, forced a general illumination, and smashed every window in the Mansion House ("even that of the Lady Mayoress's bed-chamber"—Harley, the Lord Mayor, being of the "Court" party). Any one on the street who refused to bawl "Wilkes and Liberty" ran the risk of being knocked down.

Boswell's whoring rage, in any case, would probably not have spent itself at the level of the prudent and polite debauchery he had been affecting ("a neat little lass *in armour,* at a tavern in the Strand"), but it is quite likely that the Wilkesite disturbances, which broke out again on the evening of the day he returned to London, helped to define the sordid and dangerous encounters by which he sated it. Some family censor has excised his no doubt brilliant and detailed account of his deliberate blackguarding, but has spared (or overlooked) the note on which the Journal account was based:

... Home—Sallied—Kitty—Borrowed from Mathew—Raged—Then Dun's left watch and purse and had crown wanted two like Bolingbroke got red-haired hussy went to Bob Derry's had brandy and water She went for companion; found her not. Then once—Then home with her. Watchman lighted us and *she* paid penny. Horrid room; no fire no curtains—dirty sheets, etc all night—3 here.[1]

[1] Boswell's punctuation is followed, though in two cases line-endings are counted as dashes. "Kitty" was "Kitty Brookes, as pretty a lively lass as youth need see," with whom Boswell had solaced himself on 25 March. She lived in a court off Covent Garden. "Mathew" is unidentified; he was not Boswell's servant, whose name we know to have been Anthony Mudford. "Dun," a tailor with some kind of Auchinleck connexions, had outfitted and lodged Lt. John in 1760. Boswell had had dealings with him in 1763 and 1766. "Bolingbroke" was probably Frederick St. John, 2d Viscount Bolingbroke (1734–87), a notorious rake known as "the wicked Lord

Though on decamping at 6 A.M. he had despised himself "for having been in the very sink of vice," he had by no means reached bottom. The leaves of the journal for the 30th have also been brutally thinned: twelve pages once expanded the following note, the gist of which the reader is as well qualified to unriddle as I am :

Dined Great Piazza—Sent Mathew for Black. Down to Westminster two naked ah tis the Barber hes a clever one[1]

And that was not the bottom either. The journal shows two more yawning gaps (one of fourteen pages) later than this, and this time the corresponding notes have disappeared. One cannot too much deplore the savaging of this journal, for it was, as writing, one of Boswell's very best. An undated and truncated vignette on the further brink of the second hiatus shows us the quality of what we have lost. It appears that his tireless patrolling had brought back the affliction of sore toe-nails:

He came to me this morning, and a terrible operation he had of it; and after all was obliged to leave so much of the nail in till he should get the proud flesh brought down. He was an old, formal, lean man, pretty tall, in a brown coat and red waistcoat and long light-coloured bob-wig. He actually told me that he had always a turn for this profession, and when a boy used to get apples from the maids for cutting their nails. He was a Methodist, and whined grievously, giving one no comfort but making the pain seem worse than it really was, though I do not think he had anything of a quack. But I shall know that when paying time comes.

John Dick was not the only one of his Italian acquaintances whom he was able to greet in London. Giuseppe (now generally called Joseph)

Bolingbroke." He had divorced his wife, Lady Diana Spencer, by act of Parliament on 10 March, and she had married Johnson's friend Topham Beauclerk two days later. The story to which Boswell refers has not been traced. It would not have been brought out in the divorce action, for the evidence of misbehaviour presented concerned only Lady Diana, but may well have circulated as gossip at the time. "Bob Derry's" is unidentified, but was probably a low tavern.

[1] Boswell's punctuation, one line-ending counted as a dash. "Great Piazza" was probably the Bedford Coffee-house "under the Piazza [arcade] in Covent Garden." " 'Tis the barber" is defined by Francis Grose as "a ridiculous and unmeaning phrase, in the mouths of the common people about the year 1760, signifying their approbation of any action, measure, or thing."

Baretti, who had provided the best moments of his stay in Venice in the summer of 1765, had been unable to continue his review, and after some fruitless months in Ancona and Leghorn had returned to England, where he was to spend nearly all the rest of his life. He had just published (7 March) an *Account of the Manners and Customs of Italy* which would divide the honours of the reviews with Boswell's *Account of Corsica.* The two authors had exchanged books, and Baretti, going to call, had been rudely treated at a door he believed to be Boswell's. Johnson (always a staunch friend) had spoken highly of both Baretti and his book, and Boswell on his return from Oxford had hunted Baretti up. He was able to vindicate himself (Baretti had actually knocked at the door of a Mr. Bousfield), but as Baretti's ill humour evaporated, Boswell began to develop an antipathy of his own. Baretti's manners, which he had been able to make allowance for in Venice, struck him now as brutally rough; and he found it hard to forgive the harsh things that Baretti said about the Corsicans.

We also pick up fine accounts of a call on the female Whig historian, Mrs. Catharine Macaulay ("She was very complimentative to me, but formal and affected, and she whined about liberty as an old Puritan would whine about grace") ; of a fruitless visit to the Bow Street court of the blind justice Sir John Fielding, brother of the novelist, to complain of having been cheated in some fashion which the fragmentary state of the journal leaves mysterious; and of a dinner of schoolmasters and dissenting ministers whom Dilly had collected to honour him ("The most direct compliments were paid to me without the least delicacy. . . . 'Mr. Boswell is a very respectable character!' ").

If compliments had been Boswell's sole aim, he could have got them in plenty without further fighting of the battle of Corsica. He was, however, equally concerned with getting British aid for the Corsican revolution; and half his motive for this London trip had been to organize groups to press for it. It was this persistent campaigning that had caused Johnson, whose notions about the likelihood of improving one's political lot by revolution were pessimistic in the extreme, to advise him to empty his head of Corsica. The reply that Boswell sent when he got the letter illustrates the inflated style he considered appropriate for propaganda:

Empty my head of Corsica? Empty it of honour, empty it of humanity, empty it of friendship, empty it of piety? No! While I live,

Corsica and the cause of the brave islanders shall ever employ much of my attention.

The situation was indeed critical. By 1767, France, which had entered Corsica as debtor to Genoa, had become a creditor, and had begun to adopt a firmer tone. Choiseul, the French prime minister, submitted to Paoli certain alternative terms on which the differences between Genoa and the insurgents could be accommodated. Under all of them the French were to retain bases in the island. Paoli expressed his willingness to negotiate if permanent possession by the French was not contemplated and the Corsican government could choose the sites. Choiseul (who professed to be scandalized because Paoli addressed the King of France on terms of diplomatic equality) made clear that the French would choose their bases and would hold them outright. Paoli (about the time Boswell's book appeared) replied that he could not accept such terms, for the General Consulta had solemnly sworn to enter into no treaty that did not recognize the independence of the entire island. He later said that he believed that Choiseul had never been sincere, and that nothing less than total annexation had been intended from the first.

On 6 April, following a call in *The London Chronicle* for the celebration of Paoli's birthday, Boswell organized the Corsican Club at the Queen's Arms in St. Paul's Churchyard.

James Boswell, Esq. was President. . . . The following healths were drank: the King, Queen, and Royal Family; Pascal Paoli; Success to the Brave Corsicans; May the Corsicans be Countenanced by Every State Which has a Just Value for Liberty; Lord Halifax; Lord Shelburne; Lord Lyttelton; General Conway; Horace Walpole; Dr. Franklin; Mrs. Macaulay.

The absence of Wilkes's name—and it may have taken some manoeuvring to keep it off the list—shows that Boswell and his advisers considered it very important that the Corsican movement should not be compromised by conspicuous Patriot backing.

He continued to supply the newspapers with Corsican "facts" and "inventions," the aim of the "inventions" being to shame the British people by showing that while they hesitated, others were generous and fearless. Prussia (so two paragraphs ran) was about to step forward as the guardian of liberty. Frederick the Great had held a grand review of some of his best troops. They were equipped for fighting in mountainous country, and Frederick had said to Sir Andrew Mitchell, "By and by I shall make you Englishmen blush." The Dutch were concluding a treaty with the Corsicans under which they would send a formidable fleet to their assistance. The ships which the Genoese were fitting out for the French might be used to invade England after the conquest of Corsica. Boswell also sent to the newspapers serious anonymous essays urging the military and economic importance of Corsica, and solicited similar letters from his friends. It was no doubt his plan to make these letters something like the slightly later Junius series, and to collect them in a volume.

Immediately after the meeting at the Queen's Arms, Boswell's raging caught up with him, and he paid for his greedy and reckless assaults on pleasure by the usual retirement of six weeks. It was at least a dose for Boswell if Boswell must have a dose. His surgeon, Mr. Forbes of the Horse Guards, assured him it was one of the worst he had ever seen. Percivall Pott, the foremost surgeon of the day (Pott's disease, Pott's fracture), had finally to be called in, and altogether Boswell spent more than half of his London jaunt in his elegant lodgings at Mr. Russell's, upholsterer, Half Moon Street, Piccadilly.

He was not allowed to languish in solitude. We have no notes covering the first two weeks of his confinement, but his surviving letters from the period and the scrappy record he kept for the twenty-six days from 21 April to 16 May list over one hundred calls from fifty-one different callers. We have here evidence of the sort that Johnson would have appealed to for testing the unfortunately common assumption that if Boswell met a great many interesting people, it was only because he forced himself on them in spite of their teeth and their doors. Undoubtedly, some of the fifty-one were invited, and undoubtedly some came from a sense of duty, but with all qualifications, the list is a most impressive testimony to the personal esteem in which Boswell was held in the spring of 1768. And the concentration of notables among his callers was remarkably high. Of the fifty-one, twenty-three—forty-five per cent—have gained admission to the *Dictionary of National Biography*. Surely no other private person in Britain that spring was so much sought after as James Boswell.

Of all the attentions he received, I should suppose that he would have found Lord Lyttelton's the most exciting. It was not merely that Lyttelton enjoyed a considerable reputation as an author and had been the friend of Pope, Thomson, and Fielding (imagine receiving a call from the man to whom *Tom Jones* was dedicated!) but he had also held many high positions in Government and was willing to use his influence to further the cause of Corsica. He gave Boswell permission when his book was printed again to include in it a very complimentary letter recommending British intervention, and he reported that the Earl of Hardwicke, a Rockingham Whig without office, was sympathetic to the Corsicans and disposed to help in the House of Lords. Boswell sent a letter asking permission to wait on Hardwicke when he should again be able to go abroad, but nothing came of it except the advice—relayed through Lyttelton—not to come to people's doors as though one were a minister, and not to lecture ministers, but to get properly introduced and then hint measures. Both peers clearly deprecated measures like his informal descent on Pitt two years before, and wanted him to collect solid statistics to show what Britain would gain in a commercial and military way from an alliance with Corsica. Several of the other callers came to consult seriously about the Corsican campaign. Sir John Dick dropped in no fewer than twelve times; old General Oglethorpe, whose self-introduction to Boswell has already been mentioned, brought two essays for the newspapers, and later produced a third.

Dr. John Armstrong called, Garrick dined tête-à-tête, Baretti argued against the Revolution of 1688 and said that the people of England never thought of God but with "damn" annexed. Sir John Pringle and Benjamin Franklin dined, and Franklin put the question whether infidels or Protestants had done more to pull down popery. Hume and Johnson came on the same day, but fortunately at different times. Hume, placid as usual, remarked that it required great goodness of disposition to withstand the baleful effects of Christianity, and demonstrated his own non-Christian benevolence by coming a second time on purpose to tell Boswell that the Duke of Bedford was very fond of *An Account of Corsica*. Johnson, who had been ill and was in bad spirits, said kind things about the book, but declined to review it: "People would say it was one ass scratching another." And, like Baretti, he talked roughly against popular liberty.

One can only speculate as to why there is no mention of a call from Goldsmith. He and Boswell had never been intimate friends, but Boswell had called on him both in 1763 and 1766, and he appears prominently in the three other London journals which Boswell wrote in his lifetime. Boswell's interest in him should have increased rather than diminished, for since they had last seen each other, Goldsmith had published *The*

Vicar of Wakefield and had written a comedy (*The Good Natur'd Man*) which Johnson declared to be the best in forty years. Perhaps they did meet and the record is lost—Boswell's records for this spring are riddled with gaps. Or perhaps Goldsmith was not in London during the time of Boswell's visit, and Boswell could not spare time to hunt him out in the country.

Johnson's and Baretti's strictures on liberty were occasioned by the popular tumults of the day, which, if not directly fomented by Wilkes's sympathizers, were certainly being exploited by them. "Wilkes and Liberty" had been the cry at election riots in Lancaster and Newcastle as well as in Middlesex. The coal-heavers at Wapping had struck for higher wages and had been forcibly repressed, and strikes by the sailors, sawyers, and weavers were soon to follow. After his triumph at Brentford, Wilkes had surrendered to his outlawry, as he had promised he would, and on 27 April had been committed to the King's Bench Prison. His riotous sympathizers congregated in increasing numbers in St. George's Fields, near the prison, and on 10 May proposed to release him and conduct him to take his seat in Parliament, which opened on that day. They were dispersed with bloodshed and some loss of life by a detachment of Foot Guards who unfortunately happened to be Scots. On 8 June the judges reversed the outlawry on a technicality but confirmed the convictions for libel, and later in the same month sentenced Wilkes to a fine of £1000 and two years in gaol, inclusive of the time he had already spent there. But, as we have seen, Boswell remained a spectator of these stirring events. He did not meet Wilkes again till four years later, by which time Wilkes was alderman and Sheriff of London. I have already suggested that one of his motives for this unpleasantly correct behaviour was to keep his Corsican campaign free from Wilkesite connexions. The attitude of the Government was unpromising at best, and would have hardened into downright opposition if the "Paoli and Liberty" movement had come to appear at all subservient to "Wilkes and Liberty."

Five days after the "massacre" of St. George's Fields, France signed a secret treaty with Genoa by which Genoa in effect ceded its rights in Corsica to France, and the plan to invade Corsica was avowed. The Earl of Rochford, British ambassador to France, asked for authority to demand that Choiseul declare his intentions, but the Ministry was so concerned by the riots and strikes that the authority was not immediately granted.

Meanwhile, amid all his other interests, Boswell had pushed his suit of Belle de Zuylen to a conclusion. We have seen how on the day after his arrival in London he had written to his father begging permission to go over to Utrecht to confer. Lord Auchinleck and Temple both wrote strongly against the scheme, which of course made it no less attractive to Boswell. And Belle grew actually tender. "My friend Boswell," she wrote to d'Hermenches, "has just sent me his book. . . . The heroism of that people, the great qualities of their chief, the genius of the author—it is all interesting and admirable. . . . I am going to try to translate it." Her correct taste found some parts of the book unfortunate ("Here and there it contains singularities which you will think ridiculous and I myself don't care much for"), but her tone in speaking of them is apologetic. It is evident that the reading of Boswell's charming account had shaken the bastion of her scepticism more than anything that had happened to her for a long time. She conceived a quite enthusiastic regard for Paoli ("my hero!"), and even became an ardent partisan of the Corsicans. She devoured (in an English translation) the lives of Plutarch, never having been able to get through a single one of them until Boswell put her in the Plutarchian mood. She translated, though she found translation surprisingly difficult and boring. And she began again to find Boswell odd but lovable. "My dear friend," she wrote (in English), "it is prejudice that has kept you so much at a distance from me. If we meet, I am sure that prejudice will be removed." Off went another earnest appeal to Lord Auchinleck for permission to go to Utrecht, with a promise to make no engagement but only to bring a faithful report and let him decide. "How do we know but she is an inestimable prize? Surely it is worth while to go to Holland to see a fair conclusion, one way or other, of what has hovered in my mind for years."

He had his second chance, and with tact and humility he could have had her. But the old compulsion *not* to marry her or any but one woman whom he has never yet discussed as a matrimonial possibility drove him again to trample the proud heart so trustfully exposed.

I have written to her and told her all my perplexity. I have put in the plainest light what conduct I absolutely require of her, and what my father will require. I have bid her be my wife at present and comfort me with a letter in which she shall show at once her wisdom, her spirit, and her regard for me. [Tell me that I am the severe Cato. Tell me that you will make a very good wife.] You shall see it. I tell you, man, she knows

me and values me as you do. . . . I am very ill. My surgeon, Mr. Forbes of
the Horse Guards, says my distemper is one of the worst he has seen. I
wish I may be able to go to Holland at all.

Part of the conduct he absolutely required of her he does not think it
necessary to specify. Belle, who was well along in her translation of *An
Account of Corsica,* had asked if she might make a few changes and leave
a few passages out. He peremptorily vetoed the request.

He need not have worried about the possibility that his illness would
keep him confined so long that there would not be time for a trip to Holland: his letter did the business very satisfactorily. He wrote laconically in
his notes for 2 May, "Letter from Zélide, termagant!" and a few days
later expanded for Temple:

My dearest friend, you are much in the right. . . . I told you what sort
of letter I last wrote to her. It was candid, fair, conscientious. I told her of
many difficulties. I told her my fears from her levity and infidel notions, at
the same time admiring her and hoping she was altered for the better. How
did she answer? Read her letter. Could any actress at any of the theatres
attack one with a keener—what is the word? not *fury,* something softer.
The lightning that flashes with so much brilliance may scorch. And does
not her *esprit* do so? Is she not a termagant, or at least will she not be one
by the time she is forty? And she is near thirty now. . . . I was . . . afraid
that my father . . . might have consented to my going to Utrecht. But I
send you his answer, which is admirable if you make allowance for his
imagining that I am not dutiful towards him. I have written to him, " 'I
will take the Ghost's word for a thousand pounds.' " . . .[1] As for Zélide, I
have written to her that we are agreed. "My pride," says I, "and your
vanity would never agree. It would be like the scene in our burlesque comedy, *The Rehearsal.* 'I am the bold thunder,' cries one. 'The quick lightning, I,' cries another. Et voilà notre ménage."

Belle provides the last word in a letter she wrote to d'Hermenches on
2 June:

I will with a good deal of pleasure write out what you request; it will
be a brief epitome of an interesting book which I am fond of but which I
am no longer translating. I was far advanced in the task, but I wanted
permission to change some things that were bad and to abridge others
which French impatience would have found unmercifully long-winded.

[1] *Hamlet,* III. ii. 297. The Ghost was Hamlet's father.

The author, though at the moment he had almost made up his mind to marry me if I would have him, refused to sacrifice to my taste one syllable of his book. I wrote him that I was firmly decided never to marry him, and I abandoned the translation.

Was it perhaps in the end Boswell's literary vanity that she found intolerable?

During his period of invalidism, Boswell read the Bible, as he usually did when suffering for immorality, accompanying the Scriptures this time with Lord Lyttelton's *Observations on the Conversion and Apostleship of St. Paul.* He made many moral reflections, told Temple he was positive he would never go astray again were it from nothing else but the dread of pain, and wrote to Paoli pledging his honour that he would yield no more to fleshly vice. Yet on the last day recorded in his fragmentary notes (perhaps the last day of his confinement) he confesses himself "quite in love with opposite lady," who had indicated to him by a gesture that he can write, even if he can't get out; he has sent her a note and has received a "pretty answer." "I have really a strange fortune for adventures," is his comment. The notes break off in a manner reminiscent of the *Sentimental Journey:* "But let's see_____." Whether this particular "adventure" came to anything cannot now be determined, but it is evident that neither the recollection of recent pain nor the pledge of his honour to Paoli kept him from raging again as soon as he got out. His excuse probably was that he could properly swear off only on a surfeit. At any rate, shortly before he left London (probably on Sunday 5 June) he made a vow in St. Paul's Church that he would not indulge in licentious connexions of any kind for six months. This was effective for some time, and for all we know to the contrary, may have been effective for a year. There had been nothing like that since Holland.

He had to pack a great deal into the days that remained after he was able to go abroad, but little of what he did is now recoverable. From a newspaper we learn that he went to Court and made a smart remark about General Paoli. His fragmentary notes preserve at considerable length two conversations that he had with Lord Mansfield, Chief Justice of the King's Bench, and the *Life of Johnson* records a dinner at which Johnson tossed and gored several persons. In 1768 the conversations with Mansfield were undoubtedly more important to Boswell than the dinner with Johnson. The Douglas Cause appeal would before long be decided by the House of

Lords, and Mansfield's opinion there would be of the utmost importance. There were at the time only two law lords, Mansfield himself and Lord Camden, the Chancellor; and if they were in agreement, no general vote of the House would be taken. Furthermore, as a member of the Privy Council who had twice held the seals of the Exchequer and had had a brilliant career in the House of Commons, Mansfield could if he chose be very useful to the cause of Corsica. Boswell yearned to instruct him on both issues. Mansfield (his name was William Murray) was a Scot from a Jacobite family, but he had been educated at Westminster and Oxford and had been called to the English bar, and though he and Boswell had many common acquaintances (including, for example, Mansfield's Jacobite brother, Lord Dunbar), Boswell had never met him. He seems simply to have walked in, to have been courteously received, and to have been allowed to harangue on the Douglas Cause, which Mansfield professed not to have studied. Encouraged by this, he grew so *étourdi* as to say something kind of Wilkes, whose motion for reversal of outlawry was coming up in Mansfield's own court, and who was charging Mansfield himself with having illegally altered the informations in the libel actions. Mansfield obviously did not like this, but it was Boswell's impression that his resentment was only temporary. Before he left, he also felt that he had convinced Mansfield of the importance of Corsica. He was wrong on both counts, as later appeared. He left for Scotland on 9 June, arrived in Edinburgh in the evening of the 13th, and was in Court the next morning.

We may seize the opportunity furnished by a break in the records to write Finis to the story of Belle de Zuylen.

"She and I will always be good correspondents," Boswell had said in informing Temple that Belle de Zuylen would never be his wife, but he seems never again to have written to her nor she to him. We shall hear no more of her and we shall miss her, for she was the most interesting woman and one of the most extraordinary persons Boswell ever met. She would probably have been vastly unhappy with him, but perhaps no unhappier than she was without him. In 1771 she married her brothers' tutor (a match greatly beneath her) and went to live in the manor of Colombier at Neuchâtel. Boswell, visiting the *château* of Colombier in 1764, must have looked down unknowingly upon the very house where she was to pass so many weary days and at last to die. Irony is useful for an author but is perhaps not the best state of mind for happy living. Belle's early rebellion against society turned into a scornful retreat from it. At Colombier she became a virtual recluse, declining even to know her neighbor Voltaire. She occupied herself with philanthropy, with the harpsichord, with the composition of slender novels. M. de Charrière, her husband, a good and intelligent man, loved her deeply, but he was cold and reserved. She was childless. In middle age the great affair for which she was destined came to her: a handsome but otherwise unremarkable young man, much younger than she, inspired her with profound passion and then left her for another woman, whom he married. She went through a period of deep depression, and then in 1787 (she was forty-six and he was nineteen) she met Benjamin Constant de Rebecque, nephew of her old correspondent d'Hermenches, an extraordinary red-headed youth as odd and lovable as Boswell and endowed with the kind of scornful wit which she relished. For eight years they kept up an ambiguous intimate relationship, which at times, at least, gave her great happiness. (They joked about Boswell, too, as Constant's letters show.) But in 1794 Mme. de Staël stole Benjamin. Belle withdrew even more into herself. Geoffrey Scott, whom I have been paraphrasing, should have the summing up: "Her . . . emotions, naturally profound, were tortured by her intellect; she could enchant, but more often than enchantment she inspired fear, which she could not explain, and pity, which she scorned. . . . She staked all on her intimate life, and, losing, preserved a stoical silence: a van Tuyll after all, a stickler for old-fashioned good manners, and, to the end, intolerant as Johnson himself of cant, self-deception, loose thinking and illogical speech." Though long a confirmed invalid, she outlived Boswell by ten years.

CHAPTER

XXII

When Boswell, in Edinburgh, keeps no journal and writes few letters, it generally means, not that he is idle but that he is being extremely active in a routine that neither excites nor bores him. His fee book (civil and criminal consultations during the Summer Session of 1768 and the ensuing autumn circuits) assures us that he was as much on the stretch after he returned to Scotland as he had been in London, but of his business he made no record beyond his impersonal professional registers, and of these only the fee book has come down to us.

Three concerns of the summer seemed to him important enough to report to Temple after the Session was over and he had got to Auchinleck. He had devoted a disquieting amount of time to gaming, he had purchased an imposing train of artillery for the Corsicans, and he was finally absolutely fixed in his choice for a bride.

His rage for gambling had subsided under the restrictions imposed by his agreement with Sheridan, and he had supposed that it was quite gone, but it had seized him again and must have kept him playing fiercely through his free hours during most of the Session, for he made it the chief article in his apology for letting Temple go without news for more than three months. How much harm it might have done, he says, he does not know, but after he had succeeded in reducing his losses to fourteen guineas —what shocking total they had previously reached he does not report— he had been able to quit, and he had made a resolution never to play again but for a trifle to make up a party. The resolution was as well kept as his other nevers. There is no later record of spells of gambling extending over weeks and months, but throughout the rest of his life in Edinburgh he was to be periodically plagued by the return of the gaming rage, generally as no more than an uncomfortable and unbecoming keenness in what should have been mere social relaxation, rarely by a thirst for play and more play that would keep him at cards from supper-time right around to the opening of the Court next morning. In view of his liberality concerning some of his other vices, it is surprising to find how bad a conscience he had about this one. The summer's loss of fourteen guineas made gaming an extravagant but hardly a ruinous pastime. The reason, I suppose, was that he really did have an ingrained habit of narrowness with regard to reckonings, which acted as a governor on his passion for play.

It was now known that the French had sent a force to invade Corsica. At the end of May, Shelburne had finally sent Rochford the decision of the Ministry, authorizing him to state that the annexation of territory by France could not be indifferent to England, and might endanger the peace of Europe. Rochford communicated these sentiments with great firmness. The greater part of the British nation, he said, looked upon the Corsican expedition as a violation of the treaty of Aix-la-Chapelle. The English people were deeply sympathetic with the Corsican patriots. Choiseul interrupted him "and said he knew it; that Boswell's *Account of Corsica* had made a great noise; that he had ordered it to be translated." He professed not to have expected this firmness and to be staggered by it. Had he foreseen the British attitude, he said, he would never have undertaken the business, and would now abandon it if there were any way in which he could do so and save his honour and that of France. Meanwhile he postponed the departure of Chauvelin, the commander of the Corsican expedition.

He may well have been alarmed, for the French policy with regard to Corsica was his own creation and was not supported by popular sentiment. The French people hardly yielded to the British in their admiration of Paoli (whom they now began to learn of from Boswell's book) and in their good wishes for Corsican independence. If the British government had continued to maintain a firm front and had shown it by some threatening gesture, Choiseul's enemies might well have forced his retirement and repudiated his Corsican policy. But Choiseul did not believe that the British cabinet would really stand by the instructions it had sent Rochford, and events very soon proved him right.

The ministry, to the satisfaction of the King, was divided and weak. Pitt, the nominal prime minister, was ill and in retirement, and the Duke of Grafton was actual head of the government. He had had to turn for support to the Duke of Bedford and his party, and had a bare and precarious majority in the Cabinet. The policy of Pitt and Grafton was one of firmness with France and Spain; that of Bedford (in spite of his admiration of *An Account of Corsica*), of peace with France and Spain and of strong measures against the Americans and the Wilkesites. The King was convinced that with the national debt at such a level, it was highly inexpedient to risk a war with France on the sole issue of Corsica. Lord Weymouth, Secretary of State for the Northern Department, spoke out against interference. Lord Mansfield, at the table of a minister in Paris, declared that the English ministry were too weak and the nation too wise to enter on a war for the sake of Corsica. Shelburne alone was consistently for a bold front. Grafton decided on the weak and ineffective policy of sending secret aid to the Corsicans in the form of arms and ammunition. Choiseul was soon assured that decisive action was not to be feared and dispatched Chauvelin. By August of 1768 the invasion had begun, the French attacking the Corsicans before the treaty of 1764 had expired.

The numerous group of Corsican sympathizers in Britain, frustrated by the indecisiveness of the Government, talked as though they wanted to do something. On 6 July 1768, following up an earlier proposal by "An Englishman," whose identity has not been established, Boswell published a letter in *The Public Advertiser* urging a voluntary Corsican subscription and providing practical suggestions for setting such a subscription on foot. The fact that he signed it with the initials "O. P." rather than his own name reminds us that the Proclamation of 1763 had not been repealed, and that to assist the Corsican insurgents was still criminal. The proposal was not merely notional for he and Crosbie were at the moment actually conducting a subscription in Scotland. By the time he wrote to Temple on 24 August, they had purchased for Paoli from the Carron Company over £700 worth of ordnance—thirty cannon of varying sizes, with powder and shot, "really a tolerable train of artillery," as Boswell said. The vessel on which they were embarked was driven by a storm as far north as the Orkneys and suffered such damage that the cargo had to be reshipped, but the second vessel reached Leghorn before the end of the year. Paoli wrote gratefully on hearing that the guns were on the way, and it is probable that they were landed in Corsica in time to be of some use. Since speed was of the essence, Boswell and Crosbie underwrote the purchase before they had subscriptions to anything like £700, found the money hard to collect—Sir Adam Fergusson paid his subscription twenty-two years later, and then only because of a judgement against him by the

Court of Session, Crosbie by that time being dead—and ended by putting in considerably more of their own money than either could afford.

But Boswell's chief piece of news was that at last, after all, finally his heart was fixed. One can imagine Temple's "O no!" on learning that the lady was some one he had never heard of. "I am exceedingly lucky in having escaped the insensible Miss B_____ and the furious Zélide, for I have now seen the finest creature that ever was formed: *la belle irlandaise.*" The week before, he had gone over to visit his Lainshaw cousins and had found that they were being visited by cousins from Ireland: Mr. Charles Boyd of Killaghy and his wife, their daughter Mary Anne, and Mr. Boyd's brother's wife, Mrs. Hugh Boyd.

Figure to yourself, Temple, a young lady just sixteen, formed like a Grecian nymph, with the sweetest countenance, full of sensibility, accomplished, with a Dublin education, always half a year in the north of Ireland, her father a counsellor-at-law with an estate of £1000 a year and above £10,000 in ready money, her mother a sensible, well-bred woman, she the darling of her parents and no other child but her sister. . . . I never was so much in love. I never was before in a situation to which there was not some objection. "But here ev'ry flow'r is united."

He is invited to visit the Boyds in Ireland and has promised to go in March when the Session rises. Mrs. Hugh Boyd has told him seriously that nothing can defeat his suit except his own inconstancy. He has walked with Mary Anne, he has repeated his fervent passion to her, he has carved her initial on a tree, he has cut off a lock of her hair.

This is the most agreeable passion I ever felt. Sixteen, innocence, and gaiety make me quite a Sicilian swain. . . . Maria has me without any rival. I do hope the period of my perfect felicity as far as this state of being can afford is now in view.

"But here ev'ry flow'r is united"—of course he has not forgotten that he had applied that same verse to Catherine Blair only a year before, and he is counting on Temple not to have forgotten. "I mean not to ask what you think of my angelic girl; I am fixed beyond a possibility of doubt," he writes, but as usual he can see himself quite clearly *ab extra* and he knows just how absurd his certainty is. The role of Thyrsis is delightful ("No reserved, prudent, cautious conduct as with Miss B.; no, all youthful, warm, natural") and he enters into it to the full, but it is more the feeling of himself as youthful shepherd that he savours than any genuine passion for his youthful Amaryllis. As a matter of fact, he thought her childish, and he was rather repelled than attracted by the thought of intimacies with a child. One might reasonably have supposed that his confident announcement that *here* every flower was united was emphatic confirmation of his rejection of Catherine Blair, but within a month or so after meeting Mary Anne he was at Adamton having a long talk with the Heiress beside her own wood. It may have been mere cousinly routine, or he may have gone to punish her ("I told her how I adored the fair Hibernian"), but it is much more likely that he wanted to confront Arcadia with Ayrshire and his Grecian nymphet with a handsome stately woman. He learned to his surprise that she was not to have Sir Sawney after all: neither had come up to expectation at the weighing-in. He began at once to think regretfully of lost opportunity ("Alas, what could I say to her while my heart was beyond the sea?"). Indeed, he found double cause for regret: "Were it not that I am in love beyond the salt sea, I have a notion that my neighbour Miss Gordon of Stair would be the woman. I have as good as told her so."

He had probably made his visit to Adamton during the sitting of the circuit court at Ayr in September. He reported to Johnston that he had attended the courts at both Ayr and Dumfries and said the circuit had been "riotous" (that is, hard-drinking), but gave no detail of his business.

We know, however, of one important cause that he undertook at this time: the defence of that Harris, merchant in Ayr, who had charged his clients Hay and McClure with attempted assassination. Harris was now himself indicted on the capital charge of forging bank-notes. His cause, which was appointed for the courts in Edinburgh, dragged on through many months and turned out to be one of the most spectacular that Boswell ever put his hand to, for Harris escaped from the Tolbooth in Edinburgh, was recaptured in England, slogged a turnkey in a second attempt at escape, and feigned insanity when brought to trial. I do not think Boswell liked him much or that he expended much emotion in the cause. Its chief significance for him was that it landed him at its outset in a predicament from which he had to ask Henry Dundas to extricate him; and since settled antagonism to Dundas was to become one of the more powerful passions of his later career, a biographer feels an obligation to scan all their earlier conjunctions closely. As I interpret the evidence, Boswell had sent Harris a letter of advice that was professionally indiscreet, and his letter, through a seizure of Harris's effects, threatened to fall into the hands of the Crown. Boswell asked Dundas to retrieve it from the teller of a Glasgow bank who had assisted in searching Harris's effects. Dundas acted energetically, but declined to approach Alexander (the teller) until he had assurance that Alexander really had power to produce and deliver the letter. "My reason is that it should not be entrusted in too many hands that you are in such a scrape, because when many are in the knowledge, it unavoidably gets air, which is the very thing we are so anxious to prevent." If, as seems likely, Dundas on this occasion did save Boswell from professional embarrassment, one thinks it might have been becoming in Boswell to show more than a temporary sense of gratitude. My guess is, firstly, that the favour granted was not special but was the kind of cover-up service that any advocate (including even the second law-officer of the Crown) might be counted on to perform for any other member of the fraternity whose professional zeal had got him into a fix not absolutely criminal; and, secondly, that Boswell, in asking the favour, had had to dissemble no strong feeling of aversion. He had experienced a flicker of jealousy at Dundas's spectacularly early promotion, but as yet felt no settled antagonism.

Of course he shelved Mary Anne when he learned that the Heiress was free, and went back to Adamton again. Mrs. Blair, whom Temple had tagged "the wary mother," now gave every appearance of wishing to deal without stratagem. It was, she told Boswell, his own fault that her daughter had not long since been his wife. She had shown him very particular marks of regard, and he had made a joke of their courtship. She had been piqued, and had decided that his intentions were not serious. The Nabob too told Boswell that Miss B.'s confidante had told him in the previous year that she was in love with Boswell and counted on having him. On these assurances Boswell at last quit hedging and made unqualified proposals. He knelt, he pleaded, he wrote the most passionate letters. But it turned out that the mother was not pulling the strings after all. Miss Blair remained quite cool and collected and told Boswell she did not like him enough to marry him. "Only think of this, Temple. She might have had me."

We can now cross another name off our list, for Miss Blair meant it. She took her time in choosing a husband, married her cousin Sir William Maxwell of Monreith in 1776, sold Adamton in 1783, and died in 1798.

It is not on record that she ever regretted not taking James Boswell when she could have had him.

And though Girolama Piccolomini cannot properly be said ever to have been on the list, we must now bid adieu to her too, though with more regret. Boswell had had three letters from her during 1767, and though he had reported that one of them made him cry, he let the last go almost a year before replying. When, on 5 November 1768, he did answer it, at the same time as one from the Reverend Robert Richardson, he got his letters mixed up after sealing them and sent it to Richardson at The Hague, at the same time sending to Girolama the letter intended for Richardson. Girolama (who could not read English) finally took advice and figured out what had happened, and Richardson promptly returned to Boswell the letter intended for Girolama, but Boswell seems to have thought it best to let the *contretemps* terminate a relationship which remained for him a glowing memory but was becoming increasingly unreal at the level of correspondence. Girolama died in 1792, three years before Boswell.

Not a line would the Heiress write, Aunt Boyd in Ireland sent a kind letter, all the charms of sweet Mary Anne revived. "By all that's enchanting, I go to Ireland in March."

The facetious tone which has hitherto invested all Boswell's courtships grows tedious, but Boswell himself fixed that tone irrevocably by his own journal and letters. It cannot convey to us the whole truth. Surely, though he gives us no help whatever in realizing the moments of serious feeling— of anger and bewilderment and hurt—under his pose, we must suspect such moments. Surely, when he dropped his guard and put himself without reservation in Catherine Blair's refusal, the refusal could only have stung him painfully. And it would be wrong to underestimate the anxiety concerning Corsica that he had to endure during this year and half the next. The Corsican news that was sent him for inclusion in *The London Chronicle* continued to be encouraging, but Paoli's own letters to him must have made clear, as Sir Horace Mann's to Sir John Dick were doing, that Corsica could not withstand the French force without aid from some great power.

As we have seen, the British Government, after an initial posture of firmness, became paralyzed through lack of unity. Among the active members of the Government, only Shelburne advocated strong measures with France. Grafton, at the King's urging, wrote to Chatham demanding that Shelburne be dismissed. Chatham resigned, and he and Shelburne left the Government almost simultaneously (15 and 19 October 1768). The Ministry's inactivity caused great discontent. At the opening of Parliament on 8 November, the Opposition attacked the Government on the score of its Corsican policy. Burke, Beckford, Grenville, Dunning, Sir Charles Saunders, and Isaac Barré spoke, demanding that England aid Corsica even at the risk of war. The motion, however, which the Opposition tried to push through—that the Ministry be required to lay before the House of Commons all its secret correspondence concerning Corsica since the beginning of 1767—seemed more to intend the humiliation of the Government than help to the Corsicans. Many members who were sympathetic to Corsica found themselves unable to support so dangerous a precedent, and the motion was lost. Much of the material presented in the debate to establish the importance of Corsica came out of Boswell's book. Some people, indeed, felt that the whole Corsican business had too much Boswell in it, as is amusingly shown by a frequently quoted letter which Lord Holland wrote to George Selwyn shortly before the opening of Parliament:

Foolish as we are, we cannot be so foolish to go to war because Mr. Boswell has been in Corsica, and yet, believe me, no better reason can be given for siding with the vile inhabitants of one of the vilest islands in the world.

After 17 November 1768 it was clear that Corsica would receive no open assistance from the Government of Great Britain.

Boswell's *British Essays in Favour of the Brave Corsicans,* a little book of roughly 150 pages which appeared about the first of December, seems therefore to have missed the boat so far as direct effect on political action was concerned. Why its publication was delayed past the opening of Parliament is hard to understand. Perhaps Boswell found the pickings thin and was merely waiting till he could make a respectable collection. *British Essays* consists of only twenty essays or open letters, most of them probably culled from newspapers. They assert the strategic importance of Corsica, enumerate the advantages that would accrue to England from trade with the island, and advance the claim which the cause of Corsican independence has on all lovers of liberty. A copy which Boswell annotated shows that he did not know the authors of eight of the essays. He himself wrote seven, General Oglethorpe wrote three, and Edward Dilly and Sir John Dick wrote one each. The collection lacks the bite which gives literary quality to Junius, but may not therefore have been less effective as propaganda. The most interesting thing about the book now is its engraved allegorical frontispiece. Corsica, France, and England are presented as the usual female figures with identifying emblems. Corsica seeks protection under the shield of England from France, who approaches to stab her in the back. Let Boswell's printed "Explanation of the Frontispiece" continue:

In a corner is a basso-relievo of the old fable of the Lion and the Mouse. The Lion had shown kindness to the Mouse. Some time after, the Lion was entangled in a net and could not help himself, when the Mouse came, and discovering his benefactor, gnawed the net and let the Lion escape. The fable shows that a very inconsiderable man, or a very small state, may have an opportunity of repaying a kindness to the greatest.

The mixture of humility and vanity is excessively Boswellian, as is also the primer-like unriddling of a very obvious allegory. But candour should compel even the most impatient reader to grant that Boswell is thus heavy-handed when he is writing for the masses; and secondly that without his "Explanation" most of us would have missed the prophetic dimension of his allegory, in which the Mouse becomes Corsica and the Lion England.

Though too late for the debates in Parliament, *British Essays* may have been of some assistance in the next stage of Boswell's activities—the only one left for Englishmen who wished to give some concrete assistance to the Corsican cause. Up to this time, the newspaper appeals for a subscription—some of them certainly from other pens than Boswell's—had been anonymous and abstract. After the debate in Parliament, it seems to have been generally felt that the Proclamation of 1763, though unrepealed, was no longer in force. In *The London Chronicle* for 8–10 December 1768, Boswell printed over his own signature a forthright practical appeal for funds, naming bankers in London and Edinburgh who would receive subscriptions. This long "Memorial for a Contribution in Behalf of the Brave Corsicans" leads off with four paragraphs written by some one whom Boswell calls merely "a writer of distinguished abilities." The "Memorial" was reprinted in at least three magazines, and was followed at frequent intervals by short follow-up advertisements in *The London Chronicle*. When Boswell went to Ireland in the following May, he launched a Corsican subscription there; the newspaper reports of the campaign mention £200 from the small town of Portaferry and £100 from a single contributor, "Mr. Stewart of Newtown"—Alexander Stewart, father of the first Marquess of Londonderry. A group of ladies of the first fashion and fortune were said to be conducting a subscription for Paoli in imitation of the ladies who, in her hour of need, had collected gifts of money for Maria Theresa. A theatrical company at Sunderland gave a benefit for the Corsicans. The Free Society of Artists in London put on view with an admission fee of a shilling the huge full-length of Paoli which Boswell had sent Henry Benbridge to Corsica to paint, and provided a box for further contributions. The amount of money actually paid in to the bankers named in Boswell's appeal was probably disappointing. Though *The London Chronicle* for 21–24 January 1769 reported that over £7000 had been collected, a list of contributions printed in the same paper for 8–10 June totals less than a tenth of that sum. Appeals conducted wholly by newspaper advertisement or letter always bring in much less money than the inexperienced in such matters expect, and in this case many people with a will to give must have been inhibited by a conviction that any sum raised would be too little and too late. Nevertheless, a considerable sum was collected in various ways by various people, and there were few appeals that did not ground ultimately on Boswell's book. Beckford, Trecothick, and Vaughan, with whom Boswell had been in correspondence, solicited their acquaintances in London and sent Paoli a sum credibly reported to have been £3000. The Supporters of the Bill of Rights are said to have remitted £2400. Three Englishmen at Florence—the Duke of Devonshire, Lord Algernon Percy, and Sir Watkin Williams Wynn—are credited with £2000 apiece, and other Englishmen in Florence with £900. Obviously all the figures except those of the soberly itemized acknowledgement by Boswell's bankers should be treated with some scepticism, but it can at least be said that Boswell invented none of these reports. We are more likely to underestimate than to exaggerate the amount of the practical aid to Paoli that he gave or inspired.

The Corsican cause became steadily more desperate, but the Douglas Cause at last terminated in glorious victory. On 19 January 1769, eighteen months after the decision of the Court of Session, the last stage of the historic action opened in the House of Lords. Both sides had reinforced their legal batteries. Douglas's printed case was written by a formidable young barrister named Thurlow, who would later be Lord Chancellor himself: he was so severe on the conduct of the investigation in France by the Duke of Hamilton's agent, Andrew Stuart, that Stuart called him out and the pair fought a savage but bloodless duel while the Cause was still depending. The pleadings covered eleven days, but as the Cause had to be fitted into the other business of the House, it was not until 27 February that judgement was pronounced. Everything depended on the speeches of the law lords, for it was the custom of the peers in general to vote with the law lords when they were in agreement, and, in case of disagreement, to vote with the one they respected most. Lord Mansfield, the Chief Justice, was believed (erroneously, if he told Boswell the truth) to have been a friend of Lady Jane and consequently to favour Douglas, but no personal bias was alleged for Lord Camden (the Chancellor), and he had given no hint of his opinion. Nobody paid much attention to the Duke of Newcastle, who opened with an opinion for Douglas. Lord Sandwich followed on the Hamilton side; he spoke for three hours with much humour but probably not much effect, his main object being to analyse the obstetrical evidence in such a way as to affront the bishops. Camden then rose and began to speak strongly for Douglas, declaring the Hamilton case a tissue of perjury, and saying that if he were sitting in any other court, he would order a jury to find for the appellant. Lord Mansfield followed with an impassioned speech for Douglas. Both judges made much of Lady Jane's character. The decree of the Court of Session was reversed without a division.

Ilay Campbell, one of Douglas's counsel (he was later Lord President of the Court of Session), started instantly to ride post to Scotland with the news. He took the road at about nine o'clock on the evening of 27 February and at half past seven on the evening of 2 March drew up exhausted at the Cross in Edinburgh, waved his hat, and shouted, "Douglas for ever!"

The whole city burst into violent rejoicing: bonfires were lighted and houses illuminated. Boswell, as soon as he heard the news, rushed to tell his father, who, he thought, displayed far too much phlegm. In hope of meeting more demonstrative company, he went to the Cross, where he found a crowd assembling. Operations were planned, and with Boswell at its head, the mob rushed off to break the windows of any one who would not "illuminate"—light up with candles as a sign of rejoicing. The windows of the Lord President and the Lord Justice-Clerk suffered, Boswell remarking, as the stones crashed through the dark windows of the Lord

President's house, that other honest fellows were giving *their* casting votes in their turn. After breaking the Lord President's windows, the rioters attempted to beat in his door, to the no small alarm of his family. Lord Auchinleck, and the other judges who had voted *for* Douglas, could have made themselves the heroes of the evening, but only by submitting to the demand to illuminate. When they stood by the Lord President, their windows went too. An attempt to wreck the apartment of the Duke of Hamilton in Holyrood House (he held it, as has been said, as hereditary keeper) was prevented by the soldiers on guard. The rest of the night was spent in breaking windows of Hamilton sympathizers including Andrew Stuart, whose house (which lay some distance out of town) was made the object of a special excursion of reprisal. The next day the mob insulted the Lord President on his way to the Court and threatened to pull him out of his sedan-chair. As they were clearly preparing for a second riot, the Lord Justice-Clerk appealed to the Commander-in-Chief for Scotland, who sent in a detachment of dragoons. Altogether it must have been the most sizable and satisfactory riot Edinburgh had witnessed since the Porteous affair. The magistrates, after their usual custom, offered a reward for the apprehension of the leaders of the mob.

John Ramsay says that Lord Auchinleck, with tears in his eyes, begged the Lord President to put Boswell in the town gaol. The Lord President was magnanimous, but according to Ramsay, Boswell was called up before the sheriff for examination and asked to tell in his own way what he knew about the riot. Well, said Boswell, he went to the Cross, and there he overheard a group of fellows making plans. Said one of them, "What sort of man is the sheriff? Do we need to be afraid of him?" "No, no," answered another, "he is a puppy of the President's making." Nothing came of the examination: it was always as hard to identify rioters in court in Edinburgh in the eighteenth century as it used to be to identify members of a lynching party in the United States. But outside of court Boswell made no secret of his exploits on the night of the mob, and bragged of them in very miscellaneous company. Lord Marischal congratulated him warmly on breaking his father's windows.

Boswell says that the Duke of Queensberry thanked him by letter for his services in the Douglas Cause. Archibald Douglas, as was only right, was grateful, and for a time even affectionate: he made Boswell one of the principal guests at his coming-of-age party at Bothwell Castle in the following July, engaged him as counsel in the succeeding stages of his litigation with the Duke of Hamilton, and proposed that he be his companion on a tour of Europe.

In conclusion one feels like asking how much effect Boswell's extensive activities in the Douglas Cause really had. They were certainly effective in arousing popular sympathy for Douglas and in inflaming that sympathy to a really dangerous pitch of enthusiasm. So far as the decisions of the courts were concerned, they presumably had no effect at all. It is difficult to believe that the seven hard-headed judges of the Court of Session who voted for Douglas were swayed by *Dorando* or by the public prejudice. It is equally hard to believe that either Camden or Mansfield formed his opinion from reading *The Essence of the Douglas Cause* or Boswell's printing of the *Letters of Lady Jane Douglas*. If there had been a division in the House of Lords, Boswell's popular pleadings might have gained some votes, but as things turned out, the decisions from first to last were in the hand of professional judges.

For the biographer, the episode has great values. It demonstrates, better than almost anything else in Boswell's life, the intense and generous enthusiasm which the feudal principle of Family could rouse in him. It shows, what the world has not hitherto been sufficiently aware of, his shrewdness and skill as a propagandist. He was quite capable of the kind of journalism—brilliant, protean, unscrupulous—which the economics of publishing would not make possible till a century after his death.

There was time before the Irish jaunt to cut one more matrimonial caper. George Dempster had for some months been trying to pay his court to an obdurate young lady whom he and Boswell always mask under the unriddled initial "B." It appears likely that she was one Margaret Craufford, eldest daughter of a prosperous Writer to the Signet, deceased. At any rate, she was an heiress, with property in a mine or mines, and Dempster's affairs were in such shape that her wealth would have been most useful to him. He admitted this quite frankly, but insisted—and his private letters to Boswell bear him out—that he was sincerely and affectingly in love with her. She could not bring herself to think of him as a husband, and, knowing his partiality, refused to allow him access. He thought of addressing her through a common male friend, but had formerly tried to dissuade Boswell, who was some kind of cousin of the lady's and on good terms with her, from efforts in his behalf. In February 1769 he withdrew his prohibition or Boswell persuaded himself that it had been withdrawn. Meeting "B." at supper in company with the Heiress and that Miss Gordon of Stair whom he would have courted if his heart had not been beyond the salt sea, he engaged her in cousinly conversation and fell absolutely in love.

I am positive she saw it. I cried, "Ah! this is wrong, this is wrong." There was I, in torment before this divinity. In one corner, my sweet Marianne was chiding my inconstancy in her simple, lively way. . . . In another corner my friend, like Banquo's ghost, shook his gory locks at me. I endeavoured to rage about Ireland. But I faltered.

"B." broke a rule about not dancing two nights in succession and danced with him at the next Assembly; he was in sea-green and silver and a delirium. "By all that's sacred, *ut vidi, ut perii*.[1] I never in my life was so much in love. . . . I will not see her again till I hear from you."

Dempster duly replied that though "B." had given him the strongest discouragement, he had not yet abandoned his suit. A month later he admitted that there was not a doubt of its being all over, but we hear no more from Boswell of the Lady of the Mine. The Douglas Cause riot may well have shaken him out of his delirium. If she was indeed the Margaret Crauford mentioned, she proved her ability to aim somewhat higher than mere gentlemen like Dempster and Boswell, for in 1771 she married the fifth Earl of Dumfries. She died in 1799.

On the rising of the Session, Boswell and his father went west by way of Glasgow and paused for a six-days' visit at Lainshaw. The cousins' plans to return the Boyds' visit still stood, but for some reason—possibly ill health at Lainshaw, for Boswell speaks of finding his relatives much better than he expected—the jaunt was deferred to the end of April. We have no records whatever from Boswell in the mean time. When, at the beginning of the trip, the journal is resumed, it appears that the plan has been changed and that it is now proposed that only his unmarried Lainshaw cousin Margaret Montgomerie shall accompany him to Ireland; that she has been at Auchinleck on a three-weeks' visit and that the Lainshaw chaise is there to take them on the first leg of their jaunt, but that his father is so averse to the whole scheme that she has faltered in her resolution. Boswell and Margaret are leaving Auchinleck, Boswell still firm in *his* resolution; Lord Auchinleck walks out, and there is no leave-taking. They head for Lainshaw by way of Treesbank, and at Lainshaw Margaret's

[1] "When I saw, how was I undone!" (Virgil, *Eclogues*, viii.42).

two sisters and her elder sister's husband, Captain Montgomerie-Cuninghame, at Boswell's strong urging, agree that the Irish scheme shall stand and that Margaret shall go. There is still some talk of love for Mary Anne, but it soon becomes apparent that Boswell is really in love with Margaret Montgomerie, and that this passion is of a quite different order from anything he has recorded hitherto. He has tended strongly to present all his former infatuations in the mode of comedy, but it is not possible for him to see this one as funny, even for a moment. Nor, though he will continue to strike extravagant poses, is it possible for us either to see it as funny. He does not stop posturing, but he does become very serious. This is the Real Thing.

Who, the reader may well ask, was this Margaret Montgomerie, and why have we not heard of her sooner? She was Boswell's first cousin, youngest daughter then living of David Montgomerie of Lainshaw and of Veronica Boswell, Lord Auchinleck's only sister. The Montgomeries of Lainshaw were cadets of the Montgomeries, earls of Eglinton, and had a plausible claim to the ancient peerage of Lyle. Margaret Montgomerie's grand-uncle, James Montgomerie of Lainshaw, had indeed assumed the title, but had failed to secure recognition of his claim. This James had been childless, and his heir had been his sister's son, David Laing, son of the Reverend Alexander Laing, rector of the established (Episcopal) church of Donaghadee, County Down, North Ireland. Hence the Irish cousins.

The property of Lainshaw, which lay in Stewarton parish some seventeen miles north-west of Auchinleck, was of smaller extent and value than Auchinleck, and was seriously embarrassed. David Laing (he assumed the name Montgomerie) and Veronica Boswell had had one son and four daughters, and both of them died while their children were still young. The son and the youngest daughter were by this time dead; James, the son, had died married but childless in 1766 while still a young man. From Boswell's few references to him one would infer that he was a sportsman of very limited intellectual interests who spent a good deal of time in London roistering with Lord Eglinton. Elizabeth, the eldest daughter, was now laird; she was married to Captain Alexander Montgomerie-Cuninghame, heir apparent to the baronetcy of Corsehill, and was bringing up a family of five attractive but unruly boys and one daughter. Mary, David Montgomerie's second daughter, had married, as second wife, James Campbell of Treesbank, her mother's (and of course Lord Auchinleck's) first cousin. She had one son and was to have another. Margaret, the youngest living daughter, therefore had not the slightest prospect of ever succeeding to Lainshaw, embarrassed or not. Her total fortune consisted of £1000, invested in an annuity. She was consequently, by Auchinleck standards, poor. Boswell had consistently sworn that he would marry no woman who did not have £10,000, and had been living extravagantly on the strength of that assumption.

He had of late been showing a palpitating interest in a girl of sixteen. Margaret Montgomerie was already thirty-one, more than two years his senior, and presumably in the general estimation relegated to the shelf. Boswell had also generally assumed that he could have beauty as well as fortune in a wife. Margaret, by his own description, had a good figure and a very agreeable countenance, but he did not pretend that she was what is called a beauty. (Her best feature seems to have been her eyes. A female observer once said she had at times the pleasantest look: "Her eye glistens.") Her picture shows a handsome woman with masses of black hair, a pointed chin, and considerable width of face across the cheekbones; in fact, she has a not-surprising family resemblance to Boswell himself.

Her entry into the narrative raises problems of reticence that we have hitherto not been troubled with. Boswell's journal and letters silence all a biographer's scruples: "I have a kind of strange feeling as if I wished nothing to be secret that concerns myself." Margaret Montgomerie, on the contrary, makes us feel like intruders. She has humour and brains, but she has no desire to prove it to strangers. She hated Boswell's journal, and predicted (with the sarcastic aptness in which she resembled Lord Auchinleck) that it would leave him "embowelled to posterity." She bore Boswell's extravagances patiently because she was generous and wished him to be happy in his own way, but she greatly preferred reticence and respectability. The epithet "my valuable friend" which he so often applied to her sums up perfectly the respect and affection which he preserved for her to the end of his days. Yet he called her too, and just as sincerely, "my dearest life," and it would be a grave mistake to suppose that he did not find her sexually attractive. Her person, he emphatically told Temple, was to him the most desirable that he had ever seen. She was a woman of generous physical proportions, and when he was honest with himself, he knew that to be his preference. She was "a heathen goddess painted alfresco on the ceiling of a palace at Rome," infinitely superior to "the delicate little Miss."

To have kept the winner out of sight until just before the finish must seem a piece of cheap manoeuvring for effect, but is in fact merely fidelity to the documents. It is not merely that Margaret Montgomerie plays a smaller role than one would have expected in Boswell's journal and letters up to this time; she plays no role at all. Before the spring of 1769 she is hardly mentioned, and when she is mentioned, it is generally only in the most casual manner, not as though she caused the least emotional excitement, not even as though she were a valuable friend. The only document written before April 1769 that even hints at particular intimacy is an odd and obviously jocular agreement of 8 August 1768, written by Boswell himself in full legal form and signed by her, in which she binds herself, under pain of banishment from the realm, not to marry him during 1768 nor to insist on his promise to marry her at a later date, "considering that Mr. James Boswell, advocate, my cousin, is at present so much in love with me that I might certainly have him for my lawful husband if I choose it, and the said James being of a temper so inconstant that there is reason to fear that he would repent of his choice in a very short time, on which account he is unwilling to trust himself in my company." That was about a week before he met *la belle irlandaise* and became convinced that in her every flower was united.

In the long list of women whom he at one time or another wrote down as matrimonial possibilities (Martha Whyte, Katherine Colquhoun, Miss Bruce, Margaret Stewart, Catherina Geelvinck, Isabella van Tuyll, Elizabeth Diana Bosville, Euphemia Bruce, Catherine Blair, Mary Anne Boyd, Catherine Gordon, Margaret Crauford) her name otherwise never once occurs. Yet on at least four occasions after April 1769 he explicitly stated not only that she had long been "the constant yet prudent and delicate *confidante* of all his *égarements du coeur et de l'esprit*" but also that he had always been falling in love with her and telling her that if she had money and interest, he would rather marry her than any other woman he knew. He had, it is true, so mingled these protestations of love with declarations of ardent passion for other women that she had not believed him to be serious, but he implies that he had actually been more serious with regard to her than to any one else, or at least that this love was the one to which, with all his inconstancies, he had been most constant.

There is a mystery here which I do not pretend to be able to clear up. If Boswell says that he had long been on terms of confidential intimacy with Margaret Montgomerie, we must simply accept that intimacy as a fact, for he does not tell lies about such matters. But it then follows that for years he has been deliberately excluding mention of her from his journal, and it is hard to understand why he should have done so. The obvious explanation—that she was his mistress and that he was protecting her reputation—can be summarily rejected. No one who had read the voluminous private correspondence that passed between them during this year could entertain that suspicion for a moment. But even if we did not have the correspondence, the explanation would not make sense, for Margaret Montgomerie was his cousin, and if he had been covering up an intrigue, he would still have been careful to make the appropriate amount of *cousinly* reference to her—just as he made an appropriate amount of social reference to Jean Heron and Mrs. Love. To make less than that, instead of drawing the wool over our eyes, would have been to rouse suspicion. It might be argued that he suppressed mention of his fondness for Margaret Montgomerie and his dependence on her for the same reason that he suppressed mention of good weather. But he does not otherwise take his comforting confidential relationships by any means for granted, as witness the space given first and last in his journal to John Johnston. The reticences of a man who really has a wish that nothing should be secret that concerns himself are perhaps bound to remain obscure.

One can, however, make something of the notion that to Boswell Margaret Montgomerie's comforting and invigorating presence had come to seem as of the order of nature. How he convinced himself that he could dispense with her if Catherine Blair had accepted him, I do not know. But the courtship of *la belle irlandaise,* which began at Lainshaw and continued, as it were, under Lainshaw auspices, could not fail to couple her with Margaret and to force a constant comparison. What finally brought him to a clear realization and a consequent choice he never said, but it could not have been merely the impending trip to Dublin, for he was under no necessity of going to Dublin, and (as he proceeded to demonstrate) could go there without committing himself. I fancy that the decisive factor was Margaret's extended visit to Auchinleck. He saw her there in his mother's role, except for servants the only woman in the house, a house that one day would be his, and he felt that to invade this comfortable order by putting some one else in her place would be unnatural. It was very difficult for him to give up all his gay and ambitious notions of beauty and wealth and interest; but he was somehow granted an access of sober insight and realized that more than all these he wanted the understanding and sympathy and mild affectionate subservience that he was not likely to get from any one but another Boswell.

The "access of sober insight" was not a lightning flash but a dawning. Boswell and Margaret Montgomerie left Auchinleck on 25 April and Lainshaw on the 28th. On the 27th Boswell had persuaded Captain Montgomerie-Cuninghame to join with him in one of his enthusiastic family rituals. The old tower of Corsehill, which furnished the territorial designation of the Cuninghame baronetcy, had once belonged to the family of Douglas, and Boswell proposed that they drink to DOUGLAS at that ancient spot. Reinforced with one of the Captain's principal tenants and a pot-house keeper from Stewarton who furnished the means of libation, they drank happily and huzzaed like a hundred ("Drink makes men appear numerous; we feel double as well as see double"), and Boswell was chaised home drunk. He was rude to Margaret, who was so much offended that she would have stayed at home if she could have done so without laying the blame on him. The Irish jaunt began with headache, contrition, and hurt feelings, all of which cleared on the road to Ayr. Next day, between Maybole and Ardmillan, Boswell felt himself "in love with another woman than Marianne" and "spoke of it to Margaret." This is the earliest admission in the journal of any sentimental interest in Margaret, and the information is conveyed in a solemnly mysterious manner. Margaret comforted him. On the 30th, between Ardmillan and Ballantrae, he got it into his head from something Margaret had said that "the lady" was engaged, was amazingly affected, cried bitterly and would not speak to her. She by chance discovered the cause of his misery and assured him he was mistaken. He was so much rejoiced that after she had gone to bed he got drunk again. ("I got Mactaggart the landlord to drink with me till I staggered. . . . A punster would say the landlord might be called *Macstaggered*.") On the night between 1 and 2 May they crossed from Portpatrick to Donaghadee, Boswell very sea-sick. At Donaghadee they remained four days, most hospitably entertained by Hugh Boyd and his family, and on the 6th Boswell, Margaret, Mrs. Boyd, and a niece of Hugh Boyd's set out for Dublin in two chaises. Though the journal continues to be mysterious, surviving letters written to Temple and Dempster on 3 May make the situation quite explicit.

On 2 May Margaret and Mrs. Boyd had told Boswell that they would not accompany him to Dublin. Probably they had laid their heads together and had agreed—as Margaret had felt all along—that Boswell's attitude towards Mary Anne was not what he had led the Dublin Boyds to believe it was and that the Boyds were bound to be hurt. A quarrel was imminent, and they did not wish to make it a family quarrel by seeming to support him in his inconsiderateness. Boswell was furious, and, though he said nothing, gave indications of his displeasure that affected Margaret profoundly. She allowed him for the first time to see that his professions of love to her, which she had always affected to treat as "words of course," had really had their effect: she loved him deeply though she had intended never to let him know it. Boswell at once dashed off letters to Temple and Dempster stating his quandary. Undoubtedly, what had brought his love out into the open was his discovery that his affection was returned. Characteristically, he showed Margaret the letter to Temple, with all its reasons for *not* marrying her, and she forbade him to send it. She told him her one wish was his happiness. He might marry whomever he liked best or thought most to his interest, and she would even help him. The letters were shelved and the mysterious style of the journal kept up. Boswell started off for Dublin ostensibly free to make his suit to *la belle irlandaise* but actually committed to Margaret Montgomerie.

I was received at Dublin [he wrote to Dempster] with open arms by a numerous and creditable set of relations. . . . The young lady seemed the sweetest, loveliest little creature that ever was born. But so young, so childish, so much *yes* and *no* that (between ourselves) I was ashamed of having raved so much about her.[1] I candidly told my situation: that I had come quite contrary to my father's inclination. That was enough for the present, and a genteel distance was the proper conduct. At the same time I found myself like a foreign prince to them, so much did I take, and I was assured of her having for certain £500 a year.

[1] One often has the feeling that Boswell is reaching for a quotation from an author not yet born:

> 'Tis true, your budding Miss is very charming,
>   But shy and awkward at first coming out;
> So much alarm'd that she is quite alarming,
>   All Giggle, Blush; half Pertness and half Pout;
> And glancing at *Mamma*, for fear there's harm in
>   What you, she, it, or they, may be about;
> The Nursery still lisps out in all they utter—
> Besides, they always smell of bread and butter.
>   (*Beppo*, xxxix)

The fact is that, as Boswell perhaps planned (or at least hoped), the humble trip to lay himself a suitor at Mary Anne's feet turned into a triumphal progress for the Corsican traveller. Everybody had read his book (it had had, as has been mentioned, at least three printings in Ireland), everybody wanted to meet the friend of Paoli and do him honour. He was so assiduously entertained and threw himself with such gusto into the entertainments provided for him ("Dublin is really a noble city. . . . I never in my life saw such feasting") that he had no time to record a chronology of his visit. He was apparently at Dublin or the vicinity about three weeks. He dined and spent the night with the Lord Lieutenant (Viscount Townshend) at Leixlip; "the congeniality of their dispositions united them in the most pleasant manner." He dined with the Duke of Leinster at Carton; he dined with the Lord Mayor (Benjamin Barton) at the Residence. He enjoyed the society of the Irish statesmen Lord Charlemont and Henry Flood, of the Irish historian Dr. Thomas Leland, of the celebrated Irish bookseller George Faulkner, friend of Swift and Chesterfield, whom he had often seen Foote take off as Peter Paragraph. The "relations" who received him with open arms at Dublin probably included some newly discovered members of his own family. "Mr. Boswell," he later wrote, "had a very near relation (daughter of his grand-uncle General Cochrane, whose brother afterwards succeeded to the Earldom of Dundonald), who was married to Robert Sibthorpe, Esq., a gentleman of great consequence in the County of Down. This served as an introduction to much good society." Since he made report of having seen "some beautiful country seats," it has been inferred that he also made a progress of County Down under the protection of the Sibthorpes, but I incline now to think that the Sibthorpes were his hosts in Dublin and that the country seats he referred to were those of the Duke of Leinster and the Lord Lieutenant.

The Boyds, his ostensible hosts, probably saw him only coming and going, and were pretty much thrown in the shade by the splendid company his personal fame and the Sibthorpe connexion had got him into. Aunt Boyd and Margaret turned out to be true prophets. After Boswell left Dublin, Mrs. Boyd sent him an angry letter demanding the return of a picture (probably a miniature of Mary Anne) and of a letter. Correspondence of twenty years later shows that the Boyds were angry with Margaret too, and that they never forgave her. Mary Anne was twice married and was alive in 1789, but I do not know the date of her death.

"They do not drink as they used to do," Boswell reported to Sir Alexander Dick, "though if a man chooses it, there is as much as he pleases." Reference to "one riotous evening" which Mrs. Boyd could be excused for not approving shows that on one occasion he did choose to exceed. The law of parsimony would lead one to identify this "one riotous evening" with the "one night of Irish extravagance" which Boswell later lamented. The extravagance apparently consisted of a visit to a brothel with two young Army officers and the loss of the merit of a year's chastity. Riot had the usual unhappy consequences. When we can again locate Boswell in a definite place on a definite date, it is 29 May, he is at Belfast, where the corps of one of his officer friends is stationed, six of them are starting off early next morning in three chaises for a three-day jaunt to see Lough Neagh and the Giant's Causeway, and he is ill. Margaret has apparently accompanied him to Belfast from Donaghadee, but has returned after, and perhaps because of, some "rash and most absurd passion" of Boswell's which he is writing to apologize for. They crossed to Scotland perhaps on 7 June, he stopped briefly at Lainshaw, and arrived in Edinburgh at nine in the evening of Monday 12 June, the Session due to open at nine the next morning.

And while Boswell junketed, what of Corsica? When the debate in Parliament showed conclusively that Great Britain would not intervene, the only remaining chance for Paoli rested in the new mistress of the King of France, the Comtesse Du Barry. She was Choiseul's bitter enemy, and it was generally believed that her rise would mean his fall and the repudiation of his Corsican policy. Only a court presentation was required to make her ascendancy complete. But by luck and intrigue of the Choiseul party, the presentation was staved off to 22 April 1769, and that provided time enough to settle Corsica's fate. On 8 May 1769, the day perhaps on which Boswell arrived in Dublin to bask in his Corsican glory and start projecting useless subscriptions, the Corsican resistance was crushed in the battle of Ponte Novo. I shall stop paraphrasing Joseph Foladare and let him speak directly:

Paoli, with a group of followers who preferred exile to surrender, cut through the French lines and on 13 June made his way to an English ship which hovered expectantly near the Corsican shore. Among the Corsicans who elected to stay behind and treat for peace with the French was Paoli's former adjutant, Carlo Buonaparte. His wife, big with child, had followed him in the retreat through the mountains. Now the French offered pardon to those who surrendered, and the Buonapartes were allowed to return to Ajaccio. A few weeks later a son was born. They named him Napolione.

CHAPTER

XXIII

Because he had returned literally on the eve of the Summer Session, Boswell could not shut himself up and keep quiet, but had to plunge at once into sixty days of unremitting activity in his profession. He was painfully ill, disquietingly in love, and faced with the necessity of making an irrevocable decision. At no time since Holland had he been so fretful. Boswell unhappy is sometimes more admirable than Boswell romping; he eschews the postures that, however entertaining, save him from looking deeply into himself. Yet Boswell romping is almost invariably Boswell self-critical; he shows by the very extravagance of his gestures that he knows his absurdity. During the summer of 1769 he postured extravagantly and he insisted that his postures be taken seriously.

At the end of March he had sent Mrs. Dodds £10, and he now (on 23 June) consulted with John Johnston and Dr. Cairnie about the final settlement that would be necessary if he were to marry. What arrangement was made, we do not know, but it is likely (as will later appear) that the details were reported to Margaret Montgomerie.

She had remained at Lainshaw and he was not able to get to see her again for almost two months—quite time enough, if he had still been the old Boswell, for him to succumb to another infatuation. But though he continued to be torn occasionally with regrets for all his gay and brilliant schemes of marriage ("money would enable me to buy pictures, and my Irish connexion make a pretty anecdote in my life"), he no longer had even a wish to fall in love again. He wrote frequently to Margaret, and his letters were candid and generally manly (though he tended to invoke her sympathy too much), and her answers were submissive and comforting. To all his relations but his father he mentioned her as a supposable case. Lieutenant John did not approve, but he met no other opposition.

Temple was much taken with his description of Margaret's virtues but thought the marriage would not do for family reasons; Dempster returned nothing but raillery; steady John Johnston was much Margaret's advocate.

Boswell was worried by the small crop of fees the Session was producing and torn with cruel uncertainties about Corsica. Peter Capper of the Carron Company had had a letter from Sir John Dick which represented matters as being by no means hopeless, but the news generally indicated the complete collapse of Corsican resistance.

In the midst of these distractions, Lord Auchinleck tried to talk to him of marriage, but he evaded him. A few days later he realized to his horror that his father was hinting at taking a wife himself.

Lord Auchinleck had been more deeply vexed than Boswell had realized by the extravagances of the London jaunt of 1768, by the revival of serious interest in Belle de Zuylen, and above all by Boswell's failure to win Catherine Blair. The Irish jaunt, which had been undertaken in the face of his manifest displeasure, had been the last straw. It was not merely that he did not want Boswell running around in the vacations, wasting money and getting his name in the newspapers when he should be studying law; he did not want him marrying outside the country—or, for that matter, outside the county. His demands for dowry, to do him justice, were not nearly so extravagant as Boswell's had been. His own wife had not been a great fortune, and neither had his father's. What he wanted, as his hearty approval of Catherine Blair indicates, was a comfortable, sensible, practical alliance, preferably with a relation familiar with the Auchinleck tradition, an alliance that would bring some money, some land, and—this was most important—"influence" in the shape of a good Scots vote based on an Ayrshire freehold. If Boswell had married Catherine Blair, he had planned to invite her to head his household. As a conspicuous public official he needed a woman to arrange and direct his entertaining; as an aging man with a chronic and worsening physical complaint he needed a woman to manage and nurse him; and in neither capacity could a housekeeper be really more than a stop-gap. Having waited three years for Boswell to produce a daughter-in-law whom he could accept as head of his household, he had at last not unsurprisingly decided to marry himself. He did not name the lady he had in mind, indeed seems to have handled the conference in an awkward and hesitating fashion, and Boswell had not the slightest notion as to who she might be. He was taken by surprise, cruelly hurt, and instantly retaliated by wild and childish schemes of running away and hiding himself in obscurity. That they were mostly of the order of "I'll eat worms and die, and you'll be sorry" is indicated by the fact that he talked about them so much: for weeks he showed a compulsion to discuss with everybody what he monotonously calls his dilemma. One of his earliest confidants after poor Johnston, who first and last had to absorb a great deal of violence and spleen, was a man whom he had never before felt much mental sympathy with. Lord Monboddo showed genuine concern and kindness, assured him warmly that Margaret was the woman for him, deplored deeply Lord Auchinleck's proposal to marry, and urged Boswell to hasten his own marriage so as to get a settlement fixed.

His letters to Margaret wavered and veered with each new consultant. Monboddo made him really happy with the idea of marriage, and he wrote her a grateful and committed letter; next day, after canvassing her faults with Claud Boswell's sister Elizabeth—a spinster of forty or so who had been turning up with notable frequency of late at Lord Auchinleck's dinner table—he sent one full of jealous carpings at her allegedly excessive frankness to gentlemen.

In one episode of the old glorious sort he eased for some hours the tensions of the summer. Archibald Douglas had given him a special invitation to attend the celebration of his twenty-first birthday at Bothwell Castle on Monday 10 July, had appointed him one of his regular counsel with a handsome retainer, and finally capped his favours by inviting him to accompany him abroad as his travelling companion, giving him to understand that if it detached him from his profession, the monetary loss would be made up to him. The celebration was the sort of orgulous outsize function that filled Boswell with bustle and bliss: seventy at table, sixteen excellent toasts proposed by Douglas, the Duke of Queensberry, and Boswell, Boswell himself proposing "The Family of Douglas" and the last toast of all ("May fools become wise and knaves honest") ; after each toast two pieces (a cannon and a mortar) going off as at the wassail of royal Denmark.

Two engineers attended and took charge. . . . Whenever they were charged, they made a sign with a handkerchief to a servant who was placed at the door and who gave notice to me. I then rose up and called with an audible voice, "Charged ! all charged !" Then a toast was given and I called *"Fire!"* to the servant, who made a sign to the engineers, and the artillery went off.

He was all night on the road back to Edinburgh, reaching town just in time to throw off his laced coat and waistcoat, don his black clothes and all his cares, and be on hand at nine o'clock to attend his causes in the Parliament House.

On 12 July his hopes of Corsican independence received the *coup de grâce* in a letter from Sir John Dick: the Corsican revolution was utterly crushed. Paoli was safe at Leghorn, but Boswell could not derive full comfort from this news, for Margaret had not written and he was afraid he had offended her. Sure enough, when her letter did come, it showed clear signs that her feelings had been deeply hurt.

She appeared to me so cool and indifferent that I was absolutely shocked. . . . My head turned giddy. . . . Worthy Grange represented to me that it was all my own fault, . . . and that I ought rather to be grateful to her for writing at all, and should make an apology for what I had written. He pacified me a little. But I have a wretched satisfaction in being surly. I however was much affected and could for gleams of thought have almost cried; and, had she been near me, would have fallen at her feet. Yet my obstinate, unreasonable pride still rose again. I determined not to write till I was more moderate.

Lord Monboddo assured him that his father did have thoughts of remarrying and pushed him to hasten his own marriage with Margaret; he was angry at his father, vexed with Margaret, frightened by the appearance of a very bad symptom of illness—which had been brought on (one suspects) by his junketing to Bothwell Castle and drinking sixteen toasts. His father spoke seriously to him, charging him with neglecting affairs at home and half acknowledging an intention to remarry. Boswell replied in very strong terms that if he did, he would cease to be in any way dependent on him.

It is wonderful to think how he and I have differed to such a degree for so many years. I was somewhat hurt to find myself again thrown loose on the world. But my love of adventure and hope made me surprisingly easy. My great unhappiness was thinking of M. And yet in any way she could not but suffer, for I could not think of marriage when he exposed himself at his years and forgot my valuable mother.

John Johnston begged him not to commit himself to any desperate scheme, but he remained quite determined. His surgeon, Mr. Macdonald, blooded him preparatory to treating the alarming symptom. He walked on the Castle Hill with Douglas's agent, Mr. Maconochie, and told him his dilemma; he took the stage out to Pinkie to tell Commissioner Cochrane his dilemma. The Commissioner was not at home, but as he waited for the return stage, he saw his father and Elizabeth Boswell drive past in a chaise and was chagrined by his own obtuseness. He hired a chaise and went to Prestonfield to tell Sir Alexander Dick his dilemma. His father sent for him; he would not sit down, but said a few sullen words standing.

After a wretched, feverish night I awaked in a dreadful state. I have no doubt that evil spirits, enemies to mankind, are permitted to tempt and torment them. "Damn him!" "Curse him!" sounded somehow involuntarily in my ears perpetually. I was absolutely mad. I sent for worthy Grange, and was so furious and black-minded and uttered such horrid ideas that he could not help shedding tears, and even went so far as to say that if I talked so, he would never see me again. I looked on my father's marrying again as the most ungrateful return to me for my having submitted so much to please him. I thought it an insult on the memory of my valuable mother. I thought it would totally estrange him from his children by her.

When his father tried to speak to him again, he prevented it by running away. He was determined to throw himself on the wide world.

An undated essay written about this time is exquisitely revelatory of that central Boswellian contradiction that never ceases to astonish the student of his life no matter how many times it is repeated. Flaming with rage, he sat down and wrote—obviously with intent to publish, though it does not appear that he ever did so—a cautionary periodical essay on second marriages. "A True Story in Queen Anne's Reign," with a mere change of locale (the events are said to have occurred in Berkshire), was precisely his own story as he saw it, though he carried it through to an exuberantly dismal ending. When an author chooses to express from present personal experience an attitude that is extravagant and childish, we expect him to expose himself by extravagant and childish diction. But Boswell can at will express the black scowl and unreasoning jealousy of a child in grave, precise, accomplished language, embellished with well-applied tags from Ovid and Horace.

The son, who was equally determined as he was warm, quitted his ungrateful father and retired to a distant country, where he indulged his gloomy reflections without restraint, and would upon no account listen to any terms of reconciliation. The father soon perceived that age and distemper are miserably suited for conjugal society, and, for all the art of his new wife, he saw her disgusted with his nauseous fondness. The respectable character which he had maintained was now sunk in folly and dotage. He became the subject of drunken jests, and *turpe senilis amor, peccet ad extremum ridendus*[1] were every day applied to him. None of his children would see a man, who, for the selfish gratification of at most but a few years, had exposed himself, affronted the memory of their mother, driven from his country a son who did honour to it, and ruined a family which had supported itself for ages. He died in great agony both in body and mind, and may serve to teach decorum and generosity of conduct to those who come after him.

It would be wrong to give the impression that Boswell had no case at all. Out of regard for his father and the Family, he had for three years dutifully submitted (as his essay says) "to a plan of living which he considered to be a perpetual succession of disgust." He had assumed that his father, in accepting this dutiful daily service from him, had laid himself under obligation to "pass the rest of his days with a becoming gravity and abstraction," studying "to see his heir assume in some measure the place, which, in the course of nature, he was destined one day to fill." That Lord Auchinleck should not consider himself obliged by this meritorious behaviour seemed to him monstrously unjust. He no doubt saw in Lord Auchinleck's proposed action more of an assault on his own prospects than in fact existed. His father probably did not have any very active hopes of raising a second family, and would probably not have altered the succession if he had had a second family and could legally have done so—a fundamental if which was never tested. But it was not unreasonable in Boswell to have apprehensions. His father was only sixty-two, Elizabeth Boswell little if any over forty. Lord Auchinleck had again and again expressed dissatisfaction with all three of his sons, and at one time had threatened to sell the estate, implying by his threat that he had the power to do as he pleased with it. When a respected lawyer and judge asserts a legal right that is to one's disadvantage, one cannot but be worried, however much one may suspect him of being disingenuous. And even if Lord

[1] "Sexual passion in an old man is a disgusting thing" (Ovid, *Amores,* I.ix.4); ["Turn the old horse out in time lest] at the last he stumble amid jeers" (Horace, *Epistles,* I.i.9).

Auchinleck were bound by or respected the entail in his contract of marriage, he could certainly have bequeathed to a child of his second marriage all the lands he had purchased himself—no inconsiderable portion of the estate. Finally, though Boswell should inherit the whole, his income for his entire lifetime could be very greatly reduced by a widow's jointure and annuities for her children.

Granting all this, it still seems sufficiently clear that his unyielding resistance to the idea of a stepmother had in the main very little to do with worldly self-interest, was not ultimately rational, though his lawyer's training enabled him to buttress it with rational arguments. His insistence that decency if not true love binds spouses for all eternity went beyond the demands of church no less than of civil state, and furthermore involved him in notable inconsistency. That Countess of Mar who gave him the connexion with the royal line of Scotland of which he was so proud was a second wife; his mother's mother was a third. Basic to his attitude was a passionate childish jealousy of his father's affection, a young man's instinctive disgust at elderly sexuality, and, deeper and more powerful than these, a *mystique* of Family in which anything that weakened or blurred the principle of male succession and male primogeniture was treason of the most abominable sort.

A kind letter from Margaret, taking no account of their recent rift, warmed his heart, and he wrote apologizing for his carping: "If I could behave so to such a valuable and affectionate woman as you, what a shocking temper must I have!" Appearing before his father in court, he remarked on the strange satisfaction he felt in pleading calmly to a man with whom he could have no intercourse in private. He mourned to think he must leave the Parliament House. Lord Monboddo spoke to him again and asked to be permitted to negotiate between him and his father. Lord Auchinleck had told Monboddo that what made him think of marriage was Boswell's going on in his irregular bachelor way. Boswell said he would marry, but no one but Margaret. Monboddo told him that if he would be serious and firm, he hoped to settle matters on that basis. Boswell more than once speaks of Monboddo's negotiation as a "compromise," but the concessions he himself was prepared to make were not generous. He continued violently to oppose his father's marriage, but agreed not to let it drive him into exile if he might have Margaret.

And the conclusion that he could marry Margaret after all and remain in his profession, instead of filling him with joy and the generous wish to communicate the joy, actually plunged him into a state of dissatisfaction which he called "romantic." He had played with the idea of asking her to go into exile with him, but he had not actually put the question to her, and he could not bear to think that he would never know what she would have said. He wanted, like Lovelace, to have tested his beloved to the uttermost, and like Lovelace he loved plots and stratagems. So he sent her a fine and indefensible letter:

You know my unhappy temper. You know all my faults. It is painful to repeat them. Will you, then, knowing me fully, accept of me for your husband as I now am—not the heir of Auchinleck but one who has had his time of the world and is henceforth to expect no more than £100 a year? With that and the interest of your £1000 we can live in an agreeable retirement in any part of Europe that you please. But we are to bid adieu for ever to this country. All our happiness is to be our society with each other and our hopes of a better world. . . . Think seriously of this. Give me any positive answer you honestly can. But I insist on no mediocrity, no reasoning, no hesitation. Think fully, and one way or other tell me your resolution.

Lord Auchinleck, so far as we know, first heard from Monboddo of Boswell's wish to marry Margaret. He attempted "cheerfully" (Boswell says) to discuss the proposal with him, and Boswell too tried to hold himself in, but the conference ended with both in bad humour as usual. Boswell still vacillated between possibilities: he thought of continuing at the law even if the worst happened; he thought if Margaret returned him a prudent, evasive answer, he would sail for America and become a wild Indian ("I had great thoughts of my acquiring strength and fortitude"). And, as though no compromise were on foot, he went on telling people his dilemma. Commissioner Cochrane expressed incredulity on being told of Lord Auchinleck's marriage scheme, but cut Boswell's raging short with a firmness that it would have been well if his other confidants had shown: "No. You must make the best of it."

Margaret's answer was brought to him in the Parliament House. He saw at the beginning the sentence "I accept of your terms"; his terror for marriage returned, his heart beat, his head was giddy, but as he read on, he became calm and easy in the thought that at last he was fixed for ever.

I have thought fully, as you desired, and in answer to your letter, I accept of your terms, and shall do everything in my power to make myself worthy of you. J. B. with £100 a year is every bit as valuable to me as if possessed of the estate of Auchinleck. I only regret the want of wealth on your account, not being certain if you can be happy without a proper share of it. Free of ambition, I prefer real happiness to the splendid appearance of it. . . . My heart is more at ease than it has been of a long time, though still I feel for what I am afraid you suffer. Be assured, my dear Jamie, you have a friend that would sacrifice everything for you, who never had a wish for wealth till now, to bestow it on the man of her heart.

It is to be feared that this letter did not make him as ashamed as it should have. He enclosed it in a wrapper which he endorsed in his boldest hand, "The most valuable letter of my valuable friend, which does honour to both her and me. *Vraye Foi.*"[1]

Lord Auchinleck finally managed to tell him that he would agree to his scheme of marriage, though he thought it improper and did not believe he and Margaret could live together more than six months. Boswell at once made a week-end dash to Lainshaw and he and Margaret, who had not seen each other for two months, joined hands and solemnly engaged themselves as they should answer to God. Boswell began referring to Margaret as his spouse. When he got back to Edinburgh, he sent her a long letter from Temple, just received, in which Temple made very explicit reference to his intrigues, his venereal disasters, and his "natural production" ("I hope it is in health and that you take proper care of it"). If Boswell let Margaret know about Sally's existence, he probably also informed her of the arrangements he had made for her upbringing. When he assured Margaret that he had told her everything bad about himself, he probably told the literal truth.

The Session rose that week (12 August) and Lord Auchinleck left for the country. Boswell had been genuinely very apprehensive over his illness, and had persuaded himself that he could not be properly cured unless he went to London and drank a much-advertised nostrum known as Kennedy's Lisbon Diet Drink. The problem was to convince his father that the trip was not a mere ruse for a London vacation. Suspecting, apparently, that Dr. Cairnie's authority would not carry much weight, he consulted Dr. John Gregory, Professor of Medicine at the University of Edinburgh. Gregory told him, just as Macdonald and Cairnie had, that his case was coming on well, but was willing to advise the trip if it would put his mind at rest. Thus fortified, he felt justified in telling his father that he was

[1] "True faith"—the Boswell Family motto.

under a necessity of going to London to clear his constitution. "He acquiesced," says Boswell drily. Lord Auchinleck talked not unkindly of him
and Margaret, but said they were both thoughtless and would need to
reform.

The Session over, Boswell seized the first opportunity of the summer to
shut himself up, put himself on a restricted diet, and submit to regular
medical attention. He spent two weeks at home rather pleasantly writing
law papers and sorting through a mass of printed Session papers of his
father's, selecting such as seemed worth binding.

When Lord Auchinleck got to Auchinleck, he summoned Margaret for
a conference. She was in a panic. She felt sure that her uncle was going to
try to talk her out of her engagement, and that if she opposed him and
married Boswell, he would never forgive her. It was not merely that she
brought no money, no new connexions, no "influence." More clearly than
Boswell, she realized that Lord Auchinleck considered the whole Lainshaw
tribe to be extravagant, slack, feckless—in short, Irish. Lainshaw had
been in a declining state at least from the time of her father's succession,
and Lord Auchinleck had the successful man's horror of associating himself with failure. Boswell could not be made to share her apprehensions.
Lord Auchinleck, in spite of the vexation he must have felt at the London
trip, had left Edinburgh in remarkably good humour, and had said nothing further about planning to get married himself. Boswell had been encouraged by Commissioner Cochrane to think that he might have given
up the scheme, and was considering asking Margaret and Boswell to live
with him. He wrote Margaret a long, calm, really admirable letter of advice, with a summary of the progress of their attachment which she was
to repeat to Lord Auchinleck. "I cannot help indulging hopes that before
two years are over, he may be perfectly satisfied with us, and that we may
be living together in the greatest harmony." He had not been in so happy
a frame all summer.

CHAPTER

XXIV

Boswell set out for London on 28 August in a chaise with a single travelling companion, Mr. Farquhar Kinloch, merchant in London. Since he honestly meant to be retired and perfectly economical, devoting himself solely to the restoration of his health and the purification of his blood—or perhaps since he wanted to cut himself off from temptations to be and do otherwise—he wore an old black suit, carried another black suit as a spare, and provided himself with no coloured clothes at all. But the mere escape to the south was enough to regenerate the journal. All through the summer it had been constricted, bleak, plaintive; Boswell seemed ungenial, dried out, exhausted. As he turned his face towards London, he budded as at the scent of water and brought forth boughs like a plant. The old unhurrying delighted exuberance of perception revived as he met people at inns or in the fly to which he transferred at Durham, and he jotted down characters, like sketches for a novel: Mr. Sitwell, retired ironmonger, a London cit worth £200,000, "an old bachelor, a comely old gentleman with a grey coat, large white wig, fair complexion, and linen remarkably well got up"; Mr. Howell, farmer near Darlington, "very little removed from a brute ... not ill natured but ... monstrously big, had the coarsest dress and manners, and spoke a language that could hardly be understood"; a Yorkshire farmer's wife, a good old woman with a brandy bottle in her pocket which she cordially communicated with Mr. Howell. He chatted quite freely with his companions, expecting never to see any of them again; told them he was to be married on his return from London, and took counsel with the ladies as to a posy for Margaret's wedding ring.

Dilly insisted that he live at his house instead of taking lodgings. He called at Johnson's (then in Johnson's Court, Fleet Street) and found he was at Brighton with his grand friends, the Thrales. Mrs. Williams, John-

son's blind companion, advised him to go to the Jubilee in honour of
Shakespeare at Stratford. He had resolved with especial firmness against
this temptation, but found that his approach to the metropolis had carried
him beyond the point of return within the whirlpool of curiosity (his own
figure) and that struggle was useless.

Sir John Pringle was not for Dr. Kennedy or his nostrum and wished
Boswell just to trust again to Duncan Forbes. Kennedy turned out to be
a very old gentleman (he was supposed to be ninety and was probably
seventy-seven), large and formal and tedious. He agreed that Boswell's
case was not so desperate that he might not defer treatment for nine days.
So Boswell in a characteristic about-face ("I could not resist") made a
break at the very start in his scheme of obscurity and perfect economy
and determined not only to attend the Jubilee but to make himself the
most conspicuous person there. There was to be a masked ball, and he
would appear at it as an armed Corsican chief. He had a genuine Corsican outfit in Edinburgh, but there was not time to send for it, so he
made do with such improvised accoutrements as he could pick up ready
to hand or cause to be made to his patterns and descriptions. His memorandum also calls for "a large wig and some rouge for disguise"—not, as
one might suppose, to complete the Corsican costume, but to enable him
to remain incognito at Stratford until he appeared in it. He was rather
rushed in his preparations, for he had to cram most of them into one afternoon, but Dilly obligingly scurried about and helped him in the search.

On the way to Stratford, he paused at Oxford to meet the poet William Julius Mickle, corrector of the Clarendon Press, and to write letters.
One of them was to Margaret, who had delicately hinted that he did not
love her as much as she did him, because if he did, he could not possibly
have left her with such ease and have set out on courses that might be bad
for him. His reply was a paradigm of much of their later correspondence: I
must indulge myself because it improves my spirits and consequently my
health and makes me more agreeable.

Believe me, my going to Shakespeare's Jubilee and wishing to see
many friends and enjoy many amusements ought not to be interpreted as
marks of indifference. I am forwarding the recovery of my health, I am
acquiring an additional stock of ideas with which to entertain you. I am
dissipating melancholy clouds and filling my mind with fine, cheerful
spirits. . . . I have that kind of weakness that when I looked at myself in
the glass last night in my Corsican dress, I could not help thinking your

opinion of yourself might be still more raised: "She has secured the constant affection and admiration of so fine a fellow." Do you know, I cannot think there is any harm in such a kind of weakness or vanity when a man is sensible of it and it has no great effect upon him? It enlivens me and increases my good humour.

He did not take the road till midnight, and then when he had got beyond Chapel House, he found that he had left his pocket-book in the chaise when he changed at Woodstock. One of the papers in it was Margaret's letter of acceptance, "the most valuable letter of my valuable friend." So back he posted in a fresh chaise to Woodstock and retrieved his pocket-book. But he was now hours behind schedule, it was raining heavily, and no chaise to Stratford was to be had. He arrived between twelve and one, dirty and wet, with his hair hanging about his ears, having ridden horseback part of the way without boots and protected from the weather only by a short greatcoat borrowed from a postilion. He had not had a wink of sleep and could not help entertaining some doubts as to how far he had forwarded the recovery of his health, but he says that he felt on his first view of Stratford the enthusiasm which Cicero reported in walking the streets of Athens. We who have observed his behaviour at Mantua and in the Licenza valley will not suspect him of exaggerating.

The Stratford Jubilee was what would now be called a publicity stunt of Garrick's. Though Shakespeare's plays were as highly esteemed in the 1760s as they are now, there was hardly any veneration of his relics. Few tourists visited Stratford-on-Avon, and Stratford's inhabitants had little knowledge of—and little interest in—their most famous townsman. Garrick planned a three-day festival there, the exercises to be conducted partly in the town's public buildings, partly in a huge wooden booth or "amphitheatre" jerry-built for the occasion. The program called for serenades, public breakfasts and dinners, the performance of an oratorio by Thomas Arne, a procession of Shakespeare's characters, the declaiming by Garrick of a Festival Ode of his own composition, with musical accompaniment (also by Arne) and a chorus, fireworks, horse-races, and two balls, one of them in masquerade. A huge crowd assembled, but the wits and the weather were adverse. Rain descended steadily during most of the second and third days, extinguishing the fireworks and preventing the great procession. The river overflowed the meadow where the amphitheatre and the race track were located; ladies leaving the masquerade ball had to totter into their carriages on planks, the wheels standing two feet deep in water.

Having provided himself with a bed, Boswell went straight without washing or changing to the church, where Arne's oratorio of *Judith* was being performed. He made so strange an appearance in his black suit and short postilion's duffel that people gathered and whispered. Garrick observed him, they each struck an attitude and cordially shook hands. He handed Garrick a slip of paper saying he was incognito, and Garrick told the bystanders he was a clergyman in disguise. His plan, if he had not arrived so late, must have been to put on his large wig and other make-up before showing himself, but almost at once he ran into so many people who knew him that any scheme of disguise was rendered futile. It is rather a pity, for he would have enjoyed hamming a role for two days, and his account of his adventures would have been amusing.

At the public dinner he was shocked to find himself, as he thought, falling in love with a pretty little Irish woman, Mrs. Sheldon, but he cured himself by going near the orchestra and looking steadily at Sophia Baddeley of Drury Lane ("that beautiful insinuating creature"). Mrs. Sheldon was instantly effaced.

I then saw that what I feared was love was in reality nothing more than transient liking. It had no interference with my noble attachment. It was such a momentary diversion from it as the sound of a flageolet in my ear, a gay colour glancing from a prism before my eye, or any other pleasing sensation. However, the fear I had put myself in made me melancholy. I had been like a timorous man in a post-chaise, who, when a wagon is passing near it, imagines that it is to crush it; and I did not soon recover the shock. My having had no sleep all night, travelled in the rain, and suffered anxiety on account of my pocket-book, no doubt contributed to my uneasiness. I recollected my former inconstancy, my vicious profligacy, my feverish gallantry, and I was terrified that I might lose my divine passion for M____, in which case I am sure I would suffer more than she. I prayed devoutly to heaven to preserve me from such a misfortune, and became easier.

The passage is essential Boswell. Its attitudes, its clashing areas of attention, are odd to the point of absurdity. Who but Boswell would have been so alert and curious in assessing transient shocks of young love-liking, would so have played one off against another in cool experiment, would have accompanied the experiment with fervent prayer? Yet given the attitudes, the perceptions are delicately individualized, the analysis is acute, the expression is lively and precise.

He spent most of the second day writing the "Verses in the Character of a Corsican at Shakespeare's Jubileee" which he planned to print and distribute in his masquerade costume. He had made a beginning either in London or on the road, but he had to put considerable pressure on himself to complete the forty-six lines he considered adequate. He ran with them at once to Garrick, who expressed himself pleased by the compliment to himself which they contained, and then tackled the unlikely negotiation of getting them printed. Sometime in the evening a bookseller's lad named Shank, of Scots extraction, set manfully to work on the types. Boswell must be allowed his own description of his effulgent dawning on the masquerade:

One of the most remarkable masks upon this occasion was James Boswell, Esq., in the dress of an armed Corsican chief. He entered the amphitheatre about twelve o'clock. He wore a short dark-coloured coat of coarse cloth, scarlet waistcoat and breeches, and black spatterdashes. His cap or bonnet was of black cloth; on the front of it was embroidered in gold letters VIVA LA LIBERTÀ, and on one side of it was a handsome blue feather and cockade.... On the breast of his coat was sewed a Moor's head, the crest of Corsica, surrounded with branches of laurel. He had also a cartridge-pouch, into which was stuck a stiletto, and on his left side a pistol was hung upon the belt of his cartridge-pouch. He had a fusee slung across his shoulder, wore no powder in his hair, but had it plaited at its full length, with a knot of blue ribbons at the end of it. He had by way of staff a very curious vine all of one piece, with a bird finely carved upon it, emblematical of the sweet bard of Avon.

"I was quite happy at the masquerade," says Boswell. "My Corsican dress attracted everybody. I was as much a favourite as I could desire." He wore no mask, saying that it was not proper for a gallant Corsican to hide his features, but of course it had been an essential part of his plan to be recognized from the first as James Boswell, Esq. He danced a minuet (armed) and a country dance (unarmed) with Mrs. Sheldon. Shank brought him a proof at two in the morning and hastened back to throw the broadsides off, but could not get them to the amphitheatre in time for Boswell to distribute them in costume. But Boswell probably pressed them on people afterwards, and certainly gave a parcel of them to Garrick.

The accounts of the Stratford Jubilee nearly all make it out a dismal failure. Samuel Foote said it was an ode without poetry, music without melody, dinners without victuals, and lodgings without beds; a masquerade where half the people appeared bare-faced, a horse-race up to the knees in water, fireworks extinguished as soon as they were lighted, and a gingerbread amphitheatre which tumbled to pieces like a house of cards as soon as it was finished. But it made Boswell quite happy; he was one of the child-like beings for whom festivals are appointed. Among other benefits, it greatly extended the circle of his acquaintance with theatrical people. They were all there, though most of them seem to have gone to scoff at Garrick. Besides Love, Lee, Victor, Ross, Colman, and Garrick, whom he already knew, he now made the acquaintance of King, Murphy, Lacy, Kelly, and Foote.

An act of piety remained to be performed. He went back to Holy Trinity church, now cleared of the crowd, and calmly and solemnly viewed the grave of Shakespeare. It pleased him particularly to note that Shakespeare's wife had been seven years older than her husband.

Dempster, who knew his propensities only too well, had made him promise that if he went to Stratford contrary to his original plan, he would at least not send any account of his doings to the press. Of course he broke his word—or more probably got released from it—and published over his initials in *The Public Advertiser* a letter describing the Jubilee, by no means omitting mention of his own doings there. Two weeks later *The London Magazine* reprinted this letter, giving his name in full; adding the account of the armed Corsican chief from which quotation has been made above, and the full text of Boswell's Jubilee verses. The account was accompanied by an engraved plate, J. Miller after Samuel Wale, showing Boswell full length in his Corsican costume. Wale's drawing (which has disappeared) may have had some merit, but Miller's engraving—unfortunately the best known of the six portraits of Boswell — is disagreeably dry and does not even look like him. I do not know that Boswell ever recorded his feelings about it as a likeness, but he was utterly delighted by the thought that a figure labelled with his name and accurately depicting the outfit he had worn at Stratford was to appear in four thousand copies of a popular magazine. One can imagine Lord Auchinleck's puff of exasperation on seeing that plate. My heir, he would have thought, twenty-eight years old, a member of the Faculty of Advocates, who assured me that he was going to London merely to clear his

constitution and would manage everything with perfect economy, exposing himself to the world in a piece of daft mummery as expensive as it
was shameless!

And his grief and rage must sooner or later have been increased by
report that the heir of Auchinleck was being mimed on the public stage.
Garrick decided to recoup some of his wasted preparations by putting on
as an after-piece at Drury Lane the great pageant of Shakespeare's characters which the weather had kept him from presenting at Stratford.
Colman, the manager of the rival theatre (Covent Garden), got word of
Garrick's intention and anticipated him by incorporating a Jubilee pageant into his own new comedy, *Man and Wife*. Both performances ran
many nights. At Covent Garden (certainly), at Drury Lane (possibly) an
actor impersonated Boswell in his masquerade dress. Contemporary reports indicate that the actor wore upon his hat the identifying legend
CORSICA BOSWELL, and that he briskly distributed real or specious broadsides. To this representation is due the persistent but erroneous report that
Boswell at Stratford wore his own name on his hat in large letters.

On the day of his return to London, Boswell settled to the ostensible
business of his trip: that is, he put himself under Dr. Kennedy's care and
began to drink the Lisbon Diet Drink. (Kennedy, an M.D. of Rheims
and Oxford, had been for many years physician to the British Factory at
Lisbon.) This medicine, which was advertised to cure "every species of the
scurvy, even to that of a leprosy," and was also recommended to all
"who have been injured by a certain disorder," could be had only from
Mr. Woodcock, perfumer, in Orange Street, Red Lion Square. The
course was expensive, for the medicine cost half a guinea a pint bottle,
and Boswell drank a bottle a day. He at once decided that Kennedy himself was a gaping babbler ("a gillygawpus," as he more expressively wrote
in his memoranda), but he wanted to go on believing in Kennedy's medicine. A fellow advocate assured him that Kennedy had cured him in a
few weeks after he had spent above £300 in Edinburgh in vain, and
Duncan Forbes, the very surgeon on whom Sir John Pringle wished him
to rely, testified that he had known very desperate cases cured by the Diet
Drink. Boswell, though leaving Kennedy nominally in charge, transferred
himself to Forbes's superintendence, and went on with the Diet Drink.
If, as has authoritatively been reported, it was merely a compound decoction of sarsaparilla, we can at least assume that it did him no harm. There
were other treatments, and the illness seemed to Boswell to go off very

slowly. He never explains the nature of the very bad symptom he reported on 13 July, but he arrived in London under an apprehension that some kind of surgery would be necessary. He instructed himself in a memorandum to ask Kennedy "as to operation," and also kept making memoranda to consult Percivall Pott, though he clearly did not do so. In preparation for surgery he moved nearer to Forbes, taking rooms that pleased him in Carey Street, after trying in vain to find suitable lodgings in Boswell's Court, near Red Lion Square, and Boswell's Court, Lincoln's Inn Fields.

He slept in his new rooms (which he called *Sans Souci,* the landlord's name being Careless) just one night. On 21 September, attending at St. Paul's Coffee-house a meeting of a Whiggish club he had joined when he was last in London, he was told by Benjamin Franklin that Paoli had arrived in London. Next morning he called at the splendid apartments in Old Bond Street where Paoli was lodged. The footman made difficulties, and Boswell prepared to leave a note.

His *valet de chambre* came down. Seeing something about him like what I had been used to see in Corsica, I asked him in Italian if he was a Corsican. He answered, "Yes, Sir." "Oh, then," said I, "there is no occasion to write. My name is Boswell." No sooner had I said this than Giuseppe (for that was his name) gave a jump, catched hold of my hand and kissed it, and clapped his hand several times upon my shoulders with such a natural joy and fondness as flattered me exceedingly. Then he ran upstairs before me like an Italian harlequin, being a very little fellow, and opening the door of the General's bedchamber called out, "Mr. Boswell." I heard the General give a shout before I saw him. When I entered, he was in his night-gown and nightcap. He ran to me, took me all in his arms, and held me there for some time.

The British Government had not been willing to intervene to save Corsican independence but was very willing to honour Paoli personally. The vessel to which he had escaped from Corsica, as has been said, was British, and in coming to England he must have had the encouragement of the Ministry. The Opposition felt that in justice Paoli owed them allegiance, since it was the Opposition that had advocated intervention, and several prominent members of the Patriot group had been generous with gifts of money. Paoli, however, believed that the dignity of his position required that his approach be to the first minister of the Crown. His first call in England was on the Duke of Grafton; the Duke returned the call, and Paoli was immediately granted a pension of £1200 a year on the civil list. He lived for thirty years in dignified elegance on the bounty of the Crown, serenely detached from internal British politics. He never doubted that he owed his pension in large measure to Boswell's book and he never ceased to be grateful to him.

Though Boswell had continued to counsel himself to be quiet and to get to bed in good season, he seems actually to have been packing in about the usual amount of theatre-going, dining out, and calling on people. With Paoli's arrival he abandoned all pretence of being on a retired or frugal system. After one night in Carey Street, he took rooms near the General in Old Bond Street. He ordered two suits of coloured clothes—"a genteel plain slate-blue frock suit, and a full suit of a kind of purple cloth with rich gold buttons"—and borrowed a sword from Dilly. Paoli was for the moment first-rate copy, and in the many items about him that stud the newspapers—one is surprised to find that Boswell wrote few of them himself—Boswell's name is seldom absent. On Sunday 1 October the General, accompanied by James Boswell, Esq., took an airing in Hyde Park in his coach; on Monday 9 October the General, Mr. Boswell, and other friends, went to see St. Paul's Church, the Bank, and the Tower; on Tuesday 31 October Dr. Samuel Johnson was introduced to the General by James Boswell, Esq.; some time early that same week James Boswell presented Mr. Garrick to the General.

Boswell in the *Life* apologizes for not being so assiduous in making notes of Johnson's conversation this year, and attributes his neglect, as one would expect, to his attendance on Paoli. This is somewhat misleading. It is true that he never got the journal posted to the date of Johnson's return from Brighton, which occurred four weeks after his own arrival in London, but there cannot have been more than a meeting or two for which he did not keep notes, and some of his notes were remarkably full. The year 1769 actually contains some of the best passages in the *Life:* Rousseau and the savage life (30 September); Goldsmith's bloom-coloured coat (16 October); Johnson put to the question as to what he would do if he were shut up in a castle with a new-born child (26 October). It was also the year in which Johnson for the first time really lost his temper with Boswell and visited him with angry rebuke. Two earlier rubs of this autumn may have been ominous of the explosion: 16 October, when he commiserated with Boswell for not having lived in the days of *The Dunciad* ("It was worth while being a dunce then"), and 26 October, when he advised him if he took a medicated bath, to get his head fumigated (*"That* is the *peccant part"*). In retrospect one might feel that in these sallies Johnson was working off a sense of annoyance at Boswell for his prancings at the Jubilee and for bustling about Paoli, but one could not be certain of it, for Johnson often attacked his friends out of mere unwillingness to lose an argument or mere willingness to raise a laugh. On 26 October, however, he showed unmistakable anger with no attempt to be witty, and there is no doubt as to the cause of his outburst. Boswell had kept putting miscellaneous questions (including the one about the new-born child) to him and had pertinaciously ignored his signals that he wanted an inquisition concerning the fear of death dropped. "You pursue me," he burst out, "with question after question very idly, without seeming to care about the matter." He ordered him to be silent, showed that he wanted him to go, and called out sternly as he left, "Don't let us meet tomorrow." His anger was predictably transient. Boswell disobeyed his injunction and went back next day. Johnson was complaisant, and when Boswell started to leave, stopped him at the staircase with "Get you gone *in*." And on the day of Boswell's departure for Scotland, he drove six miles over from Streatham to see him into his chaise.

This jaunt, for all that it was supposed to be a mere excursion for health, turned out to be one of the most fruitful of Boswell's life in the making of new acquaintances. Foote praised *An Account of Corsica*—"I wanted much to see you: it is manly and there is no rubbish to clear away"—and invited him to the first of a series of excellent dinners. He met Cleland, author of the notorious *Memoirs of a Woman of Pleasure,* now a government pensioner, and thought how the meeting would have struck him if it had occurred before he had met so many more important writers. Foote introduced him to the Irish actor Charles Macklin, famous for his performances of Shylock and his own Sir Archy MacSarcasm, a veteran who had been on the stage for forty-five years and would live to be a hundred. Boswell found his conversation teasing (Johnson called it a perpetual renovation of hope and disappointment), but recorded some of it. He also now met Johnson's friends George Steevens, the Shakespearian commentator, and Thomas Tyers, manager of Vauxhall Gardens. But by far the most important addition which this year witnessed to the circle of his London acquaintance was Sir Joshua Reynolds, to whom Goldsmith presented him on 26 September. Reynolds was destined to become a loyal and affectionate friend, the closest of all Boswell's London friends after Johnson and Edmond Malone, and was very properly to receive the dedication of Boswell's greatest book.

Boswell renewed many old acquaintances: with Garrick, Armstrong, Dr. John Campbell, and General Oglethorpe; with Goldsmith, whom he had not seen for more than three years, and with Colman and Sheridan whom he had not seen for six. Colman told him the *Account* was "the truest book," invited him to breakfast, and talked to him frankly as one man of letters to another. The Sheridan family had been in France to escape creditors; Mrs. Sheridan had died, and the four children (none of whom Boswell at this point names) were "surprisingly grown." Richard Brinsley was at this time a little under eighteen. Anne Elizabeth, the youngest child, aged eleven, told her daughter Alicia Lefanu many years afterwards of her recollections of Boswell in this year: "a thin, eager-looking young man in black who talked a great deal about General Paoli." Without that recollection of a child who died an old lady in 1837, we should not know that Boswell's illness had brought him sadly down from his normal plumpness.

He got on terms of intimacy with Bennet Langton, Johnson's young friend of ancient lineage, whom he had barely met in 1768. And he got really to know the Thrales, in whose family Johnson had been living much of the time since 1766. Henry Thrale, M.P., a rich brewer of university education and good social connexions, had a fine villa at Streatham, six miles from town, and a city house in Southwark. For his wife Hester, daughter of a well-born Welsh ne'er-do-well, a short, lively, clever woman about Boswell's age, Johnson had developed a more tender affection than he felt for any other person living. Boswell had met her once in the spring of 1768 when she came in her carriage to take Johnson to the country, and he was now invited to Streatham. He probably did not see enough of the Thrales this year to enable him to form much of an opinion of either of them, but he came later to entertain a high regard for Thrale's manliness and heartiness, and to feel for Mrs. Thrale a greater degree of friendliness than he commonly granted to women. It is necessary to stress this fact, for one would draw a quite different conclusion from the evidence still most generally known. Because of an unfortunate quarrel which developed seventeen years later when he and Mrs. Thrale (by that time Mrs. Piozzi) clashed as biographers of

Johnson, he subjected her throughout the *Life of Johnson* to systematic depreciation, imparting an unpleasantly condescending and captious tone to matter which in the original journal had been friendly and even cordial.

Boswell was in general admirably free from a tendency to quarrel with his friends, but this year saw an open breach between him and a man he had once been very happy to count as an acquaintance. Joseph Baretti's strictures on the Corsicans had nettled him, and he was becoming increasingly offended with the roughness of Baretti's manners. At his first call on Baretti this year, he reported him so full of himself and so assuming and really ferocious that he found himself not a little disgusted. A month later Baretti went on trial for his life at the Old Bailey. He had struck a woman of the town who accosted him, and when three men, probably her confederates, had jostled and beaten him, he had given two of them wounds with a pocket-knife from which one of them died. Baretti's distinguished friends flocked to defend him. Reynolds, Burke, Garrick, and William Fitzherbert furnished bail, and at the trial on 20 October, Topham Beauclerk, Reynolds, Johnson, Fitzherbert, Burke, Garrick, and Goldsmith appeared as character witnesses. The jury, apparently much impressed by the testimony of three commissioners of the peace who gave evidence that such gang assaults were of common occurrence in the streets of London, acquitted him on grounds of self-defence. It has not previously been known that Boswell attended the trial, but he did, and it seemed to him from the evidence that Baretti was really guilty. He freely expressed his dissent from the verdict to his and Baretti's common acquaintance till Garrick and Langton took him in hand "in a most friendly manner" and convinced him that he was wrong. He then wrote to Baretti, admitting that he had been prejudiced, and apologized for not having called on him and for having spoken to their acquaintance against the verdict. He had much better not have done it, for on further consideration he returned to his original opinion, endorsed his draft "a weak, absurd letter," and made no attempt to conceal his dislike when he and Baretti met. I fancy his feeling against the verdict was by no means all due to prejudice against the accused but reflected the habits formed by his own practice. One gets the impression that in eighteenth-century Scotland a man who killed another with a knife would never have been acquitted on a plea of self-defence, though after conviction for murder or manslaughter he might have received commutation of sentence or even a pardon. But Boswell did undoubtedly hate Baretti personally, and he hated remarkably few persons; besides Baretti I can think only of Gibbon and Horne Tooke. His hatred of Gibbon and Horne Tooke undoubtedly sprang from their sneers at the Christian religion. Baretti was an unbeliever, too, but his crude and conventional indecencies should not have bothered Boswell any more than Wilkes's did. His unpardonable offence was pretty certainly his freely expressed contempt for the Corsicans.

Wilkes was still in gaol, the center of a tremendous constitutional struggle. The House of Commons had expelled him, the electors of Middlesex had re-elected him, the House had annulled the return and two subsequent returns, and then had finally declared him incapable of being elected and had seated his opponent. Boswell still declined to call on him, though an excellent occasion presented itself. The publisher of one of the French translations of *An Account of Corsica,* not knowing Boswell's address, sent him a copy of the book in care of Wilkes, and Wilkes sent it on to the Dillys with many compliments. "I had a desire to visit the pleasant fellow," wrote Boswell, "but thought it might hurt me essentially."

The policy was questionable, but he has stated it with his usual precision. I know, he is saying, that many of the things I want to do and shall do will hurt me, but so long as I am sincerely and publicly committed to sound principles, the hurt caused by my imprudent behaviour will be ephemeral, superficial, accidental. There are always, however, emotionally charged situations in which public opinion permits no deviation from principle. Wilkes, though personally a very pleasant fellow, and even the victim of unconstitutional government persecution, is nevertheless the symbol of a popular political movement which verges on revolution, and I cannot have *any* association with him without being thought to subscribe to principles which I abhor. The hurt from that would be permanent, deep, substantial. What remains remarkable is his assumption, in the face of all evidence, that public flaunting of one's vanities and inconsistencies does one's reputation no *essential* harm. He had created what we would now call an enviable public image of himself as the eager, the devoted, the ingenuous champion of Paoli and Corsican independence. Mere *self*-advertising could not fail to hurt that image *essentially.* Yet only three days before making that remark about Wilkes, he had staged his extravaganza at Stratford, and at the moment of deciding that a call on Wilkes was too risky, he was preparing to spread the account of his cavortings over the pages of *The Public Advertiser* and *The London Magazine*. Apart from the pan-polemist Kenrick, whose attentions to him were largely incidental to an envenomed assault on Johnson, hardly any one up to this time had attacked or ridiculed him in print. He now began, not only gratuitously to invite detraction, but even to join in it himself. On 7 October, just after Miller's print had appeared in *The London Magazine,* he published in *The London Chronicle* some anonymous derisive "Verses on Seeing the Print of James Boswell, Esq., in the Corsican Dress." He informed the public, in an anonymous paragraph in the same paper, that on 18 October James Boswell, Esq., had attended the execution of six men at Tyburn, and in order to be as near as possible, had sat on the top of a hearse that was waiting to carry away the corpse of one of the malefactors. In the next issue of the paper he inserted "Verses on Seeing Mr. Boswell on the Top of an Hearse at Tyburn, by the Author of the Verses on Seeing His Print in the Corsican Dress." Both sets of verses revive the jest about the darkness of his complexion, a matter to him obviously of such continuing import that he felt others deserved to share his interest.

At Court on 25 October, unobserved or unrecognized, he had a rare opportunity to listen in on the world's reaction to his eccentricities:

Heard Sir James Calder, Colonel Grant, and an English officer talking of your being at Tyburn, etc. One said, "There was he, Sir, on a triumphal car." All wondered how people could go to see executions. Curious.

"Curious" here, as generally in such contexts in Boswell, means, "Deeply interesting as revealing the varieties of human nature." He had concluded his Tyburn paragraph in *The London Chronicle* with the first four words of Dryden's famous character of the Duke of Buckingham, " 'A man so various,' etc."

A man so various that he seem'd to be
Not one, but all mankind's epitome.

Eglinton had once told him that he had no sense of shame, but the charge was not true. He could feel shame very powerfully, but not for very long, not as a continuing or controlling emotion. Most men are perplexed or saddened or at the very least rendered uneasy by the contemplation of their own inconsistencies, but Boswell scanned the swarming variety of contradiction in his own nature with something of the pleased detachment of a naturalist watching a sectioned ant-hill. It was *curious* that the admired author of *An Account of Corsica* should like to make a show of himself, *curious* that he should have a compulsion to attend executions, and since it was curious, the world ought to know about it.

At the time he wrote *An Account of Corsica* he had a comfortable conviction that he could have it both ways:

A man who has been able to furnish a book which has been approved by the world has established himself as a respectable character in distant society, without any danger of having that character lessened by the observation of his weaknesses. To preserve an uniform dignity among those who see us every day is hardly possible, and to aim at it must put us under the fetters of a perpetual restraint. The author of an approved book may allow his natural disposition an easy play, and yet indulge the pride of superior genius when he considers that by those who know him only as an author he never ceases to be respected.

Of course, provided that *as an author* he has not himself lessened his respectable character. If Boswell had maintained normal reserve in putting his weaknesses into print, the easy play of his natural disposition would, as he says, have harmed his public image very little outside the group that came into contact with him personally. But soon after the publication of *An Account of Corsica* he did begin informing the world of his weaknesses in newspapers and magazines, and he continued the exposure in his later books. To find the distant society where the admirable image presented by *An Account of Corsica* still stands unlessened, one has to go to the Continent, where the *Journal of a Tour to Corsica* is read and the greater Johnsonian books are unknown. A Corsican biographer of Paoli refers to Boswell as a grave man; Francesco Domenico Guerrazzi, Italian publicist and patriot, made Boswell the juvenile hero of a huge historical romance. But in English-speaking countries Boswell's character as an author has from his own days been very much compromised by knowledge of his personal sins and foibles, and he himself is mainly responsible for the knowledge. He came finally, though very unwillingly, to admit that the publishing of one's follies could hurt one essentially, but it made little real difference in his reporting. We are, on the whole, very much the gainers by his lack of reticence, and should try to remember that it is upon the whole that judgements should be made. We shall consider Boswell's odd denigrations of himself a regrettable but tolerable alloy in his generally invaluable candour: something like the absurdly hyper-conservative orthography with which he chose to invest his original and vivid journal of the Corsican tour. And we may well propose to ourselves the question whether Boswell's sort of "vanity" is not inevitable in an artist who experiences in the operations of his own mind the overwhelming uniqueness and authority which subdues the more usual kind of artist to his creation.

With his "Account of the Armed Corsican Chief at the Stratford Jubilee" Boswell began a close association with *The London Magazine* that lasted for almost twenty years. The proprietors of this magazine, which had been founded in 1732 in rivalry with Edward Cave's *Gentleman's Magazine,* appear to have been Edward Dilly, John Rivington, and Richard Baldwin, Jr. On 13 October Boswell met with them in the Poultry and arranged to purchase one sixth of the ownership. He does not record what he paid, but in 1777 he evaluated his share at £240. One naturally wonders how a man whose total income was not more than £400 a year could find such a sum. The answer probably is that he took it out of moneys which he was holding to pay for Dalblair. On acquiring title to that property, he had borrowed £2000 on it by a mortgage and £500 more from Lord Marischal on his personal bond. Unfortunately, the real beneficiaries of the sale were a group of creditors to the estate, and as their claims were confused, the trustees allowed him to hold a good part of the money to be paid on demand. He may well have thought he was making a prudent investment of some of it in the mean time. I do not know whether his purchase involved also a promise to write for the magazine, but from this time forward he was a substantial contributor.

Boswell left Scotland, it will be remembered, more than half convinced that his father had given up thoughts of marrying again. Not long after he reached London, he received two letters from Lord Auchinleck which revived his fears, though they left him still somewhat in doubt as to what Lord Auchinleck intended to do. He replied "in very strong terms," "warning him of what . . . to expect." Lord Auchinleck did not write again for a month, and it was from Margaret that he learned that his father was very angry with him. Margaret's own comments upset him dreadfully: she did not take the high enthusiastic line of eternal love to which he had committed himself, but seems to have remarked that she saw nothing

wrong or even in bad taste in second marriages, and to have asked if it
was quite fair to themselves to let such high-flying views create difficulties
for their own marriage. Boswell professed himself more shocked than he
could express: "Good God, is this her idea of love? Let me return to
abandoned profligacy." He suppressed or held up the first expression of
his displeasure, but the letter he finally sent was severe enough. The most
that he would promise was that he would do nothing rash, and that he
might bring himself to *try* to live in Scotland. Temple, Paoli, and Johnson took his father's side against him: Temple scolded him and Johnson
plied him with ridicule. It is clear that he had been showing people his
"True Story in Queen Anne's Reign":

BOSWELL. "But I have been uneasy that I did not feel enough."[1]
JOHNSON. "Why, learn then by keeping good company, and read melancholy stories as how a man's father married again, and how he was driven
into foreign parts with his wife. Ha! ha! ha!" BOSWELL. "Well, but,
Mrs. Williams, is he not wrong?" MRS. WILLIAMS. "Why, 'tis strange to
us feeling people."

He reported to John Johnston that he had not come to any resolution; he was shocked and could not think rationally of what he ought to
do. A letter from Mr. Dun "on the wretched subject" probably informed
him that Lord Auchinleck had publicly announced his intention to
marry. All his unhappy feelings revived, and he resolved on France. Dilly
either humoured or rallied him ("He for France"); Dempster took the
business seriously enough to argue with him. Then finally, on Monday 23
October, being in charming spirits and enamoured of Margaret (he had
offered up intercession for her the previous day in St. Margaret's, Westminster), he received a letter from her and "all at once assumed fortitude."
He wrote to "him"—who can it have been but his father?—a sulky, defiant, but at least decisive letter: "I must resolutely endure for my family
and not run away to a warmer climate and meanly bask in sunshine while
our *house* is ruined." One cannot justify all of Lord Auchinleck's later
harshness to his heir, but one must admit that he had about as strong
provocation as can be imagined.

[1] The passage is a previously unpublished portion of the Notes for 20 October 1769,
recording the events of 19 October. Boswell and Johnson have been talking about
Baretti's trial, and discussing the question as to how much one should feel for the
distresses of others.

We have seen that on 21 September Boswell had planned for immediate surgery. But he dreaded the operation and kept postponing it; and
it appears from his notes that he was probably more insistent on the knife
than his advisers were. Finally, on 15 October Duncan Forbes "came,
and with kindness to save dire forebodings, *cut*." The operation did not
immobilize him, even for the day, for he called both on Kennedy ("nonsense") and—apparently for the first time this year—on Pott ("sensible,
neat, and fine"). And though he had counselled himself to consult with
Pott once for all, he went back to him nine days later, apparently to get
his advice about a second incision. Pott was most reassuring: told him he
might be easy as to the distemper; that there was no occasion for further
surgery; and that in marriage any abnormalities that remained would
"come right." Pott's verdict was as good as he could have obtained anywhere in Great Britain in 1769, or for that matter, for more than a century later.

After 24 October, therefore, Boswell no longer had the excuse of
health to detain him longer in London, but he wanted to see more of
Paoli, who had left London on the 12th, not to return till the 29th, and
in any case he never went back to Edinburgh more than a day or two before he absolutely had to. On the 28th he received shocking news from
Margaret: Lord Eglinton had been dreadfully wounded in attempting to
disarm an excise officer whom he suspected of poaching on his grounds,
and his life was despaired of. He had in fact died three days before Boswell received the letter. He was only forty-six years old. We have no contemporary comment from Boswell recording his feelings on this heavy
news, but years later he testified to his "emotions of most affectionate
regret" for the man who first introduced him "into what alone deserves
the name of life." He can hardly have failed to consider how fast his gay
companions of 1760 were dropping away. The Duke of York had died at
Monaco in 1767, Sterne in London in 1768, Derrick at Bath in the spring
of 1769.

Paoli came back, and he presented Garrick to him. And on the 31st
he got Paoli and Johnson to witness his signature to his marriage contract, which he had drawn himself.

The said parties do hereby agree that, in consideration of the sin-
cerest mutual love and regard, they will, on or before the holy festival of
Christmas next to come, be united to each other by marriage.

They solemnly engage to be faithful spouses, to bear with one another's faults, and to contribute as much as possible to each other's happiness in this world, hoping through the merits of their blessed Saviour Jesus Christ for eternal happiness in the world which is to come.

It had been agreed that on this trip he would pay Temple a visit in Devonshire, but he had repeatedly postponed it because of the slow progress of his cure. By the kind of scramble he enjoyed, he now managed to fit in three days at Mamhead. Set out by stage-coach to Exeter on the morning of Wednesday 1 November; rumble on day and night; arrive at Mamhead on the morning of Friday the 3d; post-coach from Exeter at one in the morning of Monday the 6th, back in London on the evening of Tuesday the 7th.

When he had suggested a visit in the spring of 1768, Temple had begged off because of the cramped and sordid accommodations of his parsonage, a small thatched cottage. "Shall we not meet?" Boswell had complained, "Have you positively no bed in your parsonage for me? But may I not come and sit up a night with you—if Mrs. Temple will allow it?" By 1769 an apartment for guests had been fitted up, or (more probably) Mrs. Temple's strong repugnance at entertaining guests had been overcome, for Boswell reported that the parsonage contained several very tolerable rooms. He was prepared to like Mrs. Temple, and thought (mistakenly) that she had friendly feelings for him; he was delighted, in the small and ancient parish church, to assume in person his obligations as godfather of his friend's first-born son, now a year old. And he was enchanted with Temple's conversation and friendly sentiment, "more valuable," as he reported to Margaret, "than I can describe without appearing to exaggerate." He had been puzzling himself again both with Dr. Johnson and with Garrick about the thorny question of God's prescience and man's free will, and was wonderfully helped by a passage in Montesquieu's *Lettres persanes* which he came upon or which Temple showed him at Mamhead on this visit.

One might have thought that he would have started for Scotland on the 8th, so as to have a day at Lainshaw with Margaret before the Session opened. But he had, as he would have said, an invitation he could not resist. On 9 November the new Lord Mayor, William Beckford, and the other City officials were being installed with the usual sumptuous ceremonials. Let *The London Chronicle* continue:

The Stationers' Company sent an invitation to General Paoli and James Boswell, Esq., to go in their barge to Westminster and back again. The General excused himself on account of his being somewhat indisposed [Beckford was a prominent Wilkesite], but James Boswell, Esq., came on board and accompanied the Company up and down the river. He was carried in a chair to Mr. Kearsley's, bookseller in Ludgate Street, where, having seen the procession pass, he went and dined with the Lord Mayor.

Beckford's public banquets are said to have been the most elaborate that had occurred in England since the reign of Henry VIII.

Boswell had been invited to sleep at Streatham that night, so that he could say farewell to Johnson next morning without requiring Johnson to come in to London. But he was "detained in town till it was too late," no doubt by his usual deferred tasks of packing and writing letters, and drove out to Streatham on the morning of the tenth. Johnson gave him good advice on marriage, and then, in a surge of affection, accompanied him back to London so as to see him off in his post-chaise. He was put badly behind schedule by the Streatham excursion, but by travelling a large part of the way without sleep, arrived in Edinburgh in time to be in Court by nine o'clock on the morning of the 14th.

He had been very faithful in writing to Margaret (by his own record twenty-seven times since 1 September, to her twenty-six), and she was touchingly grateful for his thoughtfulness, though one wonders how she managed to get much comfort out of his letters. He had lectured her severely for her insensitivity with regard to second marriages, had repeatedly disappointed her by postponing the time of his return, had worried her by reports that he was melancholy or ill with a cold, and had scared her by proposing to bring Paoli down to Scotland and having him witness the marriage.

I sincerely wish he may not come [she wrote], but if he does, and you signify to me your desire to have him, you may believe I shall agree, whatever it should cost me. Do not again take a disgust at me and think me a weak, awkward, spiritless being. Remember, with advantages vastly superior to mine, you yourself was uneasy in the presence of the illustrious chief. . . . I wish you could steal out of Edinburgh when nobody can suspect where you are going, and let the ceremony be put over as privately as possible.

It is clear from this letter and from the marriage contract that as late as 31 October Boswell had not set a day for his wedding. One might conclude from Margaret's letter that she was urging a clandestine marriage, but surely she merely meant that she wanted it quiet. A regular marriage would require the proclamation of banns in Stewarton kirk on a Sunday, at least forty-eight hours before the ceremony. Boswell, I think, learned on his arrival in Edinburgh that his father's banns were to be proclaimed on Sunday 19 November, the wedding to follow on Saturday the 25th; and either by letter or a week-end visit arranged to have his own banns also proclaimed on the 19th, and got Margaret to set their wedding for the same day as his father's. At any rate, the two weddings occurred simultaneously on that day at Edinburgh and at Lainshaw, Lord Auchinleck's at the home of his bride's mother, Boswell's at the home of his bride's sister, her parents being both long since dead.

He remained the old self-indulgent Boswell right up to the end. "I am so earnestly invited to Bothwell Castle that I cannot refuse," he wrote to Margaret. "So I shall be there [Friday] night. Your gown comes with me. You can soon put it on. Let dinner be late. We shall both dress in white before it." Peggie, then, was not even allowed a leisurely try-on of her wedding dress. He made amends—or thought he did—by bringing Archibald Douglas with him to witness her signature to the marriage contract.

At Lainshaw House, then, some time in the evening of Saturday 25 November 1769, James Boswell and Margaret Montgomerie were united in marriage. The ceremony was probably performed by the minister of the parish, the Reverend Thomas Maxwell.

Boswell took a week off for a honeymoon, the first time he had absented himself from Court in term-time when not ill since he had passed advocate. I suppose he got some of his causes deferred and arranged with Crosbie or Nairne or Maclaurin to handle the others. He and Margaret seem to have spent at least a day or two of their honeymoon at Auchinleck House. We know at any rate that *he* was there at some time during that week and that he was hurt and still seething with rage. He knelt on the ruins of the Old Castle, and, holding a crumbled fragment in his hand, swore "that if any man had the estate in exclusion of the rightful heir, this stone should swim in his heart's blood (I keep the stone)."

Such fierce language, combined with the pointed fixing of his marriage for the same day and hour as his father's, looks like the complete defiance which he had threatened, and so does a sentence in the letter of 23 November already quoted: "I cannot think of our coming to my father's house. It would be mixing gall with my honey." Yet when Boswell returned with his bride to Edinburgh on 1 December, they took rooms temporarily in the house directly above Lord Auchinleck's, which was odd if they intended to have no dealings with him, and next day—just a week after the proud and resentful gesture of the synchronized weddings—they went meekly to dine with Lord Auchinleck and his new spouse. One realizes then that Boswell would not have mentioned his and Margaret's going to stay in his father's house as a possibility if Lord Auchinleck had not invited them; and the invitation shows that the older and steadier man had refused to let himself be pushed into reciprocal defiances. He and Margaret, and probably even the new Lady Auchinleck, had all along been solicitous to preserve at least formal concord, and Boswell was a man who found it very difficult to preserve ill humour. This was not the first time that complaisance had broken in on his fierce outcries and violent gestures, and it would not be the last.

On 5 December 1769 he and his bride set up housekeeping in a house of their own in the Cowgate. Let this volume end with an entry from poor Lieutenant John Boswell's diary, recording their first serious piece of entertaining:

THURSDAY [21 DECEMBER].... Dined at my brother's betwixt three and four, my father, Mrs. Boswell, and the Balmuto family there. Drunk [tea] there too.

The Family bears scars, but it has consolidated.

NOTES,

Mainly References to Sources

Boswell assembled perhaps the most extensive and coherent mass of useful biographical documents that has ever come into the hands of a biographer, and the biographer must pay for the detailed concreteness of his narrative by a weight of annotation that may seem oppressive. If the documents were all in print and he could use the conventional concise notation of volume and page, the situation would be bad enough, but in fact the documents remain in great part unpublished, and reference to those in print is perplexed by the small number of sets of Colonel Isham's privately printed *Private Papers of James Boswell* accessible, and by the variant pagination of the American and English settings of five of the eight volumes so far issued in the trade series of the Yale editions. In any case, since the present volume is likely to be in use for a long time without revision and the Yale research edition will ultimately print practically all the documents a biographer needs to refer to, it would be misleading to label some documents published and others unpublished. The best solution until the research edition is completed is to give references that will apply equally to the printed collections and to the manuscript collections at Yale and elsewhere. Fortunately, the documents are in the main dated or datable, and in all printings they are bound to be arranged more or less chronologically. I therefore refer to journal (memoranda, notes) by date and to letters by name of recipient or sender and date. The Catalogue of the Boswell manuscripts at Yale, which is scheduled for publication in Yale's research edition in the near future, will indicate which of the documents are in the Library of Yale University. Yale's research edition, I may add, will include *all* Boswell's extant correspondence, whether at Yale or elsewhere.

As of the date of publication of the present volume, the principal printed collections of documents from Boswell's private papers are the following:

1. *Private Papers of James Boswell from Malahide Castle, in the Collection of Lt.-Colonel Ralph Heyward Isham,* ed. Geoffrey Scott and F. A. Pottle, Privately Printed, 18 vols., 1928–1934. Index vol., 1937.

2. The trade or reading edition of Boswell's papers published by the McGraw-Hill Book Company, Inc., and William Heinemann, Ltd., 8 Boswell vols. published, 1950–1963, and several more planned.

3. *Letters of James Boswell*, ed. C. B. Tinker, 2 vols., Clarendon Press, 1924.
4. *The Correspondence of James Boswell and John Johnston of Grange*, ed. R. S. Walker, Heinemann and McGraw-Hill, 1966. The first volume of Yale's research edition.

Practically everything labelled "Journ." in the following notes will be found in No. 1 or No. 2, or both. The chances of finding "Mem." and "Notes" are not so high. Of the letters cited, perhaps half will be found in one or other of the four collections. It should not be forgotten that Nos. 1 and 2, though they consist mainly of journal, do contain some letters.

References to the text of the *Life of Johnson* and to *The Journal of a Tour to the Hebrides, 1785*, when only Boswell's own text and notes are in question, are also made by dates, thus enabling the reader to use any edition.

References are omitted in the Notes when the text provides adequate identification. I have not always thought it necessary to report borrowings from previous publications of my own, especially from the editorial matter of the reading edition. In most cases of duplication, the reading edition borrowed from the present book (which was accessible to the editors in typescript), and not the other way about.

"Ibid." invariably means "the title last cited." "Op. cit." and "loc. cit." refer the reader no farther back than the note immediately preceding. Roman numerals from i to x are used to designate volumes when citations are given in the form "vi. 150," but arabic numerals are employed for all volume numbers larger than ten, and for all volume numbers preceded by the specific notation "vol."

Subjects which run over a page, whether consisting of single or grouped items, are located by the page on which the subject begins, not, as is usual with footnotes, by the page on which it ends. When annotation for a given item appears to be lacking, glance back over the notes for a page or two preceding.

The following short titles are employed:

A & W: James Paterson, *History of the Counties of Ayr and Wigton*, 3 vols. in 5 parts, 1863–1866.

Almon: *The Correspondence of the late John Wilkes ... in which are introduced Memoirs of his Life*, by John Almon, 5 vols., 1805.

A. P. S.: The Acts of the Parliaments of Scotland, 11 vols., 1814–1844. General Index, 1875.

Arnot: Hugo Arnot, *The History of Edinburgh*, 1788.

Auchinleck Memoirs: Manuscript notes on the lairds and family of Auchinleck, begun by James Boswell of Auchinleck (d. 1749) and continued by Lord Auchinleck.

Baronage: Sir Robert Douglas, *The Baronage of Scotland*, 1798.

Bergeret: P. J. O. Bergeret de Grancourt, *Bergeret et Fragonard, journal inédit d'un voyage en Italie, 1773–1774*, 1895. (Mémoires de la Société des antiquaires de l'Ouest, 2 sér., t. 17.)

Bleackley: Horace Bleackley, *Life of John Wilkes*, 1917.

Boswelliana: Boswelliana, the Commonplace Book of James Boswell, with a Memoir and Annotations by the Rev. Charles Rogers, 1874.

"Boswell's University Education": F. A. Pottle, "Boswell's University Education," in *Johnson, Boswell and their Circle: Essays presented to L. F. Powell in Honour of his Eighty-fourth Birthday,* 1965.

BP: *The Private Papers of James Boswell from Malahide Castle, in the Collection of Lt.-Colonel Ralph Heyward Isham,* ed. Geoffrey Scott and F. A. Pottle, 18 vols., 1928–1934. Index vol., 1937.

BU: *Biographie universelle, ancienne et moderne,* with supplement, 85 vols., 1811–1862.

Burke, *Landed Gentry:* Sir Bernard Burke and others, *Burke's Genealogical and Heraldic History of the Landed Gentry,* 1937 (unless some other date is specified).

Casanova: *Mémoires de J. Casanova de Seingalt . . . Édition nouvelle p.s.l.d.* Raoul Vèze, 11 vols., 1924–1932.

Chronologie J.-J. R.: L. J. Courtois, *Chronologie critique de la vie et des oeuvres de Jean-Jacques Rousseau,* 1924. (*Annales de la Société Jean-Jacques Rousseau,* t. 15.)

College of Justice: George Brunton and David Haig, *An Historical Account of the Senators of the College of Justice,* 1832.

Colonna and Villat: P. P. R. Colonna de Cesari-Rocca et Louis Villat, *Histoire de Corse,* 1927.

Comp. Baronet.: G. E. Cokayne, *Complete Baronetage,* 5 vols., 1900–1906. Index vol., 1909.

Comp. Peer.: G. E. Cokayne, revised by Vicary Gibbs and others, *The Complete Peerage of England, Scotland, Ireland, Great Britain, and the United Kingdom,* 13 vols., 1910–1959.

Consultation Book: Manuscript consultation (fee) book of James Boswell, 1766–1772, in the National Library of Scotland.

Corsica: James Boswell, *An Account of Corsica, The Journal of a Tour to that Island, and Memoirs of Pascal Paoli . . . The Third Edition, corrected,* London, 1769.

Deeds: Register of Deeds and Probative Writs (also called Books of the Lords of Council and Session), Scottish Record Office. Identification in the earlier period is by volume only, in the later by clerk's office ("Dal." for Dalrymple, "Dur." for Durie, "Mack." for Mackenzie) and volume.

Deelman: Christian Deelman, *The Great Shakespeare Jubilee,* 1964.

Dennistoun: James Dennistoun, *Memoirs of Sir Robert Strange . . . and . . . Andrew Lumisden,* 2 vols., 1855.

Dibdin: J. C. Dibdin, *The Annals of the Edinburgh Stage,* 1888.

DNB: *The Dictionary of National Biography from the Earliest Times to 1900,* ed. Sir Leslie Stephen and Sir Sidney Lee, various printings.

Donaldson's *Collection: A Collection of Original Poems by the Rev. Mr. Blacklock and other Scotch Gentlemen,* 1760 ("vol. 1"). *A Collection of Original Poems by Scotch Gentlemen,* 1762 ("vol. 2").

Douglas Cause: A. F. Steuart, *The Douglas Cause,* 1909. (Notable Scottish Trials.)

Erskine Corresp.: *Letters between the Honourable Andrew Erskine and James Boswell, Esq.,* 1763.

Faculty of Advocates: Sir Francis J. Grant, *The Faculty of Advocates in Scotland, 1532–1943,* 1944. (Scottish Record Society, part 145.)

Fasti Scot.: Hew Scott, *Fasti Ecclesiae Scoticanae,* 7 vols., 1915–1928 (unless the edition of 1866–1871 is specified).

Foladare: Joseph Foladare, *James Boswell and Corsica,* 2 vols., 1936. (Unpublished Yale dissertation. The second volume is a critical annotated edition of *An Account of Corsica.*)

French Themes: Boswell's French exercises at Utrecht, 1763–1764 (Yale MS. M87).

Gent. Mag.: The Gentleman's Magazine, ed. Edward Cave and others, 1731+.

Glasgow Matric.: W. I. Addison, *The Matriculation Albums of the University of Glasgow from 1728 to 1853,* 1913.

Godet: Philippe Godet, *Madame de Charrière et ses amis,* 2 vols., 1906.

G. R. O.: General Registry Office, Edinburgh.

History of Glasgow: Robert Renwick, Sir John Lindsay, and George Eyre-Todd, *History of Glasgow,* 3 vols., 1921–1934.

Jacobite Peerage: The Marquis of Ruvigny and Raineval, *The Jacobite Peerage,* 1904.

Johnston Corresp.: *The Correspondence of James Boswell and John Johnston of Grange,* ed. R. S. Walker, 1966.

Josephson: Matthew Josephson, *Jean-Jacques Rousseau,* 1931.

Journ.: Boswell's journal.

Kay: *A Series of Original Portraits...* by ... John Kay, 1877 (paginated as 2 vols., but often bound as 4).

Lalande: J. J. Lalande, *Voyage d'un françois en Italie, fait dans les années 1765 et 1766,* 8 vols., A Venise et se trouve à Paris, 1769. (There is another edition, Yverdon, 1769–1770, which I take to be unauthorized. It is in 8 vols., and appears to present Lalande's text, plus foot-notes and Supplement not by him, but the pagination is different.)

Letters: Letters of James Boswell, ed. C. B. Tinker, 2 vols., 1924.

Life: James Boswell, *The Life of Samuel Johnson,* originally published in 2 vols., 1791. Reference by volume and page is to the edition of G. B. Hill, revised by L. F. Powell, 6 vols., 1934–1964.

Lit. Car.: F. A. Pottle, *The Literary Career of James Boswell,* 1929.

Lond. Chron.: The London Chronicle, 1757+. (The title varies, but is *The London Chronicle* throughout the volumes to which I make reference.)

Lond. Mag.: The London Magazine, 1732–1785.

Maitland: William Maitland, *The History of Edinburgh*, 1753.

Mem.: Boswell's dated memoranda, after the autumn of 1764 generally combined with journal notes.

Memoirs: "Memoirs of James Boswell, Esq.," in *The European Magazine*, 19 (1791). 323–326, 404–407; reprinted in *Lit. Car.*, pp. xxix–xliv. Page references to both printings are provided, that of *The European Magazine* preceding.

MS. Hist.: "Boswell of Auchinleck," genealogical history of the Boswells of Auchinleck, with indication of sources, 14 folio pages in Boswell's hand. In the Hyde Collection.

N & Q: Notes and Queries for Readers and Writers, Collectors and Librarians, 1850+.

NBG: Nouvelle biographie générale depuis les temps les plus reculés jusqu'à nos jours ... p.s.l.d. J. C. F. Hoefer, 46 vols., 1853–1866.

Notes: Boswell's journal notes.

Old and New Edinburgh: James Grant, *Cassell's Old and New Edinburgh*, 3 vols., ?1881–1883.

PMLA: *Publications of the Modern Language Association of America.*

P. R. S.: Particular Register of Sasines, Scottish Record Office. Cited by county, e.g. P. R. S. Ayr.

Pub. Advt.: The Public Advertiser, 1734–1798. (The title varies, but is *The Public Advertiser* in the period for which I have used it.)

Ravenna: Leona Ravenna, *Pasquale Paoli*, 1928.

Reg. Let.: Boswell's registers of letters sent and received, 1763–1769 (Yale MSS. M251, M252, M253).

R. M. S.: Registrum Magni Sigilli Regum Scotorum. The Register of the Great Seal of Scotland, 1306–1668, 12 vols., 1814–1914.

Rousseau, *Corresp. gén.: Correspondance générale de J.-J. Rousseau, collationnée sur les originaux, annotée et commentée par* Théophile Dufour, 20 vols., 1924–1934.

R. S. S.: Registrum Secreti Sigilli Regum Scotorum. The Register of the Privy Seal of Scotland, 1488–1574, 7 vols., 1908–1963.

Scotland and Scotsmen: John Ramsay, *Scotland and Scotsmen in the Eighteenth Century*, 2 vols., 1888.

Scots Mag.: The Scots Magazine, 1739+.

Scots Peer.: Sir James Balfour Paul, *The Scots Peerage*, 9 vols., 1904–1914.

S. R. O.: Scottish Record Office, Edinburgh.

Stochholm: Johanne M. Stochholm, *Garrick's Folly: The Shakespeare Jubilee of 1769*, 1964.

Ten Lines: Boswell's dated exercises of heroic verse.

Testaments: Testaments, Scottish Record Office, cited by commissariot, e.g. Edinburgh Testaments, Glasgow Testaments, and date of recording.

Tour: James Boswell, *The Journal of a Tour to the Hebrides with Samuel Johnson,* originally published in 1785. *Tour,* 1961 (1963) is the Yale edition, ed. F. A. Pottle and C. H. Bennett, originally published 1936, revised 1961. The American and English printings have the same pagination.

Treasurer's Accounts: Compota Thesaurariorum Regum Scotorum. Accounts of the Lord High Treasurer of Scotland, 1473–1566, 11 vols., 1877–1916.

NOTES

CHAPTER I

p. 5.
"At his seat in the country."] After getting his sketch back from Rousseau, Boswell carefully inked over all those portions of it that might give a clue to the lady's identity. I have not been able to make out this sentence with complete certainty, but I am pretty sure that I can see "Il me fit venir passer [*undeciphered passage of perhaps twelve to fifteen spaces*] Campagne."

CHAPTER II

p. 7.
Auchinleck] In Boswell's time this was generally pronounced Ahfleck'. At the present time the common pronunciation, even in the neighbourhood, follows the spelling, with open Scots *ch* and stress on the final syllable: Awχinleck'. The first volume of Boswell's journal in the Yale research edition of the Private Papers of James Boswell will contain a detailed and documented genealogy. In the mean time the following may be consulted: (1) MS. Hist.; (2) *Baronage,* pp. 458–460; (3) *A & W,* i. 190–197; (4) Burke, *Landed Gentry,* 1952; (5) large folding chart, "The Parent Tree of the Boswell Family," by Jasper John Boswell, Leeds, 1900, compiled to accompany his *History and Genealogical Tables of the Boswells,* vol. 1, 1904. The projected volume of J. J. Boswell's work which would have contained the history of the Scots Boswells was unfortunately never published.

Thomas Boswell's wife descended from the Auchinlecks] She is shown by a charter of James V in her favour, 10 Feb. 1513–14 (*R.M.S.* iii. No. 7) to have been one Annabel or Anabella Campbell. *Baronage* (p. 458) and *Scots Peer.* (v. 494–495) agree in making her the daughter of Sir Hugh Campbell of Loudoun (d. 1530) and his wife Isobel, daughter of Sir Thomas Wallace of Craigie. The family of Auchinleck, however, believed her to have been the only child of Sir Hugh Campbell's father, George Campbell of Loudoun, Sheriff of Ayrshire (d. c. 1492), by his second wife, Marion Auchinleck, only daughter of Sir John Auchinleck of that ilk. Though no documentary proof of this descent is forthcoming, it is a highly plausible deduction from the documents, and was confidently asserted in a note among the Auchinleck papers by Lord Auchinleck, a scrupulous genealogist. See a learned and candidly argued anonymous document among the Boswell papers, bearing date 1859: "Notes regarding the Descent of the Boswells of Auchinleck from the Family of Auchinleck of that ilk, taken from the Family Chartulary prepared under the Direction of Lord Auchinleck."

James Auchinleck] The slaughter of Auchinleck of that ilk occurred in 1449 (*A & W*, i. 187–188; see also Samuel Johnson, *A Journey to the Western Islands of Scotland,* near the end).

Thomas Boswell] The sources are MS. Hist.; *Baronage,* p. 309; *A & W*, i. 190–191; *R.M.S.* ii. Nos. 2805, 2859; iii. No. 7; *Treasurer's Accounts,* vols. 2 and 3 *passim*. Robert Pitcairn, who extracted and published several entries concerning him from the Treasurer's books, concluded that he was one of the King's minstrels (*Ancient Criminal Trials in Scotland,* 1833, i. pt. 1, *121, *124, reprinted *Boswelliana,* p. 3). The editor of the third volume of *Treasurer's Accounts* (Sir James Balfour Paul) styles him "Master of the Wardrobe" in the index to that volume. Sir James Fergusson believes that the various disbursements made to him for buying minor articles of dress for the King and for "daunsing geir" for himself "and his complicis" indicate, as stated in the text, that he was merely a gentleman of the bedchamber or squire of the body.

David Boswell and the Battle of the Butts] Auchinleck Memoirs; MS. Hist.; *History of Glasgow,* i. 369–370. The fourth Earl of Lennox and the third Earl of Glencairn, taken prisoner by the English at the Battle of Solway Moss (1542), had been persuaded by Henry VIII to advance by force of arms in Scotland Henry's scheme to marry the infant Queen Mary to his son Edward and to get Henry himself declared Protector of Scotland. Glencairn assembled an army at Glasgow, where he was supported by the provost and citizens. The Earl of Arran, Governor (Regent) of the Kingdom, met the insurgents at what the Auchinleck documents call Glasgow Muir and modern historians the Battle of the Butts, 24 May 1544, and put them to flight with considerable loss of life on both sides. Cuninghame of Caprington, David Boswell of Auchinleck, and eight others received a remission under the Privy Seal, 6 Jan. 1553–54, for thus coming against the Governor (*R.S.S.* iv. No. 2331). This is apparently to be taken as a confirmation of a general Act of Remission granted by the Estates to Glencairn and all his adherents, 12 Dec. 1554 (*A. P. S.* ii. 450).

John Boswell, Langside] MS. Hist.; *A & W*, i. 191–192; *History of Glasgow,* ii. 17–20; Sir Walter Scott's *Tales of Grandfather,* vol. 3, ch. 7. The Battle of Langside, Queen Mary's "final and fatal defeat" (Scott), was fought at Langside, now a suburb of Glasgow, on 13 May 1568, between the Queen's forces and those of the Earl of Moray, Regent for the infant James VI. John Boswell being on the losing side, his goods and gear were escheated to the Master of Ochiltree, son of the second Lord Ochiltree, John Boswell's first cousin and already or about to become his father-in-law (Letter of gift dated 22 Aug. 1568: *R.S.S.* vi. No. 439.) Escheats were more often than not compounded (that is, operated in practice as fines), and when granted to near relations constituted a light or merely formal penalty. John Boswell lived down to about 1610, but he held the fee of Auchinleck little if any over ten years. Five years after Langside, reserving his own liferent, he made over the barony of Auchinleck to his eldest son by his first marriage, James, then not more than ten years old (MS. Hist.; Antenuptial contract between John Boswell . . . and Christian Dalzell, 22 Aug. 1562, the marriage to take place by Michaelmas: Deeds, v. ff. 315–316; Charter by John Boswell . . . to James Boswell . . . of the barony of Auchinleck, precept of seisin dated 3 May 1573: Instrumentum sasinae Jacobi Boswell baroniae de Auchinleck, dated 22 May 1573).

James Boswell, the 4th laird] MS. Hist.; Glasgow Testaments, 25 Aug. 1618; *A & W*, i. 192–193. Besides retaining a private army, he was the father of soldiers. One of his sons, Captain John, was killed in England at the battle of Seacroft Moor in the Civil War, 30 Mar. 1643. Three others (George, John, and Matthew) went abroad to fight under Gustavus Adolphus, and at least one of the three left descendants in Prussia (To Christoph Leopold von Boswell and August Ferdinand von Boswell, 10 June 1791; From August Ferdinand von Boswell, 30 July 1814; From Christoph Leopold von Boswell to Alexander Boswell, 1 Aug. 1798; From Frau E. von Boswell, 10 Feb. 1795; From Robert Boswell to Sir James Boswell, 4 Sept. 1850). Since one of James Boswell's daughters married James Law, Archbishop of Glasgow, it would appear that he supported the unpopular cause of Protestant episcopacy.

p. 8.
David Boswell, the fifth laird] MS. Hist.; *A & W*, i. 193. Richard Cameron, the covenanting leader, was slain by royal troops at Airds Moss, on or very near the Auchinleck estate, 22 July 1680, during the fifth laird's incumbency (DNB under Richard Cameron; L. R. Muirhead's *Scotland,* 1959, p. 175).

Pride and high estimation of themselves] Margaret Boswell's charge, Journ. 6 Jan. 1780.

Pride of ancient blood] *Tour,* 18 Aug. 1773.

Thomas Boswell an earl's grandson] His mother was Lady Margaret Sinclair, daughter of the Earl of Caithness (*Scots Peer.* ii. 334).

David Boswell's marriage] David Boswell was betrothed to Janet Hamilton, natural daughter of the first Earl of Arran, in the lodging of Sir James Hamilton of Finnart at Linlithgow, 13 Feb. 1531–32, the witnesses, among others, being the second Earl of Arran and Sir James Hamilton of Kincavil, Sheriff of Linlithgowshire. The marriage followed next day in the parish church of Linlithgow (Scottish Record Soc., *Protocol Books of Dominus Thomas Johnsoun, 1528–1578,* 1920, items 40, 41). This was a match with brilliant prospects, for Sir James Hamilton of Finnart, a natural son of the first Earl of Arran, was the favourite of King James V, and the young Earl of Arran stood second in the line of succession to the throne, the King as yet being unmarried. But David made nothing of his brilliant chances. The deeds of arms in which he was engaged in the 1530s were provincial and apparently sordid. Along with his mother's second husband, John Cuninghame of Caprington, and nineteen others, he was put to the horn (outlawed) and escheated for the murder of John Tod, 8 Oct. 1530 (*R.S.S.* ii. No. 750). In 1537, again along with Cuninghame and others, he had to find caution to underlie the law for the mutilation of John Sampsoune of his right thumb (Robert Pitcairn, *Ancient Criminal Trials in Scotland,* 1833, i. pt. 1, p. *201). When he did cross the page of public history in 1544, he appeared, not on the side of his brother-in-law Arran, now declared second person in the kingdom and Regent, but in the forces opposed to him.

John Boswell, the third laird] He was twice married, both his wives coming from families with turbulent histories. In 1553 Robert Dalzell of that ilk, father of his first wife, Christian Dalzell, received a most solemn and humble apology from Lord Maxwell for the slaughter of his grandfather at Dumfries; his mother, Margaret Hamilton, was murdered by Ninian Dalzell (*Scots Peer.* ii. 403-404). John Boswell's second wife was a Stewart, descended (with bend sinister) from James II. She was not, as *Scots Peer.* says (vi. 510-511), the daughter of the second Lord Avandale, but of Lord Avandale's grandson, the second Lord Ochiltree (c. 1521-1592: MS. Hist.; *Baronage;* Burke, *Landed Gentry*). Lord Avandale fell at Flodden with Thomas Boswell; his eldest son, the first Lord Ochiltree, married, like David Boswell, a daughter of the first Earl of Arran. According to Jasper John Boswell's chart, John Boswell married Katherine Stewart in the year of Langside, 1568, but it is rather more probable that he was already Ochiltree's son-in-law at the time of the battle than that he compounded his escheat by the marriage. As stated in the text, his second wife was a sister to James Stewart, the "upstart" Earl of Arran, and to Margaret Stewart, the second wife of John Knox (DNB under John Knox; *Scots Peer.* i. 394-397; vi. 513-514; Sir Walter Scott, *Tales of a Grandfather,* vol. 3, ch. 7).

James Boswell, the fourth laird] His wife was Marion Craufurd, daughter of David Craufurd of Kerse; her mother was a daughter of Malcolm, third Lord Fleming, by Janet Stewart, who was a natural daughter of James IV by the Countess of Bothwell. After Lord Fleming's death, Lady Fleming went to France to superintend the education of the child Queen, and there became the mistress of Henri II. The history of the Flemings was remarkably violent. Malcolm, the third Lord, was killed at the Battle of Pinkie (1547); his father, the second Lord, was assassinated while hawking by the Tweedies of Drumelzier; his mother, with her two sisters Sybilla and Margaret Drummond, died of poison presumably intended only for Margaret, she being the mistress of James IV (*Scots Peer.* viii. 535-540; *A & W,* i. 402; DNB under Margaret Drummond). Malcolm's second son and successor as fifth Lord Fleming (Marion Craufurd's uncle) fought at Langside with John Boswell and accompanied Queen Mary in her flight to England (*Scots Peer.* viii. 543-544).

Marriage of James Boswell, the biographer's grandfather] Detail in the text, p. 11. Thomas Bruce of Clackmannan, from whom the Bruces of Carnock, Earls of Kincardine, descended, was probably related to King Robert I, but cannot have been his son or his brother.

Royal and noble connexions of the Boswells of Auchinleck] The fact that

Boswell was absurdly vain of his ancestry does not free a biographer from the obligation of specifying it. Two of his lines of descent from the royal house of Stuart (both deriving ultimately from the Princess Mary Stuart, Lady Hamilton, daughter of James II and sister of James III) are displayed in Chart I, Appendix C, of *Boswell: The Ominous Years, 1774–1776*. The descent on his father's side (through the marriage of David Boswell with a daughter of the first Earl of Arran) is no less direct than that through the Erskines, but the Erskine descent is more brilliant as involving no illegitimate generations and reinforcing the Hamilton connexion with the great names of Lennox and Mar. Also, as the Chart shows, it provides in John Stuart, Earl of Lennox (d. 1526), a closer common ancestor with James VI and the later Stuart line than the descents from James II do. As a matter of fact, Boswell's least remote *royal* descent was another illegitimate one on his father's side, not shown on the Chart. Marion Craufurd, daughter of David Craufurd of Kerse, wife of James Boswell, the fourth laird, was on her mother's side, as has been said, a grand-daughter of Janet Stewart, Lady Fleming, a natural daughter of James IV by the Countess of Bothwell. Three of the early lairds of Auchinleck married illegitimate blood royal no more than four generations removed from the throne. Besides the second laird, David, who married a great-grand-daughter of James II, and James, the fourth, who married a great-grand-daughter of James IV, John, the third, married as his second wife a great-great-grand-daughter of James II. Boswell was descended from the Earls of Arran, Caithness, Kincardine, Lennox, and Mar, and from the progenitors of the Earls of Carnwath, the Dukes of Hamilton, the Earls of Loudoun, and the Earls of Wigtown. Among peers contemporary with himself, he was third cousin twice removed to the Earl of Buchan (1742–1829), fourth cousin to the ninth Lord Cathcart, third cousin to the third Earl Cowper, grand-nephew to the eighth Earl of Dundonald, second cousin once removed to the ninth Earl of Elgin and Kincardine, and cousin in a more remote degree (fourth cousin twice removed) to the sixth Earl of Kellie. Sir Charles Douglas, Bt., who succeeded as Marquess of Queensberry in 1810, was the grandson of his first cousin, Sir John Douglas of Kelhead, Bt. Sir James Erskine of Alva, Bt., who in 1805 succeeded as Earl of Rosslyn, was his second cousin once removed (*A & W; Scots Peer.; Comp. Peer.; Comp. Baronet.;* see also the first note for this chapter).

p. 9.
David Boswell, the fifth laird]   MS. Hist.; *A & W*, i. 193.

David Boswell, the sixth laird]   Ibid.; Auchinleck Memoirs.

James Boswell, the seventh laird]   The date of his birth has not been found, but it was apparently not earlier than 1667 and not later than 1677. His parents' antenuptial contract of marriage is dated 24 July 1666 (Recorded 2 Jan. 1678, Deeds [Dur.] 43. 370–374), and he passed advocate on 9 Dec. 1698 (*Faculty of Advocates*). From his manuscript diary and expense account kept at Leyden, 10 Sept. 1695 to 7 Aug. 1697 (Yale MS. C338), I should infer that he was then a youth of nineteen or twenty, which would place his birth-date c. 1676. He died on 21 Apr. 1749 (*Scots Mag.* 11. 206). The other sources are *Scotland and Scotsmen*, i. 160–161; Journ. 12 Dec. 1776; 19 Sept. 1778; 7 June 1779; Bond of Provision, Mr. James Boswell to Mr. Alex Boswell, his Son, dated 6 Oct. 1734, to be effective on Alexander's marriage (1738). James settled on Alexander all his heritable and movable effects as they stood at the time of Alexander's marriage, reserving a liferent of one half of the subjects. In the eleven years following, however, he could have accumulated a considerable property.

Alexander Boswell, Lord Auchinleck] Boswell's journal (28 Feb. 1777; 1 Mar. 1782) places his birthday on 1 Mar., N.S., and the Auchinleck baptismal register, now in the Register General's Office, Edinburgh, establishes 1707 as the year of his birth. Other references: Auchinleck Memoirs; *Scotland and Scotsmen,* i. 160–171; DNB under Alexander Boswell; *College of Justice,* p. 518; *Faculty of Advocates;* annual almanacs and registers, 1760–1782; "Boswell's Life of Johnson," in Thomas Carlyle's *Critical and Miscellaneous Essays,* paragraph 13. Carlyle actually says "first King's Sheriff in Scotland," but he or his informants must have misquoted. Alexander Boswell's commission was one of at least several dated 18 Mar. 1748 (S.R.O., R.M.S. unprinted [Paper Register] 19. 18, 27). "Sheriff of Galloway" is Lord Auchinleck's own expression (Auchinleck Memoirs). To W. J. Temple, 25 Sept. 1763 ("I am born to an estate of a thousand a year"; see also From Andrew Erskine, 7 July 1762). Lord Auchinleck makes brief reference to his student days in Leyden in his letters to Boswell dated c. 3 Sept. and 8 Oct. 1763. *Boswell for the Defence, 1769–1774,* and *Boswell: The Ominous Years, 1774–1776,* contain (Appendix B) an account of the Scottish courts and legal system.

p. 10.
The three houses at Auchinleck] *A & W,* i. 186–187; Helen J. Steven, *Auchinleck,* 1898, pp. 43–51; David MacGibbon and Thomas Ross, *The Castellated and Domestic Architecture of Scotland,* 1887–1892, iii. 496–497; personal observation. Sir James Fergusson, from a study of charters and sasines, concludes that the Old Castle was the place of residence of the family at least as late as 19 Sept. 1621, when David Boswell of Auchinleck signed a precept "apud castrum de Auchinleck" (P.R.S. Ayr, vol. 2, f. 265, l. 17). He concludes that the Old House (second of the three mansions) was built by David Boswell some time in the next ten years, for a charter granted by James V to David and his wife, 12 Feb. 1531–2, designates the dwelling-place of Auchinleck *turris* rather than *castrum* (R.M.S. iii. No. 1133). The Old House was inhabited at least as late as 14 Sept. 1761 (Erskine Corresp. p. 12); the New House was occupied by 17 Aug. 1762 (To John Johnston). The New House is in Adam style, but it cannot have been designed by Robert Adam, nor by William Adam unless it was a very long time building. Surviving bills paid during 1758–1760, while construction was going on, name no architect.

p. 11.
Lord Auchinleck's character] *Scotland and Scotsmen,* i. 161–177; an early chum of Boswell's called him "the greatest Whig in Britain" (From William McQuhae, 26 Apr. 1763).

Euphemia Erskine, first Lady Auchinleck; Lt.-Col. John Erskine; and Culross] First Outline and First Draft of Sketch for Rousseau, 5 Dec. 1764

(Yale MSS. L1109, L1108); Journ. 25 Sept. 1774; 17 Mar., 3 May, 4 June, 26 Aug., 3 Oct. 1780. *Faculty of Advocates,* p. 18, says that Euphemia Erskine was born on 21 Apr. 1718. I do not know the compiler's source, but the date fits. Col. John was the son of Sir Charles Erskine of Alva, Kt., and his second wife, Helen Skene, widow of Robert Bruce, Lord Broomhall (*Scots Peer.* iii. 488; v. 622). He was born in 1660 (Baptized 19 Sept. 1660, Alva Register of Baptisms, G.R.O.), and consequently was a good deal older than Euphemia Cochrane, his third wife, who was probably born in 1693 (*Scots Peer.* vii. 349: Ochiltree Register wanting from 4 June 1693 to 1 Aug. 1694). His first wife (m. 1682) was Jean Murray, daughter of John Murray of Polmaise (A. S. Gillon, "James Stuart, younger of Dunearn, and Sir Alexander Boswell of Auchinleck," in *The Stewarts, a Historical and General Magazine for the Stewart Society,* v [1926]. 124). From their daughter Helen, who married Sir William Douglas of Kelhead, Bt., the present Marquesses of Queensberry descend. His second wife (m. 1697: Alloa Register of Marriages, G.R.O.) was Lady Mary Maule, Dowager Countess of Mar, mother of the Earl of Mar who led the Pretender's forces in the Rebellion of 1715. This marriage appears to have been childless. By his third marriage with Euphemia Cochrane (Post-nuptial marriage contract 5 Oct. 1714: Deeds [Dal.], vol. 142, 28 Nov. 1737) he had three daughters, the eldest of whom, Mary, married the Rev. Alexander Webster (1707–1784). The Colonel's Close, at present generally called "the Palace of Culross," a fine old tenement with curious painted ceilings, now the property of the National Trust, consists of two closely adjoining but separate houses built respectively in 1597 and 1611 by Sir George Bruce of Carnock, the progenitor of the Earls of Kincardine. It got its eighteenth-century name from the fact that at the judicial sale of 1700 it had passed, with most of the Kincardine lands, to the Hon. Col. John Erskine, thereafter styled of Carnock. This Col. Erskine of Carnock was not Boswell's grandfather but a kinsman of his grandfather, another descendant of the prolific Earl of Mar (1558–1634). He was Governor of Stirling Castle, and Boswell's grandfather was his deputy. Tradition has it that the Hon. Colonel lived in one half of Sir George Bruce's *palatium* and rented the other half to his namesake. People in Culross distinguished them as "the black Colonel" and "the white" or "the fair Colonel," Boswell's grandfather being "the white." See *Scots Peer.* ii. 366; iii. 487 and David Beveridge, *Culross and Tulliallan,* 2 vols., 1885, *passim.* As may well be imagined, the two colonels have been frequently confused in historical and genealogical studies. Boswell's grandfather died about Martinmas 1737 (Dunblane Testaments, vol. 20, pp. 26–29).

p. 12.

Boswell's birth]   A transcript of the relevant entry in the Edinburgh Baptismal Register, 18 Oct. 1740 O.S., is printed in *N & Q,* 3d ser., vii. 197. The Register records the birth as occurring in the morning of the same day. Boswell mentions his birthday specifically several times in his journal, e.g. 29 Oct. 1777, 29 Oct. 1780, 29 Oct. 1792. He was living in the fourth storey of Blair's Land at an early age (Journ. 8 Jan. 1780). This house had been his grandfather's before it was Lord Auchinleck's (Journ. 13 Jan. 1777).

p. 13.

Edinburgh] William Maitland, *History of Edinburgh,* 1753, pp. 217–220, using the formula "population in any year is twenty-eight times the number of burials in that year," found the average population of Edinburgh in the period 1741–1747 to have been a little over 50,000. Hugo Arnot, *History of Edinburgh,* 1788, pp. 330–340, using the formula "population in any year is six times the number of families in that year" (the number of families being established by the survey of houses for the purpose of collecting road-money), estimated that by 1775 the population was more than 82,000. Application of Arnot's proportion to the number of families reported by Maitland would give a population c. 1750 of about 54,000. My topography, apart from personal observation, is based on Maitland, Arnot, the Royal Scottish Geographical Society's *Early Views and Maps of Edinburgh,* 1919, *Old and New Edinburgh,* and Tobias Smollett's *Humphry Clinker,* 1771: letters by Matthew Bramble and Winifred Jenkins dated 18 July. The remarkable structure, called by Maitland "the highest private building probably upon earth," which stood at the south-east corner of the Parliament Close, has been assigned a bewilderingly various number of storeys by those to whom it was a familiar sight, and the discrepancies are not all reconcilable by assuming that some enumerations reckon each row of windows a storey, while others exclude the basement level, or the garret level, or both. Seven storeys on the Close and twelve on the Cowgate, including garrets and basement, seems to me best authenticated, in spite of Boswell's own testimony that the building had "thirteen floors or storeys from the ground upon the back elevation" (*Tour,* 16 Aug. 1773). Edinburgh's tallest building perished in the great fire of Nov. 1824, which also destroyed the entire range of buildings on the east side of the Close (Maitland, pp. 185, 187; Arnot, p. 241; William Hunter [publisher], *The New Picture of Edinburgh, being an Accurate Guide to the City and Environs,* c. 1806, p. 80; London *Morning Chronicle,* 22, 23, 24 Nov. 1824, reprinting from *The Edinburgh Star* and *The Scotsman* of the previous week). Boswell's detail of his route home from the University (To John Johnston, 15 Feb. 1763) and his mention of the Custom House Stairs (Maitland, p. 187) show that Blair's Land stood on the east side of the Close.

p. 14.

Boswell's sister] Dr. David Cooper, minister of Auchinleck, to Lord Auchinleck, 14 Feb. 1741. John was born on 25 Sept. 1743, N.S., and David on 9 Sept. 1748, N.S. ("List of Ages" in a pocket notebook of Boswell's, 1785, formerly in the possession of Professor C. B. Tinker). For the fourth son, presumably christened Charles, see p. 25. In naming their children, the Boswells followed the custom usual in Scotland with established families: first son named for father's father, second son for mother's father, third son for father's grandfather, and so on. But an infant son's name was often used again when he died before his next brother was born.

Scott and Boswell] I have developed this theme at considerable length in *Essays on the Eighteenth Century presented to David Nichol Smith,* 1945, pp. 168–189.

p. 15.

Boswell's recollections of the year 1745] *Life,* 14 July 1763, n.; Ten Lines, 22 Oct. 1764; Journ. 3 Aug. 1782. He appears also to refer to this same house in a note recording a dream, 3 Mar. [1792 or later]: "A confused jumble of being in a garden and gathering fallen pears, being at my father's old house at Parkside, now an inn" (Yale MS. M78). I am told (letter from the late C. A. Malcolm, 4 May 1955) that there are now no houses in the Newington district that go back to 1745, but it would perhaps be possible to locate the site of the house in which Boswell lived from his information that in the summer of 1782 it was occupied by David Stewart, W.S. (Journ. 3 Aug. 1782) and that ten years or so later it had become an inn. From the account of Newington in *Old and New Edinburgh* (iii. 50–51) it seems likely that it was the small manor-house known in the nineteenth century as West Mayfield House.

Mundell's School] *Memoirs,* p. 323 (xxix); A. Cameron Smith, "The Mundells, Two Famous Schoolmasters," in *Dumfries and Galloway Standard and Advertiser,* 15 Jan. 1938; another version of the same in *Transactions* of the Dumfriesshire and Galloway Natural History and Antiquarian Society, 3d ser., 22 (1938–1939, pub. 1942). 115–128. A pamphlet (copies at Yale and in the Library of the University of Glasgow) entitled *List of Scholars educated by the Late Mr. James Mundell* was printed at Edinburgh by Mundell and Wilson, 1789, for the use of the Club of Mundell's scholars. The boys are grouped under years of admission, the name "James Boswall" appearing under the year 1746. For Boswell's references to and accounts of the anniversary meetings, see Notes, 7 Mar. 1772, 15 Jan. 1774; Journ. 21 Jan. 1775, 18 Jan. 1777, 13 and 17 Jan. 1778. Mr. Cameron Smith located Mundell's School in the West Bow by relating the Stent Rolls (tax lists), now preserved in the municipal archives (City Chambers) with the Edinburgh directories. There exist elaborate scale-drawings of the buildings on both sides of the Bow made in 1830 by Thomas Hamilton, architect (DNB under Thomas Hamilton, 1784–1858). In voluminous unpublished notes now preserved in the Ewart Public Library, Dumfries, Cameron Smith attempted to identify the very land that housed Mundell's School. He apparently did not come to a firm conclusion, but his notes seem to me to indicate that it stood about half way down the West Bow, on the east side of the street, to the north of, and immediately adjoining, the more famous Mahogany Land, which frequently appears as an illustration in books on old Edinburgh. See *Old and New Edinburgh,* i. 320: the building I mean has the sign "Anderson" over the right-hand shop on the ground floor.

p. 16.

"Spirits crushed," etc.] First Outline of Sketch for Rousseau, 5 Dec. 1764 (Yale MS. L1109).

p. 17.

Major Weir] See the sources listed in DNB under Thomas Weir, especially George Hickes, *Ravaillac Redivivus,* 1678. Add Henry Mackenzie, *The Anecdotes and Egotisms,* ed. H. W. Thompson, 1927, p. 45; Sir Walter Scott, *Letters on Demonology and Witchcraft,* 1830, pp. 329–333; Sir Daniel Wilson, *Memorials of*

Edinburgh in the Olden Time, 1873, pp. 333–338; *Old and New Edinburgh,* i. 310–314.

The Heart of Midlothian]   Chapter 4, Mrs. Howden speaking: "There was my daughter's wean, little Eppie Daidle . . . had played the truant frae the school, as bairns will do, . . . and had just cruppen to the gallows-foot to see the hanging." Scott professes to be writing of the year 1736. He himself was born in 1771, but in this matter could write from personal recollection, for the public executions in the Grassmarket were continued to 1784 (*Old and New Edinburgh,* ii. 231).

p. 18.
Boswell's attitude towards executions] *The Hypochondriack* No. 68 (ed. Margery Bailey, 1928, ii. 276–285); Journ. 4, 5, 6 May 1763.

Mr. Dun] *Fasti Scot.* iii. 4.

Sheriff of Wigtownshire] *Scotland and Scotsmen,* i. 162–163.

p. 19.
Not much of Boswell's early childhood spent at Auchinleck] The family would in any case have gone to Auchinleck only in the vacations of the courts, and would presumably have remained in Edinburgh through the spring vacations while Boswell was in Mundell's School (1746–1748 or 1749). The summer of 1745 was spent at Newington. A letter from Dr. David Cooper, minister of Auchinleck, shows that the family was in Edinburgh in September 1741 and had not been at Auchinleck recently (David Cooper to Mrs. Euphemia Boswell, 28 Sept. 1741).

Nymphs and genii at Auchinleck, Old James Boswell and Enoch] First Outline of Sketch for Rousseau, 5 Dec. 1764 (Yale MS. L1109); Journ. 20 Sept. 1777.

CHAPTER III

p. 20.
Joseph Fergusson] *Fasti Scot.* ii. 223.

Scurvy] First Outline of Sketch for Rousseau, 5 Dec. 1764 (Yale MS. L1109); Article "Scorbutus" in Robert James, *A Medical Dictionary,* 1743–1745; James Lind, *A Treatise on the Scurvy,* 3d ed., 1772; A. F. Hess, *Scurvy Past and Present,* 1920; article "Scurvy," by Laslo Kadji, in *Nelson Loose-leaf Medicine,* 1920 and later, iii. 141–160L.

p. 21.
Old James Boswell's melancholy] Besides First Draft of Sketch for Rousseau, 5 Dec. 1764 (Yale MS. L1108), Journ. 7 June 1779; 10 Sept. 1780.

Boswell's uncle James] "Finally had to be put in a strait-waistcoat" expands an elliptical but I think not doubtful passage. The French (Yale MS. L1109, 5

Dec. 1764) reads, "Ses fils un oisif—á la fin lie—melan. & au lit." Boswell's uncle John: Journ. 19 Sept. 1774; 23 Mar. 1776; 10 Apr. 1777.

Boswell's brother John]   To John Johnston, 8 Feb. 1763; Journ. 5 Jan. 1763; 9, 11, 12 Dec. 1774 and *passim*.

Moffat]   There is great need of a well-documented history of Moffat Spa in the eighteenth century. My sources, apart from present-day guide-books (e.g. L. R. Muirhead's *Scotland,* 1959, pp. 93–96) and personal observation, are John Macky, *A Journey through Scotland,* 1723, pp. 12–13; George Skene, "Account of a Journey to London" (1729), in *The Miscellany* of the Third Spalding Club, ii (1940). 123; Thomas Garnett, *Observations on a Tour through the Highlands . . . of Scotland,* etc., 1800, ii. 240–241; Agnes Marchbank, *Upper Annandale: its History and Traditions,* 1901; W. R. Turnbull, *History of Moffat,* 1871; and especially J. T. Johnstone, "Moffat and Upper Annandale in the Middle of the Eighteenth Century," in *Transactions* of the Dumfriesshire and Galloway Natural History and Antiquarian Society, 3d ser. i (1913). 191–211. That Mr. Fergusson went along and that Boswell took warm baths we learn from French Theme, c. 14 Oct. 1763.

p. 22.

Scenery about Moffat]   For an account of an excursion to the Grey Mare's Tail and Loch Skene, see J. G. Lockhart, *Memoirs of the Life of Sir Walter Scott,* under the year 1805. See also *Marmion,* end of Introduction to Canto II, and Scott's note.

"We never have such stomachs"]   To John Johnston, 15 Feb. 1763.

p. 23.

Boswell at the University of Edinburgh]   I have explored this topic in much greater detail, with full references, in "Boswell's University Education."

"Narrowness" of Boswell's education]   Discarded Portion of Sketch for Rousseau, 5 Dec. 1764 (Yale MS. L1111); Journ. 27 June, 9 Aug., 18 Oct., 28 Dec. 1764; To J. J. Rousseau, 31 Dec. 1764 (examples only). "Jeel": To W. J. Temple, 1 May 1761; 1 Feb.–8 Mar. 1767; 2 Apr. 1791; From W. J. Temple, 8 Aug. 1786.

p. 24.

Memorization of Latin verse]   To Alexander Boswell, 7 Feb. 1794.

Boswell a good Latinist]   J. G. Winter, "A Point in Boswell's Favor," *Michigan Alumnus,* 58 (24 May 1952). 236–246. The late R. W. Chapman has somewhere commended Boswell's Latin, but I cannot remember where. It may have been in a private letter to me.

p. 25.

Lord Auchinleck raised to the bench]   *College of Justice,* p. 518; *Boswelliana,* p. 5 n.; Newcastle Papers, British Museum Add. MSS. 32995, f. 24^v, Aug. 1753 ("Lord of the Session in the room of Lord Dun. Earl of Hyndford—recommends Mr. Boswell"); Auchinleck Memoirs.

p. 26.
Boswell beaten for lying]　Journ. 8 Jan. 1780.

Boswell too delicate for corporal punishment]　Second Outline of Sketch for Rousseau, 5 Dec. 1764 (Yale MS. Li110).

p. 28.
"Leaf discarded from the Sketch"]　Yale MS. Li111.

Boswell's meeting with Temple and Johnston]　Matriculation Roll of Robert Hunter's Greek class, 10 Mar. 1756, in the Matriculation Office, University of Edinburgh. Temple and Boswell in their later correspondence allude several times to Hunter and his class (see above, note on p. 23), but Boswell and Johnston never make any mention of having been class-mates or even of having been in the University at the same time. Temple clearly did not know Johnston before the summer of 1767. Yet the twenty-seventh signature in Hunter's list, 1755–1756, is almost certainly that of John Johnston of Grange, and I am inclined also to identify as his the signature "John Johnston" in Stevenson's list, ?1757–1758.

p. 29.
John Johnston's age]　See the evidence for Thomas Johnston's age collected by Professor Ralph S. Walker in Appendix I (pp. 330–331) of Johnston Corresp. The evidence—especially that of Thomas Paxton's lists—is explicit and respectable, but acceptance of the implied birth date for John Johnston produces such a cluster of chronological anomalies as in my opinion to warrant taking the evidence with a shade of reserve. I shall go into this teasing question at length in the first volume of the research edition of Boswell's journal.

Johnston's character]　See Professor Walker's perceptive introduction to the Boswell-Johnston correspondence. I do not myself see in the existing evidence any grounds for assuming that in the early stages of the friendship Johnston played generally a more dominant role than he did later. He was undoubtedly a much better-read antiquary than Boswell, and may have stimulated him and led him on in that department. For the rest he seems to me just Eeyore. The coat with a straw-coloured lining is mentioned in Boswell's letter to him, 19 July 1763.

William Johnson Temple]　Temple's character is fully revealed in his Diaries, ed. Lewis Bettany, 1929, and his voluminous correspondence with Boswell. For "Jimmy" and "Willie" see Temple's letters to Boswell of 17 June 1758 and 28 May 1766, Boswell's to Temple of 29 July 1758. See also Boswell's verse "Epistle to Temple" in Douce MS. 193 in the Bodleian Library, ff. 82, 82ᵛ; Extract, W. J. Temple to Lord Auchinleck, c. 9 Aug. 1759.

p. 30.
Boswell's introduction to Anglicanism]　Journ. 25 Dec. 1776; From W. J. Temple, 4 Jan. 1786; From Sir David Dalrymple, 10 Oct. 1764; Journ. 16 July 1769, 2 Sept. 1781. The chapel which Boswell attended was not the ancestor of Old St. Paul's, the Scots Episcopal church on the east side of Carrubber's Close whose

present handsome edifice is believed to cover the site of its eighteenth-century place of worship (Mary E. Ingram, *A Jacobite Stronghold of the Church,* 1907). There were in 1755 two kinds of Anglican chapels in Scotland. The Episcopal Church in Scotland, the direct descendant of the church established under the Stuarts, had been non-juring since the Revolution, and was the object (especially after the Rebellion of 1745) of severely repressive statutes because of its persistent loyalty to the exiled line. The priests of this church, even if they were prepared to take the oaths and pray for King George by name, were forbidden under severe penalties to officiate to congregations of more than four persons at a time besides their own families. The statutes were probably not strictly enforced in 1755, but for fear that they might be, congregations of the Episcopal Church in Scotland met quietly and obscurely. The greater number of Scots Anglicans, at least in the cities, attended "qualified" chapels served by priests in English or Irish orders, who read the liturgy of the Church of England and conducted their cures as peculiars or independents, without obedience to the Scottish bishops. Qualified chapels, though non-conformist, were perfectly legal and public, could even be fashionable, and had much more splendid appointments and ceremonial than those of the oppressed Episcopal Church in Scotland. Between 1755 and 1786 Boswell frequently attended Anglican services in Edinburgh, but, so far as is known, always in qualified chapels. The meeting-place of the qualified congregation in Carrubber's Close was Allan Ramsay's luckless theatre, finished in 1737 and closed by the magistrates almost as soon as it was opened (*Old and New Edinburgh,* i. 239). General sources: Arnot, pp. 283–289; Maitland, pp. 168–169; *Scots Mag.* ix (1747). 47, 608; 36 (1774). 505–506; Frederick Goldie, *A Short History of the Episcopal Church in Scotland,* 1951; George Grub, *An Ecclesiastical History of Scotland,* 1861, vol. 4; J. P. Lawson, *History of the Scottish Episcopal Church from the Revolution to the Present Time,* 1843; Anthony Mitchell, *A Short History of the Church in Scotland,* 2d ed., 1911; William Stephen, *History of the Scottish Church,* 1894–1896, vol. 2.

Boswell's early sexual development] Discarded portion of Sketch for Rousseau, 5 Dec. 1764 (Yale MS. L1111); First Outline for same (Yale MS. L1109); Sketch for Rousseau (above, p. 4); Second Outline for same (Yale MS. L1110). The Kinsey Report lists climbing trees as "a rather common source" of spontaneous ejaculation in adolescent boys (A. C. Kinsey, W. B. Pomeroy, and C. E. Martin, *Sexual Behaviour in the Human Male,* 1948 and later, p. 191). For Miss Mackay see Journ. 3 Jan. 1763.

CHAPTER IV

p. 31.

Internal changes] Journ. 2 June 1764.

"One of the outlines"] First Outline of Sketch for Rousseau, 5 Dec. 1764 (Yale MS. L1109).

Braddock's defeat, Highland regiments]   *Gent. Mag.* 25 (1755). 378, quoting from an article in *The London Gazette* dated 26 Aug.; *Scots Mag.* 18 (1756). 194, 302; 19 (1757). 55, 259.

Men in the Highland regiments supposed to be Highlanders]   Some of the second battalion of the Royal Highlanders (embodied 1758) were actually Irishmen who had appropriated or were given Highland names (Archibald Forbes, *The Black Watch,* 1897, pp. 59–60).

p. 32.

Boswell's Methodism]   Most of the relevant information is conveniently collected in Dugald Butler, *John Wesley and George Whitefield in Scotland,* 1898, and W. F. Swift, *Methodism in Scotland: The First Hundred Years,* 1947 (bibliography). The first Methodist Society in Edinburgh was established in 1761, John Wesley preaching in the Society's room on 9 May of that year (Swift, p. 44; Butler, p. 243). Boswell did not meet Wesley till 1779, though he may have heard him preach before that (*Life,* following 4 May 1779; Wesley's *Journal,* ed. Nehemiah Curnock, 1910, vi. 239 n. 3). Whitefield preached to enormous crowds in Edinburgh in 1741, 1742, 1748, 1750, 1751, 1752, 1753, 1756, and 1757 (Butler, pp. 21–54), and it is hard to believe that Boswell was not among his auditors on more than one of these occasions. Boswell later testified to having had "some share" of Whitefield's "pious and animated society" (*Letter to the People of Scotland,* 1785, p. 25), but does not say when or where. For Whitefield's practice of counselling, see Butler, pp. 27, 28; for Dr. Webster's support of him, ibid., pp. 32, 38, 39, 42, 45, 46. "Methodists next shook my passions" is Journ. 20 Mar. 1768. Lady Auchinleck's interest in Whitefield is inferred from a letter to her from Dr. David Cooper, minister of Auchinleck, 28 Sept. 1741. "Religion of the heart and salvation by faith" is John Wesley himself (quoted, Swift, p. 30).

p. 33.
Jaunt to Carlisle in 1757]   Journ. 21 Aug. 1778.

John Williamson]   *Scotland and Scotsmen,* ii. 327–335. Ramsay, who was four years older than Boswell, went to Moffat in this very summer of 1757 to drink the waters of Hartfell Spa, and rambled extensively with Williamson. Boswell, by comparing the scenery of St. Sulpice in Switzerland with that of Hartfell, shows that he had been at Hartfell himself (Journ. 15 Dec. 1764). The round trip from Moffat to Hartfell Spa is close to ten miles.

p. 34.
Boswell's Romanticism]   C. B. Tinker, *Young Boswell,* 1922, p. 181.

Byron and Mary Duff]   "How the deuce did all this occur so early? Where could it originate? I certainly had no sexual ideas for years afterwards; and yet my misery, my love for that girl were so violent that I sometimes doubt if I have ever been really attached since. Be that as it may, hearing of her marriage several years after was like a thunder-stroke—it nearly choked me.... And it is a phenomenon in my existence (for I was not eight years old) which has puzzled and will puzzle me to the latest hour of it" (Journal, 26 Nov. 1813, ii. 347–348 in R. E. Prothero's ed. of the *Letters and Journals*, 1898–1901). For Byron's age at the time see L. A. Marchand, *Byron*, 1957, i. 41–42.

Boswell's Shelleyanism] For Shelley consult any of the biographies. I do not mean to imply that Shelley's mild old prophet (Dr. Lind) taught him vegetarianism. He seems to have got that from books—originally, probably, from Plutarch. See K. N. Cameron, *The Young Shelley*, 1950, pp. 223–232, 374–379.

"The truth is . . ."] Journ. 11 Dec. 1762.

p. 35.
Boswell's height] Four years later he described himself as "rather fat than lean, rather short than tall" (To Andrew Erskine, 17 Dec. 1761). In his thirty-fifth year he weighed 166 pounds clothed (Mem. Wilton House, 20 Apr. 1775). He delighted all his life in allusions to the darkness of his complexion, which he perhaps considered a sign of virility (e.g., From Andrew Erskine, 11 Sept. 1761; Erskine Corresp. pp. 4, 5; *Lond. Chron.* 24–26 Oct. 1769; see above, pp. 326, 434). His hair was thick and heavy (Journ. 17 Mar. 1776). Professor A. S. Pitt, himself left-handed, told me once that he inferred that Boswell was left-handed from his habit of turning his lines down in the right-hand margin, when he was cramped for space, rather than up. I have found no documentary confirmation of this interesting suggestion.

Miss Whyte] To W. J. Temple, 29 July 1758; F. A. Pottle, "Boswell's Miss 'W——t'," in *N & Q*, 148 (1925). 80; Sir James Fergusson, "Boswell's First Flame," in *Scots Mag.* n.s. 19 (Aug. 1933). 331–334.

p. 36.
Tinker] C. B. Tinker, *Young Boswell*, 1922, p. 92.

Sir David Dalrymple] DNB under that name; To W. J. Temple, 29 July, 16 Dec. 1758.

Lord Somerville] *Life*, foot-note to the discussion, in the year 1781, of Johnson's life of Pope (iv. 50 n. 2); *Memoirs*, p. 323 (xxx); James Hutton (ed.), *Selections from the Letters and Correspondence of Sir James Bland Burges*, 1885, pp. 5–16; *Scots Peer.* viii. 33–37; John Jackson, *The History of the Scottish Stage*, 1793, pp. 14–16. Sir Walter Scott, who gave a full account of the literary sources of *The Fortunes of Nigel*, seems nowhere to have acknowledged having created Nigel Oliphaunt and his servant Richard Moniplies out of the century-later Somerville and his retainer Old Robin, but the parallels between the two narratives are too close to be accidental. Scott would hardly have needed special sources of information for so well known a story as Somerville's, but he nevertheless had them. Somerville's grandson, the fourteenth Lord, was his neighbour and intimate friend (*Scots Peer.* viii. 40–41); and seven years before the appearance of *Nigel* Scott had edited for publication the *Memorie of the Somervilles* by Somerville's great-grandfather, a labour which entailed collecting materials for a brief biographical sketch of Somerville himself (ii. 479–484). It is tantalizing, however, to find that in this sketch Scott made no mention of the particular details which I am suggesting that he borrowed.

p. 37.
Legal status of the Edinburgh theatre] Arnot, pp. 364–370; Dibdin, pp. 49–54.

Boswell's early attitude towards the stage] Journ. 14 Dec. 1762.

p. 38.
Boswell left in lodgings in the spring of 1758] Boswell twice mentions having "lodged" or "lived" in the same house in Edinburgh with a Captain Cordwell; on the latter occasion he names his landlady as "Mrs. Rainie" and places the year, though not with complete certainty, as 1758 (Journ. 30 Apr. 1763; 5 June 1786). In 1763 or 1764 he recorded an anecdote concerning a renter of rooms in Edinburgh, one "Lucky Rannie" (*Boswelliana*, pp. 217–218). The Stent Rolls for 1757 and 1758 but not later show Mrs. Rannie, a "room-setter" on the east side of Parliament Close (information furnished by the City Archivist, Miss Helen Armit, to Sir James Fergusson). There is evidence that separate rooms of a "house" or flat in the same stair with Lord Auchinleck's were regularly rented out as lodgings. On 6 Nov. 1762, having arrived in Edinburgh before his parents and finding Lord Auchinleck's house not yet opened, Boswell took a room "in Mrs. MacKenna's, in our stair, where I had formerly lodged" (Journ. 7 Nov. 1762). It is on record that in 1769 a Mrs. Guthrie, who let rooms, occupied the flat above Lord Auchinleck's (Journal of Lt. John Boswell, 1 Dec. 1769). The chances are that Mrs. Rannie, Mrs. MacKenna, and Mrs. Guthrie were successive landladies of the same lodging house in Blair's Land. The fact that Boswell occupied a room in this house does not necessarily mean that he had escaped from parental supervision. He says the room he took in Mrs. MacKenna's in 1762 was the one "where Mr. Fergusson and Davy used to sleep" (Journ. 7 Nov. 1762). This looks as though Lord Auchinleck had been accustomed to eke out his sleeping space by renting a room for the governor and one of the boys in the house above him. I feel sure, however, that if Boswell had meant that he used Mrs. Rannie's room in 1758 merely as sleeping quarters, he would not have said that he "lodged" or "lived" there. He meant that at that time he was on his own; and the date of his first period of independence is so important in the record of his early years as to justify the scanning of a body of evidence that in itself may seem trifling.

Digges and Love] DNB under West Digges and James Dance ("Love" was a stage-name); To W. J. Temple, 29 July 1758. DNB's aspersions on Digges's legitimacy are unwarranted. He was the son of Thomas Digges, Esq., of Chilham Castle, Kent, by the Hon. Elizabeth West, daughter of the 6th Lord Delawarr (Arthur Collins, *Peerage of England,* ed. Sir Egerton Brydges, 1812, v. 25).

"From nine to ten," etc.] To W. J. Temple, 16 Dec. 1758.

CHAPTER V

p. 40.

Lady Houston's play] *Memoirs*, p. 323 (xxx). John Ramsay notices the affair (*Scotland and Scotsmen*, i. 171 n.), but was probably mistaken in ascribing to Boswell some of the scenes of the play as well as the prologue. Yale has a manuscript copy of the prologue in Boswell's hand (Yale MS. M266). Lady Houston and Boswell were fourth cousins, both being descended from James Boswell, fourth laird of Auchinleck. See Chart 2, Appendix C, of *Boswell: The Ominous Years, 1774–1776*. For an account of her and her plays, see *N. & Q.* 3d ser. x. 81–83. *The Coquettes* (which has never been published) was probably a translation of Thomas Corneille's *Les Engagements du hasard*. The precise date of the performance has not yet been fixed, but I suggest with some confidence the limits January–May 1759.

Mrs. Cowper] "Methodist. Pythagorean. Companion of players. Madly in love with an actress, wanted to marry her" (Second Outline of Sketch for Rousseau, 5 Dec. 1764 [Yale MS. L1110]). Temple names her in the letter in which he expresses surprise at Boswell's transformation: "I heard an odd story here [Berwick] of you and one Mrs. Cooper" (n.d., probably early Sept. 1759). She acted at Richmond, summer 1749; was at Bath, 1750–spring 1753; Drury Lane, season of 1753–1754; Dublin, 1754–1755; Drury Lane, 1755–1757, and came to Edinburgh for the winter season, 1758–1759, remaining for the summer season 1759 (*Daily Advertiser*, 1 Sept. 1749; 27 July, 31 Aug. 1753 [Richmond]; Sybil Rosenfeld, *Strolling Players and Drama in the Provinces, 1660–1765*, 1939, pp. 187, 189, 191 [Bath]; *Faulkner's Dublin Journal*, 5 Oct. 1754 to early June 1755, *passim* [Dublin]; *The London Stage, 1660–1800*, pt. 4, 1747–1776, by G. W. Stone, 1962, pp. 382–430 *passim*, 499–599 *passim*; John Genest, *Some Account of the English Stage*, 1832, iv. 380; playbill of the Edinburgh theatre, 23 Dec. 1758, Mrs. Cowper cast as Indiana in *The Conscious Lovers*, "from the Theatre Royal, Drury Lane, being her first appearance on this stage"). Boswell called her Sylvia in writing to John Johnston, 26 Sept. 1759: "Would you believe it? The report of my affection for Sylvia has already reached the ears of my friend Temple." She acted Sylvia (clearly her best role) to Dexter's Captain Plume in Edinburgh on 11 July 1759 (*A View of the Edinburgh Theatre*, 1760, pp. 24–27: see the note immediately following this). The details as to family, marriage, widowhood, and virtue come from Temple's letter to Boswell, 25 Dec. 1759–14 Jan. 1760 (which also comments on her performance at Newcastle), and Boswell's verse "Epistle to Temple," which styles her "Lavinia" and credits her with a daughter (Douce MS. 193 in the Bodleian Library, ff. 83, 83ᵛ, 96, 96ᵛ). The evidence for her being a Roman Catholic, with additional testimony to her virtue, is given in the Appendix. I know nothing of her history after 1759.

p. 41.

Descriptions of Mrs. Cowper in contemporary reviews] *A View of the Edin-burgh Theatre during the Summer Season, 1759 ... By a Society of Gentlemen,* 1760, pp. 11, 15, 17, 26. See the note on this work below, p. 467.

Boswell becomes a Mason] Allan Mackenzie, *History of the Lodge Canon-gate Kilwinning, No. 2,* 1888, p. 85. The present age-requirement for admission probably did not come into force much if any before the beginning of the nineteenth century (information furnished by the Grand Secretary of the Grand Lodge of Scotland).

Boswell may have lingered in Edinburgh] This is suggested by the date of his initiation. Lord Auchinleck was usually at Auchinleck by 14 August. See Journ. 12 Aug. 1769, 1774, 1776, 1777.

p. 42.

Lord Auchinleck's intervention] A long letter which Boswell wrote from Auchinleck to John Johnston on 26 Sept. 1759 contains no hint that he will not be returning to Edinburgh for the coming term, which was already at hand. The manuscript of his next letter to Johnston (11 Jan. 1760) is defective but shows unequivocally that the decision against Edinburgh was Lord Auchinleck's and was unexpected. See Johnston Corresp., p. 7.

Boswell at Glasgow University] See this matter treated in much greater detail, with references, in "Boswell's University Education." The fullest and most useful description of the University as Boswell knew it will be found in David Murray, *Memories of the Old College of Glasgow,* 1927. "Possessed of 'a happy facility of manners' ": To Andrew Erskine, 8 Dec. 1761; Journ. 22 Dec. 1765; 3 Apr. 1775. Erskine Corresp. p. 41, reads "happily possessed of a facility of manners," which seems an alteration for the worse.

p. 43.

Boswell's lodgings at Glasgow University] From W. J. Temple, 25 Dec. 1759–14 Jan. 1760; David Murray, as in the note preceding this, p. 459; Alexander Carlyle, *Autobiography,* 1860, pp. 87–88; W. R. Scott, *Adam Smith as Student and Professor,* 1937, pp. 67–70, 239–254. Boswell speaks familiarly of "Tommy Fitz-maurice" in a letter to John Johnston, 29 July 1765, but the degree of their acquaintanceship is not known. William McQuhae, writing to Boswell on 27–30 Dec. 1762, reports that Mr. George Reid, minister of Ochiltree and formerly Lord Auchinleck's tutor, says that if anything should happen to Boswell, "there would be just three persons to blame for it: your father, Lord Eglinton, and —————— —————— Clow at Glasgow, whom he calls a stupid body." I see no way to explain this allusion to Clow except by assuming that Lord Auchinleck had put Boswell in his charge while he was at the University of Glasgow. Temple would hardly have inferred that Boswell was living with Smith unless Hepburn (the common friend who had informed him of Boswell's transfer to Glasgow) had said something about Boswell's being lodged in a professor's house. It does not appear to me possible from the published studies to determine just which of the professors' houses Clow occupied in 1759–1760 (Murray, pp. 368–374; Scott, pp. 415–422). Lord Auchinleck was at least supposed to have some power over Clow, for the Earl of Galloway wrote on 3 Jan. 1751 asking him to use his influence with Clow to get him to continue the charge of Lord Galloway's sons at the University of Glasgow.

He reported to John Johnston] 11 Jan. 1760. The manuscript, as has been said, is defective, and in this case the uncertainty of restoration extends to facts as well as words.

Physical beauty of Glasgow] *Tour,* 29 Oct. 1773; David Murray, *Memories of the Old College of Glasgow,* 1927, p. 41.

Social limitations of Glasgow] Alexander Carlyle, *Autobiography,* 1860, pp. 72–75.

p. 44.
The theatre in Glasgow] *History of Glasgow,* iii. 234–236; Luke Tyerman, *The Life of ... George Whitefield,* 1887, ii. 313–314.

A View of the Edinburgh Theatre] See *Lit. Car.* pp. 284–291, where the work is doubtfully attributed to Boswell. The ascription is confirmed by the evidence (not known to me in 1929) that Boswell was in love with Mrs. Cowper, and probably put beyond question by a passage in a letter from Boswell to John Johnston, 26 Sept. 1759: "I am highly diverted that a certain mock hero [probably James Dexter: see Johnston Corresp. p. 5 n. 5] has now fixed the dramatic criticisms on a different author from what he did formerly."

Francis Gentleman] DNB; "A Summary View of the Stage," prefixed to Gentleman's *Modish Wife,* 1775, pp. 12–13; Tate Wilkinson, *Memoirs,* 1790, ii. 91; *The Private Correspondence of David Garrick,* 1831–1832, i. 102–103; *Life,* beginning of 1763; Percy Fitzgerald, *Life of David Garrick,* 1868, ii. 379; Journ. 19 Sept. 1764. My suggestion in *Lit. Car.* pp. 284–291 that Gentleman may have helped Boswell with the composition of *A View of the Edinburgh Theatre* was not confirmed by the Boswell papers recovered after 1929, which include six letters from Gentleman to Boswell.

p. 45.
" 'Perhaps' or 'possibly' "] See the Appendix for the sources and an assessment of the varying degrees of certainty in the conclusions.

p. 47.
"An almost enthusiastic notion of the felicity of London"] *Memoirs,* p. 324 (xxxi).

Samuel Derrick] Ibid.; DNB; Journ. 28 Mar. 1763; *Life,* 28 July 1763; *Tour,* 1961 (1963), p. 416.

"Such authors—mainly of a theatrical cast—as allowed him access"] Certainly the great actor, manager, and playwright, David Garrick (Journ. 13 Jan.

1763), and the actor and bookseller, Thomas Davies (*Life,* Samuel Johnson to Davies, 18 June 1783, and Boswell's comment and foot-note). Boswell also met the bookseller James Dodsley on this trip (To Andrew Erskine, 1 June 1762), but I do not know that Derrick presented him.

Sally Forrester]   Journ. 21 Nov. 1762; 13 Mar., 10 June 1763. "Melting rites of love" was an unacknowledged quotation from Andrew Erskine's *The Pigs, an Elegy* (Donaldson's *Collection,* ii. 58).

Lord Eglinton's intervention]   To Sir David Dalrymple, 22 Mar. 1760; Journ. 25 Jan. 1763; Allan Whitefoord to the Earl of Loudoun, 5 May 1760: "I . . . am glad to see you have got sight of Mr. Boswell; that is all you could propose in his present keeping [i.e. while he is on his guard, as he is now]. Much was expected from Lord E——n's advice, but it's not unlikely before all is over that my neighbour [i.e., Lord Auchinleck] will not find himself so much obliged as he expected" (copied c. 1938 by Sir James Fergusson from the original, now in the possession of the Marquess of Bute). Lord Auchinleck, who was not at all intimate with Eglinton, may have sought his "advice" through his own nephew, James Montgomerie of Lainshaw, who was at the time a guest in Eglinton's house (To Sir David Dalrymple, 22 Mar. 1760).

Caldwell]   Journ. 2 June 1764.

p. 48.
Eglinton's character]   *Memoirs,* p. 324 (xxxi); Journ. 27, 29 Nov. 1762; 18, 25 Jan., 7, 20, 26 Feb., 15 Mar., 9 July 1763; *Tour,* 1961 (1963), pp. 416–417, 438–439; DNB under Alexander Montgomerie, 1723–1769; *Scots Peer.* iii. 458–459.

"The great, the gay, and the ingenious"]   *Memoirs,* p. 324 (xxxi).

The Jockey Club]   In the preface to *The Cub at Newmarket* Boswell says that he was "elected a member of the Jockey Club." The historian of the Jockey Club thinks this probably means merely that on Eglinton's recommendation he was made free of the Club's rooms during that one visit to Newmarket (Robert Black, *The Jockey Club and its Founders,* 1891, pp. 105–106). The races he attended would have been either the first or second spring, 7–11 April or 29 April–3 May (*Lond. Chron.* 8–10 Apr., 10–12 Apr., 12–15 Apr., 1–3 May, 3–6 May 1760). He mentions Grosvenor (progenitor of the Dukes of Westminster) in the letter to Eglinton which he published in *Scots Mag.* (above, p. 67) and Sedley both in that letter and the *Cub* itself. Proof that Eglinton introduced him to March and that he knew March before 1762 is furnished by a letter he wrote to March (then Duke of Queensberry), 9 Mar. 1790, and Journ. 6 Dec. 1762. For notes on all three men, see Black, pp. 54–55, 56–58, 91–93.

The Duke of York]   *Comp. Peer.;* Horace Walpole's letters, *passim.* The bit quoted is from Walpole to Horace Mann, 1 Apr. 1751.

p. 49.
Some verses]   Douce MS. 193 in the Bodleian Library, ff. 11ᵛ, 12. They are part of the epistle to Sterne mentioned in the note immediately following this.

p. 50.

A long verse letter] "A Poetical Epistle to Doctor Sterne, Parson Yorick, and Tristram Shandy," Douce MS. 193 in the Bodleian Library, ff. 7-11 (both sides), 12, 13, 77, 77^v, 79, 79^v, 80, 80^v, 87, with outlines on 13^v, 14, and 17. The portion summarized is on 80^v. See F. A. Pottle, "Bozzy and Yorick," in *Blackwood's Magazine*, 217 (Mar. 1925). 297–313. The epistle seems never to have been finished. Most of it, I should suppose, was composed after Boswell returned to Edinburgh, but at least one bit of it—a character of Lord Eglinton—was written at Newmarket (Journ. 7 Feb. 1763).

Eglinton suggests that he become an officer in the Guards] Journ. 25 Jan. 1763.

p. 51.

Lord Auchinleck's difficulties with his two sons] Lord Auchinleck to the Earl of Loudoun, 16 Jan., 3, 23 Apr., 5 May, 6 June 1760; Allan Whitefoord to the Earl of Loudoun, 1 Apr., 5 May 1760 (originals now in the possession of the Marquess of Bute; extracted 1938–1939 by Sir James Fergusson).

Lord Auchinleck comes to London] He *left* London with Boswell on 28 May (Lord Auchinleck to the Earl of Loudoun, 6 June 1760: see the note preceding this) but the date of his arrival in London has not been fixed. So far as is known, he could have set out from Scotland any time in the previous four weeks, for after attending the circuit court at Glasgow, 23, 25, and 26 Apr., he allowed his colleague, Charles Erskine of Tinwald, Lord Justice-Clerk, to go the rest of the circuit alone (Minute Books of the Western Circuit, S.R.O.).

The third Duke of Argyll] DNB; *Scots Peer.* i. 378–381; *Boswelliana*, p. 229.

The first venereal infection] Journ. 22, 25 Jan. 1763. "That distemper with which Venus...": Journ. 18 Jan. 1763.

The return to Edinburgh] *Memoirs*, p. 324 (xxxi); *Life*, beginning of 1763; Journ. 2 Apr. 1763; From W. J. Temple, 12 June 1777; Lord Auchinleck to the Earl of Loudoun, Edinburgh, 6 June 1760 (see the 4th note back): "I got safe to this place Wednesday night, but too late for writing by that post. As my son came down with me and he had had a pretty smart fever from which he was but just recovered, we travelled very slowly, and besides we went to see Cambridge and Mr. Aisleby's two seats, so that we were eight days upon the road." "Mr. Aisleby" was presumably William Aislabie, M.P., son of John Aislabie, 1670–1742, Chancellor of the Exchequer, for whom see DNB and J. R. Walbran, *Memorials of the Abbey of St. Mary of Fountains*, Surtees Soc., 67 (1878). 338–344. His principal seat was Studley Royal, near Ripon, the grounds of which are still considered "among the finest examples of Italian and Dutch formal gardening" (L. R. Muirhead, *England*, 1957, p. 476; see also J. R. Walbran, *A Guide to Ripon, Harrowgate, Fountains Abbey, Bolton Priory*, etc., 6th ed., 1856, pp. 58–65). His second seat was probably Fountains Hall, a Jacobean mansion built near to and from the stones of Fountains Abbey, the grounds of which adjoin those of Studley Royal, though on this point the authorities are in strange contradiction. Walbran (*Memorials,* p. 121; *Guide,* p. 68) avers with circumstantial detail that the Aislabies did not acquire Fountains Abbey till 1767 or 1768 but Thomas Pennant, who visited Studley Royal and Fountains in 1773, says that John Aislabie bought the property c. 1726, and both added to and improved the Hall (Thomas Pennant, *A Tour from Alston-Moor to Harrowgate and Brimham Crags,* 1804, pp. 90–91).

p. 52.
Boswell's Roman period left him only agreeable ideas] Journ. 20 Mar. 1768.

Boswell's later attendance at mass in Roman chapels] Leaving out of account the period of his Continental travels, when Roman-Catholic services were often the only ones he could have attended, see e.g. Journ. 17 Sept. 1769; 19 Apr. 1772; 17, 31 Mar. 1776. There are many more instances in the years following. For a full list, see the index of BP, article "Roman Catholicism."

Boswell's adherence to beliefs and practices generally considered popish] Imposition of ashes, Journ. 1 Mar. 1786; purgatory, *Tour,* 1936 or 1961 (1963), p. 48 n.3 (end), Journ. 22 Oct. 1782; purgatory, invocation of saints and angels, Journ. 19, 31 Oct. 1774. For attitudes characteristic of what would now be called Anglo-Catholicism, see Journ. 6 Nov. 1774; 12 Nov. 1775; 23 Apr. 1780; 10 Oct. 1782.

Not merely his right] To T. D. Boswell, 13 Oct. 1794.

CHAPTER VI

p. 55.
Lord Auchinleck and the Guards scheme] From Lord Auchinleck, 30 May 1763.

He wrote to Temple] To W. J. Temple, 1 May 1761.

p. 56.
Lord Auchinleck's youthful follies] Journ. 10 Sept. 1780; *Scotland and Scotsmen,* i. 161. Lord Auchinleck entered Edinburgh University in 1718, at the age of eleven, and matriculated in Latin (twice) 1718–1719, 1719–1720, and in Greek (twice) 1720–1721, 1721–1722. The Irish lads were said to have been named Carleton. No one of that name appears in the records (information furnished by Dr. James C. Corson). Presumably they did not remain long enough to get on the matriculation rolls, which were then made up in February or March. Lord Auchinleck was in France June–October 1729, after having spent two sessions at the University of Leyden (Auchinleck Memoirs).

p. 57.
Lord Auchinleck's coldness] For Boswell's own complaints, see p. 12 of the Index to BP, forty-five references in the article covering Lord Auchinleck's per-

sonal relations with Boswell, collected under the heading "cold (callous, harsh, indifferent, unfeeling, etc.) towards JB." For David, see From T. D. Boswell, c. 12
Aug., 1 Oct. 1766; 28 Apr., and especially 30 Oct. 1767. For John, see From Lt.
John Boswell, 10 Feb. 1766. For Lord Auchinleck's damping of conversation, see
e.g. Journ. 30 July 1769; 9 Sept. 1780.

"When my father forced me down to Scotland"]   Journ. 1 Dec. 1762.

p. 58.
The Soaping Club]   Erskine Corresp., pp. 4, 47; From Sir David Dalrymple,
10 Oct. 1764; Journ. 13 Oct., 5 Nov. 1762; 6 Sept. 1769; 31 Oct. 1775; *Memoirs*, p.
324 (xxxii); From Arthur Lee, 10 June 1768; From Edward Colquitt, "Tuesday"
[?1760 or 1761]. The names of four members besides Boswell and Erskine have been
recorded: Bainbridge, Berkeley, Colquitt, and Lee. Colquitt's letter shows him to
have been a clergyman, and Boswell (*Memoirs*) says he was assistant priest in the
English Chapel in Edinburgh. Arthur Lee (see *Dictionary of American Biography*)
studied at Eton, graduated M.D. of the University of Edinburgh in 1764, and practised medicine briefly in Virginia before embarking on a career in law and politics.
Berkeley, spelled "Barclay" in the Erskine Correspondence, and styled "Dr." in
1769 (Journ. 6 Sept.), was no doubt the "John Berkeley, Anglus," who graduated
M.D. at Edinburgh in 1762 (*List of Graduates in Medicine in the University of
Edinburgh*, 1867, p. 7). I know nothing further about him. No very plausible
identification for Bainbridge has as yet been suggested.

Boswell's second venereal infection]   To W. J. Temple, 1 May 1761; Journ.
22 Jan., 4 Feb. 1763.

p. 59.
"Shivers of genius"]   To Sir David Dalrymple, 30 July 1763. It will perhaps
spoil the phrase for some modern readers to be told that by "shivers" Boswell
meant "splinters," not "quiverings as from cold."

Boswell's announced taste in metaphor]   E.g., Journ. 5 Jan. 1763; 5 Sept. 1769
(cf. To Margaret Montgomerie, 5 Sept. 1769).

Paraphrases from Scripture]   Psalms 131, 133, 142; Jeremiah 4.9–26; Revela-
tion 20.1–5 (Douce MS. 193 in the Bodleian Library, ff. 40–42, 94, 100–103, with
all versos except 42ᵛ). Boswell made fair copies of the first three of these pieces for
his proposed "Poems on Several Occasions" (above, p. 72). I date these pieces in
1756 or late 1755 by conjecture only. Biblical paraphrases seem more characteristic
of his mind and character before he made contact with the stage than afterwards,
and we know that "he very early began to show a propensity to distinguish himself
in literary composition" (*Memoirs*, p. 323 [xxx]).

Prologue submitted to Digges]   From West Digges, dated at the top of the
sheet "April 9th, 1757" and at the bottom "Tuesday: 7 o'clock." 9 April 1757 was
a Saturday. Perhaps Digges began the note on the 9th and finished it on the 12th.
The prologue is unidentified or lost. Douce MS. 193 contains, besides the prologue

to Mrs. Sheridan's *Discovery,* later to be mentioned, prologues to *Macbeth,* Cibber's *Love Makes a Man,* and one spoken in the character of a bard disguised as an apothecary.

p. 60.
October, a Poem] Yale MSS. M264 (earlier state), M265 (uncompleted fair copy). The title-page of M265 describes the poem as "after the manner of Mr. Thomson," and bears mottoes from Lucretius and Wilkie's *Epigoniad* (pub. c. April 1757). M264 contains a grateful dedication to Lord Somerville.

An Evening Walk] *Scots Mag.* 20 (1758). 420.

Ogilvie, Home, Beattie, Macpherson] *Scots Mag.* 20 (1758). 419–420, 421, 482–483, 550–551. Ogilvie's poem bears neither name nor initials, but he showed himself to be the author by including it in his *Poems on Several Subjects,* 1762, pp. 23–28.

p. 61.
A View of the Edinburgh Theatre] Above, pp. 41, 44.

The Cub at Newmarket] Bibliographical details are given below, p. 475.

Lying down to avoid being thrown down] *Life,* 25 Apr. 1778.

p. 62.
Miss Jeanie Wells] Douce MS. 193 in the Bodleian Library, ff. 36, 36ᵛ, 47ᵛ, 48 (two copies, the second titled merely *Song;* Yale has a copy—M267—that shows some variants); Journ. 21 Nov. 1762; "An Epistle from a London Buck to his Friend," in Donaldson's *Collection,* ii (1762). 92–100. If, as seems likely, the *Epistle* concerns Miss Wells and is literal autobiography, she was the kept mistress of an M.P., "the fat brother of a lord."

p. 63.
Observations on ... "The Minor"] Mary M. Belden, *The Dramatic Work of Samuel Foote,* 1929, pp. 81–106; *The London Stage, 1660–1800,* pt. 4, 1747–1776, by G. W. Stone, 1962, pp. 801–805; *Lit. Car.,* pp. 3–5; *Observations on ... The Minor,* 1760, pp. 14–15.

Boswell's mimicry] Journ. 12 Oct., 9 Nov. 1762; 21 Mar. 1772; Notes, 10 May 1776; William Roberts, *Memoirs of the Life and Correspondence of Mrs. Hannah More,* 1834, i.213.

p. 64.
Boswell's meeting with Erskine] Journ. 10 May 1761; Erskine Corresp. p. 125. Boswell's journal of the North Circuit, Spring 1761, ends at Inverness, 16 May, with the meeting unaccomplished. It must have occurred within the next four days, for the Court sat down at Aberdeen on the 23d (*Scots Mag.* 23 [1761]. 327).

Andrew Erskine] Erskine is not in DNB, though he deserved a niche there. The fullest and best account of him at this writing (1965) appears variously as Appendix A of the unpublished Yale dissertation of the late C. H. Bennett, *Letters between the Hon. Andrew Erskine and James Boswell, Esq., 1761–1762,* 1933, and as Appendix A of J. D. Hankins's unpublished Indiana dissertation, *Early Correspondence of James Boswell, 1757–1766,* 1964, the latter of which will ultimately appear in print as a volume of the Yale research edition. The Appendix as presented by Dr. Hankins contains valuable factual revision made both by himself and by Dr. Bennett, but omits Dr. Bennett's critical study of Erskine's writings, a useful feature of the original. "Blackguard state" (not a literal quotation) is Journ. 25 Dec. 1762.

Thomas Alexander Erskine, 6th Earl of Kellie] DNB; *Scots Peer.;* life of Andrew Erskine mentioned in the note preceding this. I have not traced Foote's characterization of Kellie farther back than Robert Chambers, *Traditions of Edinburgh,* 1825, ii. 139.

George Dempster] Journ. 10 May 1761; DNB; *Letters of George Dempster to Sir Adam Fergusson,* ed. Sir James Fergusson, 1934; Sir Lewis Namier and John Brooke, *The House of Commons, 1754–1790,* 1964, ii. 313–317; Great Britain, Parliament, House of Commons, *Members of Parliament* ("The Official Return of Members of Parliament"), 1878–1891, ii. 136.

Thomas Sheridan] *Scots Mag.* 23 (1761). 389–390; Journ. 7 Jan. 1763; To Thomas Sheridan, 27 Sept., 25 Nov., 9 Dec. 1761; 9 Jan., 27 Feb. 1762; From Thomas Sheridan, 21 Nov. 1761. The lectures on elocution covered a period of four weeks, from 30 June to 24 July; they were read in "St. Paul's chapel," i.e. in Allan Ramsay's theatre at the foot of Carrubber's Close, then occupied by a qualified Anglican congregation (above, p. 461). Both Dempster and Erskine refer to dicta by Sheridan in the recommendatory letters prefixed to *An Elegy on an Amiable Young Lady.*

p. 65.
Elegy on an Amiable Young Lady] *Lit. Car.* pp. 5–6. *The Caledonian Mercury,* 8 Aug. 1761, advertised the pamphlet as to be published on 10 Aug. Boswell's letter submitting the poems to Donaldson purports to have been written from Strathaven, 28 July 1761. Strathaven, Lanarkshire, was a stage on the road from Edinburgh to Auchinleck, but it is most unlikely that Boswell was there on 28 July, for he did not go down to Auchinleck for the summer vacation till considerably later (Notes preceding 14 Aug. 1761). Demonstration that the place of dating was fictitious would somewhat bolster my suggestion in *Lit. Car.* that the "amiable young lady" was Miss Katy Young, daughter of James Young of Netherfield, a seat near Strathaven, who died at the age of nineteen on 1 July 1761. For the Scots grammar of the *Elegy,* see Sir James A. H. Murray, *The Dialect of the Southern Counties of Scotland,* 1873, pp. 209–210. Burns frequently uses this form of the verb, e.g. "And low thou lies!" in *To a Mountain Daisy. The Epistle from Lycidas to Menalcas* (the names are incorrectly reversed on the title-page) is a genuine verse-letter from Boswell to some male friend. All that can be gathered from the piece itself as to the identity of Menalcas is that he and Lycidas (Boswell) had

strolled by the banks of the silver Clyde and had read poetry together there. Dr.
Russell T. Sharpe, President of Golden Gate College, in an unpublished study of
Boswell's verses written while he was a graduate student at Harvard, 1930–1933,
makes the attractive suggestion that Menalcas was John Hamilton of Sundrum,
Ayrshire, who had been a friend of Boswell's and Temple's at the University of
Edinburgh, and matriculated with Boswell at the University of Glasgow on 14 Nov.
1759 (From W. J. Temple, 17 June 1758; 6–8 July, 25 Dec. 1759; To W. J. Tem-
ple, 16 Dec. 1758; W. I. Addison, *The Matriculation Albums of the University of
Glasgow*, 1913, p. 59).

p. 66.
Boswell's letter to Lord Eglinton] *Scots Mag.* 23 (1761).469–471. The
printed text bears the date 25 September, which was probably the date of the letter
actually sent to Eglinton. John Ramsay knew of this letter and knew that Boswell
wrote it (*Scotland and Scotsmen,* i. 172), but his editor did not know what was
being referred to and confused the foot-note references.

Eglinton's appointment to be Lord of the Bedchamber urged by the Duke of
York] Horace Walpole to George Montagu, 13 Nov. 1760.

p. 67.
List of probationary wives] From Andrew Erskine, 1 Nov. 1761; To Andrew
Erskine, 17 Nov. 1761; From Andrew Erskine, 3 Dec. 1761; To Andrew Erskine,
22 Jan. 1762; Notes, 26 Sept. 1761–6 Apr. 1762, *passim;* Journ. 30 Nov. 1762; To
John Johnston, 23 Sept. 1763; To W. J. Temple, 23 Sept. 1763.

Kitty Colquhoun] There is a poem to her by Boswell in the second volume
of Donaldson's *Collection* ("To Miss Kitty C____", p. 81); another, which I
should rather see, we know only by title, which appears to have been "To Miss
C., with Johnson's Dictionary" (Douce MS. 193 in the Bodleian Library, f. 1ᵛ and
an unfoliated scrap). She is referred to in Boswell's "Currant Jelly" (Donaldson,
ii. 89) and his "Epistle to Miss Home" (Douce MS. 193, f. 24ᵛ). Her mother, who
was sister to the 16th Earl of Sutherland, appears in *Humphry Clinker* as "Lady
H____ C____." Winifred Jenkins's spelling "Coon" indicates the pronunciation
of the name approximately; Kŭh-hoon' would be more precise. Boswell and Johnson stopped at Rossdhu, Sir James's seat on Loch Lomond, in their tour of the
Hebrides (Journ. 26–27 Oct. 1773). For genealogical details, explanation of the
baronetcy, erroneously assumed before 1786, and Lord Auchinleck's trusteeship,
see *Comp. Baronet.* ii. 294–295; iv. 426; v. 249–250 and Sir William Fraser, *The
Chiefs of Colquhoun and their Country,* 1869, i. 349, 383. For Sir Roderick Mackenzie, see *Comp. Baronet.* iv. 409.

p. 68.
Ode to Tragedy] *Lit. Car.* pp. 6–8; From Andrew Erskine, 13 Dec. 1761;
To Andrew Erskine, 17 Dec. 1761. For Boswell's admiration of Gray and Mason,
see *Life,* 2 Apr. 1775. A fuller account than perhaps exists elsewhere of the controversy then going on between the "classicists" and the "romanticists" in the drama

will be found in my unpublished Yale doctoral dissertation, *The Literary Career of James Boswell to 1785,* 1925, pp. 95–102.

Dedication of *An Ode to Tragedy*] The first sentence of the Dedication reads, "If Adam Fitz-Adam presumed to inscribe a volume of *The World* to Mr. Moore, I can see no reason why I, a Gentleman of Scotland, may not take much the same liberty with Mr. Boswell." "Adam Fitz-Adam" was the pseudonym which Edward Moore had used in conducting the highly successful series of periodical essays entitled *The World,* 1753–1756. In the collected six-volume edition of 1755–1757, Adam Fitz-Adam dedicated a volume each to five of his more distinguished assistants (the Earl of Chesterfield, Horace Walpole, Richard Owen Cambridge, the Earl of Cork, and Soame Jenyns) and the final volume to Edward Moore. This last dedication, like Boswell's, makes use of arch *double entendre* to identify dedicatee and dedicator.

Give Your Son his Will] Yale MS. M116.

p. 70.
Donaldson's *Collection*] *Lit. Car.* pp. 10–14 (full list of Boswell's contributions); *Memoirs,* p. 324 (xxxi–xxxii). Boswell and Erskine together wrote between a third and a half of the volume. See their correspondence between 1 Nov. 1761 and 20 Nov. 1762, *passim.*

B——, a Song] Donaldson's *Collection,* ii. 90–91.

p. 71.
Reviews of Donaldson's *Collection*] *British Mag.* iii (May 1762).269; *Monthly Rev.* 1st ser., 27 (Sept. 1762). 226–227; *Critical Rev.,* 1st ser., 13 (June 1762).495–499. The one-sentence review in *British Mag.* may well have been by Smollett too. The authorship of the review in the *Monthly* (Article 21 of the Monthly Catalogue, Sept. 1762) has not been established (B. C. Nangle, *The Monthly Review, 1st Ser., 1749–1789,* 1934, p. 233). Boswell's letter to Erskine, 20 Nov. 1762, containing his comment on the review in the *Critical,* "Had they said more," etc., is not among the manuscripts of the letters as now preserved, and may have been fabricated for the volume published in 1763. A passage in Boswell's letter to Erskine, 22 Jan. 1762, omitted by Boswell in publication, shows that Boswell had written to Smollett, presumably to request a review of the *Collection* in the *Critical,* and that Smollett had returned "a very polite obliging letter" saying that he reviewed "the productions of Scotland *con amore,*" and that he and his friends would do "all manner of justice to such as are to be found in the shops of the booksellers of London." Though Boswell was in correspondence with Smollett on at least one other occasion (To Tobias Smollett, 14 Mar. 1768), I know of no evidence that they ever met. Certainly there was never any extensive acquaintance between them. This apparently deliberate hiatus in Boswell's literary relationships is to me very puzzling.

The Cub at Newmarket] *Lit. Car.* pp. 16–18; Journ. 27 Nov. 1762; 25 Jan. 1763; To an unknown correspondent, 10 Feb. 1762. Since the person addressed in

this letter is a bookseller (i.e. publisher as well as vendor of books) and "the correspondent of my friend Mr. Donaldson," a plausible identification would be the
J. Richardson, Paternoster Row, London, whose name is coupled with Donaldson's
in the imprint of Donaldson's *Collection*. Boswell's instructions are to put Donaldson's name on the book as publisher in Scotland, and to add Dodsley's name as
joint London publisher if Dodsley approves. The actual imprint is "London,
Printed for R. and J. Dodsley in Pall Mall," which probably means that Dodsley
handled the entire commission himself as soon as he had assurance that Boswell
would guarantee costs. The printer was William Bowyer (John Nichols, *Literary
Anecdotes of the Eighteenth Century*, 1812–1815, ii. 400). By 24 Nov. 1762 the
piece had paid its costs and showed a profit for the author of thirteen shillings
(Journ. 24 Nov. 1762). Reviews: *Critical Rev.*, 1st ser., 13 (March 1762). 273;
Monthly Rev., 1st ser., 26 (March 1762). 233. The authorship of the review in the
Monthly (Article 8 of the Monthly Catalogue for March) is unknown (B. C.
Nangle, *The Monthly Review, 1st Ser., 1749–1789*, 1934, p. 232).

p. 72.
Boswell's plans for a volume of original poems]   Douce MS. 193 in the Bodleian Library, ff. 1, 1ᵛ and unfoliated scrap. Nothing is known of the history of
this MS. collection (over 100 leaves) before it came to the Bodleian in the papers
of Francis Douce. Douce was a friend of James Boswell, Jr., and may have had it
directly from him. More probably he purchased it at the sale of the younger Boswell's library in 1825. It is not listed in the printed catalogue of the sale, but the
catalogue is very sketchy so far as manuscripts are concerned. The *Ode on* (or *to*)
Ambition is now known only by title and two quoted lines, though Boswell clearly
thought it the best of his serious poems (Journ. 5 Jan., 21 Mar. 1763; 28 Dec.
1764).

CHAPTER VII

p. 74.
Boswell entered in the Inner Temple]   To Thomas Sheridan, 27 Sept. 1761;
From Thomas Sheridan, 21 Nov. 1761; To Thomas Sheridan, 25 Nov. 1761 (the
passage quoted is from this letter), 9 Dec. 1761; certificate of admission to the
Inner Temple, 19 Nov. 1761, in Latin, in the hand of and signed by Samuel Salt,
Sub-Treasurer, fees, £4-5-2 (Yale MS. C1582); Notes, 23 Nov. 1761. Boswell's
journal notes from 7 Sept. 1761 to 29 July 1762 were recorded in large part in the
shorthand system known as Shelton's Tachygraphy, the same system which Pepys
used. See F. A. Pottle, "Boswell's Shorthand," in *Times Literary Supplement*, 28
July 1932 (31.545).

p. 75.
Boswell elected Junior Warden]   Allan Mackenzie, *History of the Lodge
Canongate Kilwinning, No. 2*, 1888, p. 89. Dr. James Lind, author of the epoch-
making *Treatise on Scurvy*, had been elected Senior Warden that year (ibid., p. 14),
but he went abroad. Sir William Forbes, Junior Warden, was advanced to be

Senior Warden, and Boswell was elected to fill out the remainder of Forbes's term. Dr. John Cairnie, who enters our story in the summer of 1762, was elected Treasurer in 1761.

Boswell elected a member of the Select Society]   *Memoirs*, p. 324 (xxxii); Notes, 1, 8 Dec. 1761.

Lord Kames]   DNB; Helen W. Randall, *The Critical Theory of Lord Kames*, 1944, pp. 1–22; Notes, 13 Nov. 1761–25 Mar. 1762 *passim* (18 references); Materials for Writing the Life of Lord Kames (Yale MS. M135), 20 Dec. 1778, 13 Feb. 1780.

William McQuhae]   *Fasti Scot.*, 1866–1871, ii. 137–138; Journ. 26 Feb. 1763. McQuhae, who later became minister of St. Quivox, is twice mentioned with respect in Burns's *The Twa Herds*.

p. 76.
Boswell begins studying the violin]   To George Dempster, 19 Nov. 1761.

Miss Isabella Thomson]   Notes, 12 Nov. 1761–21 Mar. 1762 *passim; Register of Marriages of the City of Edinburgh, 1751–1800*, 1922 (Scottish Record Soc. Pub. No. 53), p. 702. I did not mention her in Chapter VI because, although Boswell apparently saw more of her than of Miss Bruce, Miss Colquhoun, and Miss Stewart, he appears nowhere to have recorded matrimonial inclinations towards her.

p. 77
Mrs. Love]   The prime identifying passages are Mem. 28 Nov. 1762 ("Then L.'s, as he's at Club, and try old Canongate"); 29 Nov. 1762 ("At eleven call L. and try all rhetoric old girl. . . . Concert with ϕ and vow eternal constancy and regard"); 29 Mar. 1763 ("Have nothing of that kind but with Mrs. L——— or with whom Lord Eglinton shows you"); 21 Apr. 1763 ("Stay and try Mrs. L———, yet don't go there for a month again"), and From W. J. Temple, 1–3 Feb. 1780 (as quoted). Boswell in 1769 describes her as "verging on fifty" (Journ. 18 Sept.); his characterization of her as "lively, smart," etc. is Journ. 26 Oct. 1762. For references to her as Polly, see W. H. Logan, *Fragmenta Scoto-dramatica*, 1835, pp. 20–27. Mrs. Love, whose maiden name was Hooper, married James Dance, *alias* Love, in the week preceding 27 Aug. 1739 (*Daily Advertiser* of that date), he being then in his eighteenth year (DNB). The Loves seem to have first joined the Edinburgh company when John Lee took over the management of the theatre with the season of 1752–1753 (*Scots Mag.* 16 [1754].42). They were certainly there during the season of 1753–1754 (ibid. 15 [1753].610–612; 16 [1754].41–45, 90–93, 142–143), and though they afterwards went to Dublin for at least one season (Dibdin, p. 77), appear to have been continuously in the Edinburgh company from the summer of 1756 to their departure for Drury Lane in the autumn of 1762 (Dibdin, pp. 83–113; W. H. Logan, loc. cit.; *A View of the Edinburgh Theatre during the Summer Season, 1759, 1760, passim;* To W. J. Temple, 29 July 1758). It is not known when Boswell made their acquaintance, but by the end of 1758 he considered Love his "second-best friend" (To W. J. Temple, 16 Dec. 1758).

Boswell's loans to Love]   Journ. 1 Apr., 16, 28 May, 21 June 1763; Mem.
10 Apr., 13, 16, 25, 28 May, 7, 17 June 1763; To John Johnston, 30 June 1763; To
W. J. Temple, 27 July 1763.

p. 78.
Intrigues with at least two actresses]   The Sketch for Rousseau (above, p. 5)
refers to affairs "with married actresses." When Lord Eglinton teased Boswell
(Journ. 21 Jan. 1763) for having got more than he bargained for from his current
inamorata, "Louisa," he retorted that he had had "several intrigues within these two
years," and that if he was "taken in but once in four or five times," the score was
not so bad. Assuming, as one safely can with Boswell, that his "four or five" affairs
means precisely five, including that with Louisa, we have to account for four others,
of which at least two shall be with actresses.

"A"]   Journ. 8 May 1761 ("Wrote to friends and to A_____").

Mrs. Brooke]   Boswell mentions Mrs. Brooke in Mem. 20 June 1763 ("At
night Foote's and think on Mrs. Brooke"), in Journ. 7 Sept. 1773 (surprised at
seeing a mezzotint of her in the farm-house of Coirechatachan in Skye), and in To
Edmond Malone, 27 Oct. 1785 (she lived with Richard Griffith). In revising the
journal for publication as *The Journal of a Tour to the Hebrides,* he identified her
as an actress and styled her "my fair friend," but suffered an access of caution and
deleted the personal reference in the proofs. (Yale MSS. J33; P41). Any actress
whom Boswell called "my fair friend" would fall under grave suspicion of having
been his mistress; and the only period in which Mrs. Brooke can be fitted into his
biography is the years 1760–1762. The other details of her life are from John
Taylor, *Records of my Life,* 1832, 1.31–38. Dibdin mentions her once at the end of
1761 (p. 112). I know of no way to fix her age precisely. Her husband was born
c. 1726 (*Gent. Mag.* 77 [1807], pt. 2. 1080), her son was in school with Taylor, who
was born in 1757 (DNB), and her younger daughter was married in 1774 (*Gent.
Mag.* 44.333). Boswell's association of Mrs. Brooke with Foote perhaps means that
she originally came to Edinburgh with Foote's company in the spring of 1759 (Dibdin, pp. 105–107).

Lord Kames's kindnesses]   "When I was on bad terms with my worthy father,
I was treated with great kindness by Lord Kames. His Lordship's house was a home
to me" (Journ. 27 Sept. 1764); From Lady Kames, 28 Dec. 1762. The "subsidiary
documents" are Mem. 30 Nov. 1764 and the Second Outline of the Sketch (Yale
MS. L1110).

Jean Home's marriage]   *Scots Mag.* 23.615 reports it first in the list of marriages in the November issue, without date, but followed by one dated 9 Nov. 1761.

The Heron divorce]   *Commissariot of Edinburgh, Consistorial Processes and
Decreets, 1658–1800,* 1909 (Scottish Record Soc. Pub. No. 34), p. 47 (No. 600).
Yale has an extract from the Register of Consistorial Decreets, Edin. Com. vol. 13,
23 Jan. 1772, S.R.O., giving the testimony of the witnesses in the action.

Lady Kames's account of her daughter's disgrace] Materials for Writing the
Life of Lord Kames (Yale MS. M135), 29 Nov. 1782.

p. 79.
"Angel"] "Angel" may of course be "A," and the whole "A" and "Angel"
series may refer to Mrs. Brooke, though I sense a different quality in the two
entries quoted, and cannot help connecting the "H_____" of 20 December with
the events of the 16th. The "A" series cannot refer to Mrs. Heron because of the
amicable and sensible winding up of that affair which Boswell recorded on 30 Mar.
1762 (above, p. 82).

Delicious intrigues] Journ. 14 Dec. 1762.

Temporary impotency] Journ. 2 Jan., 5 June 1763; Mem. 10 Sept. 1765.

p. 80.
Peggy Doig] Notes, 3 Jan.–14 Feb. 1762 ("Adventure with P, the most curious young little pretty, but though all out—good now! no opportunity for a long
time"); 22 Feb. 1762 ("Went P, could not get in"); 3 Mar. 1762 ("At six my
little dear P and made it out. O bravo! Two"); 25 Mar. 1762 ("Miss B[ruce] in
box; quite languish, but went to P. and cured"). The notes for 1761–1762, as has
previously been mentioned, contain many words, and groups of words, in cipher.
Boswell sometimes introduces obscurities by using the wrong symbol. "P," standing
for Peggy Doig, is always written in Shelton's character for that letter.

"Better to snuff a candle out"] From Lord Auchinleck, 30 May 1763.

Lord Auchinleck's claim to be able to disinherit Boswell] "Contract of Marriage betwixt Mr. Alexander Boswell and Mrs. Eupham Erskine," dated 21 and 27
Apr. 1738; Journ. 31 Oct. 1778.

Boswell's "renunciation"] Copy of deed by James Boswell empowering Lord
Auchinleck to vest the estate in trustees, 7 Mar. 1762 (Yale MS. M16); Journ. 21
Mar. 1772, 7 Jan. 1780; From John Johnston, 27 June 1763; To W. J. Temple,
2 Sept. 1775.

p. 81.
Lord Auchinleck formally grants Boswell an allowance] "Settlement of £100
a year, 2 April 1762" (Yale MS. C210); To John Johnston, 22 Mar. 1763.
Although the settlement was executed nearly a month after the "renunciation," the
"renunciation" speaks as though the settlement were already in force ("an ali-
mentary provision of one hundred pounds sterling yearly settled on me by my
father and which is to continue with me for life").

James Ferguson, afterwards Lord Pitfour] College of Justice, p. 527; Scotland and Scotsmen, i. 150–160.

The Duchess of Douglas] Notes, 11, 13, 16, 17, 19 Mar. 1762 (the bits quoted
are 13 and 16 Mar.); Samuel Johnson to Mrs. Thrale, 17 Aug. 1773; Sir William
Fraser, The Douglas Book, 1885, ii. 471. The Duchess left money to purchase

lands to be called Douglas-Support, which she bequeathed to the eldest son of her eldest brother and other heirs of entail, with a proviso that the heirs succeeding should always bear the surname of Douglas (ibid. i. lxxxv; Burke's *Peerage,* 1899, "Blythswood"; Burke, *Landed Gentry,* "Douglas of Mains").

p. 82.

Boswell's London ideas from autumn of 1761 centred in the Temple] To the Countess of Northumberland, 6 Jan. 1762 ("Much do I long for September next when I shall enter upon my reign over handsome chambers in the Temple").

The scheme of the Guards revived] Notes, 16, 20, 22, 24 Mar. 1762 (quotation from last date cited).

James Ferguson insists that Boswell pass his trials, Lord Auchinleck agrees to use his influence, Boswell again uncertain] Notes, 24 Mar., 2 Apr. 1762.

Leave-takings] Notes, 29 Mar. (Miss Bruce, Miss Colquhoun), 30 Mar. (Mrs. Brooke), 5 Apr. 1762 (Mrs. Love).

Conference with Ferguson and Dalrymple] Notes, 7 Apr. 1762.

Eglinton notified] Journ. 25 Jan. 1763. There is a discrepancy between Boswell's statement that he applied to Eglinton "immediately" and Eglinton's statement, as reported by Boswell, that he wrote "in May." To Andrew Erskine, 22 Apr. (misdated 22 Aug.) 1762 shows that Boswell had written to Eglinton some time before that date, consequently that "May" was mistaken.

p. 83.

"I am indulging," etc.] Erskine Corresp. pp. 104–106. The letter that went through the post, now at Yale, bears the date 9 May 1762, not 8 May 1762, as in Erskine Corresp. Presumably here, as frequently elsewhere, the "copy" that Boswell retained was actually his draft or scroll, the letter sent being a fair copy, in this instance made a day later. Boswell prepared the printed volume from his retained "copies."

Not long before] To Andrew Erskine, 22 Apr. 1762.

The Circuit Court at Dumfries] The Court sat on 14, 15, and 19 May 1762, Lord Auchinleck being the sole judge. Lord Minto had been appointed his colleague on the circuit, but he did not go to Dumfries (*Scots Mag.* 24 [1762].337; Minute Book of the Southern Circuit, S.R.O.).

"Saturday's our day"] Notes, 12 May 1767 ("Went to Dumfries at night. Curious to see town where *Saturday's our day,* etc., etc."); 13 May 1767 ("Evening, Assembly.... Played at whist. Agreeable to feel how firm since this time five years"); 15 May 1767 ("Paid several visits. Found you could talk with ease of *Saturday's our day*"). See above, p. 326.

p. 84.

Eglinton makes difficulties] Journ. 25 Jan. 1763.

Lord Auchinleck applies to the Duke of Queensberry] The Duke of Queensberry to Lord Auchinleck, 24 May 1762, endorsed by Lord Auchinleck, "In answer to a letter I wrote his Grace, desiring him to use his interest to procure an ensigncy in the Guards for my eldest son, who then had a desire to go into the Guards." The Duke fixes the date of Lord Auchinleck's letter as 12 May 1762. For Charles Douglas, 3d Duke of Queensberry, see DNB and *Scots Peer.* vii. 143–144.

Lord Auchinleck warns Boswell that the Queensberry scheme will fail] From Lord Auchinleck, 27 Nov. 1762 ("Before you left this, I told you it was in vain for you to expect a commission in the Guards"). I push Lord Auchinleck's discouraging verdict back to May by inference only.

Boswell returns to Edinburgh in bad humour] Notes, June 1762 (a review of the entire month).

p. 85.
Dr. Cairnie] Notes, 8 July 1762; From Sir William Forbes, 28 May 1791; Sir William Forbes, *Memoirs of a Banking House,* 1860, p. 68. The relevant portion of the entry in the Notes, entirely in cipher, reads, "Cairnie and I had a meeting in which we talked over Guards and different plans of life, and he gave me his advice and assistance and put me in humour with [undeciphered word]." The undeciphered word is written plainly enough, but I can make no sense of the symbols. Dr. Bennett read them doubtfully as "boy," but to me they seem rather to be ac-y, ac-g, or ac-lt. Though I can think of no word that will fit those phonetic specifications and make the desired sense, I have no doubt that Peggy Doig's pregnancy was the subject of discussion.

Meeting with the kirk treasurer] Notes, 23 July 1762; To John Johnston, 14 Dec. 1762. In his notes Boswell, using cipher, actually wrote "knk tr-s-r-r," but the letter to Johnston puts the word out of doubt.

Public rebuke for fornication] See the authorities cited in Johnston Corresp. p. 31 n. 2.

The kirk treasurer noises Boswell's secret abroad] To John Johnston, 14 Dec. 1762.

Eglinton rebuffed, new plan of courting Queensberry personally] Notes, 24, 25 July 1762; *Memoirs,* p. 324 (xxxii).

Boswell passes his trials in Civil Law] Notes, 30 July 1762; To Andrew Erskine, 23 July 1762. The Faculty's register of private examinators and examinations for 1762 is missing.

Lord Auchinleck's assurance of Boswell's aptitude for the law] From Lord Auchinleck, 30 May 1763.

p. 87.
Boswell's literary genius] I have treated this subject somewhat more fully in an essay entitled "Boswell Revalued," pp. 79–91 of C. Carroll Camden (ed.), *Literary Views,* 1964.

"I should live no more than I can record"] Journ. 17 Mar. 1776.

p. 88.
When Dr. Johnson said]   Journ. 6 July 1763.

Carlyle's contention]   "Biography" (entire) and "Boswell's Life of Johnson,"
paragraphs 16, 19–21, in *Critical and Miscellaneous Essays* (these essays originally
published in 1832.)

p. 89.
"The mysterious River of Existence"]   "Boswell's Life of Johnson," paragraph 22.

"An open loving heart"]   "Biography," paragraph 19; "Boswell's Life of
Johnson," paragraph 13.

p. 90.
Characters in "Journal of My Jaunt, Harvest 1762"]   Journ. 15 Sept. (Shaw),
11 Oct. (Coulthard), 7 Oct. 1762 (Miss Maxwell).

p. 91.
"JOHNSON . . . 'I am afraid,' etc."]   *Life,* 12 June 1784.

p. 92.
"Writing to the *moment*"]   *Clarissa, or The History of a Young Lady,* vol. 4,
letter 58 of the 3d ed. and editions adhering to it (Shakespeare Head ed. iv. 385).

Summary of the journal]   Journ. 14 Sept. (moors, mud, bullocks, duets), 15
Sept. (children, flute), 18 Oct. (Pope), 13 Oct. (apples, Punch, girl in red cloak),
12 Oct. (Lord Dumfries), 9 Nov. (Hume), 4 Nov. (giggling), 23 Oct. (need of
change), 26 Oct. 1762 (leaves Kames).

p. 93.
Jean Heron]   Journ. 18 Sept., 1, 4 Oct. 1762.

Lady Kames]   Journ. 30 Sept., 2 Oct. 1762. See also 22 Sept. 1762 ("Lady
Kames and I had a long walk in the garden and much serious conversation about
family affairs. The confidence which she reposed in me flattered me much").

Mrs. Love]   Journ. 25 Nov., 26, 27, 29 Oct., 4 Nov. 1762.

p. 94.
Boswell's uncertainty as to his real gift]   Journ. 14 Oct. 1762.

Peggy Doig]   To John Johnston, 17 Aug., 13 Sept., 24 Nov. 1762. Boswell's
jest as to the variety of his "productions" is Notes, 27 Apr. 1767.

Dr. Cairnie]   To John Johnston, 17 Aug., 13 Sept., 24 Nov. 1762.

p. 95.
Lord Auchinleck arrives, makes arrangements]   Journ. 9, 11 Nov. 1762.

Lt. John Boswell's illness]   Journ. 26 Oct. 1762; To John Johnston, 8 Feb.
1763.

Boswell absents himself from church on Sacrament Sunday]   Journ. 4, 7 Nov.
1762. See also 19 Sept. 1762 ("The family [at Kirroughtrie] went all to church, and

as I have no great opinion of the Presbyterian method of worshipping the Supreme Being, I stayed at home and read prayers").

Departure]   Journ. 15 Nov. 1762.

CHAPTER VIII

p. 96.
Entry into London]   Journ. 19 Nov. 1762.

"Mr. Addison's character ... "]   Journ. 1 Dec. 1762.

Boswell's budget]   "Scheme of Living written ... the Morning after my Arrival in London, 1762" (Yale MS. M259).

p. 97.
"Be *retenu*" (or "Preserve *retenue*")]   E.g. (a few examples out of a great many), Mem. 5, 7, 27 Dec. 1762; 2 Jan. 1763.

Boswell's lodgings]   Journ. 26, 30 Nov. 1762; 9 Feb. 1763.

"There is something to me very agreeable"]   Journ. 11 Dec. 1762.

Summary of Boswell's routine]   E.g. Journ. 9 Feb. 1763 (rising); Mem. 5 Dec. 1762; 20 Jan. 1763 (walk round the Park); Mem. 27, 28 Dec. 1762; 1 Jan. 1763 (breakfast at nine); Journ. 2, 13, 16 Dec. 1762 (Queensberry); Journ. 23, 27 Nov. 1762 (City); Journ. 3, 13 Dec. 1762 (Goulds); Journ. 30 Nov., 17 Dec. 1762 (Sheridans); Journ. 1, 4 Dec. 1762 (Macfarlanes); Journ. 26, 28 Nov. (Terrys); Journ. 15 Dec. 1762; 6, 19 Jan. 1763 (chop-house); Journ. 11, 18, 25 Dec. 1762 (Child's: the dialogue quoted is 18 Dec.); Journ. 19, 22 Nov., 8, 11 Dec. 1762; 10 Jan. 1763 (plays); Journ. 15 Dec. 1762 (cock-fight); Journ. 7, 10, 24 Dec. 1762; Journ. 7, 14, 21 Jan. 1763 (Lady Northumberland's); Mem. 3, 4, 5, 28 Dec. 1762; Journ. 10, 19, 29 Dec. 1762; 1 Jan. 1763 (early to bed, no suppers). The evidence for "next to no drinking" is of course mainly negative, but see Journ. 15 Nov., 25 Dec. 1762; 4, 19 Jan., 9 Apr., 2 June, 26 July 1763; and especially Journ. 19 Dec. 1762; 15 July 1763. For the hours spent on the journal, see Part III of the article BOSWELL, JAMES in the index of *Boswell's London Journal, 1762–1763*, 1950.

p. 98.
Boswell dines at home on bread and cheese]   Journ. 21 Dec. 1762 to 6 Jan. 1763, *passim*.

Boswell becomes a father]   To John Johnston, 14 Dec. 1762 (two letters); 30 July 1763; Johnston Corresp. p. 18 n.2. The child was presumably born about 7 December 1762.

Mrs. Love]   Journ. 25 Nov. 1762; Mem. 28, 29 Nov. 1762 (these memoranda quoted above, p. 477).

Mrs. Lewis]   Boswell, from her own account, reported (Journ. 11 Jan. 1763) that she was born of very creditable parents in London but made a heedless runaway marriage, went on the stage to support herself, and travelled in various companies. Her husband proving harsh and the marriage having been found to be invalid, they parted by mutual consent and she got into Covent Garden Theatre. In January 1763 she was just twenty-four years old (Journ. 12 Jan. 1763). Mr. C. B. Hogan has turned up in a London newspaper, *The Oracle,* 23 February 1791 (that is, some twenty-eight years after Boswell's encounter with the lady) a report of a law-suit recently decided in the Court of King's Bench which makes it possible to add some further specific details which Boswell suppressed. "Louisa's" maiden name was Anne Lewis. On 4 August 1755 she was married by publication of banns to Charles Standen, a strolling player, on which occasion she was described as of Swallow Street, London. Boswell had seen her act in Edinburgh as Mrs. Standen, but was only slightly acquainted with her (Journ. 14 Dec. 1762). The Standens did not separate until after a son was born, or at least conceived. This boy, concerning whose existence Boswell was probably ignorant, would have been quite young—not more than six—in December 1762. Mrs. Standen resumed her maiden name but continued the style of Mrs. Some time later, both she and Standen entered into second unions, she with a man named Vaughan. Standen had five children by his second wife. A Mr. Miller left a large estate "to the children of Mr. Charles Standen," whereupon Anne Lewis's son claimed the bequest. Standen gave testimony intended to prove that his marriage with her was void because it had occurred before the third publication of the banns; she testified that it occurred a week and a day after she had ascertained the second publishing. The marriage register was in order. The jury found in favour of her son.

The season of 1762–1763 was Mrs. Lewis's first at Covent Garden. She played only three "name" parts during the season: the Queen in *Hamlet* (27 September 1762 and 18 May 1763), Mrs. Ford in *The Merry Wives of Windsor* (20 October 1762), and Lady Darling in *The Constant Couple* (15 April 1763). Along with four other members of the cast she was given a benefit (*The Relapse*) on 7 May 1763. She was not re-engaged for 1763–1764 (*The London Stage, 1660–1800,* pt. 4, 1747–1776, by G. W. Stone, 1962, pp. 952, 957, 989, 995, 998).

The index to *Boswell's London Journal, 1762–1763,* furnishes a fuller résumé than is here feasible of the progress of Boswell's amour.

p. 99.
Boswell cloyed by possession] Journ. 16, 17 Jan. 1763.

Lady Mirabel] Journ. 14 Jan. 1763. Boswell was very circumspect about leaving clues for identifying this lady of quality, always employing the style "Lady Mirabel" in both the journal and the corresponding memoranda. In *Boswell's London Journal* I have suggested that she might be Lady Mary Coke (1726–1811), journalist and friend of Horace Walpole, daughter of the second Duke of Argyll and since 1753 widow of Edward, Viscount Coke, son and heir to the Earl of Leicester. She was by birth a Scot, was an acquaintance of the Earl of Eglinton, and paid marked attention to the Duke of York, to whom she afterwards tried to persuade people she had been secretly married. In his published letter to Eglinton (above, p. 67) Boswell had asked to be remembered to a "Lady M_____" (no doubt a genuine initial) whose name he juxtaposed with that of the Duke of York: "Remember me to all with whose acquaintance I have been honoured through your Lordship's kindness. It would take up the livelong day to name every one of them, from His R_____l H_____ss downwards. I must insist that you present my best respects to Lady M_____, and tell her that to hear her Ladyship's divine harpsichord for another forenoon, I would gladly serve her half a year as a down-right footman, without any mental reservation whatever" (*Scots Mag.* 23 [1761]. 471). Lady Mary Coke must have wished the reputation of being musical, for she had herself painted by Allan Ramsay, full length in white satin, standing beside a harpsichord and holding a theorbo. It is, to say the least, a suspicious circumstance that though Boswell associated Lady Mary Coke with Lady Northumberland's parties when he met and named her at the Court of Brunswick (Journ. 20 Aug. 1764), he does not mention her when he is reporting the parties themselves—and does mention Lady Mirabel.

Boswell's initials, ciphers, and pseudonyms for his various ladies are usually in some way related to their real names. I do not see how to relate "Mirabel" to "Coke" (an old spelling of Cook, and so pronounced), but it might be a telescoping of Lady Mary's maiden name: Mary [Camp]bell.

It would be less than candid, however, not to add that Horace Walpole's many letters to Lady Mary and her own voluminous journal count rather against this identification than for it. From these one would infer not only that she was not *galante* but also that she was too snobbish even to engage in smart repartee with a young commoner whom she knew but slightly. She does not record the hours of playing and practising that one would expect if she had had a real musical gift. Her relation, Lady Louisa Stuart, in fact says that the musical portrait was a fraud: that Lady Mary "had no ear" but chose to be painted with a theorbo because Lady Ancram, who did play agreeably, had been painted with an instrument (*The Letters and Journals of Lady Mary Coke,* 1756–1774, ed. J. A. Home, 1889–1896, i. lxxxi–lxxxii). But Lady Louisa is very catty and is demonstrably wrong in some of her details; and though Boswell did have a good ear (above, p. 128), his reference to Lady M_____'s "divine harpsichord" is language of compliment and does not have to be taken *au pied de la lettre.*

p. 100.
Sequel to the intrigue with Louisa] Journ. 18–20 Jan., 3, 10 Feb. 1763. The direct quotations are, in order, 19 Jan., 3 Feb., and 20 Jan. 1763. The five guineas are specified in the letter to Louisa. The black wax: To John Johnston, 25 Jan., 1 Mar. 1763; Johnston Corresp. p. 40 n.1.

The infection perhaps self-originating] Boswell says that his second infection (above, p. 58) involved epididymitis (swelled testicle) and took four months to cure (Journ. 4 Feb., 22 Jan. 1763). He may also have had an acute infection of the prostate, subsiding into a chronic gonorrhoeal prostatitis, not noticeable to himself and ordinarily non-infective, but capable of being rendered active, as suggested, by venereal excess or harsh usage. It is suggested, in short, that some of Boswell's reported bouts of gonorrhoea were not genuine new infections but recrudescences of an old one. The present case is ambiguous, but for at least one of his later attacks there seems hardly any other explanation. See above, p. 320.

"I move like very clock-work"]   Journ. 9 Feb. 1763.

p. 101.

The Discovery; coolness with Sheridan]   Journ. 28 Nov., 31 Dec. 1762; 18, 20 Jan., 8 Feb., 24 Mar. 1763; Mem. 31 Dec. 1762; 1 Jan., 11, 21, 26 Mar. 1763. The two versions of the prologue mentioned by Boswell in the journal for 18 Jan. are preserved in Douce MS. 193 in the Bodleian Library (ff. 54, 55). Mrs. Sheridan wrote the prologue actually spoken, borrowing Boswell's ideas and indeed lifting one of his couplets.

p. 102.

David Mallet; the attempt to damn *Elvira; Critical Strictures*]   Journ. 19 Jan. 1763; DNB under David Mallet; Johnson's "Life of Mallet" in *Lives of the Poets; Life,* 28 Mar. 1772; *Scotland and Scotsmen,* i. 24n.; *Gibbon's Journal,* ed. D. M. Low, 1929, pp. 202–204; Journ. 20, 21, 27 Jan. 1763; *Lit. Car.* pp. 18–19; *Critical Strictures,* Augustan Reprint Soc. Pub. No. 35, 1952, Introduction and pp. 17–20; Mem. 1 Mar., 6 Apr. 1763; *Critical Rev.* 1st ser. 15 (Feb. 1763). 160; *Life,* 25 June 1763, n. (i. 409 n. 1).

p. 103.

Reading in Hume]   Mem., *passim* (66 mentions, 30 Dec. 1762–10 July 1763); Journ. 5 Mar. 1763 (Pringle); Journ. 22, 29 Jan., 7, 20 Feb., 3 May 1763. He had finished all six volumes by 13 July 1763 (letter of that date to W. J. Temple).

A comedy . . . some essays]   Mem. 31 Jan., 1, 14 Feb. 1763; Journ. 1, 13 Feb. 1763; *Boswell's London Journal,* 1950, p. 189 n.

Details of publication of the Erskine-Boswell correspondence]   Mem. 9 Feb.– 9 Apr. 1763, *passim* (almost daily mention); Journ. 12, 13, 14 Apr. 1763; *Lit. Car.,* pp. 19–24; the date of publication is fixed by Journ. 12 Apr. 1763. The manuscripts of Erskine's letters are not known to exist. Boswell worked the published text of his own up from his retained copies, which have also disappeared. The originals of Boswell's letters after Erskine's death passed ultimately to his nephew, Brig.-Gen. Robert Anstruther, and were purchased by Yale in 1955 from Gen. Anstruther's descendant and representative, Sir Ralph Anstruther of Balcaskie, Bt. Boswell edited his own letters (and presumably Erskine's) freely for the publication of 1763, and fabricated a few that had been no part of the original correspondence.

p. 104.

Boswell's wish that nothing that concerned himself should be secret]   Journ. 4 Jan. 1776.

Boswell's characterization of himself]   Letter 13 (To Andrew Erskine, 17 Dec. 1761).

Allusions by name to Kames, Smith, Home, Sheridan, Derrick, Hume]   Erskine Corresp. pp. 149, 151; 41; 68, 149; 60, 118, 149; 107, 114, 135–137; 117 (Letters Nos. 38, 39; 10; 17, 38; 14, 30, 38; 28, 29, 34; 30).

The Laird of Macfarlane and his seat]   Erskine Corresp. pp. 23–24 (Letter No. 7); pp. 34–35 (Letter No. 9); *Tour,* 6 Sept. 1773, n.

Other indiscreet mention] Erskine Corresp. pp. 72, 81 (Letters Nos. 18, 22: "Miss C_____"); 18–19 (Letter No. 6: marriage); 33 (Letter No. 9: Donaldson's children); 149 (Letter No. 38: Sheridan, Home, Kames).

"History of Erskine and Boswell's Letters, Published Tuesday 12 April 1763"] Yale MS. M142. Eglinton's remarks were made on Thursday 14 Apr., Blair's on Friday 15 Apr.

p. 105.
Lord Auchinleck mortified] From Lord Auchinleck, 30 May 1763. The court sat down at Jedburgh on 5 May and at Dumfries on 12 May (*Scots Mag.* 25. 353).

p. 106.
Reviews of the Erskine Correspondence] *Critical Rev.* 1st ser. 15 (May 1763). 343–345; *Monthly Rev.* 1st ser. 28 (June 1763). 476–479; B. C. Nangle, *The Monthly Review, First Series,* 1934, p. 145; *Pub. Advt.* Nos. 8886 (28 Apr. 1763) and an earlier number not yet located; *Lond. Chron.* 26–28 Apr. 1763, pp. 404–405. Boswell's authorship of the review in the *Chronicle* is established by his memorandum for 21 April 1763: "Write on *Letters* for *London Chronicle*. Bid people write as good letters." The proposed admonition duly concludes the review: "Although the cynical part of mankind may accuse them of vanity, yet we will venture to say that there are few people who would not have been equally vain had they written letters of equal merit." See also Mem. 29 Apr. 1763 ("Buy another *Chronicle*"). Copies of the *Chronicle* containing Boswell's review and of the *Advertiser* for 28 Apr. turned up among Boswell's papers. I do not know whether he got copy money for the *Letters,* but the memoranda show that he tried to: e.g. 13 Feb. 1763 ("Keep Dash [Erskine] fine to elegant edition of letters, utmost secrecy and £50 apiece"); 21 Feb. 1763 ("Write letters out by degrees. It will amuse, and it will bring you gold to jaunt to Oxford and about the dusty roads round London").

Queensberry] Journ. 2, 13, 16, 26 Dec. 1762; 20 Jan. 1763; From the Duke of Queensberry, 22 Dec. 1762; To John Johnston, 22 Mar. (misdated 22 Apr.) 1763; *Memoirs,* p. 324 (xxxii).

p. 107.
Lady Northumberland] Journ. 10, 27, 30 Dec. 1762; 10 Jan., 19 Feb., 4, 11 Mar. 1763; Mem. 14 Dec. 1762; 15, 17, 22, 26 Feb., 2, 3, 11 Mar. 1763; To John Johnston, 4, 18 Jan. 1763.

Eglinton] Journ. 27 Nov., 22, 29 Dec. 1762; 5, 10, 14, 18, 21, 24, 25 Jan., 7 Feb., 9, 15, 21 Mar. 1763 (quotation from 21 Mar.); From the Earl of Eglinton, 22 Dec. 1762; Mem. 28 Dec. 1762; 10, 11, 15, 16, 17, 19, 20, 21, 23, 28 Mar., 7 Apr. 1763.

Eglinton gets the promise of a commission in a marching regiment from Bute, Boswell declines] From the Earl of Bute, 26 Mar. 1763 (endorsed, "The Prime Minister's note that I was to have an ensigncy. But as I liked only the Guards, I declined it"); To John Johnston, 22 Mar., 5 Apr. 1763; Journ. 24 Feb. 1763.

p. 108.

Lady Northumberland again] Journ. 11, 22 Apr. 1763 (quotation from the latter entry).

The sealed packets] To John Johnston, 24 Nov. 1762; 10 Feb., 22 Mar. 1763. That David Boswell came under Lord Auchinleck's displeasure is inferred from To John Johnston, 24 Nov. 1762, and From John Johnston, 24 Feb. 1763; see Johnston Corresp. p. 51 n.5. The chronology of the letters between Boswell and his father immediately before the break in relations was as follows: Boswell received letters from David Boswell and Lord Auchinleck, c. 18 Feb. 1763 (From John Johnston, 24 Feb. 1763); he sent answers to both under cover to Johnston, 19 Feb. 1763 (Mem.; From John Johnston, 24 Feb. 1763). He received a second and final letter from Lord Auchinleck, 8 Mar. 1763 (To John Johnston) and a letter from his mother, c. 12 Mar. 1763 (it is dated 7 Mar. 1763). He probably answered Lord Auchinleck's second letter the day he received it, for on that day he sent it off for Johnston to read, and on 15 Mar. 1763 (Mem.) counselled himself to "write father about bill," i.e. about the bill for £40 which Orlando Hart of Edinburgh was to draw on him (Johnston Corresp. pp. 52–53, 62, 63, 71). It does not seem as though he would have addressed his father on a business matter before answering a personal letter which he had received a week before. If, however, he did not answer that letter till he got it back from Johnston, apparently on 21 Mar. 1763 (To John Johnston, 22 Mar. 1763), his letter would have shown more feeling, for it was not till then that he learned that the seals of his packets had been broken. ("Really this was so very ungenteel and really so very hard that it pains me exceedingly. It was doing what no parent has a right to do in the case of a son who is a man and therefore an independent individual. It is equally unjust to steal his secrets as his money, especially when we consider that secrets cannot be restored, and that perhaps those of other people may be connected with them.") But though he wrote in such terms that Lord Auchinleck could say that his letter "was telling me in pretty plain language you contemned what I could say or do" (From Lord Auchinleck, 30 May 1763), it is clear that Boswell did not bring up the matter of the broken seals till some months later (To John Johnston, 20 Jan. 1764). Lord Auchinleck did not hear Mr. Reid (the minister of Ochiltree) quote from Boswell's journal till he got to Auchinleck, that is, not before 24 Mar. 1763 (From Lord Auchinleck, 30 May 1763; From Euphemia, Lady Auchinleck, 7 Mar. 1763).

p. 109.

Boswell warned of his father's threats] From Dr. John Boswell, 11 Apr. 1763; From William McQuhae, 26 Apr. 1763; From Euphemia, Lady Auchinleck, 7 Mar. 1763. One of the most interesting warnings came from James Bruce, gardener at Auchinleck, but Boswell had already sued for pardon by the time he received it: "No doubt you'll have heard before this of what my Lord talks of pretty freely as to disposing of rig and furrow, house and yard of an ancient seat" (19 May 1763).

"My father's displeasure"] To John Johnston, 17 May 1763.

Boswell writes his father "a most warm letter"] Ibid.

Pringle and Dalrymple asked to intercede] Ibid.; Mem. 16 May 1763 (quoted above, p. 112); To Sir David Dalrymple, 21 May 1763. It is somewhat surprising to find that Dalrymple had all along approved of Boswell's spending some years in the Army: "A German campaign would have done you more service than a thousand and ten thousand lectures from any of your friends" (From Sir David Dalrymple, 30 May 1763).

p. 110.

"A very kind letter"] Journ. 8 June 1763. In writing to John Johnston he called it "a most affectionate letter" (16 June 1763).

Advice of Sir David Dalrymple] From Lord Auchinleck, 18 June 1763 ("Sir David proposes you should put up at Utrecht, which is a most polite place"). Sir David, in writing to Boswell, preferred to sink his own part in the decision (From Sir David Dalrymple, 16 June 1763).

Wilkes] DNB (a remarkably good article); Almon, i. 91–124.

p. 111.

Paul Lewis] Journ. 3–6 May 1763.

p. 112.

Five convicts hanged at Tyburn] *Gent. Mag.* 33 (1763). 312. Three were hanged on 10 Feb. (ibid. p. 96), but Boswell was then confined. During the period of his first visit to London three hangings occurred. One of them involved four men, another was extraordinary in that the sufferer was a peer of England, Lawrence Shirley, Earl Ferrers (*Gent. Mag.* 30 [1760].200, 246, 248).

Boswell's admiration for Johnson and efforts to meet him] Journ. 21 Sept. 1762; *Life,* beginning of 1763; Journ. 28 Mar. 1776; 18, 25 Dec. 1762.

p. 114.

The first meeting with Johnson] Journ. 16 May 1763; *Life,* 16 May 1763.

p. 116.

Boswell meets the London wits] Journ. 24 May 1763; Journ. 6 May 1763 (Colman); Journ. 9 Feb. 1763 ("poignant acrimony"); Mem. 25 May 1763; Charles Ryskamp, *William Cowper of the Inner Temple, Esq.,* 1959, pp. 78–94 (Thornton, Colman, Churchill, Lloyd, the Nonsense Club, etc.). One greatly regrets that Boswell did not meet William Cowper, the member of the Nonsense Club who now enjoys the greatest eminence, but Cowper had already slipped into the depression preceding his first attack of insanity (ibid. pp. 145–157). For all the documentary evidence concerning further relations with the wits, see Journ. 1, 20 June 1763; Mem. 25 May, 1, 2, 9, 11, 25 July 1763; From Bonnell Thornton, ?25 July 1763; To W. J. Temple, 26 [probably 27] July 1763 ("to astonish," etc.); To Sir David Dalrymple, 2 Aug. 1763.

p. 117.

Succeeding calls on Johnson] Journ. 24 May, 14, 25 June 1763; *Life,* 24 May, 13, 25 June 1763.

"I love the young dogs," etc.] Journ. 22 July 1763; *Life*, 21 [error for 22] July 1763.

Beauclerk and Langton] DNB; *Life*, end of 1752. The grant of free warren, like most family traditions dealing with the remote past, appears to have been fabulous (*Life*, i. 540).

Boswell opens his heart to Johnson] Journ. 25 June, 14, 22, 28, 30 July, 2 Aug. 1763; *Life*, 25 June, 14, 28, 30 July, 2 Aug. 1763.

p. 118.
Joubert] "Piety is not a religion, though it is the soul of all religions. A man does not have a religion when he merely has pious inclinations, any more than a man has a country when he merely has a love for mankind. A man has a country, a man is the citizen of a community, only when he decides to observe and support certain laws, to obey certain magistrates, and to adopt certain ways of thinking and acting" (*Pensées*, I. lxi, translated).

Amorous reverie in church] Journ. 28 Nov., 5 Dec. 1762.

p. 119.
Mrs. Philips at the Green Canister] Mem. 5, 8 Dec. 1762; 30 Mar. 1763; Journ. 25 Nov. 1762; 25, 31 Mar., 9 Apr., 10, 17 May, 4 June 1763; C. J. S. Thompson, *The Quacks of Old London*, 1928, pp. 273–275.

Casual fruition] Journ. as in preceding note, beginning 25 Mar.; Journ. 19 May, 4, 18 June, 13, 16 July, 3 Aug. 1763.

Self-reproach] Mem. 26, 27 Mar., 2, 6, 16, 17 Apr. 1763.

Admonitions to give promise to Temple] Mem. 19 Apr., 21 May, 19 June 1763; Journ. 18 June 1763.

A week later, three weeks later] Journ. 26 June, 16 July 1763.

p. 120.
Heroic raking] Journ. 19 May, 4 June 1763.

"We stayed so long," etc.] *Life*, 30 July 1763.

p. 121.
He told Sir David Dalrymple] To Sir David Dalrymple, 23 July 1763.

Later sickened by his journal of 1762–1763] Journ. 3 Feb., 30 July 1780. See also Journ. 1 Sept. 1780: "Got from [James Bruce] a parcel of my letters to him at the most foolish time of my life: viz., when I was from twenty-one to twenty-three. Was sunk by viewing myself with contempt, though then a *genius* in my own eyes. Burnt all but one or two of the best. Was consoled to think that I was now so much more solid."

"You will smile," etc.] To Sir David Dalrymple, 2 July 1763.

Provision for Charles] Dalrymple owed him twenty shillings for books (To Sir David Dalrymple, 30 July, 4 Aug. 1763), Temple seven guineas, both debts payable on demand. Love owed him £20, for which Love had given bills at twelve and sixteen months (To John Johnston, 4 Aug. 1763). He had estimated his child's maintenance at £10 a year (To John Johnston, 30 June 1763).

The last of his London memoranda] Undated, following Mem. 2 Aug. 1763.

Johnson sees him off] *Life*, 30 July, 5, 6 Aug. 1763.

CHAPTER IX

GENERAL NOTE: The sources listed below are necessarily selective. For fuller documentation, consult the index of *Boswell in Holland, 1763–1764*, 1952.

p. 123.
The arrival in, and flight from, Utrecht] To W. J. Temple, 16 Aug. 1763; To John Johnston, 23 Sept. 1763.

Boswell's aim and models] Mem. following 2 Aug., 14 Aug. 1763, but mainly inferred from later memoranda, e.g. 8, 9, 10, 13, 15, 16 Sept. 1763 and *passim;* also from "Inviolable Plan," partially quoted above, pp. 127–128.

Depression at Leyden] See especially Mem. 20 Apr. 1764 ("Leyden, where you had been so horrid").

p. 124.
Boswell sends frantic appeals to Johnson, Dempster, and Temple] To George Dempster, 14 Aug. 1763; To W. J. Temple, 16 Aug. 1763; To John Johnston, 23 Sept. 1763. The letter to Johnson has not been recovered, but as it gave a "hopeless account" of the state of Boswell's mind (Johnson's characterization), must have been written at about the same time as those to Dempster and Temple. Johnson did not answer it till 8 Dec. 1763, by which time he had had another from Boswell.

Stewart, Dempster, Morgan] To W. J. Temple, 16 Aug. 1763; To John Johnston, 23 Sept. 1763; From Archibald Stewart, 7 Sept. 1763; From George Dempster, 22, 23 Aug., 29 Oct. 1763, that of 23 Aug. quoted; *Dictionary of American Biography* under John Morgan, 1735–1789.

Temple, Johnson] From W. J. Temple, 23 Aug. 1763; To John Johnston, 23 Sept. 1763; *The Rambler,* Nos. 29, 32 (quoted), 47, 72, 74, 85, 134.

François Mazerac] Mem. 8 Sept. 1763 and *passim.*

Boswell's "house"] To W. J. Temple, 23 Sept. 1763 ("I have got a neat house of my own and an excellent servant"); in his letter to John Johnston of the same date he gives his address in French as "A la Cour de l'Empereur à Utrecht." See *Boswell in Holland, 1763–1764,* Mem. 8 Sept. 1763, n.

"I am now," etc.] To W. J. Temple, 25 Sept. 1763.

p. 125.
Boswell the only British student at Utrecht, 1763–1764] To W. J. Temple, 23 Sept. 1763.

The Rev. Robert Brown] *Fasti Scot.* vii. 555; William Steven, *History of the*

Scottish Church, Rotterdam, 1832, pp. 342, 344; Mem. 27 Jan., 13 Mar. 1764; *Letters of Laurence Sterne,* ed. L. P. Curtis, 1935, pp. 121–123, 432–434; Voltaire, *La Guerre civile de Genève,* 1768, chant 1er, ll. 95–100, with foot-note (Brown had contributed, under his name, the preface to J. J. Vernet's *Lettres critiques d'un voyageur anglois sur l'article Genève du Dictionnaire encyclopédique,* 1761: see From Robert Brown, 22 Oct. 1767); Godet, i. 111 n.

Mrs. Catharine Brown and her sister Marguerite Kinloch] *Comp. Baronet.* iv. 347, 454; *The Genealogist,* 2d ser. 14. 200; From Lord Auchinleck, c. 10 Dec. 1763 (Sir James Kinloch's marriage to Mrs. Brown's mother was invalid); *N & Q,* 193 (17 Apr. 1948). 167–168.

Rose] James Rose (c. 1737—living 1794) was the second son of James Rose of Brea in Moray (*Glasgow Matric.* No. 1845), consequently grandson of Hugh Rose, 15th of Kilravock, by his second marriage, and first cousin of Hugh Rose (1705–1772), 17th of Kilravock. See Burke's *Landed Gentry* under Rose of Kilravock; James Rose does not appear there but his elder brother, Hugh Rose of Brea, does. The evidence for this identification, which my friend and colleague Professor Robert Warnock has extracted from the Rose of Kilravock papers, will appear in the appropriate volume of the research edition. Rose appears to have graduated M.A. from the University of Aberdeen before entering Glasgow (P. J. Anderson, *Fasti Academiae Mariscallanae Aberdonensis,* 1898, ii. 323) and hence to have been a man of more than ordinary learning. One would naturally assume that he came to Utrecht to continue his studies at a third university, but Boswell reported to Temple that he himself was the only British student in the University of Utrecht in 1763–1764 (To W. J. Temple, 23 Sept. 1763), and says nothing in that letter or elsewhere of Rose's having been a student at Utrecht earlier. He was ordained deacon in 1768 and priest in 1769.

Boswell arranges to dine with the Browns] Mem. 1, 4, 7 Oct. 1763; French Theme, 31 Oct. 1763; Expense Account in Holland (Yale MS. A30), 15 Oct. 1763–14 Apr. 1764).

Boswell's programme of studies] See "Boswell's University Education," pp. 250–253.

p. 126.
Ferocious time-tables] Mem. 24, 28, 30 Sept., 3, 5 Oct. 1763; To W. J. Temple, 23 Sept. 1763. That in the text is a conflation, since no single schedule covers the entire day. Time of being waked is from French Themes, c. 27 Sept. 1763; c. 28–29 Mar. 1764.

Three hours for amusement] Mem. 7 Oct. 1763.
Shuttlecock] French Theme, 2 Nov. 1763; From Charles de Guiffardière, 26 Nov. 1763.

Billiards disreputable] Mem. 24, 25 Sept. 1763.

Smoking] Mem. 12 Aug., 26 Oct. 1763; Ten Lines, 21 Jan. 1764.

French Themes] E.g. Mem. 19, 27, 28, 30 Sept., 3, 5, 15, 17, 19, 20 Oct. 1763; French Themes, 5, c. 7, c. 10, 31 Oct. 1763.

Reading in French] For references, see "Boswell's University Education," p. 252 n. 4.

Supposed to speak only French at Brown's] French Theme, 31 Oct. 1763.

Literary Society] Mem. 7, 21, 26, 27 Oct., 2, 10, 16, 17 Nov. 1763 and *passim;* French Themes, 31 Oct., 9 Dec. 1763. Manuscripts of four of Boswell's addresses are preserved among the papers at Yale (Yale MS. M89).

p. 127.
"Inviolable Plan"] Yale MS. M88; Mem. 16 Oct. 1763.

p. 128.
Scots dictionary] Mem. 20, 22, 23 Jan., 5, 7, 8 Feb. 1764; Dutch Theme, events of 6 Feb. 1764; French Themes, c. 24 Feb–c. 19 Mar. 1764; Journ. 16 Sept., 4, 6 Oct. 1764; 11 Dec. 1765; *Life,* 19 Oct. 1769. Boswell's manuscript was sold for sixteen shillings in 1825 as Lot 3172 of the sale of the library of James Boswell the younger (*Bibliotheca Boswelliana,* 1825, annotated copy at Yale, p. 101). I do not know where it is now.

Translation of Erskine's *Principles*] Mem. 29, 30, 31 Mar., 1, 2, 3, 7, 8, 10 Apr. 1764; French Theme, c. 3 May 1764. Boswell was to make the translation and Trotz was to add notes.

French Themes] c. 14 Oct. 1763 (warm baths); c. 28 Oct. 1763 (good ear); 2 Nov. 1763 (breeches); c. 17 Dec. 1763 (cousin who beat him); c. 18 Jan. 1764 (fat); c. 27 Jan. 1764 (badly educated); c. 2 Feb. 1764 (never beats his servant); c. 17 Feb. 1764 (two pillows); c. 9 Mar. 1764 (Scots authors); c. 28–29 Mar. 1764 (difficulty getting up); c. 9 Nov. 1763 (Duke of York).

p. 129.
Leonard Bacon] *Saturday Review,* 35 (26 Apr. 1952). 11.

Ten Lines] 22 Oct. 1764 (Hessians); 14 Oct. 1763 (tongs).

p. 130.
Loss of the Holland Journal] Boswell left it with Mr. Brown, with other papers, to be sent to him in Scotland after his return, but it was lost somewhere on the way. See *Boswell in Holland,* 1763–1764, pp. 258 n.7 and 359 n.5 of McGraw-Hill's edition (251 n.2 and 349 n.2 of Heinemann's).

Geoffrey Scott] BP, ii. 182.

Approving memoranda] Mem. 18, 26, 28 Oct., 19 Nov., 3, 11, 12, 14 Dec. 1763.

Andries Bart] Mem. 19 Feb. 1764; From Charles de Guiffardière, 20 May 1764. The name appears also in the address of this letter of Guiffardière's and some others received by Boswell in Utrecht, e.g. From Charles de Guiffardière, 26 Nov. 1763; From Catharina van Geelvinck, 17 Mar. 1764.

No Briton since Sir David Dalrymple] To W. J. Temple, 17 Apr. 1764 (second of that date).

Brilliant dissipation] To W. J. Temple, 23 Mar. 1764.

p. 131.

At Col. Spaen's house]   Dialogues at The Hague (Yale MS. M91), 21 Dec. 1763.

Francis van Aerssen van Sommelsdyck]   Mem. 24, 25 Dec. 1763; 6 Jan. 1764; Dialogues at The Hague (Yale MS. M91), 23 Dec. 1763.

Presentation to Prince of Orange]   Mem. 6 Jan. 1764.

Sacrament in the Church of England]   Mem. 25 Dec. 1763 ("This is Christmas day. Be in due frame. Only hear prayers at Chapel, but don't take sacrament except you can see Chaplain before"); 26 Dec. 1763 ("Yesterday you waited on Mr. Richardson, Chaplain to Sir Joseph Yorke; found him affable and decent. Took you up to his room, told you 'Our church leaves it to every man.'... Received the blessed sacrament solemnly professing myself a Christian. Was in devout, heavenly frame, quite happy. The first time I received the communion in the Church of England"). Also To John Johnston, 20 Jan. 1764.

Back to Utrecht]   Mem. 17 Jan. 1764.

Passion for Mme. Geelvinck]   Mem. 24 Jan. 1764 and following.

Hippish, gaunt, etc.]   Mem. 22 Feb. 1764.

Bad cold]   Mem. 20 Feb.–5 Mar. 1764 (first named as a cold, Mem. 26 Feb.); Dutch Theme (Yale MS. M92), c. 28 Feb. 1764. Boswell kept his bed on 29 Feb.

Happier in vice than in virtue]   Mem. 4 Mar. 1764.

Receives news of Charles's death]   Mem. 9, 10, 11, 12 Mar. 1764; Ten Lines, 8, 9 Mar. 1764; To W. J. Temple, 23 Mar. 1764; To John Johnston, 9 Apr. 1764.

p. 132.

Wail of misery]   Mem. 18, 19, 20, 24, 25 Mar., 4, 6, 7, 8, 9, 13, 18, 22 Apr. 1764; see also To W. J. Temple, 23 Mar., 17 Apr. 1764 (both letters of that date); To John Johnston, 9 Apr. 1764; From Lord Auchinleck, 2 Apr. 1764; Ten Lines, 22 Mar., 4 Apr. 1764.

No comfort from religion]   To John Johnston, 9 Apr. 1764.

Predestination, Necessity]   Mem. 11 Mar. 1764 (Hungarian); 12 Mar. 1764 (Rose); 18 Mar. 1764 (Rose and Brown); Journ. 4 June 1764; To W. J. Temple, 23 Mar. 1764; Ten Lines, 1 Apr. 1764.

"You went out to fields"]   Mem. 29 Mar. 1764.

"Show that you are Boswell"]   Mem. 22 Mar. 1764. See also To John Johnston, 9 Apr. 1764.

Boswell's melancholy]   Paraphrased from Hypochondriack Nos. 6 and 39, direct quotation from the latter.

p. 133.

Boswell conscious of his pleasures]   Journ. 8 Apr. 1781 ("Then the card table was set, and we played two rubbers at whist, hugging ourselves that we were out of the reach of Presbyterian prejudices").

Hamlet's lines]   E.g. *Hypochondriack* No. 39; Journ. 14 Feb. 1776; 4 Dec. 1777; 3 Dec. 1780; 8 Feb. 1791.

Two Dutch doctors]   To W. J. Temple, 22 May 1764 (J. D. Gaubius of Leyden); Mem. 25 May 1764; Journ. 24 May 1764 (J. D. Hahn of Utrecht).

Boswell's energy and resilience]   E.g. Journ. 10 Sept. 1773, a twenty-four mile tramp with ascent of a mountain (1456 feet), a reel on the summit and an evening of vigorous dancing afterwards.

p. 134.
Sitting up]   Mem. 14, 15 Apr., 31 May 1764.

Both melancholy and high spirits excessive]   To W. J. Temple, 17 Apr. 1764 (2d letter of that date).

p. 135.
Not merely his *right* but his *duty*]   To T. D. Boswell, 13 Oct. 1794.

Countess of Nassau-Beverweerd]   *Boswell in Holland, 1763–1764,* Mem. 25, 26 Nov. 1763, n.; Mem. 1, 2 Dec. 1763; 28 Jan., 9 Feb. 1764 ("vile spite"); 14 Mar. 1764 ("Dutch nose"); To W. J. Temple, 23 Mar. 1764 ("so-so *vrouw*").

Margaret Stewart]   To W. J. Temple, 23, 25 Sept., 9 Nov. 1763; 17 Apr. 1764; To John Johnston, 23 Sept. 1763; 20 Jan. 1764; From Lord Auchinleck, 2 Apr. 1764; Mem. 17, 23, 24 Sept. 1763; 14 Apr. 1764. The quotations are respectively from the letters to Temple, 23 Sept. and 9 Nov. 1763.

p. 136.
Mme. Geelvinck]   Catharina Elisabeth Hasselaer (1738–1792) married Lieve Geelvinck (1730–1757) in 1756. She was a close friend of Belle de Zuylen and an intermediary in her correspondence with Constant d'Hermenches (J. E. Elias, *De Vroedscap van Amsterdam, 1578–1795,* 1905, ii. 809–810, 825; *Lettres de Belle de Zuylen (Madame de Charrière) à Constant d'Hermenches, p. p.* Philippe Godet, 1909, *passim;* Portrait by Belle de Zuylen, Yale MS. C3173).

Mme. Geelvinck's son]   Lieve Geelvinck (1757–1783). He left a fortune of 650,000 florins (*Vroedscap van Amsterdam,* ii. 825).

"Love and fiery imagination"]   Mem. 10 Feb. 1764; Boswell dreams of Mme. Geelvinck, Mem. 12 Feb. 1764.

Pays court to young Geelvinck, gets invited to a party for children]   Mem. 18, 19 Feb. 1764. See *Boswell in Holland,* notes on those entries.

"How old were you," etc.]   Mem. 19 Feb. 1764, in French.

p. 137.
Delicious but impregnable]   Ibid.

Boswell enacts Troilus]   Mem. 21 Feb. 1764.

"Le sentiment est changé"]   Mem. 10 Apr. 1764.

Égarements du coeur]   The title of a tale by Crébillon fils (1736), applied by Boswell himself to his own amours (*Memoirs,* p. 404 [xxxviii]).

Belle de Zuylen]   Godet; *Lettres de Belle de Zuylen (Madame de Charrière) à Constant d'Hermenches, p. p.* Philippe Godet, 1909; Geoffrey Scott, *The Portrait of Zélide,* 1925 and later; BP, ii. 2–11. D'Hermenches's judgement on her style is given in his letter of 7 Aug. 1762 (*Lettres,* p. 9).

p. 138.
Odd and lovable]   See above, p. 142.

p. 139.
Boswell's disapproving memoranda]   Mem. 28 Nov. 1763; 18 Apr. 1764.

Boswell receives confirmation of his reward]   From Lord Auchinleck, 2 Apr. 1764. The letter is mainly taken up with expressions of sympathy and counsel concerning Boswell's melancholy.

Boswell's plans for his tour]   To W. J. Temple, 17 Apr. 1764 (2d letter of that date).

p. 140.
Delight, ecstasy, fiery vivacious blood]   Ibid.; Mem. 20 Apr. 1764.

Moral struggles]   Mem. 14 Feb. 1764 (Satan as Cupid); 22 Mar. 1764 ("Go not to Amsterdam"); 15 Apr. 1764 ("Think if God really forbids girls"); 21 May 1764 ("moderate Venus").

Hahn]   Mem. 25 May 1764.

Amsterdam, *speelhuizen*]   Journ. 26, 27 May 1764.

News that he will travel with the Earl Marischal]   Journ. 4 June 1764 ("Never was man happier"); 7 June 1764 ("I was very, very gay").

Lord Marischal]   DNB under George Keith, 10th Earl Marischal; *Scots Peer.* vi. 62–64; Edith E. Cuthell, *The Scottish Friend of Frederic the Great,* 1915.

p. 141.
A letter from Frederick]   Frederick the Great to Lord Marischal, 16 Feb. 1764 (*Oeuvres de Frédéric le Grand,* ed. J. D. E. Preuss, 1852, 15. 294–296).

Boswell drives out to Zuylen]   Journ. 10 June 1764; Mem. 11 June 1764.

The two following days]   Mem. 12 June 1764 (*"échauffée"*); Journ. 12 June 1764 (Belle's rattling, sends him her play). Belle wrote to Constant d'Hermenches on 8 June: "I am amusing myself at present by writing a comedy. If I finish it and cause it to be acted, I will notify you immediately, but do not ask to see it sooner. To show a friend a piece of writing is to ask criticism, advice, and I don't like to ask advice because I don't like to follow it" (*Lettres,* p. 59, in French). She would not have minded Boswell's criticism.

Assurance of one of their common acquaintance]   Jean Lucas Reynst, an officer in the Army (Journ. 11 June 1764).

Dr. Hahn]   Journ. 12, 15 June 1764.

Mme. de Froment]   Journ. 13 June 1764; K. A. Varnhagen von Ense, "Feldmarschall Jakob Keith," in *Biographische Denkmale,* pt. 7, 1873, pp. 37–38, 43;

Edith E. Cuthell, *The Scottish Friend of Frederic the Great,* 1915, i. 185–186, 191, 245, 266; ii. 157–159, 248–251, 308–311. I find the all-important detail of the stirrup-leather only in Mrs. Cuthell; Varnhagen von Ense says merely that Emet-Ulla was "ein schönes türkisches Kind, die Tochter eines Janitscharenhauptmanns, die er aus den Trümmern von Otschakoff gerettet hatte." I have inferred that the rescue occurred during the sack of the town, not in the siege itself. Emet-Ulla, one thinks, must have been the original of Byron's Leila (*Don Juan*).

p. 142.
Boswell takes his congé from Belle de Zuylen] Journ. 14 June 1764; Mem. 15 June 1764.

"I am affected by your departure"] From Belle de Zuylen, 14 June 1764. In French. Translation by Geoffrey Scott.

p. 143.
"Zélide said to me"] Journ. 17 June 1764. Some other bits of the passage quoted are in French in the original.

Benjamin Constant] As extracted and translated by Geoffrey Scott, *The Portrait of Zélide,* 1925, p. 100.

p. 144.
One of his French themes] 20 Apr. 1764. See the seventh note back.

Ever ready to soothe his temper and be complacent] Journ. 6 Jan. 1780.

Up all night] Journ. 17 June 1764. Besides the letter to Belle a long one to Temple survives.

A short note, Belle replies] To Belle de Zuylen, 18 June 1764; From Belle de Zuylen, 18 June 1764, both in French. Translations by Geoffrey Scott, with a few slight changes.

p. 145.
Departure from Holland] Journ. 18 June 1764.

François's letter] From François Mazerac, 17 June 1764. In French.

CHAPTER X

p. 146.
Boswell's tour of Germany] See the map on the front end-papers of *Boswell on the Grand Tour: Germany and Switzerland, 1764.*

Gilt rococo and the common *Stube*] The former hardly needs specification; for the latter, see Journ. 27 Oct. 1764; Ten Lines, 30 Oct. 1763.

The *Postwagen*] Journ. 4 Aug. 1764.

p. 147.
On the floor of a barn] Journ. 24 June 1764 (somewhere in the vicinity of Hameln); in the Palace of Brunswick, Journ. 27 June 1764.

Arrival in Potsdam]   Journ. 2–4 July 1764.

Boswell takes lodgings in Berlin]   Journ. 9, 10 July 1764.

Riding-academy]   To W. J. Temple, 23 July 1764; Mem. 17, 25, 26 July 1764; Journ. 25 July, 10 Sept. 1764.

Fencing-master]   Journ. 24 July 1764; Mem. 25 July 1764.

p. 148.
Berlin the finest city]   To W. J. Temple, 23 July 1764.

The Kircheisens]   Journ. 9, 12, 16, 18, 19, 20, 21, 25, 26, 29 July, 4 Aug., 1, 8, 10, 12, 15, 17, 19 Sept. 1764; To Caroline Kircheisen, 10 Aug. 1764; From Caroline Kircheisen, 18 Aug. 1764. Boswell gives Caroline's age (Journ. 12 July 1764), Friedrich Leopold's is provided by the *Allgemeine Deutsche Biographie*. He became a distinguished jurist and was ennobled in 1798.

Andrew Mitchell]   Journ. 8, 14, 15 July 1764.

Herr Schickler, Herr Splitgerber]   Journ. 6, 20 July 1764.

Chaise, Unter den Linden, carousel]   Journ. 29 July, 8 Sept., 22 July 1764.

"We had at ten o'clock," etc.]   Journ. 17 July 1764.

Conversations with Lord Marischal about Spain]   Journ. 23 June, 2 July 1764; Boswell quite a Spaniard: Journ. 2 July, 4 Aug. 1764; To Caroline Kircheisen, 10 Aug. 1764; From Caroline Kircheisen, 18 Aug. 1764; To Lord Marischal, 2 Sept. 1764.

"I danced a great deal," etc.]   Journ. 20 July 1764.

"I saw my error," etc.]   Journ. 9 Aug. 1764.

p. 149.
A huge letter]   To Belle de Zuylen, 9 July 1764.

"I have no subaltern talents"]   From Belle de Zuylen, 18 June 1764 (first P.S.), in French.

p. 150.
"Black girl"]   Mem. 16 July 1764. The reader must continually remind himself that each of the memoranda begins "yesterday" and ordinarily records the events of the previous day.

Berlin bawdy-house]   Journ. 3 Sept. 1764.

"Grievous was it"]   Journ. 11 Sept. 1764.

p. 151.
A discourse against fornication]   Journ. 18 Nov. 1764, recorded as having happened at Berlin. See above, p. 481, note on "Public rebuke for fornication."

Street girl]   Journ. 14 Sept. 1764; Mem. 15 Sept. 1764.
p. 152.
"It was a glorious sight"]   Journ. 13 July 1764.

"She has been handsome"]   Journ. 15 July 1764.

A week later]   Journ. 22 July 1764; To H. A. de Catt, c. 31 July 1764: two versions (Yale MSS. L357, L358), both in French.

The Queen's court at Monbijou]   Journ. 27 July 1764.

Boswell writes to Frederick's reader]   To H. A. de Catt, c. 31 July 1764, first version (Yale MS. L357). In French.

p. 153.
De Catt's answer]   From H. A. de Catt, 4 Aug. 1764.

Boswell's second visit to the Court of Brunswick]   Journ. 7–22 Aug. 1764, 12 and 21 Aug. quoted.

Bad temper]   Journ. 8 Sept. 1764 (unruly); Journ. 30 Aug., 2, 10 Sept. 1764 (fiery); Journ. 2, 12 Sept. 1764 (angry); Journ. 8 Sept. 1764; Mem. 3, 9 Sept. 1764 (splenetic).

p. 154.
The threatened duel]   Journ. 15–17 Sept. 1764.

Appeal to Rousseau]   To J. J. Rousseau, 31 Dec. 1764.

"Manage Father with affection"]   Mem. 29 June 1764.

Letters concerning the tour to Italy]   Unrecovered. Since leaving Holland, Boswell had received two letters from his father, one at Brunswick and one at Berlin, and had presumably written at least two himself. He had shown the most recent one to Mitchell before sending it off (Mem. 27, 29 June, 29 July 1764; To Andrew Mitchell, 28 Aug., 26 Dec. 1764).

Mitchell]   To Andrew Mitchell, 28 Aug. 1764.

p. 155.
The management of Lord Marischal]   To Lord Marischal, 2 Sept. 1764.

When they met]   Journ. 6 Sept. 1764.

Lord Marischal and Mitchell intercede]   From Lord Marischal, 9 Sept. 1764; To John Johnston, 10 Sept. 1764; From Andrew Mitchell, 29 Sept. 1764; Journ. 23 Sept. 1764.

Boswell's last efforts to meet Frederick]   Journ. 21, 22 Sept. 1764.

p. 156.
Tender feelings on departure]   Journ. 19, 23 Sept. 1764.

p. 157.
Coswig]   Journ. 24 Sept. 1764.

Anhalt]   Journ. 24–30 Sept. 1764.

German princes the best models]   Journ. 27 Sept. 1764; 6 Jan. 1780.

Wittenberg]   Journ. 30 Sept. 1764.

Leipzig]   Journ. 3–4 Oct. 1764.

Dresden]   Journ. 8–12 Oct. 1764. The quoted bit is Journ. 12 Oct. 1764, the conversation, as often in this tour of the German courts, recorded in French.

p. 158.
Gotha] Journ. 16–21 Oct. 1764.

Mannheim] Journ. 2–7 Nov. 1764; Ten Lines, 6, 7 Nov. 1764; To John
Johnston, 7 Nov. 1764; To ?Baron von Wachtendonck, 8 Nov. 1764 (in French);
Mem. 10 Nov. 1764.

Boswell assumes the style of Baron] Journ. 1, 21 Oct. 1764; Ten Lines, 30
Oct. 1764. Boswell's claim that his status in Scotland was equivalent to that of a
Freiherr in Germany was not without justification. In Scotland the term baron "was
applied to all those who in feudal law held immediately under the Crown, and
thus included both the nobility and the freeholders" (Robert Bell, *A Dictionary of
the Law of Scotland,* 1807, i. 68). In Scotland he was undoubtedly the son of a
baron; and German custom gave the style of baron to all a baron's sons.

Common people bowing to the earth] Journ. 1 Oct. 1764.

Muffled, in a jolting cart] Journ. 8, 27 Oct. 1764; Ten Lines, 15 Oct. 1764.

Sleeps in his clothes] Journ. 24 Aug., 3, 8, 27, 29 Oct. 1764.

Just outside a city gate] Journ. 7, 22 Aug. 1764.

p. 159.
Luggage] Journ. 30 Oct. 1764. See also Mem. 28 Nov. 1764.

"Since I have been in Germany"] Journ. 16 Nov. 1764.

Karl Friedrich of Baden-Durlach] *Allgemeine Deutsche Biographie;* Journ.
9, 15, 16 Nov. 1764. Quotations from 16 Nov.

The Order of Fidelity] Ibid.

p. 160.
"Clandestine letters keep me up too late"] From Belle de Zuylen, 19 June
1764, in French, translation by Geoffrey Scott.

"Do not tell me," etc.] To Belle de Zuylen, 1 Oct. 1764, in French, translation
by Geoffrey Scott; Journ. 20, 26 Oct. 1764; Mem. 27 Oct. 1764.

p. 161.
Paradisial fancies, sordid reality] Mem. 21 July, 7, 9, 11, 12 Oct. 1764; Journ.
10, 11, 21 Oct. 1764.

"Lesser lascivious sports"] Somewhere in the journal, but I cannot put my
finger on the passage.

CHAPTER XI

p. 162.
The meeting with Rousseau] Journ. 3 Dec. 1764. Not only is nearly all the
conversation in the Swiss portion of the journal in French, but the French of the
long and involved conversations with Rousseau is in places crabbed and obscure. I fol-

low Geoffrey Scott's skilful expanded English version in the fourth volume of *The Private Papers of James Boswell,* with slight changes here and there.

Boswell's costume]   He was wearing buckskin breeches and boots, but otherwise his costume was that shown in the portrait by George Willison which serves as frontispiece to the present volume.

p. 163.
"I am a Scots gentleman," etc.]   To J. J. Rousseau, 3 Dec. 1764, final version, original in the Public Library at Neuchâtel, Boswell's draft at Yale (L1106). In French. My translation appropriates phrases from the translation by the late Professor Chauncey B. Tinker, in *Young Boswell,* 1922, pp. 50–52.

A note from Lord Marischal]   From Lord Marischal, c. 23 Sept. 1764; Journ. 3 Dec. 1764.

Letter to M. Martinet]   Journ. 3 Dec. 1764.

p. 164.
He had prepared a letter]   To J. J. Rousseau, 2 Dec. 1764. Journ. 3 Dec. 1764 does not mention the rewriting at Môtiers.

Rousseau]   *Chronologie J.-J. R.;* Josephson.

p. 167.
Chronology of Rousseau's eclipse]   The *Lettre à Beaumont* went on sale in Geneva, 21 Apr. 1763; Rousseau renounced his Genevan citizenship, 12 May 1763; *Lettres écrites de la campagne* appeared 27 Sept., 23 Oct. 1763 (*Chronologie J.-J. R.* pp. 143, 144, 147, 148). For C. A. Boily, see Journ. 23, 24 Nov. 1763; Rousseau, *Corresp. gén.* 12 (1929). 34–35, 131–132; Ulrich Thieme and Felix Becker, *Allgemeines Lexikon der Bildenden Künstler,* 1907–1950. The remaining dates for the year 1764 are from *Chronologie J.-J. R.* pp. 158, 159.

"Creed of a Savoyard Vicar"]   To W. J. Temple, 22 May 1764; Journ. 25 Nov. 1764.

p. 168.
The preparation for Rousseau]   Mem. 27 Sept., 12, 19, 20, 21, 22, 24 Oct., 11, 13, 15, 23, 25, 26, 30 Nov., 1, 2, 3 Dec. 1764; Journ. 19, 20, 21 Oct., 10, 12, 25 Nov. 1764.

"*You* are irksome"]   End of the second interview, Journ. 4 Dec. 1764.

One of their meetings]   The fourth, Journ. 14 Dec. 1764, beginning.

A chamber-pot every other minute]   End of the third interview, Journ. 5 Dec. 1764.

Boswell has to fight for time]   First interview, Journ. 3 Dec. 1764 ("Make it short"); fourth interview, Journ. 14 Dec. 1764 ("Put your watch on the table"); second interview, Journ. 4 Dec. 1764 ("Go away"); third interview, 5 Dec. 1764 ("I don't promise to see you").

p. 169.

"Now go away"]   Last interview, Journ. 15 Dec. 1764.

Boswell courts Thérèse]   Mem. 5 Dec. 1764.

"M. Rousseau has a high regard for you"]   End of last interview, Journ. 15 Dec. 1764. I have substituted names of speakers for Boswell's "She told me," "I said," etc.

A garnet necklace]   Ibid.; To Thérèse Le Vasseur, 31 Dec. 1764; From J. J. Rousseau, 30 May 1765; Expense Account (Yale MS. A33), 1 Jan. 1765.

p. 170.

"When I speak of kings"]   Journ. 3 Dec. 1764.

"Sir, I have no liking for the world"]   Ibid.

"Is it possible to live," etc.]   Journ. 14 Dec. 1764.

"I said, 'You say nothing,'" etc.]   Journ. 15 Dec. 1764.

"I gave him . . . the character of Mr. Johnson"]   Ibid.

p. 171.

The last day]   Journ. 15 Dec. 1764.

Dinner set early]   At noon (Journ. 14 Dec. 1764, at end).

p. 172.

First interview]   Journ. 3 Dec. 1764.

Second interview]   Journ. 4 Dec. 1764.

Memorandum next morning]   Mem. 5 Dec. 1764.

Third interview]   Journ. 5 Dec. 1764.

p. 174.

A covering letter]   To J. J. Rousseau, 5 Dec. 1765. In French.

A vaunting letter to John Johnston]   To John Johnston, 5 Dec. 1764.

Letter from Lord Auchinleck received]   Journ. 6 Dec. 1764.

p. 175.

Boswell calls on Mlle. Prevost]   Journ. 8 Dec. 1764; Mem. 9 Dec. 1764.

Colombier and the manor-house; Caton]   Journ. 10, 11 Dec. 1764; Geoffrey Scott, BP, ii. 11.

Memorandum of topics to discuss with Rousseau]   13 or 14 Dec. 1764 (Yale MS. M99).

Yverdon, Sir James Kinloch]   Journ. 11, 12, 13 Dec. 1764.

The route followed by Boswell from Yverdon to Môtiers]   Boswell says only (Journ. 14 Dec. 1764) that he "passed the Mountain Lapidosa, which is monstrously steep and in a great measure covered with snow." I should like to correct my note in *Boswell on the Grand Tour: Germany and Switzerland*, where I tentatively identified "Mountain Lapidosa" (which I could not find on any map available to me) as Mont Chasseron, and suggested that Boswell went by way of Ste. Croix and Buttes. My colleague, Professor Robert Warnock, has since found "Mountain Lapidosa" under the spelling "La Pidouze," about one kilometre east of the village of Mauborget (National Survey Series, Sect. 8a, F, XI, Feuille 284). He wrote to me from Neuchâtel (13 Aug. 1954), "Score another point... for JB's accuracy. More important, this fixes the route that Boswell took from Yverdon to Môtiers. He did not go 'up the valleys by Ste. Croix and Buttes,' but took the direct route over the heights through Grandson, Fiez, Fontaines, and Mauborget which is clearly shown on eighteenth-century maps."

p. 176.
"I have read your memoir"]   Journ. 14 Dec. 1764.

"Morals appear to me uncertain"]   Ibid.

p. 177.
The Abbé de Saint-Pierre]   Journ. 4 Dec. 1764.

The true meaning of Rousseau's return to Nature]   C. W. Hendel, *Jean-Jacques Rousseau, Moralist,* 1934.

p. 179.
Another list of topics]   14 or 15 Dec. 1764, also in Yale MS. M99.

The last day]   Journ. 15 Dec. 1764; List of topics to be discussed with Rousseau (Yale MS. M99).

p. 181.
Rehearsed exit lines]   Ibid.; *Émile,* book 2, paragraph 24.

Johnson's attack on Rousseau, Boswell's defence]   Notes, 16 Feb. 1766; *Life,* 15 Feb. 1766.

p. 182.
Only if he saw it across Piccadilly]   Journ. 30 July 1790.

Sexual intercourse made him humane]   Journ. 19 Jan. 1768.

He associated love, music, and adoration]   Notes, 18 Mar. 1767.

p. 183.
"The fatal practice"]   Above, p. 30; Mem. 26 Dec. 1764; 17 Jan. 1765.

CHAPTER XII

p. 184.
Lausanne]   Journ. 21 Dec. 1764.

Boswell's dislike of Geneva]   Journ. 23, 24, 26, 30 Dec. 1764.

Letters from Rousseau and Karl Friedrich]   Journ. 22 Dec. 1764; From J. J. Rousseau, 20 Dec. 1764; Rousseau to Alexandre Deleyre, 20 Dec. 1764, 11 Feb. 1765; From Karl Friedrich, 9 Dec. 1764. Rousseau characterized Boswell as follows: "In the first letter he wrote me, he told me he was a man 'of singular merit.' I was curious to see a man who described himself in such terms, and I found that what he had told me was true. In his youth he got his head turned with a smattering of harsh Calvinist theology, and as a consequence still suffers from disquiet of soul and gloomy notions. I have advised him to devote his tour of Italy to the study of the fine arts. If you talk philosophy with him, I beg of you to restrain your own inclinations and to present moral matters to him only in consoling and tender aspects. He is a convalescent whom the least relapse will infallibly destroy" (translated).

"Voltaire! Rousseau! immortal names!"]   From W. J. Temple, spring or early summer 1759 (Yale MS. C2650); 9 Aug. 1759; W. J. Temple to Lord Auchinleck, c. 9 Aug. 1759; Journ. 29 Dec. 1764.

"I shall visit Rousseau and Voltaire"]   To W. J. Temple, 17 Apr. 1764 (2d letter of that date); To Andrew Mitchell, 28 Aug. 1764; To Lord Marischal, 2 Sept. 1764; To John Johnston, 10 Sept. 1764; Journ. 1 Oct. 1764.

Sea-green and silver]   Journ. 29 Dec. 1764.

A proper letter of introduction]   From D. L. Constant d'Hermenches, 26 May 1764 (the letter itself was presumably retained by Voltaire).

Voltaire]   Alfred Noyes, *Voltaire,* 1936; N. L. Torrey, *The Spirit of Voltaire,* 1938.

p. 185.
The first meeting with Voltaire]   Journ. 24 Dec. 1764; To W. J. Temple, 28 Dec. 1764.

"Foolish face of wondering praise"]   Pope, *Epistle to Dr. Arbuthnot,* line 212 ("And wonder with a foolish face of praise").

p. 186.
"I must beg your interest," etc.]   To Mme. Denis, 25 Dec. 1764.

p. 187.
"You will do us much honour"]   From Voltaire, 25 Dec. 1764.

"I wrote you a long letter," etc.]   To Belle de Zuylen, 25 Dec. 1764, original in French. Translation by Geoffrey Scott, slightly altered.

The second meeting with Voltaire]   Journ. 27 Dec. 1764.

Flowered velvet]   Journ. 29 Dec. 1764.

"My room was handsome"]   Journ. 28 Dec. 1764.

p. 188.
"I placed myself by him"]   To W. J. Temple, 28 Dec. 1764.

p. 190.
Remainder of Boswell's visit to Ferney]   Journ. 28, 29 Dec. 1764.

The final conversation]   Mem. 30 Dec. 1764, with some expansion. *Boswell on the Grand Tour: Germany and Switzerland,* 29 Dec. 1764, records the actual words of the manuscript and suggests a somewhat different interpretation. Boswell wrote this conversation entirely in English, which was no doubt the language used.

p. 191.
"Well, I must here pause," etc.]   Journ. 29 Dec. 1764.

p. 192.
Keats's claim]   To Benjamin Bailey, 22 Nov. 1817.

Wish to be the whinstone on a mountain]   To W. J. Temple, 1 Feb. 1767.

"I will not be baited by *what* and *why*"]   *Life,* 10 Apr. 1778.

The Chevalier de Boufflers]   Nesta H. Webster, *The Chevalier de Boufflers,* 1916 and later (including the references in her preface); *Poésies diverses du Chevalier de Boufflers, avec une notice bio-bibliographique* (by Octave Uzanne), 1886; *Oeuvres de Boufflers,* 1792. Boufflers refers to Boswell in the eighth letter of his *Voyage en Suisse,* 1771 (the "series of traveller's letters" mentioned in the text), though without naming him: "Yesterday there arrived here at [Voltaire's] an Englishman who never wearies of listening to him speak English and recite all the poems of Dryden" (translated).

p. 194.
Voltaire describes Boufflers]   Voltaire to the Duc de Richelieu, 21 Jan. 1765 (translated).

Geoffrey Scott]   BP, iv. 2.

p. 195.
"In short, I hate you"]   Rousseau to Voltaire, 17 June 1760, translated. Josephson gives a considerable extract, p. 278.

The Bailiff of Yverdon]   Journ. 16 Dec. 1764.

p. 196.
"There were a good many men here," etc.]   Journ. 24 Dec. 1764.

Dr. Tronchin]   Journ. 1 Jan. 1765.

p. 197.
He had a favour to ask]   To J. J. Rousseau, 11 May 1765.

His next letter]   To J. J. Rousseau, 3 Oct. 1765. His draft for this letter: Yale MS. L1117.

Departure from Geneva]   Journ. 1 Jan. 1765.

CHAPTER XIII

p. 198.
The Mont Cenis pass]   Journ. 6, 7 Jan. 1765; Juvenal, *Satires,* x. 166; Virgil, *Eclogues,* x. 47. Wilkes, who made the passage the next day, gives a much more detailed and interesting account in a letter to his daughter, 10 Jan. 1765 (Almon, ii. 117–123).

Geoffrey Scott]   BP, v. 8, 9.

p. 200.
Colonel Chaillet]   Journ. 8 Jan. 1765.

Young officer (the Marquis d'Aix)]   Mem. 5 Jan. 1765.

The Count and Countess of San Gillio]   Journ. 8–11, 14, 16, 18–20 Jan.
1765; Casanova, vii. 336; viii. 112–113, 304–305 (the dealings of Casanova with
Mme. di San Gillio here cited occurred in 1763: ibid. 301–302); Louis Dutens
("another observer"), *Mémoires d'un voyageur qui se repose,* Londres, 1806, i. 154–
155. Lord Charles Spencer (1740–1820) was the second son of the third Duke of
Marlborough (DNB under his father, Charles Spencer, 1706–1758). Dutens's "M.
Boothby" is perhaps too confidently identified as Sir Brooke Boothby, Bt., of Ashbourne, 1744–1824 (*Comp. Baronet.* iii. 83). I find no reference to Sir Brooke's
having been in Turin, but he knew Rousseau before 1766 and presumably had
visited him at Môtiers (Rousseau, *Corresp. gén.* 15.149–150; 16.184–185, 261–263;
Sir Gavin de Beer, "Rousseau et les anglais en Suisse," *Annales de la Société Jean-
Jacques Rousseau,* 33.283–284). Caterina Maria Teresa, wife of Vittorio Francesco
Vignati, Conte di San Gillio, lived to 1800 (Turin, documents in Biblioteca Reale;
full references will appear in the Yale research edition). Boswell invariably employs the French (or rather international) style "St. Gille(s)."

p. 201.
The Countess of Borgaretto]   Journ. 10–14, 18 Jan. 1765; To the Countess of
Borgaretto, 13 (2 letters), 14, 18 Jan. 1765 (all in French). This lady was not
nearly so prominent as Mme. di San Gillio in the society of Turin. Professor
Warnock has recovered her names (Vittoria Enrichetta) and has identified her
husband as Pietro Giuseppe Maria Bistorti, Conte di Borgaretto. She was presumably in her late twenties, having married in 1755 (Turin, documents in
Biblioteca Reale; full references will be given in the Yale research edition). Boswell invariably employs the odd spelling "Burgaretta."

The Countess of Scarnafigi]   Journ. 17–22 Jan. 1765; To the Countess of
Scarnafigi, 21 Jan. 1765. Maria Anna Teresa, wife of Filippo Ottone Ponte, Conte
di Scarnafigi, was seven years older than Boswell, and lived to 1808. Her husband
was appointed Minister to Portugal from Sardinia just after Boswell left Turin, and
was later Ambassador to France (Turin, documents in Biblioteca Reale; full
references will be given in the Yale research edition). Boswell spells the name
"Scarnavis."

p. 202.
Love, horror, devotion]   Journ. 22 Jan. 1765.

Captain Billon]   Journ. 10, 11, 14, 15, 18 Jan. 1765.

The King of Sardinia]   Journ. 11 Jan. 1765.

Opera, balls]   Journ. 8–21 Jan. 1765, *passim.*

John Turberville Needham]   DNB; Journ. 12, 14, 16, 19, 21, 22 Jan. 1765.

Wilkes] DNB; Robert Warnock, "Boswell and Wilkes in Italy," *ELH,* iii (1936). 257–260; Almon, i. 124–271; ii. 1–123; Journ. 9 Jan. 1765; To John Wilkes, 9 Jan. 1765 (two notes).

p. 204.

Boswell's itinerary, Turin to Rome] Mem. 26 Jan.–6 Feb., 14–16 Feb. 1765. The memoranda for 7–13 Feb., covering the tour from Bologna to Spoleto, if ever written, are now lost. Loreto is established by To John Johnston, 10 Feb. 1765, Spoleto by To John Johnston, 12 Feb. 1765. Rimini and Ancona are proved by Boswell's list of Dominicans (Yale MS. M111).

Bartoli, Allegranza, Dominicans] Journ. 10–12, 17, 26 Jan. 1765; To John Johnston, 11 May 1765; To J. J. Rousseau, 3 Oct. 1765; Mem. 4, 5 Feb., 22 Apr., 6, 7, 22 May, 8, 9, 23, 24 Aug., 10 Oct. 1765; "Dominicans" (Yale MS. M111, listing names of Dominicans at Milan, Bologna, Rimini, Fano, Ancona, Rome, Florence, Siena, Lucca, Pisa, and Leghorn); From Michael Brennan, Rome, 31 July 1768, sending the compliments of Messrs. Kelly, Troy, and Bodkin; From Patrick Kirwan to Dr. Tyrrell, 29 May 1765. See Louis Nolan, *The Irish Dominicans in Rome,* 1913. Fathers Bodkin, Kirwan, and Troy were prominent in the Order; Troy later was Archbishop of Dublin.

p. 205.

Parma, Deleyre, Condillac] Journ. 29–30 Jan. 1765; Mem. 30 Jan.–2 Feb. 1765; To J. J. Rousseau, 3 Oct. 1765; Casimir Stryienski, *Le Gendre de Louis XV,* 1904. I know no accounts of Alexandre Deleyre (1726–1797) more extended than those in NBG and the *Grande encyclopédie,* 1886–1902. Rousseau's letter to Deleyre, 20 Dec. 1764, appears to have been preserved only in Boswell's copy: see *Boswell on the Grand Tour: Germany and Switzerland, 1764,* Appendix 2. Deleyre to Rousseau, Parma, 18 Feb. 1765 is printed in full in Rousseau, *Corresp. gén.* 13.18–24. Deleyre sent Boswell a copy of the portion relating to himself (Yale MS. C923).

Boswell at Bologna] To J. J. Rousseau, 3 Oct. 1765, in French; Mem. 4–6 Feb. 1765. A portion of the memorandum for 5 Feb. is printed above, p. 199. There is an article on Laura Maria Caterina Bassi in BU.

Loreto] To John Johnston, 10 Feb. 1765.

Arrival at Rome, meeting with Wilkes] Mem. 16, 18 Feb. 1765.

p. 206.

St. Peter's] Mem. 17 Feb. 1765.

Races in the Corso, Guillaume Martin] Lalande, v. 194–196; Bergeret, 5, 7, 8, 9, 10, 12, 14, 15 Feb. 1774; Mem. 17, 19, 20 Feb. 1765; Thieme-Becker, *Künstler Lexikon;* É. Bénézit, *Dictionnaire ... des peintres,* etc. The French Academy in Rome was in 1765 housed in the Palazzo Mancini, on the right-hand side of the Corso facing north, almost in the Piazza Venezia, where the races ended. See J. P. Alaux, *Académie de France à Rome,* 1933, i. 80, 90, 257; Henry Lapauze, *Histoire de l'Académie de France à Rome,* 1924, i. 180–182, 187–188;

Dominique Magnan, *La Ville de Rome, 3ème éd. corrigée et augmentée*, 1783, pp. 88–89. This palazzo is now occupied by the Rome branch of the Banco di Sicilia.

Girls] Mem. 20, 25 Feb. 1765; "Argent dépensé en Italie" (Yale MS. A34), 20, 21, 22, 24 Feb. 1765. The memoranda for 21–24 Feb. 1765 are missing.

Rome to Naples] Mem. 26 Feb.–2 Mar. 1765; the second quotation combines phrases from Mem. 1, 2, 3, 5 Mar. 1765; Wilkes to his daughter, 10 Mar. 1765 (Almon, ii. 140); Louis Dutens, *Journal of Travels*, 1782, pp. 68–69.

p. 207.
Summary of the visit to Naples] Mem. 2, 3, 4, 5, 19 Mar. 1765 (Hamilton); Mem. 3, 4, 7 Mar. 1765 (Herculaneum); Mem. 19 Mar. 1765 (Pompeii); Mem. 4, 5, 19, 20 Mar. 1765 (Virgil's tomb); Mem. 13, 14 Mar. 1765 (Vesuvius); To John Johnston, 19 Mar. 1765; To J. J. Rousseau, 3 Oct. 1765; "Argent dépensé en Italie" (Yale MS. A34), 9, 14 Mar. 1765 ("peintures à Herculaneum," "deux vases étrusques"); Mem. 4 Mar. 1765 ("Guard against expensive virtu").

WEDNESDAY 6 MARCH] It must be remembered, here as elsewhere, that the memoranda all begin with the word "Yesterday," and record the events of the *previous* day. I have here permitted myself considerable latitude of silent expansion, but have very rarely changed any of Boswell's words. The reader may wish to compare with Professor Warnock's version, "Boswell and Wilkes in Italy," *ELH*, iii (1936). 262–266.

"Strada Andalusia al Mare"] So reported by Boswell in Mem. 2 Mar. 1765, but probably in error, for the eighteenth-century maps record no such street. A Dr. McKinlay, who sent him extended suggestions for his tour through Lord Auchinleck, had recommended that he put up "at the house of Giuseppe in Santa Lucia, or if he is full, at Stefano's, in the same quarter of the town" (Yale MS. C1844). Wilkes lodged at Stefano's (Almon, ii. 146).

"A large good house"] Ibid.

p. 208.
"You too like the thing"] From John Wilkes, 22 June 1765.

Wilkes assesses Boswell's gift correctly] To John Wilkes, 22 Apr. 1765 (Boswell's own expansion of Mem. 7 Mar. 1765); Mem. 18 Feb. 1765.

p. 209.
Packet of letters] Reg. Let. (Yale MS. M252), 15 Mar. 1765.

Belle replied] From Belle de Zuylen, 27 Jan. 1765. Translation by Geoffrey Scott.

p. 210.
He wrote to Temple] To W. J. Temple, 19 Mar. 1765.

Wilkes's verdict] Mem. 17 Mar. 1765.

"She has weak nerves"] Continuing the quotation from To W. J. Temple, 19 Mar. 1765.

Letter from Voltaire]   From Voltaire, 11 Feb. 1765.

p. 211.
Naples to Rome]   Mem. 21–25 Mar. 1765.

Colin Morison's course in antiquities]   Mem. 26 Mar.–23 Apr. 1765 (see also
Mem. 15, 19, 23 May 1765); "Cours des antiquités et des arts à Rome, 1765," 25 to
30 Mar. 1765 (Yale MS. M103, no more written). He paid Morison thirty sequins
(£15) on 13 June 1765 ("Argent dépensé en Italie" [Yale MS. A34]).

The Abate Dossi]   Not further identified. Boswell spells the name Dosé, Dosi,
Dosie, but Dossi seems more plausible. Mem. 27 Mar. ("Began Italian with Abbé"),
29 Mar., 1, 16, 25 Apr., 22, 28 May ("This day dismiss Dossi, as two months out"),
29 May ("Dismiss Dossi") 1765. Boswell paid him six sequins (£3) for the two
months on 13 June 1765 ("Argent dépensé en Italie" [Yale MS. A34]). To M. de
Zuylen, 23 Apr. 1765.

Feast of the Annunciation]   "Cours des antiquités et des arts à Rome, 1765,"
25 Mar. 1765 (Yale MS. M103); Lalande, v. 124–125. I find more useful accounts
of this spectacle in Bergeret, 10 Apr. 1774; Charlotte Eaton, *Rome in the Nineteenth Century*, 1820, iii. 126–129; and A. J. Hare, *Walks in Rome*, 1874, p. 484.

p. 212.
Palm Sunday]   Mem. 1 Apr. 1765. Lalande (v. 114–117) places this func-
tion at Monte Cavallo; Bergeret (27 Mar. 1774), at the Pope's chapel on the
Capitol, which appears to be a mistake. The Pope did not take up residence in the
Vatican till later in Passion Week (Bergeret, 31 Mar. 1774).

Maundy Thursday]   Mem. 5 Apr. 1765.

Easter]   Mem. 8 Apr. 1765.

He wrote to Rousseau]   To J. J. Rousseau, 3 Oct. 1765.

The Abbé Peter Grant]   The office is explained by J. A. Stothert in an account
of the Scots College at Rome which forms part of his life of Bishop George Hay
(J. F. S. Gordon, *Ecclesiastical Chronicle for Scotland,* 1867, iv. 195–196, 214–215).
The same volume, p. 560, gives a biographical sketch of Grant from the Abbé
McPherson's MS. Catalogue, and he is frequently mentioned in other parts of the
life of Bishop Hay. See especially p. 240. I originally wrote that "apparently out
of sociability and pure goodness of heart he served as a sort of ecclesiastical
cicerone to visiting Britons," a characterization for which Boswell's papers, taken
in isolation, provide ample warrant, but I find that his disinterestedness was sharply
questioned by those giving information to the official representatives of Great Britain
abroad. For example, the Abbé Giordani, Sir Horace Mann's secret agent at Rome,
said in 1766 that he "served the Pretender, assisted the English who came to Rome,
and spied on both" (Lesley Lewis, *Connoisseurs and Secret Agents in Eighteenth-
Century Rome,* 1961, p. 222; see also pp. 123–124, 144–145, 160, 216–217).

Boswell's presentation to the Pope]   Mem. 14 May 1765. The knight from
Lancashire was Sir William Farrington of Shaw Hall (W. A. Shaw, *The Knights of*

England, 1906, ii. 290), the gentleman from Derbyshire, Gibbon's friend Godfrey Bagnall Clarke of Sutton and Somersall (*The Memoirs of the Life of Edward Gibbon,* ed. G. B. Hill, 1900, p. 169; Sir Lewis Namier and John Brooke, *The House of Commons, 1754–1790,* 1964; Joseph Hunter, *Familiae minorum gentium,* 1894–1896, p. 337).

p. 213.

Frascati, Cardinal York] Special Mem. ("Frascati Jaunt"); Mem. 27 May 1765. "All the assembly, face as face of angel" is an approximate quotation of Acts, 6.15, a description of Stephen facing his accusers. Perhaps the Cardinal preached on that text. It would be not inappropriate for Pentecost: "But he, being full of the Holy Ghost, looked up steadfastly into heaven" (Acts, 7.55).

"Day, antiquities"] Mem. 25 Mar. 1765.

Roman *conversazioni*] To J. J. Rousseau, 3 Oct. 1765, in French; Mem. 17, 23 Apr. 7, 9, 16, 17 May 1765.

Boswell's election to the Collegio d'Arcadia] I have treated this matter at length, with full references, in "Boswell as Icarus," pp. 389–406 of C. Carroll Camden (ed.), *Restoration and Eighteenth-Century Literature: Essays in Honor of A. D. McKillop,* 1963.

p. 214.

Agatha Erskine] *Scots Peer.* v. 92; ix. 117; *Jacobite Peerage,* p. 213; Mem. 8 Apr.–13 June 1765, *passim;* "Argent dépensé en Italie" (Yale MS. A34); 14, 28 Apr., 5, 12, 19, 27 May, 2, 9 June 1765. There are brief but well-informed articles on Charles Erskine in both the *Enciclopedia italiana* and the *Enciclopedia cattolica.*

p. 215.

Andrew Lumisden] DNB; Dennistoun; Robert Warnock, "Boswell and Andrew Lumisden," *Modern Language Quarterly,* ii (1941). 601–607; To Sir Alexander Dick, 22 May 1765; Mem. 27 Mar.–13 June 1765, *passim.* Lumisden's reports on Boswell: Dennistoun, i. 214; ii. 33.

Lady Mary Wortley Montagu] To the Countess of Pomfret, c. Feb. 1740 (W. M. Thomas ed. 1887, ii. 61).

Boswell unpopular with the other British] "My Lord [Mountstuart]...said you was a most odd character. All the English disliked you" (Mem. 29 June 1765).

Lumisden's company like Johnson's] Mem. 26 May 1765.

p. 216.

Boswell's first jaunt to Tivoli] Mem. 18 May 1765.

The Fons Bandusiae] See the excellent brief summary by Vincenzo Ussani in the *Enciclopedia italiana* s.v. Bandusia. A *fons Bandusinus apud Venusiam* (Horace's birth-place, modern Venosa, some eighty-five miles east of Naples) is mentioned in a bull of the early twelfth-century Pope Pasquale II, and Capmartin de Chaupy (see the note following this) thought he had located the spring in question about six miles from Venosa. Some later scholars have chosen to believe that Horace named a spring on his farm after that in Puglia, and that his ode celebrates the Sabine namesake.

Horace's villa] Special Mem. "Horace Jaunt," Mem. 25 May 1765; To John Johnston, 24 May 1765; Horace, *Epist*. I. xiv. 3 (Varia); *Epist*. I. xviii. 105 (Mandela); *Epist*. I. xvi. 12 (fons idoneus); *Carm*. I. xvii. 1 (Lucretilis). The facts about the discovery of the villa are given by Domenico de Sanctis, *Dissertazione sopra la villa di Orazio Flacco*, 1761 (2d ed. 1768, 3d ed. 1784), and (at intolerable length) by Bertrand Capmartin de Chaupy, *Découverte de la maison de campagne d'Horace*, 3 vols., 1769. Chaupy accused De Sanctis of stealing his discovery and rushing it into print. See also Giuseppe Lugli, "La Villa sabina di Orazio," *Monumenti antichi*, vol. 31, part 2 (1926), Eng. trans. *Horace's Sabine Farm*, 1930; E. K. Rand, *A Walk to Horace's Farm*, 1930 (good bibliography). Lumisden's account of an antiquarian trip to Tivoli and the Sabine farm appears in Appendix 2 of his *Remarks on the Antiquities of Rome and its Environs*, 1797; it is in the form of a letter to a friend in Edinburgh and bears the date 1 Dec. 1765. I infer from this date that he had not visited Vigne di S. Pietro before he went there with Boswell.

Boswell kisses supposed Shakespeare relics on his knees] W. H. Ireland, *Confessions*, 1805, pp. 95–96.

p. 217.
Dr. Murray] Mem. 19 Apr., 5 June 1765 ("little Murray"); To John Johnston, 19 Mar. 1765; Mem. 25 Mar. 1765 ("scurvy"); Mem. 26 Mar., 19 Apr., 3, 24, 29 May, 2, 7 June 1765 (Murray dines); 30 April 1765 (a more serious ailment).

Report to Rousseau] To J. J. Rousseau, 3 Oct. 1765, in French.

"Badinages"] "Argent dépensé en Italie" (Yale MS. A34), 8, 11, 15, 27, 29 Apr. 1765. Either the last of these entries or Mem. 30 Apr. 1765 would seem to be misdated.

p. 218.
Crab-lice] Mem. 2 May 1765 ("Discovered beasts").

Murray's bill] "Argent dépensé en Italie" (Yale MS. A34), 13 June 1765.

Winckelmann] Mem. 9, 11 May 1765 (meetings); 7, 8, 14 May 1765 (other references). "Garden like spread periwig" was perhaps a conscious adaptation of Swift: "The country round appeared like a continued garden. . . . The ladies and courtiers were all most magnificently clad, so that the spot they stood upon seemed to resemble a petticoat spread on the ground, embroidered with figures of gold and silver" (*Gulliver's Travels*, First Voyage, ch. 2).

Angelica Kauffmann] DNB; Mem. 18 Feb. 1765.

p. 219.
Pompeo Batoni] [Michael] *Bryan's Dictionary of Painters and Engravers*, ed. G. C. Williamson, 1903–1905; Mem. 18 Apr. 1765; John Steegman, "Some English Portraits by Pompeo Batoni," *Burlington Magazine*, 88 (1946). 55–63: No. 44, Plate IV, C.

Nathaniel Dance] DNB; Mem. 16, 17, 18, 19 Feb. 1765; 29 Mar. 1765 ("Four, Dance: English said you despise countrymen and only with Wilkes. Be decently polite"); 13 Apr. 1765 ("Dance dined with you, too rude").

Gavin Hamilton] DNB; Mem. 20 Feb., 5, 25, 27 Mar., 4 Apr. 1765; the conversation quoted and Boswell's feeling himself a genius are also of 4 Apr.

p. 220.
Letters from his father] Mem. 4 Apr. 1765; From Lord Auchinleck, 10 Aug. 1765.

Delivery of "Mary Queen of Scots"] Journ. 18 Mar. 1776.

Virtu] "Argent dépensé en Italie" (Yale MS. A34), 24 Feb. ("Curiosité de marbre"); 5 Mar. ("Pierre gravée"); 6 Mar. ("Lave de Vésuvius"); 9 Mar. ("Peintures à Herculaneum"); 14 Mar. ("Deux vases étrusques"); 12 Apr. ("Trois pénates"); 24 Apr. ("Fruits de marbre, pénates"); 5 May ("Boîte de lava de Vésuvius"); 10 June ("Statue de Hercule"); 15 Apr. ("Ritual romain en manuscrit"); 5 May ("Cannone Historia et Vues de Pesto"); 18 May ("Office de la Vierge, MS"); 1 June ("Vestal fait par Pickler, pierre et tout [12 sequins]; pour le fair lier" [2 sequins]). He bespoke the seal on 8 May (Mem. 9 May 1765: "Found virtu growing with all its bad passions").

p. 221.
Sir Adam Fergusson] Also reproduced (Plate II,C) in Steegman's article cited under Batoni, sixth note back from this.

Willison's portrait] DNB; C. B. Tinker and F. A. Pottle, *A New Portrait of James Boswell,* 1927; Mem. 2, 3, 4 May 1765; 5, 6 May 1765 (owl recommended and debated); 6, 7 May (half length decided on and begun); 9, 10, 12, 14, 15, 16 May ("Agreed to have lines in picture, noble"); 17 May, 6, 7, 13 June 1765.

James Alves] Johnston Corresp. pp. 174–175; Mem. 31 May, 3, 4 June (sitting), 5 June (sitting), 7 June (sitting), 13 June 1765. Payments to Willison and Alves recorded 13 June ("Argent dépensé en Italie" [Yale MS. A34]).

p. 222.
Reply to Voltaire] To Voltaire, 4 Apr. 1765.

The Margrave of Baden-Durlach] To Karl Friedrich, 15 Jan., 11 May 1765. The latter letter is in the Grand-Ducal Family Archives at Karlsruhe.

CHAPTER XIV

p. 224.
Introduction to Mountstuart] Mem. 25 Feb. 1765 (Col. Edmonstone the introducer); John Wilkes to his daughter, 21 May 1765 (Almon, ii. 170); Mem. 17 Mar. 1765 (Boswell calls on Col. Edmonstone in Naples).

Intimacy with Mountstuart] Mem. 2, 4, 9, 11, 13, 14, 16 May 1765 and *passim.*

p. 225.

Tivoli]   Mem. 17, 18 May 1765.

Mountstuart talks freely about his education]   Mem. 22 May 1765.

Mountstuart invites Boswell to be his companion]   Mem. 27 May 1765 ("Col. Edmonstone had proposed your going"); 29 May 1765 ("Lumisden bid accept of Lord Mountstuart's offer"); 2 June 1765 ("Go not with him except pressed"); Mem. 3 June 1765 ("Then my Lord's, late. He again proposed . . . to travel with him. You asked him to be politician and manage Father. He will").

Mountstuart writes to Baron Mure]   5 June 1765 (William Mure [ed.], *Selections from the Family Papers preserved at Caldwell,* 1854, pt. 2, ii. 38–39).

Mountstuart's party leaves Rome]   Mem. 15 June 1765.

John Stuart, Viscount Mountstuart]   *Scots Peer.* ii. 305–306; Louis Dutens, *Mémoires d'un voyageur qui se repose,* Londres, 1806, ii. 148 (describing him as of 1779).

Col. Edmonstone]   The army career of James Edmonstone (c. 1722–1793) is summarized by J. Y. T. Grieg, *Letters of David Hume,* 1932, i. 268 n. He and Lord Auchinleck were very remotely related by common descent from the Craufurds of Loudoun, ancestors, as is believed, of both the Craufurds of Auchenames and the Craufurds of Kerse. Edmonstone's mother was a daughter of William Crau-furd, in whom the male line of the old Craufurds of Auchenames ended, and Lord Auchinleck's great-great-grandmother, Marion Craufurd, wife of James Boswell, IV of Auchinleck, was a daughter of David Craufurd of Kerse (ibid.; *Scots Peer.* viii. 540; *A & W,* i. 192, 399–402; iii. 321–325; above, p. 8. Boswell characterizes Edmonstone in Mem. 4 May 1765 ("honest"); 1 June 1765 ("hearty"); 8 June 1765 ("rough, like Scotsman; wants to be easy, rudely familiar"); 14 July 1765 ("worthy"); 27 July 1765 ("rough . . . honest, homely").

Paul Henri Mallet]   Hélène Stadler, *Paul-Henri Mallet,* 1924.

p. 226.

Memorandum not to tolerate Edmonstone's roughness]   Mem. 8 June 1765 ("Swear . . . never to allow Col. Edmonstone to be rough").

"A sad Genevois"]   Mem. 19 May 1765.

Boswell touchy and irritable]   To J. J. Rousseau, 3 Oct. 1765.

p. 227.

Jacob ill with a fever]   Mem. 5, 8 June 1765; Journ. 10 Dec. 1765. He joined Boswell at Florence (Mem. 11 Aug. 1765).

Departure from Rome, Mountstuart's reluctance to stop for sight-seeing]   Mem. 15 June 1765.

Mountstuart angry at Foligno]   Journal in Italian of tour with Lord Mount-stuart, 15 June 1765.

Boswell angry at being called "Jamie"]   Ibid. 16 June 1765; Mem. 17 June 1765. Examples of "his Excellency" and "the Baron," Journal in Italian of tour with Lord Mountstuart, 18 June 1765; Mem. 18, 19 June, 15, 27 July 1765.

The row about visiting San Marino] Journal in Italian of tour with Lord Mountstuart, 18, 21 June 1765; Mem. 18, 19, 22 June 1765; From Lord Mountstuart, 19 June 1765; To J. J. Rousseau, 3 Oct. 1765.

Dispute at Ferrara] Journal in Italian of tour with Lord Mountstuart, 21 June 1765; Mem. 22 June 1765.

Mallet cuts Boswell down] Mem. 26 June 1765.

Horace Walpole] To Sir Horace Mann, 17 July 1777.

Four days at Padua] Mem. 24–27 June 1765.

p. 228.

Giambattista Morgagni] Mem. 27 June 1765; *Encyclopaedia Britannica;* NBG.

Venice Preserved] Mem. 2 July 1765.

Strolling in a gondola] Mem. 4 July 1765.

"Those lugubrious gondolas"] To J. J. Rousseau, 3 Oct. 1765, in French.

Gen. William Graeme] Mem. 24 June 1765; Johnston Corresp. p. 171 n. 4.

Wrangles with Mallet] Mem. 28 June, 4 July 1765. For Mallet's title see Hélène Stadler, *Paul-Henri Mallet,* 1924, p. 130.

General Graeme praised] By Boswell, Mem. 24 June, 23 July 1765; To John Johnston, 13 July 1765; by Lady Mary Wortley Montagu, To Lady Bute, 23 Nov., 28 Dec. 1756.

p. 229.

Old Consul Smith] DNB; K. T. Parker, *The Drawings of Antonio Canaletto ... at Windsor Castle,* 1948, pp. 9–16, 59–62; W. G. Constable, *Canaletto,* 1961, i. 16–26; Jean François Revel, "Le Consul Smith," *L'Œil,* Nov. 1963, pp. 16–22, 64–65; Casanova, iv. 149–150, 318. Authorities differ by as much as eight years as to Smith's age. The obituary notice in *Scots Mag.* 32 (1770). 631 says that he died at Venice, 6 Nov. 1770, aged 88. Boswell confirms this by styling him in 1765 a "curious old man, past eighty" (Mem. 14 July). But both the ecclesiastical and sanitary registers of Venice, giving the same date, declare that he was 96, or about 96, when he died. This corresponds roughly with the age Lady Mary Wortley Montagu assigns him: 82 some time before the end of 1758. I have followed the official registers, but without much confidence.

Resident Murray] Casanova, iv. 120–121, 143, 312; Lady Mary Wortley Montagu to Lady Bute, 30 May 1757.

Consul Udney] Mem. 29 June 1765; John Wilkes, *Autobiography,* 1888, pp. 16, 30–31, 51–52.

Cesarotti and Sackville] BU (Cesarotti); various memoirs of Cesarotti in editions of his *Works;* Robert Warnock, "Boswell and Some Italian Literati," *Interchange Fortnightly,* i. (1940). 82–83; Mem. 25 June 1765, at Padua ("This day see Cesarotti"); From Melchiorre Cesarotti, Padua, 28 June 1765, in French, agreeing to meet Boswell at a café in Dolo if Boswell will fix a day and hour; To

Melchiorre Cesarotti, 2 July 1765 (Reg. Let.); Mem. 3, 5 July 1765. I understand Boswell to say that Sackville translated Macpherson's English into Italian prose for Cesarotti's guidance. Sackville, a natural son of the 2d Duke of Dorset (1711–1769), was a partner in the banking house of Sir Robert Herries & Co. He died at Venice on 18 Dec. 1795 (C. J. Phillips, *History of the Sackville Family,* 1930, ii. 97–98).

p. 230.
Baretti] Lacy Collison-Morley, *Giuseppe Baretti,* 1909; Norbert Jonard, *Giuseppe Baretti,* 1963; Robert Warnock, "Nuove lettere inedite di Giuseppe Baretti," *Giornale storico della letteratura italiana,* 131 (1954). 73–77; Mem. 3, 8 ("curious Italian"), 9 (Johnson's letters, Devil created man, Mountstuart introduced), 12, 13 July 1765 (Mallet and Edmonstone characterized, Johnson would have accompanied Mountstuart); *Life,* 12 Feb. 1766; From Joseph Baretti, 18 July 1765; Journ. 30 Mar. 1768; From Lord Mountstuart, 25 June 1766.

Climactic interchange between Boswell and Mallet] Mem. 8 July 1765, translated and silently expanded. Boswell recorded his final rejoinder as "M. Mallet, si vous me piquez, il faut que je vous écrase."

p. 231.
Lady Wentworth] Mem. 28 (quoted phrases from this entry), 29 June, 2, 6 July 1765; *Comp. Baronet.* iv. 160; K. T. Parker, *The Drawings of Antonio Canaletto ... at Windsor Castle,* 1948, pp. 32 and map at end. She was Angelica Kauffmann's patron (F. A. Gerard, *Angelica Kauffmann,* 1892, pp. 35ff.).

Mme. Michieli] Robert Halsband, *The Life of Lady Mary Wortley Montagu,* 1957, pp. 262, 283, 285; To J. J. Rousseau, 3 Oct. 1765; Mem. 3 July 1765 ("gay, lively, appétissante"); 4, 5, 6 July 1765 (lover and cook); 7, 8 July 1765 (never *galante:* the second of the sentences quoted precedes the first in the MS.).

"My fancy was roused," etc.] To J. J. Rousseau, 3 Oct. 1765, in French. See also To John Johnston, 19 July 1765.

p. 232.
Hardly any lessons since Rome] To J. J. Rousseau, 3 Oct. 1765.

Edmonstone reproves Boswell] Ibid.

Edmonstone's report on Boswell] *Scotland and Scotsmen,* i. 172 n. 2.

General Graeme vexed, diverted, offers country-house] To J. J. Rousseau, 3 Oct. 1765.

Old Consul Smith at Mogliano] Mem. 14 July 1765. Two views by Antonio Visentini of Smith's villa are reproduced in Sir Anthony Blunt and Edward Croft-Murray, *Venetian Drawings at Windsor Castle,* 1957, p. 10.

Mountstuart recalled] Mem. 16 July 1765.

p. 233.
Boswell vows reform] Ibid.

Boswell again in sad humour] Mem. 17 July 1765. Odoacer (c. 434–493), the first barbarian ruler of Italy, brought the Western Roman Empire to an end. Mallet was probably trying to start a new course of lectures.

Mountstuart's turn]   Mem. 18 July 1765, some expansion in the quotation.

"I shall miss you," etc.]   Mem. 23 July 1765.

Disputes and resolutions]   Mem. 26 July 1765.

The parting]   Mem. 27 July 1765; To J. J. Rousseau, 3 Oct. 1765.

p. 234.
Boswell granted four months in Italy and then a month's extension]   Journ. 6 Dec. 1764; From Lord Auchinleck, 1 Oct. 1765. Boswell received letters from Lord Auchinleck on 3 and 15 Apr. (Reg. Let.). Since he considered the letter which he received on 3 Apr. "somewhat disagreeable" (Mem. 4 Apr. 1765) but found that received on 15 Apr. "solid and kind" (Mem. 18 Apr. 1765) it was probably the latter that granted the extension.

Boswell planned to follow instructions implicitly]   Journ. 6 Dec. 1764; Mem. 4, 5, 6, 7, 10, 12 May 1765.

"There is no end nor use," etc.]   From Lord Auchinleck, 10 Aug. 1765.

"Your conduct astonishes and amazes me"]   From Lord Auchinleck, 1 Oct. 1765.

The Grassi, the Certosa of Pavia, Boscovich, the Battle of Pavia]   Mem. 27, 28 July 1765; To John Johnston, 27 July 1765.

p. 235.
Cremona]   To John Johnston, 29 July 1765.

Mantua]   Johnston Corresp. pp. 183–185; To John Wilkes, 31 July 1765. The memoranda for 30 July–2 Aug., if ever written, are now missing. There is a detached, fully written entry for 1 Aug. 1765.

"Consult all with Deleyre"]   Mem. 16 July 1765.

Second visit to Parma]   Journ. 1 Aug. 1765; Mem. 3–6 Aug. 1765; To J. J. Rousseau, 3 Oct. 1765. The quoted sentence is Mem. 4 Aug. 1765.

p. 236.
Bologna to Florence]   Mem. 10 (2 entries), 11 Aug. 1765; Lalande, ii. 132–137; John Wilkes to Mary Wilkes, 1 Feb. 1765 (Almon, ii. 127–131). The "subterranean fires" (no longer to be seen) were due to leakage from a deposit of methane (*Dizionario enciclopedico italiano*, 1955–1961, s.v. Pietramala).

Succession in Tuscany]   Sir Horace Mann to Horace Walpole, 26 Mar., 9 Apr. 1763; 24 Aug. 1765 (Yale ed. of Horace Walpole's Correspondence, 20.125; 22.330). The Emperor died on 18 Aug. and Boswell heard the news on the 23d (Mem. 24 Aug. 1765).

Lord Beauchamp]   Mem. 12 Aug. 1765. Mentioned also in Mem. 13, 16, 23 Aug. 1765 and in a special memorandum, 15 or 16 Aug. 1765.

p. 237.

Sir Horace Mann characterized]　Mem. 12 Aug. 1765 ("mighty polite"); 13 Aug. 1765 ("neat-talking," witch).

Marshal Botta]　Mem. 13 Aug. 1765 (presented); 14 Aug. 1765 (dined).

Sketched by Patch]　DNB; From Godfrey Bagnall Clarke, 17 Aug. 1765. Clarke's letter, written from Milan, indicates that he had been included in a group caricature by Patch, and assumes as a matter of course that Patch will "encanvas" Boswell too. "I soon expect a letter, which, amongst other good intelligence, will bring me that of the fate of our caricatura." Boswell makes no reference to having been painted or sketched at Florence, and, so far as I know, nowhere mentions Patch.

The Accademia della Crusca]　Lalande, ii. 400–401; Mem. 23 Aug. 1765.

Lions and tigers]　Mem. 16 Aug. 1765.

Giovanni Lami]　Lalande, ii. 424; NBG; Mem. 14 Aug. 1765.

Padre Gentili]　Mem. 16, 18, 20 Aug. 1765.

Lord Cowper]　Mem. 18 Aug. 1765; To Mme. de Spaen, 3 Oct. 1765.

Marquis Venturi]　Mem. 14 Aug. 1765 ("green neat man"); 15 Aug. 1765 (S. Lorenzo, "Gallery of Painters," i.e. the Uffizi); 16 Aug. 1765 ("wild beasts"); 17 Aug. 1765 (Uffizi, Boboli Gardens, "Marquis *quite virtuous*"); 19 Aug. 1765 ("Palais Riccardi," i.e. the Medici; Cascine); 20 Aug. 1765 (S. Maria Novella); 23 Aug. 1765 (Accademia della Crusca).

p. 238.

Jacob]　Mem. 11 Aug. 1765. Lord Mountstuart's servant Antonio had accompanied Boswell from Milan (Mem. 26, 28 July, 22, 24 Aug. 1765).

Letter from Lord Auchinleck]　Reg. Let.; Mem. 11 Aug. 1765. The depression seems to have set in on the previous day, as he left Bologna: "You're now hipped, be patient" (Detached Mem. 10 Aug. 1765).

A second batch of letters]　Reg. Let.; Mem. 12 Aug. 1765.

Unhappiness in Florence]　To J. J. Rousseau, 3 Oct. 1765; Mem. 12 Aug. 1765 ("melancholy . . . weak and young. . . . Swear conduct"); 13 Aug. 1765 ("cold and gloomy. . . . Swear behaviour solemn"); 14 Aug. 1765 ("Tired . . . dreary. . . . Swear behaviour"); Detached Mem. 15 or 16 Aug. 1765 (all fancy, etc.); Mem. 16 Aug. 1765 (free will).

Bridge, girls]　Mem. 19 Aug. 1765.

Recurrence of symptoms, Dr. Tyrrell]　Mem. 20, 22 Aug. 1765. Tyrrell had been practising at Florence for at least twenty-three years (Sir Horace Mann to Horace Walpole, 30 Oct. 1742, N.S. [Yale ed. of Horace Walpole's Correspondence, 18.87]).

Traill]　Mem. 15–25 Aug. 1765, *passim*.

Nicolaus Dothel]　Mem. 18, 20 Aug. 1765; To J. J. Rousseau, 3 Oct. 1765; F. J. Fétis, *Biographie universelle des musiciens*, 2ème éd., 1874; Robert Eitner,

Biographisch-Bibliographisches Quellen-Lexikon der Musiker und Musikgelehrten,
1900.

p. 239.
Arrival in Siena] The memoranda for 26 Aug.–8 Sept., if ever written, are
now missing. But Boswell wrote Johnston no letters from towns between Florence
and Siena, and says nothing of having halted on the way either in To John Johnston, 28 Sept. 1765 or To J. J. Rousseau, 3 Oct. 1765.

The felicities of Siena] To J. J. Rousseau, 3 Oct. 1765; "Riflessioni scritte
in Siena, 1765" (Yale MS. M108), Nos. 3, 6.

Porzia Sansedoni] To J. J. Rousseau, 3 Oct. 1765; Mem. 9, 10 Sept. 1765;
To Porzia Sansedoni, ten letters, all in French, from some date in August to perhaps
20 Sept. 1765. Quotation from what appears to be the first letter in the series.
Translation by Geoffrey Scott.

p. 240.
Girolama Piccolomini] To J. J. Rousseau, 3 Oct. 1765 (in French; all quotations from this source); Mem. 9, 10, 29 Sept. 1765 (the memoranda for 11–28
Sept. are missing). In the surviving memoranda Boswell nowhere gives Mme.
Piccolomini's full name. He refers to her twice as "Jirol" (10 Sept.), but his usual
name for her is the familiar "Moma" or "Momina." She signed one of her letters
to him in full: Girolama Nini Piccolomini (20 Mar. 1767).

Belle de Zuylen] From Belle de Zuylen, 25 May 1765 (in French, trans.
Geoffrey Scott); Reg. Let. 13 Sept. 1765.

p. 241.
Porzia characterized] The quoted phrase is from To J. J. Rousseau, 3 Oct.
1765, in French; the details about her age, children, and husband (above, p. 239)
were obtained by Professor Warnock from documents in Siena. Full references will
be given in the research edition.

Girolama's age] The evidence is conflicting. Professor Warnock found in records at Siena and Florence that Maria Girolama, daughter of Filippo Nini and
his wife Isabella, was born (or baptized) on 19 Mar. 1728, and in 1748 (marriage
contract recorded under date of 30 Apr.) married to Orazio Piccolomini, whose
birth-date was 1715 (full references will appear in the research edition). But
Boswell, in his long letter to Rousseau, 3 Oct. 1765, so often quoted in this chapter
and the preceding, makes Girolama say that she was taken out of the convent and
married at sixteen (the whole passage is quoted above on p. 242). Girolama, of
course, had motives for making herself out younger than Porzia, but as a lie,
this seems unnecessarily devious. Pending further investigation, I am willing to
entertain the possibility that she was not the child born in 1728 but another of the
same name born c. 1732. Girolama's children were Isabella (b. 1752), Giulio-
Cesare and Virginia (also 1752), and Enea-Silvio (b. 1756). Cardinal Giacomo
Piccolomini (1795–1864) was son to Giulio-Cesare (A. Lisini and A. Liberati,
Genealogia dei Piccolomini di Siena, 1900, tavola 4 and p. 55.)

"Sienese Sketch"] "Scena Sanese" (Yale MS. M109). Boswell preserved a very useful list of names of the people he met at Siena (Yale MS. M110).

Silk stockings, makings of a gown, Dante] From Girolama Piccolomini, 7 Oct. 1765; 12 Dec. 1765; 3 Oct. 1765, all in Italian.

p. 242.
She had had lovers ... she went to mass] To J. J. Rousseau, 3 Oct. 1765, in French and Italian.

"Go and visit the barbarians"] From Girolama Piccolomini, 7 Oct. 1765, in Italian.

"The good in you," etc.] From Girolama Piccolomini, 16 Nov. 1767, in Italian.

"You and that Rousseau ..."] To J. J. Rousseau, 3 Oct. 1765, in French, the bit quoted in Italian.

Boswell jealous of Girolama's lovers] Ibid.

"I wish it were over"] To Porzia Sansedoni, 6 Sept. 1765 (in French, trans. Geoffrey Scott).

"Firm though sad"] To J. J. Rousseau, 3 Oct. 1765, in French; To Girolama Piccolomini, 27 Sept. 1765.

p. 243.
Lucca] Mem. 30 Sept.–6 Oct. 1765; To John Johnston, 5 Oct. 1765.

Pisa] Mem. 7 Oct. 1765.

Keith Stewart] Mem. 13 Aug. 1765; *Corsica,* p. 292.

The Centurion, Commodore Harrison, the passport] Mem. 8, 9, 10, 11 Oct. 1765; *Corsica,* pp. 293–294; "Passport for James Boswell, Esq." (Yale MS. C1499).

Departure for Corsica] Journ. 11 Oct. 1765; *Corsica,* p. 294.

CHAPTER XV

p. 244.
"Wished for something more ..."] *Corsica,* p. 287. In my account of the composition of Boswell's book, its historical background, and Boswell's campaign in the cause of Corsican independence, I have been greatly aided by Professor Joseph Foladare's *James Boswell and Corsica,* a Yale dissertation (1936) which richly deserves publication.

Sketch of Corsican history to 1736] Ferdinand Gregorovius, *Wanderings in Corsica,* trans. Alexander Muir, 1855, i. i–129; *Encyclopaedia Britannica;* Colonna and Villat, chs. 1–15.

p. 245.
King Theodore] André le Glay, *Théodore de Neuhoff,* 1907; Ravenna, p. 18. My description of Theodore's cosmopolitan costume is a conflation of compatible details from Le Glay and Gregorovius (op. cit.). Le Glay's source was an anonymous compilation published at The Hague, *Histoire des révolutions de l'île de Corse*

et de l'élévation de Théodore I sur le trône de cet état, 1738, pp. 193–194. The frontispiece of this volume (a fancy portrait of Theodore worked up from the description; see end of Preface) has been much reproduced. Gregorovius gives only a brief general list of works consulted, and I have not found his particular source. As Mrs. Valerie Pirie well says (*His Majesty of Corsica,* 1939, p. 271), Theodore, like most Europeans who had travelled extensively in the East, had adopted a kind of mixed costume which Moors called "Frankish" and Christians "Turkish." Le Glay (p. v) denies vigorously that Theodore was valiant, but Le Glay, though scrupulous in his documentation, displays strong and tiresome French bias. Boswell, who had discussed Theodore with Paoli, calls him "a daring and desperate spirit" (*Corsica,* p. 135).

French policy with regard to Corsica]   Colonna and Villat, pp. 163–164.

p. 246.
Queen Caroline's proclamation]   12 June 1736 (*The Political State of Great Britain,* vol. 52, 1736); *Corsica,* p. 134.

Corsican history during the War of the Austrian Succession]   André le Glay, *Histoire de la conquête de la Corse par les français: La Corse pendant la guerre de la succession d'Autriche,* 1912. The diplomatic facts were more complicated than the military. Genoa was at war with the Kingdom of Sardinia, but professed to be neutral in the struggle between the Anglo-Austrian and the Bourbon parties. Sardinia was at war with Genoa and Spain, but not with France.

British proclamation against the Corsican insurgents]   29 Dec. 1763 (*Annual Register,* 1763, p. [213]).

p. 247.
Succession of chiefs, Giacinto Paoli]   André le Glay, *Théodore de Neuhoff,* 1907, pp. 9–14; Colonna and Villat, pp. 158, 162–175; Ravenna, pp. 12–24.

Gaffori, Clemente Paoli]   *Corsica,* pp. 147–152, 247–250; Colonna and Villat, pp. 182–191; Ravenna, pp. 37–38.

Pasquale Paoli's arrival, his age]   Ravenna, pp. 44, 26 n.1.

Paoli's education and training]   Ravenna, pp. 27–32; Art. "Paoli, Pasquale" by Ersilio Michel in *Enciclopedia italiana.*

p. 248.
European interest in Corsica]   See C. B. Tinker, *Nature's Simple Plan,* 1922, pp. 32–60.

p. 249.
Rousseau and Corsica]   Ernestine Dedeck-Héry, *Jean-Jacques Rousseau et le projet de constitution pour la Corse,* 1932; see Foladare, pp. 633–646 for additions and corrections. Buttafoco's first letter was dated 31 Aug. 1764.

p. 250.
Deleyre]   19 July 1765, actually dated from Monigo.

Johnston]   Same date and place of dating.

"You must see Corsica"]   Mem. 5 Aug. 1765.

Letter from Rousseau received at Florence]   Reg. Let. 11 Aug. 1765; Mem. 12 Aug. 1765. Rousseau had addressed it to Genoa, as directed by Boswell (To J. J. Rousseau, 11 May 1765), but Boswell must have arranged to have it forwarded to Florence.

Keith Stewart]   Mem. 13 Aug. 1765.

First and second treaties of Compiègne]   14 Aug. 1756, 6 Aug. 1764 (Colonna and Villat, pp. 210–217).

Boswell's uncertainty about the attitude of the French]   The Comte de Marbeuf had been named commander-in-chief of the French troops in the island in Dec. 1764, and hence had been in command of the fortified towns less than a year when Boswell appeared on the scene (ibid.).

Count Antonio Rivarola]   Mem. 10, 11 Oct. 1765. For his father, Count Domenico Rivarola, see *Corsica*, pp. 127–132, 149–151. Professor Warnock found Rivarola's reports on Boswell in the State Archives in Turin.

The passage to Corsica]   Journ. 11 Oct. 1765; *Corsica*, pp. 294–295.

p. 252.
Scarlet and gold, black]   *Corsica*, p. 393.

Boswell's luggage]   Ibid. p. 301.

Ingrown toe-nails]   See the next chapter and the chronological section of the article on James Boswell, Index to BP, under 1779 and 1780.

Whinstone on the face of a mountain]   To W. J. Temple, 1 Feb.–8 Mar. 1767.

p. 253.
Boswell's scenic descriptions]   *Corsica*, pp. 299, 304, 310–311, 312.

p. 254.
"The road, West, the road!"]   Horace Walpole to Richard West, 30 Sept. 1739. The remainder of the passage should be quoted to show how accomplished in the picturesque idiom some authors had become before the middle of the eighteenth century: "... winding round a prodigious mountain, and surrounded with others all shagged with hanging woods, obscured with pines, or lost in clouds! Below, a torrent breaking through cliffs and tumbling through fragments of rocks! Sheets of cascades forcing their silver speed down channelled precipices and hasting into the roughened river at the bottom!"

Boswell's anxiety as he approached Sollacarò]   *Corsica*, p. 314.

p. 255.
The meeting with Paoli and description of his appearance]   Ibid., pp. 315–318; Ravenna, pp. 58–59. The thinning hair, for which I do not find documentation, was probably an impression derived from Benbridge's portrait.

"Paoli became more affable"]   *Corsica,* p. 319.

p. 256.

Fanny Burney]   Mme. d'Arblay, *Diary and Letters,* 15 Oct. 1782. Editors have generally assumed that Mme. d'Arblay intended to indicate the suppression of Boswell's name in the last sentence: "Oh! _____ is a very good man" or "Oh! [Boswell] is a very good man." Surely her "Oh! is a very good man," like "of recommending him," "minte," and "espy," is part of an attempt to record Paoli's accented and unidiomatic English. In Italian the sentence would have had no expressed subject: "Oh! è un uomo molto buono!"

Mrs. Piozzi's *Anecdotes*]   G. B. Hill (ed.), *Johnsonian Miscellanies,* 1897, i. 175. She does not name Boswell, but undoubtedly meant him. He rebutted her strictures (*Life,* following 1 July 1784: iv. 343).

Professor Tinker and Geoffrey Scott]   *Young Boswell,* 1922, ch. 9; BP, vi. 19–27.

p. 257.

"Je ne puis suffrir"]   *Corsica,* p. 351. At his first meeting with Boswell Paoli spoke in French (ibid. p. 317); after that, generally in Italian. He said himself at a later date that his spoken French was not fluent (Journ. 22 Sept. 1769). He already understood English in 1765 (*Corsica,* p. 321), but spoke it haltingly even after he had lived in England for many years.

"I reached the point"]   "Arrivai al punto che quasi non mi restava più che mio fratello, e non cedei; e cederò ora che traluce qualche speranza? Ah, mi credano più onesto o più ambizioso!" Boswell's account runs, "When he was asked if he would quit the island of which he had undertaken the protection, supposing a foreign power should create him a marshal and make him governor of a province, he replied: 'I hope they will believe I am more honest or more ambitious; for' (said he) 'to accept of the highest offices under a foreign power would be to serve'" (*Corsica,* p. 328). In order to present *ipsissima verba* of Paoli I have preferred an extract from a letter of 7 Dec. 1768 in which he repeats the famous sentence in a different setting (Giovanni Livi, "Lettere inedite di Pasquale de' Paoli," *Archivio storico italiano,* 5th ser., v. 256).

"I have an unspeakable pride"]   *Corsica,* p. 320.

"I am no bigot"]   Ravenna, p. 47, translated. See also Boswell: "Talking of Providence, he said to me with that earnestness with which a man speaks who is anxious to be believed: 'I tell you on the word of an honest man it is impossible for me not to be persuaded that God interposes to give freedom to Corsica.... When we were in the most desperate circumstances, I never lost courage, trusting as I did in Providence.' I ventured to object, 'But why has not Providence interposed sooner?' He replied with a noble, serious, and devout air, 'Because His ways are unsearchable. I adore Him for what He hath done. I revere Him for what He hath not done'" (*Corsica,* p. 355).

Paoli's occasional fierceness, his visions]   Ibid. pp. 324–325, 360–363.

p. 258.
The pomp of Boswell's entertainment]   Ibid. pp. 317–319, 372.

"The English ambassador"]   Ibid. p. 340.

Corsican dress, flute]   Ibid. pp. 340–341.

Boswell's personal problems]   Ibid. pp. 329, 349, 355.

Samuel Johnson]   Ibid. pp. 356–357. He had done the same with Rousseau, and had chosen at least one of the same anecdotes for repeating: see above, p. 170. The two anecdotes in *Corsica* ("Let us count our spoons" and "They are gone to milk the bull": *Life,* 14, 21 July 1763) are of particular interest as being the first specimens of Johnson's conversation to be printed by Boswell.

p. 259.
The parting with Paoli]   Ibid. p. 372.

Boswell's illness, journey to Corte]   Ibid. pp. 372–376.

p. 260.
Corte]   Ibid. pp. 377–379. The letter to Johnson has not been recovered.

Corte to Bastia]   Ibid. pp. 380, 385.

Reception by Marbeuf]   Ibid. pp. 385–394.

Chronology of the Corsican tour]   Boswell wrote to John Johnston, 14 Nov. 1765, telling him that he had passed ten days with Paoli, and one of his paragraphs in *Lond. Chron.* (7–9 Jan. 1766: 19.32) also speaks of "ten or twelve days." The surviving documents, however, do not permit him more than eight. His Corsican passport (Yale MS. C831) is dated 18 Oct. 1765, and he left Corte for Sollacarò "next morning" (*Corsica,* p. 310). The distance being seventy miles or more, he cannot have arrived at Sollacarò before the afternoon of 21 Sept. A digest of memoirs of Paoli from his lost journal notes (Yale MS. M6: see BP, vii. 245) shows that he took leave of Paoli on 29 Oct. He arrived back in Corte on 31 Oct. (From G. M. Massesi of that date), and was confined "for several days" there with the ague (*Corsica,* p. 377). I know of no other certainly established date until he wrote to John Johnston from Bastia on 14 Nov. 1765; he is "confined by a tertian fever" which he had "carried . . . about for eleven days" before obtaining assistance "he could confide in." He says that between Corte and Bastia he "passed some days" with Matteo Buttafoco at Vescovato (*Corsica,* p. 380). In *Boswell on the Grand Tour: Italy, Corsica, and France,* Professor Brady and I have conjectured that he left Corte on 7 Nov., paused at Vescovato, 8–9 Nov., and arrived at Bastia on the evening of the 9th. He sailed for Genoa on the evening of 20 Nov. (Notes, 22 Nov. 1765).

Bastia to Genoa]   Mem. 20–30 Nov. 1765; Notes on Capraia, 22–28 Nov. 1765 (Yale MS. M113); *Corsica,* p. 257 n.

Letters from Girolama]   From Girolama Piccolomini, 3, 7, 21 Oct. 1765.

Letters from Lord Auchinleck]   10 Aug., 16 Sept., 1 Oct. 1765.

p. 261.

Padre Vasco] From P. C. Vasco, 1 May 1774 (in Italian); a second (in French), undated but later. He says that Boswell wrote to him from Genoa asking him to insert in the Bologna *Gazette* an account of his tour to Corsica; he caused it to be published in the Modena *Gazette,* from which it was copied into the other Italian gazettes. Alexandre Deleyre, 1 Mar. 1766, says he has been told that the account appeared in the Lugano *Gazette.*

CHAPTER XVI

p. 262.

"I am no longer ..."] To J. J. Rousseau, 4 Jan. 1766, in French. "Copy moderate Rousseau" in Mem. 1 Dec. 1765 does not, I think, mean "Copy the behaviour of the moderate Rousseau," but "Copy in portions of moderate length" (or "copy with some toning down") "the long letter to Rousseau which you drafted at Lucca, 3 Oct. 1765." For confirmation of this, see the undated memorandum, "Voyage to Genoa," written in Capraia: "You are to copy *Tour d'Italie à M. Rousseau,* and to write him a free, liberal, Corsican letter."

The noble force of Johnson] Journ. 20 Dec. 1765.

Holford, French *chargé d'affaires,* Genoese secretary of state] Mem. 1 Dec. 1765. The name of the *chargé d'affaires* was Michel, of the Genoese secretary of state, Gherardi (*Corsica,* pp. 393, 394).

"Do you know ..."] To John Johnston, 9 Dec. 1765.

p. 263.

John Dick] "Indeed, your not being under the necessity of putting yourself into the hands of a Genoese doctor was a lucky circumstance. I would even be cautious of having anything to say to their cooks, for your being only an admirer of this modern Numa is crime enough to render you both odious and suspected" (From John Dick, 22 Nov. 1765). "I had the greatest pleasure in receiving your kind and obliging letter from Antibes, dated the 16 instant, as was glad to find you was safe in France. I had my fears about you while you was in the other state" (From John Dick, 22 Dec. 1765).

Count Rivarola's report] These interesting reports, which Professor Warnock found in the State Archives at Turin, will be printed in full in the research edition of Boswell's papers.

Uneasiness at keeping the Doge waiting] Mem. 7 Dec. 1765. The Doge was Maria Gaetano Della Rovere.

Meetings with notables] Mem. 3 Dec. 1765 (Lalande); 6, 10 Dec. 1765 (Hessenstein); 7 Dec. 1765 (Ellis); 2, 3, 5, 6, 7, 8 Dec. 1765 (Symonds); 2, 4, 8 Dec. 1765 (Hervey).

Genoa to Noli] Journ. 10–12 Dec. 1765.

p. 264.
Toe-nails]   Mem. 8 Dec. 1765; Journ. 24, 30, 31 Dec. 1765; 2, 3 Jan. 1766;
Notes, 14, 17 Jan. 1766.

Jachone]   *Corsica,* pp. 73, 364–365, 376; Journ. 10, 11, 12, 14, 16, 17, 19, 20,
24 Dec. 1765; 1, 2 Jan. 1766; From John Nairne, 22 Jan. 1766.

Boswell beats Sandy for lying]   Journ. 8 Jan. 1780; see also p. 26 above.

p. 265.
Boswell smashes furniture]   Journ. 10 Nov. 1775.

Jacob]   Mem. 1, 10 Dec. 1765; Journ. 10, 11, 12, 18 Dec. 1765; 2, 3 Jan.
1766. "Changling" is 12 Dec.; the two quotations, 18 Dec. and 3 Jan. respectively.

p. 266.
Paragraphs in *Lond. Chron.*]   These are conveniently collected in Appendix C
of *Boswell on the Grand Tour: Italy, Corsica, and France.* Boswell's own marked
file of *Lond. Chron.* is at Yale.

p. 268.
Avignon]   Journ. 24–26 Dec. 1765; *Jacobite Peerage* under "Dunbar" and
"Inverness." Colonel Hay had also been created a Duke, but his widow seems to
have preferred the style of Lady Inverness.

Dunbar to Lumisden]   28 Dec. 1765, Stuart Papers, Royal Archives, Windsor Castle, transcribed for me in 1939 by Miss Henrietta Tayler.

p. 269.
Counsels to chastity, serious resolve]   *Corsica,* pp. 329, 371; Journ. 21 Dec.
1765.

Mlle. Susette]   Journ. 21, 22 Dec. 1765.

p. 270.
News of Rousseau, letter to him]   Journ. 3 Jan. 1766; Notes 12 Jan. 1766; To
J. J. Rousseau, 4 Jan. 1766, in French; Josephson, pp. 430–449. The Notes, 12
Jan.–23 Feb. 1766 follow the style of the memoranda in recording under each
date the events of the previous day.

Boswell in Corsica made up his mind that he loved Belle de Zuylen]   From
Belle de Zuylen, 16 Feb. 1768.

p. 271.
"Thought to offer marriage . . ."]   Mem. 1 Dec. 1765.

M. de Zuylen, Willem van Tuyll]   From M. de Zuylen, c. 1 Jan. 1766;
Notes, 14, 15 Jan. 1766; Godet, i. 5, 65.

Letter to M. de Zuylen]   The Notes (16, 17 Jan. 1766) say that it was
written on the 15th and sent on the 16th; Reg. Let. records it as sent on the 16th. It
bears date 16 Jan. 1766. Boswell probably wrote it on the 15th and made a fair

copy next day. It is in French, the passages quoted being for the greater part from the translation by Geoffrey Scott.

p. 273.

Lord Auchinleck had written] This letter has not been recovered, but Boswell gave its substance in the letter to M. de Zuylen just cited. He received it at Paris on 12 Jan. 1766 (Reg. Let.). His reply, missing but also summarized in the letter to M. de Zuylen, was written on 15 Jan. according to the Notes (15, 16 Jan. 1766) and on 16 Jan. according to the letter to M. de Zuylen. Reg. Let. records no letter sent to Lord Auchinleck between 13 and 23 Jan., but as Lord Auchinleck had received the letter in question by 30 Jan. 1766 (letter of that date to Boswell), it is probable that the Register is defective.

p. 274.

Wilkes] *Autobiography,* 1888, pp. 53–62; Bleackley, pp. 172–177; Notes, 19, 22, 24, 27 Jan. 1766.

24, 25, 26 Jan. 1766] Notes, 25, 26, 27 Jan. 1766. Professor Warnock's notes on the establishments of Mme. Hecquet and Mlle. Dupuis will appear in the research edition of Boswell's papers.

Lord Auchinleck's last letter] Summarized in From Lord Auchinleck, 11 Jan. 1766.

Lady Auchinleck's letter] Received 20 Jan. 1766. (Reg. Let.).

Boswell's behaviour under news of bereavement] Notes, 27, 28 Jan. 1766; To W. J. Temple, 26 Jan. 1766.

The dreaded letter] From Lord Auchinleck, 11 Jan. 1766, written by David.

p. 275.

Wilkes's kindness] Notes, 30 Jan. 1766; To John Wilkes, 6 May 1766.

Boswell arranges to accompany Thérèse Le Vasseur] Notes, 29, 30, 31 Jan. 1766.

Hôtel de Luxembourg, Palais Royal] Notes, 18 Jan. 1766.

Mass in two churches] Notes, 13, 27 Jan. 1766.

Robert Strange, Scots Jacobites] Notes 13, 17, 18, 20, 23, 25, 28, 29, 30 Jan. 1766.

p. 276.

Horace Walpole] To Sir David Dalrymple, 22 Mar. 1760; From Horace Walpole, undated; Notes, 22 Jan. 1766; Walpole's Paris Journals, 21 Jan. 1766 (Yale ed. of Horace Walpole's Correspondence, vii. 296); Horace Walpole to Thomas Gray, 18 Feb. 1768.

David Hume] *Letters of David Hume,* ed. J. Y. T. Greig, 1932, ii. 11, incorrectly dated 12 Jan. Greig thinks it was written in the first week of February.

Departure from Paris with Thérèse Le Vasseur] Notes, 30, 31 Jan. 1766.

p. 277.

Letters sent from Calais] Reg. Let.: Margrave of Baden-Durlach, Baron de Tuyll, Jacob Hänni on 5 Feb., Mme. Kircheisen and Robert Brown on 7 Feb. The originals of none of these have been recovered, but Yale has Boswell's draft of the letter to the Margrave of Baden-Durlach. It was originally dated 5 Feb., but the 5 has been changed to 6.

I have twice printed] BP, vii. 65–66; *Boswell on the Grand Tour: Italy, Corsica, and France, 1765–1766,* following 31 Jan. 1766.

p. 278.
Having notified Temple] To W. J. Temple, 29 Jan. 1766.

The enforced wait in Calais] The information concerning the mails has been obtained by systematic search of *Lond. Chron.* and verified by parallel search in *The Daily Advertiser.* The mail from France arrived Friday 3 Jan., Saturday 11 Jan., Friday 17 Jan., Friday 24 Jan., Friday 31 Jan., Tuesday 11 Feb., Monday 17 Feb., Saturday 22 Feb. (two mails), Friday 28 Feb., Friday 7 Mar., Tuesday 18 Mar., Monday 24 Mar., Saturday 29 Mar., Saturday 5 Apr. 1766 (*Lond. Chron.* 19.14, 40, 62, 86, 110, 144, 166, 184, 206, 230, 264, 286, 304, 328). There are many references to excessive cold (e.g. 1–4 Feb. p. 114; 4–6 Feb. p. 126; 8–11 Feb. pp. 137, 142; 11–13 Feb. p. 146), and many accounts of wrecks in the period immediately following Boswell's arrival, e.g.: "Margate, Feb. 10. For some days past we have had such a quantity of wrecks drove on shore as has not been known in the memory of man" (11–13 Feb. p. 145); "The *Augusta,* Lewis, from London to Leith, is lost near Holy Island, and all the crew perished" (ibid. p. 146); "Canterbury, Feb. 12. We hear that a large Dutch fly-boat was lost on the Goodwin Sands on Thursday last [6 Feb.]; part of her hull, with her mast, yards, etc., came ashore upon the isle of Thanet, and her rudder at Deal. It is thought the people were drowned" (13–15 Feb. p. 153); "They write from Guernsey that the French coast is strewed with pieces of wrecks from between Cape La Hogue to the Caskets" (ibid. p. 160).

Respectable authority] Rousseau's own: "When I went to live in the Rue Neuve-des-Petits-Champs, there was opposite my windows in the Hotel de Pontchartrain a clock, and I did my best for more than a month to teach her to tell time by it. She can hardly do so now. She has never been able to recite the twelve months of the year in succession, and does not know a single number, in spite of all the efforts I have made to teach her. She can neither count money nor reckon the price of anything" (*Confessions,* pt. 2, bk. 7, translated).

Walpole's characterization of Rousseau] Notes, 22 Jan. 1766.

"Quackery this"] Notes, 29 Jan. 1766.

p. 279.
Boswell's final letter to Karl Friedrich] 6 Feb. 1766.

Other letters in the correspondence] From Karl Friedrich, 9 Dec. 1764; To Karl Friedrich, 25 Nov. 1764; 15 Jan., 11 May, 30 Aug. 1765. Boswell's copy of the last named is dated 1 Sept. 1765; according to Reg. Let., it was not sent till 13 Sept.

p. 280.

"Now let us have a joke at Boswell"]   From David Boswell, 3 Feb. 1766.

p. 281.

M. de Zuylen sends Boswell's letter back]   From Robert Brown, 27 Jan. 1767. M. de Zuylen's letter of 30 Jan. 1766 was in French.

Boswell and Thérèse arrive in England]   Notes, 12 Feb. 1766.

He delivers Thérèse to Rousseau, promises not to tell]   Notes, 13 Feb. 1766.

p. 282.

He deceives Temple]   From W. J. Temple, 24 Apr. 1790. See *Boswell on the Grand Tour: Italy, Corsica, and France, 1765–1766,* 13 Feb. 1766, n.

Reunion with Johnson]   Notes, 13 Feb. 1766.

"You told him . . ."]   Notes, 16 Feb. 1766.

p. 283.

Temple, Hume, the Thirty-nine Articles]   Ibid.

Dempster]   Notes, 17 Feb. 1766.

Erskine]   From Andrew Erskine, 20 Jan. 1766; Notes, 17 Feb. 1766.

Eglinton]   Notes, 15 Feb. 1766.

Mountstuart]   Reg. Let. 3 Dec. 1765; From Lord Mountstuart, 27 Dec. 1765 (says Boswell's letter was dated 2 Dec. 1765); From Dr. John Pringle, 28 Jan. 1766 (Boswell's angry letter to Mountstuart is unrecovered, but Pringle assigns it the date 15 Jan. 1766 and summarizes its contents); Notes, 14, 15 Feb. 1766.

p. 284.

William Bosville]   Journ. 18 Apr., 30 May 1763.

Boswell meets his "chief," charmed with Miss Bosville]   Notes, 16, 17, 18, 19, 21, 22, 23 Feb. 1766.

Boswell presented at Court]   Notes, 18 Feb. 1766.

The interview with Pitt]   Foladare, pp. 25–29; DNB, William Pitt, 1708–1778; Notes, 17 Feb. 1766 (clearly misdated, for the letter, To William Pitt, is dated 15 Feb. and Pitt answered it on the 16th); From William Pitt, 16 Feb. 1766; To William Pitt, 19 Feb. 1766; Notes, 23 Feb. 1766 (misdated 22 Feb.). Boswell's cousin, Lord Cardross, afterwards Earl of Buchan, who was present during part of the interview, left a memorandum of uncertain date saying that Boswell came in Corsican dress and presented a letter from Paoli (Buchan Papers, Bodleian Library: see *Letters,* i. 88 n. 1). Both statements appear to be false.

"Only undeceive your Court"]   *Corsica,* pp. 342–343.

p. 286.

Return to Edinburgh]   To W. J. Temple, Haddington, 6 Mar. 1766. The Rev. Edward Aitken had once been tutor to Lord Auchinleck. That John Boswell was in his house at the time is shown by a receipt for ten weeks' board that he gave John on 28 Mar. 1766. For Temple's matrimonial vacillations see Notes, 12, 14, 21 Feb. 1766; From W. J. Temple, 17 Mar., 2 July 1766; To W. J. Temple, 17 May 1766. Temple protests at Boswell's interfering in the letter of 17 Mar. 1766.

p. 287.
Gains of absence, Scots accent, etc.] To W. J. Temple, 6 Mar. 1766.

CHAPTER XVII

p. 288.
Boswell and his father at Auchinleck] To John Johnston, 31 Mar., 4 May 1766; Auchinleck Memoirs. Boswell and his father arrived at Auchinleck shortly after 15 Mar. 1766 (From John Dun of that date); Claud came down soon after 5 Apr. 1766 (From David Boswell of that date). For Claud Boswell see DNB; *College of Justice,* p. 544; Journ. 29 Apr. 1769.

p. 289.
Low spirits on arrival] To John Johnston, 31 Mar. 1766.

Euphemia Bruce] To W. J. Temple, 28 Apr. 1766; Johnston Corresp. p. 215 n. 2.

p. 290.
"Scurvy spots," Moffat, a new flame] From John Johnston, 26 Apr., 10 May 1766; To John Johnston, 4 May 1766; To W. J. Temple, 17 May 1766 (quotation); Andrew Erskine to John Johnston, 2 June 1766.

Letters from Girolama] Reg. Let. 9 Mar., 11 May 1766, letters dated 14 Feb., 23 Feb. 1766.

Mrs. Dodds] Boswell's names for her, Notes 12, 13, 15 Jan. 1767, and *passim* ("Miss____"); 15 Feb. 1767 ("La Cara"); 21 Mar. 1767 ("Circe"); 22 Mar. 1767 ("Laïs"); 3 Mar. 1767 ("Mrs. Dodds"). Known to both city and Ayrshire acquantances: Notes 3, 4, 18 Mar., 13 Apr. 1767. Husband and three children: To W. J. Temple, 1 Feb.–8 Mar. 1767. Young, lively, etc.: ibid. No presents of money: ibid. I know of no proof that Mrs. Dodds followed Boswell promptly from Moffat to Edinburgh, but From W. J. Temple, 20 Nov. 1766 shows that the affair had been going on in Edinburgh for some time before that date. Of course Edinburgh may have been Mrs. Dodds's usual place of residence.

p. 291.
Examination in Scots Law] Faculty Records, National Library of Scotland.

Recurrence of malaria] From James Bruce, 19, 29 July 1766; From John Johnston, Friday [25 July 1766]; Johnston Corresp. p. 220.

Examination on thesis in Civil Law] Faculty Records, National Library of Scotland; Boswell's thesis (see the note following this), title-page.

Disputatio juridica . . . de supellectile legata] *Lit. Car.* pp. 21–26.

Correspondence with Johnson concerning the thesis] From Samuel Johnson, 21

Aug. 1766; To Samuel Johnson, 6 Nov. 1766. Boswell's letter is known only as edited by himself in the *Life;* of Johnson's the original is unreported, but the quoted sentence can be read through Boswell's deleting strokes in the copy (by Mrs. Boswell) which he sent to the printer.

p. 292.
Boswell puts on the gown]   Inscription on Consultation Book.

Boswell's first cause]   Journ. 14 Mar. 1772; Consultation Book, 29 July 1766. The cause was "Johnston & Co. against Hamilton," Boswell representing the pursuers. The judge was the newly appointed Lord Justice-Clerk, and the opposing counsel was Robert Sinclair (ibid.).

Thomas Miller, Lord Barskimming, Lord Justice-Clerk]   DNB; *College of Justice,* pp. 530–531. David Boswell wrote bitterly on 29 Apr. 1766, "I must say I am sorry to hear that Tam Miller is to be Lord Justice-Clerk for Scotland; it is a shame that such a *body,* sprung from nothing, should come before so many more worthy personages. I dare say my brother John will be almost mad at this." Boswell's own strictures are unrecovered, but we have David's approving comment on them: "Your sentiments on Tam Miller's advancement are excellent. What does Grange say upon the matter? I hope he has a proper indignation at such a strange transaction. I believe, however, you censure the D. of Grafton a little too much. ... I believe rather that the D. of Queensberry had entirely the management of the puppet show; at least, it was he that first helped Tam Miller to crawl into the office of Solicitor" (30 May 1766). Dr. John Boswell, disappointed in his hopes of being made either Professor of Medicine in the University of Edinburgh or Physician to the King in Scotland, had chimed in on 24 May 1766: "However, I think I may now be at ease, since I have got your father to keep me in countenance. I may submit to Dr. Black gaining the one and Gregory the other ... when Tom Miller is promoted over the senior Lord of Justiciary, and some of whose ancestors would not have allowed any Miller to have eat with them, etc., etc.—not to say personal merit." As a matter of fact there was nothing "strange" about Miller's appointment. He had been Lord Advocate since 1760, and it was established custom for the Lord Advocate to have the choice of vacancies occurring in the bench during his term of office.

Henry Dundas]   To W. J. Temple, 17 May 1766; From W. J. Temple, 8 Aug. 1766. "Coarse, unlettered dog" was Boswell's outburst nine years later when Dundas was made Lord Advocate (To W. J. Temple, 22 May 1775).

p. 293.
The Scots legal system]   This matter is discussed at length, with references to sources, in *Boswell for the Defence,* Appendix B, and *Boswell: The Ominous Years,* Appendix B. Boswell's estimate that half an advocate's business in the Court of Session was done by writing is in To W. J. Temple, 1 Feb.–8 Mar. 1767.

p. 294.
High Court of Justiciary]   The quotations are adapted from Sir Walter Scott, *The Heart of Midlothian,* ch. 22, a brilliant fictional account of a capital trial be-

fore the Court by a first-rate writer who was also an advocate, sheriff of a county, and one of the principal clerks of the Court of Session. Scott's father, Walter Scott, W. S., occasionally employed Boswell professionally and is frequently mentioned in Boswell's journal.

Often getting up at six] E.g. To W. J. Temple, 1 Feb.–8 Mar. 1767.

Five days a week] Monday was reserved for the studying of causes and for the business of the Court of Justiciary.

As the clock struck nine] E.g. Journ. 12 Aug. 1774.

p. 295.
Boswell's fees compared with Scott's] Consultation Book; J. G. Lockhart, *Memoirs of the Life of Sir Walter Scott,* ch. 8.

Kerr v. Thomsons] S.R.O. Dal/k2/19; Consultation Book, 4 Dec. 1766; 13, 24 Jan., 5, 11 Feb., 16 July, 5 Dec. 1767.

p. 297.
Robertson v. Storrie] S.R.O. Warrants for Acts and Decreets (Dal.), 7 Feb. 1767; Consultation Book, 27 Jan. 1767; To John Johnston, Tuesday [?27 Jan. 1767].

"Illustrious philosopher," etc.] To J. J. Rousseau, 4 Jan. 1766, in French.

Rousseau taxes him with neglect] To J. J. Rousseau, 25 Mar. 1766.

Rousseau in England, the quarrel with Hume] Josephson, pp. 449–472; F. A. Pottle, "The Part played by Horace Walpole and James Boswell in the Quarrel between Rousseau and Hume," *Philological Quarterly,* iv (1925). 351–363; v (1926). 185 (ill-informed and inaccurate, to be used with great care); R. A. Leigh, "Boswell and Rousseau," *Modern Language Review,* 47 (1952). 289–317. Deyverdun admitted the authorship of "Le Débiteur de pilules" (*St. James's Chronicle,* 24–26 Apr. 1766) in a letter to Hume, 18 Nov. 1766, pp. 297–299 of J. H. Burton (ed.), *Letters of Eminent Persons addressed to David Hume,* 1849. See also *Letters of David Hume,* ed. J. Y. T. Greig, 1932, ii. 113 n. 1, 115, 116–117.

p. 298.
"A peevish letter with strong marks of frenzy in it"] To W. J. Temple, 1 Feb.–8 Mar. 1767.

Boswell promptly writes to Rousseau and Thérèse] Reg. Let. 11 Aug. 1766. The receipt of Rousseau's letter is not recorded.

p. 299.
Boswell's gaiety of fancy] To Mrs. Thrale, 26 Apr. 1781.

Further returns of malaria] From David Boswell, 23, 30 Aug., 10 Sept., 7 Oct. 1766; From Lord Hailes, 29 Aug. 1766 (Sir David Dalrymple had been raised to the bench in the previous March, and will henceforth receive his judicial style); To Sir Alexander Dick, 23 Oct. 1766; From Dr. John Boswell, 27 Oct. 1766.

John Reid]   Yale MS. Lg4, a large mass of legal documents dealing with
John Reid's trials and of newspapers reporting them; especially Lg4:1 Indictment of John Reid for trial at Glasgow, 12 Sept. 1766; Lg4:2 Memorandum
by Reid's agent, John Johnston, Glasgow 1766, containing Reid's story of James
Wilson, who commissioned him to drive the sheep to Glasgow; Lg4:4 Boswell's
notes for his pleading on the relevancy and his appeal for delay of trial; *The
Caledonian Mercury*, 15 Sept. 1766, reporting the trial. The judges were Lords
Auchinleck and Pitfour (the respected lawyer who had witnessed Boswell's
"renunciation" in 1762, raised to the bench in 1764). Bannatyne MacLeod was
appointed counsel with Boswell (Lg4:8 Boswell's notes for his opening speech at the
Edinburgh trial), but it is clear that Boswell supplied all the energy and did most
of the speaking.

James Haddow]   S.R.O. Court of Justiciary Records, South Circuit Minute
Book, 10, 11, 13 Oct. 1766; To the Duchess of Douglas, 13 Oct. 1766; To James
Haddow, Sen., 13 Oct. 1766; S.R.O. Ayr Council Book, 1759–1767, 18 Oct., 12
Nov. 1766. On the latter date, "the Provost produced in council a reprieve . . .
advising that application having been made to the King on behalf of James
Haddow, a prisoner now under sentence of death in the tolbooth of Ayr . . . he
was commanded to signify to them His Majesty's pleasure that the execution of
the said sentence . . . be respited for three weeks from the time appointed for the
same." The judges at young Haddow's trial were the Lord Justice-Clerk and Lord
Coalston. Patrick Murray, Advocate-Depute, appeared for the prosecution, and
Charles Brown, Boswell, and Claud Boswell for the defence. Sir James Fergusson
has found no further reference to Haddow in the Council Book, but the absence
in Boswell's papers of any reference to his execution seems to me strong evidence
that the respite was in fact an absolute reprieve, and that Haddow's sentence was
commuted to transportation, which was the utmost his father hoped for.

p. 300.
Boswell's four conditions]   From Sir David Dalrymple, 10 Oct. 1764.

Boswell had expected his father to propose separate quarters]   From Sir
John Pringle, 10 June 1766. (Pringle had been made a baronet five days before
the date of this letter.)

Boswell gives up his demand for lodgings apart]   To W. J. Temple, 1 Feb.–
8 Mar. 1767.

"He must have his son," etc.]   Ibid.

p. 301.
"As to your choice," etc.]   From Dr. John Boswell, 27 Oct. 1766.

"I do assure you," etc.]   From David Boswell, 31 Oct. 1766.

"Solemn anniversaries," etc.]   Mem. Aug.–8 Nov. 1766 (Yale MS. J11.8).

Later statements]   "We were very happy. We are now friends as much as my
father's singular grave and steady temper will allow; for he has not that quick

sensibility which animates me. Since the beginning of last winter he has ceased to treat me like a boy" (Notes, 22 Mar. 1767). "At night you and Father both owned you were living very happily" (ibid. 31 Mar. 1767).

CHAPTER XVIII

p. 303.
"What strength of mind," etc.]   Notes, 18 Mar. 1767.

A dreadful winter]   From James Bruce, 23 Jan. 1767; To W. J. Temple, 1 Feb.–8 Mar. 1767.

Mrs. Dodds]   Ibid.; Notes, 14 Feb. 1767 ("Philippi").

"Be Spaniard"]   Mem. 20 Feb. 1765; Notes, 16 Jan., 18 Mar. 1767.

Mark Antony]   Notes, 17 Mar. 1767.

Fees of an entire session]   To W. J. Temple, 1 Feb.–8 Mar. 1767; Notes, 4, 7 Feb., 17 Mar. 1767.

Collecting materials for *Corsica*]   E.g. From Pasquale de Paoli, 23 Dec. 1765 (*Corsica,* pp. 395–399); Pasquale de Paoli to John Dick, 6 Dec. 1766; To W. J. Temple, 1 Feb.–8 Mar., 24 Dec. 1767; From John Dick, 1, 25 Feb., 30 May, 18 June, 26 Sept., 6, 24, 31 Oct. 1766; 7, 23 Jan., 6 Feb., 6 Mar. 1767; From Count Antonio Rivarola, 19 Sept. 1766, 18 Mar., 2 May 1767; From Richard Edwards, 26 June, 30 Nov. 1767; From Andrew Burnaby, 10 Aug., 21 Sept., 25 Oct. 1767; Mem. at Auchinleck, Glasgow, Ayr, and Dalzell, Aug.–8 Nov. 1766 (Yale MS. J11.8), pp. 4, 5; Reg. Let. 24 Apr. 1766 (To Paoli, Rivarola, Buttafoco, Dick); To Sir Alexander Dick, 9 Dec. 1766.

p. 304.
Correspondence with Chatham]   To the Earl of Chatham, 18 Sept. 1766, 3 Jan., 8 Apr. 1767; From the Earl of Chatham, 4 Feb. 1767.

Sam Jones]   *Lond. Chron.* 16–18, 21–23, 23–25 Apr. 1767; Samuel Richardson, *Clarissa,* e.g. vol. 2, letter 51 of the 3d ed. and editions adhering to it (Shakespeare Head ed. ii. 370–372); Henry Fielding, *Tom Jones,* Book 15, ch. 10. Smollett's Tabitha Bramble and Winifred Jenkins, now the best known of the comic misspellers, did not appear on the scene till 1771.

p. 305.
Signor Romanzo]   *Lond. Chron.* 22–24 Jan., 24–26, 26–28 Mar. (two items), 5–7 May, 4–6, 9–11 June 1767.

Other Corsican inventions]   *Lond. Chron.* 24–27 Jan. 1767 (Grand Duke of Tuscany); 25–28 July 1767 (quadruple alliance); 8–10 Oct. 1767 (Corsicans winning); 29–31 Oct. 1767 (King of Prussia); 16–19 Jan. 1768 (Dey of Algiers); 22–24 Sept. 1767 (Prince Heraclius).

"I do believe," etc.]   *Corsica,* p. 225.

p. 306.

Portrait of Paoli]   *Lond. Chron.* 26–28 Mar. 1767.

Island of Capraia]   Ibid. 14–16 Apr. 1767.

Two inventions]   Ibid. 31 Mar.–2 Apr., 7–9 Apr. 1767.

p. 307.

Neue Genealogisch–Historische Nachrichten]   "[Paoli] sucht mit allen Mach-
ten in guter Freundschaft zu leben, und ordnet Personen ab, die das Ansehen der
Gesandten haben. Ein solcher war der Herr Romanzo, der zu Anfang des Aprils
über Hamburg im Haag anlangte. Bald nach seiner Ankunst machte er dem
Grossbritannischen Botschafter, Herrn York, eine Visite, der sich drei Stunden
lang mit ihm unterhielte" (Part 89, 1769, pp. 283–284).

Percy and Brown's defence of the Corsicans]   Journ. 26 Mar. 1772; *Lond.
Chron.* 9–11 Oct. 1766; Andrew Burnaby, *Journal of a Tour to Corsica in the Year
1766 . . . with a Series of Original Letters from General Paoli to the Author,* 1804,
p. 40, a letter from Paoli to Burnaby dated 7 Mar. 1767.

On two later occasions]   *Lond. Chron.* 16–18 Apr. 1767; 12–14 July 1768.

p. 308.

Seneca's epigrams]   Ibid. 1–3, 3–6, 24–27 Jan., 5–7, 7–10, 24–26 Feb.,
24–26 Mar. (two items), 23–25 Apr., 30 Apr.–2 May, 7–9, 25–28 July, 13–15
Aug. 1767. Boswell's translation signed "Humilis" appeared in the issue for 23–25
Apr.

Boswell kept very throng]   To W. J. Temple, 1 Feb.–8 Mar. 1767.

Eighty-four guineas]   Consultation Book.

Pleaded a cause against Henry Dundas and Robert Macqueen]   Notes, 6, 8
Feb. 1767.

As unfair a state of the facts]   Notes, 18 Mar. 1767.

John Reid's trial in Edinburgh]   From John Rowand, Gaoler at Glasgow,
24 Nov. 1766, with account showing how twenty-eight shillings, left with him by
Boswell for John Reid, was spent; Yale MS. M125 (the inscription); From John
Reid, 13 Nov. 1766, received by Boswell 22 Nov. 1766; Yale MS. Lg4:6 (the indictment); *Edinburgh Evening Courant,* 24 Nov. 1766 (Reid brought to Edinburgh); To Sir Alexander Dick, 9 Dec. 1766; Yale MS. Lg4:8 (Boswell's notes for
his opening speech); *Edinburgh Advertiser,* 16 Dec. 1766; *Caledonian Mercury,*
20 Dec. 1766; *Scots Mag.* 28 (1766).668; S.R.O. Court of Justiciary Records, Books
of Adjournal, D.34, 15 Dec. 1766; S.R.O. Justiciary Papers, Process H. M. Advocate
v. John Reid, Edinburgh, 15 Dec. 1766; *Douglas Cause,* p. 115 ("Upon so strange
a verdict your Lordships . . . declared your opinions seriatim that this verdict was
given in the face of most complete evidence").

p. 309.

Boswell for the prosecution]   No one has thought to index this side of Boswell's practice, but the instances must be very few. Several of us who have worked
closely with his journal and notes have put our heads together and have come up

with only two causes, one of them mentioned in the *Life of Johnson* (To Samuel Johnson, 29 Nov. 1777). At the end of Nov. 1777, after once refusing, he assisted in the prosecution of John Bell, schoolmaster at Stewarton, who was being tried for indecent behaviour to his female scholars. Though he considered the offence "very criminal, if true," he nevertheless called the accused "poor Bell," and felt deeply "hurt" to be against him. He says he "spoke tolerably" but "was too tender-hearted" (Journ. 29 Nov.–2 Dec. 1777).

p. 310.

Joseph Taylor] Yale MS. Lg3 (the indictment); S.R.O. Court of Justiciary Records, Books of Adjournal, D.34, 22 Dec. 1766; 19 Feb., 9, 13 Mar. 1767; *Scots Mag.* 29 (1767). 221. Judges were the Lord Justice-Clerk, Auchinleck, Kames, Pitfour, and Coalston; counsel for the prosecution, the Lord Advocate (James Montgomery), the Solicitor General, Patrick Murray, William Nairne, and Cosmo Gordon.

Robert Hay] Yale MS. Lg6:1 (indictment), Lg6:2 (Boswell's notes for his plea); Lg6:3 (petition for clemency); S.R.O. Court of Justiciary Records, Books of Adjournal, D.35, 9 Feb. 1767; From "A friend of Robert Hay," 20 Feb. 1767 (confession of the facts); *Scots Mag.* 29 (1767). 221; Notes, 9, 10, 11, 15 Feb. 1767; Journ. 21 Feb. 1768. Boswell was assisted by Alexander Wight and Robert Sinclair. Judges were the Lord Justice-Clerk, Kames, Coalston, and Pitfour.

p. 311.

Another client of Boswell's (William Stewart, alias James Smith)] Notes, 16 Feb. 1767; *Scots Mag.* 29 (1767). 221; S.R.O. Court of Justiciary Records, Books of Adjournal, D. 35, 16 Feb. 1767. Same judges as in Hay's case. Counsel for the Crown, the Solicitor General, Patrick Murray, William Nairne, and Cosmo Gordon. George Wallace was senior counsel for the defence and according to Boswell "did ingeniously." Verdict of guilty was unanimous.

Hay's execution] From David Boswell, 25 Mar. 1767; Notes, 2 Apr. 1767.

"Why it is," etc.] Notes, 11 Feb. 1767.

Not professionally engaged at this time in the Douglas Cause] An incorrect list of the counsel printed in *Scots Mag.* for Jan. 1767 (29. 23) has been the source of persistent error. This is corrected in the Errata opposite p. 1: "*For* Mr. James Boswell *read* Mr. Alexander Murray." Boswell, writing to Temple on 22 June 1767, says, "I am not a counsel in that cause."

p. 312.

The Douglas Cause] The best concise account is that given in the Introduction of *Douglas Cause,* which also (pp. 190–245) provides a useful reprint of all the letters in *Letters of . . . Lady Jane Douglas,* 1767, a book now hard to come by. Otherwise the volume is disappointing, as instead of giving a detailed and systematic collection of the evidence, it contents itself with merely reprinting a contemporary report of the speeches of the Scots judges, plus reports of those of Camden and Mansfield in the House of Lords. Lillian de la Torre has made a thorough and accurate study of the cause and offers an ingenious solution in her lively *Heir of Douglas,* 1952. The principal sources (which I have read in large part) are the printed *Memorials* and *Proofs* for pursuers and defender, four huge quartos totalling nearly 4000 pages. Edward (later Lord) Thurlow's *Case* for Douglas in the appeal to the House of Lords is better organized and more compact than the pursuers' two volumes.

p. 313.
"Two doses of Hamilton blood"] Notes, 28 Apr. 1781.

p. 314.
"Presumptive heiress of a great estate"] Lady Jane Douglas to Henry Pelham, 15 May 1750, *Letters of . . . Lady Jane Douglas,* p. 72 (*Douglas Cause,* p. 215).

p. 315.
"Little men"] Lady Jane Douglas to Col. John Steuart, "Friday," "Saturday," "Monday," etc., *Letters of . . . Lady Jane Douglas,* pp. 37, 40, 45, 46, 67, 80 (*Douglas Cause,* pp. 203, 204, 206, 207, 214, 218).

p. 316.
Boswell's first recorded meeting with Archibald Douglas] Journ. 30 Nov. 1762; see also Journ. 22 May 1763.

Boswell meets Stuart and Nairne in Holland] Journ. 31 May–2 June 1764.

"Took care to keep the newspapers," etc.] *Memoirs,* pp. 325–326 (xxxv).

Printed memorials] The even thicker volumes of *Proofs* had been given in the previous February (*Scots Mag.* 28 [1766]. 408).

Memorials submitted] 24 Jan. 1767 (*Scots Mag.* 29.114).

Fergusson's computations] Hamilton *Memorial,* pt. 3, pp. 302–311. The seventeen-digit figure appears on p. 309.

Boswell's ballad, "The Hamilton Cause"] Notes, 14 Feb. 1767; *Scots Mag.* 29 (Mar. 1767). 119; F. A. Pottle, "Three New Legal Ballads by James Boswell," *Juridical Review,* 37 (1925). 206–209 (full text).

p. 317.
"Chaste Kilkerran"] "The Author's Earnest Cry and Prayer," l. 74; see also "Ballad Second: The Election," l. 69 ("maiden Kilkerran").

"What a variety," etc.] Notes, 15 Feb. 1767.

p. 318.
"The sound and perfect human being"] Notes, 18 Mar. 1767.

Belle de Zuylen in London] Godet, i. 117–134; *Lettres de Belle de Zuylen* (*Mme. de Charrière*) *à Constant d'Hermenches, p. p.* Philippe Godet, 1909; pp. 292–313; From W. R. van Tuyll van Serooskerken, 11 Nov.–4 Dec. 1766; From Robert Brown, 27 Jan. 1767; To W. J. Temple, 17 May 1766; 1 Feb.–8 Mar. 1767.

Mrs. Dodds makes him jealous, charms him into gaiety] Notes, 16 Jan., 15, 17, 21 Feb. 1767.

Too like a married man] Notes, 4, 5, 7 Feb. 1767.

p. 319.

"I am ... uneasy about her"]   To W. J. Temple, 1 Feb.–8 Mar. 1767 (this part written 4 Mar.).

He went to her with parting in his thoughts, she gave up the house]   Ibid. (this part written 8 Mar.). There was so much change and counter-change in the arrangements for the house that it is not clear where the one finally rented was, or indeed whether Mrs. Dodds ever really occupied it. On 4 Feb. Boswell found a house in Borthwick's Close that pleased him, and next morning went to "Mrs. Leith" and "took" it. On the 7th he learned that Mrs. Dodds had taken "other house," and resolved to give up his. Yet on the 13th he "had curious work about" his house and "was amused with the cares of it" (Notes, under dates cited). Writing on 4 Mar. to Temple he says he has taken the house and the lady has agreed to go into it at Whitsunday. Continuing his letter on the 8th, he says that she went (apparently) on the 7th and gave up the house, he went in the afternoon and secured it. On 17 Mar. he met "Miss G_____ and gave money for house, etc. Had laboured hard all winter, but now passion made you at once give up the fruits of your labour which you had carefully collected." Writing to Temple on 30 Mar., in the mistaken belief that all was over between him and Mrs. Dodds, he said that he should have a house and a servant-maid upon his hands. My guess is that the house he finally took was not that in Borthwick's Close but the one of unspecified location which Mrs. Dodds had engaged; and that she probably did live there from the end of June 1767 to at least Whitsunday 1768.

"I took her in my arms."]   To W. J. Temple, 1 Feb.–8 Mar. 1767 (this part written 8 Mar.).

The bachelor dinner and its sequel]   Ibid.

p. 320.

Surgeon, physician]   Peter Adie, surgeon in Edinburgh, on 17 Mar. 1767 (and possibly earlier; the Notes for 6–10 and part of 11 Mar. are missing); Dr. Daniel Johnston of Cumnock on 28 Mar. 1767 and at least three times later (Notes of those dates).

p. 321.

Parting with Mrs. Dodds]   Notes, 16 Mar. 1767.

Boswell takes advice]   Notes, 14 Mar. 1767 (Johnston); 16, 18 Mar. 1767 (Lady Betty Macfarlane and Andrew Erskine); 16 Mar. 1767 (Monboddo); 18 Mar. 1767 (Hailes, Blair, David); To W. J. Temple, 30 Mar. 1767 (Johnston, David).

p. 322.

Letter to Mrs. Dodds, arrival at Auchinleck]   Notes, 20–22 Mar. 1767; To W. J. Temple, 30 Mar. 1767.

Miss Blair]   Notes, 1 Mar. 1767. Boswell states her age ("just eighteen") in To W. J. Temple, 30 Mar. 1767.

Boswell likes Miss Blair more and more]   Notes, 11 Mar. 1767.

Thoughts of marrying Miss Blair]   To W. J. Temple, 30 Mar. 1767.

CHAPTER XIX

p. 323.
"I wished I could write," etc.]   Journ. 17, 18 Dec. 1784.

Boswell writes the Introduction to *Corsica*]   Notes, 23, 29 Mar. 1767; To W. J. Temple, 30 Mar. 1767.

Brown, law papers]   Notes, 28, 30, 31 Mar., 1, 3, 14, 17 Apr. 1767.

Clients]   E.g. Notes, 14, 23, 28 Apr. 1767.

Memorials in the Douglas Cause]   Notes, 31 Mar., 21, 22 Apr. 1767.

Dorando]   Notes, 14, 15, 18 Apr. 1767; *Lit. Car.* pp. 27–38, 315–316; From Robert Foulis, 24 Apr., 8 May, 29 June 1767; From William Drummond, 1 June 1767; passages quoted, pp. 39, 40, 41–43, 49 of *Dorando,* 1st ed. (pp. 35, 36–38, 43 of the reprint of 1930).

p. 325.
Dalblair]   Notes, 16, 17 Apr., 5 May 1767.

Letters about Dalblair]   To Sir Alexander Dick, 16 Apr. 1767; To Robert Dundas (Lord President), 18 Apr. 1767. Dundas's letter was dated 10 Apr. 1767.

Boswell borrows the entire purchase price of Dalblair]   Journ. 17 Nov. 1775.

p. 326.
"Black boy," "Edward the Black Prince"]   Notes, 27 Apr. 1767; To W. J. Temple, 29 Aug. 1767.

Lord Auchinleck presided]   Lords Auchinleck and Kames were appointed for the Southern Circuit (*Scots Mag.* 29 [1767].324), but Kames sat alone at Jedburgh, and Auchinleck sat alone at Dumfries and Ayr (S.R.O. Court of Justiciary Records, South Circuit Minute Book No. 12, under 13, 16, 18, 21, 22, 23, 25, 26 May 1767).

Misgivings over Jean Heron]   Notes, 12, 13, 14, 16 May 1767.

"The Douglas Cause"]   Notes, 20 May 1767; *Lit. Car.* pp. 25 (full text), 27.

p. 327.
"Scots Song"]   To John Johnston, 28 May 1767. I have noted no publication, but did not know that Boswell had composed such a song when I searched the Scots newspapers many years ago. No other manuscript text has been reported.

p. 328.
Virginia Woolf]   "The Antiquary," *New Republic,* 41 (3 Dec. 1924). 43.

Meal rioters]   Notes, 4, 21, 22, 23 May 1767; Yale MSS. Lg8 (eight documents, including Boswell's notes for his pleadings); Lg9 (five documents); S.R.O. Court of Justiciary Records, South Circuit Minute Book No. 12, under 22, 23 May 1767. Boswell won acquittals for all four of the Stewarton rioters who stood trial and for two of the Galloway rioters; two of the Galloway rioters were sentenced to 21 days' imprisonment in the tolbooth of Ayr, and three accused who failed to appear for trial were outlawed. William Nairne, Advocate-Depute, conducted both prosecutions. Boswell received six guineas as fee for the Galloway group (Notes, 21 May 1767; Consultation Book). He records no fee for the Stewarton group and may have furnished his services gratis. The men had been recommended to him by his cousin's husband, Capt. Alexander Montgomerie-Cuninghame (From Alexander Montgomerie-Cuninghame, 11 May 1767). See also From William Brown, 18 May 1767; Rev. James Maitland to Lord Auchinleck with enclosure for Boswell, 18 May 1767. From Brown's letter it appears that Boswell had advised the Stewarton rioters to abscond.

Kilmarnock necromancing Irishwoman] Notes, 23, 25 May 1767; S.R.O. Justiciary Records, South Circuit Appeal Book, 25 May 1767. Claud Boswell appeared for the Procurator-Fiscal. Lord Auchinleck reversed the sentence of the magistrates so far as it affected Nelly Barcly's family, and remitted the cause of Nelly herself to the magistrates with recommendation that if the Procurator-Fiscal insisted on a new trial, both parties were to have a proper opportunity of bringing proofs. Boswell records no fee.

p. 329.
Hay and McClure, William Harris] Scots Mag. 29 (1767). 222; S.R.O. Ayr Burgh Records, Register of Incarcerations and Arrestments, 25 Mar. 1767; From James Montgomery, 4 June 1767; From David McClure (brother of the accused), 13 June 1767; Consultation Book, Spring 1767, 2 July 1767; Johnston Corresp. p. 261 n. 7 (Harris); Scots Mag. 42 (1780). 553–554; William Roughead, Glengarry's Way, 1922, p. 70 ("Locusta in Scotland").

Boswell's visit to Adamton] Notes, 21 May 1767.

Miss Blair visits Auchinleck] Notes, 29 May–1 June 1767.

"The lady in my neighbourhood"] To W. J. Temple, 12 June 1767.

p. 330.
Arrangements for Temple's visit] To W. J. Temple, 22, 26 June 1767 (the latter quoted); From W. J. Temple, 17, 24, 27 June 1767.

Publication of Dorando] Lit. Car. pp. 34–37.

p. 331.
Isabel Walker] To W. J. Temple, 22 June 1767; Douglas Cause, pp. 19–20.

p. 332.
Puffs of Dorando] Caledonian Mercury, 17, 20 June 1767; Lond. Chron. 30 June–2 July 1767.

Prosecution of the newspapers] Arnot, pp. 449–450; Scots Mag. 29 (1767). 337–344, 411–412; Lond. Chron. 1–3 Sept., 13–15 Oct. 1767.

"I see," says "A"] Scots Mag. 29 (App. 1767). 697. "A" may well have been Hugo Arnot; compare what he says with Arnot's remarks, op. cit.

Threatening letters, etc.] *Scots Mag.* 29 (1767). 387–389; Arnot, p. 449; *Douglas Cause,* pp. 20, 184.

p. 333.
Decision of the Court of Session] *Scots Mag.* 29 (1767). 387 (the interlocutor was signed on 15 July).

Defence of the publishers] *Scots Mag.* 29 (1767). 337–338, 341–344.
"As to the ... letter from Berwick"] *Memorial for John Donaldson, one of the Publishers of the Edinburgh Advertiser,* 13 July 1767, pp. 4–5. The passage quoted appears also in *Scots Mag.* 29. 341–342. Andrew Crosbie, who was one of the counsel for the Duke of Hamilton, wrote a very fine memorial for *The Caledonian Mercury,* of which *Scots Mag.* prints a generous extract (29. 342–344).

p. 334.
Boswell's report of the proceedings] *Edinburgh Advertiser,* 28 July 1767 (reprinted *Lond. Chron.* 1–3 Sept. 1767).

"Tribunus," "Jacob Giles"] *Lond. Chron.* 1–3 Sept., 13–15 Oct. 1767.

p. 335.
"Well, I never was happier"] To W. J. Temple, 22 June 1767.

"I would not cloud," etc.] To W. J. Temple, 26 June 1767.

"You are a stranger"] Ibid.

"WEDNESDAY. ... Breakfast at eight," etc.] *Letters of James Boswell addressed to ... W. J. Temple,* 1857, pp. 98–99. The manuscripts printed by the anonymous editor of this work (Sir Philip Francis) are now in the Pierpont Morgan Library, but the sheet of instructions here quoted is not among them, and has not been reported elsewhere.

p. 336.
Mrs. Dodds and Boswell reunited] To W. J. Temple, 22 June, 29 July, 29 Aug. 1767. "My late Circe" is from To W. J. Temple, 12 June 1767.

"O Temple, what an escape!"] To W. J. Temple, 11 Aug. 1767.

Mrs. Dodds shares his misfortune] To W. J. Temple, 8 Nov. 1767.

Mrs. Dodds visits him, keeps him reasonable] To W. J. Temple, 29 Aug. 1767.

p. 337.
"Here ev'ry flower is united"] To W. J. Temple, 29 July 1767.

Temple's report of a "formal Nabob"] To W. J. Temple, 29 July, 11 Aug. 1767.

Solicits a renewal of correspondence with Belle de Zuylen] From Robert Brown, 22 Oct. 1767.

A cold and a fever] To W. J. Temple, 11 Aug. 1767.

Did not get away till 13 Oct.] To John Johnston, 9 Oct. 1767.

Edward and Charles Dilly]   From Edward Dilly, 28 July, 1, 4, 10, 15, 31 Aug. 1767; To Edward Dilly, 6 Aug. 1767. A full and interesting account of the firm will be found in Professor S. H. Bingham's unpublished Yale dissertation, *Publishing in the Eighteenth Century, with Special Reference to the Firm of Edward and Charles Dilly,* 1937. Boswell proved to be the Dillys' prime author. Others in their list included William Lisle Bowles, Hester Chapone, Richard Cumberland, Robert Lovell, Elizabeth Montagu, Thomas Nugent, Samuel Parr, John Pinkerton, Clara Reeve, Samuel Rogers, John Scott, and Robert Southey. The firm was founded in late 1754 or early 1755 when Edward Dilly succeeded to the business of one John Oswald, at the Rose and Crown in the Poultry, and it came to an end with the retirement of Charles Dilly in 1800.

p. 338.
"Of all history," etc.]   *Lond. Chron.* 25–27 Aug. 1767.

"I saw a letter," etc.]   From Edward Dilly, 31 Aug. 1767.

Corsica printed by R. and A. Foulis]   To Robert Foulis, middle of Aug. 1767 (two communications); From Robert Foulis, 21 Aug., 30 Dec. 1767, 2 Mar. 1768; From James Brown, 21 Aug. 1767; From Edward Dilly, 10, 15, 31 Aug., 10, 24 Sept., 10 Nov. 1767. At Boswell's request Dilly somewhat reluctantly allowed the Foulis name and a Glasgow imprint to appear on the title-page.

Proofs arriving by 2 Sept.]   To Sir Alexander Dick of that date; To W. J. Temple, 9 Sept. 1767.

p. 339.
The advisers on *Corsica*]   *Corsica,* pp. xx–xxi; To Sir Alexander Dick, 15 Aug. 1767; From Sir Alexander Dick, c. end of Aug. 1767; From Lord Hailes, 30 Sept. 1767 (see also To W. J. Temple, 22 June 1767); From W. J. Temple, 19 Oct. 1767; To W. J. Temple, 25 Aug., 9 Sept., 2 Oct., 5 Nov., 18 Dec. 1767; From Christopher Wyvill, 3 Oct. 1767.

Letters of Lady Jane Douglas]   *Lit. Car.* pp. 45–50; the quotations from pp. 63, 80, 48 (pp. 212, 218, 207 of *Douglas Cause*). From Edward Dilly, 31 Aug., 10 Sept. 1767, greatly strengthen the case for attributing this compilation to Boswell. Dilly hesitates to put his name to the "Douglasiana" of which Boswell has sent a specimen, but says if Boswell will send the whole, he will make the best bargain he can with some other bookseller.

Colonel Steuart confined within the Rules of King's Bench, leaves letters in a portmanteau and a cloak-bag]   *Memorial* (by Ilay Campbell) *for Archibald Douglas of Douglas,* 1766, pp. 13, 300.

Thomas Carlyle]   To Dr. John Carlyle, 19 Nov. 1860 (*New Letters of Thomas Carlyle,* ed. A. Carlyle, 1904, ii. 209).

p. 340.
Advance publicity for the *Letters*]   *Lond. Chron.* 30 June–2 July 1767 (a

letter signed "Probus" containing Lady Jane Douglas's letter to Henry Pelham, 15 May 1750, afterwards included in the *Letters*).

Copy well in hand by the end of August] His "specimen of Douglasiana" was sent to Edward Dilly on 20 Aug. 1767 (From Edward Dilly, 31 Aug. 1767).

The Essence of the Douglas Cause] *Lit. Car.* pp. 38–44.
"With a labour of which few are capable," etc.] *Memoirs,* p. 325 (xxxv).

p. 341.
Boswell and David start for Auchinleck; the message of the Duchess of Douglas] To John Johnston, 9 Oct. 1767.

The ceremony of investiture for David Boswell] Yale MS. M22, 19 Oct. 1767. The ages of James Bruce's sons have been furnished by Mrs. Laura Douglas Pfitzner of Upway, Victoria, Australia, a descendant of the eldest son.

p. 342.
Lord Auchinleck tells Mrs. Montgomerie-Cuninghame of Boswell's illness] "My father has great confidence in Mrs. Cuninghame and lets her into all his secrets. She often speaks to him about the strange way he lives in, and of the bad way he treats his children. . . . I sat with her yesterday morning half an hour and had much conversation about our family. My father had mentioned your illness to her and exclaimed against it, and do you know that she excused you by telling him that what occasioned it was now become quite common" (From David Boswell, 30 Oct. 1767).

Boswell's report on the siege of Capraia] *Lond. Chron.* 14–16 Apr. 1767.

Primus Mantuae] To W. J. Temple, 9 Sept. 1767.

CHAPTER XX

p. 343.
Plan since Aug. to go to Adamton] To W. J. Temple, 28 Aug., 9 Sept. 1767.

Letters to and from Miss Blair] Known only by his reports to Temple, 29 July, 11, 25, 28 Aug., 9, 22 Sept., 2 Oct., 5 Nov. 1767. "A strange, sultanic letter" is quoted from the last mentioned.

"I have been here one night"] Ibid.

p. 344.
Miss Blair will not own herself in the wrong, Boswell renounces her, revives Zélide] To W. J. Temple, 8 Nov. 1767.

Changes his mind next day] To W. J. Temple, 9 Nov. 1767.

p. 346.
Edinburgh obtains a patent theatre, David Ross patentee] Dibdin, pp. 140–148, 493; *Memoirs,* p. 326 (xxxvi–xxxvii). David Ross is accorded an article in DNB; his nephew was Hugh Ross of Kerse, whom Boswell calls "a young gentleman with a handsome fortune in our county" (Journ. 4 Oct. 1776; 12 Aug. 1783).

Lord Mansfield]   Journ. 20 May 1768; *Memoirs,* p. 326 (xxxvi).

Miss Blair's verbal message, assures Boswell that any quarrel between them was his own fault]   To W. J. Temple, 18 Dec. 1767.

Boswell accompanies Miss Blair to *Othello*]   To W. J. Temple, 24 Dec. 1767.

The female cousin]   Ibid.

p. 348.

Civil causes]   Advocates in Boswell's time were fee'd for the separate services they performed in an action. Boswell's Consultation Book from Nov. 1766 to Dec. 1767 records 140 "consultations" (191 guineas) in 99 civil causes. If the record were extended to include the whole Winter Session of 1767–1768, the number of causes would run considerably over one hundred.

Intense cold]   Journ. 2, 6 Jan. 1768; From the Duke of Queensberry, 5 Jan. 1768.

Political causes]   Journ. 1, 2, 9, 15, 18 Jan. 1768; *Scots Mag.* 30 (March 1768). 163–164.

Recurrence of Lord Auchinleck's complaint]   Journ. 2 Jan. 1768.

Mrs. Dodds]   To W. J. Temple, 24 Dec. 1767; Journ. 5, 10 Jan. 1768.

Belle de Zuylen]   Journ. 10 Jan. 1767; To W. J. Temple, 8 Feb. 1768; From Belle de Zuylen, 16 Feb. 1768.

p. 349.

Lord Eglinton]   Journ. 16 Jan. 1768.

He writes to the Heiress]   Journ. 22 Jan. 1768.

Street girl]   Journ. 16 Jan. 1768.

Lord Auchinleck out of humour, consultation about Raybould]   Journ. 17 Jan. 1768.

Raybould's trial]   Journ. 18 Jan. 1768; John Maclaurin (Lord Dreghorn), *Arguments and Decisions in Remarkable Cases before the High Court of Justiciary and other Supreme Courts in Scotland,* 1774, pp. 467–473.

Annual meeting of the Faculty of Advocates]   Journ. 19 Jan. 1768.

p. 350.

Boswell renews gallantry with Mrs. Dodds]   Journ. 31 Jan., 2, 5, 7, 13 Feb. 1768.

Boswell, the Nabob, and the Heiress]   Journ. 7, 8 Feb. 1768; To W. J. Temple, 8 Feb. 1768.

p. 351.

The last of Mrs. Dodds]   Journ. 13 Feb. 1768; To John Johnston, 31 Mar. 1769; To Alexander Hamilton, 31 Mar. 1769; Journ. 23 June 1769.

p. 352.

Temple consistently unsympathetic to Mrs. Dodds, Boswell states his obligations] From W. J. Temple, 7 Aug., 22 Nov. 1767; 1 Mar. 1768 ("that vulgar creature"); To W. J. Temple, 29 Aug., 24 Dec. 1767.

Peggy Doig "well taken care of"] Journ. 28 July 1763.

"The finest little girl"] To W. J. Temple, 24 Dec. 1767.

Plans for Charles] To John Johnston, 30 July 1763.

p. 353.
"Bonny wark, Colonel"] From Lord Marischal, 12 Sept. 1767.

Boswell's views as to illegitimate daughters] Journ. 22 Mar. 1776; 24 Dec. 1793.

Lord Auchinleck pays Boswell's debts] Journ. 18 Oct. 1776; see also Journ. 17 Nov. 1775. Boswell had borrowed the full purchase price of Dalblair, but had paid only part of the money over to the creditors. The money left in his hands he had treated as though it were free capital.

p. 354.
Boswell informed that *Corsica* was ready for publication] Journ. 15 Feb. 1768.

Corsica published] Journ. 18 Feb. 1768.

p. 355.
Boswell dreams of Raybould, visits him] Journ. 21 Feb. 1768. Boswell does not mention the shackle and the "gad," but all prisoners under sentence of death were so secured. See Journ. 30 Aug. 1774 and Scott's *Guy Mannering*, last chapter but one.

Raybould's execution] Journ. 24 Feb. 1768.

p. 356.
Belle de Zuylen] From Belle de Zuylen, 16 Feb. 1768, in French, except for a passage quoted from Boswell's last letter. The day of receipt is fixed by Boswell's reply ("I had yesterday," etc.).

Boswell replied] To Belle de Zuylen, 26 Feb. 1768.

"Noble" letters from Walpole, Lyttelton, Mrs. Macaulay, Garrick] To W. J. Temple, 24 Mar. 1768.

Corsica] *Lit. Car.* pp. 50–76. The uncompleted Russian translation is reported in From William Porter, 1 Aug. 1770; 20 June 1774. Boswell met Porter in London in 1769 (Mem. 11 Oct.). For the circulation of *Corsica* in America, see G. P. Anderson, "Pascal Paoli, an Inspiration to the Sons of Liberty," *Publications* of the Colonial Society of Massachusetts, 26 (1924–1926, pub. 1927). 188.

p. 357.
The reviews of *Corsica*] Full references are given in *Lit. Car.* p. 310.

The Gentleman's Magazine] To be quite precise, I should have said "more space than any other work of literary content." The longest review (eight full pages) was accorded to *The Trial of the Right Hon. Lord Baltimore for a Rape on the Body of Sarah Woodcock.* But *Corsica* was given more space than Hugh Kelly's *False Delicacy* and Oliver Goldsmith's *The Good Natur'd Man* (a combined review) or Samuel Sharp's reply to Baretti's *Account of the Manners and Customs of Italy.*

Guthrie and Griffiths] Griffiths's authorship of the review in the *Monthly* is established by B. C. Nangle, *The Monthly Review, First Series,* 1934, p. 65; Guthrie's by Boswell himself (Journ. 25 Mar. 1768).

The *Critical* and the *Monthly*] They both also agreed in giving more space to Vol. I of Clarendon's *State Papers.* With reference merely to wordage, the *Critical* rated *Corsica* below Horace Walpole's *Historic Doubts* but above Gray's *Poems* and Sterne's *Sentimental Journey.* The *Monthly* gave less space to *Corsica* than to Baretti's *Account of the Manners and Customs of Italy,* and to Sterne, but more than to Walpole.

One monthly magazine] *The Universal Magazine,* 42 (Feb.). 92–100, (Apr.). 169–174, (May 1768). 258–264; 43 (Aug. 1768). 57–63.

"We hope . . . that our author"] *Monthly Rev.* 1st ser. 39 (Aug. 1768). 150–151.

p. 358.
Deyverdun and Gibbon] In *Mémoires littéraires de la Grande Bretagne pour l'an 1768,* 1769, p. 139 (in French). Gibbon and Deyverdun wrote the *Mémoires* together and did not sign their respective articles. V. P. Helming, PMLA, 47 (1932). 1044–1046, attributes this review to Deyverdun; D. M. Low (*Edward Gibbon,* 1937, p. 204) feels sure that Gibbon had a hand in it. I know little about Deyverdun's writings, but the style of this review strikes me as being very much like that of the author of "The Pill-Pedlar" (above, p. 298).

p. 359.
Professor Lounsbury] T. R. Lounsbury, *English Spelling and Spelling Reform,* 1909, p. 219. He remarks that the *k,* of which Boswell wished to make so much "as a mark of Saxon original," does not occur at all in the "Saxon" (i.e. Old English) alphabet. As a matter of fact, the majority of the words to which Boswell wished to restore the *k* (publick, physick, musick) were ultimately of Greek or Latin origin.

As some one has well remarked] I wish some one would locate this for me. My recollection is that I came on it some forty years ago in one of the volumes of the Shakespeare Variorum edited by H. H. Furness, Senior, and that he attributed it to a German scholar.

p. 360.
"Their morals are strict," etc.] *Corsica,* p. 243.

Boswell denied the charge of adultery] To W. J. Temple, 1 Feb.–8 Mar., 30 Mar. 1767.

John Wilkes] See below, p. 565.

p. 361.

Sir George Otto Trevelyan]　*The Early History of Charles James Fox,* London, 1880, p. 153.

Two recent French books]　*Histoire de l'isle de Corse,* par M. G. D. C., Nancy, 1749 ("M. G. D. C." is usually identified as Jean François Goury de Champgrand, French Commissary of War, who served in Corsica in the years 1739–1741), and *Mémoires historiques, militaires et politiques,* Lausanne, 1758–1759, by Louis Armand Jaussin, medical officer in the French forces in Corsica, 1738–1741. Professor Foladare traces Boswell's borrowings in detail.

"What the Corsicans wished to believe"]　Foladare, pp. 150–151.

Guthrie]　*Critical Review* 25 (Mar. 1768). 178.

Johnson]　From Samuel Johnson, 9 Sept. 1769 (*Life,* ii. 70).

p. 362.
"The last part of my work," etc.]　To W. J. Temple, 9 Sept. 1767.

"After supper therefore"]　*Corsica,* p. 310.

John Wesley]　*Journal,* ed. N. Curnock, 1910–1916, v. 292–293.

p. 363.
Pitt]　Pitt was applying to Paoli, with full credit to the original author of the phrase, an encomium of the Cardinal de Retz on the Duke of Montrose (*Oeuvres,* ed. Alphonse Feillet, Jules Gourdault, and F. R. Chantelauze, 1870–1896, iii. 37). Though Boswell's notes do not record it, Pitt must have made the remark in the conversation of 22 Feb. 1766. Boswell quoted it in To Sir Alexander Dick, 23 Oct. 1766.

Paoli's occasional pungent wit]　Journ. 7 May 1781, supplementary leaf; Yale MS. M6 (BP, vii. 243, 245).

p. 364.
Edward Burnaby Greene]　*Corsica, an Ode,* 1768, 10th strophe. See *Lit. Car.* pp. xxxiv and 245 (31 Oct.). The poem is advertised in *Pub. Advt.* 21 Nov. 1768, as "by the Author of *Juvenal's Satires Imitated,*" which Greene acknowledged by signing his initials to the preface of the 2d edition, 1764. Boswell has written "By Edward Burnaby Greene" on the title-page of a copy of this edition, now at Yale. "O'erflowed with gall when Scotland is my theme" is the concluding line of Greene's paraphrase of Juvenal's Third Satire. Boswell recorded meeting Greene on 25 Sept. 1769 (Journ.).

Capel Lofft]　*The Praises of Poetry,* 1775, p. 6. Boswell later became a fairly intimate acquaintance of Lofft's, a barrister who lived to 1824 and achieved unfavourable mention in Byron's *English Bards and Scotch Reviewers.* See the Index to BP.

Anna Letitia Aikin]　"Corsica," in *Poems,* 1773, pp. 2–3.

Robert Colvill] *The Cyrnean Hero,* 2d ed. 1772, pp. 10–12. Colvill, son of a macer of the Court of Session, had been with Boswell in Mundell's School (To Sir Alexander Dick, 1 Sept. 1767).

p. 365.
Mme. du Deffand] To Horace Walpole, 15 July 1768 (in French).

James Burgh] *Lond. Chron.* 12–15 Mar. 1768, article signed "Philopaulus." Boswell identifies Philopaulus as Burgh, Journ., fragment following 30 Mar. 1768.

General Oglethorpe] *Life,* 10 Apr. 1775, n.

"Nice and romantic and bold"] See above, p. 97.

p. 366.
Deyverdun and Gibbon] *Mémoires littéraires de la Grande Bretagne,* 1769, p. 148.

Thomas Gray] To Horace Walpole, 25 Feb. 1768. I do not quote the equally well-known letter of Walpole to which this is a reply ("The author, Boswell, is a strange being, and . . . has a rage of knowing anybody that ever was talked of") because its tone of contempt seems to be directed more at Boswell the man than at Boswell the author. Gray had not met Boswell personally.

Gray's theory rebutted] I find on review that I have only repeated what Sir George Otto Trevelyan said more effectively in *The Early History of Charles James Fox,* London, 1880, p. 154 n. 1.

p. 367.
Sir John Hawkins] To W. J. Temple, 5 Mar. 1789.

"It is amazing," etc.] Journ. 31 Aug. 1769.

p. 368.
"I said to General Paoli"] *Boswelliana,* p. 328.

CHAPTER XXI

p. 369.
Conscious of a superior character] Journ. 21 Mar. 1768.

Two hundred pounds in a year] Journ. 26 Mar. 1768.

Coming heralded, etc.] *Pub. Advt.* 29 Feb. 1768; *Lond. Chron.* 27 Feb.–1 Mar., 22–24 Mar. 1768.

Mode of travelling] Journ. 16–22 Mar. 1768.

Sir George Armytage] Journ. 20 Mar. 1768.

Circumstantial metaphors] Ibid.

p. 370.
Mary] Journ. 16, 17, 20, 22 Mar. 1768; To John Johnston, 10 June 1768.

"A roaring lion"] Journ. 22 Mar. 1768.

Ceremony of investiture for John Dick] Journ. 22 Mar. 1768; To Sir Alexander Dick, 16 Apr. 1768. The account of the alleged dormant baronetcy is based on *Comp. Baronet*. ii. 448–450 and Boswell's extensive correspondence with John Dick and Sir Alexander Dick, 1766–1768, *passim*.

p. 371.
Execution of Payne and Gibson] Journ. 23 Mar. 1768; *The Hypochondriack*, No. 68; *Gent. Mag.* 38 (Mar. 1768). 140.

"Mortalis"] *Pub. Advt.* 26 Apr. 1768. More readily accessible in *Hypochondriack* No. 68, which reprints it entire.

p. 372.
Boswell meets his publishers] Journ. 23 Mar. 1768; 15 Mar. 1776; DNB; S. H. Bingham, as above, p. 541, note on the Dillys. Boswell seems first to have met John Dilly in 1773 (Journ. 7 May).

p. 373.
Wilkes] DNB; Bleackley, pp. 172–187; Almon, ii. 171–235; iii. 171–268.

Boswell taken for Wilkes] Journ. 26 Mar. 1768, recounting events of the 25th.

p. 374.
Sir John Pringle, Belle de Zuylen] Journ. 24 Mar. 1768; To W. J. Temple, 24 Mar. 1768.

Boswell still balancing Miss Bosville with Belle] Journ. 22 Mar. 1768.

Learns that Miss Bosville is engaged] Journ. 25 Mar. 1768.

Guthrie] Ibid.

p. 375.
"You have no materials," etc.] From Samuel Johnson, 21 Aug. 1766.

Boswell hears that Johnson is displeased] Journ. 26 Mar. 1768.

With Johnson at Oxford] Journ. 26, 27, 28 Mar. 1768. I give some of the "memorable dicta" in the form in which they appear in the corresponding portion of the *Life*.

p. 376.
The Middlesex election] Bleackley, pp. 189–192; *Gent. Mag.* 38 (Mar. 1768). 140.

"A neat little lass"] Journ. 22 Mar. 1768.

"Home—Sallied," etc.] Notes, 29 Mar. 1768.

p. 377.
Decamping] Journ. 30 Mar. 1768.

"Dined Great Piazza," etc.] Notes, 30 Mar. 1768.

"He came to me," etc.] Journ., undatable fragment between 30 Mar. and 20 Apr. 1768.

p. 378.
Baretti]   DNB; From Joseph Baretti, 4 Mar. 1768; Journ. 28, 30 Mar. 1768.

Mrs. Macaulay, Sir John Fielding, dinner at Dilly's]   Journ., undatable fragments between 30 Mar. and 20 Apr. 1768.

"Empty my head of Corsica?"]   To Samuel Johnson, 26 Apr. 1768, answering
Johnson's of 23 Mar. 1768.

p. 379.
Developments in Corsica]   Foladare, pp. 153–156.

Organization of the Corsican Club]   Lond. Chron. 2–5 Apr. 1768 (notice of
the meeting), 5–7 Apr. 1768. Paoli's birthday seems actually to have been 5 April
(Ravenna, p. 26 n. 1).

Corsican "facts" and "inventions"]   Lond. Chron. 16–19, 19–21 Apr. 1768
(Frederick the Great); 26–28 Apr. (Dutch and Corsicans); 30 June–2 July 1768
(ships being fitted out by the Genoese).

p. 380.
Serious anonymous essays]   Discussed in Chapter XXII.

Boswell's raging catches up with him]   To W. J. Temple, 16 Apr. 1768
(reporting that he has been ill for ten days).

Mr. Forbes]   To W. J. Temple, 26 Apr. 1768.

Percivall Pott]   Notes, 12 May 1768; DNB.

Mr. Russell's]   Journ. 22 Mar. 1768.

Lord Lyttelton]   From Lord Lyttelton, 21 Feb. 1768; Notes, 21 Apr., 3 May
1768; To Lord Hardwicke, 27 Apr. 1768.

p. 381.
Callers who came to consult about the Corsican campaign]   E.g. (besides
Lyttelton) Oglethorpe (Notes, 28 Apr., 3 May 1768), Sir John Dick (Notes, 28
Apr.–16 May 1768, passim), Edward Dilly (Notes, 24 Apr., 8, 15 May 1768).

Calls from distinguished men of letters]   Armstrong (To Sir Alexander Dick,
18 Apr. 1768); Garrick (To W. J. Temple, 14 May 1768); Baretti (Notes, 15 May
1768); Pringle (Notes, 30 Apr., 4, 14 May 1768); Franklin (Notes, 14 May 1768);
Hume (Notes, 2, 7 May 1768); Johnson (Notes, 2 May 1768). Boswell's other
callers of DNB status were Walter Anderson (d. 1800), William Bosville (1745–
1813), James Burgh (1714–1775), Charles Dilly (1739–1807), Edward Dilly
(1732–1779), Sir William Forbes (1739–1806), William Guthrie (1708–1770),
Archibald Macdonald (1747–1826), Percivall Pott (1714–1788), William Rose
(1719–1786), George Lewis Scott (1708–1780), Robert Strange (1721–1792),
George Willison (1741–1797), and Christopher Wyvill (1740–1822). At least two
others of his callers should have been noticed in the DNB: Alexander Donaldson
(d. 1794) and Archibald Hamilton (d. 1792). See Notes, 21 Apr.–16 May 1768,
passim.

Goldsmith]   He is believed to have spent part of this spring in Derbyshire, and was certainly living in a cottage near Edgeware, eight miles from London, on 7 May (R. M. Wardle, *Oliver Goldsmith,* 1957, pp. 187–188). For Johnson's comment on *The Good Natur'd Man,* see Journ. 26 Mar. 1768.

p. 382.
Tumults of the day]   *Gent. Mag.* 38 (1768). 92, 138, 197, 222–223, 241, 242–243, 442.

Wilkes]   DNB; Almon, iii. 269–282; Bleackley, pp. 195–203.

France and Corsica]   Foladare, pp. 156–158.

p. 383.
Lord Auchinleck and Temple oppose the Utrecht scheme]   To W. J. Temple, 24 Mar., 16 Apr. 1768; From W. J. Temple, 27 Mar. 1768.

Belle de Zuylen to Constant d'Hermenches]   *Lettres de Belle de Zuylen* (*Madame de Charrière*) *à Constant d'Hermenches, p.p.* Philippe Godet, 1909, pp. 326, 328, 336 (27 Mar., 28 Apr., 30 June 1768), in French. She herself blamed her previous dislike of Plutarch on having tried to read him in Dacier's translation ("le pesant Dacier").

"My dear friend," etc.; another letter to Lord Auchinleck; "How do we know," etc.]   To W. J. Temple, 26 Apr. 1768. Boswell actually wrote "How do we do."

"I have written to her"]   Ibid.

p. 384.
"My dearest friend," etc.]   To W. J. Temple, 14 May 1768; Notes 5 May 1768.

"I will with a good deal of pleasure"]   *Lettres,* as in fourth note back, p. 329, in French.

p. 385.
Boswell reads the Bible and Lord Lyttelton, makes moral reflections]   Notes, 1 May 1768; To W. J. Temple, 26 Apr. 1768.

Temple and Paoli]   To W. J. Temple, 16 Apr. 1768; Notes, 1 May 1768.

"Quite in love," etc.]   Notes, 16 May 1768, very slightly expanded.

Raging again]   To John Johnston, 10 June 1768.

Vow in St. Paul's]   To W. J. Temple, 24 Aug. 1768.

Smart remark about Paoli]   *Lond. Chron.* 28–30 June 1768.

Conversations with Lord Mansfield]   Notes, 20, 22 May 1768.

Dinner with Johnson]   *Life,* following 28 May 1768. Thomas Percy's journal, now in the British Museum, shows the date to have been 7 June.

p. 386.
Wrong on both counts]   Above, p. 390; To Lord Mansfield, 14 Feb. 1783

("I have been informed that I gave you offence several years ago by speaking too favourably in your presence of the gay and classical John Wilkes").

9 June, 13 June]   To John Johnston, 10 June 1768.

"She and I will always be good correspondents"]   To W. J. Temple, 14 May 1768.

Finis to Belle de Zuylen]   Godet, i. 149 to end; Geoffrey Scott, *The Portrait of Zélide,* 1925, pp. 48 to end; Gustave Rudler, *La Jeunesse de Benjamin Constant,* 1909, pp. 153–154.

p. 387.
"Her ... emotions," etc.]   Geoffrey Scott, BP, ii. 11.

CHAPTER XXII

p. 388.
Gaming]   To W. J. Temple, 24 Aug. 1768. For later returns of the gaming rage, see Notes, 26 Feb. 1772; Journ. 13, 21, 25, 31 Oct., 2, 11–12, 16 Dec. 1775; 9, 24 Feb., 7 Mar., 7, 12 Dec. 1776.

p. 389.
The story of Corsica]   Foladare, pp. 158–165. The quoted bit is Rochford to Shelburne, 2 June 1768 (Shelburne MSS., vol. 40, pt. 2, No. 69), Clements Library, Ann Arbor, Michigan.

p. 390.
"An Englishman"]   Boswell reprinted this proposal, which appeared in *The Public Advertiser* for 1 June 1768, as Essay 5 of *British Essays in Favour of the Brave Corsicans.* His marked copy of the book in the Johnson Birthplace, Lichfield, gives no key to the authorship. Professor Foladare (p. 176 n. 2) suggests Thomas Day.

"O.P."]   This is the style of the Dominican Order (Ordinis Praedicatorum), but it is hard to see why Boswell would have considered the suggestion of Catholic authorship useful to his purpose. He received a letter from one of his Dominican friends in Rome this summer, but not until after he had printed the appeal (From Michael Brennan, 31 July 1768). He collected the appeal as Essay 12 of *British Essays.*

Boswell purchases ordnance]   To W. J. Temple, 24 Aug. 1768; To Sir Alexander Dick, 24 Sept. 1768; *Lond. Chron.* 8–10 Dec. 1768; *Scots Mag.* 30 (Dec. 1768). 667; From Charles Gascoigne, 24 Jan. 1769. These accounts do not agree in detail, but Gascoigne's (which contains a formal bill from the Carron Company) would appear to be authoritative. He says that 30 guns, 2917 round shot, 5020 grape shot, and 38 casks (I assume of gunpowder) were sent to Leghorn in the ship *Nancy,* Capt. Hamilton, 3 Sept. 1768. Peter Capper of the Carron Company was in Corsica sometime in the spring of 1769 (Journ. 29 June 1769; To Sir

Alexander Dick, 30 June 1769), and it seems as though he would have told Boswell if his train had *not* reached Paoli, and that Boswell would have recorded his disappointment.

Sir Adam Fergusson]   *Lond. Chron.* 4–6 Feb. 1790.

p. 391.
"I am exceedingly lucky"]   To W. J. Temple, 24 Aug. 1768; To John Johnston, 21 Sept. 1768.

"Figure to yourself, Temple"]   To W. J. Temple, 24 Aug. 1768.

"This is the most agreeable passion"]   Ibid.

"I mean not to ask what you think"]   Ibid.

"No reserved, prudent, cautious conduct"]   Ibid.

p. 392.
A talk with the Heiress]   To John Johnston, 21 Sept. 1768; To Sir Alexander Dick, 24 Sept. 1768; To W. J. Temple, 9 Dec. 1768. He met Mary Anne c. 17 Aug. (To W. J. Temple, 24 Aug. 1768), and on 21 Sept. (To John Johnston of that date) spoke of his visit to Adamton as having occurred "some time ago." The circuit court sat at Ayr on 16, 17, 21 Sept. 1768 (S.R.O. Court of Justiciary Records, South Circuit Minute Book).

The circuits "riotous"]   To John Johnston, 21 Sept. 1768. The riotous behaviour of counsel at Ayr is perhaps partially explained by the fact that there was no business before the court (ibid.; *Scots Mag.* 30 [1768]. 498).

Defence of Harris]   From William Harris, 27 Aug. 1768; William Harris to James Marshall, 10 Nov. 1768; From James Neill, 30 Aug. 1768 (two letters); John Davidson to William Harris, 24 Oct. 1768; Papers in the case of William Harris, Yale MS. Lg16:1, 2, 3, 4, dates of 25 Aug. and 10 Nov. 1768.

Appeal to Dundas]   From Henry Dundas, 30 Sept. 1768.

p. 393.
Mrs. Blair]   From W. J. Temple, 8 Jan. 1768 ("the prudence of a wary mother"); To W. J. Temple, 9 Dec. 1768.

The Nabob]   Ibid.

Boswell makes unqualified proposals, is rejected]   Ibid.

End of Miss Blair]   *A & W,* i. 580; *Comp. Baronet.* iv. 311 (her father's name was David, not Adam).

p. 394.
Girolama Piccolomini]   From Girolama Piccolomini, 20 Mar., 3 May, 16 Nov. 1767; To W. J. Temple, 12 June 1767; To Girolama Piccolomini, 5 Nov. 1768; From Robert Richardson, 22 Nov. 1768; From Girolama Piccolomini, ? Dec. 1768. Professor Warnock found the date of Girolama's death (7 Jan. 1792) in the manuscript death-records in the Archivio di Stato, Siena.

The Irish scheme revived]   To W. J. Temple, 9 Dec. 1768.

Sir Horace Mann to Sir John Dick]   One letter quoted in From Sir John Dick, 30 June 1768.

Corsican affairs]   Foladare, pp. 180–189.

p. 395.
"Foolish as we are," etc.]   Lord Holland to George Selwyn, 14 Oct. 1768 (J. H. Jesse, *George Selwyn and his Contemporaries*, 1882, ii. 333).

British Essays]   *Lit. Car.* pp. 76–84. This account can now be enlarged and corrected by Foladare, pp. 174–178, and the copy with Boswell's own key which I did not know of in 1929. See the second note following this.

Most of them probably culled from newspapers]   *Lit. Car.* indicates newspaper sources (*Pub. Advt.* and *Lond. Chron.*) for Essays 1, 2, 3, 4, 5, 7, 9, 12, 15, 17, 19, 20. Professor Foladare found Essay 7 also in *The Gazetteer and New Daily Advertiser*, and Essay 9 in *The Political Register*, 2 (Feb. 1768). 110–111.
A copy annotated by Boswell]   This is in the Johnson Birthplace, Lichfield. Boswell assigns Essays 1, 6, 12, 15, 17, 19, 20 to himself, 2, 3, 4 to Oglethorpe, 9 to Edward Dilly, and 18 to Sir John Dick. Apparently he had no information as to the authors of 5, 7, 8, 10, 11, 13, 14, 16. In a begging letter at Yale, 22 Sept. 1769, one Joseph Cawthorne claims (I imagine truthfully) that he wrote Essay 18 for Sir John Dick.

p. 396.
Three magazines]   *Lond. Mag.* 37 (1768). 655–657; *Scots Mag.* 30 (1768). 625–626; *The Weekly Mag. or Edinburgh Amusement*, iii (5 Jan. 1769). 13–15. Professor Foladare (p. 190 n.) suggests that Hailes was the "writer of distinguished abilities." Another possibility would be Lyttelton.

Follow-up advertisements]   *Lond. Chron.* 7–10, 14–17, 21–24, 28–31 Jan., 9–11, 13–16, 18–20, 27–30 May, 1–3, 8–10 June 1769.

p. 397.
Corsican subscription in Ireland]   To Sir Alexander Dick, 29 May 1769; *Pub. Advt.* 7 July 1769 (a letter dated "Dublin, June 8," containing a signed appeal which is said to have "appeared in Faulkner's Journal and other public papers").

Portaferry, Newtown]   *Lond. Chron.* 20–23 May, 8–11 July 1769.

Ladies of the first fashion]   *Lond. Chron.* 18–20 Oct. 1768.

Theatrical company at Sunderland]   *Lond. Chron.* 9–11 Feb., 8–10 June 1769.

Benbridge's portrait of Paoli]   From Sir John Dick, 30 June, 12 Aug. 1768; From Isabella Strange, 28 Dec. 1768; 24 Jan. 1769; *Lond. Chron.* 12–14 May 1768; 6–9 May 1769 ("There is just arrived in London a portrait of the illustrious chief Paoli, painted for Mr. Boswell of Auchinleck. Mr. Boswell sent for this purpose to Corsica last summer Mr. Bambridge, a young American artist who had finished his studies in Italy, and amidst all the fatigues and dangers of war his Excellency was pleased to sit to indulge the earnest desire of his ever-zealous friend. . . . It is a whole-length as large as life, the canvas about seven feet by five"); 10–13 June 1769. By 10 June the Society had turned over £105 to the fund (*Lond. Chron.* 8–10 June 1769). John Raphael Smith's mezzotint from the portrait (which is still at Auchinleck) is reproduced in the present volume. There is in the Tinker Collection at Yale (No. 327) a copy of the *Catalogue* of the exhibition of the Free Society of Artists, 1769. Benbridge's painting is No. 258 in the exhibition, and a leaf added at the end reprints with some adaptation Boswell's notice of the picture in *Lond. Chron.* 6–9 May 1769 (quoted above), his signed appeal for a Corsican contribution, *Lond. Chron.* 9–11 May 1769, and a translation of a letter from Paoli, 20 Mar. 1769, to Trecothick and Vaughan, thanking them for their contribution. This also had appeared in *Lond. Chron.* (22–25 Apr. 1769). Dempster paid a shilling admission, but declined to put anything in the box (From George Dempster, 23 May 1769).

Amount paid in probably disappointing] "I am sorry the contribution has not answered your hopes. My small share was not forgot" (From Lord Marischal, 18 Apr. 1769).

Beckford, Trecothick, Vaughan] Reg. Let. 19 June 1769; *Life,* 23 Sept. 1777; *Lond. Chron.* 11–14 Feb., 22–25 Apr., 6–9 May 1769.

Supporters of the Bill of Rights] *Lond. Chron.* 4–6 May 1769.

Devonshire, Percy, Sir Watkin Williams Wynn] *Gent. Mag.* 38 (1768). 523; *Lond. Chron.* 16–18 Feb. 1769.

Decision of the Douglas Cause appeal] *Douglas Cause,* pp. 20–22 (incorporating an account by Horace Walpole), 136–177; Alexander Carlyle, *Autobiography,* 1860, pp. 511–513; *Scots Mag.* 31 (1769). 107–109. Carlyle thought Sandwich's speech "intolerable," but apparently because of its length (three hours) rather than its indecencies.

p. 398.
Ilay Campbell] *Scots Mag.* 31(1769). 109 (without the name); G. W. T. Omond, *The Lord Advocates of Scotland,* 1883, ii. 65; Alexander Carlyle, op. cit., p. 512; *Douglas Cause,* p. 187; Kay, ii (iii). 89.

Rejoicings in Edinburgh] *Lond. Chron.* 11–14 Mar., 18–20 Apr. 1769; *Scotland and Scotsmen,* i. 173; Omond, op. cit., ii. 65–66 (a letter from the Lord Justice-Clerk to Lord Rochford, 3 Mar. 1769); *Douglas Cause,* pp. 186–188 (contemporary newspaper reports); From Lord Marischal, 26 Aug. 1769 ("Most noble Colonel, I am highly delighted with your behaviour in the Douglas Cause. *Finis coronat opus.* You broke, I am told, your father's windows because they were not enough illuminate. Bravo, bravissimo!"). Dempster also seemed not too disapproving: "You have been rioting, you dog you, and have broke thy honest father's windows, as the story here tells. Nobody suspects that you have thereby broke his heart" (From George Dempster, c. 12 Mar. 1769).

p. 399.

Duke of Queensberry]   *Memoirs,* p. 326 (xxxv).

Archibald Douglas grateful]   See above, p. 413; Journ. 7 July 1769.

p. 400.

"B."]   To George Dempster, 23, 24 Feb. 1769; From George Dempster, 1 July 1768; 7, c. 12 Mar., 13 Apr., 23 May, 24 June 1769; *Scots Peer.* iii. 237. The case for identifying "B." as Margaret Crauford, which to be persuasive requires the presentation of a great many small bits of evidence, is reserved for the research edition.

p. 401.

Boswell and his father visit Lainshaw]   To John Johnston, 31 Mar. 1769.

Circumstances surrounding the departure of Boswell and Margaret Montgomerie from Auchinleck]   Journ. 25 Apr. 1769; Lt. John Boswell's diary, 4, 25 Apr. 1769.

p. 402.

Agreed that the Irish scheme shall stand]   Journ. 26, 27 Apr. 1769.

Some talk of love for Mary Anne]   Journ. 26 Apr. 1769.

Really in love with Margaret]   Journ. 29 Apr. 1769.

Margaret Montgomerie's family]   *A & W,* iii. 594–599; *Comp. Peer.* viii. 296 n.(h); *Scots Peer.* v. 556 (correct the last named by the other two).

James Montgomerie]   To Sir David Dalrymple, 22 Mar. 1760; Notes, 15, 18, 21 Feb. 1766; *Gent. Mag.* 36 (1766). 600.

The family of Campbell of Treesbank]   *A & W,* i. 655–657; Burke, *Landed Gentry;* Appendix C, Chart 6, of *Boswell: The Ominous Years.*

Margaret's annuity]   To W. J. Temple, 3 May 1769; To Margaret Montgomerie, 20 July 1769; Journ. 1 Jan. 1777, Boswell's note (BP, 12. 110 n.).

Margaret Montgomerie's age]   Boswell never reports her birthday, and at this time certainly did not know it. He wrote to James Bruce on 3 Aug. 1769 asking him to try to find out from his mother. Bruce replied on 7 Aug.: "My mother never could reckon by years (as is the case of most women) but by incidents. Miss M's birth happened in so far as I could gather in March on a Sunday's evening just that year before your father and mother married. For her mother said she intended her Eupham, but on reflection she said it looked too fond, so would prefer her aunt." (Margaret Boswell, sister of James Boswell of Auchinleck, married in 1702 Hugh Campbell of Barquharrie.) The marriage contract of Alexander Boswell and Euphemia Erskine bears the dates 21 and 27 April 1738, and the marriage occurred shortly afterwards. Bruce, I think, did not really mean "in March of the year preceding the year of your parents' marriage," but "in March of the year in which your parents married, just before their marriage." Old Mrs. Bruce's point was that the impending marriage of Euphemia Erskine to Alexander Boswell caused Veronica Montgomerie to alter her plan of naming her daughter Euphemia. In March 1737 the marriage had not been arranged and may not even have been in contemplation. Margaret Montgomerie was therefore at the very least two years and seven months older than Boswell. If she was really born in March 1737, she was three years and seven months older. Boswell more than once said that she was two years his senior (e.g. To W. J. Temple, 3 May 1769; To George Dempster, 4 May 1769).

Margaret not "what is called a beauty"] To F. C. van Aerssen van Sommelsdyck, 18 Aug. 1769, in French.

"Her eye glistens"] Journ. 4 Feb. 1784.

"I have a kind of strange feeling"] Journ. 4 Jan. 1776.

"Embowelled to posterity"] Journ. 3 Nov. 1775.

"My valuable friend"] E.g. endorsement on From Margaret Montgomerie, 22 July 1769. See illustration in *Boswell in Search of a Wife.*

"My dearest life"] To judge by the surviving specimens, the unvarying salutation of Boswell's letters to Margaret Montgomerie after their marriage. It was, by the way, Lovelace's most common salutation to Clarissa (*Clarissa,* vol. 6, letters 14, 20; vol. 7, letter 28 of the 3d ed. and editions adhering to it [Shakespeare Head ed. vi. 73, 87; vii. 91]).

Her person desirable] To W. J. Temple, 3 May 1769.

"A heathen goddess"] To George Dempster, c. 21 June 1769 (sequel to 4 May 1769).

p. 404.
Margaret Montgomerie hardly mentioned before the spring of 1769] Journ. 7, 16 Jan., 1 Feb. 1768; From Margaret Montgomerie, 22 Apr. 1766; 1 Oct. 1767. Reg. Let. records a letter received from "Mrs. Margaret Montgomerie," 25 Apr. 1766, and one sent to her 4 May 1766.

A jocular agreement] Yale MS. M20.

On at least four occasions] *Memoirs,* p. 404 (xxxvii–xxxviii); To W. J. Temple, 3 May 1769; To George Dempster, 4 May 1769; To Margaret Montgomerie, 21 Aug. 1769.

p. 406.
Boswell drinks to DOUGLAS at Corsehill] Journ. 27 Apr. 1769.

The journey and visit to Donaghadee] Journ. 28 Apr.–5 May 1769.

Letters that make the situation clear] To W. J. Temple, 3 May 1769; To George Dempster, 4 May 1769.

p. 407.
Boswell in a passion, Margaret affected] To Margaret Montgomerie, 21 Aug. 1769.

He shows Margaret the letter to Temple] Journ. 5 May 1769.

"I was received," etc.] To George Dempster, c. 21 June 1769 (sequel to 4 May 1769).

p. 408.
"Dublin is really a noble city"]   To Sir Alexander Dick, 29 May 1769.

Boswell's activities in Dublin]   Ibid.; *Pub. Advt.* 7 July 1769 (partially reprinted *Lond. Chron.* 8–11 July 1769 and *Letters,* i. 171 n. 2); *Memoirs,* p. 404
(xxxvii).

"Mr. Boswell had a very near relation"]   Ibid.

Mrs. Boyd sends an angry letter]   To Mrs. Jane Boyd, c. 11 June 1769;
From Margaret Montgomerie, 13 June 1769.

Correspondence of twenty years later]   From Mrs. Jane Charlotte McMinn,
14 July 1789.

Mary Anne twice married, alive in 1789]   Early in 1771, aged nineteen, she
married Maj.-Gen. James Gisborne (*Scots Mag.* 33 [1771].109), who must then
have been close on fifty. He died Lt.-Gen. on 20 Feb. 1778 (*Scots Mag.* 40 [1778].
111). Boswell wrote to Catharine Anne Boyd (no doubt one of Hugh Boyd's
daughters), 6 Mar. 1778, "My old flame Mary Anne is now a widow. She may
be much changed. How many children has she?" (Reg. Let.). Eleven years later
Mary Anne's cousin Mrs. McMinn (another daughter of Hugh Boyd) reported
her married to "Mr. Webster," who still remains unidentified; "they have a large
family, six little Websters and three Gisbornes." She had recently lost her eldest
son, Frederick Gisborne, and was in "a very delicate state of health" (reference in
note immediately preceding).

p. 409.
"They do not drink," etc.]   To Sir Alexander Dick, 29 May 1769.

"One riotous evening"]   To Mrs. Jane Boyd, c. 11 June 1769.

"One night of Irish extravagance"]   Journ. 14 July 1769.

Visit to a brothel with two young Army officers]   "I seldom stir abroad . . .
and should have no variety of amusement, were not some of my friends kind
enough to let me hear frequently from them and enclose me some songs and scraps
of music, of which I had a cargo from Boothby the same night yours arrived.
Sorry I am that the effects of our last interview with him have been felt more
severely and continued much longer than I imagined: *le sage entend à demi-mot"*
(From Capt. James Hoggan, 21 Aug. 1769, writing from Comlongan, Dumfriesshire, a property of Lord Mansfield's). Boswell had met Hoggan, a member
with him of Hunter's Greek Class, 1755–1756, in Ireland, where he was captain
in the 51st Foot. William Boothby (1745–1824), lieutenant in the 51st Foot,
succeeded as 7th baronet of Ashbourne Hall in the year of his death (William
Wheater, *A Record of the Services of the Fifty-First,* 1870, pp. 207, 228; Journ. 20
Mar. 1772; Johnston Corresp. p. 277 n. 5; *Comp. Baronet.* iii. 84).

Boswell located on 29 May]   To Margaret Montgomerie, Belfast, 29 May
1769; To Sir Alexander Dick, Donaghadee, 29 May 1769.

Departure from Ireland, arrival in Edinburgh]   *Pub. Advt.* 7 July 1769, paragraph dated "Dublin, June 8" saying that Boswell "is now set out on his return to Scotland"; Journ. 12 June 1769.

The last days of Corsican independence]　Foladare, pp. 194–195.

"Paoli, with a group of followers," etc.]　Ibid., pp. 195–196.

CHAPTER XXIII

p. 411.
Consultation about Mrs. Dodds]　Journ. 23 June 1769.

Torn occasionally by regrets]　Journ. 30 June 1769.
"Money would enable me," etc.]　Journ. 25 June 1769.

He wrote frequently to Margaret]　According to Reg. Let. he sent her nine letters between 17 June and 31 July and received from her thirteen between 16 June and 31 July. The Register was posted from memory and is if anything incomplete. Of the twenty-two letters, nine have been recovered: three by Boswell and six by Margaret.

He mentions Margaret as a supposable case]　Journ. 19 June 1769.

p. 412.
Temple thinks the marriage will not do]　From W. J. Temple, 1 July 1769; Journ. 7 July 1769.

Dempster returns nothing but raillery]　From George Dempster, 24 June 1769; Journ. 26 June 1769.

Johnston Margaret's advocate]　Journ. 16 June 1769.

Worried by paucity of fees]　Journ. 26 June 1769.

Dispirited on account of Corsica]　Journ. 17, 20, 26, 29 June 1769; To Sir Alexander Dick, 30 June 1769.

Lord Auchinleck tries to talk to him of marriage]　Journ. 24 June 1769.

Boswell realizes that his father has thoughts of remarrying]　Journ. 30 June, 1, 2, 4 July 1769; From Margaret Montgomerie, 1 July 1769; To Margaret Montgomerie, 4 July 1769.

p. 413.
Confides in Johnston]　Journ. 2 July 1769.

Lord Monboddo]　Journ. 4 July 1769.

A grateful and committed letter]　To Margaret Montgomerie, 4 July 1769.

Canvasses Margaret's faults with Elizabeth Boswell, writes a carping letter]　Journ. 5 July 1769.

Celebration at Bothwell Castle]　Journ. 7–11 July 1769; "Toasts," Yale MS. C1093.

p. 414.
Causes in Parliament House]　Journ. 11 July 1769. The reader is reminded that the Court of Session did not sit on Mondays. If Boswell had no cause coming up in the Court of Justiciary, he could absent himself from Edinburgh (as on this occasion) from about noon on Saturday to Tuesday morning.

Certain news of Paoli's defeat]   Journ. 12 July 1769.

Margaret offended]   Journ. 13 July 1769.

Lord Monboddo]   Ibid.

Angry, vexed, frightened]   Ibid.

"It is wonderful to think"]   Ibid.

Johnston, Macdonald]   Journ. 14 July 1769.

p. 415.
Maconochie, Commissioner Cochrane, Lord Auchinleck and Miss Betty, Sir Alexander Dick]   Journ. 15 July 1769.

Lord Auchinleck sends for him]   Ibid.

"After a wretched, feverish night"]   Journ. 16 July 1769.

Runs away when his father tries again to speak to him]   Ibid.

"The son, who was equally determined"]   Yale MS. M210.

p. 417.
A kind letter from Margaret]   Journ. 17 July 1769.

"If I could behave so," etc.]   To Margaret Montgomerie, 17 July 1769.

Appearing before his father in court]   Journ. 18 July 1769.

Lord Monboddo]   Ibid.

Boswell's references to a "compromise"]   E.g. Journ. 20 July 1769 (twice).
p. 418.
"You know my unhappy temper"]   To Margaret Montgomerie, 20 July 1769; Journ. 20 July 1769.

Lord Auchinleck speaks cheerfully of Margaret, the conference ends in bad humour]   Journ. 22 July 1769.

Boswell vacillates]   Journ. 23 July 1769.

Tells his dilemma]   Ibid. (Lady Preston, William Douglas); Journ. 24 July 1769 (Commissioner Cochrane).

Margaret's answer]   From Margaret Montgomerie, 22 July 1769; Journ. 25 July 1769.

p. 419.
Lord Auchinleck agrees to the marriage]   Journ. 4 Aug. 1769.

Week-end dash to Lainshaw]   Journ. 5–7 Aug. 1769; To Margaret Montgomerie, 21 Aug. 1769.

Boswell begins calling Margaret his "spouse"]   To Margaret Montgomerie, 21 Aug. 1769; Journ. 30 Aug. 1769; To John Johnston, 16 Oct. 1769.

Boswell sends Margaret a very explicit letter of Temple's]   From W. J. Temple, 28 July 1769; From Margaret Montgomerie, 10 Aug. 1769. The letter which Boswell sent with Temple's has not been recovered.

Boswell very uneasy over his illness, Macdonald and Dr. Cairnie reassure him] Journ. 26 July 1769.

Dr. Gregory]   Journ. 9 Aug. 1769.

Boswell tells his father he must go to London]   Journ. 12 Aug. 1769.

p. 420.
Boswell shuts himself up]   Journ. 13–24 Aug. 1769.

Lord Auchinleck summons Margaret for a conference]   To Margaret Montgomerie, 21 Aug. 1769. Margaret's apprehensions are inferred from Boswell's extended attempt to allay them.

Commissioner Cochrane]   Ibid.

A long, calm, really admirable letter]   Ibid.

CHAPTER XXIV

p. 421.
Edinburgh to Durham]   Journ. 28, 29 Aug. 1769.

Mr. Sitwell]   Journ. 29 Aug. 1769.

Mr. Howell]   Journ. 30 Aug. 1769.

A Yorkshire farmer's wife]   Journ. 31 Aug. 1769.

Boswell chats freely with his companions]   Journ. 30 Aug. 1769.

Dilly insists that he live at his house]   Journ. 1 Sept. 1769.

Johnson at Brighton, Miss Williams advises the Jubilee]   Ibid.

p. 422.
Sir John Pringle not for Kennedy]   Journ. 2 Sept. 1769.

Dr. Gilbert Kennedy]   Journ. 2 Sept. 1769. Kennedy, a Scot, M.D. from Rheims, 17 Sept. 1714, F. R. S. 1737, was for many years physician to the British Factory at Lisbon. He died on 29 Dec. 1780, the obit in *Gent. Mag.* describing him as 100 years old (51 [1781]. 46). But when he matriculated at Leyden, 20 Oct. 1712, his age was recorded as 20 (R. W. Innes Smith, *English-speaking Students of Medicine at Leyden,* 1932, p. 132).
"I could not resist"]   To John Johnston, 16 Oct. 1769.

Improvised accoutrements]   Journ. 2, 4 Sept. 1769; Mem. 3 Sept. 1769.

"Wig and rouge"]   Ibid.

Mickle]   Journ. 5 Sept. 1769.

"Believe me, my going to Shakespeare's Jubilee," etc.]   To Margaret Montgomerie, 5 Sept. 1769.

p. 423.
Oxford to Stratford]   Journ. 5–6 Sept. 1769.

The Stratford Jubilee]   See Johanne M. Stochholm, *Garrick's Folly,* 1964; Christian Deelman, *The Great Shakespeare Jubilee,* 1964.

p. 424.
Meeting with Garrick]   Journ. 6 Sept. 1769.

"I then saw." etc.]   Ibid.

p. 425.
Writing and printing of "Verses in the Character of a Corsican"]   Journ. 7
Sept. 1769.

"One of the most remarkable masks"]   *Lond. Mag.* 38 (Sept. 1769). 455.
Lond. Mag. also reprints (pp. 451–454) the "Letter from James Boswell, Esq. on
Shakespeare's Jubilee" which Boswell published in *Pub. Advt.* 16 Sept. 1769. Boswell had described the Corsican cap in *Corsica:* "A Corsican . . . wears . . . a sort of
bonnet of black cloth, lined with red frieze and ornamented on the front with a
piece of some finer stuff neatly sewed about. This bonnet is peculiar to the Corsicans, and is a very ancient piece of dress. It is doubled up on every side, and when
let down is precisely the figure of a helmet, like those we see on Trajan's pillar"
(pp. 210–211).

"I was quite happy at the masquerade"]   Journ. 7 Sept. 1769.

Boswell not able to distribute his verses in costume]   Ibid. The tradition that
he *did* hand them out at the masquerade perhaps derives from Edward Thompson's satirical poem, *Trinculo's Trip to the Jubilee,* which asserts that "Vain Boswell here stood like a Corsican dressed, / Distributing lines which he writ." It is
my opinion that Thompson is describing, not something he saw at the Jubilee
(Boswell vouches for his presence at the masquerade, *Lond. Mag.* 38. 455), but
something he saw in the later stage representation of the Jubilee at Covent Garden
or Drury Lane. See below, p. 562, note on these performances.

Gives a parcel of verses to Garrick]   Journ. 8 Sept. 1769.

p. 426.
Samuel Foote]   The famous "Devil's Definition" appeared in the newspapers in slightly varying forms. See Stochholm, pp. 113–114; Deelman, p. 272.

Theatrical people whom Boswell met at Stratford]   Journ. 6 Sept. 1769
(Love, Lee, Victor, Ross, King); 7 Sept. 1769 (Ross, King, Murphy, Colman,
Kelly, Foote); 8 Sept. 1769 (Ross); 10 Sept. 1769 (Colman, Lacy).

Visit to Shakespeare's grave]   Journ. 8 Sept. 1769.

Engagement to Dempster]   To Margaret Montgomerie, 5 Sept. 1769; see
also Journ. 2 Sept. 1769.

Publishes accounts of the Jubilee and his own doings there]   *Pub. Advt.* 16
Sept. 1769; *Lond. Mag.* 38 (Sept. 1769). 451–456.

Boswell delighted that his portrait is to appear]   Journ. 12 Sept. 1769; Mem.
14 Sept. 1769.

p. 427.
Boswell impersonated at the theatres]   For the performances in general, see
Stochholm, pp. 143–174; Deelman, pp. 276–288. That Boswell *was* impersonated

is shown by a letter of Daniel Wray to Lord Hardwicke: "I have heard the Shakespearian *Ode.* At first I thought G. too emphatical, but it could scarce be otherwise, for speaking to such an assembly is like a picture calculated for a distance. . . . In the *Jubilee,* the procession of Shakespeare's characters was an amusing spectacle, and it gratified us not a little to see in the masquerade those figures of which we had previously heard: Boswell *en Corse* and three witches who soon pulled off their masks and were the prettiest girls to be found" (John Nichols, *Illustrations of the Literary History of the 18th Century,* 1817–1858, i. 86). If Wray is speaking here of a single performance, the reference to Garrick's declamation would necessarily place that performance at Drury Lane. But Garrick's *Jubilee* did not contain a representation of the masquerade, and Colman's *Man and Wife* (the sub-title of which is *The Shakespeare Jubilee*) did; Garrick gave his Stratford *Ode* several times at Drury Lane as an afterpiece, but I cannot find that he ever combined it with *The Jubilee* (Deelman, p. 278). Wray, I think, heard Garrick declaim the *Ode* at Drury Lane, and saw Boswell *en Corse* at Covent Garden. But though Garrick's *Jubilee* does not have an amphitheatre scene, it may still have shown Boswell as a spectator of the pageant. Boswell's memoranda show him expecting Colman's man on 4 Oct., reminding himself on 8 Oct. either to call on Colman that day or to send to him next morning for "dress," and on 13 Oct. directing himself to breakfast with Garrick, pay him five guineas he had borrowed at Stratford, "and send for Corsican dress." *Man and Wife* opened on 7 Oct., *The Jubilee* on 14 Oct. (Stochholm, pp. 144, 152). It looks as though Boswell lent the costume for copying to both managers. He attended *Man and Wife* on the opening night (Mem. 7, 8 Oct. 1769) and *The Jubilee* on 17 and 21 Oct. (Notes, 17, 22 Oct. [events of 21 Oct.] 1769), but if he recorded any details, they are now lost. Of an extended journal entry for 17 Oct., only scraps and tatters now remain.

Corsica Boswell] Macaulay gave currency to this *canard* (review of Croker's Boswell, 1831), but he did not invent it. In *Gent. Mag.* 60 (1790). 1194 a correspondent who signed himself "Vigorniensis" queried whether "J.B.," who had acknowledged the authorship of certain strictures on Baretti (60. 1127), were not "the gentleman who appeared at the Stratford Jubilee *with his name written in large letters upon his cap.*"

The stage Boswell distributed broadsides] I have no evidence for this other than Edward Thompson's erroneous charge that Boswell himself did so at Stratford. As I say above, p. 561, Thompson may well have taken this detail from the stage performance, thinking that it had really happened, though he had missed seeing it.

Boswell begins his cure with Dr. Kennedy] Journ. 11 Sept. 1769.

Advertisements of the Lisbon Diet Drink] E.g. *Pub. Advt.* 7 Oct. 1769, quoted in *Boswell in Search of a Wife,* 11 Sept. 1769.

A bottle a day] "See Dr. K_____ and ask to have Drink each morn to come" (Mem. 13 Sept. 1769); "I had my Kennedy's bottle by the afternoon stage and was quite regular" ('Journ. 18 Sept. 1769); "If bottle comes not at ten, send" (Mem. 29 Sept. 1769).

Kennedy a babbler, a gillygawpus] Journ. 14 Sept. 1769; Mem. 9 Oct. 1769.

Fellow advocate, Duncan Forbes]   Journ. 14, 15 Sept. 1769.

Transfers to Forbes's superintendence]   Journ. 15 Sept. 1769.

The Diet Drink only sarsaparilla]   See J. R. Coxe, *The American Dispensatory*, 6th ed., 1825, p. 254. After a recipe for making Decoctum Sarsaparillae Compositum, D.L.A., from sarsaparilla, guaiacum wood, sassafras, liquorice, and mezereon, the article continues: "This compound decoction is an elegant mode of preparing an article once highly celebrated under the title of the Lisbon Diet Drink, which, for a long time after its first introduction into Britain, was kept a secret; but an account of the method of preparing it was at length published in the *Physical and Literary Essays* of Edinburgh by Dr. Donald Monro."

Other treatments]   "Breakfast Mr. Forbes. Consult as to plaster and camphorated friction" (Mem. 17 Sept. 1769). Kennedy had probably prescribed camphor liniment and a plaster containing a mercuric ointment, and Boswell wanted Forbes's opinion. See also Mem. 10 Oct. 1769 ("mercemplaster"), 14 Oct. ("caustic").

p. 428.
Instructs himself to ask Kennedy about operation]   Mem. 12 Sept. 1769.

Memoranda to consult Pott]   13, 21 Sept., 4 Oct. 1769.

Moves nearer Forbes]   Journ. 20 Sept. 1769; To John Johnston, 16 Oct. 1769.

Sleeps in Carey Street only one night]   Journ. 21 Sept. 1769.

Learns that Paoli is in London]   Ibid.

Club at St. Paul's Coffee-house]   Essentially a group of Benjamin Franklin's friends, called by him "The Honest Whigs" (Carl Van Doren, *Benjamin Franklin*, 1938, pp. 421–422). A few years later Boswell would have felt out of place in a club of honest Whigs and dissenting clergymen. Now he was united to them by his love of "liberty," the first word and recurring theme of *Corsica*.

"His *valet de chambre* came down," etc.]   Journ. 22 Sept. 1769.

Paoli, his pension, and the Opposition]   DNB; Horace Walpole, *Memoirs of the Reign of King George the Third*, ed. G. F. Russell Barker, 1894, iii. 257–258; Ravenna, p. 146. See also *Lit. Car.* p. 314. The newspapers of the time contain a great deal of comment on Paoli's failure to call on Mrs. Macaulay and Wilkes. See e.g. *Pub. Advt.* 11 Oct. 1769; *Lond. Chron.* 14–17 Oct., 2–4 Nov. 1769.

p. 429.
Counsels to be quiet and keep early hours]   Mem. 4, 7, 14, 20 Sept. 1769.

Takes rooms near the General, gets coloured clothes]   Journ. 22 Sept. 1769.

Newspaper items linking Paoli and Boswell]   *Lond. Chron.* 30 Sept.–3 Oct. 1769 (airing in Hyde Park, also in *Pub. Advt.* 4 Oct. 1769); *Lond. Chron.* 10–12 Oct. 1769 (St. Paul's, etc., also in *Pub. Advt.* 11 Oct.); *Lond. Chron.* 31 Oct.–2 Nov. 1769 (Johnson introduced to Paoli); 9–11 Nov. 1769 (Garrick presented to Paoli). The statement of *Lond. Chron.* that Johnson was introduced to Paoli on 31 Oct. is at variance with the *Life,* which represents them as first meeting on the 10th. Such surviving documentation as there is rather supports the dating of *Lond.*

Chron. No manuscript source for the conversation given in the *Life* under date of 10 Oct. has been found, and the memorandum for 11 Oct., summarizing the events of the 10th, makes no mention of Johnson, though it records some remarks of Paoli. On the other hand Johnson and Paoli both witnessed Boswell's signature to his marriage contract on 31 Oct. (Yale MS. M21), which should mean that they were in company on that date. Paoli left London on 11 Oct. for a tour to Portsmouth and did not return till the 29th (*Lond. Chron.* 12–14, 14–17, 21–24, 28–31 Oct. 1769).

Boswell apologizes for not being assiduous in reporting Johnson] *Life,* following 9 Sept. 1769.

Four weeks] Boswell arrived in London on 1 Sept. (Journ.) and first recorded a meeting with Johnson on 28 Sept. (Notes).

p. 430.
"Peccant part"] Pope's *Essay on Man,* II. 144. It is an odd coincidence that Pope should have figured in both these sallies.

Johnson really angry] *Life,* 26, 27 Oct. 1769. "You pursue me," etc., is a previously unpublished bit from the corresponding notes. "Pursue" is a pure guess, the rich record being now reduced to scraps.

Foote] Notes, 18 Oct. 1769 ("I wanted much," etc.); 23 Oct. 1769 (dinner). Both notes record the events of the previous day.

Cleland] Mem. 14 Oct. 1769.

Macklin] Notes, 23 Oct. 1769, recording events of 22 Oct.

"A perpetual renovation of hope"] Boswell could not remember "hope" and left a blank for it. Editors of the *Life* (1770, Maxwell's *Collectanea*) have applied this witticism to Thomas Sheridan on the dubious authority of an anonymous contributor to *Gent. Mag.* George Steevens, like Boswell, heard Johnson say it of Macklin (*Life,* ii. 122 n. 2; G. B. Hill (ed.), *Johnsonian Miscellanies,* 1897, ii. 1–2, 317).

Steevens and Tyers] *Life,* 27 Oct. 1769.

Sir Joshua Reynolds] From Oliver Goldsmith, ?24 Sept. 1769; Mem. 26 Sept. 1769.

p. 431.
Old acquaintances] Journ. 6, 7, 8 Sept. 1769; *Life,* 16 Oct. 1769; Mem. 4, 17 (events of 16) Oct. 1769; Notes 20 (events of 19), 25 (events of 24), 28 (events of 27) Oct. 1769; undatable fragment, between 29 Oct. and 1 Nov. 1769 (Garrick). Journ. 23 Sept. 1769 (Armstrong). Journ. 24 Sept. 1769 (Campbell). Notes, 26 (events of 25) Oct. 1769 (Oglethorpe).

Goldsmith] Journ. 21 Sept. 1769; Mem. 25, 26 Sept. 1769; Notes, 26 Sept. 1769.

Colman] Journ. 7, 10, 21 Sept. 1769; Mem. 29 Sept. 1769; Notes, 26 Sept. ("truest book"), 25 (events of 24) Oct. 1769.

The Sheridans] Journ. 4, 15, 16, 19, 23, 25 Sept. 1769; Mem. 4, 13, 14 Oct. 1769; Notes, 25 Sept., 18 (events of 17), 23 (events of 22), 25 (events of 24) Oct.

1769; Alicia Lefanu, *Memoirs of the Life and Writings of Mrs. Frances Sheridan,* 1824, pp. 336–337.

Langton] Mem. 13 Oct. 1769; Notes, 25 (events of 24) Oct. 1769.

The Thrales] J. L. Clifford, *Hester Lynch Piozzi (Mrs. Thrale),* 1952; *The Letters of Samuel Johnson,* ed. R. W. Chapman, 1952.

Boswell meets Mrs. Thrale] To Mrs. Thrale, 5 Sept. 1769; Journ. 30 Sept. 1769.

Boswell invited to Streatham] Notes, 30 Sept. 1769; *Life,* 30 Sept., 6 Oct. 1769.

p. 432.
First call on Baretti] Journ. 16 Sept. 1769. See also Notes, 26 Sept., 2 Oct. 1769.

Baretti's arrest and trial] Mem. 8, 14 Oct. 1769; *Life,* 19, 20 Oct. 1769; Notes, 21 (events of 20) Oct. 1769. The report of the trial from the Session Papers is conveniently reprinted in H. W. Liebert's *A Constellation of Genius,* 1958.

Garrick and Langton took him in hand] Notes, 25 (events of 24) Oct. 1769.

He writes an apology to Baretti] To Joseph Baretti, c. end of Oct. 1769. He did attempt to call on him in Newgate *before* the trial: Mem. 14 Oct. 1769.

p. 433.
Wilkes] DNB; Bleackley, pp. 204–246; Journ. 10 Sept. 1769.

p. 434.
The pan-polemist William Kenrick] *An Epistle to James Boswell, Esq., occasioned by his having transmitted the Moral Writings of Samuel Johnson to Pascal Paoli, General of the Corsicans,* by W. K. Esq., 1768. Johnson would not allow Boswell to take any notice of it (*Life,* beginning of May 1768). Wilkes had also glanced at Boswell's preference of occasional murder to frequent adultery in a letter in *The Political Register,* signed "A.B." (ii. 197; reprinted, with considerable abridgement of the strictures on Boswell, in Almon, iii. 252–253), but the passage does not go beyond raillery.

An anonymous paragraph] *Lond. Chron.* 21–24 Oct. 1769.

The next issue of the paper] *Lond. Chron.* 24–26 Oct. 1769.

At Court] Notes, 26 (events of 25) Oct. 1769.

Eglinton] "The late Lord Eglinton regretted to my father my want of shame" (Journ. 21 Jan. 1784).

p. 435.
"A man who has been able," etc.] *Corsica,* p. xxiv.

Boswell styled a grave man] Arrigo Arrighi, *Histoire de Pascal Paoli,* 1843, i. 231. I have the reference from Dr. Hill (*Life,* ii. 3).

Guerrazzi] *Pasquale Paoli, ossia, La rotta di Pontenuovo; racconto corso del secolo xviii,* 1860. See Beatrice Corrigan, "Guerrazzi, Boswell and Corsica," *Italica,* 35 (Mar. 1958). 25–37.

p. 436.
The London Magazine] Notes, 3 Oct. 1769; Mem. 14 (events of 13) Oct. 1769; Journ. 1 Jan. 1777; From Charles Dilly, 15 Dec. 1778.

Money raised on Dalblair] Journ. 17 Nov. 1775.

Correspondence with Lord Auchinleck] Reg. Let.: received from Lord Auchinleck two letters, 11 Sept. 1769; sent letters to him 11, 14, 16 Sept. 1769; To John Johnston, 16 Oct. 1769; To Margaret Montgomerie, ?2 Oct. 1769.

Learned from Margaret that his father was angry] Notes, 30 Sept. 1769; Reg. Let. 30 Sept. 1769, contents inferred from Boswell's comments.

p. 437.
"Good God," etc.] To Margaret Montgomerie, ?2 Oct. 1769; Mem. 1 Oct. 1769 ("Don't send remonstrance to M. 'Tis too much for her. Just now only hint"); 2 Oct. 1769.

Temple, Paoli, Johnson] From W. J. Temple, 13 Oct. 1769; Notes, 1 Oct. 1769; To Margaret Montgomerie, ?2 Oct. 1769.

Reported to John Johnston] To John Johnston, 16 Oct. 1769.

Letter from Mr. Dun, Dilly's advice] Notes, 21 (events of 20) Oct. 1769.

Dempster argues with him] Notes, 22 (events of 21) Oct. 1769.

Intercession for Margaret, receives letter from her] Notes, 23 (events of 22) Oct. 1769; Reg. Let. 23 Oct. 1769.

Writes to his father] Notes, 24 (events of 23) Oct. 1769. Reg. Let. records no letter to Lord Auchinleck this day, but does have one (perhaps misplaced) under 19 Oct.

p. 438.
Incision performed] Mem. 15, 16 (events of 14 and 15) Oct. 1769. Forbes had assured him some time before that the incision was "nothing" (Notes, 2 Oct. 1769). I infer that Boswell was more insistent on the knife than his advisers were because he says that Forbes performed the operation "with kindness to save dire forebodings" and because Pott was against any further surgery.

Kennedy, Pott] Mem. 16 (events of 15) Oct., 4 Oct. 1769; Notes, 18, 22, 24, 25 (events of 24) Oct. 1769. Dr. Harry Keil in 1956 suggested to Professor Brady and me that the incision was probably made to relieve a paraphimosis, "though it is possible that some form of local infection was in question." I do not know whether he would have seen reason to revise his diagnosis if he had seen Boswell's recently recovered note of his consultation with Pott, which runs as follows: "Yesterday called on Mr. Pott. Said you might be easy as to distemper; and as to the noble part no occasion for incision. By *couchant avec la même femme* all that would come right."

Pott's verdict as good as any obtainable for a century] I.e. till the identification of the specific infective bacterium by A. L. S. Neisser in 1879.

News that Eglinton had been shot] From Margaret Montgomerie, 24 Oct. 1769; Reg. Let. 28 Oct. 1769.

Boswell's tribute to Eglinton] See *Tour*, 1961 (1963), pp. 368, 416–417, 438–439.

Garrick presented to Paoli] *Lond. Chron.* 9–11 Nov. 1769; undatable fragment of Notes between 29 Oct. and 1 Nov. 1769.

Marriage Contract] Yale MS. M21.

p. 439.
Jaunt to Mamhead] Boswell arrived at Mamhead on the morning of Friday the 3d and left Exeter for London at one in the morning of Monday the 6th (To Margaret Montgomerie, 5 Nov. 1769). The other dates are inferred. Reg. Let. records the sending of seven letters on 31 Oct. (Boswell up all night as usual before a trip) and the receipt of five on the 7th (Boswell back in London).

Temple had begged off in 1768] From W. J. Temple, 1 Mar. 1768; To W. J. Temple, 16 Apr. 1768. On getting Boswell's remonstrance, Temple gave him an invitation (21 Apr. 1768) but not in such terms as to encourage acceptance: "Come and view me even in this humble state, in a poor thatched house ready to tumble about my ears, with all the marks of ruin and poverty around it. Come and view me robbed of fortune and surrounded with difficulties on every side. . . ."

Prescience and free will] Notes 27 (events of 26) Oct. 1769; undatable fragment of Notes between 29 Oct. and 1 Nov. 1769; Journ. 15 Dec. 1774.

p. 440.
"The Stationers' Company," etc.] *Lond. Chron.* 9–11 Nov. 1769. Boswell did not write this notice.

Beckford's banquets] DNB.

Departure from London] *Life,* 9–10 Nov. 1769.

Travels without sleep, arrives in Edinburgh] From Margaret Montgomerie, 15 Nov. 1769, showing that he was then in Edinburgh and had written her a note from Musselburgh which she had received on the night of the 14th. This looks as though he must have arrived on the evening of the 13th, for the mail for Stewarton left Edinburgh at 9 p.m. (*Edinburgh Almanack,* 1769, p. 161). The Session sat down on 14 Nov., 12 Nov. in 1769 falling on a Sunday.

Correspondence with Margaret] Reg. Let.

"I sincerely wish," etc.] From Margaret Montgomerie, 31 Oct. 1769.

p. 441.
Proclamation of banns] The statute called for proclamation on three successive Sundays, but a single proclamation was possible where the parties were well known to the minister, or he was satisfied that there was no impediment (*Encyclopaedia of the Laws of Scotland,* W. Green, 1926–1935, Article "Marriage"). The register of marriages for the parish of Stewarton is blank from 1750 to 1774. Lord Auchinleck's banns were certainly proclaimed on 19 Nov.

1769 (*Register of Marriages of the City of Edinburgh, 1751–1800, 1922*: Scottish Record Soc. Pub. No. 53, Prefatory Note and p. 70).

The two weddings] Lt. John Boswell's Diary, 25 Nov. 1769; *Scots Mag.* 31 (1769). 615.

"I am so earnestly invited"] To Margaret Montgomerie, 23 Nov. 1769. Archibald Douglas signed the Marriage Contract, as witness to Margaret's subscription, made on 25 Nov. 1769.

Boswell took a week off] Lt. John Boswell's Diary quoted below.

Threatenings at Auchinleck] Journ. 9 Jan. 1775, placing the oath only "in winter 1769." Temple wrote on 15 Dec. 1769: "The scene at Auchinleck was quite in character. If there should be occasion to take so desperate a revenge (which God forbid!), it will be entirely your own fault. Your father loves you and will certainly leave you his estate if you will allow him."

p. 442.
Meek return to Edinburgh] "FRIDAY 1 DECEMBER. . . . This night my brother James and his wife arrived in town from Lainshaw and took up their lodgings at Mrs. Guthrie's, the house above my father's. . . . SATURDAY 2 DECEMBER. . . . Dined betwixt three and four, my brother and his wife with us" (Lt. John Boswell's Diary).

Boswell and his wife set up house-keeping] "TUESDAY 5 DECEMBER. . . . This evening my brother James and his wife entered to a house of their own in the Cowgate, taken from Mrs. Fullarton" (ibid.).

APPENDIX

Boswell's Conversion to Roman Catholicism

[See above, pp. 45–54]

A good summary of the penal acts against Roman Catholics in Scotland will be found in the article "Roman Catholic" of the *Encyclopaedia of the Laws of Scotland,* Edinburgh, W. Green, 1926–1935; see also Robert Bell, *A Dictionary of the Law of Scotland,* 1808, section ix of the article "Treason," and Sir William Blackstone, *Commentaries on the Law of England* (consult the index under "Papists"). The latest enactment of the Scottish Parliament against papists, 1700 (*Acts of the Parliament of Scotland,* x. 215–219), confirmed and ratified all the previous Scots enactments on the subject, and by the British Treason Act of 1708 (7 Anne, c. 21, sections 1 and 23) the English law of treason became the law of Scotland, thereby making treasonable certain Roman-Catholic activities which had not previously been so defined. In strict law, a Scottish subject incurred the pains of high treason, with the penalty of being hanged, drawn, and quartered, for becoming a Roman Catholic or for procuring another to become a Roman Catholic, indeed merely for saying mass or hearing mass said; but the sanguinary provisions of the statutes had long been in abeyance, and it would be misleading to treat them as more than historical background in a case arising in 1760. Readers will find an illuminating account of the actual situation of Catholics, both priests and lay-folk, in eighteenth-century Scotland in the fourth volume of J. F. S. Gordon's *Ecclesiastical Chronicle for Scotland,* 1867, a collection of memoirs and records compiled in great part by the Roman missioners themselves.

The *Encyclopaedia of the Laws of Scotland* thus summarizes the main civil disabilities: "No Catholic could be King or Queen of the realm, and no person marrying a Catholic could take the crown. Catholics could not be governors, schoolmasters, guardians, nor factors; could not teach any art, science, or 'exercise of any sort'; could not be employed as servants; could not educate nor bring up their own children, or any of which they had been appointed guardians; could not send their children abroad to be educated; and could not hold 'any office whatsoever' in the kingdom. Catholics could not acquire real property (1) by purchase; (2) deed of gift; or (3) by trust on their behalf, such deeds being null and void. Catholics over fifteen years of age could not inherit estates; and if they failed to renounce their faith on reaching fifteen years of age, they lost their right of succession, the estate passing to the next Protestant heir." These provisions were clearly not all enforced either (e.g., Boswell for years had a Catholic manservant, Joseph Ritter), but it is quite certain that a man of Boswell's status would have suffered those disabilities mentioned in the text.

That Mrs. Cowper was a Catholic can be inferred with practical certainty from John Ramsay's statement that Boswell at this time was involved with a Catholic actress: "Not long after [the production of Lady Houston's play], he went off with an actress to London. Love, the manager, immediately acquainted Lord Auchinleck of it, telling him at the same time that the connexion was not perhaps the more safe that the woman was a papist, and reputed virtuous among *them*" (*Scotland and Scotsmen,* i. 171 n.). Ramsay, who was four years older than Boswell, was the son of a Writer to the Signet, clearly knew Lord Auchinleck well, and is seldom demonstrably wrong in what he says about Boswell. My statement that Mrs. Cowper introduced Boswell to a Catholic priest is pure conjecture. Writing to John Johnston, 26 July 1763, Boswell refers to "little Mr. Duchat, the popish priest," whom Boswell clearly has met, and who appears to be on terms of considerable familiarity with Johnston (Johnston Corresp., p. 100). The records in Gordon's *Ecclesiastical Chronicle* show that there was no Roman priest named Duchat in Scotland in 1759, but that there was one named Duguid, who had a charge in Edinburgh (iv. 542, 636). Roman priests in Britain frequently resorted to aliases. On this admittedly very slender evidence I conclude that Duchat was Duguid, that he was Mrs. Cowper's priest, and that he supplied Boswell with Catholic books.

"A Catalogue of Books belonging to James Boswell, Esq.," in Boswell's own hand, made about 1770, now in the National Library of Scotland, contains on p. 9 a cluster of titles in Roman-Catholic apologetic, listed by Boswell as follows:

> The Grounds of the Old Religion—Also
> The Touchstone of the New Religion
>   with MS Notes by Lord Auchinleck   1751
> Bossuet, Doctrine de l'Église Catholique   Paris 1751
> True Wisdom, by Father Segnery   Lond 1751

The first two titles are by Richard Challoner (1691–1781), Roman-Catholic bishop and vicar apostolic in London, author of the best Roman-Catholic apologetic works of English origin then current. Gibbon, seven years earlier, had been converted to Roman Catholicism by reading Bossuet: "I surely fell by a noble hand" (*The Memoirs of the Life of Edward Gibbon,* ed. G. B. Hill, 1900, p. 70). I have not traced any copy of "True Wisdom," but suggest doubtfully that "Father Segnery" was the famous Italian preacher Paolo Segneri (1624–1694). The fact that these four books, originally published at widely differing dates, all bear the imprint date 1751 makes one suspect that they were a special collection printed for the use of Roman-Catholic proselytizers in England. I can think of no time when Lord Auchinleck would have been so likely to annotate a book of Roman-Catholic apologetic belonging to his son as in the summer or autumn of 1759.

The statement concerning the occasional nature of Roman-Catholic services in

Glasgow rests on conclusive contemporary evidence. See Gordon, iv. 636, and J. T. T. Brown, "The Youth and Early Manhood of James Boswell," in *Proceedings* of the Royal Philosophical Society of Glasgow, 41 (1909–1910). 226. We also have Boswell's own testimony (Journ. 2 Apr. 1775) that he heard the Roman service for the first time in London.

The first published mention of Boswell's conversion to Roman Catholicism occurs in the memoir of Boswell by the Reverend Charles Rogers, *Boswelliana,* 1874, pp. 12–14, an account certainly riddled with error but perhaps based upon more documents than the one letter from Dr. John Jortin to Sir David Dalrymple which Rogers quotes. Rogers says that Boswell attended Catholic worship on Sundays in Glasgow, and before the end of the session resolved to embrace the Roman faith and to qualify for orders. Lord Auchinleck recalled him to Edinburgh. He consented to give up his plan of becoming a priest, provided that he might secure a commission as officer in the Army. In March 1760 his father accompanied him to London in order to procure for him a commission in the Guards, but the Duke of Argyll poured cold water on that scheme. Lord Auchinleck soon went home, but Boswell was allowed to stay on in London in order that his conversion might be kept quiet. At Lord Auchinleck's request, Dalrymple gave him a letter of introduction to Dr. Jortin, in the hope that Jortin, an eminent Anglican preacher and scholar, might get him at least to conform to the doctrines of the Church of England. Jortin's reply, 27 Apr. 1760, quoted by Rogers at some length, shows that Boswell called on Jortin on Maundy Thursday (3 Apr.), missed him, and did not come a second time. Rogers inferred that he soon "ceased to concern himself with ecclesiastical questions," but adds that he nevertheless stayed on in London an entire year.

As I have said, this account is riddled with error. There were in 1760 no regular Sunday services for Roman Catholics in Glasgow, as Rogers implies; Lord Auchinleck did not accompany his son to London; Lord Auchinleck did not then try to get him a commission in the Guards; Boswell did not remain in London "a whole year." The last statement was careless, for Boswell himself had said in the *Life of Johnson* (1763, beginning) that his first visit to the metropolis lasted three months; the others were mistaken inferences from scanty or ambiguous evidence. But Rogers adduces no evidence or grounds of inference for one of his more important *correct* statements, namely, that Boswell had notions of becoming a priest. The portion of Jortin's letter which he quotes shows that Boswell had become a Roman Catholic, but says and implies nothing more. I suspect that Rogers had some further source of information that he did not specify, and suggest as a likely source the archives at Newhailes, which produced the letter from Dr. Jortin. Rogers certainly had from Newhailes more than that one letter, for he quotes from a commonplace book of Dalrymple's (p. 5 n., p. 11 n.) and quotes from or refers to several of Boswell's letters to Dalrymple (pp. 30, 32, 35, 37, 39–40, 42 n.). A really thorough search at Newhailes should have turned up a letter (To Sir David Dalrymple, 22 Mar. 1760) which would have answered most of his questions, but for some reason that letter escaped the scrutiny of scholars till 1937.

Encouraged by finding one of Rogers's unsupported and by no means readily inferable statements to be true, I should like to think that he also had evidence for saying that Boswell was recalled to Edinburgh from Glasgow. A peremptory recall seems necessary to explain why Boswell had to "flee" (Sketch for Rousseau, above, p. 4), "escape" (Second Outline for the Sketch, Yale MS. L1110), "run off" (Journ. 11 Sept. 1777), "elope" (To Sir David Dalrymple, 22 Mar. 1760) to London. The precipitancy of his departure and the speed of his flight seem to show that he was afraid that if he did not leave at once, he might be forcibly restrained from leaving, and that if he did not make haste on the road, he might be overtaken and carried back. I should not have supposed that he would have feared such exercise of authority from any one but his father, or that his father would have had any reason to suspect him of meditating flight unless he had failed to put in an appearance after being ordered home. But in fine, my statements that Boswell at the end of February 1760 wrote to Lord Auchinleck telling him of his intentions, and that Lord Auchinleck "peremptorily summoned him to Edinburgh," rest on no authority other than the presumed but unreported authority of Rogers.

Boswell told Rousseau that he had turned Roman Catholic and had intended to hide himself in a convent in France (Journ. 5 Dec. 1764). The second outline for the Sketch he wrote for Rousseau is even more specific: "Madly in love with an actress, wanted to marry her. Became a Catholic. Escaped to London. Thought of becoming a priest or monk" (Yale MS. L1110).

The details of Boswell's flight to London and subsequent adventures there, unless other authority is cited, are taken from a long letter which he wrote to Sir David Dalrymple on 22 Mar. 1760. See Andrew G. Hoover, "Boswell's First London Visit," in *The Virginia Quarterly,* 29 (1953). 242–256 and "Boswell's Letters at Newhailes," in *University of Toronto Quarterly,* 22 (1953). 244–260. He went the first night (Saturday 1 Mar.) to Moffat and the second to Carlisle "with a couple of Glasgow hacks." At Carlisle he got post-horses and went "on Monday 109 miles to Wetherby, on Tuesday 131 to Buckden, and on Wednesday [5 Mar.] 61 to London." He probably rode horseback the entire way and certainly covered the distance from Carlisle to London in that fashion, as the following anecdote from *Boswelliana,* not published by Rogers, attests:

When Boswell was at Newmarket in the year 1760, he had got a circle of the Jockey Club about him and was telling that he had rode in the month of March from Carlisle to London in two days and a half. "What, Sir," cried some of 'em, "upon the same horse?" "No, gentlemen," said he, "that would be no merit of mine. But I'll tell you what is better: it was upon the same bum" (Hyde Collection).

Boswell never anywhere hints that he had a companion in his flight; in fact, he never connects Mrs. Cowper in any way with his conversion. I suppose he could have ridden horseback beside the coach in which she was a passenger, but it seems most unlikely. She was assuredly not his mistress at the time of his elopement and probably never was. Ramsay's statement that Boswell "went off *with* an actress to

London" is almost certainly erroneous. One could save the credit of the rest of Ramsay's information by assuming that Boswell ran off *to* Mrs. Cowper, that she disapproved of his breaking with his family and promptly let Love know where he was, and that Love told Lord Auchinleck.

The Lemon Tree Inn and Egan the wigmaker are reported by Boswell in his journal for 19 Mar. 1772 and 15 Apr. 1776. His one mention of Meighan, "Roman-Catholic bookseller in Drury Lane" (Journ. 4 Jan. 1763) shows that in 1760 he had left a guinea with Meighan, and had a small credit remaining in 1763. The conversion of the youthful Boswell shows so many parallels to that of the even more youthful Gibbon that I am encouraged to use Gibbon's more fully reported case as a paradigm for reconstructing Boswell's. Gibbon presented himself to John Lewis, a Roman-Catholic bookseller in Russell Street, Covent Garden, Lewis recommended him to the Reverend Bernard Baker, S.J., one of the chaplains at the Sardinian Chapel in Lincoln's Inn Fields, and Father Baker "solemnly though privately" admitted him to the Roman communion (Gibbon, *Memoirs,* ed. cit., p. 72; Edward Hutton, "The Conversion of Edward Gibbon," in *The Nineteenth Century and After,* 111 [Jan.–June 1932]. 366). Probably, as I say in the text, Catholic booksellers in London furnished the only generally known stages in the necessarily secretive route to reception. Thomas Meighan, father of the modern Catholic bookselling trade in England, was well known and a man of parts (Joseph Gillow, *A Literary and Biographical History, or Bibliographical Dictionary of the English Catholics,* 1885–1902; Gordon, op. cit., p. 17). The reader, if he prefers, may cast Mrs. Cowper in the role of intermediary. My own guess is that Mrs. Cowper, if she knew about Boswell's presence in London, tried to dissociate herself from the whole business.

Boswell tells us in his journal for 2 Apr. 1775 that he first heard the Romish service at the Bavarian Chapel. Six years earlier he had recorded going "to the Bavarian Minister's Roman-Catholic Chapel, to revive in my mind former days when, in that very place, I was so solemnly happy in thinking myself united to the grand and only true church" (Journ. 17 Sept. 1769). The Bavarian Chapel was nominally the private chapel of the Bavarian Envoy, Count von Hasslang. English law proscribed the Roman faith for Englishmen, but of course could not interfere with the religious observances of the official representatives in England of Catholic sovereigns, who maintained sumptuously appointed chapels of their own. In them mass was said publicly, these chapels in fact serving as mission churches for English Catholics in London. The Bavarian Chapel, which stood in Warwick Street, Golden Square, was gutted in the Gordon Riots of 1780, but was restored and later rebuilt on the same site, and after Catholic emancipation was continued as the Church of the Assumption. It was served by five chaplains (Alexander Rottmann, *London Catholic Churches,* 1926, pp. 65–66; Bernard Ward, *The Dawn of the Catholic Revival in England,* 1909, i. 24–26). Some day the name of the priest who reconciled Boswell to the Roman obedience may be revealed, but it will not be because Boswell himself ever provided a clue. He maintained silence obviously because he did not wish to make the priest subject to reprisals. As I have said in the text, a priest who in 1760 reconciled a British subject to the see of Rome did not run much danger of imprisonment or transportation, but he might well have been harassed and subjected to inquiry that would have been unpleasant for himself and the Bavarian Minister. Lewis, the bookseller, was summoned before the Privy Council and interrogated concerning the part he had played in Gibbon's conversion, and if Father Baker escaped questioning, it was presumably because Gibbon had been careful not to learn his name or his order (Gibbon, *Memoirs,* ed. cit., p. 72 and n. 5).

The act of submission probably occurred either at Boswell's lodgings or the priest's, not in the Bavarian Chapel. See the lists of reconciliations, 1730–1733, 1753–1756, by the Reverend Monox Hervey, Catholic Record Society, *Miscellanea,* ix (1914).369–372, 378–380. All the reconciliations in the latter group occurred in private homes or lodgings, generally in the presence of at least one witness.

Some doubts have been expressed as to whether Boswell ever more than flirted with Roman Catholicism. As I have said in the text, his speedy falling away from his new allegiance indicated that his conversion was not very profound—nothing like as whole-souled as Gibbon's—but no one should have any doubt that he was formally received into the Roman-Catholic Church. Boswell uses words very precisely, and would never have spoken of being "united to the grand and only true church" if he had not been admitted to communion. He would not have told Rousseau (a former convert) that he "had turned Roman Catholic" if he meant merely that for a time he had been greatly attracted by the Roman position. There are many other equally conclusive allusions, but perhaps the most incontrovertible is that in which he records his fears that his scruples over taking the Formula at an election in 1774 will bring out the fact of his "having once embraced the Romish faith" (Journ. 19, 31 Oct. 1774). He is speaking here as a lawyer of a *legal* status ("papist") which only formal reception could have conferred.

INDEX

This index does not provide references to sources and authorities, which can be readily located by use of the page-headings for pp. 443–568. Popes, sovereigns, and British princes of the blood are entered under their Christian names; noblemen, Lords of Session, and wives of Lords of Session, under their titles. The titles are usually those proper for the period 1760–1769. Maiden names of married women are supplied in parentheses. Titles of books are listed under the names of the authors. The following abbreviations are employed: D. (Duke), E. (Earl), M. (Marquess), V. (Viscount), B. (Baron), JB (James Boswell), SJ (Samuel Johnson).

About the Author

"My first book was my M.A. essay *Shelley and Browning,* published in 1923. In 1929 I published at the Yale Press a history of Evacuation Hospital No. 8 entitled *Stretchers: The History of a Hospital on the Western Front,* and at the Oxford Press a revision of my Ph.D. dissertation entitled *The Literary Career of James Boswell.* My choice of a subject was largely accidental: I wanted to work under Professor Chauncey B. Tinker, and he happened to mention one day that the bibliography of Boswell needed investigation. The appearance of my book in the spring of 1929 determined my later career. Lt.-Col. Ralph H. Isham had purchased the first instalment of the Boswell papers from Lord Talbot de Malahide in 1926 and 1927, and had launched an expensive limited edition under the editorship of the English essayist Geoffrey Scott. Mr. Scott died suddenly of pneumonia in the summer of 1929, and Colonel Isham asked me to complete the project. I have been working with Boswell ever since, and have brought out more volumes by or about the biographer of Johnson than I like to contemplate. Though I am known outside Yale principally as an eighteenth-century scholar, I have done considerably more teaching in the Romantic period than in the Age of Johnson. In 1941 I gave the Messenger lectures at Cornell, publishing them the same year with the title *The Idiom of Poetry* (revised and enlarged edition 1946)."

Professor Pottle is Sterling Professor and senior member of the Department of English at Yale, and is a Chancellor of the Academy of American Poets. He holds honorary doctorates from Colby College, Rutgers University, and the University of Glasgow; is a Fellow of the International Institute of Arts and Letters, and has been elected to membership in the Utrecht Academy of Arts and Sciences, the American Academy of Arts and Sciences, and the American Philosophical Society.